EVERYONE TO SKIS!

EVERYONE TO SKIS!

SKIING IN RUSSIA AND THE RISE OF SOVIET BIATHLON

WILLIAM D. FRANK

NIU PRESS

DeKalb, IL

Published by the Northern Illinois University Press, DeKalb, Illinois 60115
Manufactured in the United States using acid-free paper.
Design by Shaun Allshouse

Library of Congress Cataloging-in-Publication Data
Frank, William D.
Everyone to skis! : skiing in Russia and the rise of Soviet biathlon / William D. Frank.
    pages cm
Includes bibliographical references and index.
ISBN 978-0-87580-476-7 (cloth : alk. paper) — ISBN 978-1-60909-093-7 (e-book)
1. Skis and skiing—Russia (Federation)—History. 2. Biathlon—Russia (Federation)—History.
3. Sports and state—Russia (Federation)—History. 4. Sports and society—Russia (Federation)—
History. I. Title.
  GV854.8.R8F73 2013
  796.930947—dc23
                        2013020988

DEDICATION

Cragg Douglas Gilbert

1923–2007

farmer, patriot, mountaineer

Contents

Acknowledgments

Having lived most of my life during the Cold War era, it gives me great satisfaction to co-opt a Soviet trope by thanking the unseen collective that backed my struggle to produce this book.

Over the course of four decades, I have been privileged to study with outstanding linguists. I would be remiss if I did not acknowledge in particular the influence of Elizabeth McKee; Professors Sylvia Brown and William Moran (University of Michigan); Professors Anthony Raubitschek and T. B. L. Webster (Stanford University); Professors Laurie Moshier, Christian Schneider and Dinara Georgioliani (Central Washington University); and Professor Zoya Polack (University of Washington). Their enthusiasm for languages has been contagious and their patience with me as I struggled in their classrooms transcended the bounds of reason.

The unsung heroes of historical research are the staffs of the world's libraries and archives. I would like to express my gratitude to the hard-working Inter-Library Loan personnel at Central Washington University's Brooks Library and University of Washington's Suzzallo Library; Paul Thomas and his associates at Hoover Library (Stanford University); Harold Leich (Library of Congress); Merja Vilen (Sports Museum of Finland); Kaarel Antons (Estonian Sports Museum); and Professor Michael Biggins (Head of the Slavic and East European Section at Suzzallo Library).

I am grateful for the assistance of many scholars who had a hand in formulating my approach to Soviet sport, in particular: Professors Elena Campbell, James Felak, Guntis Šmidchens, Simon Werrett and Glennys Young (University of Washington); and Professor Roxanne Easley (Central Washington University). I would like to express my appreciation to Professors Claire Nolte of Manhattan College in Riverdale, New York, and Robert Edelman of the University of California, San Diego, for their assistance and interest; and to Professor Louise McReynolds of University of North Carolina at Chapel Hill for her cogent analysis of my original manuscript. A special acknowledgment goes to Professor E. John B. Allen for his encouragement and numerous contributions. I am indebted as well to Nadine Cohodas who critiqued with diligence and brilliance my complete first draft; and to my vigilant editors at Northern Illinois University Press, Amy Farranto and Susan Bean.

By sheer luck, I stumbled onto biathlon when it was still an obscure and misunderstood event in the United States and threw myself headlong into competing with the U.S. National Team just prior to the 1980 Winter Olympics. A finer and more dedicated group of athletes and coaches could never have been assembled: underfinanced, unappreciated, yet unrelenting in their pursuit of the sport. I am obliged to each and every one of them for accepting me into their company. Many of these individuals made significant contributions to this book, especially: William Spencer, John Morton, Peter Hale, Glenn Jobe, Russell Scott, Martin Hagen, Lyle Nelson, Art Stegen and John Ruger. I would also like to acknowledge several other members of the international biathlon and cross-country ski racing community: Nat Brown, Marty Hall, Heikki Ikola, Veli Niinimaa, Dr. Jim Stray-Gundersen, Algis Shalna, Max Cobb and the United States Biathlon Association, Julia Zisman and the Russian Biathlon Union, and Jukka Haltia and the Finnish Biathlon Association.

Many friends—too numerous to list in their entirety—have aided and encouraged my writing over the past decade; I would like to thank in particular Rick Johnson, Gordon King, Pelle Nymoen, Tom Sullivan and especially my wife, Betsy Shaw Frank, without whose unflagging support my work would never have reached fruition.

Grateful acknowledgment is made to Halvor Kleppen and Norsk Skieventyr of Morgedahl, Norway, for permission to reprint portions of my paper, "'*Proletarii, na konia!*' Bolshevism, Cavalry and the Sport of Skiing," which originally appeared in *Winter Sport and Outdoor Life: Papers presented at the Telemark Conference for Historians of Sports*, ed. Halvor Kleppen (Morgedal, NOR: Norsk Skieventyr, 2011); and to *Skiing Heritage, the Journal of the International Skiing History Association* for permission to use information that first appeared in my article "Cold Bullets, Hot Borders: The Shooting War That Russia Won" (June 2009).

Acknowledgment is due to the following institutions and individuals for permission to reproduce images in their possession: Estonian Sports Museum; Sports Museum of Finland; Arthur Stegen; University of Washington Libraries, Special Collections; University of Washington Libraries, Film Archives and Slavic Collection; Akademische Druck –u. Verlagsanstalt (ADEVA); Russian Biathlon Union; Swix Sport AS; MPI Home Video; and Contact Press Images, Inc.

Any errors, shortcomings or misinterpretations within the text are my own responsibility and should not reflect on the integrity and sincerity of the contributors listed above.

EVERYONE TO SKIS!

Introduction

BIATHLON, THAT UNLIKELY COMBINATION of cross-country ski-ing and rifle marksmanship, was a woefully underfinanced and neglected sport throughout North America in 1978, the first year I went to the Unit-ed States Olympic Training Center in Squaw Valley, California. Always on the lookout for skiers who could shoot, the National Team had extended invitations for its annual pre-season camp even to struggling neophytes like me. There, in the company of America's top competitors, I soon re-alized how much biathletes from the Soviet Union, with their fistfuls of medals, represented the sport's ultimate benchmark. "They put their pants on just like you do, one leg at a time," our coaches would tell us, hoping to boost our confidence as world-class competitions approached. I came to find out, however, that the coaches were wrong: those Soviet trousers had a different fit altogether.

No country pursued biathlon more resolutely than the Soviet Union, and no other nation garnered greater success at international venues. From the introduction of modern biathlon in 1958 to the USSR's demise in 1991, athletes representing the Soviet Union won almost half of all pos-sible medals awarded in world championship and Olympic competition. The closest rival was Norway, whose national teams gathered a distant 29 percent over the same period of time.[1] Biathletes of the USSR were so dominant that their victory was often a foregone conclusion at these major events. Yet more than sheer technical skill created Soviet superiority in bi-athlon. The sport embodied the Soviet Union's culture, educational system and historical experience and provided the perfect ideological platform to promote the state's socialist viewpoint and military might. Biathlon, in short, became much more than simply winning Olympic medals.

How the Soviet government interpreted the sport of skiing as a cultural, ideological, political and social tool over seventy years is my primary focus. I attempt to answer why success in cross-country ski racing and biathlon at the international level was so crucial to overall Soviet sport policy. Although biathlon represented only a sliver of the sporting world in the latter half of the twentieth century, its inherent characteristics, which required stamina and precision in a quasi-military setting, dovetailed with important ideological, historical and even artistic concepts promoted by the government. And though only a miniscule piece of the Soviet project, biathlon looms large in the history of global sport: it is impossible to write about biathlon, currently the most popular winter spectator sport in Europe, without considering the significant influence of the USSR. In the beginning, the Soviet Union owned biathlon, and so the stories of both the state and the event are inseparable.

To comprehend the Soviet Union's domination of this sport and why it was such an important element of the country's athletic image requires first an understanding of how modern skiing developed in Europe from the end of the nineteenth century through the late 1980s. In Russia, as in other European polities in the twentieth century, sporting events became outlets for an emotional expression of nationalism just as opera and the stage had been during the nineteenth. In the case of skiing, this dramaturgy incorporated the essential elements of virtuousness, heroism and an imagined link to a mythological past. Beyond this, four crucial factors coalesced in the latter half of the nineteenth century to further the development of skiing: the increasing need for reliable reconnaissance during large-scale military campaigns; the rise of European nationalism; for northern countries, nationalism's relationship to polar exploration; and the growth of sport as a leisure activity. At the turn of the century, all of these notions came together in the avatar of Norwegian polar explorer and scientist Dr. Fridtjof Nansen, who single-handedly propelled skiing from regional obscurity into a global phenomenon. His exploits, along with those of his fellow countryman and protégé Roald Amundsen, transformed skiing in Russia from a rural pastime associated with peasants and indigenous tribes into a nationalist trait—the latter augmented by a fascination with Arctic exploration, a concern for homeland defense, a yearning for adventure and, finally, a preoccupation with scientific inquiry and socialist ideology. This turn-of-the-century Russian nationalism wove its way into Stalinist enthusiasm for the Arctic and then, after World War II, became part of the politicized spectacle of international competition in long-distance ski racing and biathlon. Soviet athletes excelled in both disciplines and their success produced a sense of national pride for many of their compatriots while evoking imagery associated with the Russian North, the Great Patriotic War and the Soviet hero.

Cross-country skiing and biathlon were prime examples of socialist realist sport, that is, an idealized portrayal of athletic reality useful in developing socialist consciousness within the Soviet state. Skiing could be accomplished anywhere there was snow, and as a means of transportation it
had practical application in building the socialist project. In addition, tens
of millions of Soviet citizens skied every winter. Thus ski racing developed
as a spectator sport, with huge numbers of enthusiasts attending major
ski competitions as much to cheer on their favorite skiers as to observe
the subtleties of technique for their own edification. This interest among
the citizenry highlighted one of the most significant contradictions in the
Soviet sport system, pitting the proletarian concept of mass participation
(*massovost'*) in sport and physical culture for the benefit of the collective
against the need for athletes with mastery (*masterstvo*) who could compete
at the international level and gain worldwide prestige for communism.

Within this context, I have combined the arguments of several other
Soviet historians to bolster the notion that skiing was the quintessential example of socialist realist sport. Amir Weiner contends that ritual
representations of the Great Patriotic War were the revolutionary prism
through which Party leaders viewed civilian life in the decades following
World War II. The government transformed the Great Patriotic War into a
myth that defined the Soviet Union to an even greater extent than had any
other event in the canon of Soviet "great moments." The war superseded
foundation myths such as the Bolshevik Revolution and the Civil War,
which had become distant and irrelevant to a new generation of socialists.[2] In a similar vein, Mike O'Mahoney suggests that Soviet participation
in activities such as mountaineering and skiing reflected "an extension of
the stoical endurance of the Soviet population during the war," showing
the world that the capacity to persevere in the most extreme of sporting
environments was a fundamental "national" characteristic.[3]

James Riordan writes that the Soviet regime capitalized on the Second
World War's emotional impact by staging sports festivals—and naming
them after distinguished athletes who died in combat—in order to tap into
citizens' yearning for a nostalgic and mythologized past. These ritual commemorations kept the memory of the war alive in people's minds.[4] As a
result, in the post-war years the myriad cross-country ski racing events—
which at times extended from late November through early April all across
the Soviet Union—evoked the Armed Forces, the Great Patriotic War and
national defense. After the USSR joined the international sporting community in the 1950s, the government transferred these notions wholesale

to a worldwide stage at major ski competitions and the Winter Olympic Games. Barbara Keys posits that modern Western sport became "Sovietized" during this period while at the same time managing to retain a core set of values resistant to ideological transformation.[5] This phenomenon of Sovietization was especially pervasive in the sports of cross-country skiing and biathlon, where the events became a forum for socialist versus capitalist systems, a surrogate battleground, so to speak, between Cold War rivals. Reciprocal animosity across the ideological divide influenced the process by which nations came to be imagined by casting rivals on the ski track as mutual high-stakes antagonists, especially during the team relays.

The late 1940s and 1950s marked the high point of Soviet success at such international ski competitions, yet even as the women continued to dominate their events throughout the subsequent two decades, the men's teams foundered. In the male-dominated Cold War environment pride of place went to the men's competitions, especially the 30- and 50-kilometer races and the 4 x 10-kilometer relay; therefore, the continued failure of the men's ski teams to win medals at international races was particularly vexatious to the official mythmakers of the USSR. However, biathlon in the 1960s offered a new venue for Cold War competition, certainly more male-oriented and militaristic than any previous ski event and arguably more so than any other contest on the Olympic card, summer or winter. In this alternative take on ski competition, the Soviet Union was the world's predominant force: from 1958 through 1977, the top five most successful international biathletes were Soviet; and out of the top twenty-five, fully half were from the USSR. Moreover, at a still-unparalleled six consecutive Olympics, the Soviet Union never lost the 4 x 7.5-kilometer biathlon relay.

In order to delineate these broad topics, I employ a chronological and narrative approach with occasional forays into thematic discussions and biographical sketches. The first four chapters of this book provide the cultural and historical background for Soviet interest in ski racing after World War II. Chapter One introduces the reader to skiing in Russia prior to the Revolution of 1917. Beginning with archaeological evidence that points to Russia as the very source of the concept of skiing, this chapter surveys the sport's deep history across the northern reaches of the Eurasian landmass. The development of skiing was integral to people living in Scandinavian as well as Russian lands, and therefore connections between these two regions have existed for centuries. Many of these shared experiences and interests—warfare, polar exploration, winter sport—were crucial to the Russian and Soviet perception of skiing. I give an account in this chapter of

Fridtjof Nansen's impact both in Russia and abroad. Especially important is Nansen's own opinion that skiing spread from somewhere deep within Russian territory to the rest of the world. This notion fostered the belief in Russia that the sport embodied nationalist traits integral to the Russian character.

Chapter Two discusses the relationship of skiing to cavalry up to and including World War I and its development as an augmentation to military operations during the Russian Civil War. The limited effectiveness of cavalry in winter—as experienced by both sides during the Franco-Prussian War of 1870–1871—indicated that perhaps skis could substitute for horses when snow covered the ground. Belligerents on all sides of the Russian Civil War put this theory into practice as squadrons of ski troops ranged across the vast wintry expanse of Siberia. But it was Lev Trotsky who exploited the intersection of Marxist ideology and the widening gap between Alpine and Nordic branches of ski sport—the one associated with the moneyed leisure class, the other with the proletariat—as a means for excising bourgeois elements from the ranks of the Bolshevik Red Cavalry. This chapter also discusses the role of the Soviet hero whose antecedents stemmed from Bolshevik experiences during and immediately after the Civil War. One of these heroes, Toivo Antikainen, engaged in a long-distance ski trek to attack anti-communist forces during the Karelian Uprising of 1922. The Soviet regime referenced his derring-do and expertise as a skier during World War II and its aftermath. In addition, I analyze several types of races with important socialist connotations appropriated and developed by the Soviets: long-distance, or "marathon" skiing; converging races; relay races; and military patrol competitions. With an eye toward future conflicts undertaken in winter conditions, the Bolsheviks and then the Soviets incorporated these events into the athletic fabric of socialist *fizkul'tura* (physical culture).

Chapter Three analyzes skiing during Stalin's reign prior to the Winter War of 1939–1940. Of particular importance was the regime's conflation of the Stakhanovite labor movement with long-distance, multi-day ski trekking. Ski teams traversing extraordinary distances at a tremendous pace in Siberia's inhospitable climate combined a number of Soviet tropes into socialist-realist set-pieces: collectivism, concern for national defense, and sport in service to the state. Just as crucial to the Soviet Union between the wars were two programs that developed side by side during the 1930s. The first was *Gotov k trudu i oborone* (GTO), the Ready for Labor and Defense program of mass sport instruction. Among the ten mandatory test categories were cross-country skiing (or its equivalent in regions far from snow) and rifle marksmanship. The second was the Single All-Union Sports Classification System, whose intention was to motivate the best athletes to reach set standards for their particular sport. Both were designed to promote the simultaneous goals of mass participation and mastery. This chapter also considers how the development of sport in the Soviet Union paralleled that in the fascist states and the odd mix of nations on either end of the ideological spectrum participating in international ski racing prior to the outbreak of the Second World War.

Chapter Four concerns the period encompassed by World War II. The purpose of this chapter is not to recount troop movements and battle plans but, rather, to analyze the transformation of the Soviet skier into an icon of national defense just before the Great Patriotic War and during the counteroffensive against Nazi Germany in the winter of 1941–1942. In response to the success of Finnish ski troops in thwarting the Red Army during the Winter War, the Soviet Union instituted a massive ski mobilization effort that flourished between October 1940 and winter maneuvers during Operation Barbarossa the following year. This campaign to put the Soviet citizenry on skis occupied the concerted efforts of the military, the government, the educational system, industry, Communist Party organizations and the press, in conjunction with the endeavors of journalists, poets, musicians, writers, artists, filmmakers and athletes. The cumulative results had an enormous effect on the Soviet military and the development of winter sports in the Cold War era.

Chapter Five covers the immediate post-war years up to 1958, an era during which the Cold War blossomed as the Soviet Union returned to international sport competition. The Great Patriotic War decimated the USSR, and in the aftermath, ritual representations of the country's sacrifice to defeat Nazi Germany became part of the fabric of post-war Soviet life. Skiing evolved into an all-encompassing metaphor, combining patriotism with communist ideology and historical significance that harked back to the Civil War. New to the mix was the association with the suffering and endurance of the battle-hardened Soviet population during the Second World War. The stature of skiing and, in particular, cross-country racing grew as the Soviet Union adopted the sport to portray itself both domestically and internationally. The advent of biathlon in the late 1950s provided an alternative—and very Soviet—type of sport that manifested many of the important elements of this portrayal. At the end of this chapter, I detail the creation of modern biathlon and its initial development in the Soviet Union, tracing the early careers of three important figures from the first generation of world-class Soviet athletes: Dmitrii Sokolov, Valentin Pshenitsyn and Vladimir Melanin.

The next two chapters cover the period between the Second World Biathlon Championship in Courmayeur, Italy, in 1959 and the Seventh Biathlon World Championships at Garmisch-Partenkirchen, West Germany, in 1966. During this era, biathlon grew considerably—at Garmisch-Partenkirchen there were two world championship events contested for the very first time—and the skiers of the Soviet Union established themselves as the world's preeminent practitioners of the sport. Chapter Six introduces another influential Soviet biathlete, Aleksandr Privalov, destined to have a decades-long career as a major mover in the biathlon program of the Soviet Union. It also elaborates upon the conflation of the Cold War and sport, particularly at the Squaw Valley Olympic Games of 1960 and the 1962 World Ski Championships held in Chamonix, France, and Zakopane, Poland. The political turmoil that ensued at these two events foreshadowed the tone, tenor and direction of world championship and Olympic events for decades to come. In addition, experiences at these competitions were instrumental in the development of the Soviet ski and biathlon programs and their export to other Eastern Bloc nations. Integral to this growth behind the Iron Curtain was the significance of cross-country ski racing as a spectator sport, especially in the Soviet Union.

Chapter Seven follows the first generation of Soviet biathletes through a triumphant show of force at the 1964 Innsbruck Winter Olympics and a subsequent decline by the following year as changes to the rules of the sport favored faster and younger skiers. This chapter opens with a brief biography of Finland's Veikko Hakulinen, one of the most successful international cross-country ski racers of his era. He was known as "the great friend of Soviet skiers" in the USSR, even though his mediocre attempts at biathlon overshadowed those of Russia's Melanin and Privalov in the world press. I also include an interesting aside linking two of the Soviet Union's most successful high-profile endeavors—cross-country ski racing and space exploration.

Chapter Eight focuses on Aleksandr Tikhonov, one of the Soviet Union's greatest athletes. Between 1967 and 1980, Tikhonov reigned supreme in biathlon, accumulating eleven gold, five silver and two bronze medals at ten world championships and one silver and four gold medals at four Olympics. He also won the championship of the Soviet Union in biathlon nineteen times. With a larger-than-life personality, Tikhonov altered the world's perception of biathlon during the zenith of the USSR's domination of the sport. Based on the voluminous body of books and newspaper and magazine articles about Tikhonov, as well as interviews with former competitors who knew him well, I propose that Tikhonov was a high-ranking KGB agent who nonetheless garnered admiration on both sides of the Iron Curtain and extended goodwill and fellowship to the West—when it suited him—in this highly charged sport.

Chapter Nine discusses the significance of the 1974 World Biathlon Championships, which took place in Minsk, the first time that an international ski event of this magnitude had ever been held on Soviet soil. Biathletes from Finland led by Juhani Suutarinen spoiled what had been predicted as a Soviet tour de force featuring Aleksandr Tikhonov. Nevertheless, a rabid, partisan crowd whose numbers dwarfed those of any previous athletic event in the USSR helped the Soviet relay team achieve victory on the final day. I discuss the significance of sport as spectacle in addition to the revolutionary changes afoot in ski racing during this watershed year: synthetic skis; the rise of athletes from East Germany; modernized biathlon facilities; and the enormous crowds drawn to the excitement of biathlon as it evolved, incorporating breakable targets from the relay into a new 10-kilometer biathlon sprint format.

Chapter Ten details the controversy over drugs and blood doping in cross-country skiing that roiled the 1988 Calgary Winter Olympics. This international incident centered on the skiers of the Soviet Union and instigated the development of much stricter controls and testing for illegal substances and procedures that has become the hallmark of international competitions during the early decades of the twenty-first century. As background to this debacle, I discuss the development of the East German sports program, which outpaced that of the Soviet Union by the end of the 1970s. This section includes an analysis of the evolution of steroids, blood doping and erythropoietin (EPO), as well as the rise of commercialism fostered by the Olympics during the 1980s.

Note on Sources

Understanding the significance of skiing in Russia and how biathlon developed in the Soviet Union requires a grasp of cultural, social and historical trends spanning more than a century. As an introduction to these topics, my book is by necessity a vast survey. Certainly a trove of rich archival data awaits future historians interested in augmenting— and correcting—what I have written; however, I did not consider such detailed sources critical to my thesis. Rather, I have chosen to rely on the abundant newspapers, journals, books and pamphlets produced for the voracious reading public in Russia. In addition to mainstream publications such as *Ogonek, Pravda, Izvestiia* and *Trud*, I have found those of the Red Army, especially *K novoi armii, Krasnyi sport* and *Krasnaia zvezda* especially useful. In the case of sport, newspapers and magazines are compelling because they reflect discourse that intersects the interests of the reading public and the agenda of the regime. The articles in Red Army publications are crucial to the study of skiing in Russia because from the very inception of the socialist experiment, physical development and athletics were combined with military training—and cross-country skiing was the premier example of a sport with significance to the Armed Forces. Up until the 1950s, sport in general, and ski racing in particular, was of less interest to the organs of the Communist Party. The Red Army press—whose readership numbered in the millions—provided the most extensive coverage of skiing until the regime decided that sport had political as well as military importance internationally. The subsequent iteration of the Red Army's *Krasnyi sport* was *Sovetskii sport*, published from 1946 on. It was an extremely popular daily publication with circulation reaching over five million by the 1980s. It featured matter-of-fact reporting on athletic events and as a result earned a unique reputation for honesty and journalistic professionalism. In this regard, *Sovetskii sport* was the closest facsimile to Western sport journalism behind the Iron Curtain.[6]

Historical analysis depends upon primary sources, which are always subject to inherent biases and presumptions grounded in the agenda and experience of the various authors. This situation is magnified in the case of the Soviet Union because the government controlled publication, regulating how published material should reflect socialist norms and to whom a public voice should be allowed. Throughout this book I provide points of view expressed not only by individuals in the Eastern Bloc but also by those in the West and I caution the reader to consider all of them with a critical eye. I have attempted to throw in a cautionary word or two when quoting from Soviet sources, although I do allow the discourse to proceed unfiltered by my comments at times; stating the obvious—for example, the Soviet propensity toward exaggeration for propaganda purposes—becomes tedious reading after awhile. However, simply because an author or interviewee happened to be Soviet does not necessarily mean that he or she distorted the truth; nor does it necessarily follow that his or her counterpart in the West provided a more trustworthy account. Hopefully, the historical and political sketches I have included in each chapter will provide context for evaluating the reliability of each on a case-by-case basis.

Translations of source materials are mine, unless otherwise indicated.

ONE

Long Boards in the Long Nineteenth Century

LESS THAN A YEAR BEFORE the Bolsheviks seized power in Petrograd, Vladimir Lenin offered this revolutionary advice to his mistress and fellow conspirator, the French socialist-feminist Inessa Armand: "Do you ski? Do it without fail! Learn how and set off for the mountains—you must. In the mountains winter is wonderful! It's sheer delight, and it smells like Russia."[1]

It is no surprise that Lenin was enthusiastic about skiing. His short life span of fifty-four years coincided with that of Norwegian scientist and explorer Fridtjof Nansen, widely acknowledged for introducing modern skiing to the world. Lenin, who was born in 1870, was a teenager when Nansen completed his groundbreaking ski traverse of Greenland in 1888, and a young man when the Norwegian adventurer returned from the Arctic after an epic three-year exploratory voyage in 1896. Even Russia's iconic revolutionary was not immune to "Nansen-mania," a pan-European enthusiasm that swept the continent at the turn of the century and remained well into the inter-war period. That the architect of the Soviet project fused skiing with the essence of his homeland suggests the importance of this new sport to Russia during the nationalistic frenzy of late nineteenth-century Europe. His words foreshadow as well how Soviets would transform a sport that had essentially been a peasant pastime prior to Nansen's landmark trek into an embodiment of the national character, finding in skiing an anti-bourgeois mixture of militarism, Arctic heroism, scientific inquiry and socialist ideology.

Skiing developed as a modern sport between 1789 and 1914, a period Eric Hobsbawm has termed "the long nineteenth century." Historian Norman Davies defines this epoch in terms of power: technical, economic, cultural and intercontinental.[2] To gain control of these power matrices, European nations engaged in intense rivalries aggravated by diplomatic maneuvering, military development and colonial competition from the mid-1800s to the outbreak of World War I. Just as critical was the power of ideology, whose manifestations helped shape nineteenth-century Europe's geopolitical landscape. Arguably the most virulent and potent of these doctrines was nationalism, a term used to convey the idea that the optimal social system is one that divides people into nationalities having cultural and political autonomy or, preferably, independence.[3] From the very first stirrings of the romantic movement at the threshold of the nineteenth century to Franz Ferdinand's assassination at the hands of a Serbian nationalist in 1914, nationalism swept over Europe as activists strove to inculcate varying degrees of national consciousness among diverse groups across the continent. Language and culture, not citizenship in a particular state, became the determining factors of an individual's nationality.[4]

In order to establish the legitimacy of a particular nationality, nationalist intellectuals scoured history to furnish proof of a nation's separate and unique identity. Prehistoric artifacts and medieval sources were given especial credence because they established long-standing claims to nationhood. Peasant folklore was also highly valued as a living connection that joined the modern nation with its most ancient cultural roots. Interest in philology, medieval history, national literature and ethnology blossomed in the nineteenth century as ardent nationalists ransacked these sources for the glorification of their own people's achievements and cultural superiority. Wagnerian opera and the collected fairy tales of the Brothers Grimm in the German states, Serbo-Croatian studies in the Balkans and the Kalevala in Finland are just a few examples of this trend: for Norwegians, skiing was the primary cultural signifier conflating peasant roots joined to a mythical past with connotations of nationhood.

Skiing: An Ancient Solution to Winter's Problems

In regions close to the Arctic Circle or located at high elevation, skiing was often a tool of survival for people with no other means of winter transportation. Attempts to pinpoint the precise location where skiing began have inspired fierce and competing claims: a blatantly nationalist point of view has infused the study of early ski artifacts, especially among the ethnological scientists of the late nineteenth and early twentieth centuries. Although intensive lobbying by Sweden and especially Norway in the twentieth century has conveyed the notion that skiing began in Scandinavia, Russia certainly could make a similar claim. Suffice it to say that sporadic archaeological finds indicate that skiing developed all across the northern reaches of the Eurasian landmass. The most compelling argument locates the source of skiing in the Altai region, from which the concept of a long plank used for snow travel spread to the north and west via the indigenous tribes of Siberia.[5] The archaeological record, whether tracing this movement or perhaps memorializing the development of skiing in unrelated pockets, points to a prehistoric response to the exigencies of winter survival. At a site 1,300 miles east of the Urals, a pictograph known as Sunduk IV depicts two skiers armed with bows, broadly dated to a period between the third century B.C.E. and the fourth century C.E. This location is only 400 miles from the Altai Mountains, a fact that fires the imaginations of proponents of the Altai source theory. Bolstering this notion are several recent discoveries by Chinese researchers in the Altai region of Paleolithic rock paintings, pictographs and petroglyphs that appear to represent skiers or snowshoers. Other early evidence from areas far removed from Altai includes Neolithic cave art discovered at Zalavruga near the White Sea as well as an Abashevo Bronze Age shard unearthed near Voronezh, both of which illustrate hunters on skis; and a dagger discovered in excavations near Omsk with a blade engraved with a small portrayal of a skier. More intriguing than these images are the remnants of actual skis preserved in bogs that have been discovered in locations from Sweden to Mongolia. There are around 250 extant examples of such skis, which have been carbon-dated and analyzed for pollen and dendrochronological evidence. By these reckonings, a partial ski extracted from bogs north of Syktyvkar at the Vis excavations is more than eight thousand years old, perhaps the oldest in the world.[6]

Through the natural evolution of territorial defense in high latitudes, northern nations fostered the practice of skiing for military purposes. The first documented reference to combat carried out on skis dates from the end of the twelfth century. In his *Gesta Danorum*, the Danish historian Saxo Grammaticus describes ferocious tribes armed with bow and arrow and spears inhabiting regions near the Arctic Circle and travelling by ski. Grammaticus notes that the formidable forces of Danish king Ragnar Lodbrok nearly perished at the hands of fierce skiing Finns in the kingdom of Permland or Finnmark. Other sources indicate that on 6 March 1200, Norwegian king Sverre Sigurdsson fielded a company of ski troops equipped with bows and arrows at the Battle of Oslo.[7]

Anecdotal evidence gleaned from the chronicles suggests that early Russian rulers were just as keen to use skis as an efficient means of transport in support of the state. The earliest written record of skiing in Russia is a twelfth-century message from an ecclesiastical official, Metropolitan Nikifor, to Vladimir Monomakh, Grand Prince of Kievan Rus'. In 1444, when the roads from Moscow to Riazan were choked with snowdrifts, Grand Duke Vasilii II (the Blind) organized a ski raid to drive Mustafa, tsarevich of the Golden Horde, out of the region. Vasilii's son, the Grand Prince of Moscow Ivan III (the Great), equipped ski units under the command of Fedor Kurbskii with orders to wrest the regions of northwest Siberia between the Urals and the River Ob from the Tatars in 1479. His son, Prince Semen Fedorovich Kurbskii, led ski troops during the conquest of the Southern Lands in 1499. Similarly, in 1535 boyars of the Shuiskii family, acting as regents for Ivan IV, sent soldiers equipped with skis into Latvia.[8]

Descriptions of skiing in early modern Russia began to filter westward during the sixteenth century. Two sources familiar to historians of early modern Europe are the works of Freiherr Sigismund von Herberstein and Alexander Gwagnin, composed for Western European audiences during the mid-1500s. Herberstein, emissary to Moscow on behalf of the Holy Roman Empire, offered readers a glimpse of a strange steppe culture beyond Poland's borders, accompanied by a surreal illustration of skiers by Hans Sebald Lautensack, in his 1557 edition of *Commentaries on Muscovite Matters*.[9] The 1578 *Description of all Muscovite Regions* by the Polish chronicler Gwagnin used prose similar to Herberstein's to provide details of Loppia, the northernmost part of the Muscovite state.[10] Both authors adapted derivatives of an ancient Russian word, *rta*, to augment descriptive terminology for skis lacking in Latin and other Western European languages; thus Herberstein's *auf Artachn* and Gwagnin's compressed *narta*, the latter having entered Polish as "ski" and Russian as "sled."[11]

In subsequent centuries, the militarization of skiing in Western Europe increased dramatically, due in no small part to the efforts of King Gustav Vasa (1496–1560). Vasa's organizational skills led to the liberation of Sweden from the Union of Kalmar and transformed the country into a European power. He formed the first military units in Scandinavia in 1555, boasting in a letter that his mobile troops could ski 185 kilometers in a single day. Both Sweden and Russia had been vying for hegemony in the north since the Middle Ages as their armies ranged back and forth across the traditional territory of Finland. One of Vasa's forces, comprised of five hundred Swedish and Finnish skiers, defeated a far superior Russian army of five thousand on the Karelian Isthmus at Joutselka in 1555. During the Northern Seven Years' War of 1563–1570, Sweden employed Finnish ski troops under the command of Claes Fleming to invade the province of In-gria, where St. Petersburg stands today. As the Russians swept back across the Karelian Isthmus in 1590, a detachment of six hundred Finnish farm-ers on skis thwarted a potential invasion. During the Time of Troubles, a period separating the death of the last tsar of the Riurik Dynasty in 1598 from the ascension of the first Romanov in 1613, Russian commander Mikhail Skopin-Shuiskii brought five divisions of skiers to Moscow. There, they took the field against the cavalry of the Polish-Lithuanian Common-wealth at the siege of Troitse-Sergieva Lavra, one of the watershed events of the Polish-Muscovite War of 1605–1618.[12]

The seventeenth century was a pivotal period in the expansion of the Rus-sian Empire into Siberia, culminating with the establishment of a perma-nent Pacific port at Okhotsk in 1649. The legendary Cossack leader Ermak Timofeevich led the first Russian expeditionary forces deep into Siberia in the late sixteenth century, deploying skiers against Kuchum Khan of Sibir. Of the numerous service-class people and entrepreneurial contract workers who came after Ermak to explore the region's vast tracts, many used skis in their journeys, most significantly Semen Dezhnev, during his travels from the Kolyma River on the Arctic Ocean to the Anadyr River on the Pacific in 1648, and Erofei Pavlovich Khabarov, in his trek on the Amur from 1649 to 1653. Following in their footsteps during the late eighteenth century were a number of explorers, including Gavriil Sarychev, who collaborated with English Royal Navy officer Joseph Billings to search for the Northwest Pas-sage. Under the patronage of Tsarina Catherine II (also known as Catherine the Great), the Billings-Sarychev Expedition mapped eastern Siberia, the west coast of Alaska and the Aleutian Islands. Sarychev may have been the first person to ski in North America, although his attempt was inauspicious: "From our inexperience in this mode of travelling, we often sprained our [ankles], got entangled in shrubs, or fell into heaps of snow."[13]

The trend toward incorporating skis into the military continued with the advent of firearms during the modern period. Ski divisions armed with rifles played an important role during and after the Great Northern War of 1700–1721, a fact not lost on Russia's tsar, Peter I (the Great). As part of the reorganization of the Russian army, Peter incorporated special reconnais-sance units trained in ski travel, known as *Okhotniki*, or Hunters, consist-ing of four specially selected men from each company of a regiment. To one Swedish observer, the Okhotniki were part of an army with "no order in waging war." He mentions especially that the infantry was "used in a very undisciplined fashion [including] those that run over the snow on

[skis]." It is interesting to note that the first organized ski races took place around this time among guards on the Swedish border in 1767. These soldiers were, in essence, the forerunners of modern winter biathletes, because each race participant carried a rifle and shot at targets.[14]

Catherine II continued the nurturing of ski specialists in her armies. During the Pugachev Rebellion of 1774, ski troops in the army of Commander Ivan Mikhel'son battled similarly equipped rebel protagonists in the vicinity of Perevolotskoe and Chesnokovka at the base of the Urals. Colonel Aleksandr Bibikov, a veteran of the Seven Years' War of 1756–1763 who would die of cholera in the spring of 1774, dispatched his *chasseurs* on skis there to secure "all the advantageous highpoints."[15] Twenty-five years later, Field Marshal Aleksandr Suvorov employed skiers to keep his army supplied with materiel while traversing the Alps to attack Napoleon in Italy. Like Bibikov, Suvorov was a veteran of the Seven Years' War, having cut his teeth in the tsar's army as a teenaged private in Finland, a region where skiers had easily outdistanced their foe on foot. Over this same terrain and as part of the same Napoleonic conflict, Sweden and Russia again maneuvered ski troops against one another during the course of the Finnish War of 1808–1809. The commander-in-chief of the tsar's imperial army, Count Friedrich Wilhelm von Buxhoevden, incorporated skiers as advanced guards and as skirmishers on the flanks of massed cavalry during Russia's battle to wrest territory from Sweden and establish the autonomous Grand Duchy of Finland. A particularly harsh April witnessed two battles during which skiers helped carry the day. On the sixteenth of that month, General Iakov Kul'nev used quick-moving ski-skirmishers to rout the Swedish army at the Battle of Pyhäjoki while enduring temperatures of thirty below zero Celsius. The Swedes returned the favor eleven days later at the Battle of Revolax. A Swedish detachment of 150 skiers attacked the advance guard of Major General Mikhail Bulatov at three o'clock in the morning, forcing the retreat of the Russian forces and the capture of five officers, 450 troops and Bulatov himself. Sweden's Count Johan August Sandels kept the pressure on, sending ski troops to attack the rear and right flank of General Obukhov in early May near Pulkkila.[16]

With the Treaty of Paris in 1814, skiing gradually fell out of use in the military. By 1826, ski troops were no longer a part of the army in either Sweden or Norway. However, patriotic bands of Norwegians organized in 1831 and launched a campaign to revive the sport as a means of national self-defense. These efforts led to a revitalization of ski exercises in the Norwegian army to such an extent that, in 1863, Lieutenant-Colonel Oscar Wergeland published a modern ski drill manual followed a year later by a history and treatise on the use of military skiing. New developments in technique and equipment during the 1860s revived skiing in towns throughout Norway and provided the groundwork for a national sports identity known as *idraet*. This point of view evolved in reaction to foreign influences in international sports. Especially loathsome to Norwegians were the purported negative effects of the "sport-for-sport's-sake" attitude of members of the British upper class, who considered sport the domain of amateurs or simply a pleasant pastime. The Norwegian idea of sport as idraet, on the other hand, was much more serious and practical because it incorporated the concept of service to homeland defense through the development of better soldiers and the improvement of public health.[17]

As the Norwegian revival of skiing spread to other parts of Europe, the imperial Russian army was among the first to initiate concentrated training of ski troops as early as 1886. The army put special focus on the Vyborg Infantry and the Vilmanstrand 86th Regiments of the Karelian region near St. Petersburg, and the 40th Division and the Finnish Sharpshooters' Battalions. Extended ski tours, winter war games and scouting parties comprised the regimen for these soldiers. For example, in the winter of 1890–1891, a Lieutenant Wallenius covered 860 kilometers while leading a group from the Kuopio Battalion through Karelia over a period of twenty-nine days. In 1891, Okhotniki from twenty infantry divisions in the military district of Kazan carried out a ski excursion covering some 700 kilometers in ten days. War games held in the St. Petersburg military district during the winter of 1892–1893 proved that mounted troops and artillery divisions were easily outmaneuvered by ski detachments, resulting in mandatory ski training for the entire army, including the elite cavalry.[18] This led to the publication in 1893 of the Circular of the General Staff No. 193, which stated: "It is necessary to turn special attention to exercises in the use of skis extending its pursuit not only among the Okhotniki but as much as possible also among the other lower ranks of the unit."[19] By 1894, the success of the Russian army's integration of skiing into modern military operations was reflected as well in Germany and the Austro-Hungarian Empire with the adaptation of ski exercises and winter war games into the regimen of each nation's troops.

Polar Exploration and the Great Game

The European fascination with polar exploration coincided with this revitalization of skiing in the military during the last two decades of the nineteenth century. It proved to be a unique conflation of sport with militant notions of nationalism, heroism and bravery against the forces of nature, turning expeditions into arenas of relentless competition. On the world stage, national prestige hinged on the attainment of these last unknown places and imbued theoretical points on a map with something much more significant than simply another geographical discovery. The nationalism inherent in polar exploration, infused as it was with militaristic overtones, had a profound effect on the development of skiing in Russia at the turn of the century.

Great Britain was preeminent among those nations exploring high latitudes during the nineteenth century. The Royal Admiralty's decision to support polar exploration by the Royal Navy after Waterloo kindled national interest in the Arctic and Antarctic regions. By the latter half of the century, the Royal Navy took charge of all high-latitude exploration, resulting in expeditions that were increasingly expensive, bound by unwieldy rules and regulations and remarkably devoid of cold-weather savvy. Few other countries could afford to mount such cumbersome campaigns, especially the financially strapped Russian Empire. Enter Norway—to astonish the world with its school of polar exploration that would supplant Great Britain and dominate the field from 1888 through 1911. The heart of the Norwegian approach was the application of skis in conjunction with dogsleds to polar travel, a result of skiing's development as a modern sport in Norway. This method stood in marked contrast to the Royal Navy's predilection for "No ski, no dogs," which doomed British expeditions to hard slogging on foot and the man-hauling of sledges, with sometimes fatal consequences. Fridtjof Nansen's ski traverse of Greenland in 1888 propelled Europe into a frenzy of "Nansen mania," which only intensified with his return in 1896 from a three-year attempt to reach the North Pole by ski. His exploits single-handedly brought skiing to the attention of the outside world and launched it as a universal sport.[20]

Nansen was very much a product of the Norwegian ski revival of the mid-nineteenth century. Born in 1861, he grew up skiing and as a young man established his reputation in his native country as a pioneering mountain skier. An accomplished ski racer, Nansen expanded the parameters of his sport by completing two traverses across the Hardangervidda from Bergen to Christiania in 1882 and 1884 while a doctoral student of marine biology. The ability to synthesize nationalism and scientific inquiry with an athletic point of view enabled him to push the limits of skiing by undertaking the first crossing of Greenland in 1888. From 20 August to 21 September of that year, Nansen and a small band of self-sufficient skiers applied his ski touring experience to a polar environment and, in the process, revolutionized high-latitude exploration. When news of his accomplishment reached Norway, his countrymen were ecstatic. A front-page article in the Christiania newspaper *Morgenbladet* lauded Nansen for initiating a "sportsman's method" in polar exploration that had the potential for propelling Norway into the lead in the race to the North Pole, noting that the success of such an expedition would hinge on a select, small group of men inured to the difficulties of travelling over ice and snow on skis.[21] In London, the *Times* praised him as well and marveled that "such an expedition could succeed only if undertaken by experienced ski-men."[22] Nansen's ski traverse of Greenland marked the end of the era for large, expensive and ponderous expeditions that had been the style in the past; and his book *On Ski over Greenland*, a two-volume memoir of his exploits, was the stimulus that popularized skiing in Europe and made this new sport synonymous with bravery, adventure and excitement.

Nansen's remarkable tales proved the catalyst in Russia as well for renewed interest in skiing during the late nineteenth century. The notion that a small group of Norwegians using a mode of transportation with deep nationalist roots had stolen the march on Great Britain, the preeminent imperialist power of the era, was especially appealing to Russians. Defeated in the Crimean War and challenged on the sea by its nemesis, the Russian Empire had shrunk following the sale of Alaska to the United States and the abandonment of its colonies in California and Hawaii by the time of Nansen's journey. Compounding these circumstances was the steady encroachment upon areas contiguous to Russia's northern border by British polar exploration, American whaling and Norwegian fishing and sealing—activities that played the role of war among maritime nations both great and small. All of these developments were regarded as direct threats by a tsarist government preoccupied not only with the security of its borders but also with the rest of the world's perception of Russian imperial might. As a result of Russia's war with Japan in 1904–1905, claim to the Arctic reaches, especially the area between Novaia Zemlia and Novosibirskie Ostrova, gained increasing strategic value as the Imperial Navy sought shorter transit time to the Far East via the Northeast Passage.[23]

In addition, the Great Game, a determined rivalry to gain hegemony in Central Asia, kept Britain and Russia on the brink of war throughout the latter half of the nineteenth and early twentieth centuries. Together with the North and South Poles, the territories surrounding Central Asia's 8,000-meter peaks represented the last unmapped and therefore unclaimed regions on earth during the nineteenth century. The contemporary notion that these summits, especially Mt. Everest, constituted the earth's "third pole" fostered interest among adventurers striving to claim the last vestiges of unexplored territory in the heights of altitude as well as latitude. British military prognosticators, always on the alert to gain an advantage in the Great Game and aware that Russian soldiers had been training in earnest for ski maneuvers since the mid-1880s, suggested that their troops stationed in the Pamirs should have ski training in anticipation of Russian antagonists who "would not fail to take advantage of this latest innovation in the art of war."[24]

The Russian press followed the development of skiing in Scandinavia even before Nansen's Greenland expedition focused global attention on the sport. An early correspondent for St. Petersburg's weekly magazine *Niva* covered a ski competition outside Christiania (probably in Grorud) in 1871. The accompanying illustration shows skiers *en masse* descending a formidable slope, although the race was probably a combination event that tested a competitor's overall abilities on flat terrain, uphill, downhill and over jumps and obstacles.[25] In 1883, the magazine reported on another Christiania event, following with a late-December article detailing explorer Adolf Erik Nordenskiøld's plans to sponsor a long-distance ski race in northern Sweden. More than just a competition for prizes, Nordenskiøld intended that this event, held in April 1884, should demonstrate the application of skiing to polar exploration.[26] *Niva* also featured stories about Nansen prior to his departure for Greenland in 1888. However, it was Nansen's *On Ski Over Greenland*, in which he articulated the key role of Russia and Siberia in the history of skiing (indeed as the very font of the concept of skis as transportation), that enthralled the nation's reading public and altered the perception of the sport in Russia.[27]

Nansen perhaps based his theory about the Siberian source of skiing on a plethora of books written during the eighteenth and early nineteenth centuries.[28] A number of authors described indigenous tribes in Siberia who traditionally used skis for hunting and winter conveyance. Among the earliest was Stepan Krasheninnikov, who set off to explore Kamchatka and environs in 1737. In his 1755 compilation, *Descriptions of the Land of Kamchatka*, Krasheninnikov differentiates between two types of skis (*lyzhi*) used by the Kamchedal (or Itelmen). Lyzhi of the first type were made from fir wood and "similar to commonplace skis" with a length of around 1.5 meters and between twenty-two and twenty-seven centimeters in width.[29] Krasheninnikov calls the other type of ski *lapki*, or paws: however, his description further on in the book suggests that these were actually racquet-style snowshoes.[30] More accessible to northern European readers, perhaps, was Krasheninnikov's mentor Johann Georg Gmelin, a German botanist who published an account of his travels throughout Siberia, *Journey through Siberia, 1733 to 1743*, between 1751 and 1752. He describes the "lichi [lyzhi]" used by the Tungus (now Evenki) for winter travel.[31] Following them was Peter Simon Pallas, a professor of natural history at the St. Petersburg Academy of Sciences who led specimen-collecting expeditions across the reaches of the Russian Empire during the reign of Catherine the Great. His dispatches and reports were collected and published in 1776 as *Journey through Various Provinces of the Russian Empire*. Pallas mentions the use of skis by a number of indigenous tribes such as the "Ostjak" (Ostyak, now Khanty), the Koibales and the Samoyed (now Nenets). The author catalogs many words from the indigenous languages: the Nenets term for ski, for example, is notated as "Lamboi." In his account of the winter life of the Khanty, Pallas describes the "Parga or Parka," a long hooded garment that he drapes on a skier in one of his illustrations.[32]

Interest in the exploration of Siberia intensified during the first half of the nineteenth century and those who went there produced reams of documents. One of these was Adolph Erman, a German physicist with a penchant for world travel. In his journeys across Asia, he encountered the "lúija" of the Ostyak, as well as the skis of the Tungus in Siberia.[33] Russian explorer Baron Ferdinand Wrangel also took notice of the Tungus and their skis during one of his early voyages.[34] Alexander von Middendorff, a zoologist from the Baltic region of the Russian Empire, travelled extensively in eastern Siberia and published his findings in 1848 under the title *Journey in the Farthest North and East of Siberia during the Years 1843 and 1844*. He provides detailed descriptions of hunting and travel by the Tungus and the distinctive skis and poles they used. Of particular interest is the Tungus perception that European skis, perhaps similar to those used by von Middendorff himself in his travels, were "useless and clumsy as well as constructed without thought" in comparison to their own. The author concurs with this notion, declaring: "The skis of the nomadic Siberian hunter are works of art." Fearless on skis, a Tungus hunting along a ridgeline would "take off like a shot and fall to pieces in the abyss" in pursuit of game during a "lightning-fast" downhill run (an early use of the term *Schuss* in relation to skiing). Von Middendorff provides a pen-and-ink illustration of a special ski pole fitted with a crook on one end used by the Tungus "to seize hold of trees if the Schuss gets out of hand."[35] The skis of the Tungus were of interest to a number of other adventurers in the latter half of the nineteenth century as well, including Polish geographer Mikołaj Ambroży Kubalski, Richard Bush of the Russian-American Telegraph Expedition, Russian geographer Mikhail Krivoshapkin and American Methodist minister Zachariah Atwell Mudge; while the skis of the Ostiak caught the attention of German ethnographer Otto Finsch.[36] Baltic Russian zoologist and ethnographer Leopold von Schrenck studied the winter peregrinations of the Gilyak (now Nivkh) along the Amur River estuary and published his findings in *Journeys and Explorations in Amur Territory* in 1858. He provides extensive detail on native skis and associated paraphernalia with illustrations and comparisons to examples of those made by other Siberian peoples, such as the Tungus, Oltscha, Goldi and Samagírn. Notable is Schrenck's description of the ingenious use of larch wood, reindeer and elk fur, sealskin and whalebone in the manufacture of the skis.[37] Finally, in 1876, Victor Meignan of France travelled from Paris to Beijing, publishing an account of his journey the following year. Meignan describes a Votiak with bow and arrow who travels over the snow on "extremely long planks," accompanied by an illustration. This same image appears in an 1885 English translation that altered the original French text, "A Votiak in the forests of Great Russia," to "A Votiak with snow-shoes."[38]

Employing many of these sources, Nansen and a colleague developed for the first edition of his Greenland book a fold-out map that outlined the location of indigenous peoples all across Siberia. Similar to a flowchart, the map illustrated the spread of skis from deep within Russian territory to the rest of Europe. This ethnographical rendering was particularly influential in fostering the idea among Russian readers that skiing was "for the most part a Russian sport."[39] In addition, Russian authors were keen to emulate Nansen's portrayal of skiing as a national characteristic of Norway, suggesting that Russians should do the same.[40]

Pondering the possibility of attaining the North Pole after his successful traverse of Greenland, Nansen proposed an even bolder expedition based on his novel theory on the movement of currents in the Arctic Ocean. By deliberately freezing a specially constructed ship into the pack ice and drifting north over the course of two years, Nansen hoped to get close enough to 90° north latitude for making a quick foray to claim the prize. Nansen left on his voyage in the summer of 1893. Rather than man-hauling sledges as he had across the ice in Greenland, Nansen brought dogs and sleds, a recent innovation in polar travel. His practice on the ice near his ship led to the revolutionary discovery that the rate of travel for a fully laden sled pulled by dogs was the same as that of a cross-country skier.[41] With this valuable insight, Nansen began his ski tour to the North Pole on 14 March 1895. However, after three weeks of extreme cold and broken pack ice that delayed progress, it became too difficult to continue. He and his companion Hjalmar Johansen turned south, skiing 750 miles in 147 days before over-wintering on the northern edge of Franz Josef Land archipelago in a low stone hut. Finally, on 17 June 1896, the two Norwegian ski adventurers encountered English polar explorer Frederick Jackson, who sailed them home to Norway and a tumultuous hero's welcome.[42]

Interest in skiing mushroomed as a result of Nansen's miraculous return from the Arctic in 1896. From the point at which newspapers in Russia received the first telegrams from Vardø and Christiania in August, the coverage was incessant, particularly in St. Petersburg. The journalists at *Niva* had already written a number of in-depth articles about Nansen's North Pole expedition as early as 1889, speculating in one piece from the spring of 1896 that the ski adventurer had perhaps encountered a landmass and was preparing "a sportsman's dash for attaining the pole as fast as possible."[43] The daily *Journal de St. Pétersbourg*, published in French, reprinted dispatches to the newspaper *L'Indépendance Belge* from Adrien de Gerlache, a Belgian officer organizing a South Pole expedition in Christiania, which chronicled the nationalist fervor afoot in Norway in the aftermath of Nansen's return.[44] *Novoe vremia* featured Nanseniana of every variety in addition to regular daily updates on the great explorer, including lengthy essays, photographs, drawings, maps and even a reproduction of his autograph in its weekly supplement continuously from 22 August to 26 September.[45] Only ten days after his return to Norway, a Russian publishing house bought full-scale newspaper announcements offering to the reading public Nansen's biography complete with the latest details of the most recent expedition.[46] By early 1897, Nansen's *In the Land of Ice and Night*, the first in a series of biographies based on translations of Nansen's own writings, appeared, some of which went through third, fourth and, in some cases, fifth editions over the next decade.[47] Advertisements in anticipation of the publication of the first edition began in late December of

1896 and ran continually in the pages of *Novoe vremia* through the end of April of the following year.[48] A rival volume, *In the Darkness of Night and the Ice* was available for readers just a few months later.[49]

Nansen's grand tour of Russia in 1898 inspired a new round of adulation among the populace from the moment he stepped out of his railcar on 25 April to receive the Order of St. Stanislaus on the platform of St. Petersburg's train station. *Novoe vremia* breathlessly followed Nansen's every move: a private tour of the Hermitage; a gold medal, the first of its kind awarded to a foreigner, from the Imperial Russian Geographical Society; an audience with Tsar Nicholas II; a performance of *Aida* at the Mariinsky Theater. On one particularly exhausting day, Nansen and his wife, Eva, toured the Alexander III Russian Museum, visited an assortment of shops, met with Arctic specialists at the Imperial Academy of Science and dined at the restaurant *Donon*. Moscow received Nansen with enthusiasm equal to St. Petersburg's, and his tour of the country cemented his reputation.[50] Just as in the rest of Europe, Nansen's fame as a polar explorer astonishingly lasted longer than a generation; but unique to Russia was the way in which his popularity bridged the ideological divide of 1917.

The Ski Clubs of Russia

The Norwegian conceit of sport as idraet, popularized via Nansen's feats as the incorporation of service to homeland defense through the improvement of public health, found fertile ground in Russian ski clubs. The first ski clubs in Russia formed in the immediate years after publication of Nansen's Greenland book. Conventional wisdom asserts that the Moscow Club of Skiers, or MKL, organized in March 1895, was the first official ski club in Russia, although that distinction actually belongs to Frost of St. Petersburg, which celebrated its twentieth anniversary in 1913.[51] Another St. Petersburg ski club formed in December 1897, the more familiar Polar Star, which played a very active role in the growth of skiing in the country. Members built a large ski station at Iukki on the outskirts of St. Petersburg and, in subsequent years, also constructed the first jump hill in Russia there.[52]

Salutary ski opportunities abounded for the civilian populace in the form of sociable club outings and tours. Trip reports posted by the Moscow Club of Skiers in the daily newspaper *Moskovskiia vedomosti* often emphasized the wholesomeness, adventure and spiritual uplift, a form of idraet within a Russian context, found on a weekend outing: "Yes, in this storm, in this battle with nature there is a hundred times greater peace than in the struggle and storm of everyday life. This battle doesn't oppress the soul nor does it contaminate it with pessimism: rather, it ennobles a person's soul, acquiring strength for the struggle with oneself."[53] Of course, not everyone portrayed skiing with such bombast. On several occasions St. Petersburg's weekly satirical magazine *Satirikon* poked fun at the ski crowd. A cartoon from 1912 shows two skiers, one pointing off into the distance and exclaiming to his rotund companion: "Hey, partner! The lunchroom's nearby! Let's take off the skis because we need to hurry!" Another from 1910 features a man and woman skiing along the flat terrain as one muses: "I adore skiing! Especially if you could attach a seat to the back of the skis and harness horses to the front, yeah, and instead of these stupid poles—a good whip! That sport would be worth a king's ransom!!"[54]

As a natural extension of club activities, ski competitions gradually gained in popularity too. Many Russian ski historians state that the first ski race in Russia took place in St. Petersburg on 13 February 1894 over a 1/4 verst course, a distance of approximately 275 meters.[55] However, on 30 January of that year, three women and seven men had already competed in a ski race for prizes—a reindeer-skin outfit and a silver-knobbed ski staff—on the Gulf of Finland from Peterhof to Kronshtadt, a much more robust undertaking of fifteen kilometers.[56] This race pre-dates as well the 19 February 1895 first competitions organized by the Moscow Bicyclists' Club, one a 3-kilometer run through untracked snow, the other a 1-kilometer contest over a laid-out course.[57]

As the number of clubs grew toward the turn of the century, so did the desire for competition to determine the best skier from each organization, then in each city and eventually throughout the entire empire. By 1900, each infantry regiment and rifle battalion in St. Petersburg fielded large teams of skilled skiers.[58] Members of the regiments often joined in the competitions sponsored by ski clubs in St. Petersburg and Moscow, dazzling the citizen racers with their speed and technique.[59] In Moscow, the Organization of Ski Enthusiasts, or OLLS, broke away from the more stolid Moscow Club of Skiers (MKL) in the summer of 1901 to focus exclusively on ski racing, outraging conservative members of the club who preferred to promote benign ski-fellowship among the citizenry. Alarmed by the increased emphasis on competition among Moscow's skiers, MKL president S. N. Timofeev excoriated the new organization:

The main goal of [OLLS] is determining "The All-Russia Championship," "The Moscow Championship" and so on. What totally high-flown names! Such a program . . . hardly promotes the development of public sympathy for skiing and wouldn't attract many members with such measures . . . the premiership in the development of healthy winter diversions for grownups and children belongs to the MKL as Moscow's first pioneer of skiing.[60]

In the opinion of the MKL leadership, ski racing was appropriate "not so much for the determination of the speed of the run but rather for demonstrating the sport of skiing itself."[61] Particularly unacceptable was the emphasis on prizes and awards, a notion yoked to the odious vulgarity of contemporary tsarist anti-Semitism in the pages of *Moskovskiia vedomosti*: "This group of skiers presented an interesting spectacle . . . What a blend of faces, pedigrees and qualities! . . . not a single Semitic type was found among the predominantly Slavic element with faces typical of Germans, Swedes and other nations, inspired not by thirst for profit but rather by striving for nature, for its eternal and perfect beauty."[62]

Despite the predilections of the Moscow Club of Skiers, enthusiasm for ski racing grew apace in the first years of the twentieth century, reaching a crescendo of activity in 1910. That year, ten ski clubs in Moscow assembled under the aegis of the Moscow League of Ski-Runners, or MLL, and organized eighteen inter-club competitions. Soon to follow was the All-Russian Union of Skiers, or VSL, promoting inter-city competitions and a Russian "national" championship. Pavel Bychkov, a groundskeeper who worked in Sokol'niki Park, won this competition, which took place for the first time on 7 February 1910.[63] As skiing gained in popularity, ski clubs proliferated in Moscow, which boasted fourteen separate organizations by 1912, as well as in St. Petersburg, Smolensk, Tula, Ekaterinburg, Arkhangelsk and Ivanovo-Voznesensk.[64]

Ski Entrepreneurs: "A Wonderful Gift for Christmas!"[65]

Nansen's incredible exploits were a boon for the Russian ski trade. As a result of the interest in skiing generated by the traverse of Greenland in 1888, skis were readily available for purchase in the sporting-goods stores of Moscow and St. Petersburg in the early 1890s. These were limited to wide, short skis for hunting in the woods or long, narrow pointed skis.[66] However, in the wake of euphoria over Nansen's return from the Arctic in

1896, ski specialty shops began to appear that featured skis and paraphernalia imported from Finland and Norway.[67] In St. Petersburg, Gal' and
Company, B. Brenner, D. Dal'berg and E. K. Shteiner ("telephone number
3629") all vied for sales through their advertisements in the daily newspapers, maintaining a lively competition well into the 1900s.[68] In the years
leading up to World War I, V. Ort offered skis through his specialized
sporting-goods store in Kiev and, in Moscow, A. Leitner's new shop carried "genuine Finnish skis."[69]

The most enterprising purveyor of skis in Russia, however, was Konstantin Komets, who maintained a shop in St. Petersburg at 17–19 Zhdan-
ovskaia Street adjacent to Petrovskii Park from the mid-1890s to around
1913.[70] He invented and patented various ski accouterments to sell in his
store, the most famous of which were ski sails for tacking into the winds
sweeping St. Petersburg during the winter months. Fascinated by Nansen's
story of rigging tent floors on improvised masts above the sledges during his 1888 Greenland trek, Komets experimented with fabricating two
crossed bamboo poles over which he stretched a bolt of canvas. Holding
this contraption in his hands while standing on skis allowed him to capture the breeze and sail across the frozen ice on the Gulf of Finland.[71] Although Nansen had never ski-sailed as Komets envisioned it, the Russian
entrepreneur was not shy about associating his invention, as well as the
rest of his inventory, with the great Norwegian explorer: "Something new!
. . . sailing skis for running on the surface of the snow just like Dr. Nansen! . . . Received: Dr. Nansen's standard winter hats with folding earflaps
and back cover . . . New book about F. Nansen with lots of illustrations."[72]
Komets perennial best-seller was the "Dr. Nansen hat" with ear- and neck-
flaps, a constant feature of his advertising efforts well into the 1900s, in one
instance fortuitously placed just at the end of an extensive four-page article
about Nansen and his Arctic adventures that ran in an 1896 edition of the
weekly magazine *Niva*.[73]

Komets was a vociferous proponent of skiing. He authored several
books and articles on technique, the first of which appeared in the pages
of *Niva* in 1896. In his 1904 book *Skiing and Ski Sailing*, Komets opines:
"Skis give enormous scope for all manner of competition in dexterity,
quickness of the run and desperate bravery. And this sport does not demand expenses particularly, just skis, one or two poles and snow, snow,
snow."[74] As part of his efforts to promote skiing, the indefatigable Komets
instructed St. Petersburg residents in the sport. In 1899, he led ten ski-
sailing outings from St. Petersburg to Kronshtadt and oversaw practice

sessions in Petrovskii Park each Sunday.[75] He organized six ski-sailing trips for youngsters on the banks of the Niva under the auspices of the Lighthouse sport club during the winter of 1903–1904 as well as one for the Russian Organization of Tourists on the Gulf of Finland.[76] In conjunction with the Bogatyr' ski club he conducted ski and ski-sailing excursions throughout the winter of 1904–1905 and put together a two-day tour of villages along the Finnish border in the spring.[77] Judging by the wares for sale in his shop as of 1904, the ski business in St. Petersburg was booming at the turn of the century: Komets was now importing jackets from Ireland, skis from Norway and Finland, and bamboo ski-sail poles from Japan; he had his own patented ski boots, ski sails and line of ski tools; his new book and ski guide were out; and he was offering Samoyed (Nenets) reindeer mittens and clothing for both men and women.[78] Of course, the 1904–1905 war with Japan was an opportunity for Komets and other merchants to sell cold weather gear to soldiers in the capital packing up to head east. "What should an officer take on the trek to Manchuria?" advertisers asked in the pages of the newspapers, suggesting any number of rubberized sleeping bags, folding cots and cold weather gear, all available on the streets of St. Petersburg that winter.[79] With the threat of a European war looming in 1912, the "Sportsmen" sporting goods store in St. Petersburg offered "military-style skis which are used in foreign armies" to the general population in addition to its more conventional stock of gymnastics, fencing, boxing, soccer and track paraphernalia.[80]

The Sokol Movement in Russia

The rapid growth of ski clubs in Russia corresponded to the high point from 1910–1911 of international solidarity in the Sokol movement, a Slavic youth and gymnastics organization founded in Prague during the latter half of the nineteenth century. The Sokol played an important role in the development of Czech nationalism by disseminating a Czech nationalist mythology and version of history. As a result of the Austro-Prussian War of 1866, the Sokol emphasized military training and Slavic identity to distinguish it from the German Turnverein, its Western European prototype. Enthusiastically embraced by young people, both men and women, the Sokol movement had spread to Slovenia, Croatia, Serbia, Bulgaria, Poland and Russia by the late 1800s.[81] However, the amalgamation of various Czech, Croat and Serbian groups under the aegis of the Federation of

Slavic Sokols in 1908 was short-lived, illustrating the difficulty of forging unity out of the diverse Slavic world of Central and Eastern Europe.

One of the Sokol's most influential aspects was its emphasis on coordinated group activity rather than on the individual, exemplified by mass gymnastic and sporting festivals, known as *Slet*. These events provided the model for similar gatherings in the early years of the Soviet Union as a worker's alternative to the bourgeois Olympic Games. Participation at the Prague Sokol Slet grew from 1,600 in 1882 to 21,790 in 1912 with thousands more joining in as spectators.[82] In 1907, over two hundred Russian guests attended, prompting renewed interest in the Sokol when they arrived back home. The following year, Russian delegates were so enthusiastic at the 1908 Neo-Slav Congress in Prague, they donned Sokol uniforms as one exclaimed: "The Sokol is the medicine that Russia needs most!"[83]

Czech émigrés founded a few Sokols in Russia during the 1870s, but these remained isolated because the tsarist regime was concerned about the nationalist political tendencies of the movement. Cognizant that Sokol ideology was anathema to empire, the Russian government banned the organization's further expansion. However, the Czech Sokol Union raised its profile by winning gymnastic medals at the 1889 World's Fair in Paris, and Russian schools began requesting Czech trainers. By the early years of the twentieth century, Czech Slavism had acquired a new ideological direction under the guise of "Neo-Slavism," a plan for cultural cooperation through sports among smaller Slavic nations and Russia. The Sokol's fervent nationalism, fueled by the notion of Teutonic oppression of Slavic peoples, and its focus on physical fitness and military training were especially appealing to Russian teachers and military officers.[84]

After the 1905 Revolution, the government lifted restrictions on clubs and associations, including the ban on the name Sokol. The movement spread rapidly, and in 1910 a central organizing agency, the Board for the Union of Russian Sokols, came into existence, holding its first congress in Moscow in 1911 followed by a second in Kiev in 1913 with delegates from thirty-two Sokol societies. In 1913, Russian membership in the Sokol Union stood at three thousand. By the outbreak of war in 1914, the Sokol movement in Russia had grown to forty clubs manned by two hundred Czech trainers.[85] Starting in November 1910, the Russian Sokol in Moscow was involved in the promotion of skiing through the auspices of its Russian Gymnastics Association in conjunction with the Organization of Ski Enthusiasts (OLLS) and a group of ski racers based in Moscow's Sokol'niki Park, known variously as Sokol'niki Club of Skiers or Sokol'niki Club of

Ski-Runners (SKL).[86] This group played a significant role the following year in the development of a particularly Russian take on cross-country skiing: long distance multi-day ski races, inspired as much by Nansen's endeavors as by the ski competitions held among the Okhotniki regiments of the tsar's army. This genre's watershed event took place in late December 1911, over a period of twelve days when four members of SKL skied 700 kilometers from Moscow to St. Petersburg. Their trek was the template for similar events over the course of three decades, transmuting into Stalinist agit-prop set-pieces throughout the 1930s and 40s. It is interesting to note that after 1917, SKL went through a number of iterations: it became Club of the October Revolution, or KOR, in 1926, and then emerged in 1935 as Spartak, paralleling the transformation, by 1928, of OLLS into the Central House of the Red Army, or TsDKA. These two clubs, both of which started as organizations for ski enthusiasts, evolved into the two most influential sport societies in the Soviet Union.[87] In St. Petersburg, the Sokol-affiliated Bogatyr' Gymnastics Institute fielded a ski section for participation in city-wide competitions in January 1914. With a nod to romantic nationalist notions of medievalism, ancient culture and Slavic pride, this organization took its name from the Bogatyri, magical heroes out of a mythic past who served the princes of Kievan Rus'. Bogatyr' Ski Club members competed in a ski meet in February 1914, sponsored by Polar Star, now one of the largest ski clubs in Russia. The winters prior to World War I saw an increase in Sokol involvement with skiing in various locations around Russia, such as Tomsk, Voronezh and Riazan. A photograph in the Petrograd sports magazine *Gerkules* documents a Sokol group enjoying perhaps one last winter outing before the Bolshevik Revolution and the end of the Sokol movement in the midst of the Russian Civil War.[88]

Women's Skiing

Contrary to the restrictive norms governing female sporting events during the turn of the century, Russian women found ample opportunity to ski, at least in the environs of Moscow and St. Petersburg. They could thank Norway, where women had been active as skiing became a modern sport during the latter half of the nineteenth century. The dichotomy separating skating from skiing as a winter activity suitable for women provided an avenue for female emancipation via sport. Whereas skating was "lady-like," performed within the urbanized and artificial confines of an ice rink, skiing represented unfettered freedom to roam wide-open spaces. This sense of adventure associated with breaking away from societal norms imbued the sport of skiing with an aura of late nineteenth-century bohemianism.[89] Norwegian women organized their first ski club in Trondheim in 1886, followed by the conversion of the first male-only club in Christiania three years later. Although they were not allowed to compete in the Holmenkollen ski festival in Christiania, Norwegian King Oscar organized a special race event for women there in 1881. Women did compete regularly in ski races in other parts of the country, especially in the Telemark region. Outside of Scandinavia before the turn of the century, however, women's participation in skiing, especially racing, was a rarity.[90]

After Fridtjof Nansen's 1888 Greenland expedition, Russians sought to emulate the way in which Norwegians incorporated skiing into the fabric of Norway's national identity. Especially compelling was the example of Nansen's wife, Eva, who embraced the concept of idraet and became a proponent of skiing as a means of emancipating women. She was a pioneering skier who crossed the Hardangervidda with her husband in 1892. Rejecting corset, bustle and petticoat as too restrictive, Eva took to the ski trails in a pair of loose trousers covered with a long doublet and woolen skirt, a revolutionary outfit for the times.[91] Thus, an 1893 feature on winter sports in St. Petersburg's *Novoe vremia* includes a rotogravure of a female skier dressed in sporting culottes, short jacket and jaunty hat, not dissimilar to widely distributed engravings and photographs of Eva Nansen on skis, either alone or with her husband.[92] Eva remained a popular subject in Russia, admiration for her reaching a crescendo during the Nansens' tour of St. Petersburg and Moscow in 1898. As *Novoe vremia* chronicled every move the pair made during their week-long stay in St. Petersburg, the paper's noted science reporter Lazar' K. Popov (El'pe) described Eva as "a brave sportswoman."[93] The weekly magazine *Niva*, no less glowing in its praise, designated her "an example of female-heroism."[94]

Ski clubs in pre-revolutionary Russia promoted special events for women that ranged from introductory walkabouts to ski races. In fact, three women participated in the earliest recorded ski race in St. Petersburg in 1894, only three years after the first officially sanctioned ski race for women took place in Norway.[95] The enterprising Konstantin Komets led ski excursions for members of the "Organization for the protection of women's health" in St. Petersburg's Petrovskii Park, the editors of *Novoe vremia* noting that "skiing to all appearances is extraordinarily pleasing to all women."[96] The copious advertisements for sporting goods stores in

Russia's daily newspapers and weekly magazines promoted women's skis and accouterments in their advertising.[97] Photographs of various ski club outings organized by St. Petersburg's Polar Star and Sokol Bogatyr' indicate that women often constituted close to one-half of all participants.[98]

Ski Racing and *Nordiska Spelen*

Crucial to Russia's burgeoning interest in ski racing during the early twentieth century was fascination with the newly created Olympic Games and their winter counterpart, the *Nordiska Spelen* (Northern Games), both of which internationalized sport. A decade before Baron Pierre de Coubertin founded the International Olympic Committee in 1894, the Norwegian Association for Promotion of Ski Sports had sponsored local and national ski competitions, culminating in the season's most important event held in the neighborhoods of Christiania.[99] After 1891, when the Christiania events moved to Holmenkollen, this Norwegian national festival began to attract foreigners, among them tourists and even correspondents from *La Vie au Grand Air*, *L'Illustration*, *Illustrierte Zeitung* and *The Illustrated London News*. The event gained ever more interest from outside of Norway as skiing developed at the turn of the century. Soon, foreign skiers were allowed to compete, and the Holmenkollen became the most important ski event in Europe.[100]

During this period, a certain sense of pan-Scandinavianism was developing in Norway, Finland and Sweden as a result of already well-established notions of European nationalism combined with the *fin-de-siècle* Gothic revival of the late romantic era. Finland had enjoyed a somewhat amicable arrangement with Russia since 1809 but now chafed under the rule of Tsar Nicholas II, a vociferous promoter of Russification policies throughout the empire. Norway was intent on dissolving its union with Sweden, a situation viewed with alarm in Stockholm. In order to keep Norway within a Swedish-dominated block and also to offer succor to the Finns, Viktor Balck, a Swedish army captain, organized in February 1901 a sport festival in Stockholm celebrating winter events, which he named Nordiska Spelen. Balck proposed that this festival should take place at four-year intervals, just like the Olympics but in odd years. The games were soon designated "Olympic" by the French and British press, a development not unwelcome to Baron de Coubertin: he and Balck joined forces on the International Olympic Committee as the two main power brokers of international sport into the 1920s.[101]

Just as news about skiing in Russia appeared sporadically in reports to Western Europe, so mention of the international significance of Nordiska Spelen trickled slowly back to Russia. Certainly, the efforts of the All-Russian Union of Skiers (VSL) to organize national championships from 1910 onward were undertaken with the recent 1909 Nordiska Spelen in mind: the main purpose of the VSL through the winters of 1911 and 1912 was to select the best skiers in Russia to send to the competitions scheduled for Stockholm in 1913. Over the course of two seasons, the most consistent were Aleksandr Nemukhin—one of the four Sokol'niki Club of Ski-Runners (SKL) Moscow-St. Petersburg racers of 1911—and Pavel Bychkov, Russia's first national champion and a member of Organization of Ski Enthusiasts (OLLS). Although the Russian press held little hope that the nation's skiers would prevail,[102] the excitement was palpable as the pair left for Sweden in 1913 and St. Petersburg's *Novoe vremia* sent along a special correspondent to cover the races there in a series of articles.

Low snow in Stockholm that year forced organizers of Nordiska Spelen to relocate 600 kilometers further north to Östersund. Originally entered in the 90-kilometer event, held concurrently over the same course with the 60- and 30-kilometer contests, Nemukhin and Bychkov opted to switch to the latter on race day. Having never participated in an international competition of this caliber, the two Russians were overwhelmed by the abilities of the Scandinavian skiers, telling other ski racers after their return to Moscow: "They are so far beyond us—they don't ski, they fly."[103] Although neither was in the running (Nemukhin dropped out of the race, and Bychkov came in fifty-one minutes behind the winner, Jussi Niska of Finland), the race results indicate that Bychkov finished in twentieth place out of approximately a hundred competitors.[104] This was no mean achievement, considering that both Russians had stepped out of isolation from recent Scandinavian innovations in equipment, clothing and ski-waxing to compete in Sweden. Moreover, the first-place finisher, Jussi Niska, was the master of a new technique that involved a simultaneous thrust with both poles in combination with one, two or three steps on the skis, a method which increased dramatically the efficiency of the ski stride.[105]

Although the press was indignant—"beaten in a most merciless way" sniffed the St. Petersburg sport journal *Gerkules*—Nemukhin and Bychkov's participation at this international gathering impacted the development of Russian skiing well into the Soviet era.[106] Of particular interest to one young ski enthusiast were the tales they told of Scandinavian skiers who knew how to fabricate "some sort of truly magic wax" for wet snow.[107]

As a nineteen-year-old ski racer in 1913, Nikolai Vasil'ev was one of the top competitors for SKL, having won the 60-kilometer Great Race in Moscow in early February as well as the 30-kilometer Russian Championship. As a result, he was sent to St. Petersburg by the Moscow Club of Skiers (MKL) to participate in an international ski race with a field that included a contingent of skiers from Finland led by Nordiska Spelen's recent champion, Jussi Niska.[108] These athletes were among the vanguard in the art and science of ski base preparation.

In modern cross-country skiing, especially racing, good wax applied to the bottom of the ski has always been crucial. Until the early 1980s, all Nordic competitors used a diagonal stride on uphill portions of the ski course, similar to bounding off the ball of the foot at a running gait. In choosing wax, skiers face a dilemma: they want the ski to glide fast over the snow on the downhill and flat sections but also to provide grip, or "kick," when going uphill. Wooden skis work very well when the snow is cold, and if the base of the ski is a soft wood such as birch and the temperature is well below freezing, no wax is needed at all for grip. However, as temperatures approach zero degrees Celsius, the structure of the snow changes as the snowflakes' sharp points begin to melt away. The result is a slippery ski on the uphill. Moreover, as the temperature rises above freezing and snow becomes saturated with water, wooden bases start to absorb moisture, making them extremely slow. And, if a skier goes from wet snow back into cold snow, e.g., from a sunny, open field into shaded woods, skis can ice up on the bottom resulting in no glide whatsoever.

Around 1913, Norwegian skiers began experimenting with pine resin, turpentine and beeswax concoctions that worked well in thawing, granular, slippery snow that was becoming more common at ski competitions such as those at the recently completed, and relocated, Nordiska Spelen. At these races, skiers would cook up a wax potion suited to the particular conditions of the day.[109] Niska and his Finnish compatriots were obviously privy to these recent Scandinavian technological developments. To their advantage, unusually moist snow had fallen in St. Petersburg just prior to the start of the race there, and the Finns had the expertise with which to concoct an appropriate wax.[110] This was not the case for Russian skiers. Vasil'ev was unused to these conditions; with only a rudimentary pine tar-paraffin mixture on his ski-bases, he experienced first-hand the importance of proper waxing, having been outdistanced by the Finns and their well-prepared skis: "This race . . . showed me that it was possible to obtain good glide . . . over wet snow, despite what the so-called 'experts' thought—that it's impossible to ski during a thaw!"[111] He bought a piece of wax from the Finns, subsequently analyzing the contents and experimenting with his own formulations.

Vasil'ev's comments, however, are a bit disingenuous. According to Lieutenant K. B. Eimeleus, a graduate of the Russian Army's officer preparatory program at the Main Gymnastics-Fencing School in St. Petersburg and author of a military ski training manual published in 1912, Russian skiers had means available before Vasil'ev's 1913 race for maintaining glide on skis in wet snow. These were perhaps not as sophisticated as the Scandinavian wax formulations, and some were certainly more unsavory, but they were serviceable options nonetheless: "After waxing, it is possible to run on smooth skis some 50 to 100 versts. Waxing one pair of skis comes to around five kopeks . . . If there are no special waxes on hand it is possible to avail oneself of butter, stearin, lard, wax, kerosene, even herring fat and, similarly, other compositions containing fat. All of these are suitable in a cold situation, but do not last for long and after two to three versts are wiped off."[112]

Yet, there is no question that Vasil'ev's transaction with Finland's most accomplished ski racers was a watershed event. As the eldest of three ski-racing brothers, Nikolai ushered his siblings into the world of ski racing while he was fine-tuning his waxing expertise in subsequent years. The brothers Vasil'ev were a formidable relay team winning a national 3 x 5-kilometer race in 1921. The youngest, Leonid, took seventh place in the Moscow traditional 60-kilometer race of 1924. He lost his life as a member of a ski division in World War II. The middle brother, Dmitrii, captured thirteen USSR national championships over a variety of distances from 1926 through 1940; and against an international field in Norway, he placed second in the 30-kilometer race at the First Workers' Winter Spartakiada of 1928. His reputation as Russia's top ski racer resulted in national competitions held in his honor by the late 1930s. Dmitrii served as head coach for the Red Army from 1948 to 1961 and then as men's cross-country coach for the Soviet National Ski Team from 1961 to 1962. In the 1950s, the two surviving brothers were considered among "the most powerful of the powerful" ski racers in the history of the Soviet Union. Nikolai retired from racing but combined his love of skiing with a career in science, developing ski wax of the highest quality for the Soviets.[113]

A Ski Race to the South Pole

A ski race of a different sort and on a far grander scale took place in the austral summer of 1911–1912 in Antarctica, when Norway and Great

Britain went head-to-head in competition to claim the South Pole. Robert Falcon Scott, hewing to the British method of polar exploration, planned to walk to the pole and back man-hauling sledges nearly every step of the way. By contrast, Roald Amundsen approached the journey as an extended ski tour accompanied by teams of dogsleds. The consequences were tragic for Scott and his companions, who died of exposure and exhaustion on their return after reaching the South Pole a month later than the Norwegians. To the British, Amundsen remained a "base record-chaser" as opposed to their scientifically motivated compatriot.[114] For most of the world in the early years of the twentieth century, Scott became a household name in the pantheon of great polar explorers, while Amundsen's star faded. In Russia, however, and most significantly in the Soviet Union, it was Amundsen and his skiing companions who were conferred heroic status.

The attainment of the South Pole had become a global obsession during the first decade of the twentieth century. In September 1909, American explorers James Cook and Robert Perry both professed to have reached the North Pole, creating a sense of urgency among exploring nations to claim the last great prize. Scott made his first foray to attain the South Pole in the summer of 1902–1903, having reached 82°17' south latitude dragging sledges. He had only skied a little and had "an almost pathological aversion" to the sport.[115] Although the English had pioneered skiing in the Alps beginning in the late nineteenth century, they neglected and misunderstood the sport's utility as a means of transportation across vast snow-covered expanses. Great Britain viewed skiing as simply sport, a downhill frolic for the elite at Swiss mountain spas. To use the ski for energy conservation countermanded the romantic British penchant for seeing men at work, struggling against great odds on one's own two feet. Norwegian skiers such as Nansen and Amundsen called this sheer insanity.[116]

By the time Roald Amundsen set his sights on the South Pole, he had become an expert on travel in high latitudes. In 1898 as an officer on a Belgian Antarctic expedition, he experimented with different types of skis on the pack ice. From 1903 to 1906, Amundsen sailed through the Northwest Passage, during which time he developed his skills with skis and dogsleds, completing an 800-kilometer ski trek from the coast of the Yukon to the telegraph station at Eagle City, Alaska, and back in late 1905. In the seventeen years between Nansen's Greenland traverse of 1888 and Amundsen's Northwest Passage experience, the Norwegian method of polar exploration based on skis and dogs had proven its worth. The application of ski-racing methodology was Amundsen's innovation in the Antarctic.

Edward Larson points out in his most recent book on Antarctic science and exploration that Amundsen came from a completely different tradition than did Scott, whose countrymen ostensibly put a premium on scientific inquiry over the attainment of geographical firsts. Amundsen, on the other hand, while paying lip service to science, had no intention of coming in second in a race to the South Pole.[117] Among the first members he chose for his Antarctic expedition was Norwegian ski champion Olav Bjaaland, who had twice won the Nordic combined event (cross-country skiing and ski jumping) at Holmenkollen in 1894 and 1902 as well as a military ski race over 18 kilometers in Chamonix in 1908. When the Norwegians, five in number and accompanied by fifty-two dogs, finally set out for the South Pole in October 1911, Amundsen as leader and Bjaaland as pace-setter applied the psychology of ski racing to their system. With their refined, energy-efficient technique and sense of pacing, the Norwegians managed to kick and glide with well-prepared skis over 2,250 kilometers in ninety-nine days to 90° south latitude and back. They had beaten Scott and the British to the South Pole by thirty-four days: more significantly, Amundsen and his men came home alive, whereas the British perished on their return trip. Amundsen and his companions, unaware of the Britons' plight, returned to Norway considering that they completed nothing more than an extended ski tour.[118]

Amundsen's expedition was one of many polar journeys covered by the Russian press. By the end of the nineteenth century, science in general and geographical exploration in particular had become an important part of Russian culture.[119] Many of the popular scientific journals were filled with articles about world exploration. According to historian James Andrews, these stories captured the imagination of Russian readers, who were keenly interested in the adventures of both Russian and foreign explorers alike.[120] Throughout the latter decades of the nineteenth century and into the twentieth, articles on the exploits of polar travelers along with rotogravures and illustrations filled the pages of *Moskovskiia vedomosti*, *Novoe vremia*, *Niva*, *Ogonek* and *Journal de St Pétersbourg*. Besides the voluminous coverage of Nansen's Greenland traverse and subsequent journey across the Arctic Sea, there were reports, for example, of French balloon expeditions to the North Pole in the 1890s, the German Arctic Expedition of 1900, the rescue of a Swedish Antarctica Expedition in 1903, and Ernest Shackleton's 1910 lectures in St. Petersburg.[121] News of Amundsen's success was no exception. An article in *Ogonek* featured some of Amundsen's first photographs, explaining how the Norwegian explorer determined he was actually at 90° south latitude by azimuth projection and the role sled dogs played in the journey.[122] Moreover, Amundsen's exploits combined with Russian fascination for geographical exploration, and a burgeoning interest in sport inspired a new round of long-distance ski races in Russia. In 1913, a ski race idiosyncratic to Russia evolved: the converging race, in which skiers started in groups from a variety of locations and arrived at a single finish line, evocative of Scott and Amundsen's race to the South Pole from separate starting points on the Ross Sea. That year, participants left from ten different cities, with fifty-four finishers crossing the line in Moscow. The following year, Amundsen-inspired long distance ski racing continued when three skiers travelled from St. Petersburg to Moscow in twelve days, while a team of sixty-seven skiers from the Ismailvskii Battalion skied 1,000 kilometers following the Arkhangelsk Road—Petrograd, past Kargopol, Novaia Lagoda and Tsarskoe Selo—in twenty days.[123]

For most of 1912 and the first few weeks of 1913, Scott had been written off as the second-place finisher in the race to the South Pole. When news reached Europe in February 1913 that Scott and his companions had died on their return trip, the ill-fated British explorer became a sensation, reconfigured by the press as a martyr of the Antarctic.[124] Some countries now resented Amundsen for having stolen the prize from this tragic British hero. However, in Russia, Amundsen remained an avatar of the brave and competent polar explorer. After the First World War, when technological developments such as airplanes, tracked vehicles and icebreakers rendered the Norwegian method of polar travel obsolete, Amundsen embraced air travel as a means for exploring in the Arctic, becoming a transitional figure from the Golden Age of exploration to the new scientific-industrialized era of polar travel.

TWO

The First World War to NEP

THE FIRST WORLD WAR changed the map of Europe and set the stage for hostilities two decades later that resulted in Cold War polarization and, in the realm of sports, brought politics directly into the Olympic Games. Even more than Western Europe, the Great War transformed Russia, where it spawned three events that altered the makeup of the nation: the Bolshevik Revolution of 1917, the Civil War of 1918–1921 and the Great Patriotic War of 1941–1945. Throughout the 1920s, World War I framed any discussion of political work and economic planning, fostering the crucial notion among Bolshevik theoreticians that the country had to maintain a constant state of military training and preparation for the next attack, whenever it may come.[1] Given that the nation remained in a constant state of readiness, sport was an integral part of the physical training for all citizens. Thus, the conscientious growth and development of skiing in Russia during the early twentieth century became first a Bolshevik undertaking and then, with the establishment of the USSR on 30 December 1922, a Soviet mission as well.

The Great War

World War I straddled a paradoxical four years during which popular notions of warfare based on experience from the previous century coincided with the new age of industrial modernization. But one crucial nineteenth-century development in military theory resonated through this quadrennium well into the Cold War era: reliance on cavalry, or its equivalent, for mobile reconnaissance behind enemy lines. Thus, it is no exaggeration to suggest that modifications in the strategic use of horse-mounted troops during the American Civil War played a crucial role in defining Bolshevik military practice during the Russian Civil War and, subsequently, the development of skiing in the Soviet Union.

In many ways, the conflict in North America foreshadowed the Great War through the introduction of trench warfare, reliance on advanced military technology and rail transportation and, most significantly, the involvement of million-man armies. As Civil War generals maneuvered large battalions in the field, information about enemy deployment was imperative. The innovations of Confederate cavalry officer J. E. B. Stuart in particular gave the South an edge in the early stages of the war, revolutionizing cavalry tactics that had been prevalent up to and including the Napoleonic Wars. Whereas the *cuirassiers* of Bonaparte's era were heavily armed and used for frontal attacks against massed formations, Stuart's riders operated behind enemy lines as the eyes of the infantry, gathering intelligence on Union troop movements while at the same time harassing the flanks and rear and cutting off lines of communication and supply. Such operations, exemplified by Stuart's three-day "ride around McClellan" during the Peninsula Campaign of 1862, required small, mobile, fast-moving units well-versed in methods of screening, scouting, skirmishing and foraging.[2] Analysis of the conflict in the United States in conjunction with immediate post-war experiences on European battlefields altered Western military theoreticians' view of cavalry. The resulting transformation from massed shock-attack troopers to that of mobile units suited for information-gathering far afield continued throughout the latter decades of the nineteenth century and well into the twentieth. Although developments in military hardware such as barbed wire, rapid-fire rifles and machine guns proved increasingly lethal to mounted troops, cavalry continued to play a strategic role at the turn of the century.

By the outbreak of World War I, however, the advanced technology that evolved from Europe's industrialization had outpaced the belligerents' military tactics, which were remnants of an earlier era. Such innovations as breech-loading and the rifling of firearms and artillery melded with mass production in the decades following the Franco-Prussian War of 1870–1871. This new style of weaponry, together with experiences during the early conflicts of the twentieth century such as the Boer War of 1899–1902 and the Russo-Japanese War of 1904–1905, reinforced the common view that infantry on the attack would be vulnerable on a modern battlefield. Nevertheless, certain aspects of the prevailing strategy as of August 1914 still harked back to the American Civil War: massed artillery barrages would be the primary choice for attacking enemy positions; railways would play a crucial role in the rapid deployment of forces; and cavalry would be used to encircle and pursue.[3] On the Western Front, the first two prognostications proved out. And, in the early stages of the war, it appeared that cavalry would have a significant role as well: during the very first weeks, for example, French General Sordet's cavalry corps set off into Belgium to reconnoiter German positions. However, as the German advance ground to a halt in October and November, the Western Front stabilized for the next twenty-seven months into a narrow band of trenches running in a continuous line from the North Sea to the Swiss border.[4] There were no flanks and thus no chance for envelopment on these static and delimited killing fields. In such a sector, bristling with machine-guns and barbed wire, cavalry operations were rendered as irrelevant as they were foolhardy.

But World War I was a global conflict, and the land campaigns in other theaters did not parallel the extremes of trench warfare reached on the Western Front. In Africa, both sides carried out wide-ranging guerrilla actions across vast swaths of territory. In Egypt and Mesopotamia, cavalry was crucial in the October 1917 Battle of Gaza and, more famously, in the 1917–1918 exploits of T. E. Lawrence. At the Battle of Aqaba especially, Lawrence along with Bedouin leader Auda ibu Tayi employed tactics similar to J. E. B. Stuart's 1862 ride around McClellan to attack Ottoman fortifications from the rear with mounted troops after a wide-ranging desert reconnaissance expedition. In Eastern Europe, the front meandered through the Baltic states, Poland and Ukraine, with battle lines twice as long as in the west and armies dispersed more thinly over terrain with far less urban development. Just as in the Middle East, operations on the Eastern Front hinged on maneuvering around the flank of the enemy rather than breaking through entrenched and static lines.[5] The tactical element common to all of these regions was the ability to outflank and surprise the enemy.

The Italian Front offered a different set of challenges altogether. All but one-fifth of the border between Italy and the Austro-Hungarian Empire straddled the mountain ranges of the Tyrol, the Trentino Alto-Adige, the Dolomites and the Carpathian Alps. Mountain fortifications and passes were the focal point of attacks, across terrain swept nearly as often by avalanche as machine-gun. Operations in these regions involved travel far above timberline into the alpine, and personnel assigned to winter maneuvers there skied as part of their training. Skiing had already been adopted in the 1890s by both Germany and the Austro-Hungarian Empire, influenced greatly by the example of Norway. However, the armies of both nations also incorporated military skiing exercises based on those used by the Russian imperial army for troops stationed in East Prussia, the Harz, the Vosges, Hungary and Galicia.[6] During the build-up to the First World War, the armies of Russia, France, Italy, Germany and the Austro-Hungarian Empire all equipped ski divisions. The provision of these troops reflected pre-war enthusiasm among adventurous Europeans for ski touring in the high Alps. Turn-of-the-century treks on rudimentary gear across the snows of the Bernese Oberland or up Monte Rosa required ski-mountaineering skills as well as technical expertise to negotiate steep, icy descents, a precursor to the development of slalom and downhill skiing during the inter-war period.[7] Military ski competitions in the years just prior to the outbreak of war fostered camaraderie among the French Chasseurs Alpins, the Italian Alpini and the Austrian Alpenjäger, whose members treated one another with a fraternal respect far different from that found on the Western Front.[8]

Nonetheless, during the severe winter of 1914–1915, French and German skiers skirmished in the Vosges, and throughout the war ski patrols operated on both sides of the Italian-Austro-Hungarian border. In the Carpathians, German and Austrian skiers easily out-maneuvered their Russian adversaries, who did not have the same level of training in mountain warfare. The military application of mountaineering and skiing formulated on the Italian Front had a profound influence on the future development of ski troops during the inter-war years. But in the final analysis skiing proved to be of little use during the First World War, largely because of the static nature of the mountainous fronts.[9] Rather, it was in the wide-open spaces of post-revolutionary Russia that skiing truly came into its own as a dynamic military activity.

Revolution and Civil War in Russia

An exhausted Russian population, worn down by the Great War, demoralized by military defeats, pummeled by economic debacles and suffering loss of faith in the government, overthrew tsarist rule in 1917. Outdistancing their political rivals, the members of the Bolshevik Party advocated workers' control of industry, rule of the lower classes and an end to the war. Seizing power on 25 October 1917, the Bolsheviks eschewed any kind of multi-party socialist government. The outcome was a contentious Civil War from 1918 through 1921 against five distinct groups. The most potent of these coteries were the Whites, composed of former imperial army officers, property owners, aristocrats and disenchanted liberals, all of whom wanted to restore the monarchy. Equally challenging to the Bolsheviks were the foreign interventionists, including the Germans, who wanted to create their own sphere of influence in the East; the Allies, who clamored to re-establish the Eastern Front of the Great War in order to prevent the spread of Bolshevism to the West; and the Japanese, who occupied areas in the Russian Far East. In addition, bands of peasants, the Greens, sought to carve out enclaves where they would be free from government interference in Ukraine and Siberia and along the Volga. Although the Russian Civil War spread all across the former empire of the tsars, there were three major areas of contention: the south, comprising the Don region, Kuban, the North Caucasus and Ukraine; the east, including the Volga region, the Ural Mountains and Siberia; and in the northwest, the Baltic region and Poland.[10]

Arguably the greatest success of the Bolsheviks during the Civil War period was the creation of the Red Army. Unlike other European nations, which found relief from war with the Armistice of 1918, Russia experienced another three years of savagery as hostilities continued after the October Revolution. The Bolshevik Party spearheaded a party-state steeped in militarism, while it struggled to consolidate national control and build a functioning government. Starting with only a few thousand Red Guards who had distinguished themselves during the 1917 Revolution, Lev Trotsky assembled a formidable army within two and a half years through the conscription of around six million men, even though about half eventually deserted or disappeared. Although it would possibly have suffered against regular European troops of the First World War, the Red Army was effective enough in fending off the less ideologically motivated forces of the Whites and the haphazard Allied expeditionary landings.[11]

From its inception in 1918, unique circumstances forced the Red Army to follow a path of development different from that of traditional military forces. After the October Revolution, the Soviets replaced the tsarist army with a socialist militia, based on an all-volunteer army with elections of officers by the rank and file. In accordance with socialist doctrine, all ranks were equal, saluting was abolished and officers and men addressed one another as comrade. However, in early encounters, especially during the period from January through November 1919, the White armies advanced against the Bolsheviks in the northwest as well as in the south and east, prompting Trotsky to reform the Red Army. He reversed the radical democratization of the army, eliminated the election of officers and reimposed stiff discipline among the ranks. The Red Army was subject to ideological as well as military objectives, including Marxist-Leninist political indoctrination and social modernization. Each commander of every rank shared power with a Communist Party political officer, or commissar, to ensure the loyalty of the Red Army commanders, many of whom were former tsarist officers.[12]

When hostilities spread into the expanse of Siberia, opposing armies ranged over a land mass whose vastness defied comprehension. Covering an area large enough to contain the entire United States and all of Europe with room to spare, frozen under a mantle of snow in winter by the most extreme cold of any inhabited region in the world, Siberia skewed contemporary notions of dimension, time and space.[13] In these locales, it was futile to employ the tactics of the Western Front, where troops forayed across a barren no man's land to gain a few hundred yards. Instead, just as they had in the United States some sixty years beforehand, campaigns in the east hinged on mobility, spur-of-the-moment decisions and the tactics of surprise. According to Trotsky, this style of mobile warfare required cavalry adept at breakthroughs and wide, circumambulatory raids on the enemy behind far-distant lines reminiscent of Lawrence's recent successes in Jordan and Syria. Mounted units evolved as the mainstay of military operations, prompting Trotsky to exclaim in 1919: "A powerful cavalry is vital for the Soviet Republic. Red cavalrymen—forward! Proletarian, to horse!"[14]

Nevertheless, the severe winter in northern Russia made it clear that the cavalry's fulfillment of reconnaissance and pursuit would be limited, a lesson learned previously by the belligerents of the Franco-Prussian War of 1870–1871. Heavy snowfall and icy roads had choked off the use of mounted troops and wheeled vehicles. The postmortems of some armchair generals in the press suggested that the Prussians would have had more success in winter combat against *franc-tireurs*, the irregular troops of the French army, had they used "snowshoes" in northern France, along the Loire and in the Jura Mountains, based on the inability of mounted dragoons to pursue Swedish ski troops during the Napoleonic Wars.[15] During the early stages of the Russian Civil War in the northwest region, Bolshevik military theoreticians relearned some of these lessons from four decades prior. On 12 May 1918, several hundred Finnish anti-Bolshevik soldiers, "White Finns" in the parlance of Russian historians writing during the Soviet era, travelled on skis across the border to stage a full attack at Pechenga, 100 kilometers northwest of Murmansk.[16] At a latitude just shy of 70° north, this area was inhospitable to hoof and wheel alike: only skis and sledges gave troops mobility there. In the same vicinity during the following winter, Canadian, Italian, Serbian, French, English and White Finn ski troops landed in the Murmansk-Arkhangelsk area as part of the Allied intervention in North Russia.[17] The early successes by the Whites and the expeditionary forces of the Allies against the Bolsheviks in these regions prompted the Red Army to introduce ski training as part of its regular military regimen.

Well ahead of the Bolsheviks, the sport of skiing had already been incorporated systematically into the Russian military at the end of the nineteenth century. The imperial army organized a few ski units out of the tsar's cavalry during the Russo-Japanese War of 1904–1905, the subject of postcards and engravings popular in both Russia and Western Europe. Shortly before the outbreak of World War I, the Main Gymnastics-Fencing School in St. Petersburg began the preparation of ski instructors from the ranks of the officers, and the staff of the St. Petersburg region planned to open a special school of skiing. However, the declaration of war in 1914 interrupted these projects. Although commanders assigned to the north as well as in some regions in the rear began to form ski divisions and to employ them in military maneuvers in 1916 in Poland and the Carpathians, their usefulness was minimal.[18]

The Bolsheviks understood the utility of athletic training and soon after coming to power employed sport for their purposes. On 22 April 1918, a decree of the All-Russia Central Executive Committee of the Soviets of Workers,' Soldiers' and Peasants' Deputies incorporated a program of Universal Military Training, or Vsevobuch, under the administration of a central board. The Central Board's stated purpose was to popularize the idea of general military preparation and to gradually make it a part of each citizen's life.[19] In reality, it provided the hard-pressed Red Army with conscripts as quickly as possible by administering a crash physical fitness program for citizens between the ages of sixteen and forty. Recognizing the value of promoting sport as an enticement to physical fitness, the Central Board of Vsevobuch took over control of all sports clubs and societies in Russia, including the Sokols and ski clubs from the pre-revolutionary period.[20] The integration of sport into exercises for the armed forces was not a Bolshevik innovation, however. There were precedents to this phenomenon that developed dramatically in the years prior to World War I, fueled by international interest in the Olympic Games. Drilling and practicing for the Olympics, wrote the German Carl Diem just before the war, "is in the best interests of the army itself."[21] Success at the Olympic Games and other international competitions was a gauge of a nation's fitness level, its discipline and even the state of its national self-awareness. After the 1913 Nordiska Spelen, the International Olympic Committee voted to introduce winter sports into the 1916 Olympics scheduled for Berlin. Thus, the association of the militarized aspects of international competition had been well-established before the inclusion of winter events within the Olympic program.

Even though the Central Board of Vsevobuch promoted soccer and similar team games as well as other sports with military application such as boxing, wrestling and fencing, it was skiing that received special priority. In June of 1918, the Vsevobuch board took three important steps: developing and manufacturing a special military-style ski; publishing a ski manual, *Instruction Book for the Training of Ski Regiments*; and establishing ski schools in Moscow and Petrograd Military Districts for the qualification of Red Army ski instructors. By the end of 1918, Vsevobuch personnel had trained around two million citizens and organized 350 sport groups for workers, including thirty-five ski intelligence divisions by the following year.[22] As war ebbed and flowed across the Eurasian landmass during the Civil War, ski divisions from the Red Army—bolstered by Vsevobuch preparations and training—engaged similar forces from the Whites and Allied divisions in the northern regions. George Constantine Guins, administrative secretary of the Siberian anti-Bolshevik government at Omsk, recounts how White ski troops under the leadership of polar explorer Aleksandr Kolchak ranged far afield, at one particular point encountering reconnaissance forces from the Russo-Allied forces in North Russia.[23] From the Soviet perspective, a number of these ski encounters reinforced the state's official mythology surrounding the Civil War. A 1938 article in *Pravda* describes commemorative ski excursions tracing the route of Vasilii Chapaev and his 25th Rifle Division near Zavolzhe and the trail from Vitebsk through Orsha and Mogilev to Minsk made famous by the 27th Omsk Division. In a voluminous history of the Civil War published in the 1950s, Soviet historians describe the conscription of the Viatka ski battalion out of the Third Army stationed on the Karelian Isthmus for the purpose of maintaining contact with the Sixth Army along the Northern Front against the Whites and forces of the Allies. Similarly, in the more mountainous terrain of the Urals skiers of the First-Middle Siberia Corps waged a two-day battle near the train station at Kyn; and in the south, the 214th Rifle Regiment took to skis while on maneuvers against the Whites and Basmachi guerrilla bands in Turkestan.[24]

Cavalry and Skiing

A government directive issued in 1919 required the Central Board of Vsevobuch to prepare combat skiers specifically for the coming winter campaigns of 1919–1920 on the Northern and Eastern Fronts where "a lack of cavalry called for special measures . . . and the ski formations had to fill in for this shortage."[25] The relationship of cavalry and skiing had tactical as well as ideological usefulness for the Bolsheviks. Military theoreticians during the Russian Civil War understood that in winter conditions, when roads were clogged with deep snow, mounted troops could not advance. Thus, the stand-in for cavalry in its fundamental function of reconnaissance and pursuit would be the ski divisions, referred to poetically as "the riders of the snowy expanse," their skis "brisk steeds of the North."[26] A wonderful illustration of this relationship between skier and horseman is found in unissued footage from the British Pathé archives: as a line of Red Cavalry advances through the snow at a trot, a lone skier in white camouflage maintains the pace striding alongside the column.[27] Because skiers could gather information in poor weather conditions, they were considered "irreplaceable" and could operate on a smaller scale with better results than mounted riders: "Large numbers here, as in the cavalry, are unnecessary: five to ten selected and reliable scouts, brave and clever, literate, understanding maps and, although in a general way, the organization and business of the enemy, sometimes bring greater benefit than a cavalry troop."[28] Indeed, by 1929 the value of skiing as a complement to the cavalry divisions had been proven to such an extent that the Red Army newspaper *Krasnaia zvezda* asserted: "Where the climatic conditions are favorable, it is necessary from the first days of instruction of every cavalryman to get on skis and systematically carry out this training."[29]

But cross-country skiing offered more than just winter exercise for idle cavalrymen: the sport brimmed with proletarian significance which, for the Bolsheviks, was a fundamental element of Marxist-Leninist theory. Building on Karl Marx's writings, Vladimir Lenin argued that the first requirement for the formation of a socialist state was the seizure of political power by the working class from the hands of the bourgeoisie. Lenin postulated that the establishment of a dictatorship of the proletariat would be an intermediate step on the path toward complete socialism. Councils, or soviets, of workers and peasants would become the nucleus of this proletarian state, for which the trappings of capitalism, the aristocracy and the bourgeoisie were anathema. For the Bolsheviks, these reactionary and bourgeois elements had to be excised from every organization, the Red Army included. Thus, Trotsky's 1919 exhortation, "Proletarian, to horse!" was more than a sonorous slogan to inspire the Red Army. "The cavalry units from time immemorial were the possession of the privileged and titled officers," he wrote. "It's necessary that a communist becomes a cavalryman."[30]

Sport, and especially skiing at the turn of the century, reflected Trotsky's take on the Marxist dichotomy. The question of amateurism versus professionalism was at the very heart of international competitions such as the Olympics and the Nordiska Spelen from their inception. The 1896 Olympic Games adopted a broad definition of amateurism, excluding those athletes who had received money or prizes for competing or for work as sport instructors or coaches.[31] The English school and sports system with its concept of "fair play" was a huge influence on the Olympic movement, and as interest in the Games grew, class became increasingly important. For the British, the amateur world was meant for the elites: as sport historian John Allen notes, a bricklayer whose strength came from manual labor could not row a shell in the Henley regatta.[32] This point of view held sway in pre-revolutionary Russia as well. When Pavel Bychkov, the skier who later represented Russia at the Nordiska Spelen of 1913, won the Russian Ski Championship of 1910, the journal *Vsemirnyi sport i zdorov'e* (World Sport and Health) questioned his right to the title. Nekii Protopov, a member of the Moscow Organization of Skiers, wrote: "[He] worked at removing ice from roadways and swept the pavement. Inasmuch as Bychkov is a groundskeeper and, undoubtedly, as a person who has been involved in physical labor, he has an enormous advantage over competitors of the *intelligentsia*. It follows that he be reckoned among the professionals." Another journal, *Russkii sport*, began a campaign to disqualify Bychkov and at the same time to bar from competition anyone who worked with his hands as Bychkov did.[33]

This dichotomy of class carried over into British attitudes toward skiing, which developed as the elite took to winter sports at Swiss spas. These well-heeled snow frolickers preferred tobogganing and exhilarating downhill ski descents to the more mundane activity of running cross-country. Idraet—the Norwegian concept of skiing as more than just an idle pastime—was irrelevant on the slopes of Davos or St. Moritz. The version of winter sport that developed in the Swiss Alps was so bound up with wealth and tourism that it "smelled of money" and, in the view of European socialists, was the epitome of bourgeois athletics. Tobogganing, included for the first time at the Nordiska Spelen in 1922, fostered undercurrents of class antagonism in Scandinavia when sledding competitors received better prizes than skiers. As the left and liberal Swedish press pointed out, sledding carried connotations of a pleasurable diversion for the leisure class, whereas skiing was the sport of the proletariat.[34]

With more and more well-to-do vacationers flocking to the Alps after World War I, a rift developed between the bourgeois Alpine and the plebian Nordic iterations of skiing. Arnold Lunn was an early English proponent of downhill skiing and was equally antagonistic toward Nordic skiing. He argued that "sturdy mountain peasants" won cross-country races while town-dwellers were left out of the running (a class differentiation that even Mao Zedong would approve). Lunn was a fanatical promoter of the slalom, that is, a downhill run turning through gates, a popular exercise among the English on holiday in the Alps. When the Winter Games became part of the Olympic program during the inter-war years, the Nordic events retained their original sense of idraet, evocative of self-denial, strengthening of the will and enhancement of endurance and energy. Slalom and downhill skiing, on the other hand, were examples of "hotel-sport," aristocratic, elitist and expensive.[35]

The Soviets never doubted that Nordic skiing, rather than its Alpine counterpart, was the proper discipline for citizens of the new socialist order as the class division separating the two types of skiing grew greater with each passing year. Between the wars, one Soviet artist amended a ubiquitous Civil War placard that had incorporated Trotsky's famous "Proletarian, to horse!" exhortation into a ski poster reading: "Proletarian and Collective Farm Worker, to skis! Strengthen the nation's defense!"[36] In 1940, a front-page editorial in *Pravda*, the official newspaper of the Communist Party, stated that of all the winter sports in the Soviet Union that had significance in the defense of socialism, the "people's sport" of cross-country skiing was the most popular.[37] Another *Pravda* piece suggests that by participating in this sport, a citizen "trains the muscles and learns many skills that are beneficial both in peace and in war. [Cross-country ski tours] do not require expenditure of means yet at the same time can provide great profit. Ski tours on days off are excellent propaganda for ski sport. These must and should be done in the collective industrial works, in the collective farms, in the schools."[38] Alpine skiing, moreover, catered to those in a very limited age range: youth between twenty and twenty-five with "lightning-fast reactions."[39] By way of contrast, citizens of all ages could cross-country ski. A poster from 1957 shows an elderly skier with white eyebrows and moustache watching a youngster putting on his ski gear under the slogan: "Age is no hindrance to sport!"[40] *Sovetskii sport* offered its own real-life example: "There they are: old friends . . . Pavel Afanas'evich Bychkov, Russian champion 1910 and 1911; Aleksandr Niko-laevich Nemukhin, Russian champion 1912; and Nikolai Maksimovich Vasil'ev, Russian champion 1913. Even in their 70s they aren't old men!"[41] Even octogenarians who had never been sport champions could ski, nota-bly Mikhail Prishvin, the award-winning children's author.[42]

When Soviet skiers did happen to engage in Alpine skiing, according to sport historian Henry Morton, they managed to maintain a proletarian point of view. Morton relates an entertaining but unattributed anecdote about a ski competition in Switzerland during which the Soviet women's downhill team refused to ride the "bourgeois" ski lifts, preferring to hike up the hill with skis hoisted across their shoulders. Morton is alluding most probably to the Women's International Ski Tournament of 1954 held in Grindelwald, where Soviet team leader Konstantin Sorokin told *Life* magazine: "Ski lifts would not be approved in the Soviet Union. Sports without toil and sweat, without the satisfaction of self-denial and self-conquest, are nothing more than amusement. Up by chair-lift, down by gravity—what has that got to do with honest physical culture?"[43] The idea of ski-sport as amusement was a hold-over from the inter-war British up-per-class infatuation with recreation in the mountain spas of Switzerland and implied that lift-served Alpine skiing was louche and degenerate. "In the capitalist countries," wrote E. Shatrov in the early 1950s, "slalom, like tennis and boat-racing, is considered the most aristocratic type of sport, more precisely: a sport for the rich."[44] Nordic skiing, on the other hand, maintained its proletarian roots even in the West. In the journal *Sovetskii sport*, in-depth articles about top Scandinavian cross-country ski racers such as Sixten Jernberg and Hallgeir Brenden made note of the fact that it was their anti-bourgeois life-style that translated into prowess on the ski track: "Norwegian ski racers are, as a rule, either peasants or workers in timber-cutting, that is, they are people who are engaged in heavy physical labor."[45] Although Jernberg and Brenden hailed from the capitalist nations of Sweden and Norway, they were nonetheless working-class heroes wor-thy of emulation by the new Soviet man.

The Soviet Hero—Toivo Antikainen

The most outstanding feature of the true Communist was a heroism specifically tailored to Soviet ideology: a fanatical faith in the supreme goal of building socialism; the ability to transform that faith into action; and the desire to work for the common good of all rather than for individual glory.[46] During the Russian Civil War and its immediate aftermath, the Bolsheviks found many heroes conforming to these parameters who could inspire the masses. One of these was a Petrograd skier, Toivo Antikainen, whose exploits in Karelia were commemorated at special events and celebrated in both prose and poetry throughout the Soviet era.

Antikainen was born in Helsinki in 1898 to parents active in the Finnish labor movement. He joined the Finnish Social Democratic Youth Association in 1903 and was involved in labor issues through the First World War. A true believer in the socialist cause, he emigrated to Russia—along with like-minded compatriots—after the October Revolution to join the Bolsheviks. Antikainen entered the Red Army in July 1918 and a year later was among the first group of young commanders to study at the Petrograd International Military School. In the midst of the Civil War he was assigned as a battalion commissar to the Sixth Finnish Regiment, assembled from Finnish Red Guardsmen, Finns of the Petrograd Province and Karelian Soviet soldiers. The regiment's special ski detachments took part in operations on the Karelian front from Olonets on the eastern shore of Lake Ladoga to Kandalaksha, just above the Arctic Circle, a range of 680 kilometers. Antikainen returned to the International Military School as an instructor and commander of a machine-gun company through the end of 1921.[47]

By the beginning of March 1921, the Bolsheviks had subdued the opposition forces all across the former lands of imperial Russia, although over the next several years, pockets of resistance flared up sporadically. One of the earliest revolts against the Bolsheviks occurred on the Karelian Isthmus between November 1921 and March 1922, known variously as the Soviet-Finnish Conflict or the East Karelian Uprising. Realizing the need for troops who could operate in the snows of Finland and Karelia, the Bolshevik government ordered the Petrograd Military District to establish ski battalions. The International Military School was the home base for several Russian ski champions, such as Kalle Akhonen, victor in the national 30-kilometer race for juniors. These skiers formed the core of Antikainen's machine-gun detachment, which set out from Petrograd in early January 1922 for reconnaissance maneuvers behind the lines of the Finnish anti-Bolshevik forces. More than two hundred ski troops under Antikainen's direction deployed from the Maselgskaia train station on the Murmansk rail line on 7 January and headed northwest, travelling more than 1,000 kilometers to capture the station at Kimasozero a scant thirteen days later. Without benefit of resupply points and carrying full military kit, these skiers averaged a remarkable sixty-plus kilometers per day and then continued operations throughout Karelia well into February.[48]

The raid on Kimasozero became the paradigm for similar maneuvers carried out by Red Army skiers in the decades following, especially during the Great Patriotic War. Antikainen later wrote: "Our military operation was based on speed of the advance. We made a calculation on bravery and surprise as well as moral superiority. In every battle we sought to strike with force at the flank and in the rear of the enemy. . . So from the very beginning of the war, we took the initiative into our own hands. . . [and] staggered the moral soul of the enemy."[49] The notion of the superiority of the socialist system as compared to either that of the bourgeois West or fascism was a given, of course, as was the heroism of the Red Army soldier vis-à-vis the anti-communist or the German: but the descriptive prose attached to attacking behind enemy lines using the element of surprise—J. E. B. Stuart's stock-in-trade from an earlier era—defined the very notion of the Soviet skier of World War II. Time and again the Soviet media repeated this scenario in film, literature and art.[50]

Citizens of the Karelian Soviet Socialist Republic considered Antikainen one of their own, a true home-grown hero. In 1935, Aksel' Anttila and Erkka Oiala, two former soldiers who had taken part in the raid on Kimasozero, retraced the route with over sixty enthusiasts in tow with full battle gear and supplies. A special correspondent from *Pravda* accompanied the group, posting reports from various stations along the way.[51] This event proved so popular that in the following year another group of re-enactors followed the trail, establishing a tradition that continued well into the 1960s. This annual January through February trek through Karelia reflected the Soviet infatuation with long-distance multi-day ski tours, which reached a crescendo in the inter-war years. In 1968, the newspaper *Komsomolets* established a "military-sporting" ski competition for Karelian youths called "Antikainen's ski trail," which celebrated its thirteenth annual running in 1981.[52]

The fact that Toivo Antikainen was born in Finland does not negate his importance as an iconic hero of the Soviet Union. His raid on Kimasozero, imbued with significance for skiing in his adopted country, became an example of heroism, self-sacrifice and service to the masses. He was an ardent communist, having led the Communist Party's underground activities in Finland and serving as a Party representative to the Communist International (Comintern) from 1930 to 1933. In addition to being a consummate citizen of the Soviet Union, Antikainen promoted the sport of skiing in the aftermath of the Soviet-Finnish War of 1939–1940 through newspaper and magazine articles and advocating for the Soviet physical fitness program *Gotov k trudu i oborone* (Ready for Labor and Defense), or GTO.[53] Antikainen accrued perhaps the ultimate stamp of legitimacy as a Soviet citizen when he ran afoul of the Stalinist regime then died in a plane crash under suspicious circumstances in 1941. Nevertheless, he became a template for the Red Army's military scout, whose characteristics evolved during the period between the invasion of Finland and the Great Patriotic War.

Ski-Shooting and the Home Guard

The conflict on the Karelian Isthmus had an enormous effect on the development of skiing in both Finland and the Soviet Union. The Finnish government had organized a Home Guard for national defense in the spring of 1918, in order to maintain independence from Russia. The Home Guard's mission was twofold: to act as a volunteer armed defense organization in support of the regular army and to suppress the activities of the Finnish communists. Because sport was an important element of the Home Guard's military preparation, training for winter warfare received high priority. Skiing turned into the major military sport, resulting in the nation's successful maneuvers at Pechenga in May 1918. Both the general staff of the regular army and the organizers of the Home Guard advocated intensive ski practice, and when the East Karelian Uprising broke out during the winter of 1921–1922, the Finnish troops were well prepared indeed for winter operations.[54]

There were counterparts to the Finnish Home Guard in Europe during the inter-war period, especially in those Central and Eastern European nations where the possibility of internal revolution was just as frightening and real as the military threat of a resurgent Russia. Taking a cue from Finland, other Scandinavian nations, the Baltic states, Germany, Austria, Romania and Bulgaria all formed Home Guards and promoted sport for military preparation.[55] The Finnish Home Guard from the early 1920s on placed particular emphasis on *ampumahiihto*, literally "shooting-skiing," the predecessor in Scandinavia of the modern sport of biathlon.[56] In 1922,

Guard officials lobbied the government to include team, individual and senior ski-shooting events at the National Championships of 1923. The military application and purpose of this type of sport was crystal clear: targets used by the Home Guard through the mid-1920s featured half-size caricatures of Russians. Cooperation flourished between the Finnish and Estonian Guards, especially in the development of ski-shooting and cross-country ski racing, as athletes crossed the Baltic to take part in each other's competitions.[57] This did not preclude Finland's national champions from competing with the Russians, however. Dmitrii Vasil'ev writes that Finnish racers from the Finnish Workers Sport Union came to Moscow to compete in March 1923. In 1926 the best skiers from Finland travelled to the Ostankino section of Moscow to take part in a series of races over a 30- and a 60-kilometer course. The following year, Soviet skiers travelled to Finland to compete in the Workers' Sport Festival.[58]

The utility of ski competition among the Home Guard was not lost on the Bolsheviks. The Central Board of Vsevobuch, in conjunction with the Komsomol, the Communist Youth Union, actively encouraged competitive sport as a way to attract citizens to physical activity and to encourage the collective spirit that was central to socialist ideology. As in Finland and other countries, sports such as skiing, which had obvious military applications, were given special priority.[59] After the October Revolution, the All-Russian Union of Skiers (VSL) continued its program of promoting city, regional and national championships. Moscow's first ski championship under the auspices of the new Bolshevik regime took place on 28 January 1918. Competitors on the podium in this race included Nikolai Vasil'ev, the Soviet Union's future master wax technician, and A. N. Nemukhin, one of Russia's two representatives at the Nordiska Spelen of 1913 and a pioneer of the long-distance route from Moscow to St. Petersburg before the war. Other cities hosted their own ski championships as well, including Iaroslavl, Kostroma and Ekaterinburg. In Petrograd, sixty participants competed in the city race held during the 1919–1920 season. That same year, Vasil'ev won the first national championship of the Russian Soviet Federated Socialist Republic, or RSFSR, held in Moscow with competitors travelling from Vladimir, Podolsk, Rzhev, Nizhnii Novgorod, Kaluga, Kostruma and Iaroslavl to compete.[60] The government eliminated the VSL in 1923, transferring the administrative duties of ski racing to the High Soviet of Physical Culture, or VSFK, which organized the first Ski Championship of the USSR in February 1924, won by Dmitrii Vasil'ev, the younger brother of Nikolai.[61]

Women's Skiing after the Revolution

In the early decades of the twentieth century, women were excluded from ski racing at most major venues throughout the world. Although this was not the case in some Scandinavian countries—Finland, for example, held its first National Championship for women in 1911 and hosted the first officially sanctioned demonstration of an international women's ski race at the Lahti Ski Games of 1926—elsewhere gendered discrimination was the norm. After the October Revolution of 1917, however, opportunities abounded for Russian women to compete in ski racing. The inclusion of women in all aspects of the new Bolshevik order was hardly a surprise; Marxist theoreticians considered the Bolshevik Revolution an opportunity for female emancipation. After October 1917 the state removed all former legal restrictions that had placed women in an inferior position, incorporating the principle of equal pay for equal work as well as equal employment. The first Constitution of 1918 mandated equality of all citizens in the republic without regard to sex, race or nationality and stipulated the right of women to vote in elections and to hold elective office on an equal basis with men. Influenced by his association with the socialist educator Petr F. Lesgaft, Vladimir Lenin considered participation in athletics a means to social liberation for women.[62]

Thus, the Bolsheviks were eager to promote and organize women's athletic competitions, including a variety of ski championships. In 1919 Moscow held the city's first championship for women over a 5-kilometer course. Moscow's Natalia Kuzenetsova won the first women's championship for a national title in 1921, over a 3-kilometer course. The following year, Mariia Fetisova captured the national title for women on a 4.5-kilometer course. In 1923, Antonina Mikhailova was the victor in the championship race, which had been increased to 5 kilometers. The distances contested at subsequent national championships varied over the decades, alternating between 5, 8, 10, 15 and 20 kilometers. Although Mikhailova was named National Ski Champion three more times in 1924, 1932 and 1935, it is a testament to the level of interest and depth of field in women's cross-country that no one competitor dominated the competitions over the course of two decades until the era of Zoia Bolotova, who gathered twelve National Ski Championship titles from 1938 through 1949.[63]

The Soviet Union was far ahead of the rest of the world in the growth and development of women's ski racing. The first opportunity for women to participate in any type of Olympic ski race occurred at Garmisch-

Partenkirchen in 1936, an alpine event combining downhill and slalom dominated by Nazi Germany. But the first women's cross-country event— a 10-kilometer contest swept by Finland—did not take place until the 1952 Winter Olympics. The Soviet Union finally allowed its athletes to compete on an international level two years later—first at the Grindelwald International Women's Ski Tournament and then in 1956 at the Olympic Games in Cortina d'Ampezzo. By that point, women's cross-country ski racing changed radically. Soviet women emerged as the world's dominant force and remained so for almost four decades. It is interesting to note as well that women led by Bolotova raced for a national title in a form of ski-shooting in 1941, a full half-century prior to the inclusion of women's biathlon at the 1992 Albertville Olympics.

Team Events and Relay Races

The emphasis on individual success rather than on the common good, whether in ski racing or other types of sport competitions, ran counter to socialist ideology. Some theoreticians proposed altering the purpose of sport by using it to reflect notions of class struggle inherent to Marxist thought. The Bolsheviks put this theory into practice from the outset. Immediately upon its founding in 1918, the Central Board of Vsevobuch took control of all existing sports clubs and organizations, and after the Civil War, the military, trade unions and labor movements took over the country's development of physical culture. As an alternative to the Olympics and international competition with the West, the Soviet Union organized mass sporting events, the *spartakiada*, which took place on all levels of society from individual farming collectives to All-Union festivals. These gatherings had antecedents in the Sokol movement of the nineteenth century and were the forerunners as well of the traditional May Day sports display on Red Square that began in the 1930s. The First International Spartakiada was held in Moscow in 1928, ostensibly as a tournament of the international worker sport movement to demonstrate proletarian internationalism in sport and to counterbalance the bourgeois Summer Olympics in Amsterdam. A winter version of this 1928 Spartakiada drew 638 competitors. Contests included regular cross-country distances for men and women as well as downhill and ski-shooting events separated into diverse categories of participation for rural village residents, military scouts and postal workers.[64]

As befit a communist enterprise, the Bolsheviks and then the Soviets emphasized team sport as an example of socialist cooperation that could simultaneously sharpen an individual athlete's skills through competition. In skiing, this lent special significance to relay and team events, especially in the military and the collectives. In 1923, for example, a twenty-man team from Moscow's Lenin Military School of Physical Instruction won the team races held in honor of the fifth-year anniversary of the founding of the Red Army. The following year, the Leningrad Military District won the first team competition to determine the championship of the Red Army and Navy.[65] These were not isolated instances. Consider the variety of relay and team events held during the 1924–1925 winter season detailed in the pages of *Krasnaia zvezda*. In January, the High Soviet of Physical Culture (VSFK) organized a 705-kilometer, multi-day relay event for military units, collectives and sport organizations. The race was divided into eleven stages ranging from 45 to 80 kilometers, starting in Leningrad and ending in Moscow. In February, VSFK staged a combined men's and women's relay in conjunction with the USSR National Championships. A springtime race series held among skiers of the Kursk Infantry Regiment featured a 10-kilometer team race in which each skier had to compete in full battle gear. The individual contest was a far less exhausting 3-kilometer sprint. As part of the Privolzhsk Military District 1925 Championships for Regiments and Institutes of Higher Learning, a converging race similar to the one inspired by Amundsen in 1913 took place at the end of March. The Ulianovsk Red Army School prevailed over twelve other teams covering a 200-kilometer course in sixty-two hours and twenty-seven minutes.[66]

These ultra-distance ski races had another purpose, too: agitation and propaganda, or agit-prop, in remote regions of the country. Agit-prop incorporated the notion of disseminating ideas useful to the Communist Party and the Soviet state while connecting emotionally and viscerally with the intended audience. VSFK and the All-Union Central Council of Trade Unions, or VTsSPS, put together one such excursion, which was organized for a variety of relay teams during the winter season 1929–1930. Three thousand citizen and military racers started in December and covered in eighty-six days 10,000 kilometers from Khabarovsk to Moscow in celebration of the twelfth anniversary of the founding of the Red Army. Sport and civil defense organizations, the Komsomol and trade unions all sent teams to promote defense of the nation, spring planting and the government's five-year plan. At stops along the way the participants put on ski festivals to encourage participation among the rural peasants and workers.[67]

Skiing, Shooting and the Military Patrol Race

Although instruction in walking and running on skis was fundamental to winter training for national defense, the Red Army and paramilitary civil defense organizations considered rifle marksmanship, naturally, the primary goal. A poster for the Moscow Spartakiada of 1928 highlighted the connection between sport and shooting in service of furthering communism: "Every sportsman must be a sharpshooter," and "every worker-sportsman must be a soldier of the revolution."[68] In addition to the efforts of the Central Board of Vsevobuch, the Society for Assistance to Defense, Aviation and Chemical Development, or Osoaviakhim, provided shooting instruction to potential recruits for the armed forces. The majority of Osoaviakhim training centers were in urban locales where organizers put on rifle and sniping contests among fifteen thousand rifle circles and stocked more than four thousand shooting ranges by the end of the decade. Lev Trotsky, reflecting from exile on the Civil War years in his book *The Revolution Betrayed* emphasized the important role rifle marksmanship in conjunction with skiing played not only within the army but also among the general population.[69] Of course, shooting a rifle at a metropolitan range is an altogether different matter than doing so in the field. Winter weather brings certain complications, such as cold fingers, frozen equipment and the instability of firing a weapon in the snow. Assuming the standing, kneeling or prone shooting positions with skis attached to the feet adds another layer of difficulty. Therefore, Osoaviakhim arranged excursions into the countryside for its 300,000 members for the purpose of ski training, a critical element of the organization's duties: "Every rifleman must be supplied with skis. . . . Ski converging races, ski excursions which finish with shooting, must find a place in the program of winter instruction of shooting groups."[70] Illustrating one such exercise, a photograph in *Pravda* shows a female Osoaviakhim member firing from the prone position in a district ski-shooting race held in the Far East near the city of Voroshilov.[71]

Similarly, the Red Army included exercises on skis in the field with rifles, as well as digging trenches in the frozen ground or in the snow from which to practice shooting. No Red Army personnel were exempt from this requirement: the General Staff insisted that all officers and soldiers as well as all political commissars attached to the units partake in ski training and strive for the highest level of mastery. In order to "instill skiing in the midst of the Red Army masses," the Leningrad Military District included "systematic ski competition . . . undertaken two to three times per month" based on programs developed by the Finnish Home Guard, whose training exercises were conducted just a few kilometers over the border. A 1925 article in *Krasnaia zvezda* details plans for a 30-kilometer ski race with shooting, divided into separate categories for commanders, officer trainees and Red Army soldiers. The specifications at the shooting range call for "waist-figure targets"—that is, half-length silhouettes in order to simulate a partially hidden enemy. The article does not say whether these figures were caricatures of a potential foe such as those used by the Finns.[72]

The predilection of some Soviet commanders for ski-shooting races with competitors in full combat kit reflected interest in Western Europe for the military patrol race, the immediate precursor to modern biathlon as an Olympic event. The first military patrol race took place in Germany in 1902 and gained inclusion at the Nordiska Spelen of 1922. It was a demonstration sport in the Winter Olympics of 1924, 1928, 1936 and 1948 but was discontinued after 1948 because of strong international anti-military sentiments following World War II. Four-man teams consisting of an officer and three enlisted men ran on a 25- to 30-kilometer course, usually with a greater elevation gain-and-loss profile than on regular ski courses. Rules governing the competition changed over the years but, in general, conformed to the following parameters: the enlisted men carried rucksacks, the total weight of which had to be around 24 kilograms; the officer was either unarmed or carried a pistol; three competitors would shoot in the range with the option of the officer replacing one of the enlisted men if necessary; a penalty accrued for each shot missed at the firing range; and the final time was tallied when the last team member crossed the finish line.[73]

It is no exaggeration to state that of all the events that have ever been part of the Olympic program, military patrol most blatantly fused militarism and nationalism. Because entry was restricted to military personnel, it was an obvious method of comparing the level of physical conditioning and military training of each nation's army within a sporting environment. An Italian film about the military patrol race shot at the 1941 World Ski Championships in Cortina d'Ampezzo illustrates how much militaristic displays of nationalism imbued this event. The opening ceremonies for these particular competitions were nothing less than a celebration of fascist glory, the camera sweeping the flags of Spain, Bulgaria, Slovakia, Japan, Finland, Germany and Italy as well as Sweden and Switzerland fluttering alongside a black pennant displaying the fasces-bundle. During the patrol race itself, members of the teams from Italy, Germany and Sweden ski past the camera resplendent in uniforms, kepis and military regalia. In several sequences, the camera lingers on the officer leading the German team as he glides by with perfect ski technique, an Iron Cross medal dangling from his lower-left chest pocket. The semiotics inherent in these military trappings present a striking contrast to the sporting white knickers and jersey worn by Swedish cross-country racer Alfred Dahlqvist, featured in similar footage from the 1941 World Championship events.[74]

Although the Soviet Union did not participate in international contests such as those held in Cortina, the Red Army and sport organizations began to stage military patrol events in the same year as the first demonstration of the sport at the 1924 Winter Games in Chamonix. The first National Championship of the USSR, won by F. Vorob'ev, N. Pavlov, A. Il'in and A. Pashchukevich, took place in 1933.[75] The Red Army found the patrol events to be well suited to its needs because of the obvious military applications as well as the quasi-socialist team aspects, and some commanders considered ski competitions devoid of the military patrol's martial tone virtually worthless. One of them, from Iaroslavl, commented in *Krasnaia zvezda* that the niceties of modern ski racing—on flat courses with packed-out ski tracks and minus military gear—made the Red Army soldier soft and reversed the priorities of military training: "These 'skiers' on the first excursions in the field displayed all their negative qualities as *soldier-skiers*. Such a situation compelled us to radically change the formulation in competitions in order to train *skier-soldiers* . . . such competitions along unbroken, loose and deep snow in rugged country and with full trekking gear [was of] considerably greater sporting interest."[76] The opening races of the 1929–1930 ski season for the Moscow garrison perhaps took this admonition to heart: the events included a variety of categories, including two 100-meter sprints, one "in Red Army uniform (without greatcoat) on military-style skis," another in gas mask with uniform optional.[77]

Equipping the Masses with Skis

After the Civil War, the lack of equipment for skiers in the Red Army, the paramilitary organizations and the sport clubs played a major role in inhibiting mass participation in the sport. Russia had suffered severe economic hardship during the war years under War Communism: the industrial infrastructure was in a shambles and agriculture at a standstill. Widespread starvation compelled the government to requisition grain from the peasants, leading to strikes, uprisings and growing social crisis. However by spring of 1921, the external pressures on Russia eased, allowing Lenin and the Bolsheviks to focus on consolidating political control of the Party. At the same time, they replaced the earlier stringent marketplace measures of War Communism with the New Economic Policy (NEP), or state capitalism. A socialist-capitalist hybrid evolved, allowing peasants and a new entrepreneurial class to absorb agriculture, services and small businesses while finance and heavy industry remained under the control of a state ever wary of the restoration of capitalism. The plan was successful enough to foster economic recovery after the Civil War from 1921 through 1928.[78]

Nevertheless, NEP suffered from wild swings between industrial and agricultural production affecting all levels of Soviet society. In the Red Army, this meant a lack of suitable skis and equipment for the troops, certainly a matter of concern for several readers of *Krasnaia zvezda* in the midst of the NEP years. "The Red Army lacks skis," wrote Vasilii Starikov in a 1925 article, suggesting that the unsuitable ski equipment foisted by the government on the Red Army soldiers might be of better service to beginners in the rural hinterlands:

> Quite often they fill entire warehouses, to the great chagrin of supply managers and to the temptation of boiler-stokers. So what kind of skis are these? It's a hunting ski or simply a peasant model—wide, heavy, without poles, with slots for ropes for being drawn by horses. . . . For the training of the troops especially for military action these "trestles" and other "skis" are absolutely useless. . . . The Red Army doesn't lose anything, parting with these half-planks/half-skis.[79]

In the military district around Smolensk, the troops were similarly saddled with short supplies of old skis, although they gamely made repairs on the available equipment in order to train for winter maneuvers.[80] Evgenii Preobrazhenskii, a Bolshevik economist and member of the Board of People's Commissariat of Finance, weighed into the debate in the pages of *Krasnaia zvezda*. In reply to Starikov, he pointed out first of all that during Civil War operations against the White forces of General Kolchak, only special ski units were formed, whereas now the entire Red Army must be trained: therefore, more money should be allocated to ski inventories. Another problem occurred in production, which was complicated by the need for two types of skis in the Red Army: a lighter, sleeker style for racing and a more robust and serviceable type for military operations. Preobrazhenskii dated the beginning of the ski industry in the USSR to 1920, admitting that ski production at that time was expensive and the quality unsatisfactory. In the final analysis, however, the troops themselves were to blame for a lack of skis: "To my knowledge . . . the lack of skis in military units reaches up to 30–40 percent every year. One can explain such a great shortage mainly by the careless handling of the skis and only partly by quality . . . the aid of the officers is necessary . . . to inspire in Red Army soldiers a conscious attitude toward this equipment and its cautious treatment."[81]

By 1929, the government addressed the myriad problems associated with providing adequate inventories of ski equipment and other related items. At the central production conference for ski industry in the High Soviet of Physical Culture (VSFK), the plenum proposed a five-year plan for the production of two million pairs of skis per year. On the docket for the spring of 1930 was the construction of a large ski factory in the Urals with a yearly output of 200,000 pairs with three more facilities to follow in subsequent years. According to government accounts—no doubt inflated for propaganda purposes—the production of skis during the season of 1928–1929 was five times the output of the previous year. The production of ski poles, however, was more problematic: throughout the 1920s, all ski poles were imports from the West. By 1929, the government had established a special factory in Moscow for the manufacture of a proposed 200,000 ski poles each year. In addition, a new, special workshop attached to the ski factory of the economic section of the Unified State Political Department opened for fabrication of wax, with a projected yearly output of ten million pieces. But other items necessary for the sport of skiing were also in short supply. The plenum appealed to the All-Russian Council of the National Economy to organize the production of ski boots, bindings and special garments and gloves in addition to skis, poles and wax.[82]

Nevertheless, the production of ski goods continued to perplex the Soviet Union well into the 1930s. According to *Pravda*, by October 1936 the cities received 86 percent of the sporting goods produced in the country and the villages only 14 percent. The government had planned for half a million skis based on the output of its factories in Petrozavodsk, Cheliabinsk and Omsk as well as that of Moscow's Egor'ev producers' group. However, low-quality raw material reduced ski production by half. Equally deficient were the government factories in Slutsk and Sverdlovsk, the main producers of ski and skate boots. Soft goods such as ski clothing were especially disappointing: "Ski outfits that should be comfortable and beautiful are sewn in the Volodarsk factory in the city of Kalinin out of bad-quality, easily soiled material with dismal grey colors. For a long time now their styles have been out of date and defective."[83] Although the quantity of skis manufactured met production goals a month later, quality was still poor: according to a late November report in *Pravda*, Moscow's Dinamo store rejected twelve thousand pairs of inferior skis. In addition, accouterments of the sport such as ski outfits and boots remained virtually nonexistent.[84]

It is worth noting that the production of soft ski goods such as clothing—which had antecedents in the NEP years—attracted significant interest in the post–World War II era. Taking a cue from national physical culture parades and a zealous government campaign to inspire the country to take up skiing, the regime encouraged Moscow designers to challenge factories by conjuring ski apparel that was appealing to consumers as well as feasible to manufacture out of cotton. A 1946 full-color spread in the weekly *Ogonek* magazine highlighted some of their creative suggestions. The illustrations indicate that they were based on military-style garb but, for the women, offered a feminized silhouette embellished with fashionable touches.[85] Production problems and funding deficits, however, plagued the nascent ski fashion industry. In 1954, a similar compendium of ski fashions featured outfits manufactured out of woolen cloth and jersey, much more practical materials for aerobic cold weather activity, but having considerably less flair and élan. Although these particular designs were prototypes, it is apparent from a variety of contemporary photographs that Soviet ski apparel in the post-war years had advanced considerably from the drab offerings of the 1930s. In the post–World War II era, however, such sport clothing—and even the most basic ski items—were rare commodities outside of the major cities: a ski booklet for the rural collectives published in 1949, for example, provides detailed instructions and patterns for fashioning skis, poles, bindings and mittens by hand.[86]

Polar Exploration in the 1920s

Technological developments during the First World War rendered the Norwegian method of polar travel obsolete by the second decade of the twentieth century. It made little sense to travel every meter on foot over the snows and glaciers of Antarctica or across the broken pack ice in the North when air machines such as dirigibles or airplanes allowed explorers to soar just above the surface. Yet even in the industrialized age, the image of the Arctic explorer was inextricably associated with skiing.

Roald Amundsen understood that the era of dogsleds and skis was over even before the start of World War I. As he watched an airplane fly for the first time in 1913, he realized that a pilot could cover the same territory in an hour that would have taken him days of perilous effort to traverse with skis and sleds. The man who had skied to the South Pole and back in 1911–1912 received the first civilian pilot's license in Norway two years later, possessed by the idea of flying across the Arctic, a dream he fulfilled in 1926.[87] He travelled on an airship, the *Norge*, designed by Italian explorer Umberto Nobile, crewed by Italians but flown under the Norwegian flag. In 1928, Nobile returned to the Arctic (without Amundsen) piloting the airship *Italia*, a project sponsored by fascist dictator Benito Mussolini.[88] At the end of May, Nobile disappeared, and in an attempt to find him by airplane reconnaissance, Amundsen lost his life. The situation turned out well for Nobile, fortunately: the Italian adventurer was rescued by the captain and crew of the Soviet icebreaker *Krasin*, one of a number of Russian ships and airplanes deployed to aid in the search for the downed dirigible. The success of the rescue operation revealed the important role icebreakers would play in future polar exploration.[89] The Soviet Union had already anticipated the use of air travel at high latitudes as a charter member of Fridtjof Nansen's International Society for the Study of the Arctic by Means of Airships, or Aeroarctic, founded in 1924.[90] The innovation of combining sea and air exploration became the *modus operandi* of Soviet Arctic explorers throughout the 1930s.

The voyage of the *Krasin* ushered in an era of intense Soviet Arctic research based on a planned approach to science and the exploitation of natural resources.[91] In this schema, the authorities discouraged going to the North Pole for simply sporting reasons, calling such ventures frivolous. Nevertheless, true-life accounts as well as serialized science-fiction adventure novels based on explorers in the Arctic captured the imagination of Russian readers during this period. Arctic literature's underlying theme of man versus nature and the ability of "will" to transform politics and society suited communist ideals. The heroes of stories such as these, whether Soviet or from the West, persevering in the Arctic with limited means, presented a splendid source of propaganda for expressing communist doctrine in an emotionally appealing way.[92] Fridtjof Nansen, a confidant of Lenin and the recipient of the Nobel Peace Prize in 1922 for his efforts on behalf of Russians suffering from famine, was by far the most popular choice as the subject of numerous polar exploration books during the Soviet era. Nansen enjoyed a long and fruitful relationship with several other luminaries of Russia and the Soviet Union: he worked with Maxim Gorky (in conjunction with Gerhart Hauptmann of Germany) on an edition of Tolstoy's *War and Peace* and maintained friendships with many among the scientific and polar exploring community, such as Petr Petrovich Semenov-Tian-Shanskii, Vladimir Rusanov, Georgii Sedov and Aleksandr Kuchin. As interest in the Arctic grew during the 1930s, the government published Nansen's collected works in five volumes between 1937 and 1940 under the direction of Vladimir Vize, a well-known polar explorer. Vize also wrote a biography and a number of monographs about Nansen and his exploits.[93] Writing in 1923, V. Stankevich summarized why Russians considered Nansen the ultimate polar explorer: "In the history of these explorations the travels of Nansen occupy an absolutely special place. In regard to the boldness and even the audacity of the plan, to the thoroughness and systematic approach of preparation, to the ability to utilize the powers of nature . . . scarcely can the voyage of Columbus be compared with [Nansen's]." And, he suggested, for the Russian reader steeped in "the Onegins, the Oblomovs, the Raskolnikovs and the heroes of Chekov," the story of Nansen was certain to provide "vivifying relaxation."[94] In the 1930s, Nansen represented the Soviet notion of man's will conquering the environment as "one of those heroes who went forward proudly in conquests of the element of nature for the pride of all mankind."[95] To V. M. Pasetskii, writing more than half a century later, Nansen was still "one of the most outstanding polar explorers, who enriched science with a multitude of discoveries and a series of fundamental works, which glorified his name."[96]

More problematic was Roald Amundsen, whose ski tour to the South Pole represented a well-organized, calculated approach to polar travel palatable to socialist tastes on the one hand, while on the other, the obvious sporting characteristics of the trip as well as his subsequent willingness to cooperate with fascist Italy in the Arctic reflected the worst aspects of the bourgeois West. But in the days surrounding Amundsen's disappearance while searching for Nobile, M. Beliakov wrote in *Krasnaia niva*: "And if Amundsen has died, then his death inscribes in his biography an unwanted and hardly embellished page which is indicative of his exceptional generosity and responsiveness."[97] Dmitrii Vasil'ev, one of the Soviet Union's most successful ski racers, makes special note in his autobiography, *On the Ski-Track,* that on his thirty-five-day trek across Scandinavia from Moscow to Oslo in 1926, his group met a lone skier who shared the same surname with the famous Norwegian explorer. Returning to Oslo twenty-two years later, Vasil'ev visited the city's ski museum to pay special homage before Amundsen's skis.[98] Amundsen's heroic death prompted a rash of books and articles about his life, numbering seven in 1928–1929 alone.[99] He was a "brilliant star" of polar exploration, paving the way for the Soviets in the Arctic in contrast to Nobile, who "threw down the flag of the fascists and the cross of the Catholic Church," to claim the North Pole in his airship-enhanced fly-by.[100] In the 1930 publication *Conquest of the Poles*, Amundsen is "the excellent polar explorer" whose portrait graces the frontispiece.[101] Another author described Amundsen as an oblique friend of the Soviets and perhaps a socialist at heart, attributing to him as well a Soviet point of view concerning polar exploration: he was no longer journeying in the Arctic for sport; now it was in the service of science.[102]

Yet it was skiing that defined the image of the Arctic explorer. The beautifully engraved book cover and frontispiece in Stankevich's 1923 tome features Nansen's portrait surrounded by polar bears, wolves, ice floes and skis. More than fifty years later, Georgii Kublitskii wrote a volume for young readers on Nansen's life that dealt as much with relief efforts on behalf of the Soviet Union as with polar exploits; in it, he extrapolated on Nansen's ski excursions as a young boy, inventing a faithful dog as his travelling companion. In a similar vein, children's author A. Iakolev described Amundsen as a youth for whom skiing was not sport but his work. Even Robert Falcon Scott, the hapless British explorer whose Antarctic expeditions hardly depended on skiing, is pictured in his polar kit on skis.[103] The idealized notion represented by the incredible physical and mental endurance of these ski explorers who performed in the most inhospitable of climates was instrumental in tying skiing to the Stakhanovites, the heroes of Soviet labor, during the 1930s in Joseph Stalin's Russia.

THREE

Stalin and the Inter-War Years

IT IS NO COINCIDENCE that two important historians of the Soviet Union chose the same excerpt from Joseph Stalin's 1929 essay "A Year of Great Change" to introduce their respective chapters on his twenty-four-year tenure: "We are advancing full steam ahead along the road of industrialization—to socialism, leaving behind the age-old 'Russian' backwardness. We are becoming a country of metal, a country of automobiles, a country of tractors."[1] Of all the manifestations defining Stalin's reign from 1929 to 1953, his passion for industrialization is paramount. His very name, the Man of Steel, indicates that his primary goal of catching and then surpassing the West hinged upon heavy industry and manufacturing. All other aspects of the Stalinist years, such as collectivization, the Great Purges, the Five-Year Plan, the Great Patriotic War and the Cold War, were contingent upon, or the result of, this drive toward industrialization and the military-industrial complex that evolved from it.

Joseph Stalin rose from the position of political commissar on a variety of fronts during the Civil War and People's Commissar for Nationalities to General Secretary of the Communist Party in 1922. By various machinations, he had appointed himself sole ruler of the Soviet Union by 1929. One of Stalin's most significant maneuvers was establishing a permanent, institutionalized version of War Communism based on two elements: accelerating industrialization and the collectivization of agriculture. Grain and other agricultural goods would become exportable commodities and the source of funding to re-establish Russia's manufacturing infrastructure, which had been destroyed by World War I, the Revolution of 1917 and the Civil War. The means for accomplishing this goal was the Five-Year Plan, a comprehensive program for ordering all aspects of the Soviet economy. At the center of this effort was heavy industry, especially the production of coal, iron and steel in conjunction with machine tools and new factories to assemble turbines, tractors, trucks and automobiles.[2]

The industrial reconfiguration of Stalinist Russia required a new working class to operate factories, mines and machine shops. Through a forced shift from an agricultural to an industrial economic system, the government moved close to thirty million peasants from rural to urban locations during the 1930s. By the end of the decade, the Soviet Union was as economically independent and as self-sufficient as the United States— a comparison made even more compelling by the deteriorating security situation in Europe and ongoing Soviet paranoia about the threat of world capitalism. Connotations of homeland defense gave industrialization and the labor it entailed a sense of national purpose, and harnessing the Soviet Union's economic independence to the production of armaments during the latter half of the decade helped blunt the otherwise traumatic social upheaval caused by Stalin's Five-Year Plans.[3]

Low labor productivity, however, remained a major problem for the government, because the labor pool derived from a peasant base ill-equipped—both in skill and discipline—for the demands of industrial work. Economic specialists tried to quantify the normal levels of worker productivity mathematically, but it was difficult to establish norms when a continuous stream of uprooted peasants filled the positions in heavy industry. Stalin abolished equality in wages in 1931 and declared that skilled workers would receive more money than the unskilled. In 1932, bonuses and better rations accrued to the most productive laborers, known as shock workers, who were usually of working-class rather than peasant origin. Encouraged and rewarded by the state for their efforts, the shock workers strived to set production records in order to inspire their fellow laborers. But this ended up building resentment among the rank and file, who chafed at the constantly increasing work tempos.[4]

In late August 1935, local Communist Party leaders challenged a miner in the Donbass region of Ukraine, Aleksei Stakhanov, to set a new production record for extracting coal with a pneumatic drill. His performance—102 tons in five hours and forty-five minutes—was a sensation in the press. Stakhanov became the poster boy for a campaign to increase productivity based on a new iteration of the shock worker, one who would introduce radical production techniques and innovative patterns of work. The state-promoted Stakhanovite movement resulted in teams of workers across the country who reorganized their work to set new records. Stakhanovites received more pay than ordinary workers, and in some instances where superior effort meant greater rewards, the benefits included cars and huge salaries. The title soon extended to other sectors of society, such as the agricultural collectives and the Red Army. Criticism for old ways of working and for those who would not make an effort to improve productivity infused Stakhanovism with a socialist fervor.[5] "They go boldly forward," Stalin said, "breaking outmoded technical norms and creating new and higher ones."[6] The notion of improving the Soviet Union through ever-increasing levels of effort via technological progress and socialist will crossed over into other segments of society, resulting in a national mania for record-breaking from 1936 on. In sports, this engendered hierarchies that elevated individuals above the masses, a phenomenon paralleled in other societal strata. The government promoted top Soviet athletes as models worthy of emulation, and the connection between the Stakhanovite labor hero and sportsmen was explicit: Stakhanovites were encouraged to pursue sports, and top athletes visited the workplace to organize competitions.[7] Concurrently, socialist realism, a recent conceptualization of Soviet art, flourished through the direct influence of Stalin. This approach to art encouraged an ideological re-education of the masses by realistically depicting events but infusing them with an unmistakable political message that anticipated a new socialist future. First applied to literature, art and film, the concept subsequently spread to the realm of sport and spectacle. As Jeffrey Brooks suggests, socialist realism was an arrangement in which writers and journalists promoted the government's agenda by "joining in the performance" under the watchful eye of cultural bureaucrats.[8] The essence of Stakhanovism—work harder, faster and more efficiently—combined with the precepts of socialist realism, turned out to be particularly well suited to the country's new and determined attention to long-distance ski racing.[9]

Multi-Day Ski Treks and the Stakhanovites

A number of factors influenced the development of multi-day ski tours in Russia. The exploits of polar explorers such as Fridtjof Nansen and Roald Amundsen, who spent months skiing at high latitudes, had entranced Russians since the turn of the century. Moreover, the wide-open terrain that stretched endlessly across Russia fostered interest in emulating the Norwegian pair's derring-do. Indeed, the 10,000 kilometers separating Vladivostok from St. Petersburg could easily accommodate on an east-west axis the distance Amundsen travelled to the South Pole and back more than three times over. The Sokol'niki Club of Skiers (SKL) ski run of

1911 from Moscow to St. Petersburg was the paradigm for numerous other long-distance races during the pre-revolutionary period, such as Moscow to Nizhnii Novgorod in 1912 and, two years later, Iaroslavl to Moscow and Kholmogory to Tsarskoe Selo. Increasingly popular among competitors as well were single-day events covering 60, 100 and 150 versts.[10]

The pure sporting character of long-distance skiing prior to the Revolution of 1917 changed under the Bolsheviks, taking on military, scientific and educational aspects. The Soviet regime found the agitation-propaganda possibilities inherent in long-distance skiing particularly useful. Skiers on the move across vast swaths of Russian soil in conjunction with scientific, political, educational, military or even athletic goals proved a compelling combination for fashioning agit-prop set-pieces during the late 1920s and the 1930s. Such ski treks remained viable well into the post-war era.[11]

The distances covered in these types of events increased dramatically after the establishment of the USSR. In 1923, a party travelling from Arkhangelsk to Moscow traversed 1,400 kilometers. A similar excursion from Omsk to Moscow in 1929 doubled that length. On 26 December 1926, a team of four skiers set out to travel from Moscow to Oslo via Helsinki and Stockholm, a distance of 2,150 kilometers. The group included two undisputed stars: Aleksandr Nemukhin, one of the pioneer participants of the 1911 Moscow to St. Petersburg ski and Russia's representative to the 1913 Nordiska Spelen; and Dmitrii Vasil'ev, the champion ski racer and younger brother of wax technician Nikolai Vasil'ev. In Russia the skiers resembled goodwill ambassadors, visiting workers' organizations along the way. In Finland the group met Jussi Niska for dinner at his house, and in Helsinki they toured the new Karhu ski factory and signed autographs. In Sweden they prompted surprise. "We anticipated that four enormous Bolshevik-bears on skis with shaggy beards were coming," noted one Swedish reporter. "Instead four gentlemen with very good appetites showed up." They arrived in Oslo after thirty-six days on 30 January 1927. The skiers took seven rest days along the way having covered an impressive 74 kilometers for each day that they were on the ski trail.[12]

In addition to such treks undertaken by small, elite groups, the converging race that sprang up in 1913 continued to be popular after the Civil War. The converging race fostered participation among a broader segment of the population beyond top-ranked skiers such as Nemukhin and Vasil'ev. One contest of particular interest took place in conjunction with the winter Spartakiada of 1928 in Moscow. Racers from all over the country arrived in teams just in time for the opening ceremonies of the games. Twenty-five thousand skiers took part in a converging race over nine different routes ending at the All-Union Congress of 1930. Another large-scale converging race, the Relay for Labor and Defense, occurred in 1931 with teams from sixty cities converging on the capital. From 1932 through 1935, both the converging race and the relay race factored into activities organized by the All-Union Congresses of the trade unions and the physical culture collectives such as the Komsomol. By 1937, similar relay events attracted thousands of participants, drawing from tractor stations, maintenance and repair factories and machine-operator schools throughout the Moscow district.[13]

But extended adventures across the length and breadth of the Soviet Union remained the focal point of elite skiers. In addition to the Khabarovsk to Moscow itinerary completed in 1930, a 5,200-kilometer ski route from Irkutsk, on the west shore of Lake Baikal, had already been established by 1934. During the winter season of 1934–1935, three separate groups set out from the Far East on these trails to Moscow, their progress covered in detail by *Pravda*. The combination of their Herculean efforts and the publicity that ensued was a prototype for the agit-prop of the Stakhanovite movement during the latter half of the following year, a notion previously ignored in histories of this period.

In a noteworthy reversal of Amundsen's ski-to-airship transformation, one of these trans-Siberian teams, comprised of aviation specialists Vladimir Martynov, Valentin Markov, Vladimir Savchenko, Dementii Nikolenko and Sasha Karmonov, set out from Khabarovsk near the Amur River on 1 October. Five weeks later, on 7 November, a second group from the Red Army—Vasilii Itiaksov, Aleksandr Boronin, Petr Kuznetsov, Boris Druzhinin and Nikolai Leonenko—left Nerchinsk, some 600 kilometers east of Lake Baikal near the Mongolian border, sporting special jerseys emblazoned with "Nerchinsk-Moskva 7000 km."[14] The two groups met in Sverdlovsk on 13 January 1935 to great fanfare and were joined by a third ensemble—Zinaida Irdugan, Nina Ugol'kova, Klavdiia D'iachenko, Tosia Vagina [sic] and Vera Ulitina, an all-female band of Red Army skiers who had left Tiumen on 2 January. In a telephone interview from Sverdlovsk, the team leaders emphasized the extreme cold all were experiencing in the field, with temperatures reaching minus forty-eight degrees Celsius. Four days later, the skiers set off from the Sverdlovsk town square at noon, the team from Khabarovsk heading to Moscow via Gorkii, the team from Nerchinsk through Kazan. The women's team continued on the trail to the capital with one of the six commanders from the Gavriushenko battalion, who had established the Tiumen-to-Moscow ski route the previous year, in tow. The three teams reached Moscow in mid-February in time to celebrate the All-Soviet Ski Competitions scheduled for 25 February through 1 March 1935. Lauding the arrival of these "hero-skiers," a *Pravda* headline exclaimed: "Our army is fierce and indestructible!"[15] The women's group had traversed 2,130 kilometers, the Nerchinsk team 6,910 kilometers, while the Khabarovsk aviators skied 8,000 kilometers on their journey.[16]

With the advent of the Stakhanovite era, the length and speed of long-distance ski trekking increased again as one team after another endeavored to accomplish greater goals. As record mania swept the country in late 1935, successive groups made plans to cover ever longer distances at a successively faster pace during the 1935–1936 ski season: one team clocked 8,134 kilometers from Bochkarevo to Moscow, only to be surpassed by five border guards who skied 8,200 kilometers from Lake Baikal to Murmansk in 151 days. A group of eight skiers set out to ski the 1,705 kilometers separating Moscow from Perm in sixteen days, averaging 107 kilometers in each twenty-four-hour period. In March, two Red Army commanders endeavored to break a twenty-four-hour speed record on skis, one travelling 170 kilometers, the other 185, while a squad leader with two of his soldiers skied 200 kilometers in twenty-two hours and ten minutes. Yet another party of Red Army skiers (clad at all times in military uniforms and metal helmets) established a new route from Okhotsk to Khrabarovsk, travelling 3,500 kilometers in sixty-three days while enduring temperatures reaching minus sixty degrees Celsius. And five skiers from Dinamo sports club traversed 9,000 kilometers from Lake Baikal to the Barents Sea.[17]

Pravda linked the Stakhanovite workers' movement with long-distance ski racing in reports about the dozens of agricultural and factory groups crisscrossing Russia during this unusually active winter season. From December 1935 through February of 1936, the newspaper featured photographs and stories about shock-worker delegates from various district collective farms who decided to ski to the fifth regional agricultural collective Slet in Gorkii.[18] Detailed coverage began in January with a story about five Komsomol members from the Karbolit factory in Orekhovo-Zuevo who were skiing through Moscow to Komsomolsk na Amure via Sverdlovsk, Novosibirsk, Irkutsk and Khabarovsk—a phenomenal distance of 9,420 kilometers. This trip took more than six months to complete, with the final 410 kilometers accomplished on foot.[19] A ski team of trade-school students travelled the Leningrad to Moscow route in eight and one half days in January.[20] A front-page announcement in the March 5 edition praised workers of the Ob-Irtysh Government Fisheries Group who had recently trekked from Tobolsk to Moscow and informed readers that the government was awarding each of the skiers the Medal of Honor.[21] By March of 1936, such skier-workers had assumed the Stakhanovite sobriquet. *Pravda* reported that "Nine Komsomol-Stakhanovites of the Stalingrad factory Barrikady" had completed a 2,100 kilometer ski route from Stalingrad to Leningrad in March, followed by "thirty-seven Komsomol members and Stakhanovites" who finished their ski travels from Novosibirsk to Narym at the end of the month.[22] "Six Stakhanovites" from the electrical and coal-mining trades skied from Bodaibo (just northeast of Lake Baikal) to Moscow. The last part of their ninety-six-day, 7,000-kilometer effort was covered on foot as the snow disappeared in the April thaw.[23] Two years later, "twenty of the best Stakhanovites from the Petrozavodsk Industrial Works" followed the ski route of Taivo Antikainen from Maselgskaia Station to Kimasozero.[24]

Female skiers took part in the action as well. Ten women from Moscow's Kuibyshev Electrical Works set out in the winter of 1936 to improve the record set by the female commanders of the Red Army the previous season, averaging 70 to 80 kilometers each 24-hour period along the Moscow-to-Tiumen route in thirty-one days of skiing. "We weren't afraid of the distance," one of the participants told *Pravda*. "Far worse was that almost the entire way there wasn't enough snow."[25] An article in *Krasnyi sport* later that year detailed the connection between the Stakhanovite movement and athlete-skiers from this particular factory. The story suggested that the skills developed in the Kuibyshev workplace "proved useful to sport."[26] The following year, five female ski enthusiasts completed an 805-kilometer trip across Kazakhstan between Semipalatinsk and Alma-Ata.[27] The most intrepid of these groups, however, was one consisting of Liza Konstantinova, Marusia Khakhalova, Vera Liubimskaia, Sonia Tykheeva and Nastia Sunkueva, five Komosmol members from the Buriat-Mongolian People's Republic. These "courageous female skiers" travelled from Ulan-Ude to Moscow, a distance of 6,065 kilometers, in ninety-five days on the trail, the first 1,000 kilometers of which they covered on foot before putting on skis. According to a 3 March article in *Pravda*, the women undertook the trek to "bring heart-felt greetings to Comrade Stalin from the liberated people of the Buriat-Mongolian Republic." But with an explicit agenda in service to the state, they also stopped at agricultural communes, tractor stations and factories along the way to tell workers about the supreme leader's proposed constitution and the class divisions of the Spanish Civil War. Two male companions, a "team leader" and a political instructor, aided the women in their agit-prop activities. The many photographs in *Pravda* as the group neared Moscow show the men sternly eyeing the proceedings. Arriving in the capital in time for Communist Women's Day on 8 March, they met the record-setting Moscow Electrical Works team of female skiers from the previous year at the Dinamo stadium. The government honored the Buriat-Mongolian skiers by awarding them Medals of Honor, as did *Pravda* by displaying their group photograph on the front page, a distinction that had eluded other skiers of the Stakhanovite era.[28] The trip from Ulan-Ude to Moscow by the Buriat-Mongolian team was celebrated and remembered well into the Cold War era: as one journalist wrote in 1971, "the whole country followed that trek with bated breath."[29]

Citizen skiers were keen to emulate these multi-day treks on a more moderate scale. A number of books helped popularize such events among the masses, especially *Great Ski Treks in the Red Army*, authored in part by Dmitrii Vasil'ev, the well-known ski racer.[30] Mass participation routes, scaled back to between 300 and 500 kilometers, attracted thousands of participants: a 437-kilometer tour from Nizhnii Novgorod to Moscow in 1936, for example, had sixty thousand participants. That same year, the four original participants in the first long-distance ski trek from Moscow to St. Petersburg in 1911 decided to re-create their journey in commemoration of its twenty-fifth anniversary. Reversing their route, Mikhail Gostev, Ivan Zakharov, Aleksandr Nemukhin and Aleksandr Elizarov departed for Moscow from Leningrad, intent on improving the time they had set as young men. That elite skiers could become citizen racers appealed to the government as a way to foster the mass characteristic of these long-distance events. The four skiers also provided an excellent example of the way in which skiing enhanced physical fitness for citizens of all ages: even though the youngest in the group was forty-four years old, these "little old men" managed to shave four days off their total elapsed time. "Our youth has not ended" was their motto: "A true sportsman is not acquainted with old age."[31] The quartet provided agit-prop for skiing along the way by meeting with schoolchildren, industrial workers and members of the farm collectives. In honor of their efforts, the Central Executive Committee of the USSR awarded each of them the Medal of Honor.[32]

Soviet interest in long-distance skiing was codified in a number of tradi-tional ski races. A yearly 60-kilometer race began as early as 1922. Moscow's annual 100-kilometer Great Race, consisting of five loops around a 20-ki-lometer course, had its initial run in 1938, as did a four-day stage event on the Iaroslavl to Moscow route, both of which were dominated by Dmitrii Vasil'ev before the Great Patriotic War. This 230-kilometer event attracted the best skiers from sport clubs such as the Central Home of the Red Army, Dinamo, Spartak, Stalinets, Wings of the Soviets, Redfront and Locomotiv.[33] Enthusiasm for marathon skiing was greater than that shown for any other type of ski competition at the national level. At the USSR National Champi-onships of 1937, for example, only forty skiers competed in the slalom event on 24 February, less than half the number of the eighty-four competitors in the field of the 50-kilometer race at the Moscow All-Union Ski Competi-tions the following day.[34] After 1948, when the Soviet Union started attend-ing international ski races, the national ski team focused its efforts on the prestigious 50-kilometer competition, the longest distance on the Olympic docket and the oldest continuously contested event at the Winter Games.

Capping this engaging period of Russian ski development one final com-petition is worth noting. On 20 February 1938, 132 skiers lined up for the start of the opening event of the Spartakiada of the Red Army and Dinamo ski club in Moscow, a 50-kilometer event for the best rifle detachments of the Armed Forces and the People's Commissariat for Internal Affairs (NKVD). Responsible for border defense, the NKVD's border patrol rifle units were keen competitors in this race. Participants left the starting line with rifles, gas masks and rolled-up uniforms on their backs; machine-gunners carried small automatic weapons. The twelve detachments in the race left one af-ter another in a staggered start, shot at targets, then donned their gas masks to ski along a trail through a "contaminated" area. The eleven-man Moscow Military District team edged that of the NKVD for first place, finishing in five hours and twenty-four minutes.[35] This unique competition exemplified how the Soviets connected national defense and sport, combining elements of the Olympic military patrol race and 50-kilometer marathon with the Soviet inter-war predilection for gas mask training, Society for Assistance to De-fense, Aviation and Chemical Development (Osoaviakhim) marksmanship and communal participation in endurance events. In the post-war years, the intense competition between the Red Army and NKVD's successor organiza-tion, the Committee for State Security, or KGB (in association with Dinamo), produced many of the world's most successful international biathletes.

Mechanized Cavalry and Stalin's Arctic

In Arctic exploration and the military, Soviet infatuation with mechanization began to overshadow the simple act of skiing. During the inter-war years, the growing dependence of modern armies on increased fire-power and logistics, made evident during World War I, influenced the development of Soviet military dogma. "Deep Battle," a theory based on combining infantry, aviation, tanks and artillery in simultaneous frontal and flanking attacks on the enemy, became the official doctrine of the Red Army.[36] Mikhail N. Tukhachevskii contributed to the creation of the first armored divisions in 1931—four years prior to Germany—and the organization of large-scale paratroop drops during military exercises of 1935 and 1936. The concept of horse-mounted cavalry invariably shifted to that of mobile mechanized divisions that were not dependent on vast quantities of fodder.[37] Yet, integrating some form of skiing into this matrix was paramount because of the relationship of the sport to the Red Cavalry and, perhaps more important, to the difficulty of operating wheeled or tracked vehicles in snow. Newspapers of the period featured illustrations of all manner of mechanized snow travel, such as propeller-driven snow machines and even a propeller-driven backpack worn by a skier.[38] Such devices were plagued with technical difficulties, however, and the Red Army sought other solutions for mechanized winter travel. In a *Pravda* photograph from 1937, for example, a tank draws a company of skiers by attached ropes during maneuvers, at speeds approaching thirty kilometers per hour.[39] Also popular in the inter-war years was the sport of skijoring behind motorcycles: one intrepid group covered the 700-kilometer route between Moscow and Leningrad in three days.[40] The armed forces of the Soviet Union would soon learn, however, that severe winter weather could nullify the advantage of military machinery. In the aftermath of the Winter War of 1939–1940, skiing re-emerged as a worthwhile and viable military exercise in its own right.

The 1930s were formative years for the Soviets in the Arctic. Reflecting Stalin's preoccupation with technology, the state emphasized mechanical means of transportation for the purpose of economic exploitation of the region. By contrast, travelling to the North Pole for sporting reasons met with disapproval. Arctic research advanced during the inter-war period on drifting ice stations that were sometimes manned for three-quarters of a year while serviced by icebreakers and airplanes.[41] Mechanized polar travel had antecedents in Roald Amundsen's switch from ski to airship in the 1920s but also reflected the Stalinist point of view that science and technology could overcome any barrier. Industrialization under Stalin was carried out as a massive military campaign fought on several fronts, even as an expedition into the wilderness where all obstacles, both technical and natural, had to be overcome through human will. Eventually, both of these notions came together in Stalin's "Great Transformation of Nature" during the 1940s, a military-style campaign for the subjugation of the forces of nature through socialist means. In contrast, the depiction of skiing in relation to the Arctic was almost quaint in comparison and often associated with the West: one article details a British mapping expedition to Greenland undertaken the previous summer by a group of skiers with dogsleds. A picture of the cartographers' tent surrounded by skis accompanies the text.[42] As the Soviet Union prepared for war toward the end of the decade, however, interest in the Polar regions began to wane.

The return of skis to the Arctic would have to await a backlash against the mechanization of exploration—and its association with Stalinism—among adventurers of the post-war Soviet generation, most notably the mathematician Dmitrii Shparo. During the mid-1970s, he developed a penchant for self-sustained Arctic trekking and in the process became the Soviet Union's most accomplished high-latitude skier. Although he was initially vilified as a maverick, Shparo eventually garnered government approval and support in the nation's press as the archetypal Soviet explorer.[43] Active during this period as well were the all-female Metelitsa crews organized by Valentina Kuznetsova and Antonina Egorova for a variety of long-distance ski excursions from 1966 through the mid-1990s.[44] Through an exploration format, individuals such as Shparo, Kuznetsova and Egorova maintained a connection to the core values of socialism while at the same time interpreting them in ways unimaginable—or at least forgotten—by the state. There is no doubt that these last Soviet ski explorers emulated the heroes of the Golden Age of exploration in their attitude and approach to adventure. "For many polar explorers," wrote Dmitrii Shparo in 1987, "Amundsen is a teacher in the highest meaning of the word. He taught [others] how to respect and value people, to be proud and love one's country. He taught how to fight and how to win!"[45] And from his earliest expeditions in the 1970s to his most recent crossing of Greenland in 2000, it was Fridtjof Nansen to whom Shparo looked as the epitome of an Arctic explorer who set forth to forge new trails on skis over the northern ice.[46]

Gotov k trudu i oborone: Ready for Labor and Defense

Two interlinked programs focused the attention and energy as well as the hopes and dreams of the Soviet sport system on building men and women of the new socialist order in the Soviet Union: *Gotov k trudu i oborone* (Ready for Labor and Defense) or GTO; and the uniform rankings system for individual sports, or the Single All-Union Sports Classification System. Both were designed to promote the simultaneous goals of *massovost'* (mass participation) and *masterstvo* (mastery). These two concepts developed side by side during the 1930s, when the Soviets introduced sport competitions to achieve specific aims: glorifying the state and the precepts of Marxism-Leninism, improving the efficiency of production and increasing the physical fitness of the military with nationwide participation the ultimate goal.

After the end of the Civil War and the dismantling of Vsevobuch, the development of *fizkul'tura* (physical culture) became the domain of trade unions and labor movements. Nevertheless, the military never fully terminated its association and continued to support its own sport clubs and societies. During this period, the values and needs of the new Soviet state encouraged the notion of physical culture, as opposed to the more bourgeois concept of sport prevalent in the West. From the Soviet point of view, devotion to competitive sport was considered dangerous because it obscured all other social considerations. Collectivist sport, on the other hand, had a utilitarian and ideological function, primarily to prepare youth for labor and military service. The concept of physical culture was to improve the health and strength of the entire population so that every individual physical-culturalist would be better prepared to contribute to the socialist program, first through labor and the development of the industrial infrastructure of the USSR, and then through military defense of the borders. The government promoted physical culture by targeting as wide an audience as possible, incorporating it into educational programs for both students and workers. Sport was just one aspect of physical culture: it also included physical exercises, gymnastics and hygienic practices as well as industrial instruction and military training. The government saw a need for quantifiable results to determine the level of success of these sport programs, which led to the implementation of Ready for Labor and Defense (GTO) with the first Five-Year Plan in March 1931.[47]

The GTO program promoted physical culture as both a leisure activity and a civic duty. This dual aspect was fundamental to the concept of mass participation and became an integral part of the educational system from the primary grades through secondary school. The program functioned to promote participation in sport among youths so that physical culture would become a regular and permanent aspect of Soviet life.[48] Thus, adults could earn GTO awards for meeting certain athletic norms in age categories up to fifty-five. GTO also offered an introduction to military training, especially for secondary school students who planned to enter the armed forces. It set goals for proficiency in a variety of sports, in addition to knowledge of basic hygiene and first aid. Integral to the format of GTO, however, were ten mandatory test categories. Two centered on competition in cross-country skiing and rifle marksmanship.[49] The program improved shooting scores nationwide to such an extent that by 1938, Soviet competitive shooters had shattered twenty-one world records in marksmanship in a single year. GTO also generated huge numbers of skiers. By the Soviets' own reckoning, between four and twelve million skiers took part in ski events each year during the 1930s.[50] Thus, from its very inception the format of GTO encouraged the skill sets necessary for competitors in the future sport of biathlon. A refinement of the program, *Gotov k zashchite rodiny* (Ready for Protection of the Homeland), or GZR, was implemented in the mid-1960s for all military conscripts between the ages of seventeen and nineteen. The categories included norms for a 100-meter run, jumping, grenade-throwing, 1.5-kilometer cross-country run, 100-meter swim, 10-kilometer cross-country ski, marksmanship at 25- and 50-meter distances, pull-ups, cycling a 25-kilometer course and speed-marching over eight kilometers. With the exception of grenade exercises, such a regime comported with the year-round training program of the world's most competitive ski-shooters.[51]

Sports Classification System

As early as 1925, the Communist Party's Central Committee passed a resolution that promoted the development of a high-level tier of elite athletes, similar to the shock workers and Stakhanovite labor heroes of the 1930s. This unique amalgamation of work, sport and mass participation found expression on a universal factory poster of the 1930s: "Every shock worker a sportsman; every sportsman a shock worker."[52] Thus, in 1936, the Council of the People's Commissars of the USSR reorganized the leadership of athletics into the Committee for Physical Culture and Sport. Using a variety of trade union sport organizations, this governmental agency subsequently replaced the ski clubs that had functioned under the auspices of groups such as Experimental Grounds of Vsevobuch, Club in Honor of Youth of the Communist International, Club in Honor of the October Revolution, Moscow Union of Consumers' Organizations and Union of Soviet Trade Workers. The largest of these new trade union groups were Spartak, Trudovye rezervy, Lokomotiv, Urozhai, Trud, Burevestnik and Vodnik.[53]

The Soviet government developed a sports ranking system to motivate the best athletes to reach set standards for their particular sport through mastery, and to aid coaches in selecting prospective competitors. The purported goal was to encourage greater effort from less capable comrades, but in reality a tiered series of awards engendered competition among the elite athletes. The two highest honors, Master of Sport of the USSR and Master of Sport of the USSR, International Class, were honorary and bestowed for life on championship performances at the national and international levels. One higher award existed for certain internationally successful athletes, the Merited (or Honored) Master of Sport of the USSR. The state conferred this special award outside of the sports ranking system for outstanding service to the development of sport. This distinction was introduced in 1934 to honor individual highly skilled athletes, such as speedskaters Iakov Mel'nikov and Platon Ippolitov, soccer players Mikhail Butusov, Nikolai Starostin and Nikolai Sokolov, weight-lifter Aleksandr Bukharov and cross-country ski racer Dmitrii Vasil'ev.[54] Before athletes could qualify for these higher awards, they had to meet all the ranking standards for their particular sport. Results from official Soviet competitions were the basis for sport rankings 1 through 3 and were valid for one or two years only. To maintain eligibility, competitors had to renew their rankings. The qualifying standards were set high and updated regularly to maintain parity with world standards, resulting in very competitive fields in all sports.

After the Second World War, the government concerned itself with international prestige through sport and endeavored to transform Soviet athletics from a method of training for labor and combat into a missionary and diplomatic tool. Success at high-level competitions such as the Olympics demonstrated to the world the superiority of the Soviet system. As a result of this new emphasis on prizes and awards, a dichotomy between elite athletes and the citizenry ensued. Under Khrushchev, skilled athletes now found favor over physical-culturalists. The combination of state-sponsored sport development programs that arose out of GTO and the demand for athletes of the highest caliber who could represent the country internationally produced a Soviet sports apparatus geared toward one overarching goal: winning medals at the Olympics.[55]

Thus, the entire Soviet sports program of physical culture was structured to produce star athletes, yet built on a foundation that called for mass participation ostensibly available and accessible to all citizens. The mass character of skiing already afoot in long-distance ski trekking was encouraged by government efforts to combine mass participation, GTO and the educational system. The city of Gorkii, for example, offered a winter family "Olympics," held over a three-month period. Mothers, fathers and primary school children competed in cross-country skiing against members of their own age groups and gender for the title "most-sports-minded family in town."[56] But the very nature of mass sports competition created winners and losers, a notion contrary to earlier revolutionary ideals of equality and collective cooperation. Finding the proper balance between mass participation and mastery generated continual disputes within the Soviet sports system, even though proletarian service to socialism defined the concept of both. Because the socialist state considered itself free from the commercial bourgeois aspects of capitalist countries, the Soviets faced a conundrum. The emphasis on individual success through the sports ranking system and mastery was a paradoxical manifestation of the new Soviet man, who ideally preferred to remain a faceless member of the masses.[57] As eager as they were to promote excellence in sport and garner the prestige that accompanied victory in international competition, the Soviets also sought to curb the excesses of professionalism, especially among sport clubs, work unions and societies that sponsored their own teams and hoped to bring renown and rewards to their own particular association. In the dichotomy between the need for sport heroes to inspire the nation and the denigration of the West's bourgeois adulation of athletic prowess, maintaining a reasonable symmetry between mass participation and the growth of a professional elite became a critical issue in the realm of sports throughout the Soviet period.

Fascist States and International Sports

From 1917 to 1928, the Bolsheviks and then the Soviets used sport to promote "proletarian internationalism"—or, put another way, to advance world revolution by undermining bourgeois and social-democratic

authority. Although the generally accepted point of view is that the Soviet Union remained isolated from international sport competition with
the West during this period, the Soviets did have limited exposure, especially in ski races with other Scandinavian countries beginning in the
mid-1920s.[58] However, the glaring failure of the anticipated world revolution led, after 1928, to a sport policy intended to reinforce the USSR as
a self-sustained entity.[59]

During the 1930s, Soviet sport policy underwent a dramatic transformation when authorities abandoned previous hostility toward the West's
emphasis on competitive achievement. It was clear that Westerners were
keen for international sports competition, and the Soviet Union's participation would impress foreign governments with Soviet strength while
bolstering the regime's legitimacy at home. Throughout the decade prior
to World War II, fascist states demonstrated how sport could promote a
specific political ideology—a lesson taken to heart by the Soviet regime.
At the 1932 Olympics in Los Angeles, for example, Italy placed second
behind the United States in total medals won. Four years later, the Olympic Games hosted by Germany at Garmisch-Partenkirchen and in Berlin
proved a valuable instrument of foreign policy and a means to influence
public opinion abroad. By the middle of the decade, international sport
had become the catalyst for breaking the cultural isolation of the Third
Reich. The Germans understood the political aspects of sport, and teams
that represented the nation were treated as if they were auxiliary troops of
German foreign policy.[60] In addition, the culture of sport was increasingly
subsumed by a capitalist and consumer-focused orientation that placed a
higher value on elite athletes than on the class-based and collectivist iteration of sport under communism. The international proletarian sport
policy once favored by the USSR simply did not accrue the same kind of
benefits that participation in the Western sport program offered. Therefore, the Soviet regime moved toward integration with the international
sport community with which it had previously been at odds. The idea of
surpassing the West by capturing all world sport records began to appear
in the Soviet press by late 1933.[61]

The International Olympic Committee (IOC), however, was disinclined
to extend membership to nations of which it did not approve. In the case of
Russia, fear of Bolshevism meant exclusion from the Olympics, even though
the organizing committees of Paris in 1924 and, in 1932, those of Lake Placid and Los Angeles were willing to invite Russian athletes. As for Germany,
banishment from the Olympic movement was simply one more manifesta-

tion of post-war humiliation resulting from the Versailles settlement. The IOC, dominated by the French, refused to include Germany in the Games of 1920 and 1924, a particularly devastating blow to a nation whose classical scholars had devoted much time, energy and money to excavating Olympic sites in Greece. Unbowed, Germany staged the First Workers' Olympics in 1925, the precursor to the Moscow Spartakiada of 1928.[62]

Germany's example of using sport to further political ends paralleled that of the Soviet Union in many ways. The Nazi Party and other right-wing groups supported the right to use paramilitary physical training programs to subvert the provisions of the Versailles Treaty, and when Hitler seized power, physical education became centrally mandated. Physical education testing was a requirement in higher education, the rationale for participation in sport and physical education programs defined strictly in terms of service to the state. In a manner similar to the strictures of the GTO in the Soviet Union, taking part in athletics was perceived as the duty of all Germans and a contributing factor to the strength of the *Volk*; and the emphasis on mass participation in sport was a way to increase the nation's military preparedness. In addition, the usefulness of government-produced media reports as sport propaganda reached its apogee during the 1936 Olympic Games. Joseph Goebbels as Reich Minister of Public Enlightenment and Propaganda formed a working group out of his Ministry for Sport and the IOC to provide and coordinate German propaganda and Olympic press releases for the world's news organizations. Capitalizing on Goebbels' efforts, Leni Riefenstahl produced *Olympia*, a documentary about the 1936 Berlin Olympics, released in 1938. Her body of work offered a splendid prototype for the way in which sport film served propaganda purposes, a notion adopted during World War II by Soviet cinematographers.[63]

Fueled by the success of the Garmisch-Partenkirchen Olympics of 1936, a curious amalgamation of nationalism rooted in skiing developed in the late 1930s among certain European nations, creating odd bedfellows at international ski competitions. Especially supportive of the Nazi sport programs during this period were Switzerland and the Scandinavian countries. In these regions, skiing was perceived as the embodiment of dynamic nationalism and symbolic of virtuousness, manliness and the heroic.[64] These characteristics meshed nicely with Aryan notions of Nordic superiority, promoted by the Nazis through active sponsorship of international ski races. This northern European affiliation had roots in the immediate aftermath of World War I. The Swiss, Norwegians, Swedes and

Finns were sympathetic to athletes from the defeated German-speaking lands, considering them natural partners in sport. Inspired by Sweden's Nordiska Spelen, Austria, had organized Die Nordischen Spiele in the Mürzzuschlag region in 1904, at which top competitors received special "Nansen-medals" struck in gold, silver and bronze. Bavaria's Black Forest had been chosen as the location for the first Winter Olympics scheduled for 1916, abruptly pre-empted by the Great War. The pre-war Austrian ski competitions, disappointment over the thwarted Black Forest Olympics and exclusion from the international sporting community prompted Germany to initiate Deutschen Winterkampfspiele, a celebration of German unity through ski culture held three times between 1922 and 1934. For Germany, these festivals served as a template for the 1936 Winter Olympics. When Norway and Switzerland were unable to organize the Winter Games of 1940, Germany offered to host the Olympics once again at Garmisch-Partenkirchen, an offer received favorably by the IOC.[65]

Admiration for the ability of Germany to organize sport notwithstanding, the escalating threat of war in Eastern and Central Europe during the 1930s compounded the defensive instincts of the Soviet Union. Excluded from the Munich Conference in 1938, the Soviets watched with trepidation as the Germans annexed the German-speaking Sudetenland of Czechoslovakia and the Memelgebiet from Lithuania and raised demands for Danzig and the Polish Corridor. These actions encouraged the perception that the USSR was the sole bastion of communist revolution surrounded by a sea of fascist and capitalist foes. Fearing an attack by Germany and reasoning that the French and British wanted Russia to take the brunt of a Nazi campaign, the Soviet Union signed a treaty of non-aggression and friendship with Germany on 23 August 1939. The Molotov-Ribbentrop Pact stipulated that in any future territorial redistribution, the Soviet Union and Germany would divide Poland and the Baltic states. With the signing of this agreement, Soviet sport policy veered toward collaboration with the fascist bloc. The resulting division of Soviet and German spheres of influences in Eastern Europe fostered sport contests with the Baltic states, and following the German invasion of Norway in April 1940 and the establishment of Quisling's fascist regime, the parties signed a Soviet-Norwegian sports accord that stipulated an exchange of skiers to compete in bilateral competitions in December of that year.[66]

The intricate balance of political influence and military maneuvering around the Gulf of Finland as a result of the Molotov-Ribbentrop Pact had a significant impact on the Soviet Union. Soviet hegemony in this region convinced leaders in the Baltic states that the Red Army was invincible. By contrast, the Finnish government exaggerated the weakness of the Red Army, and officials in Helsinki felt emboldened to play a game of brinksmanship along the Karelian Isthmus and in the Gulf of Finland. Paramount in the minds of Stalin's staff was control of these regions, the attainment of which drove the incessant diplomatic efforts of Foreign Minister Viacheslav Molotov. In the end, Finland, Estonia, Latvia and Lithuania had little choice when confronted with these geostrategic concerns. Nevertheless, Finland's decision to defend itself against invasion in contrast to the other states' acquiescence to Molotov's demands was a watershed event in the development of Soviet skiing and the post-war sport of biathlon.

FOUR

The Winter War and the Great Patriotic War, 1939–1945

IN EARLY JANUARY 1940, a dispatch from James Aldridge, war correspondent for the *New York Times* covering the Soviet invasion of Finland, detailed a gruesome landscape along the forest roads just west of the Russian border. As he accompanied an advancing ski patrol in pursuit of survivors of the 163rd and 14th Red Army Corps, Aldridge was aghast at the carnage: "I came upon a sight I never want to see again. It was the main battle scene. It began with a smashed Russian tank, which had held up a four-mile-long super-mechanized battalion. . . . I squeezed my way along between the tanks, stepping over dead Russians and frozen horses . . . it was a kaleidoscope of bodies—bodies everywhere, tangled up with tipped-up and scattered guns, tanks, armored cars . . . and machine-guns splattered with blood."[1] The Finnish army's idiosyncratic form of guerrilla-style combat had already thwarted Stalin's proposed blitzkrieg toward Helsinki across the fortified Mannerheim Line northwest of Leningrad. Now, far to the north, Soviet military leaders were learning another costly lesson in winter warfare during the protracted Battle of Suomussalmi. Between 7 December 1939 and 8 January 1940, the Red Army lost two divisions to a greatly diminished but determined battalion of Finnish ski troops.[2] That winter, the world press heralded the Finns' well-executed series of maneuvers at Suomussalmi as a courageous and monumental display of military skill.[3] The Soviet Union only defeated a battered and isolated Finnish defensive force of 200,000 in February of 1940 after three months of devastating warfare, during which the Red Army employed the efforts of 1.2 million troops, while suffering huge casualties.[4] Although the Soviet Union ultimately claimed victory over Finland in March, its leaders realized that, in this conflict, the Finns had outmatched the Red Army.

The invasion of Finland transformed the Soviet military from an inefficient, ideologically burdened body into one of the world's most powerful fighting forces. By the spring of 1940, the Soviet General Staff began to pay careful attention to the details of the disastrous invasion, known subsequently as the Russo-Finnish War, the Soviet-Finnish War or the Winter War, and especially to the debacle at Suomussalmi. Contemptuous of the Finns in the first weeks of the campaign, the military leaders of the Soviet Union came to value the effectiveness and mobility of their ski troops. During the fifteen-month period after the peace settlement with Finland, the Red Army incorporated the Finnish methods by making general organizational and tactical changes, improving winter clothing and equipment and training ski troops with renewed fervor. Eventually, these Soviet ski troops developed guerrilla-style combat tactics on a scale unprecedented in the history of winter warfare, waging numerous successful campaigns against the Germans, especially in the winter of 1941–1942 during the counteroffensive to Operation Barbarossa. Nevertheless, the image of plucky Finnish skiers thwarting the masses of the Red Army remained a powerful trope throughout the Cold War era.[5]

Significantly, the reversal of fortunes in Finland fostered a mass ski mobilization effort in the Soviet Union beginning in the autumn of 1940. It embraced every sector of society: the military, the government, the educational system, industry, Communist Party organizations and the press, poets, musicians, writers, artists, filmmakers and athletes. The momentum generated by the ski mobilization campaign continued throughout the years of the Great Patriotic War. As one of the most successful shock movements of the Stalinist era, it had an enormous effect on the Soviet military and the development of winter sports during the Cold War.

The Winter War, 1939–1940

The quagmire that evolved in the snows of Finland from the winter of 1939 through early spring of 1940 caught the Soviet Union completely off guard. Nikita Khrushchev, Stalin's First Secretary of Ukraine during the Winter War, recalled the consensus within the Kremlin before the invasion: "All we had to do was raise our voice a little bit, and the Finns would obey. If that didn't work, we could fire one shot and the Finns would put up their hands and surrender."[6] The USSR intended to dominate the Baltic states and the bulk of Scandinavia with minimal resistance, bolstering the defenses of the country's northwestern border while receiving the accolades of the masses liberated from Western European capitalist oppression.

By all appearances, this scenario was virtually a *fait accompli* in the autumn of 1939. Two weeks after the German invasion of Poland on 1 September, under the stipulations of the Molotov-Ribbentrop Pact, Soviet troops secured Poland's eastern half and then systematically occupied Lithuania, Estonia and Latvia by the second week of October through strong-arm negotiations concluded with each nation. The USSR insisted on a similar accord with Finland, resulting in a month-long series of diplomatic meetings. With total control of the Gulf of Finland and security of Leningrad in the balance, talks reached an impasse over the key issue of placing a Soviet naval base on Hangö Peninsula, the southernmost point of Finland, just across the water from the Estonian port of Tallinn. Stalin's offer to compromise on Hangö led the government in Helsinki to conclude that the Soviets were weakening and would not dare to use military force. The Finnish negotiators were sent back to Moscow with explicit orders not to compromise on Hangö or any of the surrounding islands; if differences could not be settled, they were authorized to break off negotiations. During the last session, which took place on 9 November, the Soviets registered astonishment that the Finnish delegation remained obstinate. Within the top echelon of the Finnish government, the prevailing point of view was that Helsinki had called the Kremlin's bluff and gotten away with it.[7] However, Finland's leadership had seriously misread the intentions of the USSR. Only three weeks after negotiators walked out of the final session in Moscow, Soviet tanks arrayed along the Karelian Isthmus began to roll across the Russian-Finnish border.

The earlier success in Poland had given the Soviets confidence that they could easily invade Finland, a move of paramount importance according to Stalin's military advisors. In their judgment, the government of Finland, virulently anti-communist and cozy with fascist Germany, constituted a threat to the USSR because the Finnish border was so close to Leningrad. They convinced Stalin that a campaign in Finland would be nothing more than a glorified police action against a restive Finnish population willing to greet the Soviet troops as liberators.[8] This sanguine version of events swayed public opinion in the USSR as well. "We did not expect to meet so much resistance. We thought it would be like Poland," one Russian officer, a former Leningrad schoolteacher, told a *New York Times* reporter.[9]

Unfortunately the Soviet Union did not have enough military advisors available to analyze the true situation in Finland, because Stalin had other priorities. He wanted to increase the size of the Red Army in response to Japanese military incursions in the Far East and German rearmament in the West, while consolidating his own political power. Having abolished the Military Revolutionary Soviet in favor of a People's Commissariat for Defense under the direction of Marshal Kliment Voroshilov, Stalin subsequently sought to homogenize the Red Army's command corps. Both Stalin and Voroshilov formulated security policy based on their revolutionary enthusiasm and heroism during the Civil War. They found themselves at odds with a younger cadre of military professionals who wanted to establish a modern mechanized army staffed by highly educated and competent officers. Stalin destroyed this potential challenge to his supreme authority during the Great Purge of the Red Army in 1937. By the late 1930s, too few competent commanders remained to lead a greatly expanded pool of recruits, mobilized in response to German militarism in Western Europe and the Japanese presence on the Manchurian border. When fighting finally broke out with Japan at Kholkin Gol in July 1939, the Red Army found its best surviving supervisory talent occupied in the Soviet Far East.[10]

By this point, Germany's blitzkrieg tactics had impressed Stalin's remaining generals. This military innovation incorporated tank divisions that penetrated the enemy's main line of defense and spread havoc in the rear, followed by masses of infantry advancing with air support and artillery barrages. Soviet commanders sought to emulate Germany's successful blitzkrieg assault on Poland three months later in Finland, but they had not developed the Wehrmacht's tactical coordination between the various military branches, nor had they fostered individual initiative among frontline commanders.[11] Rather, the Red Army simply threw masses of men and overwhelming amounts of ordnance against the enemy's defenses. Described variously in the zealous Soviet press as "an iron, rumbling production-line of tanks," a "hurricane of metal" or a "steel line of tanks,"[12] the massed forces of the mechanized Red Army, representing the industrialized aspects of modern warfare, meshed nicely with Soviet five-year plans for steel production and heavy fabrication.

The Soviet regime was confident that the nation's industrialized military might would simply crush the Finnish Army and occupy Finland within a week. The forces of the USSR that gathered on the northwestern border disproportionately outnumbered the tiny Finnish Army. On the Karelian Isthmus alone, the Soviets maintained a material superiority of three to one in manpower, eighty to one in tanks, five to one in artillery and almost six to one in aircraft.[13] In the days leading up to the invasion on 30 November, *Pravda* featured numerous photographs of these Soviet armored vehicles, airplanes and artillery batteries and, in one political cartoon, represented the USSR as a tank poised on the border with Finland.[14]

However, the border territories with Finland differed greatly from the open, treeless plains that suited a German-style blitzkrieg offensive. In an unusually candid report to the Soviet General Staff on the eve of the invasion, K. Meretskov, commander of the Leningrad Military District, described the eastern regions of Finland as "split by lakes, rivers, and swamps, and . . . almost entirely covered by forests" and noted that "the proper use of our forces will be difficult."[15] Unforeseen by Meretskov were the ensuing severe winter conditions of 1939–1940. Temperatures as low as minus forty-eight degrees Celsius along with record snowfalls hampered the operations of the mechanized Red Army: artillery range decreased in cold weather and grease froze solid; the motors of automobiles, tanks and airplanes systematically failed; and tanks could not operate in snow deeper than three feet.[16] Nevertheless, Soviet commanders steadfastly believed in the Red Army's mechanized units, whose unquestioned invincibility reflected Stalinist industrial dogma. A case in point is Commander Semen K. Timoshenko's remark comparing the speed and accuracy of the gunners during an artillery barrage on the Karelian Isthmus to "the clockwork production line of a well-run factory."[17] He captured the utopian ideal of a Soviet military doctrine equating the operation of the Red Army with that of a manufacturing plant.

Glorification in the Soviet press notwithstanding, the Russian army on the Finnish front depended on raw recruits and reservists with little ski training. Compounding these difficulties were inadequate munitions and winter clothing, as well as the ponderous leadership of officers who had survived Stalin's purges. Haphazard training combined with frequent interruptions and distractions—including industrial and agricultural work for the state—left little time for the development of seasoned soldiers. Moreover, in peacetime, the Red Army did not allow troops to leave the barracks for exercise or training when the temperature fell below minus fifteen Celsius.[18] Nikita Khrushchev recalled,

> Our army encountered very mobile ski troops armed with automatic high-velocity rifles. We tried to put our own troops on skis, too, but it wasn't easy for ordinary, untrained Red Army soldiers to fight on skis. We started intensively to recruit professional sportsmen. There weren't many around. We had to bring them from Moscow and the Ukraine as well as from Leningrad. We gave them a splendid send-off. Everyone was confident that our

sportsmen would return victorious, and they left in high spirits. Poor fellows, they were ripped to shreds. I don't know how many came back alive.[19]

In bombastic style, Dmitrii Vasil'ev describes the death of one of these young ski racers, Vladimir Miagkov, the 20-kilometer Soviet National Champion of 1939. Operating as a ski scout behind Finnish lines, he and his companions encountered a well-trained enemy ski battalion. Miagkov was killed in battle, "but before he died he had time to pull out the information he had gathered from under his red national championship sweater in which he fought. [He] passed it over to his comrades and they got through to the front line."[20]

The crux of the war, as Khrushchev himself realized, was that the Finnish army travelled on skis and received specialized winter military preparation based on Home Guard training. As early as 1937, certain Soviet Commissariat of Defense publications indicated that the Finnish Army "emphasized Finland's many natural defenses" in their field exercises and that "all Finnish troops were experienced skiers trained for winter warfare."[21] Finland's land forces rejected orthodox military traditions by formulating tactics based on local conditions, using skis to move quickly across all types of terrain, avoiding frontal assaults and compensating for inferior troop strength and the lack of artillery and armor with dexterity and flexibility. Nevertheless, the effectiveness of the Finnish ski troops in foiling the vastly superior Soviet army was initially discounted in the Soviet press. Reflecting the prevailing view of the General Staff, newspapers were a riot of stories and photographs extolling the power of the mechanized Red Army leading up to and including the first week of the invasion. For example, on 4 December 1939, *Pravda* featured an interview with a distraught Finnish prisoner of war, a former factory worker from Vyborg. The captured soldier sat in a small farmhouse as tanks passed by and mumbled to the Soviet correspondent: "I don't understand, I don't understand at all . . . I didn't know . . . that you had so many machines."[22] The newspapers also indicated that Finnish soldiers were weak in comparison to those of the Red Army and thus had to resort to nefarious and underhanded tactics. *Pravda* correspondents from the front reported that the Finns fought "like bandits," employing mines and booby traps.[23] *Krasnaia zvezda*, the official publication of the Political Administration of the Red Army, featured an article under the headline "The Insidious Methods of the White Finns" on 4 December 1939: "At night, crawling into the thick forests like malicious wolves, Finnish snipers come up to the roads near our armies and, with two or three bursts of machine-gun fire, try to spread panic in the advancing columns, in order to block the roads and delay reserves for the forward lines."[24] Of course, such tactics were exactly the types of guerrilla-style activities employed successfully by the Soviets against the Germans during the Great Patriotic War, especially among partisan detachments and parachute squadrons operating behind enemy lines.[25]

By the second week of the invasion, the fortunes of the Red Army took a turn for the worse, and the number of articles devoted to military affairs in Finland dropped considerably. The Soviets came to a standstill before the Mannerheim Line west of Leningrad and, at Suomussalmi in central Finland, the mechanized divisions of the Ninth Army met increasing resistance from Finnish defenders, most of whom were deployed in ski battalions.[26] Nevertheless, *Krasnaia zvezda* insisted at the time that "the Finnish Army does not exist any more. It has fallen into ruin and has lost its fighting value."[27] Such disparaging reports about the Finnish army continued throughout the war: "In an open fight, [the Finns] could not handle the rough, strong attacks of the Red Army soldiers," *Krasnaia zvezda* proclaimed in January; but Soviet troops at the front acknowledged that they were facing a formidable foe. Commissar of Defense Voroshilov understood that the Soviet Union needed ski troops to match those of the enemy; on 24 December, he sent a directive to his General Staff ordering the immediate formation of four ski squadrons whose members should "know how to ski well and be excellent shots."[28] The soldiers in these new divisions appreciated the deadly capabilities of Finland's guerrilla-style combat: "Many of the enemy's tactics were new to us. Before us stood our mission—learn the Finns' methods as soon as possible and acquaint every commander, political officer and soldier with them."[29] Finnish anti-tank tactics in head-to-head combat were especially lethal against the Soviet's purportedly indomitable armored divisions. In addition, it is clear from reports in the Soviet press that Finnish ski detachments frequently outflanked the Soviets, operating behind the front lines to harass the enemy. Numerous accounts detail how difficult it was to defend artillery emplacements and field hospitals—often miles to the rear of the main battle sites—against groups of marauding skiers.[30]

The ingenious anti-tank guerrilla-style tactics of the Finnish army in conjunction with the stealth and mobility of its ski troops facilitated the destruction of nearly three complete armored divisions during the Battle of Suomussalmi over the course of four weeks from December to January. Heavily armored and motorized forces were at a distinct disadvantage in the dense forests of central Finland, where narrow roads limited the mobility of tanks and trucks, the hours of darkness hampered the activity of the Soviet air force, and the severe winter frost froze to death many of the ill-equipped Red Army soldiers as they hunkered in their foxholes. Members of the hapless Red Army infantry, untrained in the use of skis, were at the mercy of Finnish ski troops who, camouflaged in white and firing powerful submachine guns, attacked suddenly, then disappeared at will into the woods. As one Russian survivor of the final battle at Suomussalmi told the *New York Times*: "We couldn't see them . . . I saw one after another of my comrades killed. Still I couldn't see where the fire came from."[31] Many superstitious Soviet soldiers believed that *Belaia smert'*, White Death, stalked them through the forests of Finland during the long subarctic nights of that forsaken winter.[32]

From mid-December 1939 through the end of January 1940, Soviet daily newspapers featured more realistic reporting on the conditions in Finland and the course of the invasion in general, as the USSR attempted to justify its failure to breach the Finnish defenses during the first three weeks of the conflict. By the end of December, Soviet articles no longer belittled the Finnish army, emphasizing instead the prowess of the Red Army's foe.[33] Concurrently, articles and photographs featuring skiers, both civilian and military, appeared with increasing frequency. Ski photos had been a staple in the daily press for years during the winter months in Russia, but for the most part, these tended toward "human interest" pieces, such as school-aged skiers frolicking in the park or schussing arm in arm downhill.[34] These images soon took a more serious turn. For example, a photograph in the 27 January *Leningradskaia pravda* shows the popular image of schoolchildren skiing, but the caption indicates that they are training to fulfill the norms for GTO, the nationwide physical fitness program designed to prepare Soviet citizens for labor and defense.[35] During the same month, *Pravda* featured nine photographs of skiers, including Red Army skiers.[36] By February, the number of ski-related photographs in *Pravda* had increased to seventeen, most of them featuring Soviet ski troops on maneuvers and Red Army ski racers at long-distance ski marathons and military patrol races. And, for the first time since the arrival in Moscow of the Buriat-Mongolian ski delegation of 1937, *Pravda* displayed photographs of skiers on the front page on two separate occasions.[37] Such images were not limited to anonymous figures of the rank and file, however. In March 1940, a photograph of Viacheslav Molotov, Commissar of Foreign Affairs, training on skis appeared in *Pravda*, followed less than a year later by a similar one in *Krasnaia zvezda* featuring Marshal Semen Timoshenko, Commissar of Defense. Both of these photos mirror I. I. Brodskii's oil portrait of Marshal Kliment Voroshilov on skis in his capacity as Commissar of Defense prior to Timoshenko, completed in 1939.[38] Depicting these prominent leaders as skiers helped reinforce the notion that mastering the sport of skiing comprised the defensive duty of each and every Soviet citizen.

The surge to promote skiing among the Soviet citizenry in the later weeks of the Winter War was a direct result of the success of Finnish ski-troops against the Red Army. A front-page editorial, "Toward Standardized Ski Training of Soldiers, Divisions and Units," placed significantly just below the *Krasnaia zvezda* banner on 20 January, insisted that ski training was "an integral element of winter warfare." The article provided the example of two Russian soldiers on reconnaissance who encountered a Finnish ski patroller in the woods: "The soldiers in a flash threw off their skis, and rushed toward the observer, but . . . [sic] they got bogged down in the deep snow. It turns out, both still had not mastered skiing." The conclusion was emphatic: "Right now [ski training] must be given maximum consideration. There isn't much time remaining—every day counts. Therefore, it is impossible to delay military preparation for skiing."[39] Non-military newspapers echoed dismay over the lack of ski training throughout the country as well. Included in the *New York Times* extensive coverage after the final battle at Suomussalmi was an article under the headline "Millions Trained to Ski Demanded for Red Army," which quoted an 18 January editorial in *Komsomol'skaia pravda*, the official newspaper of Komsomol, the Communist Youth Union: "It is necessary immediately to start training millions of persons in skiing. . . . Tens of thousands of skiing centers must be organized. Every Komsomol organization must teach youths and girls the technique of military action on skis. To skis, comrades!"[40] In subsequent years, the Soviet press adopted the exhortation *Na lyzhi!* (To skis!), revoiced in this editorial, as a *cri de guerre* in preparation for defense of the Soviet Union in the period leading up to and including the Great Patriotic War.

Concurrently, *Pravda* featured a series of articles under the rubric "Stories of the Heroes of the Battle with the White Finns" that ran from 16 January to 18 February 1940. These articles highlighted the exploits of soldiers, sailors and pilots who had been awarded the Hero of the Soviet Union Medal in January. Among the medal winners who garnered front-page coverage was Commander A. M. Vasil'ev, a *boets-razvedchik*, or military scout, whose portrait on skis fills a full quarter-page.[41] The accolades heaped upon Commander Vasil'ev underscored the conclusion by front-line commanders that improved reconnaissance techniques based on the example of the Finnish ski-scout were indispensable for successful military operations. The well-trained skiers of the Finnish military, at home in their native forests, enjoyed orienteering, a popular pre-war sport in Finland. In these events, individuals raced over an unfamiliar course by day or night in any season using only a map and a compass.[42] Skills honed in such competitions proved invaluable to Finland's scouts during the Winter War. Russians at the front noted that "[Finnish] scouts skied deep into the field in extended lines, mainly choosing bad weather for their sorties."[43] With a nod to such Finnish proficiency, Second Lieutenant P. Makarov, a Soviet scout, emphasized his own map-reading skills while navigating on skis through the enemy-infested forests of Finland.[44]

The independent nature of the military scout was diametrically opposed to the production-line mentality that held sway among most of the Soviet commanders during the Winter War. Yet it was in the guise of a Red Army scout that the characteristics so closely identified with the Finns first coalesced into the quintessential image of the Soviet ski soldier during the Great Patriotic War some two years later, a process that was underway even before the end of the Winter War. Consider the comments of I. Ul'ianov, yet another ski scout designated as a Hero of the Soviet Union, who lists among the essential qualities and paraphernalia necessary for a Red Army scout these significant details: "The scout must have a pistol. Knives—they're absolutely essential. We all armed ourselves with the Finnish kind. The scout has to be an expert skier."[45] The emulation of a worthy foe among the ranks of the Soviet military scouts manifests itself in the demand for an equivalent to the enemy's deadly Suomi submachine pistol, insistence on expertise in skiing and even the choice of the *puukko*, a Finnish knife from Lapland, used with deadly efficiency in hand-to-hand combat during the Suomussalmi campaign.[46] Soon, the press rekindled Toivo Antikainen's exploits on the Karelian Isthmus during the Finnish Uprising of 1922, melding them with the experiences of the Winter War's military scout in a Soviet ski revival.

"Hurrah for Comrade Stalin!"

Ultimately, the Soviet Union amassed enough men and materiel to overpower the exhausted Finns by the end of February 1940. On 13 March, Finland accepted the harsh conditions of the Treaty of Moscow, bringing an end to the Winter War. For its unwillingness to meet the demands of the Soviet Union, Finland lost all the islands in the Gulf of Finland that had been under negotiation during the pre-war sessions in Moscow, the entire Karelian Isthmus, Hangö and additional territory totaling approximately 25,000 square miles. Out of a population of less than 4,000,000, the Finns suffered 24,923 killed and 43,557 wounded. For its part, the Soviet Union accrued around one half-million casualties. These losses resulted in a Pyrrhic victory for the Soviet Union, however, because the shore batteries at Hangö and airfields in southern Finland proved useless and impossible to defend after German troops swept through the Baltic regions in 1941 during Operation Barbarossa.[47] Although the Soviet press congratulated the Soviet military for its victory in Finland, some articles assumed a cautionary tone. An editorial in *Krasnaia zvezda* warned its readers that, despite the great victory over the Finnish "menace," the Soviet Union should continue military and political preparations: "At any moment we will be ready with Voroshilov's volleys to destroy any enemy who would dare to disturb the quiet of the Soviet population."[48]

Despite officially sanctioned enthusiasm in the press, the victory in Finland was an embarrassment for the Soviet Union and especially for officers of the Red Army. The prestige of the Soviet military plummeted in the aftermath of the Suomussalmi campaign, as worldwide press coverage cast aspersions on the army and altered perceptions of the Soviet Union's international authority. Indeed, Adolf Hitler's assessment of Soviet capabilities based on the Finnish conflict contributed to his decision to invade the USSR in 1941.[49] As Nikita Khrushchev suggested: "It doesn't take much imagination to guess what Hitler must have concluded after he watched us try to wage war against the Finns."[50]

Recently released documents from Soviet archives attest to the extent of the military's chagrin. Barely three weeks after the Treaty of Moscow, Commissar of Defense Voroshilov along with Grigorii Kulik, his Deputy Commissar of Defense, and forty-six Red Army field commanders shared their war experiences in a series of meetings with Stalin. The main thrust of this conclave was to correct deficiencies in the Red Army and to improve future performance. The critical appraisals, ranging from the impracticality of greatcoats to the need for more tactical air and ground coordination, reveal that Soviet leaders were very concerned about the state of the Red Army and the results of the war with Finland.[51]

Throughout the deliberations, the poor performance of Soviet troops vis-à-vis military skiing was a frequent complaint. During the second session of the meetings, on 15 April, S. I. Nedvigin, a brigade commander of the Leningrad Military District, admitted that his troops were ill-prepared for ski warfare and acknowledged as well that "Finnophobia" incapacitated his troops during the Suomussalmi campaign. Colonel P. Shevchenko, Commander of the 122nd Rifle Division, made a pointed comparison between the performance of the Finns and his own troops: "The Finns penetrated the flanks and rear, attacked supply convoys, logistical units, bridges and establishments, and resorted to mobile [defense]. . . . We had skis, but the majority of the division personnel were no good at skiing, and the skis were abandoned in the first battles." Shevchenko also suggested that Soviet skis should match the type used in the Nordic countries and that all troops should have white camouflage capes, similar to those of the Finns, for winter use.[52] The white camouflage promoted by Colonel Shevchenko evolved as a signature motif of the Soviet ski trooper, whose image became a regular feature of Soviet propaganda in the war's aftermath. Additionally, the government incorporated the colonel's recommendations for configuring Soviet skis while retooling the ski industry in subsequent years.[53]

More than revamping the army was on the mind of Colonel I. Rosly, Commander of the 245th Rifle Regiment. He proposed a sweeping change in the very fabric of Soviet society during the opening session of the committee meetings by emphasizing applied military arts in the schools to create an environment that fostered development of "an athlete, a good skier, a good sportsman."[54] K. Mamsurov, commander of a special ski detachment during the Winter War and Chief of the Red Army Intelligence Service, concurred with Rosly's assessment, suggesting in the Seventh Session on 17 April that sports organizations were at fault for promoting soccer matches where spectators far outnumbered athletes: "otherwise you have ten people playing and thousands merely standing and applauding. We must build up skiing and devote our main attention to the defensive aspects of sport."[55] A few months later, advocacy for Mamsurov's concerns about soccer and skiing resurfaced in the editorial columns of *Pravda*, part of a significant campaign to restructure the goals of the Komsomol in accordance with the GTO program.[56]

Although the consensus was that the Soviet Union had erred by not properly studying the organization, tactics and armaments of the Finnish army, and that the mobilization of the Leningrad District had been an appalling disaster, Stalin viewed the matter differently. During the four days of meetings, Stalin rarely spoke as his officers voiced their opinions. Only on occasions when the discussion turned to the use of heavy ordnance did he display any enthusiasm. When Colonel Rosly stated: "So, we were delivering wonderful [artillery] fire for two hours and twenty minutes. Had we a composer, he might have put it to music," Stalin interjected: "Artillery does have its music. Yes, it does."[57] In case any of the assembled commanders had missed the point, Stalin underscored his belief in the industrialization of modern warfare during his final speech at the end of the seventh session on the evening of 17 April. In his assessment of a modern army's requirements, Stalin's opinion was unequivocal: "Massed artillery . . . is the God of contemporary war. Whoever wants to reform according to new, contemporary methods should understand that artillery decides the fate of war, massive amounts of artillery. . . . Second, airplanes, masses of airplanes, not just hundreds, but thousands, of airplanes. . . . Then tanks, the third and also the decisive element. . . . Mortars are the fourth important factor." And what of his commanders' suggestions that the ski troops of Finland offered an exemplary model for thwarting just the sort of mechanized army Stalin envisioned? Again, Stalin did not mince words: "The Finns' offensive wasn't worth a damn. During three months of war, do you remember a single case of a serious massed offensive by the Finnish Army? There was no such thing."

Disregarding the costly lessons learned by the Soviet Union after three months of desperate fighting in Finland, Stalin admonished his commanders:

> What is [Finland] capable of doing that makes some of our comrades envious? Small-scale actions, for example encirclement with an attempt at the rear, or setting up obstructions: they know their own conditions, and that is all. All these obstructions can be reduced to tricks. . . . But it's not possible to live by tricks alone . . . [the Finnish army] can conduct partisan offensive operations well—it can strike in the rear, set up traps and so on—but I cannot call this army a real army.

With the purges of the previous decade undoubtedly fresh in mind and with prudence taking precedence over recent experiences in Finland, the assembled leaders of the Red Army could muster only one response to their supreme leader's recapitulation after four days of testimony: "Hurrah for Comrade Stalin!"[58]

S. K. Timoshenko and the Ski Mobilization Movement

For readers accustomed to the format of Western newspapers such as the *New York Times*, the layout of Stalinist-era daily publications looks severe.

Even during the difficult years of the 1930s, columns of hard news were leavened with the lively badinage of commercial advertising in the West. In contrast, repetitive uniform panels filled the pages of *Pravda*, *Krasnaia zvezda*, and *Leningradskaia pravda*, the solid text reinforcing the austerity incurred by five-year plans and invasion paranoia. After 1932, these publications limited the space devoted to advertising and, during the war years, dispensed with it altogether.[59] Thus it is even more remarkable to discover that *Krasnaia zvezda* carried an advertisement for ski wax manufactured by Moskhimob"edinenie (Moscow Chemical Factory) on three separate occasions during the month of October 1940.[60] This commercial "blitz," with its notable design and graphics, reflected a Soviet response to Western advertising science as an effective tool for promoting state goods.[61] The Soviets even adopted one of Madison Avenue's tried and true tactics for attracting a potential customer: associating a particular commodity with a celebrity. In this case it was the young racer who started his scientific career following a 1913 meet against the Finns in St. Petersburg, Nikolai Vasil'ev. By 1940, his name was inseparable from the very notion of ski wax in the Soviet Union, even morphing into a descriptive adjective in this example from Semen Kirsanov's poem *Na lyzhi!*: "Smoothly bend down and glide with the wind on Vasil'ev wax!"[62] With such an imprimatur attached to this series of Moskhimob"edinenie advertisements, the Soviet regime kicked off a massive, nationwide ski mobilization movement.

As a result of the Winter War postmortem conference, Stalin made one especially significant change by removing Voroshilov from the position of Commissar of Defense and replacing him with Semen K. Timoshenko, the successful front commander of the February 1940 offensive on the Karelian Isthmus. With the Red Army's dismal performance in Finland in mind, Stalin directed Timoshenko to carry out wholesale reforms of defense and mobilization planning, trusting in his judgment for restructuring and training the armed forces.[63] As a result of his experiences on the front lines in Finland, Timoshenko was well aware of the integral role played by skiing in modern winter military campaigns, stating in *Pravda*: "The war with the White Finns provides a demonstrative example of the importance we must attach to the mastery of skiing, to the training of ski troops. Without the ability to ski, it is impossible to carry out successful military operations in winter conditions."[64] Through Timoshenko's subsequent efforts, the ski mobilization movement became one of the grandest shock campaigns of the Stalinist era. The autumn 1940 ski campaign had its roots in a lecture on military ideology delivered the previous May by L. Z. Mekhlis, head of the Political Directorate of the Red Army. Although his presentation delineated Stalin's directives to form a contemporary army, Mekhlis also addressed the physical training of the individual soldier. Perhaps through the persuasion of military officers who had attended the April sessions with Stalin, Mekhlis suggested: "Today in our army, and . . . even in our nation, sport is on the backburner. In the army the inspection of physical culture is occupied with tricks, but there is no serious training. Skiing, to our shame, is completely out of mind, whereas it can and should become our national sport. And that goes for shooting as well."[65] It is noteworthy that Mekhlis' conception of skiing and shooting as "our national sport" informed the development of Soviet biathlon during the post-war era. Even at the turn of the twenty-first century, the Russian press still considered this form of competition, suffused with historical and cultural significance for the former Soviet Union, as "our national property."[66]

In early October, the push to mobilize skiers began in earnest. In conjunction with the series of advertisements for Vasil'ev's tins of ski wax in the pages of *Krasnaia zvezda*, an editorial in *Pravda* excoriated the All-Union Committee on Physical Culture and Sport for its failure to fulfill the most recent goals set by the Council of People's Commissars for the GTO program. The *Pravda* editorial specified that the results were even worse than in the previous year because fewer people had taken part, concluding with a suggestion that the All-Union Committee on Physical Culture look for "co-respondents," namely the Komsomol, to help organize sport instruction in a greater variety of venues.[67] Two days later, *Pravda* placed another editorial taking the membership of the Komsomol to task for shirking its obligation to promote physical culture. The editors complained that "many [Komsomol activists] idly chat about the benefits of sport, but they don't know how to ski, shoot accurately, hike for long distances: they continuously grumble about fatigue and lack of endurance." In addition, the editorial scolded the Komsomol leadership for failing to meet the qualification standards for GTO in sufficient numbers. To bolster this not-too-subtle message intended for the Komsomol, an article on the next page described how the schools in Petrozavodsk integrated ski instruction into their schedule in order to fulfill the GTO norms designated for skiing, in addition to developing a Be Ready for Labor and Defense (BGTO) ski program for Young Pioneers.[68] The following week, the lead article in *Leningradskaia pravda*, under the headline "Young People—Get into the Physical Culture Collectives!" encouraged all youth to undertake the study of "defensive sports" because "physical culture is an integral part of a communist education." The author also stated categorically that "a physical-culturalist must know both how to ski well and how to shoot accurately." In addition to the earlier articles from *Pravda*, this *Leningradskaia pravda* piece accentuates many important concepts related to the ski mobilization effort: the martial aspects of skiing; the mass characteristic of the movement; the integration of skiing into the educational system; and finally, the conflation of ski mastery with the very essence of being a well-rounded communist.[69] By 1942, the Ministry of Education had implemented a nationwide program for physical training with military emphasis for all elementary, middle and secondary school students. Included in these preparations were instructions on how to ski and the proper application of wax.[70]

In November, numerous articles in *Pravda* dubbed skiing "the People's Sport," reinforcing the idea that skiing was integral to socialism and Soviet society. One editorial stated that "skiing is the most popular sport in our country—it's the People's Sport. Soviet youth love skiing because, as with no other type of sport, it combines useful relaxation with endurance training."[71] A week and a half later, under the banner "The People's Sport," *Pravda* reiterated the notion of skiing's popularity among the citizenry and complained that consumers did not have a good selection of skis strong enough to survive excursions in wooded or mountainous areas.[72] The call for a sturdy and maneuverable ski suited to travel in rugged terrain was a direct result of the war in Finland; a new factory in Petrozavodsk would soon be producing just such a model.

In conjunction with the new role of skiing as the People's Sport, both *Pravda* and *Krasnaia zvezda* initiated a campaign to promote the slogan "Na lyzhi! (To skis!)" by late 1940, abbreviated from the "Proletarian and Collective Farm Worker, to skis!" slogan of the inter-war period. The lead article on the front page of the 13 November 1940 issue of *Krasnaia zvezda* featured an oversized banner font, normally reserved for war headlines, to exhort readers: "Na lyzhi!" The text from the outset declares, "Soldiers of the Red Army love skiing." The editorial details a military history of skiing in Russia, beginning with Ivan III in the fifteenth century and continuing through "the heroic exploits" of Soviet skiers against the Finns during the previous winter. Concurrently *Pravda* began a series of columns that appeared sporadically under the heading "Na Lyzhi!" or "Molodezh', Na lyzhi!" (Young people, to skis!) that recounted the efforts of the Komsomol to organize skiing events around the nation.[73]

In November 1940, both *Pravda* and *Krasnaia zvezda* reminded readers about the exploits of Toivo Antikainen's ski division and the raid against

Finnish forces at Kimasozero.[74] Antikainen himself wrote an article, later translated into Russian as "Vse na lyzhi!" (Everyone to skis!), for *Totuus* (Truth), a Finnish-language newspaper. An unflagging promoter of skiing, the hero of the Civil War and the 1922 Karelian Uprising exhorted every one of his countrymen to learn how to ski in defense of the nation.[75] A few months before his mysterious death in 1941, *Totuus* ran another Antikainen piece, "War on skis" in which he analyzed the raid on Kimasozero once again, offering this advice: "[The army] needs strong, well-trained and clever skiers. But it's possible to become one only when you continuously train and perfect the technique of skiing . . . the current winter must become at times the most active and the most mass-oriented acquisition of military ski mastery."[76]

There is no question that Antikainen's version of "Everyone to skis!" harked back to slogans of the Civil War. Front-page banner headlines of that period regularly trumpeted exhortations such as "Everyone armed, everyone to the front!" similar to Lev Trotsky's celebrated "Proletarian, to horse!"[77] Nevertheless, an imaginative editorial in *Krasnaia zvezda* suggested that during the invasion of Finland, "a frontline newspaper called for all soldiers and commanders to get on skis and operate boldly in the deep snows of the woods. . . . The military slogan 'Everyone to skis' quickly found a fervent response among the broad masses of the Red Army."[78] Variations on the phrase "Everyone to skis!" inspired a myriad of artistic works over the next two years. For example, numerous poems published in *Pravda* during the winter of 1941 included "To skis" in the text or, in one instance, even provided the title and premise of the poem itself.[79] Not to be outdone, *Krasnaia zvezda* published the words and music for "The Army Ski Song," featuring a rousing "Everyone to skis!" refrain: "To gain victory faster/ Everyone to skis, come on, to skis!/ The cry goes out to every corner/ And on their skis the soldiers fly off toward victory."[80] Graphic designers caught the slogan's spirit as well. In 1942, responding to Germany's invasion of the Soviet Union, the renowned poster artist A. Nemychin produced the placard "Everyone to skis!" Over exhortations to "Possess ski technique/ master military operations on skis/ learn how to strike the fascist invaders," a determined skier traverses a slope sporting all new equipment developed from Finnish examples obtained during the Winter War: a Soviet PPSh "burp gun" modeled after the Suomi submachine gun and Nordic-style mountain skis recently manufactured by the Petrozavodsk ski factory. Using a similar downhill ski motif, M. Nesterova-Berzina, famous for her posters of children, completed "Young people, to skis!" in 1945.[81]

Pravda, keen to promote skiing as a true socialist activity, emphasized the sport's utilitarian value to the general population in an early December 1940 editorial. Building on the supposed popularity of summer hiking among the citizenry, the article suggests that ski touring provides the same pleasurable experience in the winter. In addition, the "People's Sport" benefits socialist society: "Such trips provide the opportunity to combine the pleasant with the useful . . . a [skier] even on a short ski excursion strengthens his health, trains the muscles and learns many skills beneficial in times of peace as well as war." Moreover, skiing is suitable for the proletariat because it "requires minimal expenditure of means yet at the same time can provide great profit." In the manner of *subbotniki*, workers whose voluntary efforts on Saturdays promoted the greater good of the nation, *Pravda* suggests that "ski excursions on days off are excellent agitation for skiing. These should and must be carried out in the collective enterprises, collective farms and educational institutions . . . this is why it is necessary in every possible way to promote skiing, to do it genuinely for the masses!"[82] According to Lenin, agitation entailed motivating an audience to action by appealing to emotions, a process particularly suited to wartime or crisis situations. Because the Communist Party considered "agitational work obligatory for every communist," this *Pravda* article indicates that skiing was now transcending the boundaries of sport and entertainment to become a method of building a militant socialist state.[83]

Krasnaia zvezda was even more enthusiastic than *Pravda* about the promotion of the ski mobilization campaign during the winter of 1940 through 1941, and the efforts of the Red Army's journalists garnered special praise from *Pravda* in an editorial at the end of the ski season.[84] The military newspaper featured articles about the sport and photographs of skiers on the front page regularly during the winter months. In just one week of February, for example, six issues contained front-page lead stories about skiing.[85] On two separate occasions, *Krasnaia zvezda* devoted every column-inch and photograph on the first three pages to skiing.[86] And, with regularity throughout the winter, the editors of the paper managed to incorporate the "To skis!" battle cry into the headlines.[87]

On 27 December 1940, *Krasnaia zvezda* reported that earlier in the month, Commissar of Defense Timoshenko had addressed a letter on the subject of skiing to Komsomol members attending an annual meeting in Moscow. "Without knowing how to ski, it is impossible to carry out successful military maneuvers in winter conditions," Timoshenko wrote. He recommended that to promote proper ski training, Komsomol members in each district should "explain the significance of [cross-country ski rac-ing] without too much ballyhoo and blather, and inspire every soldier by their own personal example." The Komsomol, taking the Commis-sar's suggestion to heart, initiated plans for a series of cross-country ski races in February, intended for the benefit of the Red Army. In this article, *Krasnaia zvezda* announced that the Komsomol had elected to change the event's name from "The Komsomol Cross Country Ski Race in Honor of the Twenty-Third Anniversary of the Red Army" to "The All-Army Cross-Country Ski Race in Honor of Hero and Marshal of the Soviet Union S. K. Timoshenko."[88]

At this juncture, *"Lyzhnyi kross"* (cross-country ski race) gained promi-nence as a catch phrase in the daily newspapers. Over the next four days, both *Pravda* and *Krasnaia zvezda* featured front-page articles with this expression as the headline.[89] On 2 January 1941, the italicized banner of *Pravda*'s lead article trumpeted "Three cross-country ski races," introduc-ing the incessant coverage of the Timoshenko games that ensued during the winter months. The barrage of references to "cross-country ski race" in the press throughout January and February influenced the visual arts as well: the media frenzy surrounding the Timoshenko games of 1941 ul-timately inspired the subject and title of a post-war canvas by the accom-plished Soviet oil painter V. K. Dmitrievskii. The composition centers on a substantial crowd of ski-shod civilian spectators cheering on a group of Red Army cross-country racers who compete in full military kit while car-rying rifles on their backs.[90]

In January 1941, the Komsomol expanded the scope of the Timoshenko race series to include provisions for all levels of skiing ability, in order to increase the number of people who qualified for the first level of GTO norms in cross-country skiing. The *Profsoiuz kross* (trade-union cross-country race) was intended for "all those who know how to ski" but had not yet qualified in the ski standards for GTO. The *Komsomol'skii kross* (Komsomol cross-country race) allowed those skiers who had qualified in the norms for either GTO or Be Ready for Labor and Defense (BGTO) in cross-country skiing to advance to the second level of qualification. Fi-nally, the *Vsearmeiskii kross* (All-Army cross-country race) limited entries to soldiers and officers of the Red Army. Based on projections from Arch-angelsk, Molotov, Gorkii, Leningrad and other districts, *Pravda*'s pre-race forecast predicted "hundreds of thousands" of participants.[91]

Significantly, *Pravda* suggested that the trade-union cross-country ski race provided a unique opportunity to promote "the goal of broad propaganda for skiing, of attracting masses of workers both to the study of this important defensive kind of physical culture and to meeting the norms of GTO, and finally, of raising the level of mastery of youth in the realm of skiing."[92] This front-page article provides an excellent example of the government's attempt to reconcile the fundamental concepts of mass participation and mastery with notions of national defense, the sport of skiing and GTO. This potent amalgamation had important ramifications during the postwar era when the Soviet Union used sports, especially Nordic skiing and biathlon, to promote the benefits of socialism before a worldwide audience.

The pan-Soviet Timoshenko races were even more successful than *Pravda* had projected. An article on 25 February listed the total number of racers in the Komsomol cross-country program, separate from the other races in the series, at 4,845,000.[93] A month later, the paper reported that 1,400,000 skiers from Osoaviakhim, the national civil defense organization, took part in related military skiing competitions.[94] Dmitrii Vasil'ev, writing in 1956, put the total number of participants in the Komsomol cross-country ski race program at six million, and in 1944, more than a million skiers in the competitions organized by the agricultural collectives. In addition, the number of participants who fulfilled the GTO norms for cross-country skiing in all the divisions ranged from 73 to 93 percent, depending on the district and its proximity to snow.[95] Certainly the government inflated participation numbers and percentages for propaganda purposes, but such exaggeration illustrates the importance skiing had acquired in the eyes of the regime. The improbable statistics notwithstanding, recent tallies from the weeklong series of races held in conjunction with Sweden's Vasaloppet, the world's largest cross-country ski event, pale in comparison to even 1 percent of these stated totals.[96]

In one year, the representation of skiing in the Soviet Union metamorphosed from that of a schoolchild's diversion to a strategically viable method of waging war, on a par with the utility of a tank attack or bombing raid. The elevation of skiing to the lofty heights normally reserved for armor, artillery and aviation in the hierarchy of Soviet military might found expression in a rhapsodic editorial by Captain A. Andreev, which appeared on the front page of *Krasnaia zvezda* on New Year's Day 1941: "Faithful and trustworthy Red Army skis! How much time the soldiers and officers of the Red Army have spent with you this year, and how many bold adventures you have shared. Together with artillery, tanks and airplanes, war has made you famous."[97] Later in the year, a postal commemorative series, issued in celebration of the twenty-third anniversary of the Red Army and

Navy, included a stamp featuring a ski trooper in full stride, as if on the racecourse of the All-Army competitions. With this image, the military skier joined the ranks of other iconic heroes in the philatelic pantheon of the Soviet Armed Forces, including an artillerist, a sailor and a pilot.[98] Certainly there was no more appropriate receptacle for these stamps than a contemporary series of postcards printed to memorialize the "defense of the northwest border" by the doughty skiers of the Red Army.[99] These images transform the invasion of Finland, initially touted as a war of liberation, into a defensive operation securing the Soviet Union's northwest border from imperialist aggression, a notion useful to the government during the German-Finnish invasions of the Great Patriotic War.

Perhaps the most compelling representation of the apotheosis of Soviet skiing during the ski mobilization years was a war font- and photo-montage that ran in the 24 February 1942 issue of *Pravda*. Beneath a streamer headline that exclaims, "Under the Banner of Lenin, under the Leadership of Stalin—Forward, to the Defeat of the German-Fascist Invaders!" a photograph of ski troopers shares equal space with one of tanks, together effecting the role of stolid bookends for a quotation from Stalin during the early stages of the Great Patriotic War.[100] Images of tanks, artillery, airplanes and skiers, the modern equivalent of the Civil War's Red Cavalry, carried forward the Bolshevik notion of a military of the proletariat. These photographs filled the front pages of *Krasnaia zvezda* during this period, paired with suitably zealous headlines such as "All Power—to the Defeat of the Enemy!" and "Forward, to the West, Red Cavalry! Death to the German Occupiers!"[101] Diptychs and triptychs such as these incorporated symbolic messages of homeland defense and military prowess in combination with the legacy of Lenin and the exhortations of Stalin and the Communist Party. Thus, in addition to the semiotics of artillery, aviation and armor—still the symbols of Soviet military power preferred by the daily press—that of skiing became indelibly associated with the Soviet effort to defend the Motherland and repel German invaders from 1941 to 1945. For post-war Soviet writers, "skis became weapons of war."[102]

The Great Patriotic War, 1941–1945

On 22 June 1941, Nazi Germany unleashed a sudden and massive blitzkrieg across the border of the Soviet Union. The onslaught of three million troops and concomitant ordnance along a 2,000-mile front amounted to a mirror image of the Soviet Union's own invasion of Finland two years earlier, albeit on a much grander scale. With the tables turned, Soviet troops retreated before the advancing Germans, whose rapid encirclements of the Red Army at Minsk, Smolensk, Kiev, Briansk and Viazma eliminated from action nearly half of the Soviet Union's deployed troops. However, as autumn turned to winter, the Soviets halted the Wehrmacht's offensive a mere forty kilometers from the gates of Moscow. Having wrested the strategic advantage from the enemy, the Soviet Union mounted a winter counter-offensive that expanded from the outskirts of Moscow into a front stretching from Leningrad to the Crimea. During this campaign, the lessons of winter warfare dearly acquired in the forests of Suomussalmi paid dividends in the form of successful forays against the Germans, tailored by the Red Army to suit the immensity of the Russian steppe.

The ski battalions of the Red Army were particularly effective during the counter-offensive of 1941–1942. The guerrilla tactics of the Finns, most notably swift raids across battle lines to attack the rear of the enemy, were especially efficacious against the Germans, who were mired in severe Russian weather throughout a vast theater of war. One of the deadliest and hardest-fought campaigns took place along an 80-kilometer section of the German supply line south of Smolensk from December 1941 through March 1942. Elite mountain troops of the Wehrmacht fought desperate defensive actions against marauding Soviet ski forces and paratroopers intent on cutting supplies to the German Fourth Army on the outskirts of Moscow. After a breakthrough by Russian forces at Sininka on 13 January, a series of counter-maneuvers ensued in temperatures that dropped as low as minus forty-nine degrees Celsius. During the last half of February the daily average temperature ranged between minus thirty-five and minus forty-five degrees Celsius, while the area on both sides of the supply route from Liudkogo to Iukhnov became "a single battlefield strewn with corpses." By March the spring thaw turned the region, previously frozen solid, into a swampy bog that swallowed German supply horses up to their necks in mud. "The brutality," wrote one Skijäger officer in 1942, "tells us more than many words could possibly say against what sort of foe the German soldier has to fight here on the Eastern Front."[103]

Stories of the Red Army's successful ski operations were a regular occurrence in the press, offering a ray of hope during an otherwise dreary winter in the Soviet Union. *Krasnaia zvezda* featured glowing articles with headlines such as "A Daring Raid by Skiers behind Enemy Lines," "How a Ski Detachment Blocked the Advance of a German Division" and

"The Military Deeds of a Ski Detachment."[104] At the same time, *Pravda* assigned special correspondents to report on the activities of ski troops near the Leningrad front in a regular series of articles titled *"Na lyzhakh v tyl vraga"* (On skis to the enemy's rear), incorporating the "To skis!" slogan with the notion of guerrilla-style warfare derived from the Finnish campaign. These pieces featured tales of derring-do carried out by the ski divisions behind enemy lines, usually with details of total numbers of Germans killed included for good measure.[105] Irregular forces involved in guerrilla warfare throughout the occupied regions, collectively known as the Partisan Movement, employed the tactics of the ski divisions as well. In addition to mounting forays on skis against the enemy, the partisans effectively disrupted German lines of communication by destroying railways and bridges using sabotage and mines.[106] These tactics, first put into operation against the Soviets during the Finnish campaign, became, *mutatis mutandis*, symbols of the Russian people's resistance to Nazi occupation, especially in the copious body of literature devoted to the partisans that evolved during and after the Great Patriotic War.[107] The exploits of partisans and paratroopers operating behind enemy lines also received extensive coverage in *Krasnaia zvezda*. Photographs of these fighters in action on skis and in winter camouflage filled the pages of the newspaper throughout the winter of 1941–1942. Particularly noteworthy are photographs of female warriors posing on skis with automatic pistols draped over their shoulders. Among the rarest portrayals of women in the Red Army's official newspaper, these images imply the transformation of skiing from a leisure activity into a potent mode of defense, whose knowledge was essential for every member of Soviet society.[108]

After the outbreak of war in 1941, the General Staff of the Red Army initiated a program of collating and analyzing the details of the war, gathered into a body of work under the rubric *Collection of Materials on the Study of War Experience*. The information that resulted from these studies was much more candid and accurate than that compiled from the recollections of the Finnish campaign during the April meetings with Stalin in 1940. These working papers, focusing on the mundane functions of combat, reflect the Soviet notion that the success of grand strategic concepts depended upon how well each individual operated within the greater whole. This attention to the particular in conjunction with the enormous reserves available among the general Soviet population proved to be a successful combination. As the Red Army learned from its failures over the course of the war, it re-educated itself and emerged as a modern, potent fighting force.[109]

Of special concern to the Red Army after the winter campaign of 1941–1942 was the failure of the Soviet mechanized corps and cavalry to encircle the Wehrmacht at Moscow. However, three papers from the *Collection*, "Operational-Tactical Lessons of the Winter Campaign, 1941–1942," "Features of Offensive Actions in Winter," and "Combat Use of Ski Troops," contrast the splendid results of Soviet ski troops with other mobile forces during winter maneuvers against the Germans. The General Staff emphasized the "cross-country capability and mobility" of ski troops throughout these reports, noting that the use of ski battalions was especially beneficial because they could penetrate and strike against the enemy from the rear while disrupting lines of communication, cutting off paths of withdrawal and threatening headquarters. Just as in Finland, the Soviets found that "tanks and artillery were bound to the roads. On roadless directions covered in deep snow, not only were they of no help to the infantry, they also hindered infantry actions."[110] However, on their home turf, Soviet commanders of the ski brigades employed the tactic of cutting the opposing army's motorized columns into *mottis*, a Finnish term for the isolation and subsequent destruction of small enemy deployments.[111] Overlooked, or perhaps understated, in previous histories of the Great Patriotic War is that this scenario reads as much like a description of the Russian debacle at Suomussalmi as an outline for countering Operation Barbarossa, indicating how completely the Soviet General Staff adapted the Finnish style of warfare to a new Soviet military paradigm.

The degree to which skiing infused the Soviet conception of modern warfare during the winter campaign of 1941–1942 flickers briefly through a passage in one of the most significant literary events of the Great Patriotic War. From 24 through 27 August 1942, *Pravda* devoted page three of each edition to a serialized version of *The Front*, a play by leading Ukrainian author Aleksandr Korneichuk.[112] Amir Weiner suggests that the publication of this piece illustrates a contemporary condemnation of the way Soviet military officers of the Civil War generation had prosecuted their campaigns during the initial period of the Great Patriotic War, attacking the very foundations of pre-war revolutionary myth.[113] In one scene, Vladimir Ognev, a character representing the new cadre of young professional officers ready to reform the Soviet military, acknowledges his appreciation for well-executed maneuvers to his General Staff and praises the efforts of a ski patrol.[114] Korneichuk's dialogue employs the image of the skier, co-opted from Finnish models during the Winter War, as a symbol of this generational shift.

To the world press, the Soviet Union often furnished images of the ski trooper in winter camouflage to convey its determination in battling the Nazis. For example, the *New York Times* included a photograph of a white-clad Soviet trooper with the caption "A lesson in winter warfare on the Russian Front" in January 1943. The *Times* featured photographs of Russian parachute troops outfitted for winter combat as well.[115] The full-color cover of the February 1944 issue of *Soviet Russia Today*, a magazine intended for an American audience, portrays two ski troopers with gazes fixed determinedly on the horizon striding through the snow of the taiga, rifles slung at the ready, the winter-white camouflage of each reflecting the rays of the sun.[116]

In addition to still photographs, the main belligerents of the Second World War used motion pictures to propagandize their war efforts in movies and newsreels. Captured on film, the dramatic nature of ski troops in action proved as popular in the United States as in Germany and the Soviet Union. Using footage gathered by government cinematographers accompanying Soviet troops along the Russian front, *Artkino*, the Soviet film agency, released more than fifty war-related movies into the American market between 1942 and 1944. The number of theaters in the United States showing Soviet documentaries increased from a few dozen before the war to over 200 by 1942, bolstering the fortitude of American audiences in the months after Pearl Harbor with spectacular and victorious images.[117] Many of these films featured footage of Soviet ski troops on maneuver. In an article in the *New York Times* concerning one Soviet documentary, "The Rout of the German Armies before Moscow," the writer mentions "long columns of ski-troops in white camouflage robes going through the city."[118] The *New York Times* arts critic Bosley Crowther reviewed another 1942 release from the Soviet Union, "In the Rear of the Enemy," noting that: "[This movie is] little more than an exciting incident in the fighting on the Russian winter front . . . it is presented graphically, and some of the sequences in the forest, with the soldiers on skis are pictorially fine. But an hour is too long for such a picture."[119] In London, however, a more enthusiastic reception awaited the debut of "In the Rear of the Enemy," with two stills from the film featured in the entertainment section of the 31 January 1942 issue of the *Times*. The accompanying caption notes that the skiers, "camouflaged in white, travel quickly over the frozen snow on skis."[120]

British Pathé made extensive use of Soviet newsreels—with English commentary—for distribution in the United Kingdom.[121] One shows Soviet aero-sleds speeding across the snow at "sixty miles per hour," then purportedly disgorging ski troops to ambush the enemy. The narrator informs the viewer: "Ski troops are able to descend on the Nazis with incredible speed, following up their fire with a silent charge over the snow-covered ground to round up the enemy completely surprised by the speed of their attack. This kind of warfare was right up the Russki's street—they excelled in it."[122] The contrast in narration between newsreels such as this one, produced for the West, and those shown in the Soviet Union provides an illuminating comparison. The brisk and chipper British voiceover explains to the viewer what exactly the Soviet ski troops are doing and why their tactics are so effective, emphasizing a job well done. The more sonorous voice of the Russian narration for a film shot with the Second Baltic Front carries a much different message of suffering and duty, as skiers and mule-skinners struggle to advance through the white noise of a raging blizzard: "In the Second Baltic Front soldiers carry out their advance going to the West, covered by snow and frost, full of the notion of their many glorious deeds. Being hardened troops tempered in battle many a time they were glorified by their people. Victory comes through great labor." As the wind calms, plangent strains of Shostakovich swell and soldiers gather around a campfire for mugs of tea: "A little pause for the troops on their path."[123]

Writing during the winter of 1942–1943, German-born alpinist and skier Frank Harper critiqued the performance of Soviet ski troops based on cinematic and photographic images coming from the Russian front: "If one can judge from the few newsreels and photographs showing Russian skiers in action, great progress has been made since the Finnish campaign, and many mistakes corrected. . . . They know how to handle the skis and poles efficiently when firing rifles." Harper had one reservation, however: "It must be said that their actual ski technique seems rather poor even in simple two-step cross-country running."[124] To be sure, Soviet skiers improved remarkably on this point throughout the next four decades.

FIVE

Post-War Soviet Sports and the Birth of Biathlon

THE SOVIET UNION PAID a terrible price for the Allied victory in World War II, including the devastation of tens of thousands of cities and villages and the loss of 27,000,000 citizens. The conflagration informed virtually every aspect of Soviet life in the aftermath. As historian Elena Zubkova suggests, it is impossible to comprehend post-war Soviet history and social behavior without understanding how completely the war was ingrained into the psyche of the survivors.[1] Aleksandr Privalov, one of the premier Soviet biathletes of the immediate post-war generation, is the epitome of this experience. He was an eight-year-old child when the Nazi invasion rolled toward his home in Piatnitsa on the way to Moscow and the Soviet army passed by in full retreat. During a recent interview, the venerable Olympic medalist and coach still recalled at the age of seventy-seven the nightmarish situation after the Germans burned his village to the ground in 1941: "That was the worst. Winter got to the point where everything was used up and they sawed the meat off of dead horses. . . . Later on, Mother decided to take us away to Solnechnogorsk. The road was terrifying: there were bodies lying everywhere, arms and legs were scattered about. . . . We starved horribly. I still remember the taste of the peasant bread we ate. . . . Each crumb seemed like the most delicious thing in the world."[2] The consensus was that the country had faced the worst of the German onslaught in Europe and had made immeasurable sacrifices to free the world from fascism. The war also reinforced the belief that the militarization of physical training and sport had been essential to the Red Army, especially the use of weapons combined with skiing. A letter from a group of athletes to Stalin in 1942 makes this clear: "Soviet sportsmen taught tens of thousands of young soldiers the art of the bayonet attack and hand-to-hand combat, throwing grenades and skiing."[3] And an article in *Pravda* that year detailed various sport figures who had served in the Armed Forces, featuring in particular the military exploits of skiers Vladimir Miagkov, Fedor Ivachev and Evgenii Ivanov.[4] In the aftermath of World

War II, the Soviets continually promoted physical fitness programs, with special emphasis in the educational system and in sport societies on activities with "explicit military utility," such as cross-country skiing and rifle marksmanship.[5] "The infantry didn't know how to carry out war on skis; special ski battalions were formed only as the [Winter War] progressed," noted the Khrushchev era's official history of the Great Patriotic War.[6] The Soviet government intended that such a lapse would never occur again.

But skiing would attain more than just domestic socialist significance in the post-war years as sport became an instrument of Soviet foreign policy. For the USSR, competition on the international level became a celebration of the victory over fascism as well as a demonstration of Soviet strength. Moreover, the Soviet Union sought world supremacy in sport to enhance the status of communism abroad. The Soviets believed that success in international sport was one of the most effective means for advertising and demonstrating the superiority of the socialist way of life over that found in the decadent capitalist nations of the West.[7] Thus, the Soviet Union made a concerted effort in the immediate post-war years to rejoin the world athletic community.

However, the regime considered participation in international competition pointless if Soviet athletes did not win. "Once we decided to take part in foreign competitions, we were forced to guarantee victory, otherwise the 'free' bourgeois press would fling mud at the whole nation as well as the athletes," said Nikolai Romanov, post-war chairman of the Government Committee on Physical Culture and Sport. "That actually did happen. To gain permission to go to international tournaments I had to send a special note to Stalin guaranteeing victory."[8] After a remarkable debut at the 1952 Helsinki Summer Olympics, a new era in Soviet sport emerged with an intent focus on international victories. Following Stalin's death in 1953, Nikita Khrushchev consolidated power as First Secretary of the Communist Party and, over the course of the subsequent decade, initiated some relatively liberal reforms of the Soviet system. As Robert Edelman suggests, Soviet foreign policy under Khrushchev was more benign than during Stalin's reign, yet the relationship of the Olympic sports system to both external and internal affairs hardly changed at all.[9] Because of the national prestige victorious countries accrued at the Games, the USSR realized that this was the most advantageous venue for displaying socialist sport supremacy. Although the importance of world and European championships was a given in the arena of international sports, the Soviets found political resonance in Olympic victories.[10]

The Myth of War

As a result of the Great Patriotic War, the Soviet Union focused on skiing as both a military tool and an ideological vehicle for developing socialism. The sport combined the nationalist tropes of Scandinavia and the utilitarian pragmatism of the Nazi sports system with notions of indigenous skiing that pre-dated Kievan Rus'. The transformation of skiing into an iconic representation of Russian nationalism in the service of Soviet identity involved the entire regime. Just as Stalin invoked positive images of a whole host of Russian tsars and generals as patriotic role models for the Red Army during the war, so the propagandists used stories and imagery of Russian skiers from the reign of Ivan III in the fifteenth century forward to promote skiing. By co-opting the methodology of the Nazi sport system as a means to prepare the nation for war, the government used skiing as a potent symbol of socialist involvement among the populace.[11]

Amir Weiner notes that ritual representations of the war were the revolutionary prism through which Party leaders viewed civilian life in the decades that followed.[12] The Great Patriotic War morphed into a myth that defined the Soviet Union to an even greater extent than any other event in the canon of Soviet "great moments." It even superseded the most fundamental stories of the Bolshevik Revolution and Civil War. However, the very essence of Soviet ideology was the ongoing purification of the state and government. Initially, the Bolshevik purges targeted internal class enemies. Joseph Stalin, suspicious of the loyalties of borderland groups, transformed these purges into ethnic cleansing during the 1930s even as the USSR encouraged ethnic differentiation within a Soviet multinational state. During the war years, the dichotomies of class, so crucial to the Bolshevik project, diminished in importance as wartime behavior removed the stigma of adverse social origin and provided opportunity for the redemption of pre-war sins. Ethnicity, on the other hand, became increasingly problematic, as post-war perceptions marked certain groups as irredeemably anti-Soviet. The government portrayed the suffering that resulted from the Nazis' war of annihilation as universal and undifferentiated, denying, for example, that there was any special position for the combat service of the Jewish community during the Great Patriotic War—which in turn fueled an officially sanctioned form of anti-Semitism. At the same time, the Soviets encouraged an ethnic hierarchy of contributions to Soviet victory over Germany, with top billing reserved for the role of Russians and Ukrainians.[13]

Writing on Stalin and Russian nationalism, E. A. Rees notes that the Stalinist leadership fostered Soviet patriotism together with a commitment to Leninist internationalism. However, Stalinism allowed for only a very limited range in the expression of Russian nationalist sentiments, because the main symbols of Russian nationalism—the monarchy, the Orthodox Church, the aristocracy, the pre-revolutionary intelligentsia—had been eliminated or reduced in power.[14] Therefore, new mythologies, symbols and rituals were required for the promotion of Soviet patriotism on a worldwide stage. In the post-war years, international sport provided an opportune platform for this conceit.

Particularly useful was the association of skiing with Slavism and nationalism fostered by the Sokol organizations in the first decade of the twentieth century as well as by the nationwide ski mobilization movement of the 1940s. As Mike O'Mahoney suggests, Soviet participation in activities such as mountaineering and skiing reflected "an extension of the stoical endurance of the Soviet population during the war," which indicated to the world that the capacity to persevere in the most extreme of sporting environments was a fundamental national characteristic.[15] During the siege of Leningrad, for example, skiers of the Baltic Fleet carried out ski competitions along the Neva not only to lift their own spirits but also to show the citizenry that even though matters were serious and difficult, the city itself "was alive and would not be broken."[16]

Skiing evolved after the war into an all-encompassing Soviet metaphor. A 1951 article in the weekly magazine *Ogonek* offers a striking and highly stylized case in point. The story involves a youth of African heritage, captured by the Nazis and befriended by fellow concentration camp inmates from the Soviet Union. Liberated by the Red Army, the young man known as Sasha Demedov chose to follow his new friends to the Soviet Union rather than travel to the United States in the company of an American officer who addressed him as "boi" and "niger." Relocating in Minsk, he became a top student, studying Russian and German, history, geography, literature and chemistry with an interest in sports, music and model airplanes. The *Ogonek* correspondent describes what happens as he and Sasha leave their interview: "We went out of the children's home with Sasha. He had on a flannel ski outfit, cap with ear-flaps, warm gloves and skis on his shoulder. 'Good snow has fallen. It's a suitable day for a tour.' Then he called out to the boys who had gone ahead. And, turning to us he said, 'Excuse me. I will say goodbye to you. We've gathered for a ski tour.' Three friends, one after another, set out down quiet, snow-covered Grushevskii Street."[17] The contrast between young Sasha Demedov's life in the Soviet Union and what it might have been in the United States is unstated yet apparent: he would have had scant opportunity for advanced studies nor would he have joined white comrades such as his Belarus ski partners, shown in an accompanying photograph, for a day's outing on the ski trail.

Sasha on skis represented all that was significant to his adopted home in the Soviet Union just as, at the opposite end of the spectrum, the Soviet cross-country ski racer performing before an international audience would provide an excellent example of "patriotism, comradeship and collectivism."[18] Writing during the zenith of Soviet domination of international cross-country ski events after the 1980 Winter Olympics at Lake Placid, Soviet sport pedagogue Igor Butin detailed this point of view: "The education of skiers in feelings of patriotism has great significance. It is very important to make use of the revolutionary, military and working-class traditions of our party and nation in the education of communist ideology, ideological conviction and patriotism. The sport of skiing is familiar with many examples of the heroic conduct of Soviet skiers who saved our nation at the fronts of the Civil and Great Patriotic Wars."[19] The notion of skiing as patriotism was a recurring theme in the immediate post-war era. The oversized pages of *Ogonek* offered ample space for displaying images promoting this idea. Especially noteworthy is the 20 February 1949 issue, featuring a full-color, three-quarter-page right profile of a young border guard wearing a ski cap with earflaps and winter camouflage jacket, gripping his PPsh41 Burp gun across his chest. Opening the magazine, the viewer sees a black-and-white photograph of this young soldier's ski patrol on maneuvers with Generalissimo Stalin's supernal gaze facing from a full-page left profile portrait on page one. A similar front-cover photograph on the 18 February 1951 issue shows a young soldier in three-quarter profile clutching his automatic weapon with a slogan-bedecked red flag in the background. This image is paired with a full-color back-cover photograph of young students in their military uniforms skiing through the woods on a sunny day.[20]

Throughout the Cold War era, the importance of the Great Patriotic War never diminished, taking on a life of its own outside the historical narrative of the Soviet Union. The Soviet regime capitalized on the war's emotional impact by organizing sport festivals, similar to the Timoshenko games of the early 1940s, that would tap into citizens' yearning for a nostalgic and mythologized past. These conventionalized commemorations, named after distinguished athletes who died in combat, embodied orchestrated rituals that kept the memory of the war alive in people's minds.[21] One such competition honored Liuba Kulakova, who had defeated the formidable Zoia Bolotova in a 5-kilometer race before the war. As a member of a partisan ski division, Kulakova lost her life in an ambush near Smolensk. In 1946 a memorial statue was dedicated to her in a Moscow park, from which point a 5-kilometer ski race honoring her name started each year on 8 March, International Women's Day. Similarly, the winner of the 30-kilometer race held as part of the annual Race of the Nation's Strongest Skiers received the Prize in Honor of Vladimir Miagkov, Hero of the Soviet Union.[22] Especially evocative of the Armed Forces' defense of the Soviet Union were military patrol races, in which teams of skiers ran on a 25- to 30-kilometer course with various shooting stages along the way. Certainly these events, re-creating within the confines of a sporting environment the essence of winter warfare, prompted feelings of pride in the fighting spirit shown by the Red Army during the Great Patriotic War.[23] The rest of the war-weary world, however, had lost its taste for this event. Included as part of the Winter Games in 1924, 1928 and 1936, military patrol was run for the last time as a demonstration sport at the 1948 Olympics in St. Moritz.

One important factor contributing to the demise of the military patrol race at the Olympics after 1948 was that only military personnel were allowed to participate, and therefore the sport did not conform to the International Olympic Committee (IOC)'s ideal of competitions in which all athletes could take part. Nevertheless, military patrol remained popular among the armed forces of many nations. The Conseil Internationale du Sport Militaire (CISM), founded in 1948, promoted the event as part of its international military championships. The Soviet Union had conducted an annual national championship in military patrol since the early 1930s, and it is no surprise that interest in this type of race remained keen in the Red Army throughout the Cold War era. Such competitions followed the international military patrol format over a 30-kilometer course.[24] But in contrast to this team event, interest in international ski-shooting competitions for individuals gained momentum in 1956 when Norway sent a squad to compete in Sweden. This was followed by the announcement in 1957 that annual world championship competitions in a new sport, biathlon, would commence in 1958. The ultimate goal was to gain biathlon's inclusion as an official event at the 1960 Winter Olympics in Squaw Valley, California.

The Soviet Union and International Cross-Country Ski Racing

Unlike international sports such as shooting, speed skating or track and field where the venues, no matter the location, are relatively uniform, skiing is a hodgepodge of variables. Differences in elevation, course profile, temperature, snow structure and the vagaries of weather complicate comparisons of race results from one competition to the next. No objective indices exist in skiing, noted *Sovetskii sport*, because "conditions are unequal. Thus only in single combat can the most powerful be revealed."[25] The Soviet Union took this truism to heart and began analyzing foreign skiers in action just after the end of World War II. The goal was to develop a baseline to determine how well Soviet skiers would perform against the very best world-class competitors.

In 1946, A. G. Bychkov and Viktor Andreev travelled to the Norwegian Ski Championships to scrutinize the top Scandinavian competitors. Encouraged by their observations in comparison to results from the Soviet National Championships of 1946, the government sent downhill skier Mikhail Khimichev and Dmitrii Vasil'ev in his new capacity as coach to the Holmenkollen Games in Oslo the following year. When he returned, Vasil'ev was convinced that the Soviets would do well at the 1948 Holmenkollen Games with some diligent training, preparation and organization.[26] As a result of these various experiences, the government established a Soviet National Ski Team in the spring of 1947, comprised of sixty-two cross-country specialists, downhill skiers and jumpers.[27] The following year, ten observers from the USSR attended the 1948 Winter Olympic Games in St. Moritz. Encouraged by their analysis of the Scandinavians' performances there, the government then dispatched a team of skiers to Oslo's Holmenkollen Games, held just a few weeks after the closing ceremonies in Switzerland. Soviet athletes placed fourth, eighth and seventeenth out of a strong international field of 134 contestants in the prestigious 50-kilometer race. How the Soviet skiers waxed their skis for this contest was of particular interest to the Swedish team, although Vasil'ev and his staff completely misread the temperatures and track conditions in the subsequent 18-kilometer race.[28] Nonetheless, the results augured well and paved the way for the Soviet Union to join the Fédération Internationale de Ski (International Ski Federation), or FIS, in 1949.[29]

Vetting skiers for the Soviet National Team was an involved process, accomplished through myriad competitions all winter long. For example, in 1953, the first stage of cross-country ski races took place from 4 through

31 January for schools, industrial complexes and educational institutions among teams from workshops, departments, faculties and classes. Numerous open ski competitions put on by newspapers such as *Pionerskaia pravda, Moskovskii komsomolets* and *Sovetskii sport* introduced youngsters and interested citizens to ski racing over short distances. The second stage ran from 1 through 8 February for district championships among teams from the physical culture collectives. On 22 February, the third and final stage was a series of competitions among the district teams and collectives. These races allowed citizens to attain higher GTO classifications as well. The next level of competition involved determining championship skiers in a number of different categories leading up to the USSR National Championships, held during the first two weeks of March. In February, the Belarus, Ukrainian, Latvian, Lithuanian, Estonian, Armenian, Georgian, Kazakhstan and Karelo-Finnish SSRs each determined their regional championships, as did the cities of Leningrad and Moscow. In addition, the February competitive schedule included an All-Union Rural Ski Championship, Spartakiadas of the Physical Culture Collectives of Machine-Tractor Stations and State Farms (*Sovkhoz*), a Spartakiada of the Siberian and Far East Burevestnik Volunteer Sport Society, a ski championship of Higher Education Institutions as well as one for Industrial Trainees. Rounding out the month were championships for the Soviet Armed Forces and the sports clubs Dinamo and Spartak. In March, the Russian Soviet Federative Socialist Republic Ski Championship was held, and finally the USSR National Ski Championship, to which the top skiers from all the preceding competitions were invited. Consistent results over this exhausting winter season were the basis for selection to the Soviet National Ski Team. The very best skiers in the country competed by invitation only at the All-Union Competition of the Strongest Skiers, held in early January of each year.[30]

Although the Soviet Union took an interest in all of the FIS ski events contested internationally after the war, the focus of the National Team remained firmly fixed on the Nordic cross-country races. Certainly, glamour events such as slalom, downhill and ski jumping were worth pursuing because there were medals awarded; however, the experience of the Great Patriotic War demonstrated that cross-country skiing had "applied military significance," while in comparison ski jumping and alpine skiing seemed frivolous. Although V. Serebriakov's 1949 ski guide for rural collectives describes jumping and slalom as worthwhile diversions for the winter, only the Be Ready for Labor and Defense (BGTO) and Ready for Labor and

Defense (GTO) norms for cross-country racing are listed.[31] Consider the numbers of participants in the various disciplines in 1953: at the Moscow Ski Championships, for example, there were 373 skiers in the 18-kilometer race for men, 111 in the 50-kilometer marathon; 233 female skiers in the 5-kilometer and 129 in the 10-kilometer races. On the 60-meter jump hill, by contrast, there were only 26 competitors. At the All-Union Competition of the Strongest Skiers, held between 11 and 13 January, there were 62 racers in the men's 18-kilometer and 52 in the 30-kilometer contests, 22 women in the 5-kilometer and 21 in the 10-kilometer events. In jumping there were 28 participants and 14 in the Nordic combined. On the downhill slopes, 40 men and 12 women competed in the slalom and giant slalom events.[32]

Nevertheless, the fact that Russian downhill ski racers were lagging behind their cross-country counterparts was vexing, as indicated in this report from the Dinamo club championships of 1954: "The competitions in downhill skiing showed that many sportsmen have trained insufficiently and still possess poor modern technique for this type of sport. . . . The good organization of the work of the cross-country skiers can serve as an example."[33] As the Soviet Union re-entered international sporting competitions in the post-war era, officials focused on total medal counts. For the national ski team of the USSR, the possible medals available in the six Olympic Alpine events, eighteen in all, were equal to those awarded in the six Nordic cross-country events and thus assumed an increasingly greater significance.[34] Unfortunately, downhill skiing during the 1950s was not a "mass type" of sport in the USSR—mountainous ski areas were far removed from major population centers—and the results of Soviet downhill skiers were uniformly dismal. At the 1956 Olympic Games in Cortina, for example, the top Soviet finish in the downhill event was sixteenth, and in slalom twenty-fourth. A lack of coaches and skilled Alpine skiers hindered the training of a new, competitive cadre even though the Soviet Union had established centers for the sport's development at Zlatoust, Kirovsk, Krasnoufimsk, Krasniarsk, Ufa, Alma-Ata, Bakuriani, Karpaty and Mt. Elbrus.[35] Further restricting growth of the sport was the dearth of ski lifts available to carry skiers to the top of a run for training: "In slalom, giant slalom, downhill and ski jumping," wrote ski trainer M. A. Agranovskii in 1954, "the basic work is done in the descent. [Walking uphill] in the mountains takes away a great deal of energy and time. . . . With the goal of improving the effectiveness of training in skiing, it is high time that mechanical means are used for [such] ascents."[36] A few rudimentary ski lifts were already operating by the winter season of 1954. A January article in *Ogonek* features photographs of a t-bar style lift installed by Spartak sports club at Alma-Ata that carried skiers 1,470 meters up the hill to the start of a downhill course in only thirteen and a half minutes, compared to two hours of uphill walking. An April article that same year shows a similar ski lift at a ski resort located in Bakuriani, 75 kilometers west of Tbilisi. A photograph from 1963 shows a chairlift in operation at the village of Terskol near Mt. Elbrus.[37]

These examples notwithstanding, the construction of ski lifts to enhance training for downhill racers remained sporadic in the Soviet Union throughout the 1950s and early 1960s.[38] In addition, the rapid technological advancement of downhill skis, boots and bindings in the West required continual replacement of an Alpine racer's equipment and soon outpaced the efforts of Soviet production managers. In the United States, for example, the introduction of a composite metal and plastic ski by Howard Head in 1950 led to a frenzy of competition among manufacturers in France, Switzerland and Austria to provide bonded synthetic skis to the burgeoning ski markets of the world. By the late 1960s, the production of downhill wood skis had been completely eliminated. Cross-country ski equipment, by contrast, evolved at a much slower rate over the same period of time, as did the technique associated with the sport.[39]

Thus, cross-country skiing remained the purview of the Soviet ski team and, within the framework of the FIS Nordic Ski Championship program, there was a particular focus on team relays and the longer races of 30- and 50-kilometers.[40] Because of its emphasis on the combined exertion of three or more skiers, the relay has traditionally reflected the strength and consistency of a nation's ski program better than any other event, and at the international level it has always been a serious business. In the early 1980s, Marty Hall, head coach of the United States Cross-Country Ski Team from 1968 through 1978, noted: "When a racer puts on a bib for a relay, somehow he becomes another person. Perhaps it's pride in a nation . . . or simply the fact that two or three other people are depending on him for the team effort. Whatever the reason, the relay racer becomes an animal, particularly in international racing. There is no love lost between competitors, and the boundaries of the rules are overstepped more often than not."[41] To Vladimir Shaposhnikov, the relay was "the most nerve-wracking and emotional spectacle." And for the Soviets as a whole, the relay was the one event that most clearly reflected socialist precepts by neatly combining mass participation and mastery. Vladimir Kuzin, triple gold medalist in both relay and individual events at Olympic and world championship competitions, put it this way: "The collective helped me in training, it helped in the battle on the ski track."[42] During an interview conducted in 1987, Aleksandr Privalov, in his capacity as the Soviet biathlon team's coach, embellished this point by emphasizing the socialist aspects of Red Army and border patrol competitions: "First of all our relay team has always had four like-minded biathletes [who respect one another and] could sacrifice their personal interests for the common goal."[43] Almost an afterthought for many international ski teams in the West, the Soviets put a great deal of effort into the tactics and theory of relay competition. Soviet trainers emphasized waxing with precision for each separate stage and preparing skiers for the specific role each would play as the relay competition evolved on race day.[44]

Absent an international platform of Olympic standing for competition in military patrol, the long-distance events for individuals embodied notions of endurance and perseverance that, as an integral part of the Great Patriotic War narrative, had become part of the very fabric of the battle-hardened Soviet people. Of particular significance was the 50-kilometer marathon, an event that requires incredible stamina and mental toughness. Sweden hosted the first 50-kilometer contest in 1888; at every Winter Olympics and each of the FIS World Ski Championships since 1925, there has been a race of this length. The event has therefore attained legendary status over the years. Many Soviet sports writers extolled the 50-kilometer ski marathon as the most prestigious and interesting race of the cross-country distance events, "the most serious test," in one author's opinion, "of the ski-racer's maturity."[45] Indeed, skiing such a long course at race pace for over three hours while maintaining concentration, proper ski technique and the will to go on has augmented the mystique of the "50-K" as one of the most, if not the most, demanding events on the Olympic card.[46] By the 1960s, the 50-kilometer race was a staple at every Soviet city, regional and district ski competition as well as at the national finals.

A critical element in successful long-distance ski racing has always been proper base preparation. A marathon skier's worst nightmare would be having to depend on arm strength alone to pole around the course without benefit of skis with good glide on the flats and downhills and grip, or "kick," on the uphills. In the late nineteenth century, home-brewed concoctions of pine tar, paraffin and other ingredients were the norm at major ski competitions. But by the 1930s, a scientific approach to the production of ski wax arose as skiers began to comprehend the mechanism and physics of sliding on snow, especially the way in which friction builds up heat on the base of the ski. In 1938, a Danish industrialist working in Norway introduced four ski waxes with color-coded packaging corresponding to different snow temperatures. However, these waxes used naturally occurring compounds, and for snow transitioning from powder to wet at zero degrees Celsius, different ingredients were necessary. In the late 1930s and early 1940s, Astra, a Swedish pharmaceutical manufacturer, began to experiment with hydrocarbons and petroleum products, producing the first synthetic ski waxes under the trade name Swix in 1946. This was a technological innovation that changed the complexion of cross-country skiing by offering quality-controlled and snow-specific waxes. At the 1948 St. Moritz Winter Olympics, skiers of the Swedish National Team won all of the cross-country events, having prepared their ski-bases exclusively with Swix wax.[47]

In the USSR, meanwhile, ski wax development followed a parallel course. Nikolai Vasil'ev, the young ski racer who watched the Finns ski away from him in the wet snow of St. Petersburg in 1913, was now a chemical engineer in the Soviet Union and a lecturer at the Moscow Textile Technical Secondary School. In the 1920s, Nikolai and his brother Dmitrii began experimenting with various wax formulations. They created a successful spreadable wax for thawing, changeable snow that Dmitrii used for the first time at a 30-kilometer race in 1925. Concurrently, Pavel Gusev also concocted a series of waxes in Leningrad. In the years of the Great Patriotic War, Vasil'ev developed ski wax for the Red Army and, after the war, was producing ski waxes under several names such as Karandash, Pobeda and Uktus. Vasil'ev fabricated his wares from different combinations of pine tar, resin, beeswax, beef fat, rubber, oil, paraffin and lead, for a variety of conditions, numbered 1 through 5.[48] During the ten-year period between 1946 and 1956, other recipes for wax competed with Vasil'ev's product. One such offering came from H. G. Laptev and B. A. Sferin, which followed Vasil'ev's numerical system from 1 through 10, as well as a "22" and a "35." In addition, waxes developed by A. Novikov, A. Kovrigin, A. Riadov and V. Zinov'ev were manufactured in Tallinn under the name "TsOKB." In 1957, Riadov and Zinov'ev began experimenting with polyisobutylene as a component of their Temp wax brand. By the early 1960s, the Dinamo factories had appropriated the production of Temp, while TsOKB was taken over by the Odintsovo Chemical Works. In addition, the Tallinn Chemical Works began issuing Tallinskaia, a wax formulated by K. Lon'tech. At the same time, the Scandinavian countries were exporting their ski waxes into the Soviet Union, and such well-known brands as

Start, Rode, Swix, Rex and Bratlie were occasionally available for skiers in the larger cities.[49] However, some Soviet skiers still preferred the wax of Vasil'ev. As one skier related in a letter to *Sovetskii sport*: "The group of ski enthusiasts I belong to is not satisfied with the assortment of ski wax available in the Moscow shops . . . in our opinion, production of the well-proven wax for thawing snow conditions 'No. 1' according to N. Vasil'ev's formula should be revived."[50]

At international competitions early in the Cold War, Soviet wax proved to be the equal of Scandinavian brands such as Swix, a fact the Russians were only too happy to point out to other competitors. Still, the availability of wax for the average skier remained problematic throughout the Soviet era. Lack of raw materials hindered production, creating scarcity for this critical commodity, a situation that beset citizens of the USSR with regularity for a majority of goods.[51] One reader from Central Khazan [sic] complained to *Sovetskii sport* that "I'm a skier but, unfortunately, it's not always possible to buy ski wax. But why couldn't I make it myself? Probably it's not that complicated." In reply, the newspaper explained that manufacturing wax was quite complex, comparing the different formulations of Temp and Start; but it begged the question concerning what a skier should do without wax to buy.[52] Although wax developed by Temp and VISTI remained on the Soviet market into the 1980s, advances in the science of waxing by Scandinavian manufacturers resulted in a far superior product with much higher standards for the coefficients of both grip and glide. United States biathlete John Ruger recalls that in Minsk during the 1982 World Biathlon Championships, there was very high demand on the black market for Swix wax among Soviet skiers aspiring to qualify for the USSR National Team.[53]

But successful ski racing required more than just fast wax. With decades of experience as a Merited Master of Sport and ski coach, Nikolai Vasil'ev appreciated other variables that could make all the difference in a long-distance ski race at international competitions: "Beforehand . . . think about technical organization, tactical preparation and physical conditioning, having considered everything that is essential for winning. That glass of tea, a piece of sugar, a drink of cocoa or glucose, it's necessary to take care of these matters without fail. Many such 'trivialities' play a very large role during competition."[54] For Vasil'ev and the skiers of the Soviet Union, vast knowledge acquired before the war—when they would race in domestic ultra-distance events over several days—proved that it took more than training and conditioning to win a 50-kilometer marathon. Ski wax suited to snow that might change over the course of three hours, a well-thought-out race plan and even the proper nourishment or "feed" to eat or drink out on the course as the racer skied along might be the deciding factor in such a long competition. It was this attention to detail applied to the 20-, 30- and 50-kilometer races that contributed to Soviet success on the ski track as the national teams entered international competition starting in the late 1940s. The shorter 15-kilometer sprint for men was rarely included at major competitions held in the Soviet Union before this event's inclusion in FIS-sanctioned contests beginning in the mid-1950s.[55]

In order to maximize a skier's efficiency racing over these longer distances, Soviet physicians and scientists were among the first to analyze the physiology of skiing from a sports medicine and biomechanical perspective. In 1919, the Bolsheviks established the Institute of Physical Culture in Petrograd for the study of the "scientific-methodological fundamentals of the Soviet system of physical education." This included the publication of books and training manuals for a variety of sports including track and field, boxing and speed skating.[56] Dmitrii Vasil'ev states that he began systematically analyzing ski technique in the early years of the twentieth century with "mathematical calculations and formulas" resulting in a "new, 'engineered' approach to skiing." He found, for example, that after his 35-day trek from Moscow to Oslo in 1925–1926, his lung capacity measured 7,000 cubic centimeters.[57] A 1946 article in *Ogonek* magazine details the work of V. S. Farfel' at the Physiological Laboratory of Scientific Research Institute of Physical Culture. For many years prior to writing this article, Farfel' had been investigating the point at which long-distance ski racers found their "second wind" and how quickly the heart would recover from maximum effort, in this particular experiment over a 20-kilometer ski course.[58] The extent to which scientific methodology was applied to ski racing is evident in both M. A. Agranovskii's and B. I. Bergman's technical ski manuals published between 1954 and 1965. In addition to a variety of charts, diagrams and graphs, these volumes include formulas such as: $I = R \cos \alpha$, for calculating the amount of force (I) a skier should apply to his ski in order to climb a hill based on his weight (R) and the angle of the climb (α).[59]

In addition, the Soviets were at the forefront in the study of sport psychology. Carl Diem, who was instrumental in the organization of the 1936 Olympic Games, had opened the first psychological sport testing laboratory in Germany in 1920. Five years later, two similar facilities were established, one by A. Puni at the Institute of Physical Culture in Leningrad, the other by Coleman Griffith at the University of Illinois. Although the study of sport psychology was moribund in the West during the thirty years between 1935 and the establishment of the International Society of Sport Psychology in Italy in 1965, Puni's research continued uninterrupted in the USSR. The Soviet press noted that P. A. Rudnik was offering a course in sport psychology as of 1945 at the Stalin Central State Institute of Physical Culture in Moscow where seven thousand ski instructors had received training during the war years.[60]

Soviet Skiers Take to the International Stage

Although Dmitrii Vasil'ev had high hopes for his skiers at Oslo's Holmenkollen races of 1948, the best Soviet effort was M. Protasov's fourth-place finish—just out of the medals—in the 50-kilometer contest. The results from the rest of the Soviet squad, however, were disappointing—eighth, seventeenth and eighteenth places. This led to a reassessment of Soviet prospects at international ski competitions. The coaching staff analyzed the times of the winning skiers at the 1952 Winter Games in Oslo and compared them to those of victors at the Soviet National Championships in order to improve the squad for the 1954 World Nordic Ski Championships in Falun, Sweden. In the 1952–1953 winter season the Soviet team had captured twenty-one medals—eight of them gold—at the Tenth International Student Winter Games in Semmering, Austria, a feat that bolstered Soviet confidence.[61]

Just prior to the Falun competitions, the USSR invited a team from Finland to a dual match held in Sverdlovsk. The Soviets improved significantly upon their results from previous years: Vladimir Kuzin won the opening 30-kilometer event, with seven of his teammates coming in just behind second- and third place finishers Veikko Salo and Veikko Hakulinen of Finland. In the 15-kilometer race, Salo and Kuzin traded places, with newcomer Pavel Kolchin of the Soviet Union taking the third spot. Kuzin chose not to compete in the 50-kilometer marathon, and the race went to Finland's defending Olympic gold medalist Hakulinen. Another Soviet newcomer, Anatolii Sheliukhin, took third in this race. Teammates Kuzin and Kolchin joined veteran Fedor Terent'ev and Vladimir Oliashev to prevail over Finland in the 4 x 10-kilometer relay.[62] In their pre–world championship tune-up in Grindelwald, Switzerland, the Soviet women were equally successful, winning the 3 x 5-kilometer relay. In addition,

Valentina Tsareva took the gold medal in the 10-kilometer race (the only individual event for women until 1962).[63] Encouraged by this outcome, the USSR National Team stormed the World Ski Championships in Falun, with results that were much more satisfactory than those of 1948. Vladimir Kuzin won both the 30- and 50-kilometer events and was awarded the prestigious King's Cup before a crowd of 120,000 spectators. The men's 4 x 10-kilometer relay team took second place behind Finland. Liubov' Kozyreva became the women's champion at 10 kilometers and then helped her teammates Margarita Maslennikova and Tsareva win the 3 x 5-kilometer relay title.[64]

During the subsequent ski season, in anticipation of the 1956 Winter Olympics, Sweden and Norway sent delegations to Moscow for a series of competitions in 1955. Among the skiers in attendance were Olympic medalists Sixten Jernberg of Sweden and Martin Stokken and Hallgeir Brenden of Norway, as well as Sweden's future Olympic medalist Per-Erik Larsson. The Soviet Union's Kuzin and Terent'ev placed first and second in the 15-kilometer race. Then, they teamed up with Kolchin and Nikolai Kozlov to win the 4 x 10-kilometer relay. At the Pre-Olympics in Cortina d'Ampezzo later that year, Kuzin tied for first place with Sweden's Jernberg in the 30-kilometer race and took second behind Hakulinen of Finland in the 50-kilometer marathon.[65]

With such strong results, the prospects for the Soviet National Ski Team at the Olympic Games in Cortina d'Ampezzo were particularly bright. And indeed, Soviet skiers did not only dominate the Nordic events: the USSR won more total medals than any other nation by far. In an especially tough field of competitors in the 50-kilometer race, the Soviet team placed all four of its skiers in the top seven positions. Fedor Terent'ev won the bronze medal, less than two minutes behind defending gold medalist Veikko Hakulinen of Finland, and just over three minutes behind winner Sixten Jernberg of Sweden, to this day still venerated as one of the greatest ski racers of all time. To further demonstrate the incredible depth of the Soviet squad, the men won the gold medal in the 4 x 10-kilometer relay and Pavel Kolchin took home a bronze in the 15-kilometer race and another in the 30-kilometer event, with Soviet skiers placing fourth through sixth in the latter as well. The women took first and second in the 10-kilometer race and were silver medalists in the 3 x 5-kilometer relay. "With the coming of Soviet skiers to the winter Olympics, the Scandinavians faced formidable bidders for the top honors," the Soviet press noted with pride. "As for the Soviet women's team, it became an unchallenged leader on the ski track."[66]

To be sure, throughout the Soviet era Russian women overpowered the competition so consistently in the Nordic events that for more than three decades the world's sporting press predicted their victory ahead of time. Because international sports in general, and Olympic sports in particular, were predominantly male, it was possible for the Soviet Union to make an impact on the international stage by concentrating on the medal potential of its women.[67] Soviet books and articles of the era intended for Western consumption included full-page photo spreads featuring female gold medalists in cross-country skiing.[68] By contrast, the Western press often disparaged the Russian female skiers with gendered bias. In a 1968 article about the Swedish women's cross-country team, *Sports Illustrated* noted archly: "Her [Toni Gustafsson's] opponents on the favored Soviet women's Nordic team were all new. They were not the ones who had conquered in the last world championships—something about those sex tests it was said."[69] Interviewing Oddmund Jensen, coach of the Norwegian Cross-Country Ski Team, about the number of Olympic medals he anticipated his skiers would win, *Sports Illustrated* included another wry jab: "We do not have a chance with the women, so we can subtract those. We can compete with the Finns and Swedes, but Eastern Europe—where the Russian and Czech women do a man's work—they will produce the winning women. Our women are good, but they are charming and some of them . . . are surprisingly lady-like."[70] However, there was an abundance of fresh faces from year to year on the Soviet teams—both men's and women's— because the country's talent pool was incredibly deep, not because of failed gender tests or the travails of East European life. In a private conversation, Olympic medalist and ski coach Nikolai Anikin confided that there were so many skiers in the USSR that it mattered little if hard training burned out the stars: "there were always more to take their place and the few who survived were really, really tough."[71] By the mid-1970s, even *Sports Illustrated* had to concede the gifted Soviet skiers their due: "Here come the Russian women again, led by the unsinkable Galina Kulakova, 33, which means the rest of the female Nordics can stand aside."[72]

The Birth of Biathlon

The founder of the modern Olympic movement, Baron Pierre de Coubertin, created an unorthodox competition known as modern pentathlon for the 1912 Summer Olympics. Coubertin conceived of this event, which consists of pistol shooting, one-touch epée fencing, a 200-meter swim, stadium jumping on an unfamiliar horse and a 3-kilometer run, as a test for the ideal, well-rounded soldier-courier, albeit one firmly ensconced in the battlefield milieu of the nineteenth century. During World War II, modern pentathletes proposed to the International Olympic Committee (IOC) that a version of their event be included in the Winter Olympic Games as well. The competition would be a hybrid melding of the equestrian, fencing and pistol shooting elements of modern pentathlon with a 3-kilometer downhill run and a 12-kilometer cross-country ski race held under the rules of the International Ski Federation (FIS). In 1942, Switzerland and Sweden held a test of this curious athletic amalgamation in Gstaad; but winter pentathlon was included on the Olympic program only once as a demonstration sport at the 1948 games in St. Moritz.[73]

Nevertheless, organizers of modern pentathlon would not give up easily on the idea of a multi-sport event at the Winter Olympics. With the foundation of the Union Internationale de Pentathlon Moderne (International Modern Pentathlon Union, or UIPM) in 1948, lobbying of the IOC began in earnest to develop modern winter pentathlon. Avery Brundage, first vice president of the IOC, was inclined favorably toward this event and proposed a mixture of cross-country skiing, downhill skiing, figure skating, tobogganing and ski jumping. However, the logistics of putting on such an event appeared difficult at best; and in the post-war years, the number of sites in the world with adequate facilities was limited. Thus, the more feasible combination of cross-country skiing and rifle shooting became the IOC's preferred iteration of the winter multi-sport contest. At an IOC meeting in Rome in 1949, the notion of modern winter pentathlon was abandoned in favor of ski-shooting, renamed *biathlon moderne d'hiver*, or modern winter biathlon. In 1957, the UIPM declared itself responsible for the administration of biathlon and initiated plans for the first world championship in the sport scheduled for 2 March 1958 in Saalfelden, Austria. In May 1959, UIPM proposed to the 55th Session of the IOC that an individual biathlon race be included in the next Winter Olympic Games as an official competition, not a demonstration sport. The motion passed, with the stipulation that the continuation of biathlon as an Olympic event would be contingent on the experience of staging the first race at Squaw Valley, California in 1960.[74]

From 1958 to 1965, international biathlon competition followed a format now known as the "old program." Competitors left the start-finish area at one- or two-minute intervals and skied a continuous 20-kilometer loop, stopping to fire large-bore open-sight rifles at four separate ranges along the way. Skiers took five shots prone at each of three ranges over distances of 250, 200 and 150 meters, and then five shots from the standing, or "off-hand," position at a distance of 100 meters at the fourth and final range, for a total of twenty shots. Cardboard targets measured 30, 25, 20 and 30 centimeters in diameter respectively. Each shot missed added a two-minute penalty to the total ski time for each individual. However, the large tracts of land required to contain a 20-kilometer ski course as well as four separate shooting ranges made the old program format difficult to organize. In addition, the long distances between ranges made viewing races difficult for spectators.[75] Therefore, in 1965, the UIPM introduced a reconfigured format for the individual 20-kilometer race, with two or three 2.5 to 5-kilometer loops starting and finishing at one shooting range. Competitors alternated firing five shots prone and standing for a total of twenty shots at a standard distance of 150 meters. Paper targets measured 25 centimeters with a bull's-eye of 12.5 centimeters for the prone position and 50 centimeters for standing with a bull's-eye of 35 centimeters. Missing the smaller inner ring of the bull's-eye on the target resulted in a one-minute penalty, while missing the larger one accrued an additional two minutes of ski time. After 1976, biathletes used small-bore rifles to fire at commensurately smaller targets at a distance of 50 meters in all international competitions.

As biathlon grew in popularity during the Cold War era, UIPM devised additional formats. In 1966, it added a four-man relay to international competition. The relay featured a mass start, with each team member skiing 7.5 kilometers in succession. Targets were breakable balloons or glass (supplanted by metal knock-down silhouettes), and for each missed target, the skier had to travel around a 200- (later reduced to 150-) meter penalty loop before resuming the ski race. Each team member carried sixteen rounds of ammunition to hit five prone and five standing targets. After the first five shots at each firing stage, any necessary penalty rounds were hand-loaded into the rifle's chamber. In 1974, biathlon's governing body added a 10-kilometer sprint race based on the relay format. Biathletes started at one-minute intervals and carried ten rounds of ammunition, with one bout each of prone and standing. Each missed target resulted in a trip around a 150-meter penalty loop.[76] These three events—the 20-kilometer individual, the 10-kilometer sprint and either a team competition or the 4 x 7.5-kilometer relay—comprised the competitive structure for most international biathlon competitions, with only minor rule changes through 1991.

Biathlon in the USSR

The Scandinavian countries welcomed the addition of ski-shooting or biathlon to the Olympic card in 1960. Such competitions had been ongoing in the northern reaches of Europe since the turn of the century, and inclusion at the Olympics bolstered the number of potential medals in the Nordic column traditionally dominated by Finland, Norway and Sweden. For the Soviet Union, just hitting its stride as a major factor in international ski racing, this was a boon as well. Biathlon as conceived by the UIPM was a competition for individuals similar in format to that of races held all across the USSR for decades. In addition, the sport provided an ideal ideological forum for presenting the conflict between socialist and capitalist systems, as well as an international stage to demonstrate lessons learned and paid for dearly during World War II. "The [biathlon] race over 20 kilometers with shooting has great applied-military importance," one Soviet biathlete wrote. "Today's military studies and the experience of the Great Patriotic War show that each soldier must skillfully combine accurate fire with quick movement [on skis]."[77]

Certainly, biathlon more than any other Olympic event, embodied what historian Barbara Keys considers the Sovietization of Western sport.[78] In its written account of the 1968 Grenoble Winter Games, the United States Olympic Committee described the combination of skiing and rifle marksmanship as "a contest best-suited for the military and for frontier police in mountainous countries. As expected, the race was a duel between the Scandinavians and the Soviet Union."[79] The USSR was far and away the most successful nation ever to compete in the sport of biathlon. From the introduction of modern biathlon as an international event in 1958 to the demise of the Soviet Union in 1991, athletes representing the Soviet Union won 45 percent of all possible medals awarded at world championship and Olympic competitions.[80] To the present day, the USSR still remains the undisputed champion in the men's Olympic biathlon relay, having won six consecutive gold medals from 1968 through 1988. Even more successful than the men, the female athletes of the USSR overpowered international competition during the developmental period of women's biathlon, winning 53 percent of all possible medals. Most impressive of all, from 1984 through 1991 the Soviet women never lost a world championship biathlon relay or team competition.[81]

But this international domination of biathlon did not occur haphazardly for the USSR. During the winter of 1957–1958, the armed forces of the

Soviet Union began to promote this new version of ski-shooting in earnest. The Red Army's principal newspaper, *Krasnaia zvezda*, singled out for praise by *Pravda* for its unstinting support of skiing during the Great Patriotic War, provided the sport's main forum. An article in the 8 December 1957 edition outlined the coming competitive ski season following the UIPM criteria for the old program 20-kilometer race, including a team competition in which the combined individual times of a four-man team determined the winning squad.[82] Team competition was part of the UIPM Biathlon World Championships from 1958 through 1965, although it was not included in the 1960 and 1964 Winter Olympics. Because of the many variables in the sport of biathlon, such as changeable snow conditions on the track or capricious winds at the shooting range, the winner of a particular race was often unpredictable. The team event and its replacement after 1966, the 4 x 7.5-kilometer relay, gave biathletes another opportunity to receive medals at international meets. It also indicated the depth and strength of each nation's international squads. Therefore, the skiers of the Soviet Union were particularly interested in excelling at this format.

In the winter of 1957, the Soviet Armed Forces selected a squad of biathletes to compete with the Finnish Defensive Forces Team in a dual meet in Kuopio, Finland. Racing under the UIPM old program format, Lieutenant Petr Morozov, Sergeant Iu. Suvorov and Privates Aleksei Kuznetsov and Aleksandr Gubin gained valuable information in Finland about the sport, thus giving the Soviets a head start in the development of their National Team. "[Although we outperformed] our competitors in speed of skiing, we were, however, inferior to them in accuracy of shooting," Lieutenant Morozov reported in *Krasnaia zvezda*. "And in the [final] result they won first place." In a reciprocal race with the Finns on 28 January 1958, held in Kavgolovo, a village just north of Leningrad, the Soviet team, led by Morozov and clad in their signature winter-white uniforms, outshot and outskied the Finnish team by a combined total of just under thirteen minutes. "This year we were able to meet once more with the Finnish sportsmen . . . covering the entire distance and striking all except one target," wrote Morozov. "We took revenge, emerging as victors."[83] This delicate balance between marksmanship and skiing proved crucial in the early years of biathlon.

Unlike the modern twenty-first century iteration of the sport, the UIPM old program biathlon format provided a more equitable balance between shooting and skiing. Firing a large-bore, high recoil military rifle demanded extraordinary hand-eye coordination. The two-minute penalty for each missed shot in the 20-kilometer race placed a premium on accurate marksmanship as a counter to sheer speed on the ski track. Today's top biathlon racers such as Norway's Ole-Einar Bjørndalen are ranked among the fastest cross-country skiers in the world.[84] In accordance with current competition rules, these biathletes train to shoot knock-down silhouette targets with small-bore rifles over fifty meters at a single firing range. This type of marksmanship provides immediate feedback: if the target falls, the shooter gains positive reinforcement; if the shot misses, the biathlete can adjust the rifle's sights, realign the shooting stance or simply take more time to pull the trigger. This was not the case, however, for the world's top-ranked cross-country skiers such as Veikko Hakulinen of Finland who tried their hand at biathlon under the old program format.[85] Until rule changes after the 1964 Olympics, biathletes shot at paper targets and therefore did not know their degree of accuracy until after the race, when the targets were removed and then scored by a panel of judges. In addition, the competitors shot at four separate ranges with potentially different wind patterns, sun angles and terrain configurations. At the first world championship competition in Saalfelden (and subsequent competitions through the early 1960s), competitors were even forbidden from practicing at the shooting ranges. They were handed a sketch of the race course terrain and range location only forty-eight hours before the start. Compared with a modern biathlon range, which is equipped with the accouterments of a small-bore firing line—including mats for lying comfortably in the prone position and for standing with stability in off-hand—the old program range was a crude affair. Hardly any ground preparation on the firing line meant that a skier's elbows rested in the snow while shooting from the prone position. Such an uneven and awkward platform made it extremely difficult to hit the targets. Similarly, standing on slippery bases required digging the edges of the skis into the snow for the off-hand position, forcing some participants to remove their skis completely in order to find more solid footing.[86]

Skiing and shooting among the ranks of the Red Army took on new importance as the Soviets scoured the country for potential members of a Soviet National Team destined for the 1958 Biathlon World Championship.[87] On 10 January 1958, *Krasnaia zvezda* reported that outside of Moscow the selection trials for the Nordic World Championships in Lahti had just concluded. In anticipation of the events scheduled for Austria, for the first time, "a 20-kilometer ski race with shooting" was included that "aroused great interest."[88] On 9 January, twenty-seven racers left the starting line for a chance to gain a berth on the National Team. Although M.

Miziukaev from Dinamo sport club clocked the fastest ski time, his poor shooting left him in fourth place. Taking the first three places was a trio of skiers who eventually anchored the Soviet biathlon team through the early 1960s: Dmitrii Sokolov, a skier representing Dinamo sport club; Valentin Pshenitsyn, a junior sergeant in the Red Army; and Vladimir Melanin of the Central Sport Club, Ministry of Defense (TsSKMO).[89] Melanin would have a noteworthy career from 1959 through 1964 as the most successful biathlete in the world, leaving an indelible Soviet stamp on the sport.

To further promote the new sport of biathlon, additional competitions were scheduled for the Armed Forces Winter Spartakiada. The news about this event apparently intrigued Junior Lieutenant K. Trunichev, who wrote to *Krasnaia zvezda*: "Not long ago in the paper . . . I read that at the competitions of the Winter Anniversary Celebration Spartakiada there will be a ski race over 20 kilometers with shooting. This type of sport certainly has great applied-military significance. I am asking the editor to discuss the details of the race."[90] In reply, one of the judges for the All-Soviet Competitions, Major A. Mikhailov, described the format to be followed at the Armed Forces Spartakiada: it corresponded to that of the UIPM old program, although elements of the military patrol race were included as well: "Skiers will take the field in everyday military uniform (soldier's shirt, trousers, boots or ski-boots with gaiters, fur hat and waist-belt) having a knapsack with weight of five kilograms and a carbine."[91] However, a photograph of Valentin Pshenitsyn taken at the biathlon team selection trials held earlier in the month shows that the top Soviet racers wore lightweight knickers and tops similar to those favored by their contemporaries at international ski competitions in the West rather than the burdensome field-kit of the military patrol participant.[92]

In anticipation of the 1958 Armed Forces Spartakiada and to add interest to the competitions, a number of special prizes for races with special significance for Soviet skiing were announced in *Krasnaia zvezda* in early February. The Red Army's premier newspaper took pride of place in offering the Krasnaia Zvezda Prize to the best combined team result and to the best individual skier in the biathlon competitions. Other awards included the Prize of the Editorial Staff of *Illiustrirovannaia gazeta* for the best team in the men's 4 x 10-kilometer relay, the Prize of the Editorial Staff of *Sovetskii voin* for the best team performance in the 50-kilometer marathon and, for the individual winner over that distance, the Prize of the Editorial Staff of *Sovetskii moriak*.[93]

On 13 January 1958, the biathlon race of the Armed Forces Spartakiada took place in blustery, snowy conditions with a field of 106 competitors from various military districts around the country. As opposed to the team selection trials held in January, all racers were required to wear military garb. Among the top skiers that day were veteran biathletes Pshenitsyn, Gubin and Morozov. The race was won, however, by Viktor Butakov, a prize-winner at the USSR Military Patrol National Championships. In difficult shooting conditions, Butakov was able to hit fifteen out of twenty targets, compared to fourteen struck by his nearest competitors, A. Biriukov and Pshenitsyn. Butakov claimed the Krasnaia Zvezda Prize for best individual performance in the 20-kilometer race. In addition, he shared the newspaper's team award with his comrades from the Ural Military District: Gubin, Aleksandr Popov and the young up-and-coming athlete Vladimir Melanin, who had placed third at the National Team selection race in January.[94]

The Estonian town of Otepää was selected as the site for the USSR National Ski Championships, held in early February 1958. The first-ever national championship in biathlon took place on 6 February with the top skiers from the January team selection race in Moscow as well as from the Armed Forces Winter Spartakiada in attendance. Conditions were severe, with temperatures at race time dipping to below minus fifteen degrees Celsius. Such bitter cold can have a deleterious effect on the accuracy of rifles and ammunition, and this situation was reflected in the shooting results. Gubin was the winner of the race, but with ten penalty minutes accrued for missing five targets out of twenty. Skiers who took second and third, Butakov and V. Kozhin of Sverdlovsk, each had fourteen penalty minutes, followed by Pshenitsyn who totaled sixteen additional minutes for missing eight targets. As *Sovetskii sport* suggested: "Because the strength of the sportsmen in the race was more or less equal, so much the more did shooting play the deciding role." Gubin, however, aided his effort with the realization that the act of stepping off the ski track and onto the firing line, shooting and then returning to the race devoured precious minutes: "One must say that Gubin economized the time as well in the moment of shooting. He did not take off his skis . . . and it did not affect his accuracy."[95] Soviet innovations in a biathlete's movements during this transition period between skiing and shooting, known as "range procedure," were key elements in the USSR's early success at international competitions.

With the USSR National Ski Championships concluded and the travelling squads chosen, the odds looked good for the Soviet Union heading into international competition both at the FIS Nordic World Championships in Lahti, Finland, 2 through 9 March and the first World Biathlon

Championship in Saalfelden, Austria, on 2 March. "The USSR and Finland are the favorites in Lahti," trumpeted a headline in *Sovetskii sport*, over text that reported: "In Finland they say that the main competition will be between Veikko Hakulinen [Finland], Pavel Kolchin [USSR] and Sixten Jernberg [Sweden]. They play the major role at every distance."[96] As predicted, the combined efforts of the Soviet teams produced remarkable results in both venues with a total of one bronze, four silver and two gold medals. The Soviet women dominated their competition in Lahti, winning the 3 x 5-kilometer relay and placing first and second in the individual 10-kilometer event. However, the men's results were less satisfactory, with second-place finishes in the 4 x 10-kilometer relay, and in the 15- and 30-kilometer events. Most disappointing of all were the Soviet finishes in the 50-kilometer marathon, in which one of the pre-race favorites, Pavel Kolchin, could only manage sixth place.[97]

Meanwhile, in Saalfelden, the dichotomy between accurate shooting and fast skiing proved the undoing for Soviet biathletes. Twenty-eight participants skied through an unseasonable downpour of snow to determine the very first world champion in the sport of biathlon. Although the four members of the Soviet squad—Butakov, Pshenitsyn, Sokolov and Gubin—posted the four fastest ski times over the 20-kilometer course, their poor shooting dropped them to third, seventh, ninth and tenth respectively. Both of the first- and second-place winners, Adolf Wiklund and Olle Gunneriusson of Sweden, ran at a more conservative pace and thus accrued only three misses apiece.[98] Despite the disastrous performance at the rifle range, however, the USSR won the silver medal in the team competition, edging third place Norway by over forty-seven minutes. It was evident that the Soviet skiers had attained the highest level of competiveness on the ski track, yet it was equally apparent that the Soviet biathlon program needed to help its athletes shoot better. Commenting on the team's performance, *Sovetskii sport* opined: "Sokolov, for example, can take the field with the same success in any race for skiers. It seems his one deficiency, on account of which he lost the title of champion, is his haste at the firing line."[99] To redeem themselves at a high-profile international venue, the Soviet men's cross-country team would have to wait until the 1960 Olympics in Squaw Valley, California. For the biathletes of the USSR, however, the next opportunity would come at the Second World Championship scheduled for Courmayeur, Italy on 23 February 1959.

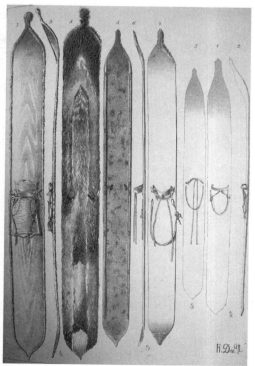

Indigenous skis and clothing.
(a) The two individuals on either side are modeling "parkas." The stylized skis pictured on the right are reminiscent of the fanciful wooden clog skis portrayed in the 1555 edition of Olaus Magnus's *History of the Northern Peoples*.
(b) Detailed drawings of a variety of Siberian skis and foot-bindings. Credit: (a) Peter Simon Pallas, *Tafelband*. St. Petersburg: Kaiserlichen Academie der Wissenschaften, 1776. Reprint, Graz, AUS: Akademische Druck –u. Verlagsanstalt (ADEVA), 1967. Reproduction courtesy of ADEVA. (b) Leopold von Schrenck, *Journeys and Explorations in Amur Territory Book III: The Peoples of Amur Territory*, plate XXXV, courtesy University of Washington Libraries, Special Collections, call no. 570.957 Sch72r v.3.

Postcard: "Skiers of the Pavlovskii Regiment on Mars Field in St. Petersburg." Images of Russian ski troops were popular in Europe at the turn of the century. Skiers of the imperial army often engaged in lengthy tours lasting several weeks, although probably without the jaunty sailor-style caps on display here. Posted from St. Petersburg to Allevard-les-Bains, France, in 1903. Private collection.

Cavalry and skiing. A single frame from Soviet footage shot during the Great Patriotic War in the catalog of British Pathé. As the cavalry canters from frame right, a lone skier in white camouflage keeps pace with the column. The imagery evokes the close relationship between the Red Cavalry and the ski divisions fostered by Lev Trotsky during the Russian Civil War. Courtesy MPI Home Video.

"Position for firing from the standing position without support" (a) and **"The 'Russian' Technique" (b).** Two line drawings illustrating the proper position for shooting standing, from Arthur Stegen's 1979 biathlon training guide and the 1945 edition of the *Red Army Ski Manual*. Credit: (a) Private collection. (b) Reproduction courtesy Arthur Stegen.

Рис. 44. Положение для стрельбы стоя без упора

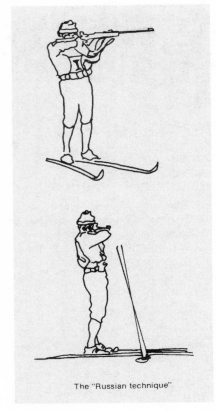

The "Russian technique"

Postcard: "Safeguarding the security of the northwestern border." As described on the reverse of this postcard printed during the Great Patriotic War, this image represents the Winter War of 1939–1940 as a campaign to secure the border between Finland and the Soviet Union from the "White Finns." Posted from Leningrad in 1944. Private collection.

Soviet skiers dominate the Fourth Biathlon World Championship. First-generation biathletes of the Soviet Union placed first, third, fourth and twelfth at the Fourth Biathlon World Championship in Hämeenlinna, Finland in 1962, establishing a precedent for their compatriots in the following decades. Credit: (a, b, c) Courtesy Sports Museum of Finland; (d) Courtesy Russian Biathlon Union <www.biathlon-rus.com>.

Vladimir Melanin (a)

Valentin Pshenitsyn (b)

Nikolai Puzanov (c)

Aleksandr Privalov (d)

Veikko Hakulinen: "The great friend of Soviet skiers." Hakulinen of Finland was one of his generation's greatest cross-country competitors. After retiring from racing in 1961 at the age of thirty-six,
he tried his hand at biathlon. In this photo, Hakulinen shoots at the final range during the Fifth
Biathlon World Championship at Seefeld, Austria in 1963. Courtesy Sports Museum of Finland.

Nikita Khrushchev honors Vladimir Melanin and Aleksandr Privalov. After the 1964 Winter Olympics, Vladimir Melanin (left) and Aleksandr Privalov receive congratulations from Nikita Khrushchev. To Khrushchev's immediate left are Anastas Mikoian, First Deputy Chairman of the Council of Ministers of the Soviet Union and Leonid Brezhnev, President of the Communist Party of the Soviet Union. Courtesy Russian Biathlon Union <www.biathlonrus.com>.

Dryland training on the tundra, ca. 1969. Left to right: Head coach of the Soviet biathlon team, Aleksandr Privalov (with pistol); Rinnat Safin; Aleksandr Tikhonov (holding rifle); and Vladimir Gundartsev. Courtesy Russian Biathlon Union <www.biathlonrus.com>.

Aleksandr Ushakov in the 10-kilometer sprint, Minsk 1974. Enormous crowds lined the tracks all week long during the Thirteenth Biathlon World Championships in Minsk. Ushakov skied the first leg for the Soviet gold medal relay squad the day after this individual race. Credit: O. Belousov and S. Luk'ianchikov. *Okhota na zoloto*, 16mm, 22 min. Belarus'fil'm: Tvorcheskoe ob"edinenie LETAPIS, 1974. Courtesy University of Washington Film Archives and Slavic Collection.

Nikolai Zimiatov in Western advertising, 1982 to 1984. Zimiatov was one of the world's best cross-country ski racers during the early 1980s. The lower-left hand corner of a poster for the 1982 World Ski Championships in Oslo produced by the Norwegian firms Swix (wax), Odlo (ski clothing) and Liljedahl (ski poles) features his portrait under a superimposed Soviet flag. Private collection. Reproduction courtesy Swix Sport AS.

Kaija Parve of Estonia. Parve—one of the USSR's most successful biathletes at world championship competition—displays her Soviet team patch on the right sleeve of her Adidas (West Germany) racing uniform while leaning on her Exel (Finland) ski poles at a 1985 world cup race in Minsk. Just weeks after the dissolution of the Soviet Union, women's biathlon finally became an Olympic event at the 1992 Albertville Games. Courtesy Estonian Sports Museum.

Moscow Parade, 2007. Soldiers dressed as ski troopers from the Great Patriotic War march in a Red Square parade arranged by Moscow's mayor, Iurii Luzhkov, a leader of the United Russia political party in 2007. The image of the Soviet ski trooper remains a potent symbol in twenty-first century Russia. Credit: Photographer: James Hill. Courtesy Contact Press Images, Inc.

SIX

Skiing, Shooting and Politics, 1960 to 1962

DIZZY WITH SUCCESS, to appropriate Stalin's famous maxim, the Soviets reveled in the prospect of repeating their 1956 Olympic performance in Squaw Valley, California, four years later.[1] What better propaganda bonus than to dominate the Winter Games again—this time on the home turf of their Cold War nemesis. Tensions that had been building between the two superpowers since the late 1940s were coming to a head by the end of the 1950s. Although the Cold War had more or less stabilized in Europe following the Berlin Blockade and the formation of the North Atlantic Treaty Organization (NATO) in 1949, the Korean War prefigured hostilities soon destined to spread around the globe. Throughout the 1960s, struggles in the Third World for political independence, cultural recognition and economic inclusion, as well as political maneuvering on either side of the Iron Curtain, led to a renewed crescendo of international tension. In addition, an arms race between the United States and the Soviet Union for superiority in thermonuclear weapons and intercontinental ballistic missiles exacerbated the division of the world into separate ideological and economic spheres. In this milieu, the political implications of success on the international stage—especially in a sport like biathlon with its unequivocally military tone—assumed a weight far greater than the simple heft of Olympic gold.

Balancing Skiing with Shooting

The results of the first world championship in biathlon sobered the organizers of Soviet sport. Certainly the skiers of the Soviet Union were on a par with the best in the world, part of the "big four" in cross-country racing along with athletes from Finland, Sweden and Norway since 1956.[2] However, sheer speed on the ski track did not always determine the winner in biathlon, and at international competitions poor marksmanship was often the bane of Soviet biathletes. With the first Olympic biathlon medals on the line at Squaw Valley in 1960, the Soviets began methodological preparation to improve their chances for success. A revamped schedule of Ready for Labor and Defense (GTO) norms proposed for the year 1959 encouraged training that would eventually pay dividends. A front-page editorial in *Sovetskii sport* called for organizers to use the 1959 winter season for increasing the number of biathlon competitors in the country.[3] Some changes were already afoot within the GTO parameters for the Armed Forces, including a second-tier set of norms for shooting with a small-caliber rifle and a cross-country race in "sport clothing" as well as a 10-kilometer ski run during the winter months.[4] *Krasnaia zvezda* suggested that officers of the Red Army should start to combine these norms and compete in biathlon during their all-around sport competitions in order to find suitable candidates for international events such as the upcoming World Championship of Biathlon.[5] The appropriation of biathlon's format created a ski-shooting awareness lacking in other nations at this time, indicating that Soviet strength in obscure Olympic events sometimes hinged on the "comparative inefficiency" in Western sport programs.[6]

Soviet National Team ski coaches understood that there were significant challenges at the Olympic venue in Squaw Valley. The first and most critical was the lung-bursting base elevation of 1,890 meters at McKinney Creek, the location of all cross-country and biathlon events, compared to 1,224 meters in Cortina d'Ampezzo four years prior. The elevation of the start-finish area was 1,921 meters for all the competitions and reached 2,048 meters at the highest point on the course.[7] Second, reports coming out of California indicated that the 20-kilometer biathlon course was quite difficult, having been laid out "through the deep ravines and along the steep slopes of the McKinney Creek forest tract."[8] The last firing range at 15 kilometers, where the athletes shot standing, came after a sustained 1.5-kilometer climb to 2,018 meters. The staff of the Soviet biathlon team had analyzed the course and targeted training programs designed specifically for this course profile. In an interview on the eve of the biathlon competition in Squaw Valley, Petr Morozov, in his new capacity as coach, explained how the team had trained for this particular race:

> The course has a large height differential, and on this account one simply cannot "recuperate" approaching the firing line. With this in mind, we have trained in shooting after exhausting uphills and attained fairly good results. We gave special attention to shooting at the fourth range, where you shoot

from standing position. Frequently you have to lower the rifle once or twice in order to choose the time between two wind gusts. And in addition, at this range there will be an especially large number of spectators and one must learn not to notice them.[9]

Morozov's words proved prescient and would come back to haunt the Soviet Union's biathletes at McKinney Creek.

In addition to the challenging course profile, wet snow conditions in the Sierra Nevada mountain range made the selection of proper ski wax notoriously difficult. Pavel Kolchin, leader of the USSR's Cross-Country Ski Team that attended the pre-Olympic race series in Squaw Valley in February 1959, recalled the nightmarish snow:

> Last winter we spent sixteen days in the mountains of the Sierra Nevada, and in that time there were often abrupt changes in the weather. At night it usually freezes, but by nine o'clock in the morning it eases off and the thermometer rises to many degrees above zero [Celsius]. . . . We took part in the American open championship at Squaw Valley and were convinced that it was difficult to find the requisite wax in "zero" weather. As is well-known, during a thaw the art of ski waxing is especially complex. And indeed many of our athletes did not know how to make use of liquid waxes.[10]

In order to simulate conditions near Lake Tahoe, the USSR biathlon team selection races for the Second World Championship in Val d'Aosta-Courmayeur, Italy were held in conjunction with the Armed Forces Ski Championships at Bakuriani in January and February 1959. This Georgian ski resort had a base elevation of 1,700 meters, only 190 meters lower than that found at McKinney Creek. Also, Bakuriani's latitude was within two degrees of Squaw Valley's, and the resulting snow conditions created the frost-freeze cycle typical of the Sierra Nevada much better than other traditional ski race locations such as Murmansk, Leningrad or Sverdlovsk.[11]

On 29 January, the Armed Forces held its 20-kilometer ski-shooting championship in Bakuriani, drawing a large crowd, *Krasnaia zvezda* reported, because "this was the selection race for the upcoming World Championship in this type of ski-sport. Therefore, besides the most powerful sportsmen of the army and navy, the best skiers of the Soviet Union took part in the race as unofficial entrants."[12] The top four finishers would be contenders for berths on the National Team and many of the nation's fastest skiers entered the race, including cross-country specialists Vladimir Oliashev (who held various national titles at 18-, 30- and 50-kilometers from 1948 to 1951) and Pavel Rodionov, as well as two veteran international biathlon competitors, Dmitrii Sokolov and Viktor Butakov, the bronze medalist at the First World Championship in Saalfelden. However, in this particular contest, the top three places went to Aleksandr Popov, Valentin Pshenitsyn and Vladimir Melanin, all experienced biathletes from the previous season. The final spot went to newcomer Aleksandr Privalov, a skier for Dinamo sport club. Over the next several decades, Privalov would play a crucial role in the development of Soviet biathlon, as both a competitor and a coach.

Ten days later, another team selection race took place in Bakuriani, an invitational competition for the best biathletes in the nation. *Sovetskii sport* noted, with a hint of criticism, that this was really a duel between two sport organizations, Dinamo (associated with the Committee for State Security, or KGB) and the Central Sport Club, Ministry of Defense (TsSKMO), because "not a single biathlete can be found in the other sport organizations."[13] Sokolov posted the fastest ski time, but inaccuracy at the last three shooting ranges kept him out of the running, a demon that had plagued him during the previous season. Nikolai Pavlovskii skied almost ten minutes slower than Sokolov but missed only one target, ending up in second place. The overall winner was B. Ban'kov, a Dinamo skier from Murmansk, who ran the third fastest time of the day with five misses. Privalov took fourth with twelve additional penalty minutes while Melanin was seventh with fourteen. Clearly, finding the proper balance between ski speed and rifle accuracy still eluded the Soviet Union's top biathletes.

Nevertheless, the capricious nature of the sport resulted in a Soviet sweep at the Second World Championship of Biathlon in Courmayeur on 23 February 1959. Temperatures close to twenty degrees Celsius and the mountain sun burning into the shooter's face at the ranges made both ski preparation and marksmanship problematic at this race. Melanin and Sokolov made up for poor shooting—out of twenty targets, Melanin hit fifteen and Sokolov sixteen—with fast skiing to take both first and second place, separated by a mere ten seconds. Their closest competitor, Sven Agge of Sweden, hit seventeen of his twenty targets, finishing over two minutes behind Sokolov. Pshenitsyn and Privalov rounded out the field, finishing in seventh and eleventh places respectively and helping their teammates capture the team competition gold medal by almost sixteen minutes over archrival Sweden.[14] Although *Sovetskii sport* praised the performance of the Soviet squad, the shooting results indicated that Sweden still had the edge in accuracy, even though the Russians were incredibly fast on the track. One certain benefit for the Soviet team had been the Bakuriani race series at elevation in the weeks leading up to the competition. "In Italy, at an elevation around 1,200 meters above sea level, we didn't need special acclimatization," Sokolov told *Sovetskii sport*. "This, of course, helped our success quite a bit."[15]

Following right on the heels of the Courmayeur World Championship was a pre-Olympic test race on the new biathlon course at McKinney Creek on 3 March. There were only nineteen competitors, all of them Americans with the exception of one Briton and one skier from Sweden, Klas Lestander. As reported by *Sovetskii sport*, biathlon's vagaries combined with the difficult McKinney Creek trail propelled nineteen-year-old Laurence Damon to first place with a disappointing seven misses but the fastest ski time: 1:34.09. This was three minutes slower than Melanin's time at Courmayeur and with two more misses accrued. In second place by only 12.6 seconds was Dick Mize, who had finished far out of the running in Italy: twenty-fifth out of thirty total competitors after a sixteen-miss fiasco at the shooting ranges. However, with a significant improvement in his marksmanship in California, Mize set a new biathlon record by hitting nineteen out of twenty targets. Almost as an after-thought, the newspaper reported that Lestander of Sweden took third.[16] His name would appear again in the Soviet press during coverage of the Squaw Valley Olympics.

Having gained the world championship crown, the Soviets had no intention of letting it go. In a report from the USSR National Biathlon Championship in Sverdlovsk on 11 March, *Sovetskii sport*'s correspondent was apoplectic when four competitors failed to show up at their starting positions for the 20-kilometer race: "The battle for the championship title began to remind us of the children's ditty: 'A' fell down, 'B' got lost, who will be—the winner? . . . Vladimir Melanin became the victor in the individual standings—there was some luck involved. But to achieve victory is sometimes easier than to retain it."[17] The race was not a complete disaster, even though it was a replay of the duel between Dinamo and TsSKMO. The relatively low elevation of Sverdlovsk facilitated faster ski times and better shooting results. Fresh from his world championship performance, Melanin won the competition by skiing a brisk 1:18.17 and hitting seventeen targets. Butakov and Popov in second and third places matched Melanin by making seventeen and eighteen hits respectively. Fourth through sixth places all hit either seventeen or eighteen of the total twenty targets and skied within five minutes of Melanin's winning time, illustrating the tremendous depth among Soviet biathletes, despite the delinquent quartet who had missed their start times.[18]

With Dinamo and TsSKMO dominating the 1958–1959 season, it was clear that the ranks of the Soviet defensive forces would fill the biathlon roster for the Squaw Valley Olympics. This was to be expected, according to *Krasnaia zvezda*: "The strength of the army's sport is in its mass characteristic. It goes without saying that every soldier should engage in skiing."[19] A similar page-one editorial three weeks later emphasized that ski-shooting races should be a fundamental criterion in appraising the preparation of Armed Forces skiers who joined the team heading for the Olympics.[20] Yet outside the battalions of the Armed Forces and the border guards, the sport of biathlon was relatively unknown prior to Squaw Valley. Even *Sovetskii sport* misunderstood the rules in these early years: a 29 January 1958 article reported that a biathlon event held in Kavgolovo was a "12-kilometer race with shooting," not a 20-kilometer event following the UIPM old program format. This error may have involved miscommunication over bad telephone lines between the newspaper's correspondent and the editorial staff, based on the similarity between "twenty" and "twelve" in Russian.[21] Nonetheless, this misprint indicates how unfamiliar the rules of biathlon were at the time. Another *Sovetskii sport* article from December 1958 detailed how the National Team would select skiers for the 1960 Games under the headline: "Comrade sportsmen! Compete for the right to take part in the VIII Winter Olympic Games. On your marks, youngsters!"[22] In the new sport of biathlon, the top ten finishers at the National Ski Championships of 1959 who hit no less than seventeen targets and finished no less than three minutes behind the fastest skier would be eligible for the Olympic Team headed for the United States.[23]

But these guidelines were lost on most citizens. One reader from Petropavlovsk wrote to ask the *Sovetskii sport* editors: "What is this 'biathlon?'" In reply V. Kamenskii, head coach for the Federation of Skiing in the USSR, outlined the rules of the event for the paper. He misinformed the letter's author that the Olympics program for 1960 would also include the World Championship in biathlon, "and consequently, the winner will be handed two medals at the same time." Implicit in the response from Kemenskii to the letter writer's question: "Who has achieved the best results?" was confidence that a Soviet biathlete would take the imaginary double award at Squaw Valley: "Soviet sportsmen . . . won first place [at the Second Biathlon World Championship] leaving behind teams from Sweden, Norway, Finland, the USA, Italy and Austria. Vladimir Melanin became world champion, Dmitrii Sokolov won the silver medal. Last year's world champion from Sweden, [Adolf] Wiklund, could only manage ninth place."[24] A companion article featured an interview with Melanin in which he detailed the preparations he and his teammates were taking leading up to the start of the competitive season: intensive training with individual skiing and shooting specialists; and re-creating the McKinney Creek course profile on a trail in the Uktus Mountains near Sverdlovsk based on film footage shot at Squaw Valley the year before.[25]

Despite the sport's obscurity, competition among Soviet biathletes for a spot on the Olympic Team was rigorous. The annual Race of the Strongest Skiers, held in late December 1959, served as just one of many team selection competitions. The contest took place at Iakhroma, a suburb of Moscow, close to a river with an elevation of only 150 meters above sea level. This proved an unfortunate site for an early season race, because low snowfall combined with warm temperatures created horrible conditions on the ski track. Much of the snow disappeared with the unseasonable thaw, exposing large swaths of dirt along the ski trail. Race directors tried to change the course but were unsuccessful. The warm snow attracted dirt from the exposed sections all along the route, creating a thin film of detritus in the parallel ski lanes. Klister wax, the glue-like substance applied to ski bases for proper grip in such warm conditions, collected grime from the track. As the athletes circled the course, the accumulation of dirt reduced ski glide with every step, slowing the race to a crawl. The winner of the competition, Valentin Pshenitsyn, finished with a sluggish ski time of 1:44.48, leading a Red Army sweep of the first three slots with teammates Butakov and V. Makarov. Dinamo skiers Sokolov and Privalov finished behind in fourth and sixth places respectively, with Melanin taking fifth.[26]

That the top three places at any given biathlon race in the USSR were always up for grabs—as in Iakhroma—indicates once again not only the sport's topsy-turvy character but also the incredible rivalry among the nation's biathletes. This phenomenon continued throughout the Soviet era, resulting in national races that were often more competitive than major international events.[27] Consider the selection process for the five biathletes named to the 1960 Soviet Olympic Team. With powerful and seasoned competitors to choose from, the Soviet coaches had the luxury of picking those athletes who displayed a certain level of consistency. The staff passed over Iurii Vorob'ev, the recent victor in January at the Armed Forces Ski Championships, preferring three Red Army veterans: Pshenitsyn, with two team-competition medals from as many world championships;

Melanin, the defending world and national champion from the previous season; and Butakov, the second-place finisher at Iakhroma, with two medals from the First World Championship of 1958 and several Armed Forces championship titles to his credit. Two other experienced racers from Dinamo with awards from the Second World Championship of 1959 completed the squad: Sokolov, the individual silver medalist; and Privalov, his gold medal team-competition compatriot. Needless to say, this group of skiers constituted the best biathlon team in the world.[28]

The Eighth Winter Olympics: Squaw Valley, California, 1960

That politics would play a part on the ski tracks at Squaw Valley was evident during the run-up to the pre-Olympic competitions held there in February 1959. The previous October, the United States Ski Association had invited skiers from the German Democratic Republic (GDR) to attend the North American Open Ski Championships in California, held as a test of the Olympic courses at McKinney Creek and Squaw Valley. Waiting for the flight out of Berlin on 4 February, however, the German squad received a telegram—the German Ski Union had submitted information about team members from the GDR too late: therefore, they could not compete in Squaw Valley. The East Germans sent an appeal to Avery Brundage, now the president of the International Olympic Committee (IOC) and to Marc Hodler, president of the International Ski Federation (FIS). Hodler deferred to the IOC, which determined that East German skiers could compete at Olympic competitions only under the aegis of the United German Team, as they had in 1956. The Associated Press reported an announcement from the State Department saying that the eight members of the East German Ski Team were Communists and could not receive a visa for entrance into the United States because the government did not recognize East Germany as a separate nation. East German officials appealed to President Eisenhower to help expedite visas for five skiers, but their efforts were in vain. The apparent discrimination against athletes from behind the Iron Curtain was unacceptable to the Soviet Union; the furor that erupted over these developments was a harbinger of the increased politicization of sports during this intense period of the Cold War.[29]

East Germany remained the focus of State Department sanctions leading up to the Olympic Games of 1960. On 12 February, East German sports writers were banned from admission into the United States because

State feared "[they] would inject a political note into their reporting of the games."[30] East Germany's press agency, *Allgemeiner Deutscher Nachtrichtendienst* (ADN), filed a protest with the IOC: however, President Brundage stated that his organization had no control over the granting of visas to the press. Three days later, the IOC issued a statement disagreeing with the State Department's refusal that barred members of the ADN. Nevertheless, State remained unmoved, claiming that issuing these visas was not in the best interests of the nation.[31]

Thus, on the eve of the Squaw Valley Games, the Soviet press emphasized the peaceful aspects of the Olympics on the one hand ("in the ice arena, Soviet and American sportsmen stand in ranks shoulder to shoulder and the spectators love this neighborliness") but still couched the competitions in Cold War terms on the other ("the contest for first place in everyone's opinion will unfold between the two sporting powers of the world—the USSR and the USA").[32] Certainly the Soviet Union's many special correspondents brought their own preconceived notions of life in America, which they relayed in daily reports to their Russian readers. A surprise to one reporter, especially in light of the previous season's dust-up over the East German Ski Team and the more recent exclusion of that nation's press, was the warm reception Eastern Bloc skiers received in the United States: "One must say that the interest displayed toward our sportsmen is very great. As soon as one of our athletes appears on the streets of Squaw Valley tourists encircle him immediately asking for autographs, taking pictures, tying him up with friendly conversation."[33] In addition, American journalists heaped so much praise on Russian athletes that *Pravda* quoted comments about the Soviet team straight out of magazines such as *Sports Illustrated*.[34]

Though the Soviet journalists seemed to be fascinated by how many Americans skied, they misinterpreted what this really meant. After Soviet skiers Mariia Gusakova, Liubov' Baranova and Rad'ia Eroshina swept all three medals in the 10-kilometer race on the second day of events—with fourth place Alevtina Kolchina just off the podium into the bargain—*Pravda*'s V. Petrusenko wrote: "The victory of the Soviet female cross-country skiers made a huge impression in America. This type of sport is extremely popular in the USA. Around four million Americans regularly take part in it."[35] And indeed, Americans were amazed at the performances of the Russian women, but not because of their enthusiasm for the sport of cross-country skiing. "Soviet Women Mix Marriage, Sports," read the headline in the *Reno Gazette* two days after the women's individual event. Of interest to

Nevada's main newspaper was that gold medalist Gusakova, silver medalist Baranova and their teammate Kolchina were all between twenty-nine and thirty years old, "an age when most U.S. women athletes have retired to suburbia and are bringing up children."[36] Belying Petrusenko's notion that millions of Americans participated in a sport in which Russians had just taken all three medals, there were no entries from the United States in this 10-kilometer race, and attendance was a "sparse crowd of fifty" that emitted no shouting or cheering.[37] To be sure, cross-country skiing was, for the most part, a moribund activity in the United States. The sport had been transplanted from Scandinavia by immigrants at the turn of the century but found little support compared to more dynamic modes of skiing such as jumping and downhill. By the early 1960s, Nordic skiing was virtually unknown to most Americans as a competitive event outside of a few isolated regions.[38] This was astounding to seasoned cross-country competitors who were used to boisterous crowds in Europe. Swedish biathlete Klas Lestander thought that perhaps "the shooting would be what most interested the Americans," but not even gunplay could attract an audience to the Nordic venues: "When I was collecting my start number I saw from the corner of my eye that there were quite a few empty seats in the arena. The biathlon races would suffer pretty much the same lack of attention as when the [cross-country] ski races were held."[39]

In the Soviet Union, by way of contrast, the week leading up to the first three days of the Squaw Valley Olympics was designated "Ski Week" all across the nation. From 14 through 21 February, the All-Russian Council of Sport Organizations in conjunction with the All-Russian Federation of Skiing organized a series of races: 3- and 5-kilometer sprints for girls and women; 5- and 10-kilometer contests for young men sixteen to eighteen years old; and for men, 10- and 15-kilometer events.[40] As reported by *Pravda*, the enthusiasm for Ski Week was enormous: "Early in the morning on the platforms of the Moscow train stations a 'forest of skis' sprang up." In Leningrad, more than fifty thousand racers arrived at the various ski stations to participate on the first day. In Novosibirsk, harking back to an earlier era, "one could see the slogan 'Everyone to skis!' on every industrial work site, in the institutions and on the streets."[41] Because the festivities attracted so many participants, the Presidium of the All-Russian Council of Sport Organizations extended the week through 1 March to coincide with the end of the Olympics on 28 February.[42] Apparently, the Olympics belonged as much to the masses back home as to the Soviet Union's representatives in Squaw Valley.

The Russian women's triumph in the individual race on 20 February bode well for Soviet prospects in the first Olympic biathlon the following day. America's *Sports Illustrated* had predicted the outcome of this race in its Olympic preview edition: "The Russian team is the best in this unique shooting-cum-skiing contest. . . . The current world champion, is unsurprisingly, Vladimir Melanin. His countrymen confidently predict a gold medal for him or teammate Alexander Privalov."[43] On 21 February, these two set off at one-minute intervals from the starting line at McKinney Creek, along with twenty-eight other competitors. It was Privalov who had the right combination of skiing and shooting that day, and through the first fifteen kilometers of the race, it appeared that he was destined for first place. His ski time was a full minute faster than his nearest competitor, Antii Tyrväinen of Finland. In addition, Privalov shot "clean"—that is, he hit all fifteen of his targets at the first three ranges. However, Petr Morozov's prediction that the last shooting stage would be the crux of the race came true: the 1.5-kilometer climb to the highpoint of the course preceding the final shooting range proved Privalov's undoing. The final five targets were 100 meters away from the firing line, facing north. Each shot was taken from the standing position at a point in the race where limbs are the most exhausted and breathing difficult to control. Nevertheless, Privalov had run an excellent race and could afford to miss two targets and still maintain his gold medal position. Unfortunately, a sudden wind change negated his rifle's sight alignment. He hurried his shooting tempo and missed three of his last shots, dropping him from first to third place. His teammates fared no better at this difficult stage of the contest: Melanin missed four times and Sokolov placed all five of his shots "in the milk."[44] Sweden's Klas Lestander, who had skied in the pre-Olympic trial race on the McKinney Creek course the previous year, ran at a more conservative pace than Sokolov by almost five minutes but did hit every one of his twenty targets to take the gold medal. Tyrväinen of Finland missed two targets to finish in second place. The incredible ski tempo of the Soviet team members made up for a great deal of poor marksmanship nonetheless: Melanin placed fourth, Pshenitsyn fifth and Sokolov sixth.[45]

The astonishing conclusion to this race obscured the fact that had it been held in accordance with UIPM guidelines followed in Saalfelden and Courmayeur, the four Soviet skiers would have received gold medals based on the team's combined finishes, boosting the total medal count for the USSR: "If this were a world championship," Semen Bogachev, an official for the Soviet Ski Federation, told the *Reno Gazette*, "we would be team champions. But this is an individual competition, so our men merely fin- ished third, fourth, fifth and sixth."[46] A bronze medal and a theoretical win based on mathematics was cold comfort for the Soviet press, how- ever. *Pravda* could only say: "What bad luck! . . . they ran the race well, but achieved poor results in shooting."[47] *Sovetskii sport* buried the results from the biathlon race deep within an article about speedskater Lidiia Skoblikova, who set a world record and won a gold medal in the 1,500- meter race held on the same day.[48] Only after the closing ceremony would *Krasnaia zvezda* mention the meltdown at McKinney Creek, lumping the unfortunate performance of the biathletes in with the debacle suffered by the Nordic combined and men's ski teams.[49] In a similar recap of Olym- pic events, *Sovetskii sport* gave space to Nikolai Romanov, the leader of the Soviet Olympic Team, who stated: "Our sportsmen Privalov, Melanin, Pshenitsyn and Sokolov didn't perform too badly in the biathlon race. They took third through sixth place. All that's necessary to say is that they had the opportunity to do more. You know, a breakdown took place in shoot- ing even though these athletes usually are distinguished by outstanding marksmanship." Romanov repeated his commentary in *Pravda* the next day, although with his critical comments removed.[50] Yet, eleven years later, this humiliating display of poor shooting at the final range still rankled the *Novosti* Press Agency: "The impossible happened: [Privalov] missed again and again, until he lost his chances of winning even second place. The other [Soviet biathletes], all of whom were excellent marksmen, also got jittery and kept missing the target."[51]

Adding to the woes of the Soviet Olympic Team at Squaw Valley, the male cross-country skiers performed far below their potential. Team leader and top racer Pavel Kolchin became ill with "a malicious California flu" just prior to the opening ceremonies and could not compete.[52] The only individual medal was bronze, awarded to Nikolai Anikin in the 30- kilometer race. The men's team was able to capture the bronze medal in the relay, but this offered little solace to the disheartened ski contingent. Only the brilliant efforts of the women—their medal trio also took silver in the 3 x 5-kilometer relay—maintained the Soviet Union's parity with the Scandinavian countries and saved its reputation as a skiing powerhouse.[53]

One other disconcerting aspect in the aftermath of the 1960 Winter Games was the division of total medal results between East and West. Ac- cording to Soviet calculations based on points awarded for gold, silver and bronze medals, the USSR's 146.5 total far outpaced the United States and Switzerland's 62 points each as well as the combined German team's 58.5.

However, the Eastern Bloc People's Republics of Poland with 16 points and Czechoslovakia with 11 lagged far behind Finland with 54 and Norway with 45. The Soviet press trumpeted that "the results of the Soviet Union and the countries of the socialist camp exceeded the achievements of the athletes of many of the capitalist governments." Despite such rosy pronouncements, however, any calculation comparing unofficial points based on the Cold War divide, even with the GDR's contribution factored in, indicated that the Eastern Bloc was badly outmatched by the West at the Winter Olympics.[54] Therefore, the Soviet Union initiated two new programs to increase opportunities for socialist nations to gain experience in international competition, especially in the ski events. With an eye toward the 1962 FIS World Nordic Ski Championships in Zakopane, Poland, the Red Army proposed the First Winter Spartakiada of Friendly Armies as a pre-championship dress rehearsal. These competitions, scheduled for 5 through 12 February 1961, would bring together teams from the armed forces of Bulgaria, Hungary, the GDR, Poland, Romania and the USSR on Zakopane's ski courses, located between 850 and 1,000 meters above sea level. The events conformed to FIS and Olympic standards for the 15-, 30- and 50-kilometer distances, the 4 x 10-kilometer relay, biathlon, downhill, slalom, giant slalom and jumping. In addition, this Spartakiada program included a military patrol race.[55]

To coincide with the Nordic World Championships in Zakopane, the government also scheduled an all-encompassing winter Spartakiada series throughout the entire Soviet Union for 1962, based on the Winter Spartakiada of the Russian Soviet Federative Republic (RSFSR) held for the first time in 1958.[56] The Second Winter Spartakiada of the RSFSR had been scheduled for 1961; it would complement the following year's First Winter Spartakiada of the USSR. This was a series of spartakiada competitions throughout all of the SSRs (including the RSFSR) culminating in a grand finale to determine a national champion in March.[57] As ski racer Alevtina Kolchina explained in *Pravda* prior to the start of this final event, the guiding principle of the winter spartakiadas was mass participation: "Thousands of competitions in the districts and cities of our nation helped expose new, talented sportsmen, who joined the National Team of the USSR. Mass participation is one of the absolutely very highest conditions of subsequent growth of the mastery of our athletes."[58] Spartakiadas such as these endured for decades as systematic dragnets to find the best young winter sport talent in the nation. The Second Winter Spartakiada of the USSR in 1966 coincided with the Biathlon World Championships held in Garmisch-Partenkirchen and Oslo's World Nordic Ski Championships. Seventy thousand physical culture collectives representing some nine million Soviet athletes took part in these contests.[59] By the mid-1970s, spartakiadas attracted around twenty million skiers, skaters, sledders and hockey players. In 1974, at the finals of the Third Spartakiada of the USSR, 1,344 athletes contended for the top prizes in what had become a "domestic Olympics."[60] As points of comparison, 1,008 competitors from thirty-five countries were on hand in Sapporo, Japan for the 1972 Winter Olympics; and 1,129 athletes came to compete in Innsbruck, Austria for the 1976 Games.

Revamping Biathlon

To the three *Sovetskii sport* correspondents covering the All-Union Ski Championships in Sverdlovsk a month after the Soviet Ski Team returned from Squaw Valley, it was clear that a new regime was in order for biathlon. A chastened Aleksandr Privalov, fresh from having the gold medal snatched from his grasp at McKinney Creek, shot a perfect twenty hits out of twenty to win the championship title; and second place finisher Viktor Butakov chalked up a respectable nineteen hits. In fact, the top seven finishers shot no worse than three misses apiece. However, the rest of the field failed miserably from the firing line. Evgenii Repin, skiing for Trud sport club, clocked a brisk 1:24.31, twenty seconds faster than Privalov, but gave up five hits for an extra ten minutes of penalty time and ninth place. N. Arkilov skied the course in 1:25.05, good enough for second place had he shot clean, but with the addition of thirty penalty minutes for missing fifteen targets, he finished in thirty-third place. The *Sovetskii sport* journalists were merciless in their condemnation of this poor showing at such an important race and found the root of the problem in the military patrol race: "On the course, any sort of mutual aid was allowed—even taking a comrade by the hands. And it used to be that the three classes of racers literally dragged along after them one excellent shot who 'covered' their targets at the firing line. . . . But it's high time to understand that on the modern biathlon course each person answers for himself."[61]

As Melanin had intimated in his December 1959 interview with *Sovetskii sport*, biathlon in the early years separated skiing and shooting into two categories, each with separate coaching staffs. Most biathletes were well-trained and capable cross-country ski racers with an interest in marksmanship. However, the results from Squaw Valley indicated that the crucial element in biathlon was the integration of these two very different disciplines. A third of the Olympic competitors at McKinney Creek missed more than half the targets, many of them hitting only two or three.[62] Rifle coaches for biathletes in these early days came from a background in competitive shooting, where a steady pulse and slow-fire pacing on the range are key elements.[63] However, biathlon requires just the opposite: the competitor enters the range in an aerobic deficit and must fire five accurate shots as quickly as possible in order to return to the ski race. The debacle on the fourth shooting range at McKinney Creek provided a case study for coaches and athletes in these differences, demonstrating that biathlon was much more than merely the sum of its parts.

From 1960 to 1964, Soviet biathletes propelled the sport to new, previously unimagined heights, aided in no small part by the development of a systematic and comprehensive training regimen based on combining skiing and shooting into a unified whole. B. I. Bergman, an instructor at the P. F. Lesgaft Government Institute of Physical Culture as well as an associate of the Scientific Research Institute of Physical Culture in Leningrad, included a detailed account of this program in *Lyzhnyi sport* (Skiing), a technical manual written for university students. It involved specialized shooting and ski training regimens as well as tactical preparation tailored specifically to the sport based on old program parameters. In subsequent decades, many of these ideas formed the basis for biathlon development programs all around the world.[64]

Ski training for biathlon was fundamentally the same as that undertaken by cross-country specialists with a few minor modifications. Bergman points out that the rifle carried by a biathlete can amount to 7 to 10 percent of his total weight. Therefore the length of the ski stride would necessarily be different than for athletes in regular cross-country ski races, especially on the uphills.[65] Soviet coaches designed specific ski exercises to accommodate these differences and increased the amount of dryland training on roller skis, devices similar to elongated skates with a ratchet mechanism on the front wheel. Roller skis allowed athletes to train for the specific movements of skiing during the off-season. These implements, in conjunction with increased rifle practice, provided an opportunity to hone the unique skill sets required for attaining high-level performances in biathlon before the first snowfall.[66] Soviet coaches formulated carefully prepared year-round ski and shooting training programs for individual biathletes according to detailed daily and monthly charts, meticulously recorded in each racer's diary.[67]

Bergman's volume indicates that the Soviets focused on several elements crucial to biathlon's idiosyncratic style of marksmanship. Fundamental to the sport was accurate shooting accomplished through practice with both large- and small-bore rifles in a variety of exercises. No matter what level of proficiency the athlete had attained, each incorporated "dry-firing" the rifle—practicing trigger pull, sight alignment and proper breathing techniques without actually firing live ammunition—into daily workouts all year long. The athletes received instruction in assessing the variables encountered at the shooting range such as temperature, wind, lighting and the appearance of the targets. Additional exercises focused on finding equipoise between rapid firing and accuracy. This involved the integration of a training regimen that included aiming the rifle, breathing rhythmically and squeezing the trigger, all with an elevated pulse. Experience has shown that although an increased demand for oxygen due to the stress of cross-country skiing accelerates the pulse rate and respiratory cycle, controlled and concentrated deep breathing as the shooter approaches the range helps to reduce these to manageable levels. In addition, if the biathlete holds his breath before each shot, a phenomenon known as the Valsalva effect lowers the pulse rate significantly for a few seconds before resuming its accelerated rate. A good shooting rhythm that combined all of these elements became the holy grail of biathletes during these formative years.[68]

A second factor related to accurate and rapid shooting was range procedure, or the way a biathlete prepared for firing his rifle during the transition from skiing to shooting then back again. Vladimir Melanin recommended that a biathlete "hurry as little as possible at the range and perform as quickly as possible all the movements necessary to cross over from the range to the ski track—put on the rifle sling, buckle up the cartridge belt, grab the ski poles."[69] Soviet trainers were at the forefront in analyzing all the movements of this phase of the race with an eye toward maximum efficiency and time reduction. In addition, exercises that improved balance and equilibrium while handling a rifle with skis on through each stage at the shooting range were part of a biathlete's regimen.[70] In the 20-kilometer race, this transition occurred four times, and crucial seconds or even minutes were gained or lost there. Moreover, if the mechanics of range procedure and the shooting process became ingrained responses, the biathlete would have more time to concentrate on the mental preparation necessary for shooting.

The psychological framework required to handle the stress of shooting became a focal point of the Soviet biathlon program. In the heat of competition, there is a natural tendency at the firing line to physically force a shot before its proper time. Not giving in to this phenomenon takes discipline and mental control. Eliminating all other thoughts not related to firing the rifle accurately combined with concentration on precise shooting procedures can only be developed with copious practice and race experience. Every biathlete faces the same conundrum: as desire increases for each bullet to hit the target, attaining that goal becomes more difficult. Sport psychologist Daniel Gilbert notes that close attention to every aspect of a task is essential when it is done for the first time, or if it is very complex, but can be destructive when the task is simple and well-practiced.[71] In the act of firing a rifle there is a fine line between a lack of focus and trying too hard to make each bullet find the mark. This middle ground, found somewhere in the athlete's subconscious, is perhaps the most crucial element in the sport of biathlon. The biathlete's every shot must exist within its own sphere without interference from recollecting the previous shot or anticipating the one to follow. With each bullet fired at the range, the competitor must keep himself "in the moment," like a Zen master who is oblivious to space and time. Fulfilling this endeavor at a major event such as a national championship or the Olympics compounds the mental tension: in Gilbert's words, "when stakes go up, performance goes down."[72] Only continuous exposure to high-pressure competition affords the opportunity to develop these skills, thus explaining the dense and complex winter-season racing schedules that Soviet biathletes endured.

Ski Racing as a Spectator Sport

In comparison to the paltry crowds attending the cross-country events at McKinney Creek, the numbers of spectators reported by the press at important ski races in the Soviet Union were staggering. "Thirty-five Thousand Spectators in the Uktus," reads the subheading in *Sovetskii sport's* article about an international 30-kilometer race near Sverdlovsk where Russia's Pavel Kolchin and Nikolai Anikin went head-to-head with Scandinavian ski greats Veikko Hakulinen and Harald Grønningen in January 1959.[73] For the opening of the 1962 Winter Spartakiada in Sverdlovsk, *Pravda* reported that there were over 130,000 spectators on hand as well as an unspecified number who watched the proceedings on television.[74] Even at a more pedestrian All-Union cross-country ski race, the number of people in the crowd was enormous as "[competitors] rushed through a living corridor of spectators."[75] Photographs in the Soviet press illustrate just such a scene time and again in the post-war era: by the early 1980s, crowds at international ski races held on Soviet soil could number in the hundreds of thousands.[76] For the spectators at these events, there was a certain amount of pomp and ceremony on display, packed with symbolism that any post-war Soviet crowd would appreciate. Consider Dmitrii Vasil'ev's description of the 1946 National Ski Championships:

> The Uktus Mountains looked especially solemn and festive on that March day 1946. At the foot of the pine forest-covered hill rows of skiers got into formation, sport banners streaming above them. The red sweaters of the skiers of Moscow stood out like bright spots in the snow—the victors of last year's championship. The first champions of Russia were invited that year—[Pavel] Bychkov, [Aleksandr] Nemukhin and [Nikolai] Vasil'ev. The honor of carrying the flag of the competition was bestowed upon them. . . . There they stood, the youth of the Soviet nation, more powerful, better trained than before the war. And right next to them stood the most powerful skiers in Russia, who began the battle on the snow many years ago and as a team transferred their own mastery and knowledge to the next generation of Soviet sportsmen.[77]

A photograph from the 1953 All-Union Competition of Rural Skiers in Iakhroma illustrates a similar scene. Ranks of skiers, formed into squadrons, are on parade with skis carried vertically over their shoulders. As they pass by rows of spectators, large banners and flags flutter above them.[78] Another photograph from this competition shows the enormous crowds attending the event and the festive atmosphere under the banners. "The citizens of Iakhroma have an eye for skiing," reads the caption, indicating that this rural audience knew how to watch a ski race.[79]

To the Soviet government, events such as track and field reflected the scientific approach to sport better than any other discipline, in addition to having close ties to military fitness. However, track and field competitions generally attracted only a limited audience in the USSR due, perhaps, to the sterility of the events: although running was a universal activity, nearly all of the field events were relevant only within the confines of a meet with scant utility outside the stadium. This was not the case for skiing. The sport could be accomplished anywhere there was snow and had practical application as a means of transportation as well as defense. And the tens of millions of skiers who competed in ski racing in the Soviet Union from before the war through the 1970s confirm the sport's popularity.[80] These eager participants, moreover, transitioned into enthusiastic spectators at ski events throughout the country. The government encouraged spectator-ship at sporting events as a worthwhile activity; however, with few excep-tions, Soviet citizens were not required to attend these sporting events.[81] Certainly one of their most crucial functions was to acclimatize athletes to boisterous audiences, thus inuring racers to the stage fright inherent at Olympic and world championship competitions. This was an especially important factor at the shooting range in biathlon, as Petr Morozov point-ed out in his interview before the Squaw Valley Olympics. In the case of ski racing one further observation can be made: the attendees came to watch these races for their own self-improvement, creating an idiosyncratic bond in the sport of skiing between the individual spectator and the skiers on the track. To be sure, the fans of ski racing were a breed apart from those of any other sport in the Soviet Union.

The ski mobilization effort during the Great Patriotic War in combina-tion with the Ready for Labor and Defense (GTO) program significantly increased the number of active skiers in the USSR. After the war, the gov-ernment's promotion of ski culture continued unabated in a stream of po-ems, short stories, paintings and sculpture, whose reproductions filled the pages of the general Soviet press from November through March, as well as occasionally during the off-season.[82] Dmitrii Vasil'ev writes that mil-lions of skiers took part in cross-country ski races in the midst of World War II, with six million participants in the winter of 1941 alone; and hun-dreds of thousands of citizens continued to ski race every year in the im-mediate post-war era.[83] For these athletes, learning the proper technique of cross-country skiing was of paramount importance.

Although it appears easy, the motions needed to move efficiently over the snow on narrow Nordic skis are quite complex and vary according to terrain, weather and snow conditions. In the diagonal stride, the basic component of a ski racer's arsenal of techniques, opposite arms and legs work alternatively in pairs. Each push or "kick" with a leg corresponds to a push via the ski pole held in the opposite hand. Balance, physical fitness and muscle-memory all play a role in maximizing the efficiency of this ski stride. Other techniques, such as double-poling, running uphill and negotiating downhill slopes, all require different sets of skills and a great deal of training and practice to perfect. Explaining each of these processes is difficult because of the limitations of language and the simultaneous nature of the many movements needed to perform the various techniques. Moreover, there are subtle nuances that must be ingrained in order to ex-ecute each of the different techniques efficiently. Although words and even photographs can be useful, they do not adequately impart these details to a developing athlete.

After the war, there was an upsurge of interest in improving on these aspects of ski technique, and therefore Soviet newspapers and magazines provided how-to-ski articles during the winter months. *Sovetskii sport* featured ski advice columns that ran the gamut from maintaining balance through corners on a fast downhill to developing a dryland training program.[84] "Many of our readers are interested in ski technique," reads one of these articles with an accompanying action-sequenced series of pictures showing Pavel Kolchin on an uphill climb. "Today we continue to present the best skiers moving over various segments of a ski track utilizing this or that style of running."[85] "For you, skiers!" gushes a front-page headline for yet another *Sovetskii sport* compendium just prior to the opening of the 1961 ski season, providing detailed suggestions for cross-country training regimens from national and Olympic ski team members Kolchin, Vladimir Kuzin and Nikolai Anikin.[86] Readers provided some inspiration for these pieces, with questions on a variety of ski-related topics. One *Ogonek* ski-fan wrote: "I'm asking for details about what one needs for training . . . to schedule a day's regime. Please help me. I love skiing very much. I'm nineteen years old."[87] Another ski enthusiast asked *Sovetskii sport* "How do you select skis?" eliciting a full-page response from the paper.[88] "How do you wax skis correctly and look after them?" one Sverdlovsk skier inquired.[89]

Despite good advice and helpful tips from experts in the sport, skiing is a dynamic activity that has to be seen to be appreciated, and no amount of reading or studying still photographs can possibly substitute for observing a skier in motion. In *Langrennsteknikk*, a Norwegian manual filled with action-sequenced photo-montages of the world's best cross-country ski racers circa 1981, the authors qualify their own work by suggesting that studying film and video in combination with photographs produces better results.[90] Certainly Soviet filmmakers understood the value of their craft in assisting all manner of skiers to learn the fine points of the sport. By the early 1960s, enthusiasts could watch documentaries such as "Learn to Ski," "Tourists on Skis" and "On the Ski Tracks in Kavgolovo."[91] Observing how the very best skiers in the world negotiate the same course and in the same snow conditions, though, provides the optimum milieu for developing one's own technical mastery. Assimilating good ski technique requires serious analysis of a skilled racer's rhythmic movement and then the application of continuous mental imagery as one imitates these movements on snow.[92] For exactly these reasons, citizen skiers of the Soviet Union flocked to ski races of their own volition, just as their counterparts in the Scandinavian countries had been doing for years. "The average Norwegian skier," asserts former United States Olympic Coach John Caldwell, "studies [cross-country] skiing as closely as our sports fans assess the fine points of baseball and pro football."[93] Occasional photographs in the Soviet press featured Scandinavian crowds lining the course at world championship races: as if to illustrate Caldwell's point, one famous photo of Vladimir Kuzin skiing to victory at Falun during the 1954 World Championships in Sweden shows spectators standing shoulder-to-shoulder behind a rope barricade as he strides past.[94] Similar photographs from events in the USSR reveal throngs of people on either side of the ski trail—a "corridor of spectators"—as the country's top athletes compete.[95]

With so many Soviet citizens actively involved in ski racing after the war, it is no surprise that attendance at ski races started to grow. In a number of articles, sports writer Viktor Viktorov suggested that prior to the war, ski competitors generally ran their race far from the view of spectators who found it difficult to trudge through deep snow and follow the course; but now, with so many good skiers in the country, races had become more accessible. Viktorov notes that the rabid ski enthusiasts of the Soviet Union had their own special way of spectating quite dissimilar to that of "passive" audiences sitting in the stands at basketball, soccer or ice hockey matches:

> The ski fan is a fan of a particular type. In order to observe the contest on the course he must move around along the track, and to move here and there in deep snow is impossible without skis. And the spectators, familiarizing themselves with the course of the track beforehand, and having jotted down the numbers of the most powerful skiers, rush to those places where the contest will be the most intense. They cluster along the difficult climbs—the "heaves of the sea" as skiers call them—and at the steep, looping downhills. They meet their favorites there and afterward cross over to a new place so as not to miss a thing . . . besides skis, the fans are armed with stop-watches. They are very well oriented to the race and determine the leaders without a mistake according to tempo.[96]

Because ski races generally involved completing a series of passes around a 5- to 10-kilometer loop, it was relatively easy for a ski enthusiast to move to and fro, following racers as they circled the course. Even for more sedate race fans, a spot at the start-finish area afforded views of the competitors at both the beginning and the end of the race as well as once each time the skiers completed a loop of the course.

This was not the case, however, at biathlon races run according to old program parameters, and this somewhat diminished the enjoyment for potential fans. Because the course was one 20-kilometer loop with four separate shooting stations, it was impossible for spectators to follow a race as competitors left the start-finish area at one or two minute intervals then moved in a single direction around the track. In order to cover a biathlon race for *Sovetskii sport*, for instance, it took three journalists to track the racers: one stayed at the finish line while the other two set out in different directions on the ski course.[97] Perhaps the most exciting aspect of biathlon occurs at the firing line, yet even if a fan had the wherewithal to traverse the course to one of the ranges, only one of the four shooting bouts was visible: the racers progressed to subsequent ranges and then finally to the finish line out of sight of spectators at the various firing lines. Yet even watching the action at the range would ultimately prove unsatisfying: the biathletes shot at paper targets, and unless the spectator had a spotting scope or binoculars and a practiced eye, it was impossible to tell the degree of accuracy for each marksman. Finally, the abstruse nature of biathlon scoring detracted from the spectator's enjoyment because, in the words of *Sovetskii sport*, "this arithmetic is a problem with quite a few uncertainties—any further and you're talking about algebra."[98] Targets from each of the four ranges had to be gathered and scored, and then the information collated, in order to calculate the total penalty minutes added to each competitor's ski time. Arcane rules were also a factor: at one particular race, Nikolai Pavlovskii, well on his way to a top-three finish, was disqualified because one of the judges at the first shooting station thought that he was using a snow ridge on the firing line as a rest for his rifle. He was removed from the competition results only after the race was over.[99] Consulting with officials, analyzing targets and adjusting scores meant that the announcement of the winner took place long after the competitors had finished.

Observers from the International Olympic Committee (IOC) noted these details at Squaw Valley, where the viability of biathlon as an event in the next Games hung in the balance. Even before the closing ceremonies had taken place, the prospects were not favorable: "The man who wins the gold medal will probably endure as the Olympics' only biathlon champion," reported *Sports Illustrated*. "It has just been voted out of the next Winter Games in 1964."[100] At the 56th IOC Congress held in San Francisco, California, in early February, voting members cut biathlon from the Olympic program because they considered it too militaristic. But such decisions were always open to debate during official IOC deliberations. At the next Congress just prior to the 1960 Summer Games in Rome, the Soviet Union made an unsuccessful bid for reintroducing biathlon as an Olympic event. Nevertheless, the USSR won concession for further discussion about biathlon's fate the following year. At the 58th IOC Congress in 1961, the International Modern Pentathlon Union (UIPM) pleaded for reinstatement, to which the Olympic Committee acquiesced on one condition: biathlon's governing body should make the event more interesting—by converting it to a winter pentathlon.[101] To satisfy the IOC without completely changing the nature of the sport, UIPM scuttled the old program in favor of a more spectator-friendly format after the Innsbruck Olympics of 1964. Gone were the four separate ranges spread over a continuous 20-kilometer loop. Instead, UIPM consolidated all the shooting stages into a single range inside an arena with the start-finish area close at hand: this allowed spectators to follow a biathlon race from a single vantage point. The introduction of breakable targets in the mid-1960s intensified the experience of watching a biathlon race by providing an instantaneous and visual indication of how each athlete would fare in the final results. In the USSR, these changes fostered boisterous scenes captured on one particular occasion in a photograph described by Russia's Aleksandr Tikhonov, the most successful biathlete of the twentieth century:

> There it is: the genuine love of the people. It's a typical start-area at Kirovo-Chepetskii and these are very typical spectators. Of course one has to love biathlon and its important heroes in order to act like this—in a united rush to pick up the winner right at the finish line and pass him from hand to hand through the entire stadium! Who knows: perhaps it is precisely at this moment you begin to understand that patriotism is not simply a nice-sounding, beautiful word. Rather, it's a simple and sincere affection toward one's own people.[102]

This potent blend of patriotism, ski racing and marksmanship within a stadium environment generated enormous crowds in the Soviet Union.[103] Russian enthusiasm for the event set a precedent for other nations, playing an important role in the way spectators viewed a race. One striking example is the roar of the crowd as each bullet finds its mark on a breakable or knockdown target; another is the rhythmic chanting that encourages biathletes as they climb the uphills out on the course. Such viewer involvement has elevated biathlon to the position of Europe's most popular winter spectator sport as of the early twenty-first century.[104]

Zakopane, Poland and Umeå, Sweden, 1961

The First Winter Spartakiada of Friendly Armies attracted military teams to Zakopane, Poland in February 1961 from all across the Eastern Bloc as well as a delegation of eighteen skiers from the People's Republic of China and representatives from Mongolia. Expectations for the event were tremendous: organizers planned for three hundred competitors from Bulgaria, Poland, Romania, East Germany (GDR), Hungary, Czechoslovakia and the USSR, along with thirty thousand spectators for each day's events.[105] Geopolitics had a part to play in this extravaganza as well—the focus was clearly on the East-West divide that was widening almost daily in 1961. *Pravda* summed up the events in Zakopane by noting: "Every day of the Spartakiada is marked by new friendly meetings of sportsmen with the workers of the Polish People's Republic. They pass by in exceptionally warm, comradely surroundings and further even greater consolidation of friendship between the peoples of all countries in the socialist camp."[106]

In the Soviet Union, preliminary team selection trials for Zakopane began during the first weeks of January. At the Armed Forces Championship in Skiing held in Leningrad, the biathlon competition determined the field from the military invited to selection races for the National Team travelling to Poland in early February, then on to the Third Biathlon World Championship scheduled for 25 February in Umeå, Sweden. At this early season competition, Valentin Pshenitsyn took top honors with a fast ski time and nineteen hit targets. Behind him finished veteran Aleksandr Popov and B. Moskvin, a skier from the Far Eastern Military District. Several biathletes proved they were capable special skiers in other events too at these Armed Forces Championships. Both Vladimir Melanin and Aleksandr Gubin ran medal-winning legs in the 4 x 10-kilometer relay, and in the 50-kilometer race Gubin placed first while Popov also finished high in the rankings, helping his teammates win medals in the team competition.[107]

Just a week before the Armed Forces Ski Team left for Zakopane, a series of international competitions took place in Kavgolovo. Although teams from six other nations attended, only Soviet skiers took part in the ski-shooting race on 28 January, the field selected from the strongest biathletes in the USSR. The up-and-down fortunes of Dmitrii Sokolov on the shooting range were favorable this day: he had the second fastest time by a mere ten seconds but also shot clean to win the race over Nikolai Pavlovskii, who had skied faster but accrued two misses. Veterans Vladimir Melanin, Viktor Butakov and Aleksandr Privalov rounded out the top five places.[108] Zone competitions of the Second Winter Spartakiada of the RSFSR ran concurrently with the Armed Forces Spartakiada in Zakopane during the second week of February. For those athletes who were not part of the Armed Forces Ski Team competing in Poland (such as biathlete Sokolov, who skied for Dinamo sports club), these races were crucial for maintaining fitness prior to the Umeå World Championship of Biathlon on 28 February, a scant two weeks away. According to *Sovetskii sport*, Sokolov was holding his form well, having won the Ufa zone championship with a smart 1:25.31 and only one missed target. The results of other biathlon competitions, however, came in for a blistering tirade from the Soviet Union's leading sports journal. The winner of the Moscow zone race shot well, but *Sovetskii sport* explained the extenuating circumstances: "[Nikolai] Meshcheriakov . . . didn't put his bullet 'in the milk' even once. Really, this result depended upon the character of the course. Remember, at last year's national biathlon championship the course aroused a great deal of criticism—it was literally flat as a tabletop. The organizers of the competition in the Moscow zone took it even further: the course . . . was flatter than flat." The paper decried the poor shooting results from other regions as well. *Sovetskii sport* offered these suggestions to improve the prospects of the Soviet biathletes in the midst of a week of intense competitions, both domestically and abroad: "The results of the zone competitions in biathlon prompt this conclusion again and again and again: marksmanship training and once again marksmanship training—painstaking and every day—is necessary for raising the general standards of our biathletes. Moreover, it's imperative to make the character of the course difficult."[109]

Dmitrii Sokolov weighed into this debate a month later. In his opinion, biathlon was first and foremost a ski race: "[In other countries] they are recruiting biathletes from shooters, but I think that our way is actually better. It's easier to teach a racer to shoot than a shooter to ski." What the Soviet Union needed was to develop a cadre of coaches who specialized in biathlon marksmanship, especially in shooting quickly at the range. More often than not, Sokolov suggested, Soviet biathletes took too long to fire their rifles—around two to three minutes—waiting for perfect conditions before pulling the trigger: "But the benefit from this is doubtful and time is racing by. No, one and a half minutes at the firing line—that limit should become the law."[110] Sokolov was prescient on this point, but rare indeed was the biathlete who could achieve this kind of speed combined with accuracy, especially with the variety of distances and range conditions inherent in the old program format. It was not until the mid-1970s, after rule changes stipulated a single range and the development of a new approach to the sport, that top biathletes were consistently firing five shots in under forty seconds.[111]

According to *Krasnaia zvezda*'s correspondent covering the military ski races at the Winter Spartakiada in Zakopane, the biathlon race on 7 February was the high point of the week, indicating an upsurge of enthusiasm for the sport among the USSR's Eastern Bloc allies: "Interest among sport fans was exceptionally great for this [event]. On the streets and in the squares . . . stood close to one hundred loudspeakers and the progress of the competition had uninterrupted coverage on the radio." Butakov, Pshenitsyn, Popov and Melanin represented the Soviet Union in this race. Once again, they had mixed shooting results: Melanin missed five targets, Pshenitsyn one and Butakov four, finishing third, second and first respectively. The surprise of the day, however, was the strong showing by two skiers from East Germany (GDR), Horst Nickel and Wolfgang Heider, who took fourth and fifth places.[112] The biathletes of the GDR proved formidable adversaries to those of the Soviet Union within a decade, and in the years just prior to the collapse of communism, East German skiers were dominating the sport.

Two days later, Zakopane biathlon enthusiasts had the opportunity to watch another ski-shooting competition, this time in the format of a military patrol race. Reminiscent of an earlier era, each participant was required to wear a white camouflage cloak over his racing outfit as well as a rucksack and ammunition belt. The official poster of this Spartakiada featured an image of a military patrol team competing with just such accouterments.[113] *Krasnaia zvezda* noted that there was a great deal of interest in this ski-shooting race as well, especially since the newspaper offered its eponymous prize to the winning team based on the best combined results in both biathlon and military patrol. Although the teams of Bulgaria and Poland did their best, it was the powerful team of Pshenitsyn, Fedor Terent'ev, Iuri Titov and A. Martynov from the Soviet Armed Forces who won the military patrol race. Combined with their first- through third-place finishes in the earlier biathlon, there was no question about who would take the Krasnaia Zvezda Prize.[114]

Interest in biathlon was on the rise in the rest of Europe as well. Two weeks after the closing ceremonies at Zakopane, forty-one competitors started the 20-kilometer race of the Third Biathlon World Championship in Umeå, Sweden, an increase of 37 percent over the number of racers at Squaw Valley the previous year. In addition to the four-man team from the Soviet Union, eight skiers from Poland and the GDR represented the Eastern Bloc. Aleksandr Privalov ran a respectable 1:29.07, good enough for a silver medal ahead of Finland's third-place finisher Paavo Repo; but his three misses were too much to overcome the fast-skiing gold medalist Kalevi Huuskonen of Finland, who hit nineteen out of twenty targets. Pshenitsyn also missed three targets to finish in fourth. Dmitrii Sokolov, perhaps adhering to his "law" that limited each shooting bout to ninety seconds, skied one of the fastest times of the day but missed a total of five targets, leaving him in sixth place; his teammate Nikolai Pavlovskii finished the race in twelfth place with five misses. The Soviet team lost the gold medal in team competition by a little less than six minutes to Finland. The results from this world championship indicate that competition in biathlon was intensifying, especially between Finland and the USSR: Klas Lestander of Sweden, who shot clean to win the gold medal at Squaw Valley in 1960, missed two shots in Umeå, dropping him to ninth overall. However, had he hit every target in this race, he would only have managed to claim fourth place. In addition, the team results were becoming more competitive. The time differential between the two top teams at Umeå had been effectively cut in half in comparison to those at Saalfelden in 1958 (just under twelve minutes) and Courmayeur in 1959 (just under sixteen).[115]

Biathletes of the Soviet Union had one more opportunity to take on an international field in late March at the traditional three days of races for Skiers of the Defensive Forces of Finland and of the Soviet Army held in Kuopio, Finland. Fedor Terent'ev, Vladimir Melanin, A. Martynov and Iuri Titov comprised the Soviet military patrol team that competed on a 25-kilometer course with one bout of shooting. The Soviets needed eight shots to hit their five targets to the Finnish team's seven, losing the race by five minutes. In the 4 x 10-kilometer relay, part-time biathlete Aleksandr Gubin skied the third leg to help his team beat the Finns by just under four minutes. Once again, the Soviet skiers demonstrated that they were on a par with their counterparts in Finland on the ski tracks, but improvement on the shooting range remained elusive.[116]

The World Ski Championships of 1962: *"La guerre froide et le sport"*[117]

The town of Zakopane had welcomed the International Ski Federation (FIS) World Championships twice before, once in 1929 and then a decade later in February of 1939. The political milieu in Central Europe was just as difficult during the 1962 World Championships as it had been during those of 1939, held the winter prior to Germany's invasion of Poland and the start of World War II. The Cuban Missile Crisis was eight months into the future, but these were still fraught times. East Germany had begun construction of the Berlin Wall in August of 1961. In October, the United States committed additional advisors and helicopters to support and transport South Vietnamese troops in battle with the Northern communists, placing American personnel and resources directly into combat. In early January 1962, the Soviet Union and Cuba signed a trade pact, followed by an economic embargo of Cuba by the United States on 3 February. Reflecting global geopolitics taking place across an ever-widening ideological divide, the year 1962 also marked the first time FIS designated two separate sites on either side of the Iron Curtain as hosts for the World Ski Championships. Since these were the first events of their kind ever held in a communist country, the propaganda potential of the Zakopane competitions nearly outpaced that of the Squaw Valley Olympics.

Up until 1958, one country had sponsored the FIS ski championships each biennial period, although sometimes in separate locations. For example, during the 1950 World Championships, held in the United States, the Alpine events took place in Aspen, Colorado, while the Nordic events were split between Lake Placid, New York (jumping), and Rumford, Maine (cross-country). However, improvements in equipment, slope grooming and technique in Alpine skiing meant that steeper and longer courses with more technical difficulties were necessary to challenge the competitors. Therefore, while the Nordic World Championships took place in Lahti, Finland, in 1958, the Alpine competitions were held in Badgastein, Austria. Squaw Valley had been an ideal location for the Olympics two years later because the cross-country tracks at McKinney Creek were just nineteen kilometers to the south of the steep courses on Squaw Peak, KT-22 and Le Papoose, the main peaks at this California resort. In 1962, FIS split the races between two nations again: the Alpine events in Chamonix, France, from 10 to 18 February, followed immediately by the Nordic competitions in Zakopane, Poland, from 18 to 27 of that month.

Prior to the Chamonix races, a sporting crisis occurred that foreshadowed the highly politicized Olympics of the next two decades. The Allied Travel Office in West Berlin refused to issue visas to the Alpine Ski Team from the GDR. These athletes needed special documents to travel to France because NATO member nations did not recognize East German passports. Moreover, the Allied Travel Office made no attempt to deny that this was an overt reprisal for building the Berlin Wall. The situation threatened the very existence of the 1962 World Ski Championship. "The championships are in danger. [FIS] rules state that all countries which want to participate must be permitted to do so. There are no provisions for exceptions," said FIS President Marc Hodler.[118] East Germany protested the ban to FIS on the grounds that when the Alpine competitions were awarded to Chamonix, the government of France had made assurances there would be no restrictions on FIS member-nation teams; and furthermore, the events surrounding the World Championships had been organized long before the construction of the wall.[119]

This Cold War melodrama was one of the first to involve both FIS and the International Olympic Committee (IOC), with governments on either side of the Iron Curtain in seeking a politically palatable solution. FIS ruled that there would be no Alpine World Championships unless East Germany could travel to Chamonix, citing its constitution, which forbade staging a world championship unless all member nations could compete. As precedent, FIS member Rolf Hohantahl of Finland noted that the results of the 1941 Cortina Games had been nullified because not all of the federation members could compete during World War II.[120] The French Foreign Office claimed that it could do nothing to help the East German athletes because this was a decision made by the Allies, not by France alone.[121] The Allied Travel Office in West Berlin remained adamant: it would not allow East German athletes to receive the necessary documentation. The East German Ski Federation insisted that its skiers wanted to compete, even though prospects for medals were remote. This impasse forced an emergency FIS plenary session on Sunday, 4 February, in Bern, Switzerland, where representatives voted on whether to cancel the Chamonix events. However, because of the short notice, many member-nations—including the Soviet Union, the Eastern Bloc nations and the Scandinavian countries—could only attend by telephone. These phone-in delegates, representing the major Nordic skiing powers, all voted to cancel the Alpine championships.[122] Having little recourse for countermanding this decision, the executive committee renamed the competitions the FIS World Games.[123] The *New York Times* lamented that the World Ski Championships were now "doomed by an entanglement with politics."[124]

FIS desperately wanted to hold the Alpine competitions as a world championship, as did the event's French organizers, who had invested a great deal of time, money and effort: "The Berlin Wall Will Cost Hundreds of Millions at Chamonix," read the headlines in the nation's daily newspaper *France-Soir*.[125] Troubling as well were suggestions that the Alpine events should be relocated to Italy or Austria in order to accommodate the East Germans. France protested to FIS that its plenary session in Bern had been illegal, because the organization's charter required members be present to vote, nullifying the call-in balloting. FIS conjured what it considered a viable solution: the East German athletes and coaches, whose passports were valid in Switzerland, would fly to Geneva. Then, with a "safe conduct pass" in hand signed by both FIS and the IOC, the delegation could cross the French border and travel the ninety-odd kilometers to Chamonix. Marc Hodler sent telegrams to French President Charles de Gaulle, British Prime Minister Harold Macmillan and United States President John Kennedy asking for their personal intervention in this matter—to no avail.[126]

The Soviet Union, in the meantime, called for a change in venue of the World Amateur Ice Hockey Championships scheduled for March in Colorado Springs, Colorado, because East German athletes were unable to obtain visas for travel in the United States. East Germany's *Neues Deutschland* in addition to *Sovetskii sport* unleashed a barrage of articles that called into question not only the events in Chamonix and the Colorado hockey competitions but also the World Championships of track scheduled to take place in the United States and the European Table-Tennis Championships set for West Berlin.[127] The Soviets then orchestrated a mass withdrawal among the Eastern Bloc nations from the Alpine competitions on 7 February. "There is no world championship in Chamonix," said one of the Soviet delegates, "so there is no reason to go there."[128] During the run-up to the controversy over the competitions in Chamonix, the Nordic events in Zakopane appeared immune to disputation, much to the chagrin of the editors of *Le Monde*: "It's just too bad that the World Ski Championships, both Nordic and Alpine, aren't grouped in the same place . . . these decisions have been taken so as not to bruise sensitivities."[129]

Without a "World Championship" designation, the Alpine races in Chamonix were unraveling. The day after the Russian skiers departed, Austria threatened to pull its team as well.[130] As the qualifying heats were taking place, the delegates of FIS held another conference in Chamonix in order to "break" the decision made in Bern. Stanley Mullin, a vice president of FIS and self-professed "smart lawyer" from Los Angeles, flew to Chamonix and made a pitch to his fellow delegates: if the Alpine races there were not world championships, then neither were the Nordic competitions in Zakopane.[131] *Sovetskii sport* took Mullin to task on this point:

"Strange logic! Everyone knows that the government of the Polish People's Republic—unlike France—opened the doors of the nation hospitably for every athlete who might want to take part in the competitions."[132] Without a doubt, the Eastern Bloc nations wanted the events in Zakopane designated world championships in order to legitimize what was sure to be a socialist cakewalk. *Pravda* quoted V. A. Andreev, chairman of the USSR Federation of Skiing and vice president of FIS: "Needless to say, some people tried to rob the championships of the title world championship. However, the majority of [FIS] did away with these intrigues announcing that Poland fulfilled all its obligations by granting visas to athletes of all governments without exception and did not breach sporting statutes, as happened just recently with the French, who denied visas for the team from GDR to the Alpine Championships."[133] Mullin's lawyerly arguments, which included a reiteration of the illegality of the 4 February vote at the plenary session in Bern, carried the day by the end of the week's competitions, allowing the reinstatement of the title "Alpine World Championships" to the Chamonix races.[134] Absent the Eastern Bloc, the Western countries of Austria, France, the United States and Italy and a team representing West Germany dominated the competitions; but with focus shifting to the Nordic events in Poland, expectations were high that the Soviet Union would take the lion's share of medals.

Anticipation for these Nordic World Championships had been building in the Soviet press for over a year, beginning with the extensive coverage of the First Winter Spartakiada of Friendly Armies in the early months of 1961. A report from Finland in December 1961 about the opening of that nation's training camp characterized it as "Zakopane in miniature."[135] Under a banner headline conflating skiing and cavalry as a metaphor for modern winter competition—"The Snow Cavalry Is on the Attack"— *Sovetskii sport* reminded readers that time was growing short until the most important ski events of the season.[136] "The Last Test before Zakopane," read the headlines in *Krasnaia zvezda*, above an article about a Soviet ski-jumping trial set for the first week of February.[137] On the eve of the competitions, another article listed the members of the Soviet team taking part in the World Championships in Zakopane, predicting victory for the mighty skiers of the USSR, especially Olympic bronze medalists Genadii Vaganov and Aleksei Kuznetsov.[138] Veteran ski writer Viktor Viktorov noted that the first two times world championships took place in Zakopane, the cross-country events had been dominated by Finland, Sweden and Norway, but this year, "the contest will go head-to-head between not three but four countries."[139] Even as the controversy over the Alpine competitions in Chamonix raged, the Soviet and Eastern Bloc press continued to stoke the enthusiasm for the Nordic events.[140]

During the week of the World Championships, Soviet national television broadcast special reports with highlights taken from Polish news sources. These ran on the First Program channel for twenty minutes during prime time at ten o'clock in the evening.[141] The Soviet Union certainly had ample opportunity to cheer on the National Team during these shows. The brilliant squad of women who had performed so well in Squaw Valley two years before—Baranova, Gusakova, Kolchina and Eroshina—managed to improve on their spectacular results by taking all possible medals this time, sweeping both the 5- and 10-kilometer individual races as well as winning the gold medal in the 3 x 5-kilometer relay.[142] "Our Skiers are the Heroines of Zakopane," exclaimed the Soviet daily newspaper *Trud*.[143] But there were no such headlines associated with the men's performance, which was even more disappointing than it had been at the Olympics in 1960. In the premier events, the top Soviet finishers managed only seventh place in the 30-kilometer and tenth in the 50-kilometer races. Equally galling was the fact that the Italians were performing better than the Soviets—one of them even taking the bronze medal in the 30-kilometer race. The Italians gave the Soviet team a run for their money in the men's 4 x 10-kilometer relay, but in the end, the USSR prevailed, crossing the finish line ahead of fast-closing Norway by a hairsbreadth for third place.

The political brouhaha surrounding the FIS World Ski Championships was a disconcerting development in the world of international sports. The precedent set in Chamonix carried over to Oslo's Holmenkollen Games held one month later. The Norwegian Foreign Office refused to grant visas to ski jumpers of the GDR, a group that included Helmut Recknagel, recently the gold medalist on the large hill jump at Zakopane, but also the Olympic gold medalist in Squaw Valley and winner at Holmenkollen in 1957 and 1960.[144] As a coda to the end of the winter competitive season, the IOC issued a statement expressing regret that the East German team had been excluded from the Alpine World Ski Championships in Chamonix. It stated that the Olympic Games would only be held in cities that would guarantee free access to all recognized international competitors. In no uncertain terms, the IOC said it opposed the use of sports "as a political instrument or weapon." The exclusion of East Germany was an inexcusable violation of Olympic principles: "Occurrences of this kind are most regrettable and may have more and more violent repercussions that will threaten the very existence of organized international amateur sport and the Olympic games."[145]

Hämeenlinna, Finland: Fourth Biathlon World Championship, 1962

The hubbub surrounding the 1962 Alpine and Nordic World Championships obscured the biathlon season in most of the world's press—administration by the UIPM kept biathlon separate from and impervious to the high-profile posturing that was now the norm at such FIS competitions. Prior to the international furor over the East German Ski Team's ban from entering France, the biathlon squads of the GDR and Sweden travelled to Finland for a mid-January tune-up race. *Sovetskii sport* took pains to note that the previous year's world champion, Kalevi Huuskonen, who had beaten Privalov by almost three minutes in Umeå, missed eight targets and finished in eleventh place.[146] Concurrently, a race for the best biathletes of the Soviet Union, with arguably a more competitive field than that assembled in Finland, took place in Kavgolovo. The shooting results had improved remarkably for the Soviet skiers, with the top five finishers totaling just nine missed targets. In the opinion of the *Sovetskii sport* correspondent covering this race, Vladimir Melanin managed the "requisite average," posting the best ski time and missing just a single target at the last range. Privalov, on the other hand was still struggling to find the golden mean: "He got nervous and, trying to make up for lost time on the course, was less attentive standing eyeball to eyeball with the target." Melanin's closest rival, Nikolai Puzanov, shot clean to take second place, even though he required a full three minutes to clear his targets at the final range.[147]

In preparation for the Biathlon World Championship in Hämeenlinna on 4 March, each of the athletes chosen to represent the Soviet Union had taken part in fourteen to eighteen biathlon and cross-country ski races.[148] The most important of these were the team selection races held in the Estonian village of Kääriku near Otepää on 31 January on the second day of the USSR National Team competitions. Valentin Pshenitsyn edged Vladimir Melanin for first place, with Nikolai Puzanov close behind in third. The daily newspaper *Izvestiia* commented on the continuing hard-luck saga of Aleksandr Privalov: "He almost fell prey to his own carelessness. Shooting at the second range, [Privalov] forgot to set his sights for 200 meters and missed: however, just in time he remembered and subsequently his shots were accurate."[149] Privalov salvaged his race to finish fourth, with Evgenii Repin rounding out the World Championship Team in fifth place.

As the Zakopane World Nordic Championships were winding down on 27 February, the Soviet biathlon team arrived in Finland for a week of training prior to their own competition.[150] Interest for this event was high in Hämeenlinna, and on race day, according to *Sovetskii sport,* more than ten thousand fans attended.[151] The championship race was an incredibly close contest—the top three competitors were separated by a scant forty-seven seconds. Vladimir Melanin, with two misses, maintained a lead of thirty-eight seconds over Squaw Valley silver medalist Antti Tyrväinen of Finland, with Valentin Pshenitsyn third by nine seconds, both of whom accrued a single miss. Melanin's meticulous range procedure had served him well: he told *Sovetskii sport* that "although at every range it took some time for me—between a minute and a half and a minute and forty-five seconds—I usually got out on the track again faster than all the foreign skiers who started firing at the same time as me."[152] Nikolai Puzanov had four misses, which was good enough for fourth place, besting team leader Aleksandr Privalov, who accumulated six misses for a distant twelfth-place finish. Nevertheless, the one-three-four combination of the USSR's top three positions enabled the Soviets to reclaim the team competition gold medal, which they had lost to Finland the year before. The Soviet Union's calculated margin of victory was just over eight minutes.[153] "The performance of the Soviets on the ski track," commented the Finnish newspaper *Uusi Suomi,* "was considerably better than expected."[154] As reported in the Soviet press, this outcome offered a welcome contrast to the recent discouraging news from Zakopane.

Returning home from Finland as victors, the world-championship members of the Soviet National Team competed in the biathlon race of the First Winter Spartakiada of the USSR held only six days after the race in Hämeenlinna. Melanin in particular had trouble adjusting due to the rapid transit through four time zones.[155] A sizeable crowd was on hand in Sverdlovsk to watch the nation's world champions. To keep ski fans up to date on the progress of the race, radio messages were relayed back to the finish line from all four of the shooting ranges. Whereas the Soviet National Team had competed in a field of forty athletes in Finland, in Sverdlovsk sixty competitors took to the line on the morning of the race. The surprise of the day was that the USSR's world championship team gold medal biathletes—including second place finisher Vladimir Melanin and third place finisher Nikolai Puzanov (as well as Privalov and Pshenitsyn who were out of the running)—came in behind Nikolai Meshcheriakov, a young athlete skiing for Dinamo. This was the same skier who, as *Sovetskii sport* reported a year earlier, had prevailed in the Moscow District Zone Race by shooting clean on a pancake-flat course.[156] Here was a new hero who had confounded the experts by winning the national title in biathlon, a worthy complement to the world championship contingent with whom he had raced. "I'm really happy for my comrade Nikolai Meshcheriakov," Melanin told *Sovetskii sport*. "For a long time we've lived in each other's pockets [i.e., side by side] with him. And here he is: he's finally become first among us."[157] Delighted with this turn of events, Russia's daily sports journal could not pass up the opportunity to tweak Privalov for his poor performances both in Hämeen-linna and Sverdlovsk: "His movements were fluid, although outwardly he seemed sluggish . . . [in biathlon] a great inner composure is necessary, and today Privalov doesn't feel it. He evidently didn't recover himself after the bad luck in Finland . . . in these competitions Privalov didn't even fulfill second-class norms [for the All-Union Sports Classification]."[158] The results from the First Winter Spartakiada of the USSR demonstrated once again two important aspects of Soviet biathlon: first, victory on any given day could never be predicted; and second, there was a wealth of talent in the sport just waiting to be discovered all across the country.

SEVEN

The Triumph of Soviet Biathlon, 1963 to 1966

EARLY IN 1963, VIKTOR VIKTOROV, *Ogonek*'s die-hard ski enthusiast, reminisced about the golden glory days of the Soviet Union at the 1956 Cortina Olympics in comparison to the National Team's more recent world championship showing in Poland: "Bronze medals," he grumbled, "that's all they were able to achieve at Zakopane."[1] Noticeably absent from Viktorov's account, of course, were the brilliant results of the women's squad. That the USSR virtually owned the women's 5- and 10-kilometer distances and 3 x 5-kilometer relay was all well and good; but the world's sport journalists were predominantly male, and their obtuse comments about Soviet women—especially in the West—hardly reflected shock and awe: "Maria Gusakova of Russia, an amazingly attractive girl, slogged more than six miles through the snow to lead a USSR sweep in the first ladies' cross-country event, and then, after hastily applying lipstick, proceeded to charm several hundred members of a curious and unbelieving press."[2] In such a gendered Cold War environment, pride of place went to the men's competitions, especially the 30- and 50-kilometer races and the 4 x 10-kilometer relay, whose military connotations were still vivid for the Soviets. However, biathlon in the 1960s offered a new forum for Cold War competition, arguably even more male-oriented and more militaristic than any previous ski event—unlike Gusakova in the 10-kilometer race, biathlon was "masculine and serious," according to *Sovetskii sport*—and by 1963, it was evident that in this style of racing the Soviets were predominant.[3] Just two weeks after Viktorov's article appeared, Vladimir Melanin and his Soviet teammates gathered up the gold at the Fifth Biathlon World Championship in Seefeld, Austria, a small village just outside of Innsbruck. *Krasnaia zvezda* featured a portrait of Melanin heroically posed with his rifle, a fitting homage to the accomplishments of the nation's biathlon program.[4] Melanin was world champion for the third time, the Soviets had taken the team title for the second year in a row and biathlon was well on its way to becoming the USSR's "national possession." All that was lacking was an Olympic gold medal.

Seefeld, Austria: Fifth Biathlon World Championship, 1963

Russia's first biathlon hero, Vladimir Melanin, would turn thirty years old in 1963, with a contingent of younger skiers snapping at his heels. As an older athlete, he desperately missed his family when travelling to ski races both within and outside of the Soviet Union, and homesickness, by his own admission, may have affected his concentration levels during the USSR National Championship of 1962.[5] Nevertheless, he was still one of the Soviet Union's fastest biathletes during the early season of 1963. In addition, his maturity and extensive experience in competition were important assets in an event that required tremendous mental discipline.

There was significant concern in the Soviet press in 1963 about the ability of the nation's biathletes to defend their world title from the previous year. Reports out of Finland that Veikko Hakulinen had switched from his specialty, long-distance skiing, to biathlon contributed to the journalistic angst. Hakulinen was an anomaly of sorts during the Cold War era: arguably the greatest cross-country ski racer of his generation, this three-time Olympic champion maintained an amicable relationship with rival athletes on the other side of the Iron Curtain for decades. He was born in 1925 in Kurkijoki, a small village roughly 150 kilometers northwest of St. Petersburg. This region, known as West Karelia, was an area of contention between Finland and Russia for centuries. Five years prior to Hakulinen's birth, the Bolsheviks had conceded West Karelia to Finland in the aftermath of the Finnish Civil War via the Treaty of Tartu. When Hakulinen was fourteen years old, the territory was incorporated into the Karelo-Finnish Soviet Socialist Republic—a result of the Moscow Peace Treaty signed by Finland in 1940 after the Winter War.[6] As a defeated former ally of Nazi Germany, Finland was forced to cede territory to the USSR after World War II and pay reparations of 300 million dollars. Like other Eastern European nations bordering the Soviet Union during the late 1940s, Finland was on the brink of a communist takeover and eventual subjugation to the USSR. In 1947, Stalin proposed a mutual assistance pact similar to that offered to Romania and Hungary. But Finland was able to negotiate a different arrangement: the nation maintained an independent parliamentary democracy with a Western-oriented capitalist system while at the same time coordinating its foreign policy with the interests of the Soviet Union.[7] The close relationship that developed between Finland and Russia during this period assumed the pejorative epithet "Finlandization" in the early 1960s. Hakulinen's association with athletes of the USSR reflected this curious geopolitical amalgamation during its earliest stages across a border that was often fluid and subject to sporadic change.

Hakulinen was already an eight-year veteran of international racing when he travelled to the Soviet Union for the first time to compete at Sverdlovsk in 1954. He made another trip in 1959. The ski-obsessed Russians admired his technical expertise and speed on the track over all distances, and Hakulinen's performances became the benchmark against which top Soviet racers compared themselves. To the Soviets, he was one of the "two giants of skiing," along with Sweden's formidable Sixten Jernberg; both received extensive coverage in the Soviet press during the 1950s and early 1960s.[8] Hakulinen reciprocated by showing great respect for Soviet skiers, telling *Ogonek*: "For a long time I've anticipated the debut of new names in the Soviet Union. I know that they train there just as much and just as persistently as in other countries."[9] Hakulinen was so venerated in the Soviet Union that he earned the moniker "king of the ski track" as well as "the great friend of Soviet skiers" when he retired from racing in 1961.[10] His friendship with Pavel Kolchin, cultivated at the Sverdlovsk competitions of 1954 and at subsequent international events throughout the decade, bolstered his standing in the Soviet press well into the 1970s.[11]

Hakulinen's rationale when he left behind "pure" Nordic racing in 1961 was that thirty-six years of age was the upper limit for a good skier. He had therefore decided to get out of the way of a younger generation of competitors.[12] But cross-country skiing is much more of a lifestyle than most other types of sport, especially for those who compete at its highest levels. Certainly, to those unfamiliar with the regimen, cross-country skiing sounds unimaginably austere, as described for an American audience by *Sports Illustrated*: "The real loneliness comes in training. Men like [Finland's Eero Mäntyranta] condemn themselves to a kind of solitary confinement in the great, gusty outdoors, going out day after day to slip through the forest for long hours without meeting a soul."[13] To aficionados of the sport, however, this type of endeavor is no condemnation at all but, rather, a satisfying form of exercise carried out in beautiful natural surroundings. Cross-country skiing can be addictive; and so too can its competitive aspects. Hakulinen "in retirement" still outdistanced a majority of the top racers in Finland in 1962 and, when he tried his hand at biathlon, found that he was consistently beating members of the Finnish National Team in time trials by over five minutes and top international competitors by three to four minutes over a 20-kilometer course. Hakulinen had trained with the Finnish biathlon squad all summer, and in his early January starts at the team selection trials he posted some respectable times, his best a third place finish with seventeen targets hit out of twenty. Despite his sometimes erratic shooting—he made only eleven hits at a race in Lahti—and an overall ranking of tenth after the selection races, Hakulinen secured a berth on the National Team headed to Seefeld, Austria, for the Fifth Biathlon World Championship on 3 February 1963. As reported in *Sovetskii sport*, this was a tactical stroke based on his renown as one of the world's fastest ski racers: "The very name of this competitor will make a huge impression on his rivals."[14] If he shot well, Hakulinen posed a serious threat to the USSR's claim as home to the most powerful biathlete in the world.

In the wake of the 1962 World Championship, the Soviet Union had expanded the country's biathlon program beyond Moscow and Leningrad to some twenty different cities including Murmansk, Omsk, Perm, Krasnoiarsk, Riga and Kiev. Forty athletes from these regions received invitations to attend an early-season biathlon race in Leningrad on 8 January as part of a week of international ski competitions. Because the next biathlon world championship was scheduled more than a month earlier than in the previous year, the normal six- to eight-week buildup to the event was compressed, and this particular January race took on much greater significance. There were quite a number of young racers in attendance, and with an eye toward Seefeld, the coaching staff of the National Team scrutinized each of them throughout the week. However, the old guard still held the advantage, as V. Antipenko, head administrator of the Soviet biathlon program, explained to *Sovetskii sport* on the eve of the race: "Six sportsmen are going to Austria and perhaps one could name them almost without error right now. Really the choice isn't so large. There won't be miracles—in a difficult type of sport like biathlon masters of the highest class don't spring up suddenly. You have to prepare them carefully and patiently."[15] On race day, Antipenko's comments proved clairvoyant as one unseasoned biathlete after another skied into the range too fast and missed his targets. However, some of the veterans demonstrated that experience did not necessarily guarantee victory either: Melanin ran one of the fastest times of the day but missed four targets, dropping him to sixth place. Nikolai Meshcheriakov, the young prodigy who became the USSR National Champion of 1962, skied equally well but missed only one target to win the race just in front of Aleksandr Privalov.[16]

Meshcheriakov continued his winning ways, securing a berth ahead of Privalov on the National Team bound for Seefeld along with Melanin, Valentin Pshenitsyn and Nikolai Puzanov. *Sovetskii sport* proposed on the day of the 20-kilometer event that prospects were good for the Soviet skiers, with the speed and sharpshooting of Meshcheriakov rivaling Olympic bronze medalist Privalov's own significant talent. And even though Melanin had struggled in the early season, he was famous for his composure at major competitions: "Everyone knows that Melanin knows how to shoot more accurately when the glow of a gold medal blinds the other athletes."[17] These musings read like a script as the day's events unfolded. Adapting splendidly to the incredible pressure that accompanied the defense of his world championship title, Melanin was in top form, once again out-skiing his main rival from the previous year, Antti Tyrväinen of Finland, by an impressive one minute and forty seconds. The Soviet contingent bolstered Melanin's gold-medal performance: Meshcheriakov placed fourth, while Pshenitsyn and Puzanov finished in seventh and eighth place behind Finland's Hakulinen, whose blistering tempo on the ski track was tempered by six misses (and twelve penalty minutes) at the shooting ranges. This one-four-seven-eight finish by the USSR edged Finland's two-three-six-eleven effort in the team competition calculation by a slight 5.8 seconds, resulting in a gold medal sweep by the Soviet team.[18]

Melanin's individual gold medal—in addition to those from Hämeenlinna one year before and Courmayeur in 1959—vaulted him into that rarified stratum of individuals who had won a world championship title three times, a difficult feat even among the talented athletes of the Soviet Union. *Pravda* published news of Melanin's victory within twenty-four hours—unusual in that paper's coverage of skiing events.[19] In praise of his accomplishment, *Izvestiia* marveled at Melanin's success, noting that it was difficult enough to win a world championship, let alone win another the very next year.[20] "As everyone knows," *Krasnaia zvezda* told its readers, "in any kind of sport you can count on one hand a three-time champion of the world."[21] But this was not Melanin's victory alone: that Soviet biathletes repeated their success from Hämeenlinna in team competition was significant as well. Modern biathlon had only been in existence for six years, but in this time the Soviet Union had won three gold medals in the team category, and for the second year in a row, the country's biathletes had swept all the world championship gold medals. "Once again," read the banner headline accompanying *Sovetskii sport*'s front-page article, "it's a golden double."[22] Here, perhaps, was the beginning of a dynasty, and Russia's premier sports daily adopted biathlon wholeheartedly. In the aftermath of the Seefeld World Championship, coverage of every aspect of biathlon, previously the domain of *Krasnaia zvezda*, became a fixture of *Sovetskii sport*.

Photographs of biathletes appeared regularly, along with articles on topics running the gamut from Red Army competitions to the Estonian biathlon championships and even a lengthy interview with the winner of a local spartakiada event.[23]

But the Soviet team had little time to rest on its laurels. A few weeks after returning from Seefeld, Soviet biathletes who skied for the Red Army travelled to Romania for the Friendly Armies of the Socialist Countries Applied-Military Ski Competitions. It is significant that the men's 4 x 10-kilometer relay was included among the applied-military events along with biathlon and military patrol during this meet. *Sovetskii sport* noted that both Melanin and Puzanov acquitted themselves well in this relay, although the Soviet team came in second to Poland and then behind Romania in the military patrol race. In the 20-kilometer biathlon race, a Romanian skier placed third among Soviet skiers Puzanov, Vladimir Makarov and Pshenitsyn, who were first, second and fourth respectively. Their world championship teammate Melanin, however, was out of the running after the first shooting stage, where he managed to place all five shots on another skier's target.[24] Winning performances by athletes from Poland and Romania at these competitions indicated an upsurge of interest in biathlon and cross-country skiing among Eastern Bloc nations. Back in the Soviet Union, Melanin returned to form the following week at the USSR Armed Forces Championships, taking third place behind Aleksandr Popov, who shot clean, and Makarov, whose tempo on the track resulted in the fastest ski time of the day.[25] Forty-two biathletes affiliated with KGB-sponsored Dinamo finished the season at their club championship in early March in the Uktus Mountains. For Red Army skiers, there was another round of military ski competitions with Finland a week later at Hämeenlinna. In the biathlon race, Pshenitsyn, Melanin and Makarov finished first, second and third.[26]

The Ninth Winter Olympics: Innsbruck and Seefeld, Austria, 1964

The significance of the 1964 Winter Olympics to the Soviet government cannot be overstated. The political nature of international sporting events had increased substantially in the four years since Squaw Valley, morphing into theatrical posturing such as that of the 1962 FIS World Ski Championships in the interim. The pronouncements of Nikita Khrushchev, First Secretary of the Communist Party and Chairman of the Council of Ministers of the Soviet Union, illustrate how communist ideology infused Soviet perceptions of the Olympics during this period. On the eve of the opening ceremonies, one of his themes was world peace, a curious juxtaposition in the midst of the nuclear arms race. Cognizant of the world stage, Khrushchev exhorted the athletes of the USSR: "Be worthy of the times we live in, the magnificent times of the building of communism."[27] Another was the role sport played in the development of communist society: "Sport is the source of courage, cheerfulness, capacity for work and long life. The progress of society in sizeable steps depends on the training of a new man who harmoniously combines spiritual richness and moral purity with physical development."[28] Inherent in this notion was that even though the country's top athletes represented the USSR at the Olympics, mass participation in sport was essential to the development of the state. Thus, the Communist Party introduced a new slogan beginning in early December 1963 that associated the Games as much with the common citizen as with the elite athlete: "The Olympic year is not just for Olympians."[29] *Sovetskii sport*, which had started its coverage of the 1964 Winter Olympics in October 1963, featured this new slogan through a host of articles organized under a stock heading from December on. Subheadings counted down the months, weeks and days as the Games approached. To engage its audience the sports journal challenged readers to an Olympic-themed contest, posing questions such as: "Which biathlete will prove the best shot and what place will he take in the competition?"[30]

In the week leading up to the Innsbruck opening ceremonies and during the Games themselves, Soviet press coverage was incessant. As events unfolded at the Olympics, *Sovetskii sport* as well as other major newspapers, such as *Pravda* and *Izvestiia*, filled the pages with Olympic reports and published charts totaling the number of medals won by each country with an unofficial point count calculation each day.[31] These daily tallies did not disappoint: the Soviet Union gathered eleven gold, eight silver and six bronze medals at the Innsbruck Games, more gold and a larger total than any other nation by far. Conjuring the emotion as the Olympic flag was lowered on the last day, a headline in *Pravda* declared that Innsbruck was "a triumph of Soviet sport."[32] In high-profile events such as speed-skating and ice hockey, the teams from the USSR were outstanding. Lidiia Skoblikova became the first woman to win all four speed-skating events in a single Olympics, matched by the female cross-country skiers, who among themselves accounted for two bronze, one silver and three gold medals, or six out of a possible seven total medals awarded across three events. Close behind them were the nation's biathletes, capturing two out of three top prizes in their one race.

"Repetition of a Legend"[33]

Perhaps no world champion has garnered more success in his or her event yet labored in greater obscurity than biathlete Vladimir Melanin. Those who knew him well in 1964 considered him a man of few words, slow-moving and particular, a husband on the cusp of his fourth decade who doted on his nine-year-old son. To the editors of *Sovetskii sport* he was "simply Melanin."[34] It is no surprise that he was virtually unknown in the West, overshadowed by the larger-than-life Alpine skiers of his era such as Austria's Karl Schranz, France's Jean-Claude Killy and Americans Buddy Werner, Jimmy Heuga and Billy Kidd, all of whom were youthful free-wheeling rapscallions by comparison. These downhillers were the darlings of the Western sports press, dashing and newsworthy in contrast to the staid and tedious athletes who toiled at the Nordic events, especially the anonymous skiers of the USSR.[35] In 1962, for example, newspapers such as the *New York Times*, West Germany's *Die Welt* and France's *Le Monde* and *France-Soir* devoted multiple columns if not full pages to the Chamonix Alpine World Championships, then relegated coverage of the Nordic events in Zakopane to a desultory paragraph or two during the following week.[36] Moreover, Melanin's specialty was "the strange biathlon event," a sport at the far end of the ski spectrum even in the estimation of the most ardent Nordic cognoscenti.[37]

In the run-up to the 1964 Winter Olympics, even this small group of ski enthusiasts discounted the three world championship titles held by Melanin, Russia's premier biathlete. Rather, most prognosticators—swayed in the West perhaps by anti-Soviet sentiments—considered Veikko Hakulinen the overwhelming favorite to win the Olympic biathlon gold medal. After his debacle at the Biathlon World Championships in 1963, Hakulinen returned to Finland and won his homeland's national title. He spent the following summer under the tutelage of Vilho Ylönen, a world champion and Olympic medalist in marksmanship. Hakulinen's name was familiar to the American editors of *Sports Illustrated*, and it was he whom the magazine chose as the likely winner of the Olympic biathlon, a designation duly noted in *Sovetskii sport*.[38] *Krasnaia zvezda* took issue with this prediction, using the record of the country's female skiers as its standard for excellence: "Just like our women, Soviet biathletes are considered the primary contenders for victory." This bold statement was qualified, however, with an acknowledgment of Hakulinen's potential: "His threatening weapon is speed."[39] As Finland's biathlon coach Ivo Kauranen told *Sovetskii sport*: "If Hakulinen hits eighteen [targets] at the Olympics I think the gold medal will be his for sure."[40]

There was no question about the women's ski events in the weeks leading up to the opening ceremonies at Innsbruck. The consensus in the sporting press on either side of the Iron Curtain was that Soviet women would collect all the Nordic medals. Even *Sports Illustrated* predicted a Soviet gold medal sweep of the women's 5- and 10-kilometer individual races as well as the 3 x 5-kilometer relay. That America's premier sports journal, oblivious to cross-country ski racing except in the weeks prior to each Winter Olympics, could forecast so accurately the outcome of the women's races indicates the overwhelming strength of this Russian squad.[41] "Our golden ski girls" would compensate, in the opinion of *Ogonek*'s Viktorov, for the dismal record of the nation's male skiers, who were regularly off the awards pedestal at international competitions ever since the World Championships in Zakopane. "To put it simply," sniped *Krasnaia zvezda*, "[our men] have annoyed the nation's sports fans."[42]

The Innsbruck Olympics were scheduled early in the winter of 1964 from 29 January through 9 February; thus the Soviet team selection trials came early in the year as well. The coaching staff scheduled the Race of the Strongest Skiers in mid-December at Zlatoust, 1,385 kilometers due east of Moscow in the southern Urals. I. Bulochkin and Evgenii Polikanin, coaches for the biathlon team, knew that it would be dangerous for the racers to peak too early: there was still a month and a half to go until the Olympics. Nonetheless, they helped install courses near this small village in the southern Urals matching those found at Seefeld and organized the biathlon race in cold and windy conditions on 16 December 1963. It proved a good test for firing from the standing position, which Bulochkin and Polikanin in particular had emphasized during pre-season training. Vladimir Melanin had a good start but fell just before the last shooting range, clogging the barrel of his rifle with snow. He was only able to hit two of his targets from the off-hand position and had to settle for ninth place. The rest of the field shot well, validating the team's coaching efforts: first- and second-place finishers Boris Ivanov and Aleksandr Privalov both shot clean, as did Valentin Pshenitsyn and Iurii Zabaluev in fifth and sixth positions. Nikolai Meshcheriakov hit a respectable nineteen out of twenty to place third followed by hard-charging Nikolai Puzanov who missed three targets.[43]

The ski team returned to Zlatoust for the USSR National Ski Championships three weeks later. On 6 January 1964, Privalov won the biathlon title. He combined a quick ski run with clean shooting, a testament, according to *Sovetskii sport*, to the work the coaching staff had accomplished with him as well as to Privalov's own character, which was "balanced and even a bit self-possessed."[44] Puzanov finished behind him, followed by Vladimir Makarov. Noticeably absent among the top skiers were Meshcheriakov, whose poor shooting precluded his finishing even among the top ten competitors, and the ill-fated Melanin, who once again was having trouble staying upright on his skis. Russia's premier biathlete took a tumble on the first loop and damaged his rifle before firing even one shot. He continued the race using a spare firearm but was unaccustomed to its idiosyncrasies. Like Meshcheriakov, Melanin shot poorly and finished out of the running. Significant in this competition were the top-ten results of Evgenii Repin, representing Trud sport club, and G. Shagin from Burevestnik, one of the few times that multiple biathletes not affiliated either with Dinamo or the Red Army had competed at such a high level.[45] "Not without reason," surmised the editors of *Krasnaia zvezda*, "we expect that [Soviet biathletes] will return from Innsbruck with medals."[46]

In order to gain some high-altitude conditioning before heading off to Seefeld, the biathletes of the Soviet National Team travelled to a competition in Le Brassus, Switzerland, in mid-January. This race was scheduled exactly two weeks prior to the Olympic biathlon, and most of the squad performed quite well. Pshenitsyn and Privalov both hit nineteen out of twenty targets and Puzanov made up for his three misses by skiing the best time of the day. The results did not bode well, however, for the struggling Melanin, who missed five targets to finish a distant fourth, although he did maintain a full eight-minute lead over the closest Swiss racer.[47]

In the weeks leading up to the start of the Games, Austria was experiencing its warmest winter in fifty-eight years. As of the opening ceremonies, ski conditions could not have been worse—rain continually washed away Seefeld's minimal snow coverage and made the cross-country tracks exhaustingly slow.[48] The biathlon race was scheduled for Tuesday, 4 February, at which point the Soviet Cross-Country Ski Team had achieved mixed results after the first three events. In the men's 30-kilometer race on 30 January, the best Soviet finish was Pavel Kolchin's sixth-place effort. Two days later, Igor Voronchikhin won a bronze medal in the 15-kilometer contest.

On the same day, however, the women gathered up all three medals in their 10-kilometer race, led by Klavdiia Boiarskikh, who would also take gold in the 5-kilometer race later in the week.

The rain-saturated snow of the Tirol changed dramatically on the eve of the Olympic biathlon. A post-sunset thaw on Monday was followed by a morning freeze that turned the biathlon course into a skating rink. These conditions demanded extraordinary technical skill as the athletes negotiated the icy track on narrow wooden-edged racing skis.[49] For skiers of the Soviet Union, however, these difficulties were to their advantage. The majority of training and competitions for the National Team members had taken place on courses designed to mimic the profiles at Seefeld and in states of thawing and freezing ice similar to those the Soviet coaches had expected to encounter.[50] Nevertheless, it was still an extremely difficult race. Stating the obvious, *Sovetskii sport*'s special correspondent wrote: "The icy ski track did not herald a 'pleasant ski excursion,' although all in all, it was much faster than the previous day."[51] First out on the course for the Soviet Union was veteran racer Valentin Pshenitsyn, the most consistent marksman on the team. However, his many years of experience in major competitions inexplicably failed him on this particular day. At the first range he fired only four shots, but one of the range officials insisted he had made five. Pshenitsyn appealed to the head official, who allowed him to chamber a fifth bullet. The confusion broke his concentration and it appeared that this shot ended up off the target, further fueling his nervousness. On the icy tracks beyond the third range Pshenitsyn took a tremendous fall, scattering bullets helter-skelter from his carrying pouch. By the time he got to the final shooting stage it was clear from his face that he was dazed and confused. Igor Nemukhin of *Sovetskii sport* was watching as Pshenitsyn came into the range:

> Something wasn't going right. Pshenitsyn shouts into the crowd surrounding the firing line: "Is anyone here from our team? I've lost five bullets!" But who could help him? Even if somebody had extra bullets, giving them to a competitor is useless. According to the regulations they can [disqualify] you for that. Pshenitsyn had three extra bullets in his cartridge belt. He took three shots and after a futile and incomprehensible attempt to get two more bullets he headed off to the finish.[52]

This was certainly an inauspicious start for the Soviet team; but Pshenitsyn was not the only competitor struggling at the range that morning. Veikko Hakulinen dropped two shots at the first shooting stage and proceeded to miss another four for a total of twelve penalty minutes added to his course ski time, which had been the fastest of the day. After all the buildup in the press, he delivered only a fifteenth-place finish.[53]

Melanin, Privalov and Puzanov were on the track next for the Soviet Union, and fortunately for them Pshenitsyn had absorbed all the bad luck. Melanin posted the field's third fastest ski time, one minute and eleven seconds behind Hakulinen. In addition to this brilliant performance as a ski racer, Melanin managed to tap his reserve of quietude to hit all twenty of his targets and win the gold medal. His next closest competitor was Privalov, who also shot clean but skied over three minutes slower than Melanin, good enough for silver. Pshenitsyn and Puzanov rounded out a magnificent Soviet effort, finishing in seventh and tenth places respectively. After the race, Privalov told *Sovetskii sport*: "[In biathlon] it's necessary to know your own optimum pace."[54] For Melanin, the pacing he maintained throughout the race could not have been better: it was slow enough to allow a steady hand at all four shooting stages yet quick enough to stay within striking distance of Hakulinen. Even if the Finnish national champion had been able to hit nineteen targets, one more than the best-case scenario his coach proposed in *Sovetskii sport* at the end of January, Melanin would still have won the gold medal by over a minute that day.[55]

News of the one-two finish by Melanin and Privalov prompted celebration in the Soviet press. Above the *Sovetskii sport* masthead of 5 February, headlines blared "Biathlon: The Gold and Silver Are Ours" next to Melanin's formal portrait on page one.[56] Constraints governing glossy magazine production meant that *Ogonek*'s coverage was delayed by several weeks, yet the journal gushed as if the story were new: "Victory! Not a single miss! So shot Vladimir Melanin, the best biathlete in the world."[57] Echoing this sentiment, the government authorized a special commemorative biathlon postage stamp with the inscription "Soviet biathletes are the best in the world."[58] Not only was this a great victory in a sport the Soviets had made their own: Melanin's win tweaked experts on the other side of the Iron Curtain as well. "[Melanin's performance] cancelled the very predictions of many Western specialists and journalists," crowed *Krasnaia zvezda*.[59] "Soviet biathletes confirmed that they are the best in the world," wrote *Pravda*. "Remember that the sport prophets of the Western press allotted to Melanin at the very most second place, putting Finland's Veikko Hakulinen ahead of everyone."[60] *Sovetskii sport* was pleased to report that Sweden's newspapers, disheartened at the loss of the biathlon gold medal to Russia, were now lamenting the dominance of the USSR.[61] If three-time world champion Melanin had been an unknown before the Games in Innsbruck, his gold-medal-winning persona was now on everyone's radar. On the last day of the Olympics, *Krasnaia zvezda* conducted a poll of correspondents from Austria, Czechoslovakia, Poland, the United States, Italy and thirteen other nations concerning the week's events. To the question "who in your opinion displayed the greatest desire to win at the IX Winter Olympics," thirty-seven of the fifty people responded with Melanin's name.[62]

On the heels of Melanin and Privalov's effort, the Soviet women took gold and bronze in their 5-kilometer event the next day and then the gold medal in the 3 x 5-kilometer relay by the end of the week. However, the Soviet men's team continued to struggle. Not one of the USSR team members cracked the top ten in the 50-kilometer marathon held the day after the biathlon, and in the 4 x 10-kilometer relay the Soviets had to settle for third place.[63] For the officialdom of the Soviet Union, the contrast was unacceptable: "Our entire country knows the names of our hero-Olympians [such as] the skiers Vladimir Melanin and Klavdiia Boiarskikh," wrote Iurii Mashin, chairman of the Central Committee of Sport Clubs and Organizations of the USSR, in *Pravda* on the last day of the Olympics: "As to the feeble performances of our male skiers . . . the reason first and foremost is in the slow reorganization of the training process and the absence of a proper system for preparing athletes."[64]

Nevertheless, Mashin announced the next day that Moscow was planning a hearty welcome for the returning Olympians. A huge crowd gathered at Sheremet'evo Airport on 12 February to greet the team with speeches, fanfare and singing.[65] One week later there was a reception at the Kremlin to honor the Innsbruck medal winners attended by members of the Communist Party Presidium as well as Italian Communist Party General Secretary Luigi Longo. Aleksandr Privalov and Vladimir Melanin received special commendation in front of the assembly, a moment memorialized in photographs on the dais with Nikita Khrushchev, as Leonid Brezhnev, Andrei Kirilenko, Dmitrii Polianskii, Aleksandr Shelepin, Anastas Mikoian and others looked on.[66] In a recent interview, Aleksandr Privalov described meeting Khrushchev at this event: "[Melanin] and I were standing with the defense minister of the USSR Rodion Malinovskii—even though I competed for Dinamo and [Melanin] for the Red Army club . . . Khrushchev saw us and said to Malinovskii: 'Bring the guys over here.' We poured champagne and he said: 'Well done, fellas! You shot good and straight. If one of our enemies makes it across our border, shoot him right in the forehead!' We remembered those words for our entire life."[67]

Just prior to these Moscow festivities nearly 400 of the nation's best skiers who served in the army and navy competed in the Ski Championships of the Soviet Armed Forces. These annual competitions took place in Kavgolovo from 15 through 21 February; and it is all the more astounding to consider the performances, with only a few days of rest, of Olympians Aleksandr Gubin and Nikolai Puzanov. Gubin, who had placed fourteenth in the 50-kilometer race at the Olympic Games, was victorious over the same distance here by a three-minute margin. Puzanov shot clean in the biathlon competition to outdistance by over six minutes his closest competitor, perennial runner-up Iurii Zabaluev, who also hit twenty out of twenty targets.[68] Puzanov almost repeated this perfect performance at the USSR Team National Championships at the end of the month, hitting nineteen of his twenty targets to edge his clean-shooting rival Boris Ivanov by just under three minutes.[69]

These excellent results notwithstanding, the question of how to maintain the nation's position as the top winter sports power in the world, especially in biathlon, consumed the Soviet sport press after the 1964 Olympics. While applauding the sharpshooting of Puzanov and Zabaluev, the two leaders at the Armed Forces Championship in Kavgolovo, *Krasnaia zvezda* berated the rest of the field for weak marksmanship. "For instance," wrote General-Major Z. Firsov, "Junior Sergeant I. Romanov of the Zabaikale Military District hit only three targets with twenty shots, and Senior Lieutenant G. Ushakov of the Northern Fleet—only two. Little wonder that both of them could not fulfill the norms of the third rank [of the All-Union Sports Classification] at the championships."[70] *Sovetskii sport*'s correspondent at the USSR Team National Championships was appalled by some of the poor marksmanship displayed there. "Here are the targets of a biathlete from Armenia, R. Sarkisiian . . . four hits out of twenty shots! He himself makes his own appraisal: 'Shooting on a hope and a prayer!'" This did not bode well for future international competitions, in the author's estimation: "Indisputably, we have a solid group of genuine biathlon masters. Indicative of this would be that the positions of the Olympians at the competitions in Kavgolovo underwent resolute and successful attacks. But among those who managed to make the top ten, there was essentially not one new name."[71] As this first echelon of Soviet biathletes reached retirement age, the recruitment of younger skiers became the ski team's number one priority.[72]

The Last of the Old Program Competitions: Elverum, Norway, 1965

The winter of 1964 through 1965 was the last season during which international biathlon competitions followed the old program format, culminating with the Sixth Biathlon World Championship in Elverum, Norway, the third week of February. For the years to follow, International Modern Pentathlon Union (UIPM) rules stipulated a 150-meter range for all of the shooting—now two prone and two standing stages—and a new scoring system that allowed either a one- or two-minute penalty to accrue for different distances from the center of the target.[73] Despite these proposed changes, *Sovetskii sport* understood that old program parameters would dictate biathlon competitions for the immediate future and therefore considered variations in shooting patterns at the four separate ranges as one of the "problems of the season" for 1965. In a guest opinion piece, Evgenii Polikanin, head coach of the National Team, offered an analysis of Melanin, Pshenitsyn and Puzanov's poor marksmanship at the first prone range at 250 meters during the 1962 World Championship and the 1964 Olympics. He proposed that shooting at this range was easier, yet the scores were consistently worse than at the other three. Polikanin's explanation was nerves, which were an especially bothersome problem before a major competition. He suggested that biathletes needed a warm-up in order to get into the rhythm of the race, perhaps by running on foot for one and a half to three kilometers, then skiing intervals before coming to the starting line.[74]

First-range nervousness, however, was neither Melanin's nor Privalov's bête noir at the 1965 season opener in Kavgolovo, where the biathlon team competed against skiers from Poland and Finland in early January. At the second range Privalov forgot to adjust his sights from 250 to 200 meters, and Melanin fired all five of his shots onto another's target at the third. As a result of their mistakes, both former Olympians placed far out of the running. Nikolai Puzanov continued his string of top finishes from the end of the previous season to win the competition, followed by teammates V. Kozhin and V. Sukhanov. The Finns could only place a skier in fifth, rationalizing that their best competitor, Veikko Hakulinen, remained at home, yet all the while hinting to the press that he was contemplating a return to international racing at Elverum in February.[75]

Following immediately after these races, the armed forces of Finland and the Soviet Union met in Kavgolovo for a series of competitions consisting of a 4 x 10-kilometer relay, a 20-kilometer biathlon and a 25-kilometer military patrol race. In the biathlon race, Puzanov led the field again as Melanin struggled at the range, accumulating four misses at the first two shooting stations. Puzanov maintained his lead to take first place followed by Finland's Asko Marttinen in second and Aleksandr Popov of the USSR in third. Slightly less than ten minutes separated the two squads in team calculations. At the end of the week, Puzanov led the Soviet's Team Number One to victory in the military patrol contest, edging Finland's top unit by one and a half minutes.[76] Melanin and Privalov fared better in a dual meet with East German biathletes at the end of the month, taking first and second place followed by Puzanov in third.[77]

The significant number of races against Finnish competitors scheduled by the Soviet biathlon team indicates that the USSR still viewed Finland as its top rival at major international skiing events in the wake of the 1964 Olympics. At the Innsbruck Games, Finnish athletes had taken ten medals, eight of them in skiing. In biathlon, Finland and the Soviet Union had alternated dominance at the World Championships from 1961 through 1963, although the Finnish team was shut out of medals in 1964. Finland's national coach, Veli Saarinen, told *Sovetskii sport* that the biathlon squad was one of the weakest groups on the Finnish Olympic Team. The poor showing at the Olympics, however, did not deter the Soviet Union's top sporting journal from covering the 1964 and 1965 Finnish Biathlon Championships as well as other races in that country. Of special concern was the makeup of the 1965 World Championship Team headed to Elverum and whether Hakulinen would be a member. At the Finnish National Championships in Lahti, Hakulinen skied a blistering pace to beat his closest teammate by over two minutes but accrued twelve penalty minutes to end up in fourteenth place. A few days later his fortunes improved when he won an international race against biathletes from East Germany and Sweden, missing only three targets.[78] Once again, Hakulinen was a viable threat with the potential to interrupt Melanin's three-year string of consecutive world championship and Olympic titles in 1965. All he had to do was hold his shooting together in Elverum.

The forty-nine competitors who took to the starting line at the Sixth Biathlon World Championship on Sunday, 21 February, enjoyed beautiful weather and well-prepared ski tracks. Instead of four separate shooting areas, the four different-length ranges were arranged side by side at one location. This facilitated the monitoring of the race and provided spectators with a central vantage point to watch the athletes shoot throughout the entire event. This new arrangement in combination with near-perfect conditions resulted in some superb marksmanship: the top three biathletes missed only two targets out of sixty possible. This high standard of accuracy resulted in an incredibly close race: Olav Jordet of Norway edged Nikolai Puzanov for first place by twenty-two seconds, while Finland's clean-shooting Antti Tyrväinen ran third by a mere six-tenths of a second. However, the rest of the Soviet contingent accrued only one other top-ten finish: Melanin in seventh place with three misses, Vladimir Makarov fifteenth with four and Privalov crossing the finish line in sixteenth with three misses. Veikko Hakulinen missed seven targets, accumulating fourteen penalty minutes to take thirty-first out of forty-eight finishers. In pointing out this disheartening result for Finland's top skier, *Sovetskii sport* was keen to note that on this occasion, Hakulinen had not even skied the fastest time of the day.[79]

As part of the Elverum competitions, the UIPM held a test relay race on 20 February in anticipation of the event's official debut at the Seventh Biathlon World Championships in Garmisch-Partenkirchen the following year. The format designated that four team members would ski a 7.5-kilometer course in succession with two bouts of shooting, one from the prone position and one from standing. The five targets for each stage were balloons placed behind cutouts in a target frame whose arrangement resembled dots on a dice face. For each unbroken balloon the skier had to negotiate a 200-meter penalty loop before returning to the course. Each competitor was allowed to use eight bullets (five loaded into a cartridge plus three loose) to hit his five targets at both stages. Rather than interval departures the relay featured a mass start, with biathletes skiing and shooting head-to-head, the winner of the race determined by the first team across the finish line.[80] At this initial contest Norway placed first, followed by Sweden and the USSR. The Soviet team put Valentin Pshenitsyn in the first leg, then Melanin and Privalov. These three skiers had the gold medal in sight, having missed only one shot out of thirty possible when the hand-off went to Puzanov for the final leg. However, a silver medal in the individual race did not guarantee a similar result in the relay: Puzanov hit all of his targets prone but missed three standing, dropping his team to third place. Nevertheless, *Sovetskii sport* was enthusiastic about this new event, anticipating its inclusion at the next Winter Olympics planned for Grenoble, France, in 1968.[81]

The relative success of the Soviet biathlon team at the 1965 World Championships stood in stark contrast to the irregular efforts of the men's cross-country ski team. On the eve of the USSR National Ski Championships, *Sovetskii sport*'s chief ski correspondent, Igor Nemukhin, noted that "only the biathletes pulled off a medal at a world championship this season." Although the International Ski Federation (FIS) Nordic World Championships only took place every two years (with the next one scheduled for Oslo in 1966), the nation's cross-country skiers had been participating in international races in Europe throughout the season with only spotty results. "Our male skiers are 'running a fever,'" wrote Nemukhin. "One time they're going head-to-head with the medalists from the Olympic Games and with world champions, the next thing you know they lose to them in a way that even an ordinary Master of Sport would not." He continued his critique by pointing out that Soviet skiers I. Utrobin and N. Arshilov placed in the medals at Lahti, Finland, but a week later could finish no higher than eighteenth at the Holmenkollen Games in Oslo, Norway: "To make a prognostication on the day before the first start [of the USSR championships] is a thankless task."[82]

In truth, the results from the international competitions in which Soviet skiers participated held greater interest for Nemukhin because they provided an indication of what future world championships held in store. Such was the case at an early March biathlon race in Kavgolovo, where the Soviet Union hosted the Championships of the Friendly Armies of the Socialist Countries. Vladimir Melanin set the best ski time of the day but dropped three shots to end up in third place behind Poland's clean-shooting Józef Gąsienica-Sobczak. Although Nikolai Puzanov eked out a victory with only one miss, skiers from Poland and Romania were close behind the Soviets in the team calculations.[83] Competition in biathlon was gathering intensity, and in 1966 the Soviet Union would have one of its worst international showings ever at the World Championships in Garmisch-Partenkirchen, West Germany.

"Sport Is the Cosmonauts' Assistant"[84]

Along with international sport and the arms race, a dominant motif of the Cold War era was the competition between the United States and the Soviet Union to land a man on the moon. Nikita Khrushchev considered the Soviet space program a preeminent example of the state's technological progress, and the USSR astonished the world indeed with the launching of the first Sputnik satellite in 1957. As the Soviet Union continued to accumulate one major achievement after another—including the first unmanned landing on the moon in 1959 and Iurii Gagarin's unprecedented orbital flight in 1961—the likelihood that the Soviets would dominate space became a political factor in the West. "Russia will try to land a man on the moon in 1967, at least a year ahead of the United States, according to the way the space race timetable for the rest of the decade shapes up," wrote American science journalist Walter Wingo just six days prior to President John F. Kennedy's assassination. "There remains the possibility that the two nations will accept [Kennedy's] suggestion that they join hands in putting both a Russian and an American on the moon at the same time."[85] However, Soviet progress in space reinforced Khrushchev's and subsequently Leonid Brezhnev's belief in the superiority of the Soviet system. Cooperation with the United States, whether in rocket science or sports, appeared to be an unnecessary concession for the Soviets throughout the mid-1960s.[86]

The week of the 1965 USSR National Ski Championships, from 21 through 27 March, followed yet another sensational development in the Soviet space program, the flight of Voskhod-2, resulting in perhaps the first and only conflation of extraterrestrial travel and skiing on record. Over the course of twenty-six hours, cosmonauts Pavel Beliaev and Aleksei Leonov piloted the Voskhod 3KD spacecraft into orbit and conducted the world's first spacewalk on 18 March. Their safe return electrified the nation; *Sovetskii sport* devoted the first three pages of each edition from 19 to 27 March to coverage of events surrounding the flight, spacewalk and return to earth. Several issues included pictures of Beliaev and Leonov participating in a variety of sports—basketball, ice hockey and, on two separate occasions, skiing.[87] The text accompanying one of these ski photographs declares: "Sport is the true and dependable helper of the cosmonauts."[88] This sentiment was not peculiar to the Voskhod-2 mission, however. In a telephone conversation from Otepää, Estonia, site of the Soviet Union's Ski Championships that week, head coach Nikolai Anikin recalled an earlier meeting at the Innsbruck Games with cosmonaut Pavel Popovich, the sixth man to orbit earth:

> We talked for a long time with the cosmonaut. It appeared that we had a lot in common. Both cosmonauts and skiers carry out great physical loads in periods of training. It's true, Popovich told me, that cosmonauts have somewhat of the same character. He himself, as well as all the cosmonauts, pay a lot of attention to skiing. "Of course," Popovich said "it isn't necessary to attain your mastery on the ski track. But we incorporate much of the skiers' training into our preparation for space flight."

For Anikin and the ski team, the admiration was mutual, conforming to socialist precepts: "The flight of the crew of the spacecraft 'Voskhod-2' inspired the sportsmen who are participating in the USSR championships of skiing and biathlon."[89]

The extent to which Soviet biathletes competing in Otepää were truly motivated by the success of Voskhod-2 is unknown of course, but their shooting scores at the USSR National Championships were certainly inspirational in their own right. Among the top ten finishers, all shot with either eighteen or nineteen hits. Rapid fire and range procedure played a crucial role in this race, foreshadowing developments in subsequent versions of single-range biathlon competition. Aleksandr Privalov, for example, hit five out of five shots at the first range in one minute and ten seconds. Nikolai Meshcheriakov set a Soviet record for cumulative speed on all four ranges, managing eighteen hits in six minutes and twenty-five seconds.[90] This event was the last major old program competition ever held, and it attracted a huge field of sixty-one competitors. To initiate the race, with a pair of skiers leaving the starting line at three-minute intervals, required a full two hours. The time and effort necessary to put on such an event limited the opportunities for newcomers to become acquainted with biathlon, according to head coach Evgenii Polikanin: "No one wants to mess around with the labor-intensive organization associated with this sport."[91] In Polikanin's opinion, this limited the opportunities for neophytes to learn about biathlon, and indeed this particular race belonged to the veterans. The oldest competitor in the field and a crowd favorite was Trud's Evgenii Repin, who took third place. Privalov won the national championship title, followed by World Championship Team member Vladimir Makarov representing the Red Army. Rounding out the top ten were many familiar names, such as Meshcheriakov, Privalov's old Dinamo teammate V. Sukhanov and the Red Army's dependable warhorse Valentin Pshenitsyn. But the list included some newcomers as well, most significantly eighth-place finisher Viktor Mamatov, a twenty-eight-year-old skier from Siberia who competed for Lokomotiv sport club.

Biathlon's New Epoch

Biathlon's updated format as of the 1965–1966 competitive season slanted the competition toward faster skiers. In the individual 20-kilometer race, there were now two bouts each of prone and standing. To be sure, doubling the number of shots taken off-hand increased the degree of shooting difficulty. But without having to adjust the rifle to account for variations at four separate ranges that differed in length, sun aspect and wind direction, the biathlete could concentrate on just one set of parameters with only minor adjustments necessary for firing from either position.[92] In addition, new rules governing proximity to the center of the target allowed for gradations of penalty time awarded. The black circles at which the biathletes now shot included an extra ring beyond the bull's eye. If the bullet hit the center of the target, no penalty was assessed. If it landed within the first ring, one minute of penalty accrued to the shooter. If the bullet missed the target rings completely, a two-minute penalty was the result. The all-or-nothing two-minute penalty of the old program yielded to a more generous method of rewarding a "pretty close" shot, thus reducing to a certain degree the importance of meticulous marksmanship that had been the hallmark of biathlon. With the penalty for a shot near but not in the bull's-eye essentially cut by half, a subtle shift occurred in the race results as speed on the track gained in importance over steady shooting at the range.

In comparison to Norway's biathletes, the older and more experienced skiers of the Soviet Union were at a disadvantage in this new style of biathlon. In a report about the Norwegian National Ski Team prior to the start of the important world championship year of 1966, *Sovetskii sport*'s correspondent noted that the average age of that nation's biathletes was twenty-three, compared to over thirty in the USSR.[93] At the first selection race in Otepää to determine members of the National Team headed to Garmisch-Partenkirchen for the 1966 Biathlon World Championships, the first three prize-winners in the individual 20-kilometer race were two thirty-three-year-old veterans, Vladimir Melanin and Aleksandr Privalov, followed by Nikolai Puzanov, a relative youngster of twenty-eight. The veterans were also medalists on their respective teams in the 4 x 7.5-kilometer relay a few days later.[94] At Smolensk in mid-January, the irrepressible Evgenii Repin, at this point in his early thirties, posted an incredible win over a mixed field of veterans and newcomers. In horrific conditions where the temperature dipped to minus twenty-one degrees Celsius and the tracks turned to sheets of ice covered by grainy snow, Repin shot only one penalty minute. This veteran beat biathletes in their late twenties such as Puzanov, who accumulated five minutes, and Viktor Mamatov, who added eight. But head biathlon coach Evgenii Polikanin was more enthusiastic about some of the younger skiers in the race, such as Vladimir Goncharov and especially twenty-one-year-old Vladimir Gundartsev, who he thought had the potential to become a top international athlete. Polikanin understood the team needed a new cadre of skiers who could compete against the younger and faster athletes emerging from the Scandinavian countries.[95] Two of the fresh faces in this race who came of age during the transitional phase of biathlon, Mamatov and Gundartsev, would gather between them four Olympic and eight world championship medals from 1966 through 1972.[96]

Garmisch-Partenkirchen, West Germany: Seventh Biathlon World Championships, 1966

The sport's many rule changes meant that the outcome of the Seventh Biathlon World Championships in Garmisch-Partenkirchen was anyone's guess, a nerve-wracking situation for athletes and coaches alike. The Soviet skiers had competed according to the new rules in their selection races at Otepää and Smolensk but worried about performing in a major international competition, especially in pursuit of the first-ever world championship title in the 4 x 7.5-kilometer relay.

While maneuvering to gain a psychological edge over other competitors had always been part of the world championship scene, at Garmisch-Partenkirchen the intrigue reached new levels. "The start had not been given," wrote *Sovetskii sport*'s special correspondent at the races "but the battle was already begun, a battle of a purely psychological nature. The coaches of several teams are trying to introduce panic into the ranks of the competitors with their statements that are fraught with meaning." One rumor, started by the head coach of the Swedish delegation, suggested that Sixten Jernberg, the Swedish ski racer who had won nine Olympic and six world championship medals, the bulk of them gold, was in Garmisch-Partenkirchen as both an assistant coach and an alternate racer. Speculation was rampant that Sweden would place him in the 20-kilometer individual race on 4 February and perhaps on a leg in the relay two days later. To be sure, Jernberg was no Veikko Hakulinen, according to Swedish sources: "It was modestly stated that the veteran [Jernberg] has been comfortable around rifles for a long time, and in training he hit the 35-centimeter target ten times out of ten." For its part, the Norwegian coaching staff touted a twenty-seven-year-old athlete named Jon Istad. As Norway's head coach informed *Sovetskii sport*, Istad was a top racer and crack shot who was "not especially worried" about the Russian biathletes—and that included Vladimir Melanin.[97]

As if these mental games by the coaches had not added enough drama to the proceedings, on the first day of competition a bank of fog that seemed to rise and fall over the shooting range "like a theater curtain" transformed the individual 20-kilometer race into "a raffle in the mist."[98] Whether by luck of the draw or athletic skill, the top prize-winners were all newcomers to the world championship podium. Norway's Istad was first, with four penalty minutes. Second was Poland's Józef Gąsienica-Sobczak, followed by the USSR's youngest entrant, Vladimir Gundartsev, who accrued only one penalty minute. In a telling outcome, the Soviet Union's old guard could not even crack the top ten: Aleksandr Privalov, in his last world championship race, placed eleventh; Nikolai Puzanov finished in thirteenth place and Vladimir Melanin was twenty-first after shooting eleven penalty minutes.[99] Although it was reasonable to blame the random nature of the fog in the individual race, conditions were ideal and thus equal for every competitor in the relay race two days later. Still the Soviet Union's fortunes did not improve. Buoyed by Meshcheriakov's clean shooting on the first leg, Puzanov and Gundartsev followed suit, garnering only one penalty loop apiece. As the anchor on the fourth leg, however, Melanin missed three targets and had to run an extra 600 meters, dropping his team to a distant fourth-place finish behind Sweden and Poland and nearly eight minutes off the gold medal pace of Norway.[100] Never had the Soviet biathlon program failed so miserably, Gundartsev's bronze medal notwithstanding. "The championships that have just concluded," wrote *Sovetskii sport*, "have put an end to the hegemony of the 'big four' (USSR, Norway, Sweden and Finland) in this type of sport. The biathletes of Poland and Romania took part . . . with some bit of luck. It's clear that at the [1968] Olympic Games the competition will be even more intense."[101]

Compounding the disheartening news from Garmisch-Partenkirchen were the results from the Nordic World Championships in Oslo a few weeks later, where the best showing by the men's team was a fifth-place finish in the 4 x 10-kilometer relay. Once again, the women's squad salvaged the Soviet Union's standing among the most powerful ski nations, capturing one bronze, two silver and three gold medals, accounting for six out of a possible seven pedestal positions in the 5- and 10-kilometer individual races and the 3 x 5-kilometer relay.[102] Not that the women's results mattered so much to *Sovetskii sport*'s Igor Nemukhin, however: "So this world championship is over," was his laconic assessment at the end of the week, "the first championship which did not yield a single medal for our men."[103]

Running concurrently with the World Championships in both Garmisch-Partenkirchen and Oslo was the Second Winter Spartakiada of the USSR, an enormously popular event with five million participants registered by mid-February.[104] Regional races took place throughout the Russian Federation and other SSRs with finals scheduled for the beginning of March at various sites across the nation. The competition at these events was ferocious as world-class athletes, many of whom had not been named to the various national teams travelling outside the country to the world championships, vied for honors. Regional selection trials for the finals of the Russian Federation's Biathlon Championship took place in several locations held less than two weeks after the Garmisch-Partenkirchen races. At the Siberian and Far Eastern races in Novosibirsk, sixty racers took to the starting line on Sunday, 13 February. While the skiers were out on the track, *Sovetskii sport*'s special correspondent made the rounds of the coaches and team leaders to inquire about the Russian Federation's biathlon program in the wake of Garmisch-Partenkirchen. His report offered a rather bleak assessment. The major complaint was that most of the competitors only had one or two opportunities to participate in a biathlon race prior to the Spartakiada final. Another problem was a shortage of rifles and ammunition. A. Kuz'menkov of the Irkutsk delegation noted that the biathletes from his region had lived at training camp for fifteen days without firing a single round because there were no bullets available. B. Plotnikov, senior instructor at the Tomsk Polytechnic Institute, stated: "Training has been very little and very poor. Not a single organization in Tomsk has acquired rifles, although they have a right to weapons. For the biathlon team they haven't earmarked even one pair of skis." But Feodor Zaitsev, a Dinamo coach from the Far East region, had a different point of view: "In Magadan we have everything: excellent natural conditions, prepared tracks and plenty of rifles and ammunition." In consideration of the difficulties faced in some of the districts with groups not affiliated with Dinamo or other major clubs, it is no surprise that three National Team members who were skiing on their home turf took the top three places: Novosibirsk residents Viktor Mamatov and Valentin Pshenitsyn and winner Boris Ivanov from relatively nearby Krasnoiarsk. Two skiers from Kamchatka were also among the top five.[105] The Novosibirsk team went on to take the 4 x 7.5-kilometer relay a few days later in weather so severe that the balloons in the target frames "burst like soap-bubbles."[106] At the same time, the North-Western Regional Competitions occurred in Petrozavodsk from 13 to 15 February, led by skiers from Murmansk, Kirov and Leningrad. At these races, Vladimir Melanin anchored a first-place relay team from Kirov. *Sovetskii sport* noted, however, that even though there were several younger skiers present, not one of them was able to compete reasonably with the veterans.[107]

The final Biathlon Championships of the Spartakiada were held in Novosibirsk the second week of March with an enormous group of competitors. Whereas there had been fifty-four racers at the starting line for the individual 20-kilometer race in Garmisch-Partenkirchen a month prior, ninety individuals participated in Novosibirsk, with an equally competitive field. National Team biathletes Vladimir Melanin, Viktor Mamatov and Aleksandr Privalov placed first, third and fourth respectively, followed by their teammates Nikolai Puzanov and Valentin Pshenitsyn, both of whom finished out of the top six. Evgenii Repin raced as well, capping off his twenty-first season as a ski racer. One surprise was the second place result of a dark horse from Perm, A. Shvetsov, whose ski time was not even among the top fifteen posted but who did manage to clean all of his targets.[108] The championship relay race took place on 12 March, expanded to a 4 x 8.5-kilometer contest because the rifle range near the Novosibirsk ski station required an extra kilometer for each loop. First place went to a team representing Moscow comprised of National Team veterans Privalov and Meshcheriakov in combination with the two younger skiers who had performed so well in the early season, Vladimir Goncharov and world champion bronze medalist Vladimir Gundartsev.[109]

Despite the sharp competition throughout the Second Winter Spartakiada, the Soviet biathlon program had reached a critical juncture in 1966, made all the more apparent by the National Team's results at Garmisch-Partenkirchen. The famous biathletes who cut their teeth on the old program and then went on to dominate that form of the sport were getting too old to compete at the highest international level.[110] The performance of Vladimir Gundartsev was auspicious, but as the team returned home from the Seventh World Biathlon Championships to compete in the Second Winter Spartakiada it was clear that the recruitment of new biathlon talent was essential. Curiously, athletes from the Red Army sports club were not contenders at the ski events in the Soviet Union that season, even in biathlon: Dinamo was the new powerhouse in the sport. It is perhaps no coincidence that the Ready for Protection of the Homeland (GZR) program came into existence for military inductees at this time. The GZR's combination of skiing, shooting, cycling, running, hiking and swimming was in essence the prescription for a well-rounded biathlete's training regime.[111]

For many of the old program veterans, this was the last season of their competitive careers. However, Vladimir Melanin continued to compete for the Red Army through the following season and skied in the team selection trials for the 1968 Olympic Games. He would often travel with the biathlon team to the Olympics, acting as a consultant to the coaching staff, and in later years he was instrumental in developing his sport in the Kirov region.[112] The Red Army's Valentin Pshenitsyn became a coach and waxing specialist, preparing skis at most major international biathlon competitions through the 1980 Winter Olympics.[113] Dinamo's Aleksandr Privalov was appointed head coach of the national biathlon team in 1966 and served as either senior coach or team leader at the 1968, 1972, 1976, 1980, 1984 and 1988 Olympic Games. Privalov had announced his retirement as of the end of the 1965–1966 racing season in anticipation of joining the biathlon coaching staff for the following year. He was scouring the nation for potential athletes while still a competitor and as a starting point began to track the results of the Spartakiada with interest. One promising candidate was making his mark in the Siberian and Far Eastern Regional races of 1966. He was a nineteen-year-old Novosibirsk resident who went on to capture the national 10-kilometer junior title at the final Spartakiada Championships on 5 March. His name was Aleksandr Tikhonov, and in just one year, he was on the threshold of becoming the most famous biathlete in the history of the sport.[114]

EIGHT

The Era of Aleksandr Tikhonov

AT THE OPENING EVENT OF THE 2010 United States Summer National Biathlon Championships in Seattle, Washington, two rifles stood side by side on a gun-rack. Each bore a distinctive white sticker with "Alexander Tikhonov & MA" embossed in a black Latin-letter font. One rifle-owner explained to me the import of the stickers: they were used to mark firearms after trigger-weight testing at the 2009 World Summer Biathlon Championships in Oberhof, Germany. "Tikhonov was a really famous Russian biathlon skier," the young man added, a helpful tone in his voice.

As the sitting vice president of the International Biathlon Union (IBU), Aleksandr Tikhonov had paid between 800,000 and 1,000,000 euros in 2009 for the right to sponsor the Oberhof competitions. And his name was everywhere: on the rifle-stickers, the programs and the stadium walls— even though he had not competed at an international biathlon race in twenty-nine years.[1] Yet as the young biathlete in Seattle made clear, Tikhonov's name recognition among those involved in the sport had not diminished one iota. It was a testament to his remarkable career. Between 1967 and 1980, Tikhonov accumulated twelve gold, four silver and three bronze medals at ten world championships, one silver and four gold medals at the Olympics, and won—no mean feat—championships of the Soviet Union nineteen times. Beyond that, the Soviet government awarded Tikhonov the Order of Lenin, the Order of the Red Banner of Labor and the Order of the Red Star as well as medals "For Labor Valor," "For Outstanding Sport Achievement" and "For Labor Distinction." But in his own estimation, one of the greatest honors that accrued to him was designation as flag-bearer on American soil for the Soviet Union's Winter Olympic Team at Lake Placid in 1980, his fourth and final trip to the Games.[2]

Tikhonov's life story in the twenty-first century reads like a pulp novel set in Russia's post-Soviet "Wild East." After retiring from ski racing in 1980, Tikhonov busied himself with coaching, competing in equestrian events and pursuing a variety of business opportunities. In 2000, he and his younger brother Viktor were charged with plotting the murder of Aman Tuleev, governor of Kemerovo *oblast'*, by offering two professional assassins 179,000 dollars to do the deed. Viktor was sentenced to four years in prison in 2002 and served out his term, while his older brother fled into exile in Austria. Russian prosecutors resumed their case against him in 2007. Tikhonov was convicted at trial but then immediately released under an amnesty law passed by the Russian parliament in 2000. More recently, Tikhonov represented the IBU at the 2010 Vancouver Olympics and claims that he is the head consultant for biathlon for the 2014 Winter Olympics in Sochi.[3] Despite his legal problems and resulting efforts by several international union and national federation officials to curtail his involvement (reports have circulated about athletes blood doping under his watch as president of the Russian Biathlon Union through 2008), Tikhonov remains closely associated with the sport. His thirteen-year stint as an active competitor helped define the world's perception of biathlon in the subsequent three decades, perhaps more than that of any other individual.

"Sasha Tikhonov from Novosibirsk"

Aleksandr Tikhonov was born in Uiskoe some 125 kilometers southwest of Cheliabinsk in 1947. His father, Ivan Tikhonov, was an accomplished ski racer who introduced his son to the sport at an early age. His first race, as for many young Soviet skiers, was a local 2-kilometer contest sponsored by the newspaper *Pionerskaia Pravda*.[4] By the time he was fifteen, Tikhonov had placed second in the USSR Junior Championships 10-kilometer race, and the following year he earned the designation Master of Sport. At the age of nineteen he qualified for the finals of the Second Winter Spartakiada of the USSR. As Tikhonov explained to a new generation of sports journalists almost four decades later, many Soviet citizens considered these competitions to be on a par with the Olympics, and they thus carried enormous cachet in the USSR.[5]

As he readied himself to run in the 10-kilometer race in Sverdlovsk on 5 March 1966, the correspondents from *Sovetskii sport* were not particularly impressed: "Number 43, Sasha Tikhonov from Novosibirsk takes off from the starting-line—a little puny guy, kind of emaciated. In the beginning, we didn't really pay much attention to him." By the end of his ski, however, Tikhonov had posted a decisive win, outdistancing his closest competitor by twenty-six seconds to take top honors and the first gold medal awarded in the Soviet Union's most prestigious athletic event; and a few days later, he also added the junior 15-kilometer title to his portfolio.[6] So impressive were his finishes that the coaching staff for the Novosibirsk team put Tikhonov into the senior 4 x 10-kilometer relay race on 10 March. "The young sportsman did not let down the collective," wrote Igor Nemukhin for *Sovetskii sport*, "as his leg assured the silver medal for his team."[7] The two victories in the junior competitions in conjunction with this creditable finish in the relay caught the attention of the press: the Sverdlovsk newspaper *Na smenu!* (On Change!) awarded Tikhonov a prize as best junior of the Spartakiada; and all the attention warranted an article in *Sovetskii sport* focusing on the background of this amazing young star.[8] His success in Sverdlovsk capped an already remarkable career as a junior racer in the Soviet Union, as well as marking the first step on his path to greatness in the sport of biathlon.

Tikhonov on many occasions has credited Aleksandr Privalov with introducing him to biathlon, although his father, Ivan, was no stranger to ski-shooting. The elder Tikhonov taught his son how to use a rifle for hunting and in 1966 had competed in the Southern Ural regional biathlon competitions of the Spartakiada at the age of fifty-plus.[9] In the aftermath of his string of victories at the finals in Sverdlovsk, the younger Tikhonov was in pursuit of a berth on the national cross-country ski team. However, in the summer he injured his knee and could only maneuver on crutches while at a training camp in Otepää. It happened that the biathlon team was training there too, and Privalov suggested that he try shooting a biathlon rifle as long as he was laid up with an injury. Tikhonov, who under the tutelage of his father had become an avid hunter and marksman, hit five out of five targets at the shooting range using Privalov's rifle.[10]

In 2002, Tikhonov stated that making the transformation from the men's cross-country team to the biathlon squad was hard: "The composition of our national biathlon team was very strong in those days. Olympic champion Vladimir Melanin, [Nikolai] Puzanov, [Viktor] Mamatov, [Vladimir] Gundartsev: all of them were experienced and authoritative athletes in biathlon. To push your way onto that team was very difficult."[11] But in fact the Soviet biathlon team was struggling in 1967 at international races leading up to the Eighth World Championships in the East German village of Altenberg and there was ample opportunity for Tikhonov to make a bid for inclusion on that squad.

Early season races in the Soviet Union had been curtailed due to weather and organizational issues. In addition, small niggling details seemed to bedevil the team: Puzanov was having trouble with his arm and struggled to shoot from the standing position, and Melanin's rifle was giving him problems.[12] Rivalry among National Team members had been keen at Leningrad's domestic biathlon competitions when the season started in the second week of January. Newcomer Rinnat Safin lost the 20-kilometer individual contest by two seconds to a forty-year-old Dinamo skier from Novosibirsk, Boris Ivanov, with Nikolai Meshcheriakov following close behind in third. In the relay USSR Team Number One (Safin, Meshcheriakov, Melanin and Puzanov) edged USSR Team Number Two (Anatolii Kol'ev, Vladimir Makarov, Mamatov and a skier identified only as Mal'kov) by twenty-three seconds.[13] But Soviet race results against international fields were disappointing. In preparation for the upcoming World Championships, members of the USSR National Team travelled to Oslo for a dual meet with their Norwegian counterparts in late January. The outcome was sobering: Norway took all of the top spots save fourth place, which was filled by Mamatov. The rest of the Soviet racers—Meshcheriakov, Makarov and Vladimir Goncharov—took ninth, tenth and twelfth respectively.[14] At the end of the month, a different contingent from the national squad competed in Oberhof, East Germany (GDR), as part of the Red Army's team at the Ski Championships of the Friendly Armies. Although Puzanov won the individual 20-kilometer biathlon race, the next best finish was fifth place by Kol'ev. Two Polish skiers finished close behind Puzanov in second and third positions, while Melanin crossed the line a distant fifteenth.[15] A pre-Olympics test of the jumping venues and cross-country trails in Grenoble, France, held just prior to the Biathlon World Championships in Altenberg, yielded only one top-ten finish for Soviet skiers in the 20-kilometer biathlon with Vladimir Gundartsev placing eighth, Kol'ev fourteenth and Vladimir Gorchakov twenty-first. The young biathletes of Norway were the best of the field, taking first, second, fourth and seventh places. In the 4 x 7.5-kilometer relay, the team from the USSR could only manage fourth behind Finland, Norway and Sweden. "Admittedly biathlon (especially the shooting part) is a very capricious type of sport," was *Sovetskii sport's* lugubrious mid-February assessment.[16] On the eve of the Eighth Biathlon World Championships the prospects for the team from the Soviet Union were looking quite slim indeed.

Back in the USSR in the beginning of February, the first All-Union Biathlon Competitions for juniors took place in Otepää, featuring a 15-kilometer individual race and a 3 x 7.5-kilometer relay. These contests were in anticipation of the first Junior Biathlon World Championships (for racers between nineteen and twenty-one years of age) held in conjunction with the Biathlon World Championships in Altenberg. Skiing for Dinamo's First Team, Tikhonov set the fastest time of the day in the relay, beating his closest competitor by a full half-minute.[17] In Tikhonov's opinion, it was the 200-meter penalty loop that worked to his advantage in the relay race: the team was desperate for fast skiers, and no one could catch him racing head-to-head over the extra distance.[18] Tikhonov's phenomenal speed propelled him out of the junior ranks and onto the senior squad headed for Altenberg along with Puzanov, Mamatov and Safin. Vladimir Melanin accompanied the team as an assistant coach.[19]

Privalov's decision to advance twenty-year-old Tikhonov out of the junior category paid dividends at Altenberg. On the day of the 20-kilometer individual race on 17 February the shooting conditions were horrid. Although temperatures hovered around four to five degrees below zero Celsius, violent gusts of wind wreaked havoc on the firing line. Tikhonov posted the fastest ski time of the day but shot nineteen penalty minutes, to finish in a still respectable ninth place. Also appearing in his first international race, twenty-six-year-old Rinnat Safin, ran well too while accumulating an extra thirteen penalty minutes, good enough for fourth, a mere five seconds behind Norway's Jon Istad in third. The overall winner was Viktor Mamatov, with only six minutes of penalties, one of the best shooting scores of the day. Only second-position finisher Stanisław Szczepaniak of Poland out-gunned Mamatov with five penalty minutes.[20]

The weather had not improved much for the 4 x 7.5-kilometer relay race held a few days later. Gusting winds alternated with snow showers to challenge the marksmen. Privalov chose Tikhonov as first man out for the Soviet team, and in that position the youngster showed his mettle. Missing only one prone target, Tikhonov was penalized with a single 200-meter penalty loop, the same as Sweden's lead-off skier. But Tikhonov was running much faster than the rest of the field, and when he handed off to Nikolai Puzanov for the second leg, he delivered a robust lead of two minutes and forty-two seconds. However, Puzanov had two disastrous turns at the shooting range on his leg for a total of eight penalty loops, amounting to an extra 1,600 meters of skiing. When he tagged Safin at the third stage, Norway's Olav Jordet, Olympic bronze medalist at Seefeld in 1964, had pulled ahead of the Soviets by one minute and five seconds. It took a tremendous effort by Viktor Mamatov on the final stretch to hold on to second place over the fast-closing Swedish team.[21]

At the tender age of twenty, Aleksandr Tikhonov had won his first world championship medal, outskiing the entire relay field into the bargain. His closest competitor that day was Jon Istad of Norway, double gold medalist at the previous world championship in Garmisch-Partenkirchen and winner of the bronze medal in Altenberg, just a few days before, in the individual 20-kilometer race. Tikhonov's time was almost a minute faster than that of the former world champion. Coupled with Mamatov's win, Tikhonov's surprising performance breathed life back into the Soviet biathlon program, evident in the resurgent coverage of biathlon on the pages of *Sovetskii sport* in the aftermath of the World Championships. The travails of the Soviet biathlon team in the early season had been relegated to sparse articles printed in small type through mid-February. A distinctive "biatlon" logo that had accompanied articles about the sport the previous year disappeared altogether from the newspaper during the months of January and February 1967. It reappeared on 7 March with coverage of the final biathlon races of the Sixth Winter Trade-Union Spartakiada in Gorkii, held less than two weeks after the Altenberg competitions.[22]

Three weeks later Kavgolovo hosted the Best Biathletes of the Nation race series, where the highlight of the week was competition in the relay events. Various groupings of National Team members had raced against one another since early January both in the senior 4 x 7.5-kilometer and the junior 3 x 7.5-kilometer relays. Nevertheless, results at the World Championships in Altenberg had been mixed: the junior relay squad finished out of the medals in fourth; and the senior team with the addition of Tikhonov had placed second. With the first-ever Olympic biathlon relay gold medal on the line in less than a year in Grenoble, the Soviet team wanted to ensure that the nation's biathletes were accustomed to the idiosyncrasies of the event. Thus, there was an increase in the number of relays on the race schedule across the USSR. This proved beneficial, because National Team members were challenged by lower echelon athletes particularly at the regional level, eliminating any sense of complacency. At the Sixth Winter Spartakiada finals, for example, a relay team from Ukraine defeated the more experienced Novosibirsk contingent featuring Mamatov in the anchor position. Certainly very few countries had enough biathletes to stage truly competitive relay events such as this one. At the Sixth Winter Spartakiada sixteen regions fielded teams for the Biathlon Championships; less than five minutes separated first from sixth place.[23] By comparison, at the Biathlon World Championships of both 1966 and 1967, thirteen teams competed in the 4 x 7.5-kilometer relay, where first place was was 5:45 and third place was just over 12 minutes.

In Kavgolovo, Tikhonov competed as a junior. In the 15-kilometer race, the recent world champion silver medalist accumulated nine penalty minutes to finish fourth, almost four minutes out of the lead position. In the senior 20-kilometer individual race, Nikolai Puzanov ousted the recently designated World Champion Viktor Mamatov from the number one spot, with Rinnat Safin just behind in third. Tikhonov managed a top podium finish skiing for the Dinamo Number One team in the junior 3 x 7.5-kilometer relay a few days afterward. It is interesting to note that Boris Ivanov, a fellow Novosibirsk resident and Tikhonov's senior by twenty years, anchored the first place Dinamo Number One team in the senior 4 x 7.5-kilometer relay.[24]

These final relay races of the 1967 season illustrate how important this event was in the eyes of the Soviet coaching staff. *Sovetskii sport*'s correspondent, Stanislav Tokarev, noted that there were graduate students from the physical education institutes on hand to observe and analyze the races as they progressed, with special attention given to the psychological quirks of each contestant. Whether from talking with these experts or through his own intuition, Tokarev offered an insightful critique on the biathlon relay: "What's necessary for victory in the relay? Ski fast and shoot straight—that much is clear. And one more thing: fire with a rapid tempo. It's a paradox: sometimes it's better to risk missing the target and waste forty seconds on the 200-meter penalty loop than to get hung up standing or lying there for forty seconds and still perhaps miss the target."[25] The key to success in the biathlon relay was speed: fast on the track and fast on the range. This was a far different sport from the 20-kilometer race, which placed a premium on the mental control necessary for maintaining a proper pace and having confidence in one's ability to place each shot into the paper target. The relay was more visceral: each stage was a head-to-head contest against other racers, with immediate feedback from the bank of breakable targets at each shooting bout.[26] The short 7.5-kilometer distance of each leg meant that every team member was in a dead sprint from start to finish. This proved such a popular version of biathlon competition that a 10-kilometer individual race based on the relay format was introduced at the 1974 Biathlon World Championships in Minsk.

The Tenth Winter Olympics: Grenoble, France, 1968

The first ski event of the Tenth Winter Olympics was a shock to long-suffering Viktor Viktorov, now in his twenty-second year as a ski journalist for the weekly magazine *Ogonek*. Franco Nones, a postal official from Italy, won the men's 30-kilometer race on 7 February 1968 in Grenoble, causing a huge sensation: this was the first time that a non-Scandinavian or non-Russian had won an Olympic gold medal in a Nordic event. One of Viktorov's favorite Soviet skiers, Vladimir Voronkov, whom he had touted in an article just a few weeks before, missed the podium altogether, finishing in fourth place. Two days later, another blow fell: the Soviet women were completely out of the medals in the 10-kilometer race. The weariness and disappointment in the veteran writer's prose is palpable: "Our rivals have imitated us quite a bit in the organization of sport and in the preparation of athletes. And somewhere we, evidently, have kind of been delayed in our forward movement . . . not only the men but even the women. The skiers up to now can't find a way to return to confidence in themselves, which would allow them to become Olympic champions like they did once in Cortina d'Ampezzo."[27] The ski heroes of the Soviet Union were failing miserably on the eve of the 20-kilometer biathlon as twenty-one-year-old Aleksandr Tikhonov prepared for his debut at the Olympics.

Just one month earlier, Tikhonov had finished second to Nikolai Puzanov at the All-Union Biathlon Team Selection Races in Vorokhta, a small village in the Carpathian Mountains of Ukraine. Two fellow Novosibirskians also qualified for the top four slots on the Soviet Olympic Biathlon Team: Viktor Mamatov and Boris Ivanov, now well into his fifth decade. Nevertheless, it was twenty-four-year-old Vladimir Gundartsev who made the final cut, replacing the older Ivanov before the team headed to Grenoble.[28] Because Tikhonov and Gundartsev were the youngest and least experienced biathletes on the Soviet team, they were placed among the first groups out on the track for the 20-kilometer individual race on 12 February.

In ski racing it is the responsibility of the coaching staff to "seed" skiers according to relative starting positions based on a random draw conducted the day before the competition. The field is broken into groups, and coaches select individual racers to fill slots within each section. For example, if there are forty racers registered for a competition, there might be four groups with starting positions one through ten in the first section, eleven through twenty in the second and so on. Drawing lots, the coaching staff might receive position number five in group one, position number fourteen in group two, number twenty-seven in three and thirty-five in four. The staff then chooses which four racers on the team will take these spots within the start field based on a number of variables such as each skier's competitive experience, the race day weather forecast and the track conditions. Generally, the most advantageous position for a racer is among the final group: this allows the coaching staff the opportunity to analyze who is leading the race and to pass this information on to the athlete as he or she is competing. The younger or more inexperienced skiers fill the earlier slots, though an early start can be beneficial, especially when weather conditions are deteriorating as the day progresses.

Tikhonov wore bib number 1; he was the very first racer out of a field of sixty to start on the course the morning of the 20-kilometer race. After Tikhonov came Gundartsev in the second grouping, then the more seasoned Puzanov and finally Mamatov, the defending world champion. Along with Tikhonov in the first group were Magnar Solberg, an unknown thirty-one-year-old police officer from Norway, and Poland's thirty-four-year-old Stanisław Szczepaniak. These three skiers were leading the field as the last racers left the starting line. However, the weather began to change abruptly, with a cold rain transforming the snow into a sluggish wet mush. Those skiers who had started earliest had the advantage of skiing when the tracks were the fastest: Tikhonov finished just behind the race-winner Solberg, with Gundartsev edging Szczepaniak for the bronze medal by twenty-nine seconds. The two Soviet veterans, Puzanov and Mamatov, finished in sixth and seventh places respectively.[29] Tikhonov's silver medal for second place at Grenoble was as close as he ever came to achieving the one goal that eluded him throughout his career: to become an Olympic gold medal champion in an individual race. Although he took top honors in five world championship races and second place twice between 1969 and 1980, Tikhonov never again attained such a high level in a non-relay event at the Olympics. Nonetheless, his performance in this race during the first half of the 1968 Winter Games was inspirational: "Our skiers need to get tuned up with the silver tuning-fork of Aleksandr Tikhonov," admonished *Pravda*.[30] "Maybe this is the day that represents that turning point we've been waiting for?" wrote a hopeful Viktorov.[31]

The Olympic Biathlon Relay

The introduction of the biathlon relay into the Olympic Games at Grenoble started a legacy that endured right up to the disintegration of the Soviet Union: from 1968 to 1988, a span of six Olympics, the Soviet Union never lost the gold medal in this event. But the record is even more impressive when considered within the event's total context. From the first biathlon relay at Elverum in 1965 through the last race in which a Soviet team competed in early 1992—a period embracing twenty-eight possible world championship and Olympic competitions—the USSR won fifteen, placed second in six and third in four. In short, the 4 x 7.5-kilometer relay became the Soviet Union's signature winter display of teamwork, the biathlon squad's "crowning item." According to Aleksandr Privalov, a competitor and then head coach throughout most of this period, the relay turned into more of an "emotional experience" than the individual race.[32] The ideological reasoning behind this was clear: for ski enthusiasts of the Soviet Union, the efforts of the biathlon relay team were synonymous with those of the collective.[33]

At Grenoble, the odds that the Soviet team would take the gold medal in the relay were extraordinarily favorable. All four of the Soviet team members had finished in the top seven of the 20-kilometer individual race only three days before, and they were clearly one of the two favorites. Their main competition came from the Norwegian team, made up of three members who were on the gold medal squad from the 1967 World Championships along with Olympic gold medalist Solberg. Fog on the day of the race required a delay of several hours because the targets were not visible from the firing line. When the weather finally improved, fourteen teams left the starting line led by Tikhonov, Lars-Göran Arvidsson of Sweden and Ola Wærhaug of Norway. Tikhonov handed off to Puzanov for the second leg with a two-and-a-half minute lead over his rivals, and the Soviet team never looked back, outshooting the Norwegians to finish decisively in first by one minute and forty-eight seconds.[34]

The final results of this race illustrate Tokarev's "relay paradox": the biathletes of the USSR missed two targets and skied an extra 400 meters to win the race over the second place Norwegians, who had four misses requiring an extra 1,600 meters. The team from Sweden shot clean, avoiding the penalty loop altogether but only managed a third-place finish two minutes and thirty-six seconds behind Norway. Clearly, speed was the crucial factor in the relay: fast skis, quick range procedure and an accelerated tempo on the track. Many of the top competitors from the 20-kilometer individual race had incredible races in the relay: Solberg hit every target and finished his leg in 32:26.4, the fastest of the day; less than seven seconds behind were Gundartsev and then Szczepaniak in 32:50.8. Two other competitors who would challenge the Russians in the coming years were also in this race: Dieter Speer of East Germany, who became a close friend of Tikhonov's, even lending his ski in the midst of a near-disaster during the Sapporo Olympics relay four years later; and a young skier from Finland who proved to be the Soviets' nemesis on their home turf in 1974, Juhani Suutarinen.[35]

The performances of the rest of the Soviet skiers at Grenoble improved somewhat during the second half of the Games. Galina Kulakova took the silver medal in the 5-kilometer sprint, followed by her teammate Alevtina Kolchina in the third top spot. With Rita Achkina, the two Soviet medalists added another bronze in the 3 x 5-kilometer relay. In the 50-kilometer race, Viacheslav Vedenin posted a brilliant silver medal finish, a mere seventeen seconds behind the winner, Ole Ellefsæter of Norway. But this offered little solace to the Soviets covering the Games: the nation's skiers had let down the country, allowing Norway to accumulate the greatest number of medals. "Out of the twenty-seven medals won by [our] men and women," wrote Viktor Viktorov after the Olympics, "our skiers accounted for only seven, and out of these one was gold. At the same time the Norwegians merely received some five gold medals on the ski track!"[36] Lev Kassil', a noted Soviet author attending the Grenoble Games, offered this opinion in *Pravda*: "I'm not a ski specialist, but I dare say that our skiers today have already conceded a little to their foreign rivals—but there once was a time . . . [sic] It's really great that V. Vedenin won the silver medal in the ski marathon, the 50-kilometer race. But one would like to think that we hold the cards for success as well on ski tracks of other lengths. It's a good thing that the Soviet biathletes justified our expectations."[37] What were these expectations? Certainly the most important one was that a winning Soviet team would showcase the superiority of communist society before an international audience. Vedenin's performance was remarkable: a Soviet skier had not medaled in the Olympic 50-kilometer race since 1956, and he was just seconds out of first place. Biathlete Tikhonov had won a silver medal in his individual event as well, the margin of victory a few millimeters one way or the other on a paper target. But being runner-up did not have the prestige of winning the Olympic champion title, and for this reason alone the Soviet biathlon relay team was lionized. It was evident to the world that the gold medal in the biathlon relay indicated the pinnacle of accomplishment in the sport.

But for observers from the USSR the relay victory represented more than the mere act of winning: it was infused with symbolic connotations. In his 1990 biography, Tikhonov related a story that demonstrates this point. Celebrating with the Soviet team at the finish line after winning the relay race at Grenoble, he saw an old man with burns on his hands and face approaching him. Somehow, this fellow had made it all the way from the Soviet Union to France to watch the relay and then—even more improbably—through the crush of people at the finish line to congratulate his compatriots. He told Tikhonov that he fought with a tank battalion in the Great Patriotic War, during which time he sustained burns to most of his body. This veteran thought he had experienced and seen everything in his life, but the victory in the relay had special meaning for him: "You won that medal today not just for you, but for all of us . . . we all need your victories."[38] Whether apocryphal or not, the fact that Tikhonov included this story in his biography indicates the significance of this particular sport ritual to the ordinary citizen, a phenomenon well understood by the Soviet Union's star Olympic medalist. As a biathlete performing before an international audience during the Cold War, Tikhonov was the avatar of Soviet military might. Indeed, the martial connotations of biathlon were implicit on both sides of the Iron Curtain: one spectator at Lake Placid, New York, asked a competitor after an international biathlon race held in sub-zero weather: "What do you guys do in a real war?"[39] In a sense, the Cold War was nuanced kabuki theater, performed in an environment where no conflict would actually be fought but for which preparation was nonetheless constant.[40] The sport of biathlon was ideal for this, both on the track and off. In an article about Don Nielsen, a member of the United States Olympic biathlon team in 1980 and 1984, an American writer discussed Nielsen's search for money to support his training program: "Nielsen talked Boulder [Colorado]-based *Soldier of Fortune* magazine into funding part of his training. The magazine liked the anti-Soviet feel of the biathlon, and Nielsen said he liked walking along the Downtown Mall in his Soldier of Fortune T-shirt."[41]

For the Soviet Union in particular, biathlon knit together several important historical themes, from Trotsky's revision of the Red Army to the defeat of the Nazis in World War II. The conflation of this legacy with the brilliant success of Soviet biathletes before an international audience illustrates Amir Weiner's thesis that the myth of the Great Patriotic War transcended the confines of the Bolshevik foundation mythology to take on a life of its own during the Cold War era.[42] Furthermore, this iconic representation of the Soviet paradigm in the sport of biathlon has outlasted the regime itself, existing to this day outside of its original historical context: within the annals of the Olympics, no nation has come close to improving upon the USSR's unbroken string of gold medal performances in the biathlon relay.

Tikhonov in the Limelight

Aleskandr Tikhonov was accustomed to newspaper coverage back home in the Soviet Union, so when his silver medal at the Grenoble Olympics vaulted him into the international limelight he was a well-versed and natural performer before the world's press corps. In the 20-kilometer individual race Tikhonov had a faster ski time than Norway's Magnar Solberg, but he accrued two one-minute penalties to the Norwegian's perfect shooting. Had he made one less shooting error, Tikhonov would have been the gold medalist, a point alluded to in his first Olympic press conference. When asked what place he expected to take in the next Olympic biathlon race, he immediately replied, "First place, of course"; then, waiting for the murmurs in the conference room to subside, he continued with the timing of a comedian working a small club: "—if the International Federation of Modern Pentathlon and Biathlon decides to increase the diameter of the bulls-eye by one centimeter."[43] His playful banter with the press increased his popularity and put a distinctive and personable face on the otherwise austere Soviet biathlon program. Yet he suffered to a certain degree from notions of superiority, in the opinion of Aleksandr Privalov, and could be maddeningly full of himself before a room of correspondents. Prior to the 1973 World Championships in Lake Placid, he was asked at an international press conference who he thought would win medals and take top honors in the races: "In the interest of saving time I'll answer both of your questions immediately. I'll be first, and besides me Soviet biathletes will also be in the medal group. You can write that down and translate it in your newspapers today. And add one more thing: Soviet biathletes will win the relay."[44] His insolence was notorious, often infuriating to those who competed against him. One outstanding example occurred the night before the 1969 World Championships in Zakopane. Still smarting from his loss of the gold medal at Grenoble, Tikhonov walked into Magnar Solberg's room and told him in broken German: "I want to congratulate you ahead of time for your medal, although it won't be gold . . . because I'll be first!"[45] Such antics did not endear Tikhonov to his teammates, who often wrangled with him almost from the moment he joined the National Team.[46] Viktor Mamatov, for one, considered this prank at Solberg's expense an inexcusable breach of etiquette: "You're a loudmouth," he allegedly told Tikhonov the next day.[47] Rather than an embarrassment for himself, Tikhonov's braggadocio and egregious displays of poor sportsmanship were points of pride, providing his first biographer, Aleksandr Burla, the title for his book, *I Will Be First . . .*

John Morton, an American biathlete who cultivated a close friendship with Tikhonov during the 1970s, recalls an illuminating vignette from the 1972 Winter Olympics in Sapporo, Japan. Of particular interest to athletes from either side of the Iron Curtain during the Cold War era was the exchange of goods and souvenirs in after-hour sessions, especially Levi's jeans for Russian vodka, or Soviet rifle harnesses for nylon cartridge belts and aluminum ski poles manufactured in the West. These trading sessions were especially intense during the closing days of a competitive series, and it was here that the American biathlete observed Tikhonov at his worst. To understand the implications of Morton's story, however, requires some additional background information: in Sapporo, the last event on the biathlon schedule was the 4 x 7.5-kilometer relay, and even though the Soviet Union won the gold medal, it was in spite of, not because of, Tikhonov's performance.

That Aleksandr Tikhonov had lost the Olympic gold medal by one penalty minute to Magnar Solberg in Grenoble only intensified Soviet efforts to win the 20-kilometer individual event in Sapporo four years later. The outlook was propitious: even though Tikhonov took second place at the 1971 Biathlon World Championships in Hämeenlinna, Finland, behind Dieter Speer of East Germany, he was able to finish ahead of Solberg in third. This was an extremely competitive race: the adjusted time separating the gold medal from the bronze was one minute forty seconds. In addition, Viktor Mamatov and Rinnat Safin finished in the top six. A decisive victory in the relay a few days later bolstered the confidence of the Soviet team.[48] In Sapporo, the Olympic 20-kilometer race was set for 8 February 1972, a day that brought unseasonable rain and severe winds to the biathlon venue. Despite these conditions, the course officials decided to start the race, then with a majority of competitors out on the course, abruptly canceled and rescheduled for the next day. "I think," wrote Aleksandr Privalov after the Games, "that because of this our biathletes suffered more than the others. The psychological rise of our team and the mood for winning of all its members was at an extraordinary height . . . but to get it together twice, as every specialist knows, is really, really difficult." The restart was especially hard on Tikhonov, who had been leading the aborted race of 8 February. At the conclusion of the competition the next day, Tikhonov finished out of the medals in fourth place, with Mamatov, Biakov and Safin behind him in seventh, twelfth and nineteenth respectively. Especially galling for the Soviet team was that Sweden, East Germany and Norway took the three pedestal spots. For Tikhonov in particular it was devastating that his nemesis, Magnar Solberg of Norway, had now won his second straight Olympic gold medal in the 20-kilometer biathlon event.[49]

The disastrous results from the individual race increased the significance of the relay for the biathletes of the USSR, and consequently the level of performance anxiety. On the day of the competition, the coaching staff appointed Tikhonov to ski in the lead-off position. All went well during the first stage of prone shooting, but when he returned to the firing line for standing, Tikhonov only hit three out of five targets and had to take two penalty loops. Having slipped into fifth place from first, Tikhonov was in pursuit of the leaders on the final stretch when he broke a ski. As he hobbled toward the exchange area, East Germany's Dieter Speer was out on the course warming up to run the third leg of the relay; he immediately offered one of his skis as a replacement. Tikhonov skied to the finish and just managed to hand off to Rinnat Safin in an uncharacteristic ninth place. Safin unleashed a remarkable effort to take the lead by fifty-five seconds. With a brilliant performance by Viktor Mamatov on the last leg, they salvaged the gold medal for the Soviet Union. However, the entire Soviet squad was indebted to Speer for this impressive gesture of sportsmanship.[50] That evening, Morton observed Mamatov and Safin celebrating in the athletes' dining hall. After the meal the American led a few others to the Russians' quarters to negotiate some trades. The Soviet minders waved them past, and as Morton made his way down the corridor, "I could hear Tikhonov shouting in Russian through an open door. Mamatov and Safin were standing at attention, thumbs down the crease of their pants, and Tikhonov, who was much shorter than they were, was slapping them in the face with his open hand. We decided that this was probably not a good time for a visit."[51]

Morton's recollection is indicative of Tikhonov's temperamental and at times imperious attitude. Occasionally this irritable haughtiness could backfire. In 1978, after he placed out of the medals in all three events at the World Championships for the first time in eleven years, one writer asked him why he did not win. "I didn't want to," Tikhonov snapped. The follow-up article read "Tikhonov didn't want to win the World Championships."[52] The flashy showmanship that he enjoyed was sometimes imprudent as well: finishing the final leg of the relay at the 1977 World Championships, the last time large-bore firearms were used in biathlon, Tikhonov took his rifle off before crossing the finish line and threw it barrel-first into the snow. This antic could have disqualified his team because he had not carried his rifle the entire distance of the race course.[53]

Nevertheless, Tikhonov remained an energetic self-promoter, always conscious of the mystique he generated among biathlon's cognoscenti and the public at large. Posturing as a man's man in one of the world's most masculine sports, he was fond of "quoting" the American novelist Ernest Hemingway with concocted snippets such as: "A real man should know how to shoot."[54] The government and the Soviet press worked together to encourage his macho image. In one particular instance worthy of its own Hemingway sketch, Tikhonov's derring-do earned him the Order of the Red Star, awarded by the government for bravery in service to the state. Returning on the train from Kirov to Novosibirsk after the USSR National Championships of 1969 and fresh from his victory over Solberg at the Zakopane World Championships, Tikhonov and fellow biathlete Vladimir Mel'nikov apprehended an escaped convict who had harmed several passengers. Various versions of this story appeared in the press, all equally thrilling. The criminal, armed either with a single knife or sometimes with two blades, one in each hand, had inflicted wounds on a number of railway workers and fellow travelers. In one rendition, Tikhonov and Mel'nikov heard shouts for help from the restaurant car; in another they were roused from sleep by a knock on the door of their compartment and the screams of a woman lying in the corridor covered with blood. TASS News Agency reported that Tikhonov was afraid of striking innocent bystanders with rounds from his firearm, the obvious choice of weaponry in such a situation; he therefore armed himself with the rifle's cleaning rod instead. It is worth noting that the cleaning rod for a rifle is most often a flexible piece of equipment similar to an old-style car antenna, perhaps not the best selection for facing an opponent with a knife. Relating this story to Stanislav Tokarev in 1976, Tikhonov more plausibly suggested that he found a crowbar in the kitchen before approaching the criminal. No matter the choice of truncheon, a struggle ensued during which the criminal kicked out a window and leapt from the train. Tikhonov pulled the emergency brake and jumped down in pursuit, with Mel'nikov close behind. They grabbed the fugitive and returned to the train, handing him over to the authorities at the Kungur train station. In appreciation of their "manly actions" the government awarded both Tikhonov and Mel'nikov the Order of the Red Star.[55]

To many observers, Tikhonov appeared to function outside of the normal strictures imposed by the government on international athletes, in marked contrast to Soviet biathletes of an earlier generation such as Privalov and Melanin. He was outgoing and eager to associate with athletes from the West, even accompanying Finnish athletes out to restaurants while attending training camps in Finland.[56] Never shy about making his wishes known, Tikhonov hinted to John Morton over the years that he wanted to acquire an American-made Winchester sport rifle with mounted scope. For the 1976 Olympic Games, Morton and head coach Bill Spencer arranged to have one prepared for him with a special inscription in Russian. "Several of us presented the rifle to Tikhonov in our hotel in Seefeld, during the Olympics," Morton recalls, "and he had tears streaming down his cheeks."[57] The story of the Winchester rifle appears in Tikhonov's 2006 biography, *Aleksandr Tikhonov's Penalty Loop*, which details how he smuggled the firearm back into the USSR hidden in his ski bag.[58] That there was no search of Tikhonov's luggage as the team returned home indicates that the Soviet government accorded Tikhonov extraordinary privileges, beyond those extended even to the nation's top athletes. At the Lake Placid Biathlon World Championships in 1973, Tikhonov borrowed United States currency from Morton in order to buy several pairs of blue jeans to take back home and sell on the black market, returning the loan during the Biathlon World Championships at Minsk in 1974. Both Morton and Martin Hagen recall that Tikhonov ferried them around Minsk several times in his own personal Lada automobile unaccompanied by any other government official. On another occasion Morton and several other United States athletes observed Tikhonov at the stadium in Minsk dressing down a young soldier who had the temerity to demand that he remove his vehicle from a restricted parking area.[59]

The apparent ease with which he operated around foreign athletes without interference from government agents, in conjunction with his humiliation of Mamatov and Safin in Sapporo and the Red Army parking attendant in Minsk, suggests that Tikhonov was a high-ranking KGB official. Tikhonov's ability to smuggle a rifle from the West back into Russia in the mid-1970s corroborates this opinion: customs service came under the aegis of KGB and the police, and because these security forces sponsored Dinamo, the club's athletes were exempt from border customs control.[60] Tikhonov was forthright about his association with KGB in a private conversation he had with Morton. On one of the Minsk car excursions, the American asked him about his military rank and in which branch of the armed forces he served. "Police," was Tikhonov's reply. "You mean military police, keeping soldiers in line?" Morton pressed. "No. Secret Police."[61] Despite his affiliations, Tikhonov was not reluctant to offer an iconoclast's view of the Soviet system. After retiring from active racing in 1980, he served as coach for an "experimental" national biathlon team. "I've always been against the strict limitations that are accepted in our sport," Tikhonov said in a 1989 interview. "Many times I've observed this scene: before the women's relay the Norwegian skiers are having a good time, while our girls are each in their own rooms, isolated under unrelenting supervision, 'making up their mind' for victory. The next morning the Norwegians win and we make a mess of it."[62]

It should be noted that Tikhonov expressed his oblique opinion of the USSR's sport policy nearly a decade after retiring from active biathlon competition, during the era of Mikhail Gorbachev's policy of openness and transparency, or *glasnost'*, just prior to the disintegration of the Soviet Union. Yet in his heyday as the world's foremost biathlete, during the Brezhnev decades, Tikhonov was the consummate communist, the very embodiment of the socialist camp's notion of the sport, and arguably one of the most recognizable athletes in the Soviet Union: "I don't think," recalled Olympic diver Vladimir Aleinik, "that in Soviet times there was even one person in the nation who didn't know who Aleksandr Tikhonov was."[63] It was in this capacity that Tikhonov received the ceremonial keys to the world's most advanced biathlon complex at Raubichi on the outskirts of Minsk in February 1974, for the purpose of opening the Thirteenth Biathlon World Championships. This was the first ski event of such magnitude ever held within the borders of the Soviet Union. Media coverage had started more than a month before the opening ceremonies and expectations for the nation's team were high. At the time nine Olympic and world championship medals accrued to Tikhonov's credit, and his resume needed no varnish. But without a doubt the world's most successful biathlete was now dealing with extraordinary pressure in a sport that already required nerves of steel.[64]

NINE

Minsk
Thirteenth Biathlon World Championships, 1974

In late February 1974, the Soviet Union's decades-long drive for recognition as a major ski power soared to a new level when two skiers from the USSR placed first and third in the junior men's 15-kilometer biathlon, winning the first medals ever awarded at an international world championship ski race on Soviet soil. Headlines in *Sovetskii sport* had been trumpeting the fact that these were the first races of such magnitude ever held in the USSR, and after the opening competition *Pravda* summarized the significance in one headline: "And a GTO Badge on His Chest: The First Victory at the Biathlon World Championship." The gold medal winner was Sergei Khokhulia, a junior racer representing the Novosibirsk club Chkalovets who hailed from the same region as biathlon greats Viktor Mamatov and Aleksandr Tikhonov. "His character?" said Tikhonov after the race. "His character is Siberian." The Ready for Labor and Defense program had saved the Soviet Union during the Great Patriotic War, and now GTO proved remunerative once again as a third generation of athletes prepared to follow in the footsteps of two of the nation's most successful athletes, Tikhonov and Mamatov, in a sport they helped define. "The new champion of the world [Khokhulia] traversed the ski track wearing a gold GTO badge on his chest," wrote *Sovetskii sport*'s correspondent Stanislav Tokarev, echoing *Pravda*. "Of course it's one of his own. And how fortunate."[1] With such an auspicious start, the Thirteenth Biathlon World Championships were certain to be a socialist *tour de force* played out before a supportive and enthusiastic home crowd.

1974: The Year of Change

The World Championships in Minsk were a watershed event in the sport of biathlon beyond their significance for the Soviet Union. Just one week earlier at the Nordic World Championships in Falun, Sweden, two Austrian ski manufacturers, Fischer and Kneissl, revolutionized cross-country ski racing by introducing synthetic fiberglass skis into international competition. On 17 February, Thomas Magnusson of Sweden won the opening race over 30 kilometers on a pair of Kneissls. The results electrified the ski world: "Today's newspapers are returning readers to the subject of Thomas Magnusson's victory in the 30-kilometer race," wrote *Pravda* two days later. "Many correspondents are emphasizing that the Swede's success was partly due to a novelty—plastic skis which, it turns out, eight of the fifteen best skiers used in the competition."[2] Although Norwegian Magne Myrmo won a world championship title in the 15-kilometer event on wooden skis a few days later, he was the last male competitor ever to do so. Only .52 of a second behind Myrmo that day was Gerhard Grimmer of the German Democratic Republic (GDR), on fiberglass skis that also carried him to victory at the end of the week in the 50-kilometer race just ahead of Magnusson.[3]

The results from Falun were the harbinger of change in cross-country skiing and biathlon for a number of reasons. First and foremost, it was apparent that the era of wooden skis was over, and ski manufacturers, racers and coaches were frantic to adapt to the new technology. Biathletes preparing for the Minsk World Championships—scheduled to start just a few days after Falun—scrambled to lay their hands on fiberglass skis. Film footage and photographs from Minsk reveal that Aleksandr Tikhonov skied on a pair of Fischers during the 20-kilometer race and perhaps on Kneissls during the 10-kilometer sprint; and Finland's Juhani Suutarinen had Kneissl skis for all the events. John Morton remembers that as Suutarinen crossed the finish line at these races, his coaches would remove his fiberglass skis and replace them with a pair made by Järvinen, Finland's premier manufacturer of wooden racing skis. But the advent of fiberglass skis sounded the death-knell for Scandinavian companies such as Järvinen that had crafted skis from wood for almost half a century: during the 1975 competitive season, every racer in Europe was using fiberglass skis; by the following year there were no wooden skis found at any major ski competition anywhere in the world.[4]

Due to the increased speed of fiberglass skis, the technique of Nordic skiing underwent a tremendous change too. The camber of these skis created a "pocket" under the foot that lifted the grip wax out of the snow as the ski was in its glide phase. On either side of this grip wax pocket, on the tips and tails of the ski, skiers began to apply speed wax that Alpine racers used to increase glide on their slalom and downhill skis. But fiberglass cross-country skis were stiffer than wooden models and thus required a more pronounced application of force under the ball of the foot to drive the grip wax into the snow when the skier needed purchase on an uphill. Double poling with the grip wax out of the snow now proved more efficient than diagonal stride for a skier travelling over a greater variety of terrain. Because of the different combinations of grip and glide wax employed on these types of skis, the science of base preparation for cross-country racing took a giant leap forward in the years after Falun. In addition, new technological processes were introduced into the manufacture of other articles of ski equipment, such as carbon-fiber ski poles and plastic-soled boot and binding combinations.[5] The ultimate result of these faster fiberglass skis, more sophisticated waxes, stiffer poles, boots and bindings and greater emphasis on double-poling was the adoption of ski-skating technique in the early 1980s.

Another significant but less noticed result of the Falun races was the success of the East German Ski Team, whose members won the most medals. As the USSR's most proficient students of socialist sport, the East Germans were on the threshold of dominating cross-country ski racing in 1974 after a disastrous turn at the 1972 Sapporo Winter Games.[6] Although the skiers of the Soviet women's cross-country team continued to capture the bulk of the medals in their events at Falun—Raisa Smetanina took bronze in the 5-kilometer race behind gold medalist Galina Kulakova, the victor in the 10-kilometer contest and anchor of the USSR's winning effort in the 4 x 5-kilometer relay—the world's male-oriented sporting press remained fixated on the men's races. In this realm the Soviet National Team came up short in comparison to the skiers of the GDR, especially Gerhard Grimmer, who took away one silver and two gold medals. Vasilii Rochev captured the Soviet Union's sole individual medal, a bronze in the 15-kilometer race, and the relay team lost the gold medal to the East Germans at the finish line by just over nine seconds. "Has the National Team of the USSR just now lost its leadership role in the world of skiing?" M. Zubko, *Izvestiia*'s special correspondent in Falun asked his readers in response to this East German display of power.[7] Just as American Bill Koch would fuel a surge of interest in cross-country ski racing all across North America after his silver medal performance in the 30-kilometer race at the 1976 Innsbruck Olympics, so Grimmer's success in Falun inspired a new generation of world-class skiers in the GDR.[8]

In biathlon, the notion that the Soviet Union could lose its supremacy seemed preposterous at the time: from 1958 through 1977, the top five most successful biathletes in the world were Aleksandr Tikhonov, Viktor Mamatov, Nikolai Kruglov, Rinnat Safin and Vladimir Melanin; and out of the top twenty competitors on the list over half were from the Soviet Union. Dieter Speer was the sole East German even close to this elite group at number twenty-two. Yet Zubko proved prescient, because by the end of the decade, the GDR's biathletes began to displace those of the Soviet Union as champions in the ski-shooting sport: from 1978 through 1998, six of the top twenty most successful biathletes were East Germans compared to only four from the USSR.[9] Although East German skiers were officially "sportsman-comrades" of the Soviets, a certain degree of animosity existed between the two groups. In an unguarded moment of conversation with John Morton, Tikhonov acknowledged the mutual dislike the Germans and Russians had for one another, stemming from World War II hostilities. Art Stegen recalls that one East German biathlete confessed to him that "the Russians are supposed to be our Communist comrades, but they still see us as their enemy."[10] Thus, the rise to prominence of East Germany in cross-country skiing, biathlon and other international sports that developed in the mid-1970s concerned the Soviet Union on more levels than just a superficial one defined by medals and athletic prowess.

The inclusion at Minsk of the first 10-kilometer sprint ever contested at a world biathlon championship also prefigured a transformation of the sport by the end of the century. The sprint was a hybrid event developed in East Germany that incorporated the regimen and fast pace of the relay with the interval start format of the 20-kilometer race. From its inception in the late 1960s, the 10-kilometer sprint was an immediate success: at Minsk, even on a Thursday morning in February, the 10-kilometer event for juniors attracted around ten thousand spectators. "The [biathlon] sprint and the relay," opined *Sovetskii sport*, "are the most exciting and emotional events."[11] The popularity of this type of race paved the way for significant changes in the rules of biathlon by the end of the 1970s. Just as in the relay, biathletes shot at five breakable targets, once from the prone position and once from standing (for a total of ten), which gave spectators a thrilling show at the range and provided the athletes with immediate feedback concerning their marksmanship. Glass discs suspended on nails had superseded balloons by 1974 as targets for both the sprint and the relay, but inventors were busy designing metal knock-down silhouettes that became the standard after the 1980 Olympics. The heavy metal fabrication necessary for withstanding the force of a large-bore rifle made this type of target impractical and contributed in no small way to the switch from large-bore to .22-caliber rifles as of the 1976 through 1977 ski season. By 1982, knock-down targets had replaced paper in the 20-kilometer race as well, completing a total makeover of the sport of biathlon. No longer was it a "double contest" split equally between rifle marksmanship and ski racing; rather, biathlon had become simply a ski race that included shooting.[12]

Finally, the state-of-the-art biathlon facilities that the Soviets constructed at Raubichi, a village twenty-six kilometers outside of Minsk, were unprecedented in 1974. "The new site," effused Horst Schiefelbein of East Germany's *Neues Deutschland*, "presents in its modernity and practicality absolutely the *non plus ultra* for biathletes."[13] Athletes, coaches and officials from the West were equally impressed, and the Raubichi grounds influenced the development of other complexes in Europe. Subsequent World Championships at Antholz-Anterselva, Italy, in 1975, Hochfilzen, Austria, in 1978 and Ruhpolding, West Germany, in 1979 included many of the updated features, such as an electronic reader board, automated target systems and a commodious arena utilized in the Soviet Union. These advancements marked a significant turning point in the ability to host the larger crowds that eventually adopted biathlon as a popular winter spectacle by the late 1980s. That a biathlon race could attract huge numbers of fans was perhaps the greatest legacy of the Minsk World Championships, a fact not lost on officials of the International Modern Pentathlon and Biathlon Union (UIPMB) in attendance there.[14]

Sport as Spectacle

"In the Soviet Union," wrote sport sociologist N. I. Ponomarev in 1981, "sport has become an important part of public life. Therefore the sports spectacle has become a meaningful social phenomenon."[15] Although sport spectacles were common enough in the Soviet Union, beginning with the Spartakiada of 1928 and Stalin-era parades through Red Square during the 1930s, the growth of sport in the Soviet Union as a spectator event was a post-war phenomenon. Robert Edelman suggests that initially Soviet audiences may have been somewhat indifferent to the sports in which the teams of the USSR were excelling. However, the cumulative effect of victories across a variety of sports year after year, combined with a continuous barrage of media coverage, instilled a sense of patriotic pride in the

Soviet populace.[16] Arguably the greatest factor contributing to the growth of sport as a part of the social fabric within Soviet society was the Cold War. For the Soviet government, international competition at the very highest levels had a relationship to the complexities of world diplomacy, and high-profile events such as the Olympics played a crucial role in the foreign relations of the nation. The superpower struggle that played out at international sporting events heightened the visibility and popularity of such competitions as they evolved into a surrogate for the military rivalry between the Eastern Bloc and the West. Within this matrix, the Biathlon World Championships at Minsk were perhaps the most significant international competitions ever held in the Soviet Union until the Moscow Summer Olympics of 1980.

As a commentator on sports viewed through a Marxist lens, Ponomarev is keen to point out that sports events in the capitalist countries of Europe and the United States had been subsumed by rampant commercialism, obscuring the "educational essence" of sport. Crucial to this concept is that sports spectacles performed a number of functions in socialist society, including education in the moral code of communism and constant improvement in socialist social relations. Most important of all, however, is that sport demonstrated "the socially valuable qualities of the individual" such as "collectivism, courage, daring, initiative, discipline, friendliness to teammates and respect for them, selflessness [and] staunchness when facing an opponent."[17] And in this respect, the Soviet sports hero connected the socialist citizen with success in the international arena: "We live in our sports heroes," wrote journalist Stanislav Tokarev, "and they in us. They are together with us."[18] The Minsk World Championships provided ample demonstration of these socialist precepts as they unfolded before a massive Soviet audience crowding the ski tracks of Raubichi.

"Accept Flowers, Guests of Minsk!"[19]

The notion of spectacle certainly infused the Minsk festivities. The region had been promoting itself as the center for Belarus ski activity since the late 1940s, hosting national, regional and municipal biathlon competitions beginning in 1958. For this unprecedented international gathering, the Minsk sports committee officials pulled out all the stops. In the week leading up to the opening ceremonies, the committee organized a program for visitors to attend a variety of events around the city at museums, theaters and other sites. These activities ran the gamut, from a visit to the site of the Katyn Massacre to an evening at the circus. On 23 February the world's greatest biathlete, Aleksandr Tikhonov, received a ceremonial key to the Raubichi biathlon complex. Before a bank of photographers and journalists he cut a ribbon to open the firing range and ski course to foreign skiers and coaches.[20] Tikhonov had personally gone to the Minsk airport earlier in the week with film crew in tow to greet the contingent from the United States upon its arrival. "We had to remain on the tarmac inside the Aeroflot plane," remembers John Morton. "Then Soviet officials came on board and told everyone to wait while I was escorted down the stairs to meet Tikhonov. He made a big show for the cameras welcoming his friend from America."[21] The official opening ceremonies on 25 February were billed as a "sport-theatrical celebration" to be held in the brand-new Minsk Palace of Sport. The gala affair was completely sold out by seven o'clock in the evening. As projectors flashed images of the flags of the participating nations on the walls, strains of "The March of the Biathletes," a composition written by I. M. Luchenok especially for the occasion, resounded through the hall. After a procession of athletes into the Palace of Sport and a round of speeches by the chairman of the Union of Belarus Ministers and UIPMB president Sven Thofelt, a variety of performances took place: an artistic presentation by Olga Shutova; songs from Valerii Kuchinskii; music by the ensemble Pesniary; and a presentation of "The Biathletes" from a Minsk pantomime troupe. The highlight of the evening was a demonstration of floor exercise gymnastics by the most famous international sport celebrities in Belarus, Olympic individual– and team–gold medalist Olga Korbut and her team–gold medal compatriot Antonina Koshel.[22]

Throughout the week at the biathlon complex in Raubichi, the festival atmosphere was enhanced by pomp and circumstance each day as giant samovars dispensed hot tea for thirsty spectators. A variety of dignitaries visited the site as the week progressed, including USSR Sports Minister S. P. Pavlov, Politburo member Pavel Masherov and cosmonaut Viktor Gorbatko.[23] On the day of the first race, rockets soared into the air to signify the start of the world championship series. The results of the junior 15-kilometer event on that opening day followed the presumed socialist script: the Soviet Union owned the podium with the nation's gold and bronze medals (while two other USSR skiers and a Pole made it into the top ten as well), aided by veteran biathletes Vladimir Melanin and Vladimir Gundartsev who radioed information to head coach Privalov as his racers circled the course. *Pravda* summed up the day's results: "All-in-all one can say that on the initial day of the championship, the sun of victory beamed on our sportsmen." All eyes were now focused on the following day's event, the men's 20-kilometer race.[24]

For biathletes of the USSR the 20-kilometer race was "'their' distance."[25] Since the initial World Championship in 1958, Soviet skiers had captured twenty-two out of a possible forty-eight world championship and Olympic medals in this contest as of 1973. After his silver medal at the 1968 Olympics, Tikhonov himself had won the race at the world championships three times and placed second once in the subsequent five years. The prospects for winning again were favorable, according to Privalov, because the entire Soviet squad was showing signs of improvement: "In the past, frankly speaking, Tikhonov was head and shoulders above his teammates. At this point, Tikhonov hasn't become weaker, it's just that his teammates have gotten better too, and are approaching his level."[26] But earlier in the season, Tikhonov had been struggling. At a January race in Raubichi for the USSR Cup in biathlon, he shot five penalty minutes in a 10-kilometer sprint event, allegedly having problems adjusting to a new rifle. Leaving nothing at risk, Privalov had Tikhonov return to his old rifle for the races in Minsk, assisted by a group of technicians from the Bio-Energy Laboratories of the All-Union Scientific-Experimental Institute of Physical Culture and an inventor from Izhevsk who had fashioned a special light filter for the rifle sights to aid in shooting during stormy conditions.[27]

A special apparatus for poor light was unnecessary on 27 February, however, the day of the first men's event. Unseasonably warm weather had reduced the ski tracks to a thin band of snow wending its way over the ski course under bright sunshine. Thousands of Red Army soldiers assisted in moving snow around the Raubichi complex to fill in the race tracks, which had turned to ice through the continuous melt-and-freeze cycles. Just as they had in Falun the previous week, the hard, icy tracks proved an ideal medium for the new fast fiberglass skis.[28] The situation could not have been more propitious for Tikhonov: he had his feet clipped onto a pair of Fischer skis and bib number 27 about his torso, a good omen since it was the twenty-seventh of February. In addition, he had won his first world championship race in Zakopane five years before wearing that same number. Tikhonov was skiing on his home turf before a large, supportive crowd. This race was his to lose.

Tikhonov started well that morning. He cleaned his targets at both the first prone and standing bouts, dazzling onlookers with his signature twirl of the rifle as he removed it from his back in preparation for shooting, and the fans voiced their approval. "From the starting line," wrote *Sovetskii sport*'s special correspondent, "one could tell exactly at which place he was out on the course by the deafening roar of the spectators."[29] But matters took a turn for the worse as the race progressed. At each of his last two trips to the firing range Tikhonov accrued two minutes of penalty, for a final total of four, leaving him in fifth place. "It's clear the Soviet sportsman completely lost his nerve," was *Izvestiia*'s post-race analysis.[30] His teammates fared no better: Ivan Biakov placed seventh, while Gennadii Kovalev was sixteenth, followed by Nikolai Kruglov in seventeenth. "Up until now," lamented *Sovetskii sport*, "biathletes of the Soviet Union had never performed so badly." Perhaps it was the vociferous crowd that threw Tikhonov and his teammates off their game. His personal trainer, Evgenii Glinskii, told *Sovetskii sport* that Tikhonov unwittingly increased his ski tempo as he hurtled through "the continuous corridor of spectators."[31] This phenomenon affected other racers as well: "It was difficult skiing there because the crowd was yelling and encouraging you the entire way around the track," recalls Art Stegen who represented the United States in this race. "[There was] no place to 'back off' the pace."[32]

The day belonged to the Soviet Union's arch-rival Finland. Surprising almost everyone in attendance, thirty-one-year-old Juhani Suutarinen shot only one minute of penalty to win the world championship title ahead of another dark-horse contender, Gheorge Girnitsa of Romania. The bronze medal went to Norway's Tor Svendsberget, just ahead of Suutarinen's teammate Heikki Ikola in fourth.[33] Out of the top ten finishers, three were Finns, all of whom were on fiberglass skis or wood-plastic hybrids. "I remember the astonishingly fast speed of the Finns on the downhills before the shooting range," wrote three-time world champion biathlete Vladimir Melanin after the race. "The Finnish biathletes, calmly saving their energy, descended smoothly." Melanin expressed alarm that in sheer track-speed alone, Ikola had outdistanced Tikhonov in the 20-kilometer race by nineteen seconds; and over the final 2.5-kilometer loop, Ikola, Suutarinen and Svendsberget had all skied faster than the USSR's top biathlete.[34]

Melanin's commentary was more than just an analysis of a ski race however: it went to the heart of the Cold War's fraught environment. The policy of Finlandization made for a tense association between the USSR and Finland after World War II, tinged with old Winter War memories and new Cold War anxieties. During the era of détente in the late 1960s and early 1970s, tensions between the United States and the Soviet Union relaxed to a certain extent. However, this relaxation encouraged Czechoslovakia to assume a more independent stance, culminating in a Soviet-led

Warsaw Pact invasion in 1968. Concurrently the USSR tightened its hold on Finland when it no longer recognized Finnish neutrality. By exploiting contemporary youth's infatuation with student radicalism and the Left's increasing influence, the Soviet Union hoped to produce a gradual transition to communism in Finland. With the violent end to the Prague Spring in 1968, however, many Finns began to fear a Soviet occupation of their country, producing a swing back to a more conservative agenda during the early 1970s. Over the next decade, this uneasy balance fostered a biathlon rivalry between the two nations that was legendary as each vied for superiority in this sport-as-war surrogate. In Minsk, Finland was in the process of unleashing a concerted effort to dethrone the Soviets as gold medalists in biathlon, a policy that was reaping abundant rewards.[35]

The morning after the debacle in the men's 20-kilometer race, the juniors were back on the track for their 10-kilometer sprint and the excitement was palpable: "Every day the competitions in biathlon are attracting more and more fans," wrote V. Nemenov, *Sovetskaia Belorussiia*'s special correspondent to the World Championships. "Early in the morning today Minsk residents arrived in Raubichi and filled the special viewing areas, from which there is a beautiful vista of the shooting range and various parts of the ski course . . . this time there were around ten thousand spectators."[36] Although the inflation of statistics was endemic to Soviet journalism, independent observations corroborate these numbers. Two of the competitors in the 10-kilometer race were Martin Hagen and Russell Scott, junior racers from Jackson Hole, Wyoming. Both were astounded by the number of people on hand. Scott's recollection is that the spectator count as reported in this article was too low: "There were tens of thousands in the crowd that day, four to five deep, right up to the edge of the track. They would reach out and touch you on the shoulder." Scott, who was having an exceptionally good race that morning, recalls that one of the Soviet coaches ran out into the track to push him up and over one of the last hills. "We were treated very well in Minsk," Scott says. "There was never any interference and the crowd was cheering for everybody."[37] The final results were only a slight improvement over the previous day for the Soviet Union. East Germany's Steffen Thierfelder won the race less than three seconds ahead of Erkki Antila of Finland. "By profession he's a border guard, like the majority of Finnish biathletes," sniffed *Sovetskii sport*. Igor Gruzdev of the USSR managed to capture the bronze medal, but Sergei Khokhulia, his teammate and gold medalist from the 15-kilometer event at the beginning of the week, placed a distant thirty-second. "It always happens to me," he told the press. "After the joy there are always *hu-u-ge* disappointments." A twelfth- and twentieth-place finish for the other two Russians entered in this event rounded out a disconcerting end to the day. "They say that the sprint is a lottery," was *Sovetskii sport*'s assessment of the race. "Perhaps this new distance takes a new type of biathlete, one especially feisty and determined."[38]

The next event on the docket was the junior 3 x 7.5-kilometer relay held on 1 March, predestined by the Soviet press to be a "battle for the prizes" among the teams of Finland, the Soviet Union and the GDR.[39] This day however, turned out to be the low point of the week for the Soviet biathlon team: the relay trio finished out of the medals in fourth place behind a surprisingly strong surge by Poland for the bronze medal and East Germany for silver. The clear winner in the event was the team from Finland, which led the field for most of the race and finished more than half a minute ahead of the pack. "Our guests are getting all the awards," was the baleful headline in *Sovetskaia Belorussia* after the mid-point of the week's events, acknowledging the superiority of Finland's athletes throughout the bulk of the competition: "It's not necessary to say much about the Finnish sportsmen. The two gold and two silver medals speak for themselves."[40] This was more than the staff of correspondents from *Sovetskii sport* was willing to concede, however. For these reporters, the comrade-skiers of the GDR were Russia's chief rivals in Minsk.[41]

Sovetskii sport was philosophical in the aftermath of the junior 3 x 7.5-kilometer relay. "After a knockdown, of course, you can't beat yourself up," the paper editorialized, although the pages in the days following became a forum for analyzing the dismal performance of the current generation of Soviet biathletes in Minsk. For Vladimir Melanin, it was psychological pressure on the shooting range that had been the junior racers' undoing in the relay.[42] Nikolai Puzanov and Vladimir Gundartsev, gold medalists along with Tikhonov and Mamatov at the 1968 Olympic biathlon relay, focused on the skiing. "In my opinion, [Sergei Khokhulia] simply 'burned out' and was beaten by his rivals long before the start," declared Gundartsev. The Finns and Norwegians were skiing well, he continued, but "the biathletes of the GDR have made the greatest impression on me."[43] For Puzanov, it was the inability of the Soviet team to adapt to the new exigencies of ski racing presented at the current World Championships: "The tracks are fast and difficult at Raubichi, so one has to go as energetically as possible, you have to accelerate and accelerate."[44] Even East Germany's Dieter Speer, now a coach for the GDR National Team, was allotted space for his viewpoint, one that must have given pause to the readers of *Sovetskii sport*: "The track here is tough and we love it like that. When our head coach Kurt Kintz arrived in Raubichi he said to us: 'This is our course.'"[45]

On the eve of the final individual race, the men's 10-kilometer sprint, the USSR had won only three medals out of a possible ten awards during the week—and only one of these was gold. Pressure on the Soviet senior team was enormous: so disappointing were the results at Raubichi that *Pravda* dropped its coverage from Minsk the day after the opening race. Because the new 10-kilometer race format was so similar to that of the 4 x 7.5-kilometer relay, the Soviet Union, in theory, would field the world's best sprint specialists in the competition—since the Winter Olympics of 1968 through the 1973 World Championships in Lake Placid, New York, the Soviet Union had never lost the biathlon relay. Therefore, the coaching staff chose the most experienced relay racers on the squad for Saturday's race. Aleksandr Tikhonov, of course, was a double gold medalist at the Lake Placid World Championships the year before. Ivan Biakov was his teammate on the gold-medal Soviet relay team at the 1972 Sapporo Winter Olympics; he had also shot only two penalty minutes in his 20-kilometer individual race earlier in the week at Minsk. Aleksandr Ushakov owned one world championship gold medal from the relay at the 1970 World Championships in Östersund, Sweden. He had also posted top-ten finishes in both the 1970 and 1971 World Championship 20-kilometer individual race, although he slipped to sixteenth in that event at Lake Placid in 1973. Rounding out the field was newcomer Nikolai Kruglov, a metalworker from the Gorkii factory Krasnoe Sormovo who had taken up biathlon while serving with the Ural district air defense and continued his training in Gorkii with Trud sport club. In his first world championship start earlier in the week he shot five minutes of penalty to finish seventeenth.[46]

The race was scheduled for Saturday morning and once again a large crowd made its way out of Minsk to the race site: "On the day of the championship streams of transport vehicles on the streets of Minsk flow into the single arterial connecting the city with the arena . . . the appearance of the best biathletes in the world is never met with indifference. Tourists and excursion groups are making corrections in their routes and including one more stop—Raubichi."[47] Film footage and photographs from Saturday's race reveal an incredible number of fans and spectators in the stands and lining areas along both sides of the ski track, in some places five and six deep, in others mere inches from the point where the racers were planting their poles.[48] But the day turned into one of disappointment for these masses gathered at Raubichi. Perhaps they could not have expected matters to take a turn for the worse after the junior relay the day before: yet the best Soviet finish was Kruglov in sixth place, with the rest of the Russians finishing far out of the medals: Tikhonov was eleventh, Ushakov fourteenth and Biakov ended up at the bottom of the list, in fortieth place out of fifty-six competitors. This was far more discouraging than the Soviet effort in the 20-kilometer race earlier in the week. Worst of all, the Finn Juhani Suutarinen had taken another individual gold medal and an East German, Günther Bartnick, had captured silver. Sweden's Torsten Wadman crossed the finish line in third for bronze.[49]

"We ask the forgiveness of our readers for calling attention to quite a few numbers right from the start [of the article]," wrote *Sovetskii sport* the next day. "But we ask as well that you scrutinize these numbers carefully, since one of the main causes of our sportsmen's failure lies at the bottom of them." Statistics from the sprint event revealed the vast differences between the 20-kilometer race, in which competitors shot at paper targets and were penalized with either one or two extra minutes added to the total ski time for each missed shot, and this new iteration of biathlon with breakable targets and a penalty loop. The paper's analysis indicated that Suutarinen had taken thirty-three seconds to fire five bullets from the prone position and only twenty-eight to complete five shots standing, for a total of sixty-one seconds, with just two penalty loops as the result. Bartnick's performance was seven seconds faster overall but with four penalty loops; however, his errors in marksmanship may have stemmed from a tremendous fall on the first downhill after which he entered the range with face and knees covered in blood. By comparison, Kruglov was six seconds slower than Suutarinen firing prone and nine seconds slower standing, totaling seventy-six seconds, but he still missed four shots, resulting in an extra 600 meters of skiing. Tikhonov spent an additional five seconds shooting prone and seventeen seconds for his standing shots for a total of eighty-three seconds, yet accrued five subsequent trips around the penalty loop. Ushakov, who had taken 110 seconds for his ten shots at the range, came in for particularly blistering criticism from the paper:

> Staring at the stopwatch after Aleksandr [Ushakov] pulled the trigger for the third time we couldn't believe our eyes. Raising and then lowering the barrel of his rifle, he wasted fifty-five seconds between shots. We note, by the way, that the best were circling the penalty loop in around twenty-eight seconds and the majority of biathletes in around thirty. Consequently, in

the time he was spending, Ushakov could have run around that unfortunate loop twice.[50]

Whether intentionally or not, a cartoon that appeared in *Sovetskaia Belorussiia* on the same day as this *Sovetskii sport* article lampoons the disastrous results of the Russian biathletes at Raubichi's shooting range. In the first panel, a competitor has abandoned his rifle for a slingshot; in the next, he has replaced a ski pole with his ostensibly useless rifle; and in the third, the hapless biathlete has placed his rifle in the snow, thrown both poles at the target and removed one of his skis to launch like a javelin in the same direction.[51]

The conclusion for Soviet observers was that the Finnish and East German skiers had fired their rifles faster and more accurately than the top biathletes of the Soviet Union, who could not make up the difference over the shorter, 10-kilometer sprint distance after multiple trips around the penalty loop.[52] Methodical and careful shooting such as Ushakov displayed was worthwhile in the longer race, but in the sprint, firing more quickly and more accurately than anyone had thought possible was the key to victory, as Juhani Suutarinen had just proven. For Tikhonov, Suutarinen's performance throughout the week was especially unnerving: "His fine, technical skiing and accurate and devilishly quick shooting startled the world."[53]

Only the men's 4 x 7.5-kilometer relay remained on the card at Minsk and if the Soviet Union failed to capture a medal on Sunday, 3 March, Tikhonov and his senior teammates would leave these prestigious races without anything to show for their efforts. The narration of the film *Okhota na zoloto* (The Hunt for Gold) captures the essence of Tikhonov's thoughts on the eve of the last event: "Tikhonov lost for the first time in many years. What is it? Bad luck or exhaustion? He knows there are no secrets or tricks to being first. There is only the uncompromising fight."[54] Despite the poetic license of the film's script (Tikhonov actually had been defeated in the individual race for two years in a row prior to his win at the Lake Placid World Championships in 1973), clearly the stakes were high for the relay. In this event, the Soviet Union had an unbroken string of victories stretching all the way back to the Grenoble Olympics of 1968, and Aleksandr Tikhonov had been a member on every single one of those winning teams.

The journalists of *Sovetskii sport* were perhaps speaking for the ski fans of the Soviet Union by the end of the week: "On the evening of the day before the start [of the relay]," they wrote, "our mood was, to put it mildly, despondent."[55] Yet a remarkable event was about to unfold during Sunday's relay race, one that would illustrate the relationship between spectator and participant that was the quintessential element of the socialist sport experience. The correspondents of *Sovetskaia Belorussiia*—normally the first to arrive in Raubichi prior to the competitions—realized that something unusual was brewing early in the morning that day: "Long before the start of the race, cars and buses filled with fans pulled into the complex in a never-ending stream. Before the start of the competition spectators filled up every possible—and impossible—observation point: the stands; the slopes adjacent to the track; the roofs of the busses; the tops of the ridges and the scaffolding of the jump-hills. And the automobiles kept coming and coming."[56] By eleven o'clock, more than 100,000 spectators had arrived to watch the start of the race. Heikki Ikola, formerly a sports analyst for the Finnish national broadcasting company YLE, commented in 2011 that he had never seen so many people at a ski race either before or since.[57] The masses were boisterous in their enthusiasm for the biathletes, especially at the shooting range, where each shot that found its mark was greeted with roars of approval.[58] "The crowd was so supportive," remembers John Morton, who skied the last leg for the United States relay team that day. On one of the steep uphills "the spectators were standing several deep along the trail shouting rhythmically. During the race, I wasn't aware of what they were shouting, since I assumed they were cheering all the athletes up the tough hill, but after the event one of my teammates asked if I heard them shouting 'Jun . . . Jun . . . Jun.'"[59]

The coaches of the Soviet National Team knew that they were facing a serious predicament if there were no medals in this final event. At the latest, the decision about who would ski in the relay had to be made thirty minutes prior to the start of the race. Privalov joked with the press corps later in the afternoon that he had made up his mind about the team at "five hours, thirty-five minutes and thirty seconds in the morning," but the truth of the matter is that he and his staff were shuffling and reshuffling all possible combinations almost until the very last minute.[60] Biakov was slated to ski the first leg of the relay, but his poor performance on the previous day made him nervous and he had been up all night worrying about his start. Privalov assigned the first spot instead to Ushakov, who unleashed perhaps the finest race of his career that morning, setting the pace for a gold-medal performance by the rest of his teammates. Shooting without penalty, he out-skied the rest of the field by a full minute to hand off to Tikhonov, who left the starting line for the second stage minus his customary white racing cap. Tikhonov skied with a vengeance on his leg, running the second fastest time of the day and shooting without penalty: only Suutarinen skied faster than he did, by four seconds. In the opinion of Norway's daily newspaper *Aftenposten*, it was this leg of the relay that proved the key in determining the final outcome.[61] Hatless and determined, Tikhonov tagged Iurii Kolmakov for the third stage. Kolmakov had been a member of the gold-medal relay team at the 1973 Lake Placid World Championships, where he had skied in the third position as well. He did not disappoint the crowd in Raubichi, cleaning his targets and handing off to Nikolai Kruglov with a solid two-minute lead over Finland for the final 7.5-kilometer stretch.

With such a lead, the outcome appeared to be a foregone conclusion. But Kruglov was racing against Finland's Heikki Ikola, a fierce and dogged competitor. Kruglov came into the range for his first bout of shooting and missed three targets from the prone position as Ikola made up time from behind and hit five for five. The two skiers left the range area at about the same time and skied the second loop almost step-for-step. The savvy spectators, understanding full well that in the relay the first skier to cross the finish line won the race, were now in a frenzy as the competitors circled the course. Kruglov was ahead of Ikola entering the range area for the second stage and thus had a bit more time to concentrate on each shot fired offhand. But both skiers missed a target apiece, and from this point on it was a mad dash to the finish line. As Kruglov passed by just seconds ahead of Finland's anchor, the spectators edged closer onto the tracks behind their countryman. Crossing in front of Ikola, the crowd at times was only a meter in front of his ski tips, thus hindering his progress and limiting his ability to relax and concentrate on the race.[62] At various points along the course, individuals in the crowd were throwing pine needles and branches in front of the Finn's skis, knowing that such detritus would catch on klister wax and thus slow Ikola's glide in the icy tracks. Art Stegen was watching the race among a throng near the ski jumps at the last big uphill before the finish. From his vantage point, he observed blatant interference as enthusiasts blocked the ski lanes: "The crowd moved back as Kruglov passed and then closed in, close to the track as Heikki tried to make his way through the crowd that lined the track." With an aggressively partisan audience to help him, Kruglov crossed the finish line one minute and twenty seconds ahead of Ikola for the gold medal. "I feared for my life that day," Ikola told Morton and Stegen after the race. "I was not to win."[63] The celebratory crowd, oblivious to the last teams completing the race, was trampling the race course and obstructing the approach to the finish line: "I remember the spectators laughing in surprise when they realized that we were still racing, attempting to force our way through the crowd . . . after the leading teams had finished," recalls Morton as he battled to keep the United States out of last place.[64]

The Soviet media went into production to create a socialist scenario worthy of Ponomarev immediately after this gold-medal performance. *Pravda* was ostensibly back on the scene to report on the race, idealizing the emphatic participation of the fans and spectators: "More than one hundred thousand Minsk residents were longing ardently for this triumph, holding hands in a continuous wall around the entire course." As Kolmakov took off at the start of his leg, "the spectators led their countryman onto the track with a thundering 'Hurrah!'"[65] With his remarkable performance in the first stage of the relay, Aleksandr Ushakov had redeemed himself virtually overnight in the eyes of the press: "Let us say straight away," wrote *Sovetskii sport*, back-tracking from its assessment of him the previous day, "that the choice [to replace Biakov with Ushakov] seemed, as they say, one hundred percent on target."[66] *Izvestiia* elevated the praise even further: "Without exaggeration one has to name [Ushakov] the hero of the day."[67] Perhaps *Izvestiia* was not far from the mark, because Ushakov was more than just a sports hero who had performed well in his event: in front of one of the largest crowds ever assembled for a ski race, he had fulfilled the educational precepts of Ponomarev's thesis on sport. The narration of *Okhota na zoloto* explains how this was so: "He started to cry when he won the first hand-off. When he was in the individual races he lost often, but he found will and bravery and re-established himself. Aleksandr Ushakov set an excellent example for his team. His selflessness awakened his team to strive for victory."[68] Collectivism, courage and sublimation of the individual to the greater good were Ushakov's "socially valuable qualities" on display before the biathlon fans at Raubichi that day. Similarly, as Tikhonov circled the course to complete the next stage of the relay racing against Henrik Flöjt of Finland in second place, the relevance was not lost on the correspondents from *Sovetskii sport*. They utilized imagery harking back to the Winter War to make clear what was at stake on the ski tracks that morning: "Usually Tikhonov drops his ski hat onto the snow after the first firing range, but here today he took off bare-headed straightaway and it appeared symbolic: there was nothing to lose, there was nowhere to retreat."[69]

The duel between Kruglov and Ikola over the final 2.5-kilometer loop inspired a variety of descriptions in the press. "I don't know what he was thinking about out on the track," wrote *Komsomol'skaia pravda*'s correspondent, "but I'm certain about one thing: Kruglov remembered that since 1968 our team has never lost the relay."[70] Both *Izvestiia* and *Sovetskii sport*'s versions have both skiers hurtling with matched pace toward the finish line, the two Cold War rivals joined in a contest of Homeric proportions: "Everything was on the line, both of them put all they had into the battle, every bit of reserved strength that still remained in those two mighty bodies."[71] Rather than this neck-and-neck contest, *Sovetskaia Belorussiia* reported that Kruglov was on the course far ahead of Ikola for the last loop.[72] For *Pravda*, it was a super-human effort on the part of Kruglov that sealed the victory: "Never, probably, has Nikolai Kruglov skied so fast on a final loop."[73] Poland's *Trybuna ludu* suggested that Kruglov "appeared to be a much better runner" than Ikola as he crossed the finish line "unthreatened."[74] *Ogonek*'s recap provided a bit more drama: "The trail to the finish upon which Nikolai Kruglov was running was difficult. . . . However, Nikolai showed his genuine killer instinct, he didn't waver and finished first."[75] Needless to say, interference from the spectators was never mentioned in any of these accounts: they were simply "warm and cordial."[76] For filmmakers O. Belousov and S. Luk'ianchikov, who had initially approached the Minsk World Championships as an encomium to Tikhonov, the final result was praise for the collective. Captured in slow motion at the end of *Okhota na zoloto*, Kruglov completes the race to the strains of heroic music as the narrator's voice booms: "They were four: Aleksandr Ushakov, Aleksandr Tikhonov, Iurii Kolmakov, Nikolai Kruglov. They were four: they shared the same hope, will and bravery for winning."[77] In the penultimate scene, oversize banners with hammer and sickle insignias wave in the breeze as the victorious Soviet team receives the gold medal.

Disregarding the mythology that arose out of this last race at Minsk, statistics show that the week-long event was a huge success. Combining junior and senior events, ninety-nine competitors from eighteen countries participated in the six-race series. The final tally of spectators exceeded 150,000 for the week. Members of the press corps numbering 147 spent 900 minutes in telephone conversation with news services in Moscow, Warsaw, Stockholm, Berlin, Oslo and other cities and sent telexes totaling 1,400 minutes from Raubichi.[78] These figures were far greater than those from any other previous biathlon world championships. When Minsk hosted the Junior Men's Biathlon World Championships in 1976, 100,000 spectators once again lined the tracks in Raubichi for the 3 x 7.5-kilometer relay. Eight years later, when the 1982 World Championships returned to Minsk, the members chosen for the USSR's National Team were selected out of some 30,000 Soviet skiers who competed in biathlon. Over 500,000 spectators attended these events, with estimates ranging from 150,000 to more than 200,000 fans overflowing the courses and stands on the day of the relay alone. Attendance records such as these dwarf the numbers for individual soccer, hockey and basketball games, cited by Robert Edelman as the Soviet Union's most popular spectator sports, indicating that biathlon of this era was indeed *bol'shoi sport*.[79] In subsequent decades, it would become *bol'shoi biznes* as well.

TEN

The Fifteenth Winter Olympic Games
Calgary, Canada, 1988

The Norwegian delegation's team leader offered a few words of solace to readers of *Sovetskaia Belorussiia* as the world's biathletes departed Minsk in 1974: "The 'reshuffle' in biathlon is a natural phenomenon," he proposed. "Every sportsman, every team alternates between 'peaks' and 'valleys.' So one can say right now the Russian team appears to be in a valley, ceding the peak to the Finns. I think that we won't have a long wait before the Soviets climb back up."[1] In years to follow, the USSR's biathlon program did in fact return to form: from 1975 through 1977, biathletes of the Soviet Union, led by Aleksandr Tikhonov, captured twelve out of eighteen possible medals at world championship and Olympic individual competitions, four of them gold. In the sprint event, the team's new specialty, the Soviets relinquished only one medal out of a possible nine to a non-Soviet skier over the 10-kilometer distance during this time. And the USSR won two out of three biathlon relays, which capped a streak of nine wins and only two runner-up positions over an eleven-year period that began in 1967.[2]

Yet by 1978 the primacy that Soviet biathletes had enjoyed for two decades began to ebb away. Certainly an increase in the number of nations sponsoring internationally competitive teams contributed to this decline. The roster of biathletes worldwide swelled after the 1976 Winter Olympics once the International Modern Pentathlon and Biathlon Union (UIPMB) instigated the switch from large-caliber to small-bore rifles the following year.[3] In Minsk in 1974, fifty-seven skiers took part in both of the men's individual races. Four years later, ninety-six biathletes competed in the 20-kilometer race and ninety-four in the sprint at the Seventeenth World Biathlon Championships in Hochfilzen, Austria, an average increase of about 66 percent. In the 4 x 7.5-kilometer relay, there were twenty-four teams vying for the pedestal, up from fourteen in Minsk. Against an expanded field, the biathletes of the USSR were shut out of the medals in every event for the first time in the twenty-year history of the sport at this

1978 meet. The team from East Germany was in the forefront, capturing five out of six possible medals in the individual races and taking the gold in the relay. These results were representative of the surge created by the much-vaunted East German sports program that commenced with the Summer Olympics of 1972. Although biathletes of the Soviet Union continued to win individual medals over the next ten years, taking twelve out of sixty-six possible from 1979 through 1989, they ran a distant second to those of East Germany, who garnered twice as many podium spots during the same period.[4] But by the late 1980s other nations were also challenging the perennial powerhouses for medals. Valerii Medvedtsev, the Soviet Union's top biathlete at the Calgary Games of 1988, told Canadian television channel CTV: "I'm convinced that the level of competition is increasing . . . now, along with countries known for their biathletes such as East Germany, Norway, West Germany and Austria, the competition for medals includes American and Czech athletes."[5] No nation, however, could loosen the USSR's stranglehold on the relay event, in which the total Soviet haul was three bronze, two silver and six gold medals over the course of the decade.[6]

Ironically, as the fortunes of the biathlon team slipped in the last years of communist rule, those of the Soviet men's cross-country squad finally improved, especially at the Olympics, where it managed six gold, five silver and two bronze medals across three Games. At Calgary in 1988, the swan song of Soviet skiing at the Olympics, the combined efforts of the men's and women's cross-country teams along with those of the biathlon squad accounted for nearly two-thirds of all possible medals awarded in their events, precipitating a media donnybrook over the most pressing issue of the day in international sport: doping of athletes to improve performance.[7]

The resurgence of Soviet skiing at the Olympics, however, belied an undercurrent of general disillusionment among many ordinary citizens with bol'shoi sport—that is, the sum total of high-profile international athletic events in which the USSR demonstrated superiority over the world's most advanced capitalist nations. A disastrous campaign in Afghanistan from 1979 through 1988 was the political backdrop to this final period of Soviet history, during which disenchantment with the nation's policies affected a significant portion of the younger generation.[8] This incursion led to a covert proxy war with the United States over most of the decade. In the last year of his presidency, Jimmy Carter imposed a grain embargo on the Soviet Union and declared a boycott of the 1980 Moscow Olympics. The Soviet Union responded in kind four years later when the Summer Games moved to Los Angeles. Just days before the opening ceremonies of the 1988 Winter Olympics in Calgary, Soviet Communist Party General Secretary Mikhail Gorbachev announced a ten-month gradual withdrawal of troops from Afghanistan to commence on 15 May.[9] These international developments coincided with Gorbachev's attempts at domestic reform, or perestroika, a restructuring of the Russian economy through decentralization, monetary incentives and the stimulation of individual initiative. Hand in hand with this restructuring was a nationwide policy of openness, or glasnost', whose purpose was to publicize the problems afflicting the socialist system in order to inspire creative solutions among the populace. This process led to a re-examination between 1987 and 1988 of the entire Soviet past, including the economics of Marx and the politics of Lenin, and the result was a radical alteration of the population's consciousness. Recapitulating this final era of the Soviet project, Martin Malia writes: "In two years a whiff of *glasnost* demolished the ideological work of seven decades."[10]

Thus, at the end of the decade a sense of introspection and analysis concerning life in the USSR and the country's role on the world stage pervaded the Soviet Union; and in sport, the regime's monomaniacal focus on the Olympic Games highlighted all that was wrong with contemporary Soviet policies. The era of glasnost' revealed that the government's purported emphasis on mass participation over mastery was fraudulent: only 8 percent of men and 2 percent of women engaged in athletics on a regular basis. Furthermore, the number of citizens who could meet the Ready for Labor and Defense (GTO) standards was abysmal. As James Riordan reported in 1990, only forty-one out of seven hundred Moscow school children at a city sports tournament passed the minimum, and even among men in the armed forces, up to a third failed the GTO norms. After Moscow State University sponsored a survey of students who were attending mandatory first-year physical education sessions, the final report concluded that such compulsory sport participation had resulted in "resistance and anti-sport sentiments."[11] Riordan also delineated a migration toward sport popular in the West, such as baseball, golf, Grand Prix auto racing and even American football.

In this climate, many individuals of the last Soviet generation rejected activities in a variety of venues specifically promoted by the state, which they identified as part of the USSR's culture. As Alexei Yurchak argues, the more the government reiterated the rituals and discourse of socialism, the more reality appeared disconnected from official statements for many citizens. This allowed diverse and unanticipated shifts in late Soviet culture.[12]

Participation in physical culture—and skiing was one of its most important subsets—came to represent ideological and uncritical collective conformity with the Soviet regime. From 1985 to 1990, officially sanctioned sport organizations such as Young Pioneers and the Komsomol lost over six million members.[13] A number of negative factors—including politics and ideology, hypocrisy, paramilitary coercion, Russian dogmatism, drug abuse, the exploitation of children and immorally distorted priorities—exacerbated the demise of physical culture in the USSR.[14] Although such problems were endemic to the Soviet sport system, they were nonetheless inextricably linked to the rise of the East German sports machine in the 1970s.

The East German Sports Program

East Germany competed for the first time as an independent entity during the 1968 Winter Olympics in Grenoble, France, and the Summer Games in Mexico City after twelve years under a combined German flag. Although the GDR had a mediocre tenth-place finish in the medals count in France that year, East German athletes took home twenty-five total awards for fifth position behind Hungary, Japan, the Soviet Union and the United States in Mexico. Four years later, the GDR scooped up sixty-six medals, for third place behind the USSR and the United States at Munich's Summer Games, and fourteen winter medals in Sapporo for second place behind the Soviet Union. East Germany's athletes improved on this record in 1976: they were second again in total medals to the Soviet Union in the winter events at Innsbruck, then ousted the United States from second place behind the USSR with forty gold, twenty-five silver and twenty-five bronze medals at Montreal. The Moscow Summer Games of 1980 and those in Los Angeles four years later were subject to reciprocal boycotts between East and West. When all nations finally competed together at the Seoul Summer Games of 1988, the last before the collapse of communism at the end of the decade, the GDR maintained its second-place position in total medals behind the Soviet Union and ahead of the United States. During the 1980s there were no Winter Olympics boycotts, which amplified the political significance of these competitions. East Germany alternated with the Soviet Union between first and second place in total medals during the 1980 Lake Placid, 1984 Sarajevo and 1988 Calgary Games.[15]

The remarkable record of East Germany spanning twenty years of Olympic competition is all the more astounding considering that the nation's population was only around seventeen million, slightly less than that of the state of New York for the comparable period. Greatly influenced by the Soviet Union's state committee- and trade union–based sports system, the East Germans fine-tuned their government-sponsored program into a medal-winning juggernaut, often compared to a sports factory, a foundry or a machine. The GDR used local sport clubs under the aegis of the German Gymnastics and Sports Union to channel talented young athletes—selected according to ideal body types for a particular sport as early as kindergarten—into specialized boarding schools where they were subjected to stringent and often brutal training regimens. For those scientists with an interest in athletics, the government established the German College of Physical Culture (also known as the Leipzig Sports Institute), the world's leading university for the application of science to high-performance sport. Students spent four years studying sports science, biomechanics, natural science, psychology, math and computer science in addition to courses on coaching and training. East Germans destined for coaching positions across a broad spectrum of events took the same classes and learned the same techniques. In addition, because of the heavy course load in science and mathematics, the graduates were able and willing to work in conjunction with team physicians who were in daily contact with the nation's elite athletes. By the end of 1979, more than 8,000 professional coaches had graduated from the Leipzig Institute, working with 200,000 volunteer coaches on the municipal and regional levels and manning an advanced medical research system throughout the nation dedicated to the analysis of athletics.[16]

This approach to the development of athletic talent was not lost on Aleksandr Privalov, who explained to *Sovetskii sport* in the aftermath of the Minsk debacle that the USSR's problem was a lack of specialized sport schools for biathlon. This was a concern not only for the biathletes themselves but also for coaches who had no programs in which to enroll at the nation's physical culture institutes and were by necessity self-taught. The example of the East German system propelled competition in all sports to new levels during the 1970s as the Soviet Union and other nations sought to match the GDR's stunning advancements in the science of sport. During this period, the Lokomotiv sports club opened a school for children and youths dedicated to biathlon in Novosibirsk under the direction of Mikhail Durnev. By 1980, the USSR had established five thousand specialized sport schools such as Durnev's through which the government funneled two million potential athletes.[17]

Steroids, Drugs and Blood

The most controversial aspect of the East German program was the use of drugs, especially anabolic steroids, to enhance the performance of the nation's athletes. Steroid use became the hallmark of any discussion concerning Eastern European sports during the last decades of the Cold War. Although the misappropriation of drugs to improve athletic performance has always been a part of sports—in some instances pre-dating the modern era—verifiable documentation of such abuse has only existed since around 1929: stimulants such as amphetamines, cocaine, nitroglycerine and caffeine, for example, were common in multi-day bicycle racing throughout the first half of the twentieth century.[18] But in the early 1950s, rumors circulated that Soviet scientists were experimenting with something completely different in the form of hormonal enhancement. This boost to the body was accomplished through the use of steroids, particularly androgens, a basic component of the male hormone family. Agents such as testosterone trigger puberty in boys and, when applied to a mature adult as a supplement, enable the body to retain more protein and thus increase muscle growth. A physician travelling with the United States delegation to the 1956 World Games in Moscow observed some Soviet athletes using urinary catheters, a tell-tale sign of an enlarged prostate resulting from testosterone use. These observations accelerated research in the West to match the Soviets' use of athletic pharmaceuticals. The result was the development of Dianabol, the first mass-produced anabolic-androgenic steroid. By the 1960s this type of product found wide acceptance in sport. However, the deleterious side effects of anabolic steroid use were legion: the drug causes disturbances in carbohydrate and lipid metabolism leading to the advancement of arthrosclerosis, heart disease and strokes; when used by prepubescent children, premature sealing of bony growth plates occurs, resulting in physical underdevelopment; because anabolic steroids increase muscle mass without a parallel growth of tendon strength, strenuous exercise can produce torn ligaments. In consideration of these and similar problems, as well as for the purpose of fostering a sense of fair play, the International Olympic Committee (IOC) banned the use of steroids in April 1975, putting in place systematic drug-testing protocols at all competitions beginning in 1976.[19]

Stimulants are not a normal component of the body's chemistry, and therefore it had been easy enough to develop test procedures for their detection. The situation was far different for anabolic steroids, since hormones are a naturally occurring substance in humans. Thus, testing focused on abnormally large amounts of testosterone or comparable substances, generally through an analysis of an athlete's urine. However, athletes easily avoided discovery because it was possible to take steroids for months and benefit from the increase in muscle mass then pass the urine test by stopping the intake of the drug just a few days prior to competition.[20] Besides the increase in muscle mass, steroids aid recovery from training, allowing an athlete to endure greater amounts of effort at a higher level of intensity. This was especially beneficial in cross-country skiing, because innovations in ski equipment such as polyethylene ski bases, carbon-fiber poles and synthetic waxes considerably enhanced the speeds at which skiers could travel. By the early 1980s, the tempo sustained by cross-country racers intensified as skiers double-poled and skated around courses that had been packed solid by specialized snow-grooming machinery. As ski times dropped, athletes adopted more stringent training regimens in order to inure the body and ski faster. The physical toll on these skiers increased as well. *Sovetskaia Belorussiia* either misconstrued or deliberately obfuscated this situation in its coverage of the 1990 Minsk Biathlon World Championships, where high-speed skating was now the only ski technique used in the sport and doping was on everyone's mind: "The doping problem in biathlon isn't as acute as it is in other types of sport. This is easily explained: it's known that a little bit of anabolic stimulant is able to impart strength in the course of the race. But, biathletes have to shoot as well. . . . Taking into account the stress load in training and competition that puts the 'snow shooters' to the test, for them the use of prohibited preparations is suicide."[21] Anabolic steroids per se did not make athletes better skiers or biathletes: they did, however, make them stronger and therefore capable of enduring a higher level of effort, or as here, "the stress-load in training and competition" suited to the recent technological advances in ski equipment. The effect of the drugs on shooting accuracy was irrelevant, other than the fact that a biathlete using steroids could sustain greater amounts of training and thus would experience less fatigue while racing. This allowed a steadier skeleto-muscular platform for holding a rifle at the firing line. This article also disregarded a much more widespread and controversial phenomenon that had superseded steroid use as a cause for concern in athletics by the end of the 1980s: blood doping.

The manipulation of an athlete's blood had antecedents in East Germany's elite sports training programs. Scientists incorporated into the athletic regimen cutting-edge medical research protocols such as blood tests, muscle biopsies, electrocardiograms and bone x-rays along with the injection of enzymes, minerals and vitamins. Interest in these types of sports-related medical advances was paralleled in the West, particularly in Finland. Experiments with Finnish endurance athletes like Olympic gold medalist Lasse Viren allegedly resulted in the development of blood doping through intravenous transfusion during the early 1970s, with the first documented case occurring at the 1980 Moscow Summer Games. There are two types of transfusion procedures: homologous, in which one person's blood is put into another; and autologous, in which an athlete's own blood is removed, frozen for storage and then reinfused just before an important competition. The loss of blood through transfusion stimulates the bone marrow to form more red blood cells. When the stored blood is reinjected into the athlete, the extra red cells increase the oxygen-carrying capacity of the cardiovascular system and thus the amount of oxygen available to the muscles. Initially, several research projects carried out during this period indicated that blood doping could boost endurance by 17 to 30 percent. Dr. Jim Stray-Gundersen, team physician for the United States Cross-Country Ski Team at the 1988 Winter Games, takes issue with this assessment, proposing that the increase in red cell mass conferred a more modest 1 to 4 percent improvement in endurance. No matter the amount, even a slight boost in red blood cell count proved to be a huge advantage in a sport such as cross-country skiing.[22] As John Underwood, a physiologist for the United States Biathlon Team, explained to ABC Sports in February 1988, a blood-doping skier could shave nearly two and a half minutes off his or her time in a 10-kilometer race, making "the difference between a medal and twenty-fifth [place]."[23] This process was initially considered a legitimate alternative to the use of drugs, and by the late 1970s and early 1980s blood doping was prevalent at the elite levels of not only cross-country skiing but also other endurance events, such as cycling and marathon running. However, blood doping carried inherent risks: homologous transfusions had the potential to transmit bacterial and viral infections and create life-threatening immunological reactions; autologous transfusions increased the chance of thrombosis, which can cause heart attacks, strokes and other clotting problems. The IOC banned the process after the 1984 Olympic Games.[24]

In the 1980s, scientists researching a treatment for anemia patients synthesized erythropoietin (EPO), a naturally occurring hormone made primarily in specialized kidney cells that stimulates the production of red blood cells in bone marrow. Utilizing recombinant gene technology, the human therapeutics firm Amgen synthesized EPO in ovarian cells of hamsters. "It is the most effective performance enhancing agent ever developed," according to Dr. Stray-Gundersen.[25] The availability of this substance resulted in a black market among elite endurance athletes, who saw a way around the medically dangerous and now illegal blood-doping regime. An athlete would take EPO starting eight to ten weeks prior to a major competition and build up the number of circulating red blood cells. However, use of EPO thickens the blood and increases the risk of life-threatening clots and strokes in an athlete whose red blood cells have already reached an elevated number. Rumors circulated among international skiers that in 1984 at the Sarajevo Games the Czech Ski Team had used a drug similar to EPO. These innuendos flared again at the 1988 Calgary Olympics when stories of EPO use in sport surfaced in the press.[26] As the drug became more readily available after 1988, demand for EPO created a doping epidemic and led to its inclusion on the list of substances banned by the IOC in April of 1990. It has only been in the last decade that scientists have formulated a reliable test for the detection of EPO.[27]

Big Sport, Big Business

Marxist-Leninist ideology, bolstered by the parallel development of performance-enhancing drugs and technologically advanced athletic equipment throughout the last decades of the Cold War era, powered the "win at all costs" mentality pervading sports programs of Eastern Europe. Paradoxically, this coalesced with an increase in Western investment in the region throughout the 1970s. The Soviet Union had subsidized East European countries by exporting fuel and raw materials to them at prices below those of the world markets and importing manufactured goods from them at inflated prices. However, as the USSR reorganized these trade and payment arrangements during the 1980s, it sold more materials to the West in order to earn hard currency, resulting in an ineluctable trade imbalance. The increase in commercialism permeating the Olympics during the late 1970s was also a part of this odd mix.[28]

One of the first major commercial stars of the Winter Olympics was triple gold medalist Jean-Claude Killy. On the podium at Grenoble in 1968, Killy clutched his Rossignol Alpine skis before the television cameras with logo in plain view, a high-profile endorsement that side-stepped IOC protocols banning professionalism. Over the next decade, ski manufacturers courted the world's best skiers with increasingly lucrative sponsorships, prompting International Ski Federation (FIS) president Marc Hodler to remark in 1978 that he simply did not know how to control downhill skiers who were receiving under the table payments from ski companies.[29] Interest in cross-country racing experienced a burst of growth after the 1976 Olympics and major manufacturers of ski equipment such as Fischer and Kneissl of Austria, Excel of Finland and Adidas of West Germany eagerly sponsored East German and Soviet skiers and biathletes with the expectation that their products would be seen worldwide when the East Europeans climbed the winner's pedestal. Advertising of the era often featured photographs of Soviet skiers and biathletes in action at international competitions using skis, boots and poles manufactured in the West. This was not always to the benefit of the athletes: one enthusiastic proponent of her sponsor was Soviet cross-country skier Nina Gavryliuk, who was disqualified after the women's 20-kilometer race at the 1988 Winter Games for wearing a headband with an oversized Adidas logo.[30] Manufacturers offered cash incentives for medals won at major international competitions, making cross-country skiing and biathlon a remunerative career choice for top athletes. The Soviet government offered a five-thousand-dollar bonus to each gold medalist at Calgary in 1988. Additional rewards that accrued for athletes behind the Iron Curtain were enticing as well. For successful skiers, winning medals in international competition, especially the Olympics, meant special privileges beyond cash payments such as foreign travel, apartments and *dachas*.[31] One Scandinavian ski journal noted that the Soviet Union rewarded its Olympic medalists by allowing them to spend money in the West: "This year in Ramsau [Austria] the Russians bought, among other things, Volvo and Mercedes cars, which they drove home some 3,600 miles to Moscow."[32]

With so much money on the line—not only for the athletes but also for the cash-strapped regime—the pressure to partake in drug use and blood doping was intense. And these disreputable activities were certainly carried out with the knowledge and consent of the Soviet sports federations. Chess master (and political gadfly) Garry Kasparov summed up the situation succinctly in a 1989 interview: "The demand for doping crops up where a harsh 'governmental' task is set before athletes, a task which must be endured at whatever cost."[33] As in the GDR, the state provided drugs as part of the athletes' development through officially sanctioned sports medicine programs, along with nutritional supplementation, exercise physiology and biomechanical studies. Because testing procedures were inadequate and administered only sporadically at international events, Soviet coaches, scientists and officials had a cynical attitude about doping and drug use. One top-level Soviet scientist specializing in pharmacological research stated: "Basically, the question of a drug test's result has no meaning whatsoever . . . if a test is negative it only means that the pharmacological preparation was done correctly. If it is positive, then the coach is an idiot."[34] Although the government vehemently denied charges of drug use throughout the Soviet era, in the early 1980s two deputy sport ministers detailed the prescription of anabolic steroids as part of the regimen for Soviet cross-country skiers. Moreover, the documentation contained the particulars for a program to test for the effect of steroids and for research into methods for avoiding detection.[35] In 2003, Michael Kalinski, a professor at Kent State University, went public with a thirty-nine-page document he had received in 1972 in his former position as chairman of the department of sport biochemistry at the Kiev Institute of Physical Culture. This classified report, "Anabolic Steroids and Sport Capacity," was one of 150 copies printed and labeled "for limited use." It provided guidelines for steroid use by elite athletes based on top-secret experiments at the USSR's premier sport-research laboratories. In one study, a group of unnamed biathletes training at altitude took Dianabol for twenty days. They experienced increased muscle size, greater oxygen-carrying capacity and faster recovery times from hard exercise than the control group.[36]

In addition, the practice of blood doping was widespread and accepted. Extensive blood-doping research was carried out at the highest levels in sports institutions of the USSR, including the Central Institute for Physical Culture and the Central Institute of Hematology and Transfusiology in Moscow. The clandestine government-sponsored program established protocols for blood doping as early as 1976, although results were not made public until 1990. Recent research documents how elite competitors on the Soviet national cross-country skiing, biathlon, cycling, rowing, swimming and skating teams all used blood-doping procedures at the 1976 and 1980 Olympic Games.[37] It should be noted, however, that the athletic success of the Soviet Union's skiers cannot simply be explained away by citing the use of performance-enhancing drugs and blood doping. No matter the level of drugs or high-count red blood cells in a cross-country skier's system, nothing can replace sport-specific specialization through talent-screening, along with the development of good technique and a well-planned training regimen, the three fundamental aspects of the USSR Ski Team's program.[38] As three time Olympian and current Canadian

National Nordic Team Head Coach Justin Wadsworth remarked recently: "You can't dope technique. You can't dope ski feel. That's one of the very cool things about our sport."[39]

Nevertheless, the stigma attached to drug use for the majority of sports fans on either side of the Iron Curtain took the sheen off athletic success. By the 1980s, journalists began to question the ethics and ethos of Soviet sport, deriding the win-at-all-costs mentality that fostered acceptance of drug use as a prerequisite for elite-level athletic performance. Veteran sports journalist Stanislav Tokarev foreshadowed the 1988 Calgary Olympics in an article the year before that excoriated Soviet athletic organizations for their clandestine proclivities, singling out a pair of weightlifters for illicit drug use: "They got caught outside the country, too—in Canada. They got caught for what they took there—according to speculation—a substantial dose of a preparation comprised of anabolic steroids, doping. Yes, they got punished. But they should have been punished publicly and in the open. And thereby wash away the stain from our sporting banner."[40] Working under the direction of *Ogonek*'s Vitalii Korotich, a liberal editor appointed by Gorbachev in 1986 to ramp up glasnost' in the wake of the Chernobyl nuclear plant disaster, Tokarev offered a point of view that reflected a sea-change in his own perception of the country's outlook on sport, and perhaps some of his fellow citizens' as well. After the Seoul Olympics of 1988, Soviet track and field coach Igor Ter-Ovanesian launched a well-publicized campaign to eliminate drugs in Soviet sports.[41]

The Winter Olympics: Calgary, 1988

By the late 1980s, the amount of money generated by the Olympics was staggering. The Los Angeles Summer Games of 1984 were the first "corporate Olympics," with multi-national companies such as Coca-Cola, 3M, Kodak and others involved in major marketing campaigns tied to the events. The organizing committee under the direction of Peter Ueberroth amassed a surplus of 215 million dollars, a marked contrast to the 1.1 billion dollar deficit accrued by Montreal eight years before. The Calgary organizers had no intention of repeating the Montreal fiasco and welcomed a new global marketing effort called the Olympic Program (TOP), which immediately yielded enormous amounts of revenue. By the time of the opening ceremonies in Calgary, TOP had accumulated around 125 million dollars and, with the corporate sponsorship of the U.S. Olympic

Committee thrown into the mix, worldwide support of the 1988 Olympics, both winter and summer versions, eventually came to around 400 million dollars. "We do business in 140 countries," said Donn Osmon, vice president of marketing and public affairs for 3M, "and we were looking for a unifying theme, something apolitical that everybody could support."[42]

Television became one of the major venues for disseminating the Olympic themes of these corporate sponsors. Interest in the events of the Winter Olympics grew during the 1970s as a result of exposure on television, a phenomenon duly noted in the Soviet press: "Austrian television promises to devote 6,970 minutes to the [1976] Winter Olympics," Alevtina Kolchina reported in *Ogonek*. "With television's help the Olympic Games will receive an immense, truly worldwide audience." The final tally published by the journal *Smena* was 800 million television spectators. By the end of the 1980 Lake Placid Olympics, global viewership of the United States' ABC transmissions had exceeded 900 million.[43] Throughout the 1980s, media coverage mushroomed as ever greater numbers of television viewers stimulated larger markets for advertising revenue, especially during the broadcast of glamour events such as figure skating, ice dancing and ice hockey. The amount of money expended for the rights to broadcast the Olympics increased exponentially during this period. ABC paid 15.5 million dollars to cover the Lake Placid Games in 1980, 91.5 million for Sarajevo four years later, and by the end of the decade, a record 309 million dollars for Calgary. In addition, the American corporation invested another 100 million dollars in production costs. Canadian CTV's contribution added another 45 million dollars. Because there was so much at stake financially (ABC averaged 285 thousand dollars for a 30-second commercial), the company finagled an expanded schedule from the IOC for the Calgary Games. The result was almost one hundred hours of television broadcasting, a number matched by Canadian, European and Soviet networks. With every advertising slot filled, ABC still projected a loss of around 40 million dollars.[44]

Newspaper coverage followed a growth trajectory that paralleled television, and in Calgary international correspondents relayed reams of information to fill daily columns on both sides of the Iron Curtain. Reuters, United Press International (UPI) and Associated Press (AP) fed stories to affiliates throughout the world. European newspapers such as West Germany's *Frankfurter Allgemeine Zeitung*, East Germany's *Neues Deutschland*, Norway's *Dagbladet* and *Le Monde* of France had their own correspondents on the ground in Canada. The *Calgary Herald* enlisted dozens of journalists and staff spread across every venue from Calgary to Canmore, covering all the events in detail for the paper's daily Olympic supplement: for the opening ceremonies alone, editor-in-chief Kevin Peterson dispatched twenty-seven reporters and thirteen photographers. Soviet newspapers *Trud, Pravda, Sovetskii sport, Izvestiia, Komsomol'skaia pravda* and *Krasnaia zvezda* as well as the TASS News Agency all had crews of reporters and photographers covering the Games for domestic consumption as well as for other readers in the Eastern Bloc. In addition, around 1,600,000 spectators flooded into Calgary, overwhelming the local population of some 651,000. Although the majority of these fans packed the ice hockey and figure skating venues, downhill skiing attracted approximately 240,000 devotees and 180,000 spectators watched ski jumping on the outskirts of the city. Even the cross-country events, including Nordic combined and biathlon, drew some 120,000 fans to Canmore, a small mountain village a ninety-minute drive to the west of Calgary. With hundreds of millions of dollars in corporate funding, worldwide broadcasts, incessant newspaper coverage and enthusiasts flocking to Canada from around the globe, the Games of Calgary demonstrated that by 1988 the Winter Olympics had become big business indeed.[45]

The socialist states dominated all three of the Winter Olympics held during the 1980s, a period during which interest in these un-boycotted events reached an all-time peak. At Lake Placid in 1980, the Soviet Union finished in a virtual dead heat with East Germany for total medals. These results were a triumph for the Eastern Bloc: both the athletes of the USSR and GDR out-performed those of the third-place United States on their home turf. The disappointment for neighboring Canada was even greater: that nation's athletes won a total of only two medals, one bronze and one silver. In cross-country skiing, the Soviet men's squad had more success than the women's team for the first time ever, gathering one bronze, one silver and two gold medals in the individual races and winning the 4 x 10-kilometer relay. Raisa Smetanina was the sole female individual medalist, winning the women's 5-kilometer sprint. East Germany's team edged that of the second-place Soviets for gold in the women's 4 x 5-kilometer relay. In biathlon the Soviet Union and East Germany were evenly matched, with each nation's team winning one gold, one silver and one bronze medal in the two individual events. In Aleksandr Tikhonov's final Olympic race, the USSR's relay team outshot the East Germans to win the gold in the Soviet Union's premier event by almost one minute.[46]

Four years later, in Sarajevo, the Soviet Union and East Germany again were separated by only a hair's breadth in total medals, but both teams fell off considerably in cross-country skiing as Sweden and Finland dominated the top positions. Only the indomitable Raisa Smetanina kept the women's squad on the podium, with two silver medals in the individual races. Nikolai Zimiatov and Aleksandr Zav'ialov finished first and second in the 30-kilometer race and then added a silver medal to their collections in the relay race. Soviet biathletes were shut out of the medals in the individual races yet were able to maintain their unbroken golden streak in the 4 x 7.5-kilometer relay, edging Norway by less than thirteen seconds at the finish. "This latest Olympic victory," gushed the Soviet team's sponsor, Austria's Fischer Ski Company, "meant that the Russians had succeeded in winning all five Olympic relay events since 1968, an Olympic record that will not be broken easily."[47]

In 1988, the Winter Olympics returned to North America for the second time in the same decade. The Nordic events had undergone tremendous change in the interim. The Lake Placid Olympics were the last in which every athlete competing in cross-country skiing and biathlon used classic, or diagonal, stride technique. America's most accomplished Nordic ski racer, Bill Koch, had participated in a 30-kilometer speed race on a frozen river in Sweden in 1980 where he observed a competitor skiskating on the perfectly flat course.[48] This one competition changed the sport of Nordic ski racing forever. Koch, who had won a silver medal at the 1976 Winter Olympics, did not ski up to his potential four years later in Lake Placid. Perhaps one of the most innovative skiers ever in the sport of cross-country, Koch was constantly searching for ways to gain an edge against his European competitors and get back on the podium. By 1981, Koch had perfected a technique known as "marathon skate" in which he would keep one ski in the groove of a prepared ski track and use the other to push off at an angle, propelling him forward on the flats. The next year he employed this new skating technique to win the first-ever overall World Cup title in Nordic ski racing, and elite competitors around the world hastened to emulate Koch's style.[49] By the time of the 1984 Olympics in Sarajevo, even though competitors were still using diagonal stride to ski on the steep uphills, many had adopted skating technique on rolling terrain.[50] By the following season, diagonal stride had virtually disappeared from the Nordic ski racing scene on the elite level. At the 1985 Nordic World Championships in Seefeld, Austria, all the top finishers were skating around the entire course, leaving those who adhered to diagonal stride far behind.

Almost overnight the new technique was readily embraced by biathletes, who found that skating was not only faster but also kept the rifle better balanced while carried on the back. "The extent to which skating technique is now being used in international biathlon came as a surprise to all of us," wrote U.S. Biathlon coach Bill Spencer in the spring of 1985. "We certainly didn't anticipate that all the top competitors would be glide waxing the full length of the ski and skating the entire course."[51]

During the 1985 through 1986 ski season, all the top international ski racers had abandoned diagonal stride, causing concern in the Scandinavian countries that traditional skiing was doomed. The International Ski Federation (FIS) convened a special meeting and determined that measures were necessary to preserve diagonal stride as a viable form of ski racing. This notion met with derision from skiers such as Koch, who felt that the sport was evolving naturally and that the Scandinavians were propping up the traditional manner of Nordic skiing by artificial means. Nonetheless, FIS proposed two types of competitions, separated into classic or diagonal stride only and freestyle, or skating, categories. The International Modern Pentathlon and Biathlon Union (UIPMB), on the other hand, decided at the end of the season that all biathlon events would allow skating, a resolution that was reconfirmed by the organization in 1988.[52] The Calgary Games, therefore, were the first in which two types of cross-country events were included on the card. For the men, the 15- and 30-kilometer individual races were designated classic or diagonal stride–only events; the 50-kilometer marathon and 4 x 10-kilometer relay were freestyle or skating. For the women, the 5- and 10-kilometer events were traditional; the 20-kilometer individual and the 4 x 5-kilometer relay were freestyle. Biathletes were free to skate all of their races.[53]

The race courses for the Nordic events were laid out at a brand-new 17.5-million-dollar facility in Canmore, Alberta, on some of the most challenging terrain ever encountered at an Olympic venue. As described by Canadian journalist Kevin Cox, the courses were "monsters," with "a punishing, mile-long vertical climb and a descent where skiers can hit speeds of up to 80 kilometres [sic] an hour—just before they negotiate the hairpin turn at the bottom."[54] After the first Olympic events at Canmore, *Pravda*'s correspondents reported that virtually every competitor was complaining about the courses. For example, American Dan Simoneau called the track "the hardest course I've ever raced," and Jochen Behle of West Germany concurred: "The course is simply too difficult."[55]

Complicating the situation was the snow upon which these courses were set. The state-of-the-art machinery used to prepare the ski tracks at Canmore tilled the snow into a fine powder. When this substance was repacked, the structure of the snow crystals metamorphosed from a naturally occurring type of snow into an artificial one, creating havoc for many of the wax technicians working there. The Soviet team allowed that they were frantic prior to the starting gun for the 30-kilometer race: "The coaches told us that they debated variations of ski wax all night and early in the morning," wrote the correspondents from *Komosmol'skaia pravda*, "testing the snow by feeling it—and maybe tasting it too?"[56] Panic ensued during the 15-kilometer competition as well: "We had six different waxes at first," Simoneau explained after his poor showing that day. "We finally got it down to three just before the race, and I had to make my decision and practically run to the starting gate."[57] In the opinion of *Frankfurter Allgemeine Zeitung*, the first week's events boiled down to a game of "wax-roulette."[58]

The Soviet Ski Team was quite aware of the challenges that the Canmore trails would present. The government invested in a new, ultra-modern high-altitude ski training center in the Altai Mountains; and in the autumn months prior to the Olympics, coaches and athletes prepared themselves at the national ski training center at Bakuriani, where the team constructed ski courses modeled on those in Canmore. In addition to practicing on the course, waxing specialists could study snow conditions at an elevation and latitude similar to Alberta's.[59] The team leaders also understood the importance of cultivating specialists for both classical and freestyle events. The Russians instituted a two-year intensive program that would reach its peak just in time for the Olympics in Calgary: "We have consequently trained the same amount in both styles," team member Aleksei Prokurorov told *Neues Deutschland* in 1988, "one thousand kilometers each month of the winter."[60]

Details of this Soviet training program were of great interest to ski aficionados, who tried to fathom how the Russians had managed to perform so well in 1988. Erik Røste, a correspondent for the Norwegian magazine *Ski Sport*, accompanied two coaches from Sweden and one from East Germany to participate with the Soviet team at their final dryland training camp in the fall of 1988, the season after the USSR's successful Olympic showing. There he found a difficult 4.5-kilometer roller ski course and a 3.2-kilometer interval loop designed specifically to mirror the Canmore ski tracks. In Gorbachev's Soviet Union glasnost' was the operative mode, and Røste conversed freely with Viktor Ivanov, the USSR's head coach, and his nine assistants, as well as the six doctors, six masseurs, two physiologists and full-time video technician assigned to the team. He learned that Vladimir Smirnov, the 1988 Olympic bronze and double silver medalist at Calgary, had logged over 10,000 kilometers of training through running, roller-skiing and snow skiing prior to his departure for the Games. The other elite squad members put in between 9,000 and 9,500 kilometers during the same period. While at the training camp Røste observed two test races over the 3.2-kilometer interval trail during which the Soviet medical staff monitored each athlete's pulse rate and blood lactate levels. The training loads for both men and women at this camp were prodigious, with morning and afternoon workouts totaling between twenty-eight and fifty kilometers per day.[61] Former United States Olympic Coach John Caldwell also attended a dryland camp at Bakuriani and was impressed by the amount and intensity of the Soviet training. In his opinion, these had been the critical factors contributing to the Soviet team's success at the Calgary Olympics: "The pace of the workouts was about one-half a stage more intense than any I have witnessed during the past 15 to 20 years. I was astounded that they could keep this up day after day. At the time, they were training about 30 hours per week."[62]

After a substantial early-season program similar to this one, the USSR's top skiers participated in some World Cup races in December 1987. But rather than continuing to follow the ongoing European World Cup "circus" in the weeks just prior to the Olympics, the Soviet team returned home to host a series of domestic World Cup point races on 9 through 10 January: a 30-kilometer classic and 4 x 10-kilometer relay for men in Kavgolovo, and a 5-kilometer classic individual race and 4 x 5-kilometer relay for women in Leningrad.[63] With athletes reaching their carefully charted athletic peaks and a coterie of well-practiced coaches, waxers, ski technicians and medical assistants in tow, the Soviet Ski Team took the Canmore courses by storm from 14 to 27 February.

In the opening race on Sunday, the women's 10-kilometer classic, Vida Vencienė and Raisa Smetanina won gold and silver. Four of the first five finishers in this race were Soviet women.[64] The following day, Aleksei Prokurorov and Vladimir Smirnov took first and second places in the 30-kilometer race with teammate Mikhail Deviat'iarov just out of third by less than twenty seconds.[65] Both of these contests were restricted to diagonal stride, and ski base preparation played a crucial role in the outcomes. Conditions were complex for the wax technicians: the snow, which estimates placed at 80 percent artificial, maintained a one- to two-degree Celsius differential between air temperature and track surface. The proper mix of good grip wax underfoot and fast glide paraffin on the tips and tails was complicated by a recent innovation in ski preparation: structuring of the polyethylene ski bases with rilling tools designed specifically for each of a variety of snow conditions. This process impressed a pattern on the base that reduced suction between the ski and the surface of the snow during the skier's glide phase. The quest for the best combination of wax and base structure was especially problematic during the men's 30-kilometer race, when the air temperature hovered between minus two and zero degrees Celsius, the most challenging of all waxing ranges. The dirt content of the reprocessed snow as well as variations in compaction added other confounding factors into the equation. To illustrate the difficulties involved in juggling all of these variables, consider that Canada's premier cross-country racer, Pierre Harvey, had a team of twenty technicians and coaches preparing a stable of sixteen pairs of skis for him in anticipation of Monday's competition. The permutations of glide and grip wax combinations, base structure and ski selection made the job of the team technicians a nightmare.[66]

A majority of the journalists covering the Nordic events believed that the Soviet Union's wax specialists had concocted the perfect mixture for the conditions during both the women's 10- and men's 30-kilometer races.[67] For fans out on the course, especially during the men's race on 15 February, it was obvious that the Soviet team members had the best skis of the day: the grip was tenacious while skiing uphill, yet the glide was meteoric on the flats and downhill. Harvey of Canada expressed surprise to the *Calgary Herald* at how well the Russian's skis performed given the tricky wax conditions. His teammate Al Pilcher said that a Soviet racer sped past him on one of the downhills with unbelievably fast skis.[68] Both *Pravda* and *Sovetskii sport* crowed over the success of the nation's technicians: "It looks like our waxers 'hit the wax.'"[69] *Komsomol'skaia pravda* exulted, "And they guessed it right!"[70]

So well did the Russians ski that rumors circulated about a "secret wax" procured by the Soviet squad. The methodical testing of new products by waxing experts from the Soviet Union may partially explain this. One of the technical innovations available at the Calgary Olympics was a new type of wax discovered in Italy that increased glide on the bases of both Alpine and Nordic skis. These were hydrophobic waxes formulated from fluorocarbons that could be ironed into polyethylene ski bases at high temperatures. In 1988 this type of fluorocarbon wax had been in existence for less than two years, but tests subsequent to the Calgary Games revealed that it improved ski glide by around 2 percent over the best non-fluorocarbon combinations.[71] In the waxing trailers at Canmore, however, few understood the proper way to use these new waxes. "It was the dawn of Cera F," waxing specialist Nat Brown recalls, using the commercial name for fluorocarbon wax marketed by Swix in 1990, "and *no one* knew how to use the stuff."[72] It is likely, however, that the technicians of the USSR did. In addition, the Soviets employed an innovative device to assist in their testing protocols. This was a spring-wound "egg-beater" with interchangeable polyethylene discs upon which technicians applied a variety of test waxes. At various points out on the race course, a wax tester would wind up the egg-beater, place it on the snow disc-side down and pull a trigger cable. As the discs rotated, the number of revolutions indicated the relative friction associated with each of the different waxes. This allowed technicians an easy and consistent way to test waxes anywhere on the racecourse in a matter of minutes as opposed to the time-consuming process of carting multiple pairs of skis around the track.[73]

Prokurorov realized that the Soviet staff had found the magic formula for ski base preparation.[74] He also believed that his early start was a benefit: "If Vladimir [Smirnov] had had my start number 28 and had been able to go out earlier, he would surely have been the winner. For those in the back the track was progressively more powdery, because the artificial snow didn't bind to the natural snow."[75] Start numbers were irrelevant, however, for top skiers from Scandinavia such as Sweden's Gunde Svan and Torgny Mogren, who had been leading the World Cup circuit prior to the Games. Swedish waxing specialists had badly misjudged ski preparation for both skiers that day. Slippery grip wax plagued not only the Swedes but also a majority of competitors attempting to ski the difficult ascents leading out of the spectators' area.[76] Expending an enormous amount of energy to negotiate the steeps on slick bases, these racers found their skis sluggish on the downhills and flats, rendering their ski technique inefficient and exhausting. "Today Svan wasn't in top form like he usually is," Smirnov told an interviewer after the race, "and when the coaches said to me that he was losing big, I wasn't surprised."[77] But with bad wax, it was more than even the best skiers in the world could muster to ski proficiently on the demanding Canmore course, and the highly favored team from Sweden could only produce a tenth-place finish. "This is an endurance track," said West Germany's Behle, "custommade for the Soviets."[78] After just two cross-country ski events in as many days, the Soviet Union had gathered four out of six possible medals. In an off-the-cuff answer to a journalist's question after the 30-kilometer race, a

Canadian Nordic Team coach groused: "This is not the Russian champion-ships."[79] By the end of the week, his follow-up comments had inspired an absolute furor in the world press. "Canada's head coach Marty Hall," stated Norway's leading daily *Dagbladet,* "for a few days has been the most exciting man at the Olympics."[80]

"I've Created What They Say Is an International Incident"[81]

Described variously as a "loud-mouthed trouble-maker," a "blunder-buss," "no stranger to controversy" and "never one to shy away from tack-ling tough issues," Marty Hall has been one of the most influential indi-viduals in the history of North American cross-country skiing over the past forty years.[82] He served the United States Cross-Country Ski Team in a variety of positions from 1968 to 1978, coaching American ski racers when they accumulated some of their best Olympic finishes to date, most notably Bill Koch's silver medal at the 1976 Innsbruck Games. His con-troversial coaching methods led to a parting of the ways with the United States Ski Team in 1978. Four years later, he moved to Canada to assume the head coaching position for the nation's cross-country ski team, re-maining until 1989. In that time, he improved the international ranking of Canada's Nordic Team from fourteenth to seventh place. One of Hall's charges, Pierre Harvey, won several World Cup races under his tutelage.[83]

Over the span of three decades Hall had often travelled behind the Iron Curtain, and each time he became increasingly suspicious that Eastern European skiers were involved in illicit drug use and medical procedures. In the opinion of Canada's iconoclastic head coach, both the IOC and FIS were culpable for the rampant spread of drug use and doping. Hall was on record prior to the 1988 Games as FIS President Marc Hodler's antagonist. In the midst of blood-doping allegations and countercharges at the 1987 World Championships in Obertsdorf, West Germany, FIS had publicly berated a West German doctor and revoked his ski accreditation for two years after he sprayed champagne on three of the nation's athletes who had just won a gold medal on their home turf. "You should be ashamed," Hodler indignantly scolded Dr. Heinz Liesen, for allowing athletes and alcohol to appear together on television. FIS needs "to get its head out of the sand," was Hall's own indignant response.[84]

As Canada prepared for the 1988 Games, Hall was afraid that the East Germans and Russians as well as other communist bloc nations would gather all the medals at Calgary through illegal means.[85] However, the applied technology of doping prevalent among athletes and their coaches far outpaced that of the drug-testing protocols at international races, including the Olympics. In the late 1980s, the only "test" for blood doping was an examination of the skin for needle-marks. With detection difficult and the margin of victory at international competitions measured in mere seconds, no nation's athletes were immune to the attraction of blood doping: although Finnish coaches vociferously denied that their athletes were involved, Aki Karvonen, who won one silver and two bronze medals in Sarajevo in 1984, later admitted to *Sports Illustrated* that he had received the treatment there; and just one month before the opening races in Canmore, FIS suspended an American Nordic combined skier, Kerry Lynch, along with some of his coaches, from all competitions in 1988 because of his admission to blood doping.[86] It is worth noting that both Karvonen and Lynch came forward of their own volition to confess to blood doping rather than having been compromised by enforced drug testing. It was Lynch's naiveté, *Le Monde* of France suggested cynically, that had kept him out of the Olympic Games: "Today once again there are those who are calling the unfortunate Kerry 'Candide.'"[87]

Because the high-profile events of the Winter Olympics such as figure skating and ice dancing were scheduled to begin later in the week, an expanded press corps hungry for news to fill their daily quotas followed the first events on the Nordic tracks of Canmore. Many of these correspondents, unaware of the myriad complexities involved with international cross-country ski racing, expressed surprise that the Soviets were so strong on the first two days. A Reuters News Agency story from Calgary picked up across North America two days after the initial races encouraged this point of view with the erroneous statement that Prokurorov had finished in only sixty-second place in the previous year's World Cup. Mike Moran, chief spokesman for the United States Olympic Team, told Reuters that he considered Prokurorov and Smirnov's first- and second-place finishes "unexpected performances by unknown competitors."[88] These pronouncements were ill-informed and quite misleading: gold medalist Prokurorov was certainly no dark horse in the 30-kilometer race, having finished sixth, not sixty-second, during the 1987 World Cup season.[89] His teammate, the new silver medalist Smirnov, had placed just ahead of him in fifth during that same season. The year before that, Smirnov was third in the overall World Cup standings after three consecutive seasons on the circuit, while Prokurorov accrued enough points to finish eighteenth, a marked improvement from his 1984 World Cup ranking of fifty-fourth. In the World Cup races of December 1987, just two months prior to the Calgary Games, both Smirnov and Prokurorov had acquitted themselves quite admirably among a competitive international field during a 15-kilometer classical race in Davos, Switzerland, and a 30-kilometer skating event held in Castelrotto, Italy.[90]

During these first days of competition at Canmore, Marty Hall's group of skiers had not fared so well: in the women's 10-kilometer event, the top Canadian finisher placed thirtieth. He was furious that his top racer, Angela Schmidt-Foster, had altered the wax on her skis just before her start, against the advice of the team technicians: "It was a lousy day," Hall said in his press conference after the race. "It's embarrassing. It's like somebody forgot to tell [the Canadian women] the Olympics have started."[91] The next day, Pierre Harvey, who had taken seventh-place overall World Cup honors just a few points behind Smirnov and Prokurorov in 1987, came across the line at the end of the 30-kilometer contest in fourteenth. Hall was annoyed: "[The Soviets] could be this great," he told the press after the men's race. "They have a helluva program. But you just have to wonder when you come to a championship like this, an Olympics like this. This isn't the tiddlywinks tournament. Everyone is here."[92] Could the difference possibly have been the superior waxing capabilities of the Soviet specialists? Not according to Hall: "It's not the wax on the bottom. It's the body on top of the skis. There's been a lot more drugging going on in this sport than people realize. Don't take that out of context, but there are more problems than FIS lets on."[93] Reports of EPO use by athletes were making headlines in Calgary that week, and sensing a story, reporters asked Hall whether the success of the Soviet team could be attributed to blood doping. "That's the most logical thing," Hall replied, adding as an afterthought: "I'm going to get in trouble for this because I'm a loudmouth in the international scene."[94] He was absolutely correct on this final point: the response was immediate and overwhelmingly negative.

Marty Hall had unleashed a firestorm during his Monday afternoon conference. Afterward, Roger Jackson, president of the Canadian Olympic Association, demanded that Hall issue an apology, a move the incensed ski coach initially refused to make.[95] In a hastily assembled press conference the following day, representatives from the IOC, Canada, the United States and the Soviet Union issued statements castigating Hall. Michele Verdier, IOC's spokeswoman, informed the press that his comments had "absolutely no substance," although she offered no facts to substantiate her claim. Jackson's criticism carried a much harsher tone: "The stupidity is [Hall] made an accusation he has absolutely no ability to back up. I don't understand why he made such comments. He has absolutely no evidence to make such accusations and I think it was really ridiculous."[96] Jean Grenier, Canada's Chief of Mission, told the press that the Canadian team would not support Hall's accusations. Mike Moran of the United States offered that it was wrong to make unproven allegations against East European countries that had consistently fielded top athletes. Vitalii Smirnov, a Soviet member of the IOC's executive board, expressed the sentiments of the USSR's Olympic Team: "Of course we're upset by this. It's unfair to make such statements." However, his assertion that Soviet athletes had not blood doped was just as unfounded as Hall's accusation: "All the athletes were checked for blood transfusions, including the medalists, and there were no marks found." Firing back at Hall, Smirnov suggested: "In my opinion, it would be better for him to be a better coach than to criticize the best athletes in the world."[97] He added that it was work and hard training that accounted for the success of the Soviets. A doctor for the Soviet Olympic Team, Aleksei Kuznetsov, disingenuously stated: "We came here well prepared. We don't need blood doping, and also we don't have the techniques for it." Raymond Gafner of Switzerland, who served as IOC administrator, summed up the conference: "It's stupidity. When you are the host team, the host nation, you don't behave like this."[98]

By Wednesday an international crisis was brewing, and Canada's Federal Sports Minister, Otto Jelinek, felt compelled to step in and defuse the situation. He spoke personally with Soviet Sports Minister Marat Gramov in Calgary, expressing regret for the controversy and distancing the Canadian government from Hall's statements. Jelinek announced that he and Gramov intended to resolve the doping situation in sports with an accord committing the two countries to fight the use of performance-enhancing drugs. Prince Alexandre de Merode, chairman of the IOC medical commission, condemned Hall as well, demanding that the Canadian coach issue an apology, since a doctor had examined the athletes under suspicion for needle punctures without finding a single incriminating mark.[99]

The pressure on Hall from Jelinek, Jackson, Grenier and the rest of the Canadian government to apologize was enormous. Conceding to their demands, Hall worked with Brent Rushall, sport psychologist for the Canadian team, to formulate a retraction suitable for presentation to the press—but the coach was adamant that the criticism directed at him was unwarranted.[100] His final, carefully worded product was included in a note sent on Tuesday afternoon to former biathlete Viktor Mamatov, now the Soviet Chief of Mission in Calgary. In this missive, Hall enumerated several alternative reasons for the Soviet skiers' success: "I made it clear that no accusations [about blood doping] were being made since there was no evidence available." At a news conference in Canmore on Wednesday, Hall insisted that his comments earlier in the week had been taken out of context and that he was merely explaining his statements and not apologizing.[101]

The press, both foreign and domestic, was quick to pick up on the international controversy after the Wednesday press conference. Kevin Cox of the *Globe and Mail* queried Hall on the continued success of the Soviet skiers after Tamara Tikhonova and Vida Venciene won silver and bronze medals in the women's 5-kilometer sprint. The previously effusive Canadian coach was circumspect in his response: "We see these kinds of results from them on the World Cup circuit all the time."[102] The *Boston Globe* pressed Hall on his accusations against the Soviet skiers: "I'm saying doping is going on. But I never said the Russians. You guys [the press] had to make that inference. Yes, I think it's happening, but I have no evidence, nobody does."[103] In a televised interview outside the Canmore Nordic Center, Hall told CTV that the results from a race in Lahti the previous year proved that something nefarious was occurring in Canada, because even though Prokurorov had won that race, no other Soviet skier made the top ten: "You don't see shutouts like this [in Calgary], especially in the men . . . I made no accusation about the Russians blood doping, [but] those are pretty damn good results."[104] For a segment concerning the blood-doping controversy aired on Canadian Broadcasting Corporation (CBC) News, Hall stated: "They're good—there's no doubt about it, and to have those kind of results two days in a row? You know, you can't say anything because there's no way you can prove it." The program featured a theatrically bemused Viktor Ivanov, head coach of the Soviet Cross-Country Ski Team, scoffing at the suggestion his athletes were involved with blood doping. In response to footage of the IOC's Michele Verdier addressing the morning press conference, an exasperated Hall told the camera: "They [IOC] haven't done anything—haven't done anything! And I think they have a responsibility . . . to spend some money, do some research."[105]

The variety of opinions on Hall was as mixed as the number of correspondents furnishing comment. The *Calgary Herald* ferreted out Soviet athletes for their reaction to Hall's blood-doping allegations. "Taking into account it was not true, it did not make us angry," silver medalist Tikhonova said through an interpreter. "I consider it very silly information," was the reaction from her teammate and bronze medalist Venciené. The *Chicago Tribune* cornered cross-country racer Dan Simoneau of the United States, who suggested that Hall was merely stating out loud what many people assumed was true.[106] An article in Australia's *Sydney Morning Herald* quoted the deputy head of the Soviet Olympic delegation, Viacheslav Gavrilin, in reply to Hall's charges: "He does not produce any evidence. As soon as Soviet athletes achieve success some people turn up who try to belittle their accomplishments. Sometimes it is done for the sake of concealing one's own blunders in the training technique . . . for instance, Pierre Harvey: he has impressive victories to his credit. If Harvey were trained as thoroughly as his Soviet counterparts he could become a prize winner at the current Olympics."[107] Other accounts in the Western press accelerated the dispute. The normally staid *Frankfurter Allgemeine Zeitung* quoted Aleksii Kuznetsov's incendiary comeback to the accusations: "It's an obscenity."[108] A bold-type headline directed at Hall in Norway's *Dagbladet* screamed: "Shut Up—For Now, Only Bad Losers Are Talking." In the paper's opinion, Hall's theory about blood doping was "a more effective means for poor losers rather than for dishonest winners."[109]

By Saturday, 20 February, the plodding staff of ABC Sports finally caught up with the blood-doping scandal that had rocked Canmore earlier in the week. Its perfunctory exposé emphasized the sensational aspects surrounding the controversy, such as the denigration of Kerry Lynch and the lurid details of the doping process. ABC's sports medicine expert, Dr. Ken Forsythe, delivered a simplified explanation of the blood extraction phase, seated on a hospital gurney with a tube in his arm and a nurse technician in a white lab coat at his side manipulating the attached plasma bag. In a sit-down interview with Pekka Vähäsöyrinki, the head coach of the Finnish Cross-Country Ski Team, the network's Mike Adamle asked about Soviet blood-doping allegations made by Finland's own coaching staff. Clearly perturbed by Adamle's line of questioning, his reply was terse: "A misunderstanding, maybe by newspapers." Adamle fared no better with Lev Markov, team physician for the USSR Cross-Country Ski Team. Instead of pressing him with pointed questions, Adamle tossed out vapid queries that Markov easily parried. Was Markov upset by the doping allegations? "Me personally, I am not displeased," replied the doctor with the help of a struggling translator. "I am not upset, it is simply funny for me. The same guys who told it to us claim that we are trying to put a fire on the Olympic Games." ABC's correspondent continued: Do you test your athletes for blood doping? "We are conducting the tests concerning blood doping strictly according to IOC recommendations . . . if there is some new method we are going to implement it immediately." Adamle followed with a hypothetical query: What if the IOC said today that they wanted to test every racer? Would the Soviet Union agree? "Each competitor? Certainly we agree. But it costs very much so it would be very complicated up to now." Adamle's final question, delivered with an investigative journalist's incisive flair, completely missed its intended target: "You have nothing to hide?" With a chortle, Markov replied: "No. We have nothing to hide."[110]

Behind the Iron Curtain, the reaction to the Canmore brouhaha was one of predictable outrage. "Unfortunately, the fourth day of the Olympics didn't manage without a very unsavory episode," lamented *Pravda*.[111] "This totally unsubstantiated and boorish declaration," wrote *Trud*'s correspondent, "rang out in an interview that was conspicuously published on the spot. It's clear that such rash words don't become the Canadian coach—they blemish sport."[112] *Izvestiia* was blunt: "We have a saying that's almost become a proverb: 'You have to know how to lose, too.'"[113] A *Sovetskii sport* editorial titled "The Logic of Envy" cited the careful preparation the USSR's National Team endured in Bakuriani on specially built courses prior to the Games and the experienced waxing specialists who assisted the skiers. The paper made note of the poor results of the Canadian skiers during the first two days of competition and quoted Pierre Harvey's comments after his finish in the men's 30-kilometer race about the vital role ski preparation and waxing played in the outcome.[114] *Krasnaia zvezda* bristled that the *Calgary Sun* had printed a front-page article under the banner: "Russians Accused of Blood Doping."[115] The following day, Bulgaria's *Robotnichesko delo* expanded upon *Sovetskii sport*'s "Logic of Envy" theme, while Poland's *Trybuna ludu* quoted Roger Jackson's comment as a sub-headline: "It's Stupidity."[116] The Polish Communist Party's official publication also took the *Calgary Sun* to task for its editorial on the blood-doping allegations aimed at the USSR, printing Viacheslav Gavrilin's response: "The accusations should be treated as an ordinary category of slander . . . there is no doping and never will be."[117] In Budapest, *Magyar nemzet* considered Hall's accusations a case of "sour grapes," referencing statements by West Germany's Manfred Donike, an expert in combating drugs in sport, who opined that blood doping could not significantly increase athletic performance.[118] On the following day, *Krasnaia zvezda* chimed in again: "The atmosphere around the ski competitions has heated up to the max." So implausible were Hall's statements about blood doping, the newspaper suggested, that there could be no guarantee the next morning's edition might not carry a report that teenaged Soviet figure skater Katia Gordeeva "arrived at the Olympics on the back of a white bear."[119] In a Friday recap of the comments by representatives of the IOC, Canada and the United States, *Sovetskii sport* predicted the worst for Marty Hall: "He risks bringing trouble on himself."[120]

Less than twenty-four hours later, the ominous prognostication of the Soviet Union's premier sports journal came true when Marty Hall received an official letter of reprimand from the federal Government of Canada. The contents of the letter were transmitted by Otto Jelinek to Soviet Sports Minister Gramov, who could not resist taking a jab at the besieged Hall. In response to a question from a member of the Canadian press, he said: "A coach has to be a coach, not only by training but by avocation. . . . Our coach told me that if he had his hands on [Pierre] Harvey, he'd be a world champion in two years."[121] At the time, it was hard to argue with Gramov's boast: Soviet skiers dominated the full gamut of diagonal stride sprint races that week. In addition to the Soviet women's silver and bronze medal finish in the 5-kilometer sprint on Wednesday, Mikhail Deviat'iarov took first place in the men's 15-kilometer race two days later on 19 February. His teammate, 30-kilometer silver medalist Vladimir Smirnov, added a bronze medal to his Calgary collection of hardware. Even the Soviet press expressed surprise at this outcome: "We expected Smirnov to win," one journalist said to John Husar of the *Chicago Tribune*. "He is much stronger."[122] Pierre Harvey crossed the finish line in a disappointing seventeenth place.[123]

The USSR's show of force continued into the second week as well. Soviet women swept all three pedestal spots in the 20-kilometer freestyle event and took gold in the 4 x 5-kilometer relay.[124] However, the Soviet men did not fare as well as the women in their final races. Snow conditions were more consistent by the second week with less complex ski preparation, leveling the playing field to a certain extent. Sweden edged the USSR for the gold medal in the men's 4 x 10-kilometer relay by a mere twelve seconds at the finish line.[125] Still, *Sovetskii sport* delighted in passing on to its readers a UPI report stating that with only the 50-kilometer marathon remaining, Soviet skiers had already won thirteen out of seventeen medals. "Reuters also notes the performance of Raisa Smetanina," the paper continued. "The bronze medal [in the 20-kilometer race] of the thirty-five-year-old sportswoman has allowed her to join the Swedish skier Sixten Jernberg with a collection of nine Olympic medals."[126] At what was destined to be the Soviet Union's last appearance at the Games, a Russian skier competing in her fourth Olympics had finally equaled the record of the twentieth century's greatest cross-country ski racer.

In biathlon, a certain level of frustration clouded the individual efforts of the Soviet skiers. Before the largest crowd ever assembled for an Olympic biathlon event, Valerii Medvedtsev out-shot East Germany's Frank-Peter Roetsch but still lost the gold medal by twenty-one seconds in the 20-kilometer race on Saturday, 20 February. *Sovetskii sport* remained hopeful, however, for the outcome of the 10-kilometer sprint and 4 x 7.5-kilometer relay: "In the final results the Soviet biathletes were closer, or as marksmen might say 'more tightly grouped,' than those of East Germany: second, fourth, fifth and twelfth for us, while theirs were first, seventh, ninth and sixteenth. Although changes on the teams are to be expected, there's still some kind of clue about the upcoming biathlon sprint and relay competitions in this arithmetic."[127]

The 10-kilometer sprint on 23 February produced two more medals for the Soviet Union: a second silver for Medvedtsev and bronze for his teammate Sergei Chepikov. But once again it was Roetsch at the top of the pedestal: "Of course we were really counting on gold here," senior coach Aleksandr Privalov told *Sovetskii sport.* "But Roetsch upset all our plans. He simply did a phenomenal job preparing for the Olympics. I have nothing but good to say about Medvedtsev and Chepikov. The guys did well, they gave it all they could. But their competitor did just a little bit better."[128] Of greater concern were Roetsch's East German teammates, who finished in fourth, fifth and sixth positions. This did not bode well for Saturday's biathlon relay: "One can imagine," wrote *Komsomol'skaia pravda*'s correspondents, "but in no way divine, what kind of intensity—sharper than a blade—the battle in the relay holds in store now."[129] The reporters from *Sovetskii sport* expressed not only dismay for the team's prospects but also a bit of irritation with their nation's biathletes: "After the race we went up to the boys in order to congratulate the medalists and find out from the others how they explained their bad luck today. But all four evaded answering: we're not allowed, they say, to talk with journalists. By whom is it not allowed? Why? We didn't obtain answers to these questions either. Don't you think that's a strange conspiracy of silence in an era of glasnost'?"[130]

Despite the newspaper's misgivings, the Soviet relay squad pulled off a stunning victory on Friday, 26 February 1988. East Germany was out of the hunt right from the start after lead-off skier Jürgen Wirth left three targets untouched after the first bout of shooting. The Soviet Union took the lead by the second leg and never surrendered the front spot, crossing the finish line ahead of West Germany by a comfortable margin of one minute and seven seconds.[131] With this victory the USSR now owned six consecutive biathlon relay medals, and the Soviet press was justifiably exuberant. "A Golden Tradition," read *Pravda*'s headline on 27 February. Under the banner "The Weighty 'Gold' of Calgary," *Krasnaia zvezda*'s subheading dubbed the Soviet relay team "The Magnificent Four." "Shoulder to Shoulder toward the Dream" blared *Sovetskii sport*'s front-page headline, with an additional rejoinder below the fold: "How wonderful when it's springtime in your heart."[132] This final gold medal capped a week of brilliant Soviet performances in the three cross-country relay events, providing an opportune moment for the press to tout old-school socialism in the topsy-turvy era of glasnost' and perestroika. The Red Army's *Krasnaia zvezda* suggested: "In the relay there is the highest manifestation of comradeship and collectivism, when the hearts of the sportsmen beat in unison and all thoughts are directed at the achievement of an important goal. Only then does victory arrive."[133] Conflating both the gold medal hockey team and biathletes of the USSR, *Sovetskii sport* rhapsodized: "In each of them the pulse of one heart, of one living organism is felt—they are teams. It's the pulse of twenty-three knights of hockey and four ski-shooters."[134] Head coach Privalov stressed—with a dash of hyperbole—the importance of the socialist paradigm in Soviet biathlon: "In the relay the power was already on our side. It's the power of the collective, united by one dream, by this dream of existence."[135] Cognizant of the fact that only three more Games remained in the twentieth century, *Trud* noted the significance of this unbroken string of victories: "[It's a] record that athletes will be able to repeat only in the next century."[136]

Calgary's Aftermath

Throughout the Calgary Games, Marty Hall retained a handful of allies in his anti-doping camp, such as former Canadian head coach Anders Lenes, who had seen first-hand doctors and coaches transfusing blood into Finnish ski racer Aki Karvonen at the 1984 Olympics in Sarajevo.[137] Nevertheless, the consensus was that Canada's coach was a loose cannon with an even looser tongue, lashing out in frustration before a hometown crowd. Even as Hall's imbroglio began to fade from the front pages after his formal reprimand from the Canadian government, the controversy over drugs and blood doping remained a topic of interest for the duration of the

Winter Olympics. The concerns about EPO raised during the first week of competition continued throughout the Games as additional drug scandals broke in other sports. Speculation ran rampant that three Romanian speed skaters who were sent back to Bucharest before the start of their competitions had failed drug tests. A pair of Czech figure skaters returned home after team officials discovered that one of the athletes took a headache pill containing codeine. A Polish hockey player failed his requisite urine test with elevated levels of testosterone, attributable, according to Polish officials, to the unwitting athlete falling victim to a malicious perpetrator.[138] By the time of the closing ceremonies, the debate initiated by Hall's doping allegations spurred Otto Jelinek to announce that Canada would host a three-day international anti-drug conference in Montreal. On the agenda for the June meeting was the formulation of uniform sanctions and testing procedures for all subsequent international athletic competitions.[139] Hall found vindication for the charges leveled at him by Jelinek in the controversy over Canadian sprinter Ben Johnson's infamous steroid scandal just a few months later. "I hate to say I told you so," he told reporters. "I feel sorry for Ben, but I feel happy for sport."[140] Marty Hall continued in his role as an unapologetic and implacable foe of drug use in athletics throughout his tenure as a ski coach. He remains so to this day. Only in recent decades, after extensive work by researchers in East German and Soviet archives, has it been possible to appreciate Marty the Mouth's perspicacity concerning the use of banned substances and procedures by Eastern Bloc athletes during the first week of the Calgary Olympics.[141]

The culture of blood doping, unfortunately, remains ingrained in the sport of cross-country ski racing, and nowhere is it more prevalent than in post-Soviet Russia.[142] In 1992, Russian biathlete Sergei Tarasov wound up in the intensive-care unit in Les Saisies, France with a serious viral infection just prior to the Albertville Olympics. Cross-contamination during a blood-doping procedure was the probable cause: "It's a big temptation to grab a unit of blood off the shelf on your way to the Olympics," said the United States' Nordic Team doctor, Jim Stray-Gundersen, at the time. "We think it was some food we brought from home. I don't know of any cases of blood doping in the former Soviet Union," was the assessment of Aleksandr Privalov, at this point serving as head coach of the Russian Unified Team. A curious *non sequitur* from another veteran of the Calgary Games, Dr. Lev Markov, implied that the intravenous saline solution hooked into Tarasov's arm may have given the public a wrong impression: "That might lead some people to think there were some illegal blood transfusions."[143]

Two female Russian skiers, Larisa Lazutina and Olga Danilova, were disqualified at the 2002 Olympics in Salt Lake City and banned from competition for two years after testing positive for EPO. Rather than returning home in disgrace, the pair were met by cheering fans and a military band at Moscow's Sheremet'evo Airport. President Vladimir Putin hailed both women as heroes and excoriated the Russian Olympic Committee (ROC) for not doing enough to defend them against charges brought by the IOC. Russian vice premier Valentina Matvienko told the press that despite the forfeiture of her gold medal, Lazutina deserved to receive the fifty-thousand-dollar award bestowed upon all the other Russian Olympic champions by the government.[144] Prior to the start of the Vancouver Olympics of 2010, eight Russian cross-country skiers and biathletes failed tests for EPO and were sidelined from the Games. The nation's cavalier attitude toward illegal use of drugs and doping resulted in a warning from Jaques Rogges, current president of the IOC, and John Fahey, president of the World Anti-Doping Agency, stating that Russia must sort out the drug problem before the Sochi Olympics of 2014. In June 2010, FIS cautioned Deputy Prime Minister Aleksandr Zhukov that Russian athletes would be banned from competing in their own country if the ROC did not incorporate new drug and blood-doping policies well in advance of the Sochi Games. Zhukov, who also served as president of the ROC, immediately fired eight coaches and established a Russian anti-doping agency. As a result of these actions, Gian Franco Kasper, president of FIS, rescinded his organization's threat in November 2010.[145] That FIS has found it necessary to resort to such a stringent course of action indicates the degree to which the ephemeral "logic of envy" proposed by the Soviet Union in 1988 has so thoroughly dissipated in the twenty-first century.

Afterword

Just three months after the closing ceremonies at the 1988 Calgary Olympics, President of the United States Ronald Reagan received a standing ovation as he entered Moscow State University's main auditorium. He was in the Soviet Union at the behest of Mikhail Gorbachev for a series of wide-ranging discussions on bilateral treaties and strategic arms limitations. Addressing the assembly from a stage beneath a huge bust of Lenin and a red-and-gold banner emblazoned with the hammer and sickle, Reagan was interrupted frequently with applause during his lecture on the importance of freedom of thought and information. "It was a very good speech, filled with humor," one student told Reuters. "Really, I like your president very much. It's very rare for a small man like me to meet a president."[1] Reagan's visit to the Soviet Union changed the perception of the citizenry toward the United States dramatically: by the end of his trip, over half the Muscovite population indicated in response to a poll that they admired Reagan more after his visit. The threat posed by the United States had diminished considerably in just a few short days, as had the reason for blind allegiance to the Soviet regime. Although it would be simplistic to attribute the demise of the USSR to Reagan's appearance before a Soviet audience, it is indicative of a major paradigm shift in the country, one that had significant impact. In less than a year, elections of representatives to the Congress of People's Deputies, initially promulgated by Gorbachev himself, ushered in a period of radical political democratization, first in the Soviet Union and then in Eastern Europe: in May of 1989, the barbwire on the border separating Hungary from Austria came down; on 4 June, Solidarity swept national elections in Poland; on 9 November, the Berlin Wall was dismantled; and on 25 December, the overthrown ruler of Romania, Nicolae Ceauşescu, was executed. The disintegration of the entire Soviet bloc was now close at hand. By the second half of 1989, the parties in favor of radical change in the Soviet Union had left the more conservative

Gorbachev far behind. His former allies were now backing Boris Yeltsin, an unstinting reformer who called for the very abolition of the USSR's political system. From 1990 through 1991, two major crises faced the Soviet Union: reviving the economy and keeping the union together, neither of which Gorbachev was able to resolve. On 21 December 1991, eleven of the Soviet republics issued a statement creating the Commonwealth of Independent States (CIS) to replace the USSR. Four days later, Gorbachev resigned as president of the now defunct Soviet Union.[2]

Yet the dissolution of the USSR had little effect on the elite skiers who came of age under the Soviet regime. At the 1992 Albertville Olympics, which opened six weeks after Gorbachev left office, the women of Russia's Unified Team performed magnificently. In the first-ever biathlon events for women, athletes from the CIS placed third in the 3 x 7.5-kilometer relay, and they took home a total of three individual medals: Anfisa Reztsova won gold in the 7.5-kilometer sprint, followed by Elena Belova for the bronze; and Svetlana Pecherskaia placed second in the 15-kilometer race. In special cross-country skiing, Russian women accounted for eight out a possible twelve individual medals. In her fifth Olympics, the ageless Raisa Smetanina ran the second leg for the CIS team's gold medal performance in the 4 x 5-kilometer relay. In men's biathlon, less than twenty-three seconds was the margin between reunified German gold and post-Soviet Russian silver in the 4 x 7.5-kilometer relay, ending a gold medal streak that had endured since the 1968 Grenoble Winter Games. Nonetheless, Evgenii Redkin posted a first-place finish in the 20-kilometer individual race.[3]

Medals won by Russian athletes at the 1992 Winter Olympics belong to the CIS in name only: the awards redound to the credit of the incredibly successful Soviet sports juggernaut, its many flaws notwithstanding. Certainly, the Soviet regime's decades-long commitment to cross-country skiing laid the groundwork for Russia's continued excellence in skiing and biathlon. Subsequent to dissolution, Russia has maintained its position as a potent force at International Ski Federation (FIS) competitions, winning a total of seventy-one medals at Nordic World Championship cross-country skiing events from 1993 through 2013. Russians accounted for 33 percent of all possible medals in the women's events.[4] Russian biathletes have won ninety world championship and twenty-five Olympic medals between 1992 and 2013. In the biathlon relay, the Russian women have taken three gold, one silver and two bronze medals over the last five Olympics, eclipsing the three silver and two bronze medals of the men's squad during the same period. On any given day the biathlon relay—whether the men's, the women's or the recent mixed men's-and-women's format—is still Russia's to lose.

On a broader scale, the influence of the USSR's athletic program on the development of international sport is unmistakable in the twenty-first century. A 2008 article in the *Wall Street Journal* remarked: "Now, characteristics of the old East bloc are apparent in the Olympic programs of countries like Australia and Japan. By pouring money into a limited number of medal-promising disciplines, these countries already have gotten results."[5] The significance individual countries attribute to winning Olympic and world championship medals has only increased as a major motivating factor over the last three decades, reflecting how politics continues to infuse sports. In addition, the USSR's example improved elite standards for women, making their events an integral part of modern national sports policies. Unfortunately, a hold-over from the Cold War era is a twenty-first-century "arms race" to find ever-more powerful—and untraceable—athletic bio-enhancers. Although cyclist Lance Armstrong's fall from grace in 2013 has recently reinforced a backlash against doping in Nordic ski racing, the financial rewards for discovering products that improve athletic performance while mimicking natural substances in the body may once again prove too much of a temptation. In the future, controlling these developments will require constant vigilance by the governing bodies of athletic associations throughout the world.[6]

The tumultuous course followed by Russia since dissolution has encouraged some citizens to re-evaluate the Soviet era: general polls taken in 2006 found around 60 percent of the respondents expressing nostalgia for life under communism. These numbers remain virtually unchanged as of late 2011.[7] President Vladimir Putin has certainly promoted this point of view. In his 2005 State of the Union Address, Putin called the breakup of the Soviet Union "the great geopolitical catastrophe of the twentieth century."[8] Recent efforts to rehabilitate the reputations of Stalin, Brezhnev and even the KGB have recast the past in dulcet revisionist tones while a new type of antagonism toward the West in general and the United States in particular has gained appeal across a broad political spectrum throughout the country. It is likely that the militaristic nationalism of a resurgent Russia will assume new meaning vis-à-vis sport in the aftermath of the 2008 South Ossetia War. Russia's border with South Ossetia, Abkahzia and Georgia is barely thirty kilometers from the Russian resort town of Sochi, site of the Twenty-Second Winter Olympics scheduled for 2014. Cold War dynamics still shroud events in this locale.

Putin, currently serving his second stint as president of Russia, has long enjoyed Sochi as a recreational destination, and in July 2007 he made a personal pitch to the IOC to have Russia host the Winter Games there. When the Black Sea city received the bid, a contributing factor was his promise to invest twelve billion dollars of government money in developing the region. Putin himself has quite a lot riding on the success of this venture: "Sochi is his personal city," remarked Fiona Hill of the Brookings Institute in a 2013 interview, "in many respects the way Peter the Great made St. Petersburg his own imperial project."[9] The ski area above the town has served as a backdrop for Putin's ski exploits, documented in carefully scripted videos bolstering his multi-faceted "man of action" persona. In 2008, Vladimir Makarenko, deputy director of Gazprom, the state-run conglomerate overseeing a good portion of the construction, accompanied a reporter from the *New York Times* up a brand-new ski-lift high above Sochi. Makarenko had served as guide for Putin when he visited the newly opened ski resort in April of that year, and the experience was taxing: "He skied there," Makarenko said, "and there, there too, and there, also there. I was tired, I couldn't keep up. What a tempo!"[10] With current Russian prime minister Dmitrii Medvedev in tow, Putin has taken to the Sochi slopes for the cameras most recently during a World Cup competition in February 2011. That same month, just weeks after Medvedev unveiled a fifteen-billion-dollar plan to establish five ski resorts in the Caucasus Mountains, terrorist attacks destroyed cable cars used to transport climbers and skiers on nearby Mt. Elbrus. More ominous have been alleged plans to assault Sochi itself and the 2014 Olympic Games, thwarted in May 2012 when Russian authorities seized a cache of weapons in neighboring Abkhazia and arrested three suspects with possible links to Doku Umarov, a Chechen rebel leader.[11]

That terrorists have plotted to strike Putin's playground and Russia's first Winter Olympic site—and managed to carry out at least one successful attack at an established ski area less than 250 kilometers away—reinforces the notion that skiing remains a significant cultural and ideological metaphor in the region. This is often manifested in imagery that evokes themes inherited from the Soviet era and stokes overt yearning for the former regime's military might. Dmitrii Peskov, Putin's current press secretary, recently compared the Olympic site development in Sochi to the reconstruction of cities destroyed in the wake of World War II. In addition, photographs from recent events, such as a 2007 political parade arranged by Moscow's mayor Iurii Luzhkov in support of the United Russia Party, as well as one in Red Square in 2009 marking the sixty-eighth anniversary of the departure of the Red Army to meet the German invasion of 1941, illustrate that the image of the ski-trooper of the Great Patriotic War is still a potent trope in Russia. In both parades, soldiers dressed in winter-white camouflage uniforms marched smartly before the Kremlin walls with skis and poles hoisted over their shoulders and rifles slung across their backs. Ski-troopers on the march are now a regular feature of similar commemorative events in Russia.[12] The association with Soviet biathlon is implicit in these patriotic displays.

Without a doubt, biathlon has become international bol'shoi sport and bol'shoi biznes: as of 2008, the International Biathlon Union (IBU)'s operating budget was just over 10.5 million euros. The total value of contracts with IBU partners and suppliers, without factoring in arrangements with individual athletes and national federations, amounted to 500,000 euros in 2007.[13] "Biathlon has become a mass event," writes Uwe Jentzsch, sports editor at *Deutsche Presse-Agentur* (German Press Agency), "and the marketing machine par excellence among ice and snow-based sports."[14] The recent interest of Russian billionaire Mikhail Prokhorov has surely upped the ante for biathlon programs throughout the world. Prokhorov, named head of the Russian Biathlon Union in 2008, pledged support for another twenty-six sport schools and nineteen biathlon complexes in Russia for the 2011–2012 ski season, augmenting the organization's funds with an infusion of 16.7 million rubles. With the biathletes of Russia struggling at international competitions as of late, and the potential for twenty-six individual and three relay medals on the line at the Sochi Olympics—more than in any other event—the pressure on Prokhorov is building at home. Thus, in addition to his busy schedule as founding member and head of a new Russian political party, the Civic Platform, as well as owner of the National Basketball Association's New Jersey Nets, Prokhorov has been writing his own biathlon training manual for the Russian National Team based on Norwegian and German examples.[15]

Biathlon's recent growth as a spectator event has tempered its military connotations somewhat, with the help of electronic targets, split-screen video technology and innovative new events: currently, biathlon maintains status as the most popular winter sport in Europe, attracting over 500 million television viewers each season.[16] Conceding to the commercial considerations of the global community, medals struck in 2003 for the Thirty-Eighth World Biathlon Championships in Khanty-Mansiisk featured the image of a modern biathlete juxtaposed with that of a very unmilitary indigenous skier on wide hunting skis drawing a bow and arrow.[17]

Similarly, one of the Sochi commemorative silver three-ruble coins minted by the Bank of Russia in April of 2011 displays a biathlete firing from the off-hand position with a full-color Pitsunda pine cone and branch positioned just under the Olympic rings.[18] These iconic symbols reinforce the contemporary Russian point of view that biathlon is "our national property, which we have perceived for a long time as an established tradition, like a gift from on high."[19] Certainly, the notion of exceptionalism in relation to biathlon informs Russian perception of the sport. "The achievements of biathletes from the Soviet Union and Russia were the pride of the sport nationally and internationally during the entire course of modern biathlon's development," wrote Aleksandr Kurakin, Russia's technical delegate to the IBU, in 2008.[20] In an interview that same year, the Russian ski journal *Lyzhnyi sport* posed a question to the nation's patriarch of biathlon, Aleksandr Privalov: "You stood at the source of our country's biathlon. How great is the role of tradition in sport?" The former coach and two-time Olympic medalist replied: "This depends on the resources of the country as well as on how they are utilized. There isn't one country that can potentially compare to us."[21]

Privalov's statement is more than an old Olympic warrior's self-gratulatory musing, however. Skiing in general and the sport of biathlon in particular, remain the epitome of socialist sport; and in an era when many Russians view their Soviet past through a nostalgic lens, the specifics of biathlon can still conjure notions of self-defense, proletarian rootedness, national pride, historical mythology, collectivism and sporting prowess within a concise theatrical display. Although many other events were celebrated as examples of socialist sport, it was biathlon that best represented this notion of athleticism in service to the state. The idea that human will, bolstered by Marxist-Leninist ideology, could overcome the forces of nature was inherent in long-distance cross-country ski racing, with a long tradition in Russia that pre-dated the Revolution. Biathlon combined this potent trope with rifle marksmanship, the quintessential expression of the country's defense. In addition, the Soviet biathlon program incorporated two other socialist strengths—scientific experimentation and technological analysis, running the gamut from psychological testing to blood doping—in order to win medals on the international stage. The result was an unbroken string of gold medal victories over six Olympic Games in the biathlon relay, perhaps the most powerful metaphor for socialist collectivism in the realm of sport. Privalov had it right: no other nation has managed to attain a record comparable to this one at the Olympics.

The contrast between this Russian perception of biathlon and that of the West, especially in the United States, illustrates the degree of importance each society attached to the sport. Even as recently as 2009, an editorialist on the opinion pages of the *New York Times* wrote: "Generally speaking, there's nothing wrong with adding peripheral sports to the Olympics: They have a competition in which athletes fire guns while on skis, after all."[22] The general attitude expressed here was certainly no different during the Cold War era. For United States athletes of that time, participation in biathlon was an exercise in futility in a marginalized event, with scant recognition outside of Olympic years and little remuneration. A *New York Times* profile of Lyle Nelson, a four-time Olympian chosen as flag-bearer for the opening ceremonies in Calgary who devoted more than two decades of his life to the sport, represents this American point of view: "It's hard to believe that someone like Lyle Nelson still exists. Someone who at age 39 competes . . . for what he calls [biathlon's] 'dedication to excellence' . . . who described his being chosen as the American flag bearer as 'the ultimate accolade' of his life. 'More so than a gold medal?' he was asked. 'For the team, the gold medal would be better,' he said. 'But for my own individual sake over a lifetime, carrying the American flag at the Olympics is more important to me.'"[23]

Biathletes Lyle Nelson and Aleksandr Tikhonov, separated by eight years, shared the honor of carrying their nation's flag at the opening ceremonies of the Olympics, and both were deeply moved by the experience. But unlike American biathletes, those of the Soviet Union were regularly lionized in the press and received largesse unavailable to the masses behind the Iron Curtain, while participating in an event understood by nearly everyone in the nation. Soviet culture considered all participants in biathlon, whether at regional spartakiadas or the Olympic Games, the very essence of the Soviet citizen: selfless, mindful of his proletarian roots, committed to both the socialist cause and defense of the homeland. Victory in biathlon during international competitions provided the perfect ideological platform from which to promote the superiority of the socialist system and its military might. But most of all, for the Soviet generation that had lived through the horrors of the Great Patriotic War, the quasi-military nature of biathlon was a reminder of the sacrifices endured by the USSR. Nelson, in an interview with *Newsweek* magazine prior to the Lake Placid Games of 1980, observed, "Being [number one] in the biathlon is not that important. You don't want to crawl into your grave saying you won a gold medal."[24] Biathletes of the Soviet Union, backed by twenty-seven million victims of twentieth-century fascism, perhaps thought otherwise.

Notes

Introduction

1. Based on individual, relay and team competition medals awarded at senior men's and women's world championships and the Winter Olympic Games held between 1958 and 1991. A nation could potentially win three medals out of three in each individual race, although only one medal was possible in a team or relay event. In discussing athletes who represented the Soviet Union, it is important to keep in mind that ethnic Russians constituted only 50.8 percent of the country's total population (as of 1989). In e-mail correspondence dated 15 November 2012, Algis Shalna of Lithuania, a Soviet gold medalist in biathlon at the 1984 Sarajevo Winter Games, remembers: "I never felt discrimination [as a member of the Soviet team] and was well-respected. Even these days Russians consider me as part of their Olympians." Although it is somewhat inaccurate to lump all Soviet athletes into the category of "Russians," the term is nonetheless a conventional shorthand.

2. Amir Weiner, *Making Sense of War: The Second World War and the Fate of the Bolshevik Revolution*, 17, 20. The term "Great Patriotic War" refers to the period from 22 June 1941 (the start of Operation Barbarossa, Germany's invasion of the USSR) to 9 May 1945, Victory in Europe Day. It reflects a particularly Soviet ideological perspective on events that took place in the USSR and Europe during World War II. From a Western, or non-Soviet, point of view, the Great Patriotic War forms a subset of World War II, conventionally described as the period between the German invasion of Poland on 1 September 1939 and the surrender of Japan on 2 September 1945.

3. Mike O'Mahoney, *Sport in the USSR: Physical Culture—Visual Culture*, 165.

4. James Riordan, *Sport in Soviet Society: Development of Sport and Physical Education in Russia and the USSR*, 159.

5. Barbara J. Keys, *Globalizing Sport: National Rivalry and International Community in the 1930s*, 3–4, 160.

6. Robert Edelman, *Serious Fun: A History of Spectator Sports in the USSR*, xii.

1: Long Boards in the Long Nineteenth Century

1. Vladimir Il'ich Lenin, "I. F. Armand," in *Lenin: Polnoe sobranie sochinenii*, Vol. 49, 5th ed., 341.

2. Norman Davies, *Europe: A History*, 759.

3. Paul Robert Magocsi, *A History of Ukraine*, 351.

4. Lonnie R. Johnson, *Central Europe: Enemies, Neighbors, Friends*, 2nd ed., 130–34.

5. Fridtjof Nansen popularized this theory in his writings at the turn of the century. John Allen suggests that responses to unrelated local and regional needs for snow transportation were more likely. See Fridtjof Nansen, *The First Crossing of Greenland*, 86, 88–89; Nansen, *Through Siberia, the Land of the Future*, 89, 347–48; E. John B. Allen, *The Culture*

and Sport of Skiing from Antiquity to World War II, 20; Shan Zhaojian and Wang Bo, eds., *The Original Place of Skiing—Altay Prefecture of Xinjiang, China*, 169–361.

6. Allen, *Culture and Sport*, 10–12; Roland Huntford, *Two Planks and a Passion: The Dramatic History of Skiing*, 4, 7; Zhaojian and Bo, 194–96, 199, 234–39, 241–43, 245–63, 288–89, 320–31.

7. Saxo Grammaticus, *Gesta Danorum*, Book V, "The Nine Books of the Danish History of Saxo Grammaticus" [http://www.ealdriht.org/saxo5ii.html]; V. A. Firsoff, *Ski Track on the Battlefield*, 13; Jacob Vaage, "The Norse Started It All," in *The Ski Book*, 194; Robert Readhead, "Soldiers on Skis," in *Mountain Panorama: A Book of Winter Sports and Climbing*, 107; Huntford, *Two Planks*, 358.

8. K. B. E. E. Eimeleus, *Lyzhi v voennom dele*, 132–33; A. Artsikhovskii, "Lyzhi na Rusi," 10; M. A. Agranovskii, *Lyzhnyi sport*, 18; T. I. Ramenskaia, *Lyzhnyi vek Rossii*, 14; "Na lyzhi!" *Krasnaia zvezda*, 13 November 1940; "Lyzhi na sluzhbe armii," *K novoi armii*, nos. 14–15 (1920).

9. Sigmund Von Herberstein, in Bertold Picard, ed., *Description of Moscow and Muscovy*, 86.

10. Alexander Gwagnin, *Opisanie Moskovii*, 54.

11. *Na rtakh* [on skis] appears in the 1444 manuscript *Nikonovkaia letopis*.' More common to the ski vocabulary of Russian writers is the term *lyzhi*, used from the twelfth century on.

12. Huntford, *Two Planks*, 365; Readhead, 107; Firsoff, 13; Artsikhovskii, 11–12; Ramenskaia, 14; Ted Bays, *Nine Thousand Years of Skis: Norwegian Wood to French Plastic*, 29; Barry Gregory, *Mountain and Arctic Warfare: From Alexander to Afghanistan*, 12.

13. Ramenskaia, 14–15; "Na lyzhi!"; Daniel Gottlieb Messerschmidt, *Forschungsreise durch Sibirien, 1720–1727: Tagebuchaufzeichnungen Jan. 1723–Mai 1724*, 126, 144; Gavriil Andreevich Sarychev, *Account of a Voyage of Discovery to the North-East of Siberia, the Frozen Ocean, and the North-East Sea. By Gawrila Sarytschew, Russian Imperial Major-General to the Expedition. Translated from the Russian, and Embellished with Engravings*, 17–18.

14. Huntford, *Two Planks*, 366; Ramenskaia, 97; Veli Niinimaa, *Double Contest: Biathlon History and Development*, 1.

15. Aleksandr Pushkin, "*Istoriia Pugacheva*," in *A. S. Pushkin, Polnoe sobranie sochinenii v shesti tomakh*, ed. M. A. Tsiavlovskii, Tom IV, 468, 471.

16. Eimeleus, 133–34, 136; Agranovskii, 18; Ramenskaia, 14–15, 97; Niinimaa, 1; Huntford, *Two Planks*, 366; S. V. Bezobrazov, "Lyzhnaia rat'," in *Entsiklopedicheskii slovar' Tom XVIII*, 129; Carl J. Luther, *Schneeschuhläufer im Krieg*, 26–27; "Der Skilauf im Russischen Heer," *Der Winter* 9 (January 1915): 49–50; "Na lyzhi!"; "Lyzhi na sluzhbe armii."

17. Firsoff, 16–17; Einar Sunde, "Oscar Wergeland: An Apostle for Skiing," in *2002 International Ski History Congress: Selected Papers from the Seminars Held at Park City, Utah, January 20–24, 2002*, 207; Matti Goksøyr, "Skis as National Symbols, Ski Tracks as Historical Traits: The Case of Norway," in *2002 International Ski History Congress*, 198.

18. Luther, 26–27; "Snowshoes in Warfare," *The Graphic* 3 (March 1894): 248; "Der Skilauf im Russischen Heer," 49–50.

19. "Tsirkuliar Glavnago Shtaba za no. 193," excerpted in Eimeleus, 134.

20. Edmund J. Larson, *An Empire of Ice: Scott, Shackleton, and the Heroic Age of Antarctic Science*, 169; Roland Huntford, *Shackleton*, 66; Huntford, *Nansen: The Explorer as Hero*, 146.

21. "Norsk Nordpolsexpedition," *Morgenbladet*, 12 December 1888.

22. *Times,* 25 May 1889.

23. Pier Horensma, *The Soviet Arctic,* 14, 19; Roland Huntford, *Scott and Amundsen,* 41.

24. "Snowshoes in Warfare," 248. See also Peter Hopkirk, *The Great Game,* 332; Jennifer Siegel, *Endgame: Britain, Russia and the Final Struggle for Central Asia,* xv; Horensma, 19.

25. *Niva* 6 (1871): 85, 87–88. Compare Huntford's description of a race in nearby Huseby attended by Nansen in 1881: Huntford, *Nansen,* 14–15. *Niva* was a very popular magazine published in St. Petersburg from 1870 to 1918. It had a circulation of over 200,000 by the first decade of the twentieth century.

26. *Niva* 12 (1883): 285; 51 (1883): 1244. Five years prior to Nansen's famous journey, Nordenskiøld explored Greenland accompanied by two Lapps, Pava Lars Tuorda and Anders Rossa, whom he sent on skis into Greenland's interior to see how far the ice extended. After a fifty-seven-hour excursion with four hours of rest, the two skiers had covered just over 450 kilometers. Upon their return to Scandinavia, skeptics questioned whether such a pace was even possible. To assuage the doubters, Nordenskiøld organized a 220-kilometer race in Sweden to prove that skiers could cover such immense distances quickly. E. John B. Allen, "The Longest Race, 3–4 April 1884," 32; Huntford, *Two Planks,* 128–31.

27. *Niva* 3 (1888): 86; 35 (1888): 877–78; Nansen, *The First Crossing of Greenland,* Vol. 1, 90, 91, 93.

28. Although Nansen does not discuss his sources in the Greenland book, he cites Alexander von Middendorff and Leopold von Schrenck extensively in his 1914 work, *Through Siberia, the Land of the Future,* on pages 88, 89, 93, 97, 100, 101, 104, 120, 160 and 236.

29. Stepan Krasheninnikov, *Opisanie zemli Kamchatki: v dvukh tomakh,* Vol. 1, 244.

30. Krasheninnikov, *Opisanie zemli Kamchatki,* Vol. 1, 74; Vol. 2, 59 (also illustrations between 58 and 59; 77 and 78). Krasheninnikov informs the reader that *lapki* are a type of ski (*lyzhi*) in a footnote on page 74, Vol. 1. These were the only terms available to the author to describe what he saw in the eighteenth century, mirroring the "snowshoe" and "ski" conundrum in English during the late nineteenth century. The Russian term for snowshoe, *snegostup,* did not enter the language until mid-twentieth century. Krasheninnikov's book was translated into an abridged English version in 1764, German in 1766 and French in 1767.

31. Johann Georg Gmelin, *Voyage en Sibérie: contenant la description des moeurs & usages des peuples de ce pays, le cours des rivieres considerables, la situation de chaines de montagnes, des grandes forêts, des mines, avec tous les faits d'histoire naturelle qui sont particuliers a cette contree,* 303. Krasheninnikov was officially an *uchenik* (apprentice) under the supervision of Gmelin on an early trip to Kamchatka in 1733 with Vitus Bering. See B. P. Polevoi, "Predislovie," in Krasheninnikov, *Opisanie zemli Kamchatki,* Vol. 1, 4, 16.

32. Peter Simon Pallas, *Reise durch verschiedene Provinzen des Russischen Reichs,* Vol. 3, 39–40, 49, 74, 91, 377; Pallas, "Pallas Reisen.Tom.III.Tab.I.und.II," in *Tafelband,* 40; Pallas, *Voyages en différentes provinces de l'empire de Russie,* Book 4, 66, 99, 122–23, 542.

33. Adolph Erman, *Reise um die Erde durch Nord-Asien und die beiden Oceane in den Jahren 1828, 1829 und 1830 ausgeführt von Adolf Erman: Zweiter Band: Reise von Tobolsk bis zum Ochozker Meere im Jahre 1829,* 335; Adolph Erman, *Travels in Siberia: including excursions northwards, down the Obi, to the Polar Circle, and southwards, to the*

Chinese frontier, Vol. 1, 433.

34. Ferdinand Petrovich Wrangel, *Le Nord de la Sibérie: voyage parmi les peuplades de la Russie asiatique et dans la mer Glaciale*, 17.

35. Alexander von Middendorff, *Reise in den äussersten Norden und Osten Sibiriens, Band IV: Übersicht der Natur Nord- und Ost-Sibiriens, Theil 2*, 1234, 1348–51, 1370, 1378; also 1478, 1483.

36. Mikołaj A. Kubalski, *Voyages en Sibérie recueillis par N.-A.* [sic] *Kubalski*, 80; Richard J. Bush, *Reindeer, Dogs and Snow-Shoes: A Journal of Siberian Travel and Explorations Made in the Years 1865, 1866, and 1867*, 166, 198–99; Mikhail Krivoshapkin, *Eniseiskii okrug i ego zhizn*, 28–29; Zachariah Atwell Mudge, *Fur-clad adventurers; or, Travels in skin-canoes, on dog-sledges, on reindeer, and on snow-shoes, through Alaska, Kamchatka, and Eastern Siberia*, 241; Otto Finsch, *Reise nach West-Sibirien im Jahre 1876*, 530.

37. Leopold von Schrenck, *Reisen und Forschungen im Amur-Lande Band III: Die Völker des Amur-Landes*, 472–78, 630. See also Zhaojian and Bo, 231–32.

38. Victor Meignan, *De Paris à Pékin par Terre: Sibérie-Mongolie*, 81 and engraving between 80 and 81; Meignan, *From Paris to Pekin over Siberian Snows*, 89 and engraving between 90 and 91. "Ski" had not yet attained common use in Western Europe at the time of the English edition, thus the use of the term "snow-shoes." For centuries, the linguistic concept of "snowshoe" had been applied to any device affixed to the foot to walk over the snow, whether in reference to snow boots, skates, skis or racquet-style snowshoes. Because of the simplicity of its conceptualization, "snowshoe" suited the needs of modern European writers until the publication of English and German editions of Fridtjof Nansen's book, *The First Crossing of Greenland* in 1890. His use of the Norwegian word "ski" began to supersede all other terms from that point on. See E. John B. Allen, *From Skisport to Skiing: One Hundred Years of an American Sport, 1840–1940*, 8–9.

39. *Moskovskiia vedomosti*, 5 December 1896.

40. E.g., *Niva* 6 (1896): 134–35; *Novoe vremia* 18 (30) January 1897; O. N. Popova, *Geroi poliarnoi nochi i vechnykh l'dov Fritiof Nansen*, 17.

41. Huntford, *Nansen*, 215; Huntford, *Two Planks*, 265–66.

42. Fridtjof Nansen, *Farthest North, being a record of a voyage of exploration of the ship "Fram" 1893–1896, and of a fifteen month's sleigh journey by Dr. Nansen and Lieut. Johansen, Volumes 1 and 2*. See also Huntford, *Nansen*, 137–383.

43. *Niva* 21 (1889): 546; 10 (1891): 236; 30 (1893): 687, 690–91, 692; 39 (1893): 882; 27 (1896): 685, 688–90; 33 (1896): 839; 45 (1896): 1125–28.

44. *Journal de St. Pétersbourg*, 10 August (22) 1896; 19 August (31) 1896; 20 August (1 September) 1896.

45. *Prilozhenie k gazete Novoe vremia*, 10 August (22) 1896; 17 August (30) 1896; 24 August (5 September) 1896; 31 August (12 September) 1896; 7 September (19) 1896; 14 September (26) 1896. *Novoe vremia* (New Time) was one of Russia's most popular liberal newspapers, published from 1868 to 1917. At its peak in 1915, the paper had a circulation of 80,000 with street sales of 6.2 million.

46. *Novoe vremia*, 11 August (23) 1896; *Moskovskiia vedomosti*, 12 August 1896.

47. E.g., Popova; also, V. Semenov, *Sredi l'da i nochi*; A. Annenskaia, *Fritiof Nansen i ego puteshestviia v grenlandiiu i k severnomu poliusu*, 4th ed; Annenskaia, 5th ed.

48. *Novoe vremia*, 29 December 1896 (10 January) 1897; 3 January (14) 1897; 7 January (19) 1897; 10 January (22) 1897; 17 January (29) 1897; 22 January (3 February) 1897; 25

January (6 February) 1897; 31 January (12 February) 1897; 4 February (16) 1897; 8 February (20) 1897; 25 February (9 March) 1897; 3 March (15) 1897; 27 March (8 April) 1897; 1 April (13) 1897; 3 April (15) 1897; 10 April (22) 1897; 17 April (29) 1897.

49. *Novoe vremia,* 9 March (21) 1897; 13 March (25) 1897; 8 April (20) 1897; 12 April (24) 1897.

50. *Novoe vremia,* 14 April (26) 1898; 15 April (27) 1898; 16 April (28) 1898; 18 April (30) 1898; 19 April (1 May) 1898; 20 April (2 May) 1898; *Moskovskiia vedomosti,* 16 April 1898; 17 April 1898; 18 April 1898; 19 April 1898; *Vladivostok,* 19 April 1898.

51. *Gerkules: Zhurnal sporta,* 25 November 1913: 29. That the Moscow Club of Skiers (MKL) was the first official ski club in Russia has been an accepted and unchallenged notion for more than half a century. For example, a short introductory history of skiing in a pamphlet published for the 1948 USSR National Ski Championships makes this claim. See *Programma pervenstva SSSR po lyzhnomu sportu 1948 g.,* 3. Sixty-three years later, D. Beliukov and N. Ershova of the Velikie Luki Sports Academy reiterate this notion. See D. Belyukov [sic] and N. Ershova, "Skiing Development in Russia in the Beginning of XX Century," in *Winter Sport and Outdoor Life: Papers presented at the Telemark Conference for Historians of Sports,* 289. MKL was distinguished, however, by having Fridtjof Nansen himself as an honorary member. See Dmitrii Vasil'ev, *Na lyzhne,* 6.

52. Tat'iana Andreeva and Marina Guseva, *Sport nashikh dedov: Stranitsy istorii rossiiskogo sporta v fotografiiakh kontsa XIX–nachala XX veka,* 164. The foreign community used Iukki as a ski area as well. See John F. Baddeley, *Russia in the 'Eighties': Sport and Politics,* 253–54.

53. *Moskovskiia vedomosti,* 4 December 1901.

54. "Sportsmeny [The Sportsmen]," *Satirikon* no. 9 (1912): 4 and "Sportsmenskaia dusha [The Sportsman's Soul]," *Satirikon* no. 3 (1910): 2 in I. B. Khmel'nitskaia, *Sportivnye obshchestva i dosug v stolichnom gorode nachala XX veka: Peterburg i Moskva,* 128–29.

55. Agranovskii, 20; Ramenskaia, 17; Andreeva and Guseva, 164. A *verst* at this time was equivalent to 3,500 feet or 1.07 kilometers.

56. *Novoe vremia,* 1(13) February 1894.

57. "Pervye lyzhnyie gonki v Rossii," *Ogonek* no. 10 (1187), 5 March 1950: 30. *Ogonek* was a popular weekly magazine in the years before the Revolution with circulation reaching 700,000 in 1914. In the twentieth century, the magazine under a different guise was a large-format pictorial weekly with circulation between 500,000 and 1.3 million by the late 1980s.

58. "Lyzhnyi sport v armii," *Moskovskiia vedomosti,* 11 February 1900.

59. *Moskovskiia vedomosti,* 20 February 1901; *Der Winter* 4 (1915): 49–52.

60. *Moskovskiia vedomosti,* 16 November 1901.

61. *Moskovskiia vedomosti,* 15 February 1900.

62. Ibid.

63. *Moskovskiia vedomosti,* 2 December 1910; 17 December 1910; 5 January 1911; 8 January 1911; 11 January 1911; "Lyzhnomu sportu 50 let 1896–1946," *Ogonek* no. 4 (973), 27 January 1946: 29; "RU14" no. 6 (1079) 8 February 1948: inside cover; Agranovskii, 21–22. A detailed account of this race, including a point-to-point description of the 30-kilometer course, can be found in D. Vasil'ev, *Na lyzhne,* 7–9.

64. *Moskovskiia vedomosti,* 2 December 1912; Agranovskii, 21; Ramenskaia, 18.

65. *Niva* 50 (1896): 1250z.

66. "Aus Moskau." In *Allgemeine Sport-Zeitung* no. 95 XV Jahrgang, 8 December 1894: 1334; Konstantin Komets, "Lyzhi: vybor lyzh," *Gerkules: Zhurnal sporta*, 10 January 1914: 14–16. See also "Zimnii perekhod okhotnich'ei komandy, no. 2," published by Scherer, Nabholz and Co., Moscow 1904 [postcard], where the Okhotniki troopers are carrying both types of skis over their shoulders.

67. *Novoe vremia*, 11 November (28) 1895; 24 November (6 December) 1895; 8 December (20) 1895; 15 December (27) 1895; 22 December (3 January) 1896.

68. *Novoe vremia*, 17 November (29) 1896; 12 December (24) 1896; 19 December (31) 1896; 21 December 1896 (2 January 1897); 24 December 1896 (5 January 1897); 19 November (1 December) 1897; 6 December (18) 1897; 15 December (27) 1897; 21 December 1897 (2 January 1898); 23 December 1897 (4 January 1898); 28 December 1897 (9 January 1898); 16 December (28) 1898; 20 December 1898 (1 January 1899); 23 December 1898 (4 January 1899); 1 January (13) 1899; 5 January (17) 1899; 6 December (18) 1899; 12 December (24) 1899; 15 December (27) 1899.

69. *Moskovskiia vedomosti*, 6 December 1907; *Ogonek* 43: Sunday 21 October (3 November) 1912; 49: Sunday 2 December (15) 1912; 51: Sunday 16 December (29) 1912; 3: Sunday 20 January (2 February) 1913; 11: Sunday 17 March (30) 1913.

70. *Novoe vremia*, 9 November (21) 1896; Andreeva and Guseva, 176.

71. A hand-held sail for use while ice skating was popular at the turn of the century. However, sailing on ice skates was generally confined to lakes and prepared rinks. Sailing on skis, especially on the vast Gulf of Finland, was an entirely different matter. See "Katan'e na kon'kakh s parusami v Amerik," *Novoe vremia*, 30 January (11 February) 1893; "Zimnii sport," *Novoe vremia*, 27 November (9 December) 1893. Sailing on ice skates was also an event at the *Nordiska Spelen* in Sweden. See Åke Jönsson, *Nordiska Spelen: Historien om sju vinterspel i Stockholm av Olympiskt format 1901 till 1926*, 108–9.

72. *Niva*, 42 (1896): 1057; 45 (1896): 1128; 50 (1896): 1250z; *Novoe vremia*, 9 November (21) 1896; 30 November (12 December) 1896; 25 November (7 December) 1897; 27 November (9 December) 1897.

73. *Niva*, 45 (1896): 1128.

74. Konstantin Komets, "Lyzhi," *Gerkules: Zhurnal sporta*, 5 November 1914: 15–16. Excerpted from his book.

75. *Novoe vremia*, 21 December 1899 (2 January 1900); 22 December 1899 (3 January 1900).

76. *Novoe vremia*, 8 January (21) 1904; 13 January (26) 1904; 20 January (2 February) 1904; 31 December 1904 (13 January 1905).

77. *Novoe vremia*, 25 January (7 February) 1905; 1 February (14) 1905; 11 February (24) 1905; 25 February (10 March) 1905; 1 March (14) 1905.

78. *Novoe vremia*, 7 November (20) 1904.

79. *Novoe vremia* 22, February (6 March) 1904; 29 February (13 March) 1904; 1 March (20) 1904; 18 December (31) 1904.

80. Eimeleus, back cover.

81. David R. Jones, "Forerunners of the Komsomol: Scouting in Imperial Russia," in *Reforming the Tsar's Army: Military Innovation in Imperial Russia from Peter the Great to the Revolution*, ed. David Schimmelpenninck van der Oye and Bruce W. Menning, 64.

82. *Gerkules: Zhurnal sporta*, 10 November 1913: 10.

83. Quoted in "Sokolstvo na sjezdu slovanském," *Sokol*, Vol. 34 (1908), 173. Cited in

Claire E. Nolte, "All for One! One for All! The Federation of Slavic Sokols and the Failure of Neo-Slavism," 130.

84. Jones, 64; Claire E. Nolte, *The Sokol in the Czech Lands to 1914: Training for the Nation*, 163.

85. *Gerkules: Zhurnal sporta*, 10 November 1913: 10; Nolte, "All for One! One for All!" 130; Jones, 65.

86. *Moskovskiia vedomosti*, 7 November 1910; 19 November 1910; 23 November 1910; 24 November 1910; 27 November 1910; 1 December 1910; 2 December 1910; 14 December 1910.

87. Edelman, 29. In 1953, all sport groups of the Moscow Military District came under the aegis of TsSKMO (Central Sports Club, Ministry of Defense).

88. *Gerkules: Zhurnal sporta*, 10 February 1914: 29–31; 25 February 1914: 29 [photo series]; 19 February 1916: 13 [photograph].

89. Allen, *Culture and Sport*, 186; Huntford, *Two Planks*, 168, 172.

90. L. F. K. von Thiele, "The Norwegian Olympic Games," in *The Wide World Magazine* Volume IX May 1902–October 1902: 473; Marianne Singsaas, "Laying the First Tracks: Female Skiers at the Turn of the 19th Century," in *Winter Sport and Outdoor Life*, 91–92; Allen, *Culture and Sport*, 148–52. Suvi Kuisma of the Lahti Ski Museum in Finland writes that a women's ski race took place in Impilahti, Karelia, in 1886. See Suvi Kuisma, "Womanly Light and Easy on Ski Track—Women's Ski Races in the Lahti Ski Games between 1923 and 1952," in *Winter Sport and Outdoor Life*, 121.

91. Huntford, *Nansen*, 138; Huntford, *Two Planks*, 173–74; Allen, *Culture and Sport*, 149.

92. *Novoe vremia*, 27 November (9 December) 1893; Huntford, *Two Planks*, 173; Huntford, *Nansen*, photographs between 306 and 307.

93. *Novoe vremia*, 16 April (28) 1898. El'pe is quoting from page 15 of D. N. Anuchin's recently released book *Frit'of Nansen, ego podvigi i otkrytiia*.

94. *Niva* 16, (1898): 320; also *Prilozhenie k gazete Novoe vremia*, 31 August (12 September) 1896; *Novoe vremia*, 14 (26) April 1898; 15 (27) April 1898; 16 (28) April 1898; 16 (28) April 1898; 18 (30) April 1898; 19 April (1 May) 1898; 20 April (2 May) 1898; *Moskovskiia vedomosti*, 16 April 1898; 17 April 1898; 18 April 1898; 19 April 1898; 21 April 1898; *Sanktpeterburgskiia vedomosti*, 16 April 1898.

95. *Novoe vremia*, 1 (13) February 1894; Huntford, *Two Planks*, 167.

96. *Novoe vremia*, 21 December 1899 (2 January 1900).

97. *Moskovskiia vedomosti*, 5 December 1896; 20 February 1901; *Novoe vremia*, 21 December 1896 (2 January 1897); 18 (30) January 1897; 23 December (4 January) 1898; 21 December 1899 (2 January 1900); 7 (20) November 1904; *Ogonek* 43: Sunday 21 October (3 November) 1912; 49: Sunday 2 (15) December 1912; 51: Sunday 16 (29) December 1912; 3: Sunday 20 January (2 February) 1913; 11: Sunday 17 (30) March 1913.

98. *Gerkules: Zhurnal sporta*, 10 February 1910: 29; 25 February 1910: 29; 24 December 1914: 10; Andreeva and Guseva, 165, 166–67. The groups in these photographs, however, are small, numbering from twelve to thirty-five people. In Moscow at the turn of the century, between seven and thirty skiers would take part in the various excursions sponsored by the Moscow Club of Skiers (MKL). See *Moskovskiia vedomosti*, 15 February 1900; 6 February 1901; 20 February 1901; 13 November 1901; 20 November 1901; 23 November 1901; 27 November 1901; 4 December 1901; 11 December 1901; 18 December

1901; 25 December 1901; 1 January 1902; 4 January 1902; 8 January 1902; "Aus Moskau," *Deutscher Wintersport* nr. 16 Jahrgang 15 (16 February 1906): 213. By 1910, events held by Sokol'niki Club of Ski-Runners (SKL) with a paying membership of around one hundred, were attracting close to fifty participants. See *Moskovskiia vedomosti*, 14 December 1910. Women comprised less than 10 percent of the total members of Russian sport clubs responding to a pair of surveys conducted in 1913; and of those clubs, only 5 percent were involved with winter sports. However, these figures only represent around 13 percent of the country's sport club membership. See Khmel'nitskaia, 317.

99. From 1879 to 1891, the Christiania competitions were held in the Husebyrennet neighborhood.

100. Allen, *Culture and Sport*, 182–83.

101. G. de Lefreté, "Les 'Jeux du Nord,'" in *La Vie au Grand Air*, 10 February 1901: 85; von Thiele, 465; Allen, *Culture and Sport*, 182–83; Huntford, *Two Planks*, 317–23.

102. *Gerkules: Zhurnal sporta*, 25 January 1913: 23–24.

103. Nikolai M. Vasil'ev, "Porazhenie, ravnoe pobede," 62; Jönsson, 163–64, 169.

104. *Novoe vremia*, 1(14) February 1913; 5 (18) February 1913; 7(20) February 1913; 8 (21) February 1913.

105. Eimeleus discusses some variations on ski technique familiar to Russian skiers circa 1912: "simple three-step (two steps without poles)," "simple two-step on the same foot," "simple two-step on different feet" and "complex three-step," illustrated with four action-sequenced photographic montages on pages 53–54 and back page insert, figures 49, 50, 51 and 52. For a more detailed discussion of the development of different ski techniques used by Russian, Norwegian and Finnish skiers at international competitions during the early decades of the twentieth century, see D. Vasil'ev, *Na lyzhne*, 90–97.

106. *Gerkules: Zhurnal sporta*, 10 March 1913: 29.

107. N. Vasil'ev, 62.

108. *Gerkules: Zhurnal sporta*, 25 February 1913: 29; D. Vasil'ev, *Na lyzhne*, 12–17.

109. Huntford, *Two Planks*, 313–15.

110. Andreeva and Guseva, 173.

111. N. Vasil'ev, 69.

112. Eimeleus, 34–35.

113. N. Vasil'ev, 69–70; *Pravda*, 13 January 1937; V. Viktorov, "Sport: brat'ia Vasil'evy," *Ogonek* no. 4 (973), 27 January 1946: 28–29; L. Libkind, "Na lyzhne," *Ogonek* no. 5 (1182), 29 January 1950: 28; V. Viktorov, "Lyzhnaia gonka," *Ogonek* no. 2 (1283), 6 January 1952: 28–29; *Krasnaia zvezda*, 25 January 1959; D. Vasil'ev, *Na lyzhne*, 24–25, 35, passim; Ramenskaia, 25, 26, 29, 53.

114. Larson, 23.

115. Huntford, *Two Planks*, 276. At the time of his 1901–1904 Antarctic expedition, Scott had very little experience with skis. When he returned to the south six years later, he took along a Norwegian ski instructor, Tryggve Gran, and used skis on the Polar Plateau in his push to the South Pole. However, pulling heavy sledges on skis would have been an exhausting exercise, especially at the Plateau's high elevation: Scott's team frequently experienced temperatures below minus forty degrees Celsius, which considerably reduced the glide of their skis and sledge runners. It was the combination, perfected by the Norwegians, of skiing alongside fully laden dogsleds that allowed Amundsen to succeed where Scott failed. See Roland Huntford, *The Last Place on Earth*, 162–63; Larson, 83, 278–79. For a

view of Scott that contrasts with Huntford's, see Tryggve Gran, *The Norwegian with Scott: Tryggve Gran's Antarctic Diary, 1910–1913*.

116. Huntford, *Shackleton*, 66, 110, 170; Huntford, *Two Planks*, 276; Huntford, *Scott and Amundsen*, 275; Allen, *Culture and Sport*, 90–91.

117. Larson, xi, 15, 234.

118. Huntford, *Two Planks*, 280–81; Huntford, *Scott and Amundsen*, 447.

119. Loren R. Graham, *Science in Russia and the Soviet Union: A Short History*, 3, 24, 53.

120. James T. Andrews, *Science for the Masses: The Bolshevik State, Public Science, and the Popular Imagination in Soviet Russia, 1917–1934*, 88.

121. *Novoe vremia*, 8 (20) February 1892; 29 November (12 December) 1903; *Prilozhenie k gazete Novoe vremia*, 6 April (18) 1896; *Moskovskiia vedomosti*, 11 January 1900; *Ogonek* 4: Saturday, 23 January (5 February) 1910 [no page number].

122. "Otkrytie Iuzhnago poliusa," *Ogonek* 11: Saturday, 10 (23) March 1912 [no page number].

123. Agranovskii, 25.

124. Huntford, *Shackleton*, 353.

2: The First World War to NEP

1. Peter Holquist, "'Information Is the Alpha and Omega of Our Work': Bolshevik Surveillance in Its Pan-European Context," 446, 450. Also Sheila Fitzpatrick, "The Civil War as a Formative Experience"; Fitzpatrick, "New Perspectives on the Civil War."

2. Douglas Southall Freeman, *Lee's Lieutenants: A Study in Command*, Vol. 1, *Manassas to Malvern Hill*, 282–302.

3. Davies, 902.

4. John Keegan, *The First World War*, 182–83.

5. Hew Strachan, *The First World War*, xvii, 43, 47–48, 83, 90–93, 131,137, 140.

6. "Snowshoes in Warfare," 248; K. Komets, "Beg na lyzhakh," in *Niva* 6, 1896: 135. For the Norwegian influence on the German and Austrian armies, see *Deutscher Eissport II* 8 (14 December 1893): 52; *Der Winter* 2 (October 1935): 18; *Illustrated London News* 106 (9 February 1895): 163, 172; "Major Oscar Schadek," *Allgemeine Sport-Zeitung* XIV (1 January 1893): 27 and (5 February 1893): 127–28.

7. Robin Fedden, *Alpine Ski Tour: An Account of the High Level Route*, 11–12; Fritz Hartranft and Franz Königer, *Skiführer Haute Route*, 18–19; Eric Roberts, *High Level Route Chamonix-Zermatt-Saas*, 2nd ed., 16–18; Denis Bertholet, *Die Walliser Alpen auf Ski: die 100 schönsten Skitouren und Abfahrten*, 6–14; Morten Lund, "Arnold Lunn and the Birth of International Downhill Racing in the Bernese Oberland," 1, 4–15.

8. *Illustrated War News*, 17 March 1915 [Part 32], 31[photo and text].

9. Allen, *Culture and Sport*, 151, 162; Strachan, 155; Firsoff, 28–29.

10. Ronald Grigor Suny, *The Soviet Experiment: Russia, the USSR, and the Successor States*, 72–73.

11. Martin Malia, *The Soviet Tragedy: A History of Socialism in Russia, 1917–1991*, 120–21.

12. Roger Reese, *Stalin's Reluctant Soldiers: A Social History of the Red Army, 1925–1941*, 79–80, 128–30; Suny, *Soviet Experiment*, 77–78, 183.

13. W. Bruce Lincoln, *Red Victory: A History of the Russian Civil War*, 230–32.

14. L. Trotsky, *Kak vooruzhalas' revoliutsiia (na voennoi rabote)*,Vol. 2, Book 1, 287–88. See also Vol. 3, Book 1, 50: "*Proletarii, na konia!*"

15. "Snowshoes in Warfare," 247.

16. John Wendell Long, *Civil War and Intervention in North Russia, 1918–1920*, 59.

17. Allen, *Culture and Sport*, 162.

18. Eimeleus, 147–48; "Lyzhi na sluzhbe armii," 18; Firsoff, 29.

19. A. Miasnikov, "Vseobshchee Voennoe Obuchenie: znachenie vsevobucha," *K novoi armii* no. 1 (1920).

20. Agranovskii, 26; Riordan, *Sport in Soviet Society*, 69–71; O'Mahoney, 126.

21. Carl Diem, "Aufgaben für 1916," *Fussball und Leichtathletik* 14 (1913): 4654, cited in Allen, *Culture and Sport*, 187.

22. Riordan, *Sport in Soviet Society*, 72, 78; "Kratkie itogi raboty Vsevobucha," *K novoi armii* no. 16 (1920); "Lyzhi na sluzhbe armii."

23. G. K. Gins, *Sibir', soiuzniki i Kolchak*, Vol. 2 (Peking: Tipo-litografiia Russkoi Dukhovnoi Missii, 1921), 127; Lincoln, 250.

24. N. Kryzhkov, "Ledianoi pokhod," *Pravda*, 17 March 1937; "Po sledam legend-arnykh pokhodov," *Pravda*, 22 February 1938; S. F. Naida et al., *Istoriia Grazhdanskoi Voiny v SSSR*, 354, 357.

25. E. I. [sic], "Dva goda Vsevobucha," *K novoi armii* no. 5 (1920); "Kratkie itogi raboty Vsevobucha."

26. Ul'ias Vikstrem, *Toivo Antikainen, dokumental'naia povest'*, 78. For the conflation of skiing and cavalry, see also *Zimniaia kavelariia* [winter cavalry], *Krasnaia zvezda*, 15 February 1974; *Snezhnaia kavelariia* [snow cavalry] in I. M. Butin, *Lyzhnyi sport*, 9–18; *Snezhnaia kavelriia idet v ataku* [snow cavalry goes on the attack], *Sovetskii sport*, 26 December 1961.

27. "(Russo-Finnish War 1940)," British Pathé [no issue date], unused/unissued ma-terial, 2:16 min., canister: UN226E, film ID: 626:13, tape: *PM0626* [http//www.british-pathe.com/record.php?id=50917] According to British Pathé, this is unused footage from the Soviet campaign during the Winter War in Finland, 1939–1940; however, it is more probably from the Great Patriotic War, 1941–1945, since the Russian narrator references a fascist German, as opposed to a Finnish, foe.

28. "Lyzhi na sluzhbe armii."

29. V. Tereshchenko, "Osobennosti podgotovki voiskovoi konnitsy zimoi," *Krasnaia zvezda*, 7 December 1929. Over a quarter century later, the newspaper still touted the rela-tionship between skiing and the cavalry, reporting that the much-vaunted tank corps, the new mechanized cavalry, was benefiting from ski training and competition. See "Cherez trudnosti—k boevomu masterstvu!" *Krasnaia zvezda*, 8 February 1957.

30. Trotsky, *Kak vooruzhalas'*, Vol. 2, Book 1, 288.

31. Keys, *Globalizing Sport*, 32. In pre-revolutionary Russia, these restrictions applied even to those who had taken part as a passive participant in a professional athletic event, for example as a judge or a timekeeper. See "Sportivnye s'ezdy," *Artist i stsena* 5 (1911): 20.

32. Per Jørgensen, "From Balck to Nurmi: The Olympic Movement and the Nordic Nations," 81; Allen, *Culture and Sport*, 191.

33. Excerpted in "Lyzhnomu sportu 50 let: 1896–1946," *Ogonek* no. 4 (973), 27 Janu-ary 1946: 29; Iu. Khromov, *Lyzhnyi sport v SSSR*, 2. "Intelligentsia" refers to the educated and privileged members of pre-revolutionary Russia.

34. Allen, *Culture and Sport*, 157, 188.

35. Huntford, *Two Planks*, 340; Allen, *Culture and Sport*, 185, 188, 193–94; Lund, 10–15.

36. "Proletarii i Kolkhoznik na lyzhi! Krepi oboronu strany!" See "Lot # 308, 'Prole-tariat, On Your Skis! Fadeev'" [http://www.postersplease.com/index.php?FAFs=75333d9b 6a90d1907e539b7c971996f5&FAFgo=/Auctions/LotDetail&LotID=132&sr=102&t=C&ts =&AID=4] Poster Auctions International website.

37. "Zimnii sportivnyi sezon," *Pravda*, 4 December 1940. See also "Lyzhnyi sport—v massy!" *Pravda*, 13 November 1940; N. Klimenko, "Narodnyi sport," *Pravda*, 23 November 1940.

38. "Na lyzhakh—v turistskii pokhod," *Pravda*, 11 December 1940.

39. "Zimoi na gornykh sklonakh," *Ogonek* no. 49 (1382), 6 December 1953: 29.

40. "Vozrast—sportu ne pomekha!" [http://www.originalskiposters.com/new/poster.php?ID=288] Original Ski Posters website. This site lists the poster erroneously as "Sport: No Handicap to Age!"

41. "Pozdravliaem vas, veterany!" *Sovetskii sport*, 20 February 1960.

42. L. Maliugin, "Zdrov'e, bodrost', optimizm!" *Sovetskii sport*, 3 March 1959. No-table as well is *Ogonek*'s back cover photograph of an elderly gentleman with flowing white beard scarcely able to contain his grin as he frolics on skis with a comely young woman. See *Ogonek* no. 4 (1701), 24 January 1960: back cover.

43. Henry M. Morton, *Soviet Sport: Mirror of Society*, 31; "'Toil and Sweat' Win Out Over 'Amusement,'" *Life* 36, no. 4, 25 January 1954: 128–29. The same year, however, M. A. Agranovskii wrote about the need for ski lifts in the mountains for properly training Alpine ski racers. See Agranovskii, 524. At Grindelwald the Soviet women raced only in the cross-country events and, despite Sorokin's statement, did ride on the chairlifts to watch other teams compete in the slalom.

44. E. Shatrov, "Na trasse Sidorovy," *Ogonek* no. 7 (1184), 12 February 1950: 29.

45. L. Frenkin, "Khallgeir Brenden," *Sovetskii sport*, 11 January 1958; Frenkin, "Siksten Ernberg," *Sovetskii sport*, 8 January 1958. See also K. Smirnov, "Na lyzhne Veiko Khakulinen," *Sovetskii sport*, 28 February 1958; "Siksten Ernberg," *Sovetskii sport*, 12 February 1959.

46. Andrei Sinyavsky, *Soviet Civilization: A Cultural History*, 115–16, 142.

47. Vikstrem, 41, 48, 55, 60.

48. Agranovskii, 27; Vikstrem, 66–93; "So sportom—cherez vsiu zhizn'," *Krasnaia zvezda*, 4 January 1968.

49. Vikstrem, 97.

50. E.g., the Soviet film *In the Rear of the Enemy*, produced for Western audiences during the Second World War. See *Times*, 31 January 1942: 8; also, I. Brazhnin, "Na lyzhakh po tylam vraga [On skis toward the rear of the enemy]," *Pravda*, 15 December 1941; L. Vysokoostrovskii, "Smelyi reid lyzhnikov v tyl vraga [A skiers' brave raid on the rear of the enemy]," *Krasnaia zvezda*, 4 March 1942; L. Ganichev, "Na lyzhakh v tyl vraga [On skis at the rear of the enemy]," *Pravda*, 18 January 1942. Antikainen's trek inspired Santeri Mäkelä's 1922 poem *Molchalivym bortsam* and Genadii Fish's 1932 story *Padenie Kimasozera*.

51. "Po sledam legendarnogo pokhoda k Kimasozeru," *Pravda*, 26 January 1935; "V puti," 26 January 1935; "Po sledam legendarnogo pokhoda k Kimas-ozeru," 29 January 1935; Po sledam legendarnogo pokhoda k Kimas-ozeru," 30 January 1935; "Po sledam legendarnogo pokhoda na Kimasozero," 2 February 1935.

52. "Po sledam otriada Antikainena," *Pravda* 7 (February 1938); Vikstrem, 220–22; Y. Lukashin, *USSR Skiing*, 4–5; Aleksandr Valentik, "Lyzhnia Antikainena," *Avrora* no. 4 (April 1981): 147–53.

53. Vikstrem, 219–21.

54. Erkki Vasara, "Maintaining a Military Capability: The Finnish Home Guard, European Fashion and Sport for War," 157.

55. Ibid., 163, 170.

56. Also *skiskyting* in Norwegian, *skidskytte* in Swedish, *lyzhnaia gonka so strelboi* in Russian. The term "biathlon" did not gain currency until the late 1950s.

57. Vasara, 159, 164.

58. Agranovskii, 29; D. Vasil'ev, *Na lyzhne*, 29, 58; Ramenskaia, 25.

59. Riordan, *Sport in Soviet Society*, 78; Agranovskii, 27; N. Rakitin, "Za massovyi sport," *Krasnaia zvezda*, 11 November 1925.

60. Agranovskii, 27; Riordan, *Sport in Soviet Society*, 78.

61. Viktorov, " Brat'ia Vasilievy"; Ramenskaia, 22.

62. Alice Schuster, "Women's Role in the Soviet Union: Ideology and Reality," *Russian Review* 30, no. 3 (July 1971): 260; Suny, *Soviet Experiment*, 186; Riordan, *Sport in Soviet Society*, 49, 64; A. Semenov and S. Ksenofontov, "Uchenyi, pedagog, obshchestvennyi deiatel'," *Sovetskii sport*, 11 December 1959.

63. "Zakonchilas' vsesoiuznye lyzhnye sorevnovaniia," *Pravda*, 14 March 1938; "Ikh znaet vsia strana," *Ogonek* no. 32 (951), 12 August 1945: 8–9; "Chempiony minuvshego sezona," no. 1 (970), 6 January 1946: 28–29; Zoia Bolotova, "Ran'she i teper'," nos. 10–11 (979–800), March 1946 [sic]: 42; Igor' Solntsev, "Khoziaika lyzhnoi gory," no. 10 (1031), 9 March 1947: 30; E. Vasil'ev, "Sportivnyi Ural," no. 3 (1076), 18 January 1948: 29; "Sportivnoe obozrenie: Lyzhnye gonki v Bakuriani," no. 5 (1078), 1 February 1948: 30; "Sportivnoe obozrenie," no. 10 (1083), 7 March 1948: 30; Lukashin, 7; Agranovskii, 29–30; Ramenskaia, 27–28. Zoia Bolotova, the "mistress of the Uktus Mountains," worked as a ski instructor for the Red Army and also served as a coach for the Soviet National Ski Team throughout the 1950s and early 1960s. See Zoia Bolotova, "Sovetskie lyzhnitsy v Sveitsarii," *Ogonek* no. 3 (1388), 17 January 1954: 16.

64. Agranovskii, 29; Riordan, *Sport in Soviet Society*, 95, 111, 136; Morton, 73; O'Mahoney, 126; Edelman, 37–41, 149.

65. Agranovskii, 29.

66. "Bolshoi lyzhnyi probeg Leningrad–Moskva," *Krasnaia zvezda*, 1 February 1925; 17 January 1925; 31 January 1925; 21 February 1925; 26 March 1925; 31 March 1925.

67. "10,000 kilometrov na lyzhakh," *Krasnaia zvezda*, 14 December 1929; A. M. Esaian, ed., *Fizkul'turniki VII s"ezdu sovetov*, 14–16. See also "Karnaval na snegu," *Krasnaia niva* no. 2 (8 January 1928): 15.

68. Gustav Klutsis, "Spartakiada Moskva 1928," in *The George Costakis Collection: Russian Avant-Garde Art*, ed. Angelica Zander Rudenstine, 221. See also V. Tsitovich, "Kak stat' metkim strelkom?" *Krasnaia niva* no. 29 (15 July 1928): 8.

69. Esaian, 45–46; A. Fedorov, "Osaviakhimu—dvadtsat' let," *Sovetskii sport*, 25 January 1947; G. F. Krivosheyev, "Preparation of Trained Reserves for the Soviet Army in the Prewar Years and during the Great Patriotic War," *Soviet Union Military History Journal* no. 1 (January 1988): 30; Leon Trotsky, *The Revolution Betrayed*, 155.

70. L. Krymov, "Krepi obornu SSSR! Rabota osoaviakhima," *Krasnaia zvezda*, 12 November 1929.

71. *Pravda*, 9 January 1936.

72. I. Rakitin, "Sport v chastiakh," *Krasnaia zvezda*, 17 November 1925; A. D. Borisov, "Zimniaia ucheba v pole," 24 November 1925; "Okruzhnye lyzhnye sostiazaniia," 20 December 1925; Ia. Gorelik, "Budem sberegat' lyzhi," 9 October 1929; "V zimnikh usloviiakh," 2 November 1929.

73. Arthur Stegen, *Biathlon*, 10; Niinimaa, 17; Jönsson, 240–42.

74. "Vertigine Bianca," MPEG-2 XA_TF10-5113; and "Stafett 4 x 10 km," MPEG-2 XA_TF10-5115, National Library of Sweden Film Archives.

75. Aleksandr Kurakin, "O biatlone: istoria razvitiia biatlona" [http://www.biathlon-rus.com/biathlon/story/] Russian Biathlon Union website.

76. Ia. Gorelnik, "Opyt proshloi zimy," *Krasnaia zvezda*, 26 November 1929.

77. "Otkrytie lyzhnogo sezona," *Krasnaia zvezda*, 21 December 1929.

78. Stephen F. Cohen, "Bukharin, NEP, and the Idea of an Alternative to Stalinism," 75; Suny, *Soviet Experiment*, 136–38; Malia, 145–47.

79. Vasilii Starikov, "Lyzhi—sel'skim kruzhkam," *Krasnaia zvezda*, 24 November 1925.

80. V. Usachev, "Fizkul'tura i sport: zimnii sport v ZVO," *Krasnaia zvezda*, 10 December 1925.

81. Preobrazhenskii [sic], "Kak izzhit' lyzhny golod," *Krasnaia zvezda*, 31 December 1925.

82. A. Tarasov, "Osmotri lyzhi: tekhnika material'noi podgotovki," *Krasnaia zvezda*, 6 November 1929; "Sport: 3 milliona par lyzhi v piatiletku," *Krasnaia zvezda*, 29 November 1929.

83. "O zimnem sportivnom inventare," *Pravda*, 1 October 1936.

84. "Lyzhi i kon'ki," *Pravda*, 26 October 1936; "Zimnii sportivnyi sezon nachalsia," 23 November 1936. The production of ski goods was an ongoing problem throughout the Soviet era. See L. Naumov, K. Livenus, B. Moskvin and Iu. Danilov, "Novyi sneg—starye problemy," *Sovetskii sport*, 11 November 1965; D. Dembo, "Neukliuzhie lyzhi: reportazh iz sportivnogo magazina," *Sovetskii sport*, 17 November 1965.

85. "Kostiumy dlia sportsmenov," *Ogonek* no. 50 (1019), December 1946: 40 and inside back cover.

86. *Ogonek* no. 52 (1437), 26 December 1954: 31 and back cover. For full-color examples of Soviet ski fashion—real or imagined—during the period between 1946 and 1954, see the front and back covers of *Ogonek* from December through March. For production problems, see I. Kazakov, "Myshinyi tsvet," *Sovetskii sport*, 27 November 1948; "Novyi sneg—starye problemy"; D. Dembo, "Neukliuzhie lyzhi: reportazh iz sportivnogo magazina," *Sovetskii sport*, 17 November 1965. Handbook for rural collectives: V. Serebriakov, *Lyzhnyi sport*, 34–39.

87. Huntford, *The Last Place*, 553.

88. *Krasnaia niva* no. 20 (13 May 1928): 22; no. 21 (20 May 1928): 17.

89. "Na pomoshch' Nobile," *Krasnaia niva* no. 26 (24 June 1928): 3; M. Beliakov, "Poiski ekspeditsii Nobile," no. 27 (1 July 1928): 8; "'Nobilesse' oblige . . ." no. 32 (5 August 1928): 23; N. Bobrov, "Sluchai s Chukhnovskim," no. 34 (19 August 1928): 14; "Geroicheskii pokhod ledokola 'Krasin,'" no. 38 (16 September 1928): 1, 19.

90. John McCannon, *Red Arctic: Polar Exploration and the Myth of the North in the Soviet Union, 1932–1939*, 26.

91. L. Rimskii, "Za poliarnym krugom," *Krasnaia niva* no. 24 (10 June 1928): 8–9; "Led pobedil," no. 23 (12 August 1928): 20; Horensma, 37–38.

92. Andrews, *Science for the Masses*, 94; Horensma, 171.

93. V. M. Pasetskii, *Frit'of Nansen: 1861–1930*, 8–10. See also A. M. Gor'kii, "Perepiska A. M. Gor'kogo s F. Nansenom," in *Arkhiv A. M. Gor'kogo Tom VIII: Perepiska Gor'kogo s zarubezhnymi literatorami*, 290–93.

94. V. Stankevich, *Frit' of Nansen: Puteshestviia cherez grenlandiiu, k severnomu poliusu i v sibir'*, 7.

95. L. Bat' and A. Deich, *Frit'of Nansen (zhizn' i puteshestviia)*, 150.

96. Pasetskii, 327.

97. M. Beliakov, "Roal'd Amundsen," *Krasnaia niva* no. 34 (19 August 1928): 16. See also no. 32 (5 August 1928): 6.

98. D. Vasil'ev, *Na lyzhne*, 56, 141.

99. See V. M. Pasetskii and S. A. Blinov, *Rual Amundsen: 1872–1928*, 201–2.

100. A. Iakovlev, *Rual Amundsen*, 198; A. Garri, *Po sledam Amundsena*, 11.

101. E. K. Pimenov, *Zavoevanie poliusov*, 237.

102. Garri, 11, 96, 105. See also E. Zinger, "Znak Amundsena," *Ogonek* no. 15 (1868), 7 April 1963: 32.

103. Georgii Kublitskii, *Frit'of Nansen ego zhizn' i neobyknovennye prikliucheniia*, 50–55; Iakolev, 24; Pimenov, 201; also I. P. Magidovich, *Ocherki po istorii geograficheskikh otkrytii*, 602.

3: Stalin and the Inter-war Years

1. J. V. Stalin, "A Year of Great Change: On the Occasion of the Twelfth Anniversary of the October Revolution," 445; Malia, 177; Suny, *Soviet Experiment*, 233.

2. Malia, 182, 201, 202; Suny, *Soviet Experiment*, 217–18.

3. Malia, 208–10.

4. Suny, *Soviet Experiment*, 242, 243, 248.

5. Jeffrey Brooks, *Thank You, Comrade Stalin! Soviet Public Culture from Revolution to Cold War*, 85–89.

6. I. Stalin, "Rech' na pervom vsesoiuznom soveshchanii stakhanovtsev" (17 November 1935), cited in Sheila Fitzpatrick, "Stalin and the Making of a New Elite, 1928–1939," 393.

7. Edelman, 35–36.

8. Brooks, 109, 112–13; Suny, *Soviet Experiment*, 270–72; Malia, 237–38.

9. On the Stakhanovite movement, see Lewis H. Siegelbaum, *Stakhanovism and the Politics of Productivity in the USSR, 1935–1941*. On the relationship between sport and the Stakhanovite movement, see Barbara Keys, "Soviet Sport and Transnational Mass Culture in the 1930s," 420; Edelman, 10, 35–36.

10. Ramenskaia, 31.

11. *Ogonek* no. 9 (1186), 26 February 1950: front cover; ibid., V. Pushkin, "Dobro pozhalovat', gosti dorogie!": 29–30; T. Utkina, "V podshefnyi raion," no. 10 (1187), 5 March 1950: 29; no. 7 (1340), 15 February 1953: photographs between 8 and 9; "U nas v gari-

zone," no. 8 (1341), 22 February 1953: 4; no. 7 (1964), 14 February 1965: 28–29 [photo]; no. 9 (1966), 28 February 1965: inside cover and 1; "Lyzhnyi perekhod Leningrad-Moskva," *Pravda*, 12 March 1962 [photo]; 4 February 1963 [photo]; *Krasnaia zvezda*, 8 March 1967; Agranovskii, 222–28.

12. A. Nemukhin, "Iz Moskvy v Oslo na lyzhakh," *Ogonek* no. 15 (1296), 6 April 1952: 28–29; D. Vasil'ev, *Na lyzhne*, 44–57; I. Nemukhin, *Lyzhnia pokoriaetsia smelym*, 9–10; Agranovskii, 30; Ramenskaia, 31. This Moscow to Oslo trek was re-enacted in 1967 as part of the celebration of fifty years of skiing in post-revolutionary Russia. See "V chest' 50 letiia: dorogoi ottsov," *Sovetskii sport*, 10 February 1967; "Pervye kilometry pozadi," 11 February 1967; 19 February 1967; 22 February 1967; 24 February 1967; 26 February 1967; 3 March 1967; 5 March 1967; 7 March 1967; 10 March 1967; 11 March 1967; 12 March 1967; 14 March 1967; 15 March 1967.

13. Esaian, 14–16; Ramenskaia, 31; "Moskovskaia oblastnaia zvezdno-lyzhnaia estafeta," *Pravda*, 7 March 1937. These types of races continued in the post-war era as well. See S. Krasotkin, "Zvezdnaia estafeta," *Sovetskii sport*, 19 March 1960; G. Abdulkhanov and B. Erzakov, "Zvezdnaia lyzhnaia . . . v chest' velikogo 50-letiia," *Sovetskii sport*, 22 February 1967.

14. "Uchastniki lyzhnogo perekhoda Nerchinsk-Moskva," *Pravda*, 24 December 1934.

15. "Nasha armiia gorzna i neskorushima! Finish lyzhnykh perekhod Khabarovsk-Moskva i Nerchinsk-Moskva," *Pravda,* 13 February 1935.

16. "Vsesoiuznye kon'kobezhnye i lyzhnye sorevnovaniia," *Pravda*, 15 December 1934; "Na lyzhakh iz Perchinska v Moskvu," 28 December 1934; "Nerchinsk-Moskva," 4 January 1935; "Lyzhnye perekhody Dal'nii Vostok-Moskva," 14 January 1935; "Ot Amura do Moskvy na lyzhakh," 15 January 1935; "Lyzhniki idut v Moskvu," 18 January 1935; "5,400 kilometrov za 59 dnei," 22 January 1935; "Nerchinsk-Moskva," 28 January 1935; "Khabarovsk-Moskva: Uchastniki lyzhnogo perekhoda pribyli v Kazan," 28 January 1935; "Lyzhniki Khabarovska vyshli iz Kazani na Moskvu," 31 January 1935; "Nerchinsk-Moskva: proideno na lyzhakh 6,291 kilometr," 1 February 1935; "Nerchinsk-Moskva," 2 February 1935; "Iz Nerchinska v Moskvu na lyzhakh: kak my shli," 3 February 1935; "Komanda lyzhnits vyshla na Moskvu," 6 February 1935; "10 fevralia—v Moskve," 9 February 1935; "Lyzhniki-dal'nevostochniki pribyli v Arzamas," 9 February 1935; "Pobediteli snezhnykh prostranstv," 10 February 1935; "Vsia nasha zhizn' prinadlezhit rodine," 10 February 1935; "Lyzhnyi pokhod zhen komandirov Krasnoi Armii: proideno 2,000 kilometrov," 21 February 1935; "Zhena komandira: lyzhnyi pokhod Tiumen'–Moskva zakonchen," 23 February 1935; D. Vasil'ev, *Na lyzhne*, 82–83.

17. Ramenskiaia, 31; Lukashin, 5; D. Vasil'ev, *Na lyzhne*, 83; "Skrostnyi lyzhnyi probeg Moskva-Perm'," *Pravda*, 8 January 1936; "Lyzhniki prolozhili novuiu trassu," *Pravda*, 1 March 1936; "Lyzhnye perekhody komandirov i boitsov," *Pravda*, 5 March 1936.

18. B. Aristov, "Na s'ezd [sic]—na lyzhakh," *Pravda*, 14 December 1935; 29 January 1936 [photo]; "Delegaty na lyzhakh: segodnia v Gorkii pribivaiut pervye delegatsii kraevogo s'ezda [sic] kolkhoznikov," 11 February 1936; 12 February 1936 [photo]; 13 February 1936 [photo]; "Gorkii kolkhoznikov," 15 February 1936.

19. "Na lyzhakh v Tiumen' i Komsomol'sk," *Pravda*, 2 January 1936; "Lyzhnyi perekhod iz Orekhovo–Zueva v Komsomol'sk-na-Amure," 9 March 1936; "Perekhod Orekhovo-Zuevo-Komsomol'sk-na-Amure," 3 June 1936; "Finish zamechatel'nogo perekhoda," 13 June 1936; Ralph Izard, *The Soviet Olympic Team and Soviet Athletes*, 18.

20. "Lyzhnyi perekhod studentov instituta vneshnei torgovli," *Pravda*, 1 February

1936.

21. "O nagrazhdenii uchastnikov lyzhnogo perekhoda Tobol'sk-Moskva," *Pravda*, 5 March 1936; A. Starostin, *Sport in the USSR*, 27.

22. "Na lyzhakh iz Stalingrada v Leningrad," *Pravda*, 6 March 1936; "Zakonchilsia lyzhnyi perekhod Novosibirsk-Narym," 1 April 1936.

23. "Uchastniki pesho-lyzhnogo perekhoda Bodaibo-Moskva," *Pravda*, 4 April 1936; L. Brontman, "Bodaibo-Moskva: 7.000 kilometrov peshkom i na lyzhakh," 17 April 1936.

24. "Po sledam otriada Antikainena," *Pravda*, 7 February 1938.

25. "Na lyzhakh v Tiumen' i Komsomol'sk," *Pravda*, 2 January 1936; "Blestiashchii perekhod: lyzhnitsy elektrozavoda prishli v Tiumen'," 9 February 1936; "Khronika sporta," 10 February 1936; "Lyzhnitsy elektrozavoda vernulis' v Moskvu," 29 February 1936. See also D. Vasil'ev, *Na lyzhne*, 84.

26. *Krasnyi sport*, 15 November 1936, cited in Edelman, 36.

27. "Pokhod piat' lyzhnits," *Pravda*, 9 January 1937.

28. "Peshe-lyzhnyi perekhod Ulan-Ude-Moskva," *Pravda*, 4 December 1936; "Lyzhnyi pokhod devushek-buriatok," 1 February 1937; "Otvazhnye lyzhnitsy Buriat-Mongolii," 4 February 1937; "Ulan-Ude-Moskva na lyzhakh," 25 February 1937; 3 March 1937 [photo]; "Poslednii etap," 3 March 1937; 7 March 1937 [photo]; "6.065 kilometrov peshkom i na lyzhakh," 7 March 1937; "Vstrecha v Moskve," 7 March 1937; 10 March 1937 [photo]; "O nagrazhdenii znak pocheta," 10 March 1937; "Lyzhnitsy Buriat-Mongolii vozvratilis' v Ulan-Ude," 31 March 1937.

29. Lukashin, 5.

30. Ramenskaia, 32.

31. D. Vasil'ev, *Na lyzhne*, 85.

32. "Lyzhnyi probeg 'starikov,'" *Pravda*, 10 December 1935; Aleksandr Nemukhin, "Na lyzhakh iz Moskvy v Peterburg," *Ogonek* no. 4 (727), 7 February 1941: 22; A. Nemukhin, "Lyzhnaia gonka Moskva-Peterburg," *Ogonek* no. 12 (1241), 18 March 1951: 20; "Pozdravliaem vas, veterani!" *Sovetskii sport*, 20 February 1960: 8; I. Nemukhin, 11; Agranovskii, 33–34. In 1937, Moscow skiers over the age of thirty-five raced for a prize named in honor of Nemukhin. See "Lyzhniki stolitsy otkryli sezon," *Pravda*, 2 January 1937.

33. "Bol'shaia lyzhnaia gonka," *Pravda*, 28 December 1937; "Lyzhnaia gonka Iaroslavl'-Moskva," 14 January 1938; "Bol'shaia lyzhnaia gonka," 16 January 1938; "Bol'shaia lyzhnaia gonka," 17 January 1938; "Segodnia finish lyzhnoi gonki," 18 January 1938; "Bol'shaia lyzhnaia gonka zakonchilas," 19 January 1938; S. Bogachev, "Vsesoiuznaia marafonskaia," *Sovetskii sport*, 18 February 1961; D. Vasil'ev, *Na lyzhne*, 26, 30, 105–18, 120–24; Agranovskii, 35–36.

34. "Sorevnovaniia po slalomu," *Pravda*, 24 February 1937; "Pobeda Vasil'eva: zakonchilis' vsesoiuznye lyzhnye sorevnovaniia," 25 February 1937.

35. "Spartakiada krasnoarmeitsev, krasnoflottsev i pogranichnikov," *Pravda*, 20 February 1938; "Iubileinaia Spartakiada RKKA i 'Dinamo,'" 21 February 1938.

36. Carl Van Dyke, *The Soviet Invasion of Finland, 1939–1940*, 42.

37. Robert A. Doughty and Ira D. Gruber, *American Military History and the Evolution of Warfare in the Western World*, 271, 377. On the eve of the Battle of the Marne during World War I, the horse-drawn heavy artillery of Germany could not keep up with advancing columns of infantry due to the lack of adequate fodder.

38. E.g., *Krasnaia zvezda*, 14 December 1929; *Pravda*, 25 February 1933.

39. *Pravda*, 6 February 1937.

40. *Pravda*, 7 January 1936. Russian motorcycle ski-joring still had practitioners in the latter half of the twentieth century. See Viktor Borod'ev, "Derzhas' za 'khvost,'" *Smena* no. 1 (1143), January 1975: 28–29.

41. Vladimir Snegirev, *On Skis to the North Pole*, trans. George Watts, 184.

42. *Pravda*, 6 February 1935.

43. Snegirev, 16, 22, 26–27; Dmitrii Shparo, "Dvadtsat' chetyre dnia na lyzhakh po dreifuiushchim l'dam arktiki," 126; Shparo, "To the North Pole on Skis," *Soviet Union* 3 (276) 1973: 55; "Skiing across the Bering Strait," *Explorers Journal* 76 (1) 1998: 10–13; "Dmitri Shparo—30 let vokrug poliusa."

44. "Zdravstvui, 'Metelitsa!'" *Komosomol'skaia pravda*, 18 March 1969; V. Kuznetsova, "'Metelitsa' idet po ostrovam," *Ogonek* no. 44 (2677), 28 October 1977: 20; B. Sopel'niak, "'Metelitsa'—v Arktike," *Ogonek* no. 26 (2711), 23 June 1979: 22; Marina Popovich, "'Metelitsa' v Arktike," *Ogonek* no. 52 (2841), 26 December 1981: 30, back cover; Arkady Martynov, "'Metelitsa's Last Address: The Antarctic," *Soviet Woman* 4 (1990): 25–27; "From Pole to Pole," *Soviet Shipping* 3 (91): 33; "Pamiati Valentiny Kuznetsovoi, glavnoi Metelitsy strany."

45. Dmitrii Shparo, *K poliusu!*, 164. See also Snegirev, 190.

46. Shparo, "Dvadtsat' chetyre," 124; Dmitrii and Matvei Shparo, *Challenging Greenland (The Epic Russian Crossing of Greenland)*, 24–27, 91.

47. O'Mahoney, 16, 17, 126.

48. Riordan, *Soviet Sport*, 46.

49. "Novye normy ispitanii na znachok 'gotov k trudu i oborone,'" *Pravda*, 11 December 1934; "Voenizirovannym lyzhnym pokhodom," 12 January 1936; "Sdacha norm na znachok 'gotov k trudu i oborone,'" 17 January 1937; Sergei Kournakoff, "The Soviet High School Curriculum," *Soviet Russia Today*, June 1947: 16; "Novyi kompleks GTO," *Sovetskii sport*, 9 January 1959; "The Physical Culture Program in the Secondary Schools," *Yessis Review of Soviet Physical Education and Sports* 2, no. 1 (March 1967): 28–35, 69–83; "The Physical Culture Program in the Secondary Schools," ibid., 2, no. 4 (December 1967): 84–112; I. T. Osipov, "A New Battery—A New View," ibid., 5, no. 1 (March 1970): 24–27; "Requirements and Norms for the All-Union Battery of Physical Perfection 'Prepared for Work and Defense of the Country," ibid., 5, no. 2 (June 1970): 50–55; Bernard Cooper, "Health through Sports and Knowledge," *Soviet Life* 8 (August 1972): 48–49; *Yessis Review of Soviet Physical Education and Sports* 7, no. 3 (September 1972): 79–83; Mark Tatrakovskii, "Chtoby byt' muzhchinom," *Smena* no. 6 (1124), March 1974: 30–31.

50. Hy Turk, "Sports Steeled the Soviets," *Soviet Russia Today*, October 1944: 12.

51. "Stal'nye muskuly rodiny," *Sovetskii sport*, 5 December 1965; B. I. Bergman, *Lyzhnyi sport*, 320–29; Riordan, *Sport in Soviet Society*, 292.

52. Edelman, 10, 42.

53. Ramenskaia, 34–35, Izard, 17. Smaller sport clubs also involved with skiing included Dzerzhinets, Avangard, Metallurg and Torpedo, as well as regional organizations such as Sel'mashevets in Frunze, Fili in Moscow and Olimpiia in Kirovo-Chepetskii.

54. Riordan, *Soviet Sport*, 48; D. Vasil'ev, *Na lyzhne*, 82.

55. James Riordan, "Soviet Sport and Foreign Policy," 322–43; Riordan, *Soviet Sport Background to the Olympics*; Riordan, "The Rise and Fall of Soviet Olympic Champions," 26.

56. William M. Mandel, *Soviet Women*, 158.

57. Sinyavsky, 117; Victor Kuprianov, "To Train Champions or to Make People Healthy? The Sports and Physical Fitness Program," *Soviet Life* 8 (August 1972): 42–45.

58. D. Vasil'ev, *Na lyzhne*, 29, 36, 58, 60; Agranovskii, 29, 35; Ramenskaia, 25.

59. James Riordan, "The Sports Policy of the Soviet Union, 1917–1941," 67.

60. Arnd Krüger, "Sport in German International Politics, 1918–1945," 92; Keys, *Globalizing Sport*, 129.

61. Keys, *Globalizing Sport*, 159, 164–65, 179.

62. Ibid., 169; Krüger, 81.

63. "Voennoe vospitanie molodezhi," *Pravda*, 14 December 1940; Keys, *Globalizing Sport*, 124–26; Krüger, 88; E. John B. Allen, "Leni Riefenstahl and Her Skiing World," 221–30.

64. Sverker Sörlin, "Nature, Skiing and Swedish Nationalism," 150.

65. Gerd Falkner, "The *Deutschen Winterkampfspiele*, German National Winter Olympics," in *2002 International Ski History Congress*, 183–84.

66. Riordan, "Sports Policy," 67. In 1938, skiers from the Norwegian Worker's Union participated in the USSR National Championships. See "Sport," *Pravda*, 5 March 1938; and Agranovskii, 35.

4: The Winter War and the Great Patriotic War

1. *New York Times*, 12 January 1940.

2. Anthony F. Upton, *Finland, 1939–1940*, 52–57; Allen F. Chew, *The White Death: The Epic of the Soviet-Finnish Winter War*, 97–125.

3. *New York Times*, 17 January 1940; Chew, 124–25. The invasion of Finland and the campaign at Suomussalmi received intense press coverage. See *The Official Index to the Times October–December 1939*, 94–99; *The Official Index to the Times January–March 1940*, 101–16.

4. Chew, 212; William R. Trotter, *A Frozen Hell: The Russo-Finnish War of 1939–1940*, 263.

5. For example, see Kevin Cox, "Biathlon," 28–29.

6. Nikita Khrushchev, *Khrushchev Remembers*, 152.

7. N. I. Baryshnikov, V. N. Baryshnikov, B. G. Fedorov, *Finlandiia vo vtoroi mirovoi voine*, 62; Olli Vehviläinen, *Finland in the Second World War: Between Germany and Russia*, 38–39, 45; Trotter, 21; Upton, 40, 43; Van Dyke, 20.

8. Khrushchev, 151; Trotter, 34, 36; Chew, 21.

9. *New York Times*, 12 January 1940.

10. Van Dyke, 40–41; Reese, *Reluctant Soldiers*, 134–35; John J. Stephen, *The Russian Far East: A History*, 235.

11. Trotter, 36.

12. *Pravda*, 4 December 1939; S. Kovtynenko, "Nakanune," in Gurevicha et al., *Boi v Finliandii: vospominaniia uchastnikov*, Vol. 1, 26.

13. Van Dyke, 40.

14. E.g., photographs of tanks: *Pravda*, 6 November 1939; 18 November 1939; 20 November 1939; 29 November 1939; 30 November 1939. Political cartoon: *Pravda*, 28 November 1939.

15. Chew, 256, footnote 6.

16. *New York Times*, 18 January 1940; Van Dyke, 107.

17. Van Dyke, 150, 181, footnote 65.

18. Roger Reese, *The Soviet Military Experience: A History of the Red Army, 1917–1991*, 60; Reese, *Reluctant Soldiers*, 33–40; H. Shukman, "Introduction," in E. N. Kulkov and O. A. Rzheshevsky, *Stalin and the Soviet-Finnish War, 1939–1940*, xxiii. Lack of adequate winter clothing was a perennial problem in the Red Army. See Nikolai Denisov and Nina Vatolina's 1941 poster of a ski trooper, "Grazhdane Sovetskogo Soiuza, sdavaite teplye veshchi dlia Krasnoi Armii, muzhestvenno srazhaiushcheisia s fashistskimi bandami! [Citizens of the Soviet Union, hand over warm items for the Red Army, which is courageously joining battle with the fascist gangs!]," in N. I. Baburina et al., *Plakaty voiny i pobedy*, fig. 63.

19. Khrushchev, 153.

20. D. Vasil'ev, *Na lyzhne*, 130–31.

21. *Finliandia i ee armiia*, cited in Chew, 256, footnote 6.

22. *Pravda*, 4 December 1939.

23. *Pravda*, 3 December 1939.

24. *Krasnaia zvezda*, 4 December 1939.

25. Alexander Hill, *The War behind the Eastern Front: The Soviet Partisan Movement in North-West Russia, 1941–1944*, 8, 12, 133.

26. James Anzulovic, "The Russian Record of the Winter War, 1939–1940," 108, 112, 120; Van Dyke, 86.

27. *Krasnaia zvezda*, 11 December 1939.

28. *Krasnaia zvezda*, 26 January 1940; K. Voroshilov and B. Shaposhnikov, "*Prikaz no. 0672*, 24 December 1939," in Volkovskii, ed., *Tainy i uroki zimnei voiny 1939–1940*, 238.

29. G. Aksel'rod, "Oznakomlenie s taktikoi protivnika," in Gurevicha et al., Vol. 1, 269–70; S. Gudziuk, "Batal'on lyzhnikov," in Gurevicha et al., Vol. 2, 489.

30. Anti-tank tactics: K. Simonian, "Vsegda pomogat' tovarishsham!" in Gurevicha et al., Vol. 1, 96–98; *New York Times*, 18 January 1940: 5. Outflanking on skis: B. Korenskii, "Vysota 'Znamenitaia,'" in Gurevicha et al., Vol. 1, 192; G. Laptev, "Zharkaia skhvatka," in Gurevicha et al.,Vol. 1, 248; *Pravda*, 9 February 1940; *Krasnaia zvezda*, 2 February 1940.

31. *New York Times*, 11 January 1940.

32. Chew, 28, 110.

33. Anzulovic, 145–47.

34. Arm-in-arm skiers: *Pravda*, 28 December 1938; school boys frolicking: *Pravda*, 31 December 1938.

35. *Leningradskaia pravda*, 27 January 1940.

36. *Pravda*, 2 January 1940; 6 January 1940; 7 January 1940; 8 January 1940; 10 January 1940; 14 January 1940; 28 January 1940; 29 January 1940; 30 January 1940.

37. *Pravda*, 2 February 1940; 7 February 1940; 10 February 1940; 11 February 1940; 12 February 1940; 13 February 1940; 14 February 1940; 15 February 1940; 16 February 1940; 22 February 1940; 23 February 1940; 25 February 1940; 27 February 1940; 29 February 1940.

38. *Pravda*, 10 March 1940; *Krasnaia zvezda*, 25 February 1941; Plate 196: "The People's Commissar for Defense, Marshal of the Soviet Union K. E. Voroshilov, out Ski-ing [sic]," Matthew Cullerne Brown, *Socialist Realist Painting*, 183.

39. *Krasnaia zvezda*, 20 January 1940.

40. *New York Times*, 19 January 1940.

41. *Pravda*, 11 February 1940. See also *Krasnaia zvezda*, 4 February 1940. No relation to the brothers Nikolai, Leonid and Dmitrii.

42. Chew, 28.

43. Aksel'rod, "Oznakomlenie," 269.

44. P. Makarov, "Sviazisty-lyzhniki," in Gurevicha et al., Vol. 2, 381.

45. I. Ul'ianov, "Razvedchik," in Gurevicha et al., Vol. 1, 150.

46. Chew, 45, 46. The Suomi machine-pistol or submachine gun was so effective in the Winter War that the Soviets copied it in the design of the Pistolet-Pulemyot Shpagina (PPSh) "burp gun," exported to Soviet bloc countries until the advent of the AK-47 assault rifle in 1949.

47. Trotter, 263–64.

48. *Krasnaia zvezda*, 14 March 1940.

49. A. O. Chubaryan, "Forward," in Kulkov and Rzheshevsky, *Stalin and the Soviet-Finnish War, 1939–1940*, xvi–xvii; Firsoff, 124; Upton, 160; Chew, 212–13. Chew, however, takes issue with the notion that Hitler miscalculated Soviet strength because of the Winter War.

50. Khrushchev, 156.

51. David M. Glantz, "Preface," in Kulkov and Rzheshevsky, *Stalin and the Soviet-Finnish War, 1939–1940*, xiii; Mark von Hagen, "From 'Great Patriotic War' to the Second World War: New Perspectives and Future Prospects," in *Stalinism and Nazism: Dictatorships in Comparison*, ed. Ian Kershaw and Moshe Lewin, 244; Chubaryan, in *Stalin and the Soviet-Finnish War, 1939–1940*, xvii.

52. Kulkov and Rzheshevsky, *Stalin and the Soviet-Finnish War, 1939–1940*, 106–7.

53. E.g., "V chest' slavnoi godovshchiny [photo]," *Leningradskaia pravda*, 26 February 1940; "V boiakh za obespechenie bezopasnosti severozapadnykh granits SSSR. Na Karel'skom peresheike 1939–1940 gg. Lyzhniki v pokhode," Leningrad: Iskusstvo, [no date] [postcard]; "Iugo-Zapadnyi front," *Pravda*, 24 February 1942 [photo]; "Zapadnyi front," *Krasnaia zvezda*, 22 February 1942; "Sovetskii aviadesant," *Krasnaia zvezda*, 14 January 1942 [photo]; "Partizany miniruiut zheleznodorozhnyi put'," in V. Liventsev, *Partizanskii Krai*, 305 [photo]; *Krasnaia zvezda*, 14 January 1942; cover, *Soviet Russia Today*, February 1944; "In the Rear of the Enemy," *Times*, 31 January 1942. Also see photographs in Gurevicha et al., Vol. 1, 279, 109 and a companion line drawing on page 263; *Pravda*, 22 November 1941.

54. Kulkov and Rzheshevsky, *Stalin and the Soviet-Finnish War, 1939–1940*, 15–16.

55. Ibid., 237.

56. *Pravda*, 11 October 1940.

57. Kulkov and Rzheshevsky, *Stalin and the Soviet-Finnish War, 1939–1940*, 14, 255. Stalin also offered an ardent interjection during the testimony of N. Voronov, Chief of the Red Army Artillery. To the artillerist's statement, "I should say that anybody wishing to fight successfully needs shells and mortars," he exclaimed: "Yes, yes."

58. I. V. Stalin, "*Vystuplenie*, 17 April 1940," in N. S. Tarkhova et al., "*Zimniaia voina*": *rabota nad oshibkami aprel'–mai 1940 g.*, 37–38, 40–41.

59. Randi Cox, "All This Can Be Yours!" 156.

60. "Lyzhnuiu maz'," *Krasnaia zvezda*, 9 October 1940; 18 October 1940; 22 October 1940.

61. Randi Cox, "'NEP without Nepmen!' Soviet Advertising and the Transition to Socialism," 147.

62. Semen Kirsanov, "Na lyzhi!" *Pravda*, 23 December 1940; P. Lebedev, "Vydaiush-chiisia lyzhnik," *Sovetskii sport*, 18 January 1947. See also N. Vasil'ev, "Porazhenie, ravnoe pobede," 59.

63. Robert E. Tarleton, "'Bolsheviks of Military Affairs': Stalin's High Commands, 1934–1940," 334; David M. Glantz, *Stumbling Colossus: The Red Army on the Eve of World War*, 89; Reese, *Reluctant Soldiers*, 172. It is unclear how, or even if, Stalin's opinion of Finnish ski troops and tactics changed during this period, but he relied on Timoshenko's instincts. A post–Soviet Russian biography of Timoshenko includes an undocumented conversation in which Stalin says to his new Commissar of Defense: "First of all take care of discipline and training in the army. The commonly accepted wisdom is unimportant." See R. M. Portugal'skii et al., *Marshal S. K. Timoshenko: Zhizn' i deiatel'nost'*, 109.

64. *Pravda*, 14 December 1940.

65. L. Z. Mekhlis, " Doklad nachal'nika Politicheskogo upravleniia Krasnoi Armii L. Z. Mekhlisa o voennoi ideologii, 10 May 1940," in Tarkhova et al., *"Zimniaia voina,"* 340.

66. Konstantin Boitsov, "'Zolotoi zalp v Khanty-Mansiiske," *Ogonek* no. 12 (4791) March 2003: 50.

67. *Pravda*, 9 October 1940.

68. *Pravda*, 11 October 1940. The Young Pioneers recruited children between the ages of eight and fifteen to join a Party-approved program based on the Boy Scout movement.

69. *Leningradskaia pravda*, 17 October 1940.

70. "Programma voenno-fizicheskoi podgotovki uchashikhsia nachal'nykh i I–IV klassov nepolnykh srednykh i srednykh shkol," Narkompros RSFSR, 1942 [pamphlet]: 19, 20, 26, 28.

71. *Pravda*, 13 November 1940.

72. *Pravda*, 23 November 1940.

73. *Krasnaia zvezda*, 13 November 1940; *Pravda*, 25 November 1940; 27 November 1940; 8 December 1940; 11 December 1940; 17 December 1940; 21 December 1940; 23 December 1940; 28 December 1940; 4 December 1941; 9 December 1941.

74. *Krasnaia zvezda*, 13 November 1940; *Pravda*, 23 November 1940.

75. Toivo Antikainen, "Vse na lyzhi!" *Totuus*, 29 November 1940, cited in Vikstrem, 222. *Totuus* (the Finnish equivalent of the Russian *Pravda*, or "Truth") was a Finnish language newspaper published in Petrozavodsk from 1940 to 1955.

76. Toivo Antikainen, "Voina na lyzhakh," *Totuus*, [ ] February 1941, cited in Vikstrem, 222–23.

77. "Vse pod ruzhbe, vse na front!" *Pravda*, 7 October 1919; Trotsky, *Kak vooruzhalas' revoliutsiia*, Vol. 2, Book 1, 287; Trotsky, Vol. 3, Book 1, 50. For other "vse na . . ." examples from the Russian Civil War, see *Pravda*, 10 July 1919; 10 October 1919; 21 October 1919; 11 January 1920; 17 February 1920; 21 February 1920.

78. *Krasnaia zvezda*, 1 January 1941.

79. E.g., S. Kirsanov, "Na lyzhi!" *Pravda*, 23 December 1940; M. Ryderman, "Dobryi put'," *Pravda*, 9 February 1941; A. Syrkov, "Nashi normi—ne dlia formi!" *Pravda*, 30 December 1940.

80. "Armeiskaia lyzhnaia," words by V. Levedev-Kumach, music by A. Novikov in *Krasnaia zvezda*, 22 February 1941.

81. A. Snopkov et al., eds., *Shest'sot plakatov*, 151, 157–60.

82. *Pravda*, 11 December 1940.

83. Matthew Lenoe, *Closer to the Masses: Stalinist Culture, Social Revolution, and Soviet Newspapers*, 28; E. Babachenko, "Kazhdyi communist—agitator," *Pravda*, 1 March 1935; "Agitation," in *The Great Soviet Encyclopedia: A Translation of the 3rd Edition*, 138.

84. *Pravda*, 26 March 1941.

85. *Krasnaia zvezda*, 6–9, 11–12 February 1941.

86. *Krasnaia zvezda*, 9 February 1941; 26 March 1941.

87. E.g., "Na lyzhi!," *Krasnaia zvezda*, 13 November 1940; "Na lyzhi, voiny Krasnoi Armii!" 27 December 1940; "Voitsy i komandiry Krasnoi Armii! Na lyzhi!" 8 February 1941; "Ves' polk na lyzhakh!" 26 March 1941.

88. *Krasnaia zvezda*, 27 December 1940.

89. *Krasnaia zvezda*, 28 December 1940; 29 December 1940; 31 December 1940; *Pravda*, 28 December 1940; 29 December 1940.

90. *Pravda*, 2 January 1941; V. K. Dmitrievskii, *Lyzhnyi kross* (Moscow: "Sovetskii khudozhnik" [no date]) [postcard]. A far from comprehensive list of *Pravda* issues featuring *Lyzhni kross* headlines and captions includes: 3 January 1941; 6 January 1941; 10 January 1941; 13 January 1941; 15 January 1941; 19 January 1941; 20 January 1941; 21 January 1941; 30 January 1941; 3 February 1941; 4 February 1941; 10 February 1941; 13 February 1941. See also "Lyzhnye krossy," *Ogonek* no. 4 (727), 7 February 1941: 22; "Vzvod—pobeditel'," no. 6 (729), 25 February 1941: 3; no. 7 (730), 5 March 1941: 2.

91. *Pravda*, 2 January 1941.

92. *Pravda*, 29 December 1940. The article includes the terms *massovost'* [mass participation] and *masterstvo* [mastery or prowess].

93. *Pravda*, 25 February 1941.

94. *Pravda*, 29 March 1941.

95. D. Vasil'ev, *Na lyzhne*, 132, 134; *Pravda*, 25 February 1941.

96. The 90-kilometer Vasaloppet attracted 15,806 competitors on 4 March 2012.

97. A. Andreev, "Lyzhniki," *Krasnaia zvezda*, 1 January 1941.

98. This 1941 series of stamps is reproduced in D. Karachi and V. Karlinski, *Pochtovye Marki SSSR (1918–1968)*, 77–78.

99. "V boiakh za obespechenie bezopasnosti severozapadnykh granits SSSR. Na Karel'skom peresheike 1939–1940 gg. Vo bremia boev s belofinnami v raione Teriok." Leningrad: Iskusstvo, [no date] [postcard]; ibid., "Lyzhniki v pokhode."

100. "Pod znamenem Lenina, pod voditel'stvom Stalina—vpered, na razgrom nemetsko-fashistskikh zakhvatchikov!" *Pravda*, 24 February 1942.

101. *Krasnaia zvezda*, 22 February 1942; 14 January 1942. The concept of skiing as cavalry was a metaphor that continued throughout the Soviet era. See *zimniaia kavelariia* [winter cavalry] in *Krasnaia zvezda* 15 February 1974; and *snezhnaia kavelariia* [snow cavalry] in "Snezhnaia kavelariia v ataku," *Sovetskii sport*, 26 December 1961; and Butin, *Lyzhnyi sport*, 9–18. For the association of skiers with tanks, see *Pravda*, 14 January 1937 [photo]; L. M. Torich, "Krepche udar po vragu!" in I. V. Selivanova and N. N. Shkol'nyi, *Leningradskie "Okna TASS" 1941–1945 gg.*, 95 [poster]; K. Palamarchuk, "Nash zolotoi fond," *Krasnaia zvezda*, 8 February 1957; 24 February 1976 [photo]; 26 February 1988 [photo].

102. V. Viktorov, "Pocherk slalomista," *Ogonek* no. 11 (1084), 14 March 1948: 26; D. Vasil'ev, *Na lyzhne*, 133.

103. Gustav Fochler-Hauke, *Schi-Jäger am Feind! Von Kampf und Kameradschaft*

eines Schi-Bataillons in der Winterschlacht in Osten 1941/1942, 36–37, 64, 72, 73, 84, 88, 161, 175, Figure 28, Map Insert; Georg Gunter, *Die deutschen Skijäger von den Anfängen bis 1945*, 28–40, 289–98; Firsoff, 146–53; P. N. Pospelov et al., eds., *Istoriia Velikoi Otechestvennoi voiny Sovetskogo Soiuza, 1941–1945*, Vol. 2, 276, 278, 279, 290, 319, 320.

104. "Smelyi reid lyzhnikov v tyl vraga," *Krasnaia zvezda*, 4 March 1942; "Kak lyzhnyi otriad pregradil put' nemetskoi divizii," 14 February 1942; "Boevye deistviia lyzhnykh otriadov," 16 January 1942.

105. E.g., *Pravda*, 15 December 1941; 18 January 1942.

106. Hill, *The War behind the Eastern Front*, 132–33.

107. E.g., Liventsev, *Partizanskii krai*; P. P. Petrov and L. M. Subotskii, *Partizanskie byli*; V. E. Bystrov, ed., *Sovetskie partizany*. See also the photograph of mining the railroad tracks in *Krasnaia zvezda*, 14 January 1942, as well as *Times*, 13 February 1942, to illustrate the work of Russian parachute troops dropped behind enemy lines.

108. *Krasnaia zvezda*, 14 January 1942; 7 March 1942; 9 March 1942. Another female skier, Aleksandra Ivanova, was remembered in the 1970s as a "fearless scout" as well as an instructor for a ski battalion. See V. S. Murmantseva, *Sovetskie zhenshchiny v Velikoe Otechestvennoi voine*, 171–72. See also Susanne Conze and Beate Fiesler, "Soviet Women as Comrades-in-Arms," 211–34; Iurii Strekhnin, "Dvenadtsatyi prizhok," 244–72; R. Chernoglazova, "Zhenshchiny Belorussii v Velikoi Otechestvennoi voine," 186–210.

109. Harold S. Orenstein, trans., *Soviet Documents on the Use of War Experience*, Vol. 1: *The Initial Period of the War, 1941*; Vol. 2: *The Winter Campaign, 1941–1942*; Vol. 3: *Military Operations, 1941 and 1942*.

110. Orenstein, *Soviet Documents on the Use of War Experience*, Vol. 2, 35, 34.

111. Ibid., 17.

112. *Pravda*, 24–27 August 1942.

113. Weiner, 43–46.

114. *Pravda*, 25 August 1942.

115. *Times*, 13 February 1942; *New York Times*, 4 January 1943. Other examples from the *New York Times* include: "Sergei, Red Fighter," 4 January 1942; 1 March 1942; 2 March 1942. Also popular were photographs of propeller-driven sleds used by Soviet ski troops: "The Aero-Sled Joins the Russian March against the Nazis," *New York Times*, 23 January 1942; "Airsled—It Travels Faster than the Fleeing Nazis," 17 March 1942.

116. *Soviet Russia Today*, February 1944: cover. This photograph previously appeared in Gurevicha et al., Vol. 1, 109.

117. Thomas Doherty, *Projections of War: Hollywood, American Culture, and World War II*, 202. For examples of Soviet ski film from the Great Patriotic War, see M. Iurev and V. Semeniuk, *World War II Russia: The Russian Front*, VHS format, 30 min.

118. *New York Times*, 17 February 1942.

119. Bosley Crowther, "'In the Rear of the Enemy,' Soviet Film, Opens at the Stanley," *New York Times*, 10 October 1942.

120. *Times*, 31 January 1942.

121. See "Latest from the USSR," British Pathé, 1942 [issue date: 26 March 1942], 1:59 min., canister: 42/25, film ID: 1322.01, tape: *PM1322* [http://www.britishpathe.com/record.php?id=22542]; "March of Time—One Day of War—Russia," British Pathé, 1943, 20:19 min., canister: DOCS, film ID: 2723.01, tape: *PM2723* [http://www.britishpathe.com/record.php?id=84457]; "West of Voronezh," British Pathé, 1943 [issue date: 25 March

1943], 2:10 min., canister: 43/24, film ID: 1079.10, tape: *PM1079* [http://www.british-pathe.com/record.php?id=12203]; "Russian Ski Troops," British Pathé, 1943 [?], 1:51 min., canister UN230G, film ID: 1623.20, tape: *PM1623* [http://www.britishpathe.com/record. php?id=6065]. This is a Russian newsreel, "Pomoshch' ranenym zimoi [aid for the wounded in winter]," shot by I. Veinerovich about evacuation of injured troops over the snow, although there is no skiing shown; "Russo-Finish [sic] War—1940 (aka Bryansky Front)," British Pathé, [no date], 2:09 min., canister: UN228D, film ID: 628.06, tape: *PM0628* [http://www.britishpathe.com/record.php?id=50928]. The British Pathé title and date are misleading. This is a newsreel in Russian, "Brianskii Front," shot by A. Solodokov and M. Prudhikov; the SKZh (*Sovetskii kinozhurnal*) date on the reel is 1944.

122. "Russia," British Pathé, 1942 [issue date: 6 July 1942], 1:46 min., canister: 42/54, film ID: 1328.24, tape: *PM1328* [http://www.britishpathe.com/record.php?=22934].

123. "Russian [sic]Overcome Winter" [Ia. Marchenko et al., eds.] British Pathé, 1944 [?], 2:02 min., canister: UN231D, film ID: 1623.24, tape ID: *PM1623* [http://www.brit-ishpathe.com/record.php?id=60609]. This is footage unused by British Pathé shot by Ia. Marchenko, M. Prudnikov, Ia. Smirnov and K. Shironin, cinematographers of the Second Baltic Front, 1943 through 1944, with the original Russian soundtrack intact.

124. Frank Harper, *Military Ski Manual: A Handbook for Ski and Mountain Troops*, 346.

5: Post-War Soviet Sports and the Birth of Biathlon

1. Elena Zubkova, *Russia after the War: Hopes, Illusions, and Disappointments, 1945–1957*, 12, 20; Melvyn P. Leffler, "The Cold War: What Do 'We Now Know'?" 513. As a point of comparison, consider that the United States suffered around 420,000 military and civilian deaths during the Second World War.

2. Ekaterina Novikova, "Pervyi i edinstvennyi."

3. "Pismo Tovarishchu Stalinu ot uchastnikov antifashistskogo mitinga sovetskikh sportsmenov v Moskve," in *Antifashistskii Miting Sovetskikh Sportsmenov v Moskve*, 34. See also 3–5, 35–37, passim.

4. Platon Ippolitov, "Sportsmen v shineli," *Pravda*, 1 April 1942.

5. Riordan, *Sport in Soviet Society*, 159.

6. Pospelov et al., Vol. 1, 276.

7. Riordan, *Sport in Soviet Society*, 59, 364.

8. N. N. Romanov, *Trudnye dorogi k Olimpu*, 57, cited in Victor Peppard and James Riordan, *Playing Politics: Soviet Sport Diplomacy to 1992*, 63.

9. Edelman, 125–26. Edelman suggests as well that the policies remained the same throughout the Brezhnev era and even after Gorbachev came to power in 1985.

10. K. Platanov and S. Groshenkov, "O professional'noi sportivnoi orientatsii uchashcheisia molodezhi," *Teoriia i prakitika fizicheskoi kul'tury* 5 (1968): 42, quoted in Peppard and Riordan, 71. See also P. Sobolev, "Mezhdunarodnye sviazi sovetskikh sports-menov," *Sovetskii sport*, 27 December 1949; O'Mahoney, 166.

11. E.g., "Na lyzhi!" *Krasnaia zvezda*, 13 November 1940.

12. Weiner, 17, 20.

13. Ibid., 32, 61, 138, 208–9, 213. The literature on Soviet ethnicity and nationalism is voluminous. A very partial listing includes: Yuri Slezkine, "The USSR as a Communal

Apartment, or How a Socialist State Promoted Ethnic Particularism," *Slavic Review* 53, no. 2 (Summer 1994): 414–52; Francine Hirsch, "Toward an Empire of Nations: Border Making and the Formation of Soviet National Identities," *Russian Review* 59, no. 2 (April 2000): 201–26; Terry Martin, *Affirmative Action Empire: Nations and Nationalism in the Soviet Union, 1929–1939*; Ronald Grigor Suny and Terry Martin, *A State of Nations: Empire and Nation-Making in the Age of Lenin and Stalin*; Eric Weitz, "Racial Politics without the Concept of Race: Reevaluating Soviet Ethnic and National Purges," 1–29.

14. E. A. Rees, "Stalin and Russian Nationalism," 101.

15. O'Mahoney, 165.

16. Vladimir Gankevich, "Estafeta pod artobstrelom," *Avrora* no. 5 (May 1974): 60.

17. S. Vershinin, "Sud'ba negritianskogo mal'chika," *Ogonek* no. 5 (1234), 28 January 1951: 11.

18. I. A. Nemukhin, *Lyzhi—sport sil'nikh i smelykh*, 29–30.

19. Butin, 85.

20. *Ogonek* no. 8 (1133), 20 February 1949: cover, inside cover and 1; no. 8 (1237), 18 February 1951: cover and back cover. According to Nikita Khrushchev, Stalin boasted of his own prowess on skis as well as his flawless marksmanship. See *Khrushchev Remembers*, 302–3.

21. G. D. Kharabuga, *Sovetskaia sistema fizicheskogo vospitaniia* (Leningrad: [no publisher] 1970), 13, quoted in Riordan, *Sport in Soviet Society*, 159; Weiner, 8.

22. "Lyzhnitsa—geroinia," *Ogonek* no. 9 (1030), 2 March 1947: 30; "Zavtra v Moskve," *Sovetskii sport*, 6 March 1948; V. Viktorov, "Lyzhnaia gonka," *Ogonek* no. 9 (1238), 25 February 1951: 29. Miagkov was the 20-kilometer national champion of the USSR in 1939. He died on 6 March 1940 during the final days of the Winter War, receiving the posthumous designation Hero of the Soviet Union on 21 May 1940. The stadium at the Lenin Institute in Moscow was named in his honor. In response to a letter from three female students who reported that there was no statue, portrait or information about Miagkov in the stadium, *Sovetskii sport* initiated an inquiry that led to placement of a memorial there. See D. Vasil'ev, *Na lyzhne*, 130–31; A. Bazhenov, "Student, chempion, geroi . . . ," *Sovetskii sport*, 16 October 1959.

23. *Krasnaia zvezda*, 29 December 1956; 11 February 1958; Bazhenov, "Student, chempion, geroi."

24. "Pervenstvo Vooruzhennykh Sil po lyzhnomu sportu," *Krasnaia zvezda*, 9 February 1957. See also *Krasnaia zvezda*, 23 January 1957; 27 February 1957; 6 March 1957; 30 October 1957; 2 March 1958.

25. "Rasstanovka sil: obozrenie," *Sovetskii sport*, 1 March 1958.

26. D. Vasil'ev, "Khomenkollenskie gonki," *Sovetskii sport*, 22 March 1947; 25 March 1947; D. Vasil'ev, *Na lyzhne*, 138. Vasil'ev also observed military patrol competitions taking place at nearby Hovseter.

27. A. G. Bychkov, "Sport: lyzhniki," *Ogonek* no. 47 (1068), 23 November 1947: 30–31.

28. D. Vasil'ev, *Na lyzhne*, 141–43. The 1948 Holmenkollen Games were considered an "unofficial" world championship having fallen in an Olympic year. Nordic world championships officially sanctioned by the FIS were held annually from 1925 through 1939 (the Winter Olympics of 1928, 1932 and 1936 included). Although a world championship took place in Cortina d'Ampezzo in 1941, the results were officially expunged from FIS records in 1946. From 1950 to 1978, the world championship was contested every two years, alter-

nating with the Winter Olympics. Since 1980, the events have taken place every two years.

29. Soviet insistence that Spain be rejected from FIS in 1949 led to a small crisis, causing Sir Arnold Lunn, the British delegate, to resign in protest. Delegates also demanded that Russian become one of the official languages of international sport. See Robert Creamer, "Of Greeks—and Russians," *Sports Illustrated*, 6 February 1956: 32.

30. "Sportivnaia zima," *Ogonek* no. 50 (1123), 12 December 1948: 30; *Programma pervenstva SSSR po lyzhnomu sportu 1948 g.*, 1–16; E. Vasil'ev, "Zimnii prazdnik u timiriazevtsev," *Ogonek* no. 7 (1288), 10 February 1952: 29; N. Komkov, "U nas v Iakrome," no. 8 (1289), 17 February 1952: 29; "Rezerv chempionov," no. 10 (1395), 7 March 1954: 29; V. A. Serebriakov, *Lyzhnyi sport v SSSR: spravochnik za 1952–1954 gg.*, 5–149; V. Shaposhnikov, *Na lyzhnoi trasse*, 73–86; "Gonki sil'neishikh," *Sovetskii sport*, 4 January 1958; "Pobezhaiut veterany," 7 January 1958, 8; Iu. Bel'skii, "Poedinok dvukh kollecktivov," 8 January 1958; "Latviiskie lyzhi idut v drugie respubliki," 12 January 1958; V. Parshenkov, "Vse—na lyzhnyi kross!" 14 January 1958; V. Ratsek, "V kanun zimnei spartakiady armeitsev," 11 February 1958; A. Ivliev, "Novye sily," 14 February 1958; "Zimniaia Spartakiada narodov RSFSR," 12 March 1958.

31. Z. Firsov, "Razvivat' lyzhnyi sport v voiskakh," *Krasnaia zvezda*, 27 February 1957; Serebriakov, *Lyzhnyi sport*, 29–32, 43–45.

32. Serebriakov, *Lyzhnyi sport v SSSR*, 77–78, 87–89.

33. Ibid., 111.

34. An additional six medals were available in jumping and Nordic combined.

35. A 1931 poster promoting the winter sport facilities at the Moscow Park of Culture and Leisure touts a downhill ski station, an "American ice slope," skeleton and bobsled runs as well as Moscow's first jump hill. See El. Lessitzky and V. Akhmet'ev, "Poster Advertising the Skiing Facilities of the Moscow Park of Culture and Rest, 1931," in Elena Barkhatova, ed., *Russian Constructivist Posters*, 145.

36. Agranovskii, 524.

37. L. Vil'dt, "Lyzhnyi pod"emnik," *Ogonek* no. 3 (1388), 17 January 1954: 21; V. Zakharchenko, "Priezhaite Bakuriani," no. 16 (1401), 18 April 1954: 28–29. Film footage of Alpine ski racers shows a t-bar lift (probably the one located at Alma Ata) in operation in the late 1950s. See "USSR Mountain Ski Championships," British Pathé, 1959, 53 sec., canister: UN3209D, film ID: 2716.27, tape: *PM2716* [http://www.britishpathe.com/record.php?id=64199]. Film footage from the Serebrianyi Edel'veis downhill ski competition of 1962 shows skiers following a course next to lift towers. See "Skiers Compete for 'Silver Edelweiss' Prize," British Pathé, 1962, 1:18 min., canister: UN3578I, film ID: 2639.21, tape: *PM2639* [http://www.britishpathe.com/record.php?id=62710]. "Spartakiada shesti millionov," *Ogonek* no. 11 (1864), 10 March 1963: 6–7; no. 15 (1972), 11 April 1965: back cover; Elina Semenova, "Vesnoi na lyzhakh," no. 19 [ ] May 1966: 16; no. 38 (2151), 14 September 1968: photographs between 8 and 9 [Chegeta near Mt. Elbrus]; no. 10 (2227), 7 March 1970: back cover [Zailiiskii Alatau, Kazakhstan]; Agranovskii, 524–26; Bergman, 433–37.

38. Iu. Probrazhenskii, "Prichiny otstavaniia gornolyzhnikov," *Sovetskii sport*, 8 January 1958; German Popov, "Dalekoe blizkoe Kavgolovo," *Avrora*, March 1976, no. 3: 77.

39. S. Anisimov, "'Strela' otpravilas' na eksport," *Sovetskii sport*, 24 December 1965; "Sportivnoe obozrenie: Lyzhnye gonki v Bakuriani," *Ogonek* no. 5 (1078), 1 February 1948: 30. The Dinamo factory in L'vov began production of synthetic slalom skis under the Strela

brand-name in late 1965. See "Lyzhi iz polietilena," *Sovetskii sport*, 11 December 1965.

40. I. A. Nemukhin, *Lyzhi—sport sil'nikh i smelykh*, 19–20; "Otsenki, prognozy, deistvitel'nost'," *Sovetskii sport*, 7 March 1958. World Championship and Olympic Nordic competitions during the period 1948 through 1991 generally included: 18-kilometer and 50-kilometer individual races for men until 1952, after which the 18-kilometer race was replaced by 15- and 30-kilometer events; 5- and 10-kilometer individual races for women; men's 4 x 10-kilometer relay; women's 3 x 5-kilometer relay (4 x 5-kilometer from 1974 on); men's Nordic combined (15-kilometer ski race and ski jumping); men's normal and large hill ski jumping. FIS did not administer military patrol and biathlon.

41. Marty Hall and Pam Penfold, *One Stride Ahead: An Expert's Guide to Cross-Country Skiing*, 193.

42. Shaposhnikov, 53, 65.

43. *Biathlon in the USSR*. However, competition between individual competitors was inevitable. See "Sportivnoe obozrenie: Lyzhnye gonki v Bakuriani," *Ogonek* no. 5 (1078), 1 February 1948: 30. Text that accompanies a photograph of the Moscow District Championships lists the individual winners of the 30-kilometer military patrol race. See *Sovetskii sport*, 6 March 1948: 4. See also Aleksandr Kruglov, "Pervyi iz pervykh."

44. See Shaposhnikov, 34–35, 53; Pavel Kolchin, "Khorosha taktika, prinosiashchaia pobedu," *Sovetskii sport*, 16 March 1960; I. Nemukhin and L. Nikolov, "Lyzhnia polna neozhidonnostei: xxx iubileinaia lyzhnaia estafeta na priz gazeti 'Sovetskii sport,'" 28 December 1965.

45. V. Viktorov, "Lyzhnia vedet v Kortina d'Ampetstso," *Ogonek* no. 3 (1492), 15 January 1956: 24; I. Nemukhin, "Snova Anatolii Sheliukhin," *Sovetskii sport*, 9 February 1958; "Oni budut v Lakhti," 19 February 1958; Nemukhin, *Lyzhi—sport sil'nikh i smelykh*, 20.

46. B. H. Nilsson, *Competing in Cross-Country Skiing*, 138; Hall and Penfold, 191–92; Bob Woodward, *Cross-Country Ski Conditioning for Exercise Skiers and Citizen Racers*, 79–81.

47. For a detailed history of the development of ski wax, see Huntford, *Two Planks*, 307–18.

48. Number 1 was for wet, icy snow and skied-in wet tracks; 2, for fresh-fallen wet snow at the beginning of a thaw from zero to minus two degrees Celsius; 3, for new-fallen snow and skied-in tracks to minus twenty degrees Celsius; 4, for flat or slightly rolling terrain at temperatures minus fifteen to minus twenty degrees Celsius; and 5, for severe cold at temperatures below minus twenty degrees Celsius. V. Viktorov, "35 let na lyzhne," *Ogonek* no. 10 (1031), 9 March 1947: 30; D. Vasil'ev, *Na lyzhne*, 35–36; Agranovskii, 503, 506–7.

49. "Bloknot sportsmena," *Ogonek* no. 5 (728), 15 February 1941: 23; "Lyzhnaia maz'," *Sovetskii sport*, 2 February 1948; N. Laptev, "Bol'she lyzhnykh mazei," 17 November 1949; "Plokho smazhesh', khorosho ne proidesh'," 12 December 1958; Agranovskii, 502–4; Bergman, 451–61. "TsOKB" is an acronym for *Tsentral'noe opytno-konstruktorskoe biuro sportivnogo oborudovaniia i inventariia*, or the Central Experimental-Construction Bureau of Sport Equipment and Inventory.

50. "Pochemu net mazi?" *Sovetskii sport*, 14 February 1959.

51. Ia. Dairedzhiva, "Tormoza na lyzhne," *Sovetskii sport*, 18 January 1962; Igor Nemukhin, "Takogo ne byvalo," 24 February 1962.

52. B. Sferin, "Chtoby lyzhi skol'zili," *Sovetskii sport*, 19 January 1963.

53. I. B. Maslennikov and V. E. Kaplanskii, *Lyzhnyi sport*, 19; John Ruger, interview

by author, 5 August 2010. VISTI is an acronym for *Vserossiiskii proektno-tekhnologicheskii i eksperimental'no-konstruktorskii institut po sportivnym i turistskim izdeliiam*, or the All-Russian Production-Engineering and Experimental-Construction Institute for Sport and Tourism Goods.

54. N. Vasil'ev, "Porazhenie," 69.

55. Serebriakov, *Lyzhnyi sport v SSSR*, 167; Dmitrii Vasil'ev, "Lyzhnaia gonka," *Ogonek* no. 8 (977), February 1946 [sic]: 27–28; D. Vasil'ev, *Na Lyzhne*, 98; P. Kolchin, "Khorosha taktika, prinosiashchaia pobedu," *Sovetskii sport*, 16 March 1960; S. Bogachev, "Vsesoiuznaia marafonskaia," 18 February 1961; N. Nemukhin, "Maz' vyruchaet i . . . podvodit," 7 March 1961.

56. I. Nikiforov, "God rozhdeniia—1920 . . . ," *Sovetskii sport*, 1 December 1960.

57. D. Vasil'ev, *Na lyzhne*, 32, 58.

58. V. S. Farfel', "100 metrov do finisha," *Ogonek* no. 5 (974), February 1946: 29; "Nauka i sport," *Sovetskii sport*, 5 November 1946.

59. Bergman, 119. This example is one of the simpler calculations. For other formulas see 85, 125–26, 137, 260, 264–66, 273, 274; Agranovskii, 51–55, 114, 118, 135–36. See also Shaposhnikov, 87–91; V. A. Manzhosov and I. G. Ogoltsov, "Optimal Movements in Cross-Country Skiing under Certain Conditions," *Theory and Practice of Physical Culture* 2: 20–23, 1973, in *Yessis Review of Soviet Physical Education and Sports* 10, no. 4 (December 1975): 85–90.

60. M. Martynov, "Kak rozhdaetsia sportivnoe masterstvo," *Ogonek* nos. 48–49 (967–968), 9 December 1945: 17–19; I. Nemukhin and L. Nikolov, "Ukroshchenie skorosti," *Sovetskii sport*, 8 January 1966; Diane L. Gill, "Sport and Exercise Physiology," 297–300. See also L. F. Egupov, "Takticheskie ustanovki slalomistov," 206–41; ibid., "Zapominanie slalomnoi trassy," 154–205.

61. Serebriakov, *Lyzhnyi sport v SSSR*, 5; Holmenkollen Skimuseet, e-mail correspondence 21 June 2013..

62. V. Viktorov, "Mezhdunarodnaia lyzhnaia nedelia," *Ogonek* no. 4 (1389), 24 January 1954: 12; D. Vasil'ev, *Na lyzhne*, 152–59; Shaposhnikov, 51–56. Skiers from Czechoslovakia and Poland also took part in these races. Terent'ev was a champion skier from the Karelo-Finnish SSR in 1946 and 1947. See Al. Svetov, "'Pervyi lyzhi Severa,'" *Ogonek* no. 15 (1036), 13 April 1947: 29.

63. Zoia Bolotova, "Sovetskie lyzhnitsy v Shveitsarii," *Ogonek* no. 3 (1388), 17 January 1954: 16; Agranovskii, 39–40; Ramenskaia, 39–40. In 1964, a 5-kilometer event for women was added to the Olympics. This shorter race was introduced to international competition at the 1962 FIS World Championships in Zakopane, Poland.

64. Nedelia sportivnykh pobed," v Falune," *Ogonek* no. 9 (1394), 28 February 1954: 19; V. Viktorov, "Chempion mira," no. 13 (1398), 28 March 1954: 28–29; D. Vasil'ev, "Nashi lyzhniki," no. 2 (1439), 9 January 1955: 28–29; D. Vasil'ev, *Na lyzhne*, 161–66; M. I. Aleksandrov and Iu. A. Ranov, *Fizicheskaia kul'tura i sport v SSSR*, 186–88; Nemukhin, *Lyzhi—sport sil'nikh i smelykh*, 30–40; Agranovskii, 40; Ramenskaia, 40; Shaposhnikov,

65. Hakulinen and Kuzin are featured skiing this 50-kilometer race in "Sweden-Russian Wins Ski-Contest," British Pathé, 1954, 1:14 min., canister: 54/18, film ID: 14432, tape: *PM0144* [http://britishpathe.com/record.php?id=31669]. The King's Cup was presented by Norway's King Oscar in 1888 to the winner of the first 50-kilometer ski race in Huseby, Sweden, after which it became a "floating" trophy. See Huntford, *Two Planks*,

114. Despite Kuzin's auspicious precedent, the only other Soviet gold medal winner in a 50-kilometer event held at an FIS Championship or Olympic venue was Nikolai Zimiatov at the 1980 Lake Placid Games.

65. V. Viktorov, "Lyzhnia vedet v Kortina d'Ampetstso," *Ogonek* no. 3 (1492), 15 January 1956: 24; D. Vasil'ev, *Na lyzhne*, 168–69; Shaposhnikov, 84–85.

66. Aleksandrov and Ranov, 188–92; Lukashin, 7.

67. Jennifer Hargreaves, *Sporting Females: Critical Issues in the History and Sociology of Women's Sports*, 224.

68. E.g., "Soviet Winter Sports," *New World Review* February 1954: 24–25; *UdSSR Der Wintersport/SSSR Zimnii sport* (Moscow: Fizkul'tura i sport, 1963).

69. "In Sped the Ancients," *Sports Illustrated*, 26 February 1968: 12.

70. "Norway Will Run—and Jump—Away with the Nordic Events," *Sports Illustrated*, 5 February 1968: 4.

71. Nat Brown, e-mail correspondence, 4 July 2011. Nikolai Anikin won one gold medal in the 1956 Cortina Winter Games and two bronze medals at Squaw Valley four years later. He spent twenty-seven years as an instructor for Soviet national ski teams before emigrating to the United States in 1990. He was active in American cross-country ski programs near Duluth, Minnesota, until his death in 2009.

72. "Cross-Country," *Sports Illustrated*, 2 February 1976: 45. For views on Soviet women and gender testing in sport according to newspapers in the United States, see Stefan Wiederkehr, "'We Shall Never Know the Exact Number of Men Who Have Competed in the Olympics Posing as Women': Sports, Gender Verification and the Cold War," 556–72. For a Soviet perspective on gender stereotypes in the American press, see S. I. Gus'kov, *V atake dollar (mezhdunarodnyi sport i ideologicheskaia bor'ba)*, 247–48.

73. Sandra Heck, "'A Superfluous Appearance?' The Olympic Winter Pentathlon 1948," 184–92; Niinimaa, 3.

74. Niinimaa, 3–4; "Extract of the Minutes of the 55th Session of the International Olympic Committee," 25–28 May 1959 (Munich): 75, 78–79.

75. For the layout of an old program course, see "Skiing Championships near Sverdlovsk" [Russian title: "Na lyzhne pod Sverdlovskom (On the ski tracks near Sverdlovsk)," ed. A. Istomin, Iu. Leongardt, N. Shmakov] British Pathé, 1959, 2:45 min., canister: UN32166, film ID: 2720.23, tape: *PM2720* [http://britishpathe.com/record.php?id=64256]; "The Ski Events: Biathlon," *Sports Illustrated*, 14 February 1960: 21.

76. In 1968, the UIPM was renamed the *Union Internationale de Pentathlon Moderne et Biathlon* (UIPMB). For more information on biathlon rules and regulations, see Stegen, 10–14; Niinimaa, 17–22; Josef DeFlorian, "Heavy Calibre or Small Bore Biathlon?" *Union Internationale de Pentathlon Moderne et Biathlon Bulletin* no. 27 (January 1975): 21–22; Edgar Fried, "What Is Biathlon?" no. 37 (December 1977): 27–29; Günther Swatz, "Biathlon—With Small-Bore toward Success," no. 46 (May 1981): 16–17; John Moore, "UIPMB—Biathlon Technical Committee Meeting 1981," no. 47 (December 1981): 23.

77. P. Morozov, "Na trekh distantsiiakh," *Krasnaia zvezda*, 11 February 1958.

78. Keys, *Globalizing Sport*, 160.

79. Frederick Fliegner, ed., *1968 United States Olympic Book* (Lausanne, SUI, and Stuttgart, FRG: International Olympic Editions, 1969), 399.

80. Niinimaa, 73–81, 98–99. Norway, the Soviet Union's closest competitor, accounted for 29 percent.

81. Zdeněk Kašper, "Biathlon—Also for the Ladies," *Union Internationale de Pentathlon Moderne et Biathlon Bulletin* no. 46 (May 1981): 18–19; Battista Mismetti, "Junior and Ladies' Biathlon World Championships 1984," no. 52 (June 1984): 12–13; Zdeněk Kašper, "Applause to Our Ladies!" no. 52 (June 1984): 14; Zdeněk Kašper, "Minsk, Once Again Super," no. 54 (July 1985): 15; V. Černý, "Ladies' and Juniors' Biathlon World Championships in Switzerland," no. 54 (July 1985): 14; Antero Huttunen, "Naisten ja nuorten ampumahiihdon MM-kisat," *Ampumahiihtäjä* no. 3 (27 March 1987): 1, 3–4; Jack Hanna, "Women Regarded as Poor Sisters of Biathlon," *Calgary Herald*, 16 February 1988; Niinimaa, 80–81; Zdenek Kasper [Zdeněk Kašper], "The female athletes go down in biathlon history," in Lehotan et al., *50 Years of Biathlon: 1958 to 2008*, 71–79; Kaija Helinurm and Viktor Mamatov, "Two Great Biathlon Women from the Soviet Union," in ibid., 180–83. The first international events for women took place in the Eastern Bloc countries in 1970. Competition expanded to include female biathletes in the West at the first World Championship in 1984; however, women's biathlon did not become an Olympic event until 1992.

82. "Sportivnye sostiazaniia v 1958 godu," *Krasnaia zvezda*, 8 December 1957.

83. "Vstrecha armeiskikh lyzhnikov," *Sovetskii sport*, 29 January 1958; Morozov, "Na trekh distantsiiakh"; Z. Firsov, "Vstrechi prinosiat druzhbu," 23 February 1958. For information on Kavgolovo as a training site for biathlon and cross-country skiing, see German Popov, "Dalekoe blizkoe Kavgolovo," *Avrora* no. 3 (March 1976): 75–77.

84. Bjørndalen won a gold medal in an officially sanctioned FIS Nordic World Cup cross-country ski race on 18 November 2006. After winning two medals at the 2010 Vancouver Winter Olympics, Bjørndalen is currently the most successful biathlete in the history of the sport. Whether he deserves the title of Best Biathlete in the History of the Sport is subject to controversy, based on the increased number of events included in biathlon world championship and Olympic competitions since the Soviet era. See Elena Kopylova, "Aleksandra Vasil'evicha Privalova—s iubileem!"

85. N. Nemukhin, "Zeefel'dskie mitvy," *Krasnaia zvezda*, 23 January 1964; Aleksei Orlov, "Terpi, Rinnat!" *Avrora* no. 2 (February 1973): 75; "Streliaiushchie lyzhniki," *Sovetskaia Belorussiia*, 8 January 1974.

86. V. Gavrilin, "Lyzhnaia gonka so strel'boi," *Krasnaia zvezda*, 13 February 1958; Arthur Liebers, *The Complete Book of Winter Sports*, 64–67; Nikolai Puzanov, "Srazu posle finisha," *Sovetskii sport*, 14 January 1965; Leopold Rehard, "1958: Inaugural WCH in Saalfelden," in Lehotan et al., *50 Years of Biathlon: 1958 to 2008*, 28; Herbert Kirchner, "Episodes in East German biathlon: carrying bayonets into the woods," in ibid., 359. At the 1960 Olympics in Squaw Valley, Aleksandr Privalov took off his skis for all four shooting bouts. See Alexandr [sic] Privalov, "A test of nerves passed successfully," in Lehotan et al., *50 Years of Biathlon: 1958 to 2008*, 141. In film footage from the same competition, Klas Lestander of Sweden fires from the prone position with one ski removed, then puts his ski back on before exiting the range at minutes 3:01 to 3:20 in Hermann Ohletz and Roggi [sic], directors, "50 Jahre Faszination [50 Years of Fascination]," DVD included on *50 Years of Biathlon: 1958 to 2008*. Portions of Ohletz's film as well as footage from the 1959 USSR National Championships at Sverdlovsk illustrate the rudimentary nature of early old program biathlon ranges. See "Skiing Championships near Sverdlovsk."

87. A. Terekhov, "Sportivnye uspekhi voinov," *Krasnaia zvezda*, 17 December 1957.

88. "Sorevnovaniia sil'neishikh lyzhnikov strany," *Krasnaia zvezda*, 10 January 1958. "Ski race with shooting" (*lyzhnaia gonka so strel'boi*) or "winter double-contest" (*zimnoe dvoebor'e*) were the common descriptive phrases for biathlon in *Krasnaia zvezda* and *Sovetskii sport* in 1958. The word for "biathlon" in Russian (*biatlon*) did not gain currency in the Soviet press until February 1959. See "Lyzhnia, vedushchaia v Skvo Velli," *Sovetskii sport*, 10 February 1959; *Pravda*, 24 February 1959; and *Krasnaia zvezda*, 25 February 1959. This was apparently the result of world-press coverage of the pre-Olympic events in Squaw Valley and the success of Soviet skiers at the 1959 World Biathlon Championship in Courmayeur, Italy.

89. N. Nemukhin, "Bystrota i metkost'," *Sovetskii sport*, 10 January 1958.

90. *Krasnaia zvezda*, 24 January 1958.

91. "Lyzhnye gonki so strel'boi," *Krasnaia zvezda*, 24 January 1958.

92. Iu. Shapovalov, "Mladshii serzhent V. Pshenitsyn v gonke so strel'boi," *Krasnaia zvezda*, 10 January 1958.

93. "Spetsial'nye prizy—luchshim lyzhnikim," *Krasnaia zvezda*, 8 February 1958. *Sovetskii voin* (Soviet Fighting Man) was a publication of the Red Army from 1947 to 1992. Originally, from 1919 to 1947, its title was *Krasnoarmeets* (Red Soldier). The journalistic counterpart for members of the Soviet Navy was *Sovetskii moriak* (Soviet Sailor), originally *Krasnoflotets* (Red Fleet Sailor). *Illiustrirovannaia gazeta* (Illustrated Newspaper) was a publication of *Pravda* initiated in 1938.

94. V. Gavrilin, "Lyzhnaia gonka so strel'boi," *Krasnaia zvezda*, 13 February 1958; Z. Firsov and V. Gavrilin, "Zimniaia iubileinaia spartakiada," 14 February 1958; G. Popov, "Uspekh prikhodit v bor'be," *Sovetskii sport*, 13 February 1958.

95. "Pervyi chempion v zimnem dvoebor'e," *Sovetskii sport*, 7 February 1958. Aleksandr Kruglov incorrectly places this race in January 1958. See Kruglov, "Pervyi iz pervykh."

96. N. Smirnov, "'SSSR i Finliandiia—favority v Lakhti," *Sovetskii sport*, 27 February 1958.

97. "Pervye starty lyzhnikov v Lakhti," *Pravda*, 3 March 1958; 4 March 1958; 5 March 1958; "Uspekh sovetskikh lyzhnits," 6 March 1958; "Pobeda sovetskikh lyzhnits," 8 March 1958; 9 March 1958; V. Viktorov, "Kolchin—Khakulinen," *Ogonek* no. 6 (1651), 1 February 1959: 22–23.

98. "Skvoz' snezhnuiu pelenu," *Sovetskii sport*, 4 March 1958. Rather than the V notch arrangement of an open sight, as was standard on a military rifle, the Soviet biathletes used sophisticated diopter sights at this competition. The diopter has an adjustable pinhole aperture, allowing for a more accurate sight-picture when viewing the target, and is especially advantageous during a snowstorm. See Riikka Salokannel, "Heikki Ikola: The third coup," in Lehotan et al., *50 Years of Biathlon: 1958 to 2008*, 158. Sokolov skied the course in 1:19.21 with 11 missed targets, or 22 penalty minutes; Gubin ran in 1:22.12 with 10 missed targets, or 20 penalty minutes; Butakov in 1:22.46 with 6 missed targets, or 12 penalty minutes; and Pshenitsyn in 1:23.14 with 7 misses, or 14 penalty minutes. Sweden's Wiklund covered the course in 1:27.41 with an additional 6 penalty minutes; Gunneriusson ran in 1:28.13 with an additional 6 penalty minutes. Butakov can be seen skiing and shooting at this race in the Ohletz and Roggi film "50 Jahre Faszination," minutes 1:17 to 3:00.

99. "Skvoz' snezhnuiu pelenu."

6: Skiing, Shooting and Politics

1. On 2 March 1930, Stalin published an article titled "Dizziness from Success" in the aftermath of a disastrous campaign to collectivize the peasants initiated in January of that year. See Malia, *Soviet Tragedy*, 196–99.

2. V. Viktorov, "Prolog okonchen," *Ogonek* no. 7 (1704), 14 February 1960: 27.

3. "Novyi kompleks GTO," *Sovetskii sport*, 9 January 1959; "GTO," 30 January 1959.

4. "Novyi kompleks GTO," *Krasnaia zvezda*, 11 January 1959.

5. D. Gulevich and P. Ershov, "Vozrodit' ofitserskoe mnogobor'e," *Krasnaia zvezda*, 22 March 1959.

6. Edelman, 124.

7. N. Anikin, "Eto bylo v Makkini-Krik," *Sovetskii sport*, 4 January 1960. Currently, FIS rules state that the maximum elevation at any point on a cross-country ski course cannot exceed 1,800 meters.

8. "Na olimpiiskoi trasse biatlona," *Sovetskii sport*, 5 March 1959.

9. V. Viktorov, "Vspykhnul olimpiiskii ogon'," *Ogonek* no. 8 (1705), 21 February 1960: 28.

10. V. Viktorov, "Vstrechi na lyzhne," *Ogonek* no. 3 (1700), 17 January 1960: 28. The liquid wax Kolchin refers to is klister, a runny, spreadable formulation with the consistency of model-airplane glue. It is used for snow with high moisture content as a result of rain or a cycle of melting and freezing.

11. "Lyzhniki vstupaiut v bor'bu," *Krasnaia zvezda*, 25 January 1959.

12. "Vsearmeiskie lyzhnye sorevnovaniia," *Krasnaia zvezda*, 30 January 1959.

13. G. Akopov, "Lyzhnia, vedushchaia v Skvo Velli," *Sovetskii sport*, 10 February 1959. Representatives from Trud and Burevestnik participated in the All-Union Biathlon Ski Championship on 15 March 1960. Evgenii Repin of Trud placed ninth. See Iu. Matiukhin, L. Nikolov and S. Tokarev, "Arifmetika i algebra dvoebor'ia," *Sovetskii sport*, 16 March 1960.

14. In a recent interview with the Russian Biathlon Union, Privalov explained that he was hindered at this race by his rifle's warped wooden stock, for which there was no replacement. See Novikova, "Pervyi i edinstvennyi."

15. "Pobeda sovetskikh sportsmenov," *Pravda*, 24 February 1959; "Vladimir Melanin—chempion mira po biatlonu: 'Srazhenie' v doline Aosta," *Sovetskii sport*, 24 February 1959; "Sovetskii voin—chempion mira," *Krasnaia zvezda*, 25 February 1959; I. Nemukhin, "Oni vernulis' s pobedoi," *Sovetskii sport*, 26 February 1959.

16. "Na olimpiiskoi trasse biatlona," *Sovetskii sport*, 5 March 1959.

17. "'A' upalo, 'B' propalo . . ." *Sovetskii sport*, 12 March 1959.

18. "Zolotye medali armeiskikh lyzhnikov," *Krasnaia zvezda*, 13 March 1959; *Sovetskii sport*, 13 March 1959 [photo]. Brilliant film footage of this event by A. Istomin, Iu. Leongradt and N. Shmakov features Melanin, Butakov and Popov skiing the flat course at Sverdlovsk and shooting at the first three ranges. See "Skiing Championships near Sverdlovsk."

19. "Vyshe uroven': sportivnoi raboty v voiskakh," *Krasnaia zvezda*, 24 November 1959.

20. "Na lyzhni, druz'ia, na kon'ki!" *Krasnaia zvezda*, 20 December 1959.

21. "Vstrecha armeiskikh lyzhnikov," *Sovetskii sport*, 29 January 1958.

22. "Tovarishchi sportsmeny!" *Sovetskii sport*, 9 December 1958.

23. "Usloviia otkrytogo konkursa," *Sovetskii sport*, 9 December 1958.

24. V. Kamenskii, "Biatlon? Eto—sovremennoe zimnee dvoebor'e," *Sovetskii sport*, 3 November 1959. In skiing, the Winter Olympics have only served as world championships for the Alpine events during Olympic years between 1948 and 1982.

25. *Sovetskii sport*, 3 November 1959. The army already had a well-established training center for biathlon in the Uktus region. See A. Kochurov, "Na Uktusskikh gorakh," *Krasnaia zvezda*, 27 December 1958.

26. I. Nemukhin, "Doma i gory pomogaiut," *Sovetskii sport*, 30 December 1959.

27. In a 2007 interview, Aleksandr Tikhonov, the greatest biathlete of the twentieth century, described his last Olympic ski race in 1980: "I prepared to shoot my last round thinking that I could not make a mistake. I knew that if I did not hit [the last remaining target], that would be the end of my exceptional career in Soviet sports. That's the way the system was in the Soviet Union." See Ivor Lehotan, "Four Olympic Games—four Golds," in Lehotan et al., *50 Years of Biathlon: 1958 to 2008*, 161.

28. N. Arakcheev, "Na lyzhne—sil'neishie," *Krasnaia zvezda*, 14 January 1960; "Iz Moskvy v Skvo Velli," 7 February 1960.

29. *New York Times*, 6 February 1959; 17 February 1959; A. Grigor'ev and A. Gurkov, "Politicheskii fil'tr v Skvo Velli," *Sovetskii sport*, 1 March 1959.

30. "German Reds Assail U.S. Olympic Curb," *New York Times*, 12 February 1960.

31. "Germans Protest to Olympic Group," *New York Times*, 13 February 1960; "Free Press Gets Olympic Support," 16 February 1960; "Ban on Writers Stands," 17 February 1960; "US Explains Ban on East Germans," 19 February 1960; "Extract Minutes of the 56th Session of the International Olympic Committee," 52.

32. V. Petrusenko, "Pod olimpiiskim fakelom," *Pravda*, 19 February 1960; Petrusenko, "Belaia olimpiada nachalas'," 20 February 1960.

33. V. Gavrilin, "Gorit olimpiiskii ogon'," *Krasnaia zvezda*, 20 February 1960.

34. V. Petrusenko, "Pered bol'shimi startami," *Pravda*, 18 February 1960. Compare with "All Set for the Games!" *Sports Illustrated*, 15 February 1960: 14–15.

35. V. Petrusenko, "Na lyzhnykh trassakh i katke," *Pravda*, 22 February 1960.

36. "Soviet Women Mix Marriage, Sports," *Reno Gazette*, 22 February 1960.

37. "German, Soviet Girls Star," *Reno Gazette*, 20 February 1960. Photographs from McKinney Creek show that the cross-country and biathlon races were poorly attended. See *Sports Illustrated*, 29 February 1960: 20; V. Viktorov and I. Nemukhin, "Sneg i sekundy," *Ogonek* no. 5 (1754), 29 January 1961: 30–31; Niinimaa, 13.

38. Allen, *From Skisport to Skiing*, 54, 62.

39. Patrik Jemteborm, "Klas Lestander's triumph without a single miss," in Lehotan et al., *50 Years of Biathlon: 1958 to 2008*, 48.

40. K. V. Krupin, "14–21 fevralia—'Nedelia lyzhnogo sporta,'" *Sovetskii sport*, 10 February 1960.

41. "Startuiut lyzhniki," *Pravda*, 15 February 1960.

42. "Nedelia lyzhnogo sporta prodlena," *Krasnaia zvezda*, 16 February 1960.

43. "Ski Events: Biathlon."

44. "Za molokom," that is, outside the center black circle on the white part of the target card for a time penalty. Also "v moloko."

45. "Russians Happy with Domination of Biathlon Run," *Reno Gazette*, 22 February 1960; V. Petrusenko, "V bor'be pobezhdaiut silneishie," *Pravda*, 23 February 1960; Lu-

kashin, 11; Niinimaa, 73.

46. "Russians Happy with Domination of Biathlon Run."

47. Petrusenko, "V bor'be pobezhaiut sil'neishie."

48. *Sovetskii sport*, 22 February 1960.

49. V. Gavrilin, "Ubeditel'naia pobeda sovetskikh sportsmenov," *Krasnaia zvezda*, 1 March 1960.

50. N. Romanov, "Dostizheniia olimpiady," *Sovetskii sport*, 1 March 1960; N. Romanov, "Olimpiada zakonchilas', druzhba prodolzhaemsia," *Pravda*, 2 March 1960.

51. Lukashin, 11.

52. V. Viktorov, "Tri? Net, chetyre!" *Ogonek* no. 3 (1804), 14 January 1962: 22–23.

53. V. Viktorov, "Ulybki i tsifry," *Ogonek* no. 10 (1707), 6 March 1960: 26–27. See also N. Nemukhin, "Chetyre v chetverke: traditsiia sovetskikh lyzhnits torzhestvuet," *Sovetskii sport*, 22 February 1960; "Rasskazy o chempionakh: naslednitsa," 22 February 1960; *Reno Gazette*, 25 February 1960; 26 February 1960.

54. *Sovetskii sport*, 20 December 1960; "Olimpiada v tsifrakh," *Pravda*, 1 March 1960; "'Sovetskii sport zasluzhivaet samoi vysokoi otsenki,'" 1 March 1960; N. Romanov, "Dostizheniia olimpiady," *Sovetskii sport*, 1 March 1960.

55. V. Sinitsyn, "Na 'priz druzhby,'" *Krasnaia zvezda*, 28 January 1961.

56. Ivliev, "Novye sily"; "Zimniaia Spartakiada Narodov RSFSR."

57. S. Bogachev, "Kazhduiu nedeliu—start!" *Sovetskii sport*, 7 January 1961.

58. Alevtina Kolchina and Viktor Kosichkin, "Prazdnik sportivnoi zimy," *Pravda*, 4 March 1962.

59. Iurii Mashin, "Kryl'ia krepnut v polete," *Sovetskii sport*, 15 March 1966.

60. V. Viktorov, "Bogastva spartakiady," *Ogonek* no. 13 (2438), 23 March 1974: 4–5, 6. See also V. Viktorov and A. Bochinin, "Zimniaia narodnaia . . . ," no. 12 (2231), 20 March 1971: 30–31; V. Viktorov, "Shagi Spartakiady," no. 12 (2489), 15 March 1975: 20; A. Pozdnaev, "Flagi nad Eniseem," *Nedelia (Izvestiia)* no. 10 (1042), 8–14 March 1982: 4.

61. Matiukhin, Nikolov and Tokarev, "Arifmetika i algebra dvoebor'ia." The statement "three classes of racers" refers to the makeup of a military patrol team: an officer, a noncommissioned officer and enlisted men.

62. Niinimaa, 39–40.

63. "Pul'," *Ogonek* no. 39 (1320), 21 September 1952: 16; V. Pukhnachev, "Sibirskii strelok," no. 6 (1339), 8 February 1953: 29.

64. For example, see calculations for comparing skiing with and without a rifle in Stegen, 32; also the "Russian technique" for firing from the standing position, ibid., 46. Instructional manuals such as Bergman's had antecedents in the publications produced for Red Army ski training during World War II. See L. V. Gavrichkov, *Lyzhnik-boets*; D. P Markov and V. G. Kalashnikov, *Lyzhi*; E. Shchadenko, *Nastavlenie po lyzhnoi podgotovke krasnoi armii*.

65. Bergman, 320, 329.

66. Niinimaa, 40. Footage from a sports parade honoring Stalin on Red Square in the mid-1930s features motorcycles drawing roller skiers, followed by another troop executing synchronized diagonal stride. See "Soviet Sports Parade (aka Cultural Parade in Red Square)." See also "A. Bazhenov, "Pochti kak na lyzhne . . . ," *Sovetskii sport*, 14 October 1958; G. Sergeev, "Na lyzhakh po asfal'tu," *Sovetskii sport*, 13 November 1958; *Sovetskii sport*, 8 September 1960; 16 October 1960 [photograph]; "Russian Skaters and Skiers at

Training"; E. P. Boechin and B. L. Merkulov, "A New Machine for Training Skiers," in *Yessis Review of Soviet Physical Education and Sports* 4, no. 2 (June 1969): 41–42.

67. Bergman, 321–22, 325–27; I. F. Mokropulo and O. I. Sazhin, *Trenirovka lyzhnika-biatlonista*, 16–32.

68. "Chto skazali lyzhnia i mishen'?" *Sovetskii sport*, 11 March 1962; Bergman, 318–20; Mokropulo and Sazhin, 13, 33–59; Stegen, 48, 49, 53.

69. Vladimir Melanin, "Pora zrelosti," *Sovetskii sport*, 11 March 1962.

70. Bergman, 320, 328; B. Bikbov, "Skorost' i tochnost': reportazh s ognevykh rubezhei," *Sovetskii sport*, 24 March 1965.

71. Daniel Gilbert, "The Weight at the Plate."

72. Ibid.

73. I. Nemukhin, "Blestiashchaia pobeda Nikolaia Anikina," *Sovetskii sport*, 13 January 1959. Film footage from this event features crowd scenes, action sequences of Nikolai Anikin, Pavel Kolchin, Vladimir Kuzin and Veikko Hakulinen in the 30-kilometer race as well as extensive coverage of the women's 10-kilometer race. See "Men and Women's Ski Race" [Russian title: "Druzheskie vstrechi sportsmenov (Sportsmen's Friendly Meet)"], British Pathé, 1959, 2:20 min., canister: UN31886, film ID: 2764.31, tape: *PM2764* [http://www.britishpathe.com/record.php?id=65067].

74. "Khronika spartakiady," *Pravda*, 4 March 1962.

75. E. Shatrov, "Lyzhnia ukhodit za okolitsu," *Ogonek* no. 12 (1293), 16 March 1952: 27.

76. "Novaia vysota biatlona," *Sovetskii sport*, 16 February 1982; Zdeněk Kašper, "Anniversary World Championships Raubichi 1982," *Union Internationale de Pentathlon Moderne et Biathlon Bulletin* no. 48 (June 1982): 16.

77. D. Vasil'ev, *Na lyzhne*, 135–36.

78. Serbriakov, 90. For other ski competition parades see "Snezhnaia kavaleriia idet v ataku," *Sovetskii sport*, 26 December 1961; N. Il'inskii and V. Shirokov, "Na starte—tysiacha sportsmenov," *Pravda*, 5 March 1962; *Sovetskii sport*, 13 March 1962; 2 March 1966; V. Viktorov and A. Bochinin, "Zimniaia narodnaia . . . ," *Ogonek* no. 12 (2231), 20 March 1971: 30–31.

79. O. Shmelev, "Gonki v Iakhrome," *Ogonek* no. 13 (1346), 29 March 1953: 29.

80. Riordan, *Sport in Soviet Society*, 156; V. Viktorov, "Bogastva spartakiady," 4–5, 6; Viktorov, "Shagi spartakiady," 20. On track and field, see Edelman, 75–77.

81. O'Mahoney, 167; Edelman, 14.

82. Especially during the winter months from 1946 through 1961, the pages of *Ogonek* and *Sovetskii sport* were positively brimming with all manner of ski-related entertainment for readers (far too many to list here), including full-color and grey-tone photographs, cartoons, short stories, reproductions of paintings, ceramics, wood carvings and sculptures, children's art, poems, pen-and-ink illustrations and essays.

83. D. Vasil'ev, *Na lyzhne*, 132–34; "Lyzhnye krossy," *Ogonek* no. 4 (727), 7 February 1941: 22; E. Vasil'ev, "Sportivnyi Ural," no. 3 (1076), 18 January 1948): 29–30. Interest in cross-country skiing remained high throughout most of the Soviet period, with ten million participants as of 1987. See Eric Evans, "Powers That Will Never Be," 50–51.

84. E.g., V. Smirnov, "Oseniaia trenirovka lyzhnika," *Sovetskii sport*, 26 October 1946; A. Nemukhin, "Zabytaia forma trenirovki," 12 November 1946; V. Kharitonov, "Tonkosti poperemennogo khoda," 24 December 1946; "Trenerovka k krossu," 28 December 1946; N. Alferov,

"O lyzhnike-dvoebortse," 11 January 1947; "Prav li trener Kharitonov?" 15 February 1947; N. Fedosov, "Trener po lyzham," 27 December 1947; A. Donskoi, "Na lyzhne—M. Galiev," 10 January 1958; V. Smirnov and V. Sinev, "Pervye trenerovki na snegu," 9 December 1958; B. Bergman, "Aktivnyi otdykh nuzhen," 13 February 1959; A. Donskoi, "Ne otstupat' ot rezhima" and "Gotov'sia k sezonu," 23 October 1959; N. Fedosov, "Nachinaiushchii lyzhnik na distantsii," 8 January 1960; A. Nemukhin, "So skorost'iu ne shutiat," 23 November 1961; 15 December 1961; "Khod poperemennyi," 20 November 1964; I. Voronchikhin, "Effectivnye melochi," 14 January 1965; V. Naumov, "Ne tol'ko na lyzhne," 14 November 1965; B. Bikbov, "Naputstviia pered lyznei," 24 December 1965; B. Bikbov, "Lyzhnia i ee sekrety," 14 January 1966; N. Anikin, "Kak dostaiutsia sekundy: v pomoshch' uchastnikom spartakiady," 10 February 1967.

85. *Sovetskii sport*, 10 January 1959. Action-sequenced photography was a familiar tool utilized in twentieth-century books on skiing in Russia and the Soviet Union. The 1912 ski manual of K. B. Eimeleus featured sequence photographs demonstrating four different ski techniques in a large format fold-out section after page 148. Similarly, diagrams and photographs of ski champions A. Borin and V. Smirnov fill the pages of P. N. Liudskov's *Lyzhnyi sport*.

86. "Dlia vas, lyzhniki!" *Sovetskii sport*, 3 December 1960.

87. A. Donskoi, "Kak khodit' na lyzhakh," *Ogonek* no. 8 (1289), 17 February 1952: 29.

88. "Sovet korotok—pol'za velika," *Sovetskii sport*, 25 November 1958.

89. P. Zhukov, "Lyzhnia kosmetika," *Sovetskii sport*, 2 December 1961.

90. Halldor Skard and Olle Larsson, *Langrennsteknikk*, 11–12. By 1988, a full-time video technician assisted the coaching staff and athletes of the Soviet National Cross-Country Ski Team. Erik Røste, "'Dear Countrymen: We Wish You to Be the Best,'" *Ski sport* no. 9 (1988), excerpted in "The Soviets: A Special Report," 2–3.

91. G. Blinov and I. Prok, "Sport glazami kino," 109–10, 113.

92. M. Michael Brady, *Nordic Touring and Cross-Country Skiing*, 3rd rev. ed., 73; Hall and Penfold, 137.

93. John Caldwell, *Caldwell on Cross-Country: Training and Technique for the Serious Skier*, 119.

94. *Ogonek* no. 13 (1398), 28 March 1954: 29; D. Vasil'ev, *Na lyzhne*, 161. See also V. Viktorov and B. Svetlanov, "Lakhti—gorod lyzhnyi," *Ogonek* no. 14 (1555), 31 March 1957: 30–31. Other crowd scenes from Scandinavia: Genrikh Gurkov, "Spor lyzhnykh korelei," *Ogonek* no. 9 (1862), 24 February 1963: 30–31; Dimitrii Vasil'ev, "Razmyshchleniaia u lyzhni," no. 2 (2011), 8 January 1966: 26–27; *Sovetskii sport*, 16 March 1962; 8 January 1964; 19 January 1964.

95. Serebriakov, *Lyzhnyi sport v SSSR*, 151; *Sovetskii sport*, 7 January 1958; 18 January 1962; 2 February 1962; 10 March 1962; 11 March 1962; 19 March 1962; 7 March 1963; 8 March 1963; 14 February 1964; 7 March 1964; 24 December 1964; 7 January 1967; 10 January 1967; V. Viktorov, "Lyzhnia poveselela," *Ogonek* no. 5 (2066), 29 January 1967: 30–31; V. Viktorov and A. Bochinin, "Zimniaia narodnaia . . .," no. 12 (2231), 20 March 1971: 30–31; "Bolel'shchiki," no. 4 (2325), 22 January 1972: 32 and inside back cover; V. Viktorov, "Bogastva spartakiady," 4–6; V. Viktorov, "Shagi spartakiady," 20; N. Il'inskii and V. Shirokov, "Chempiony, rekordy, medali . . . ," *Pravda*, 7 March 1962; "Koroleva lyzhni," 8 March 1962; G. Il'in, "Medali—u armeiskikh lyzhnikov," *Krasnaia zvezda*, 7 March 1962.

96. V. Viktorov, "Lyzhnaia gonka," *Ogonek* no. 9 (1238), 25 February 1951: 29; V.

Viktorov, "V den' lyzhnoi gonki," no. 4 (1337), 25 January 1953: 29. See also I. Efimov, "Nedelia lyzhnogo sporta," no. 14 (1295) 30 March 1952: 14. For passive spectators, see Edelman, 70.

97. Matiukhin, Nikolov and Tokarev, "Arifmetika i algebra dvoebor'ia."

98. Ibid.

99. "Tsena vyderzhki," *Sovetskii sport*, 14 January 1962.

100. "Ski Events: Biathlon."

101. "Extract of the Minutes of the 57th Session of the International Olympic Committee," 22–23 August 1960 (Rome): 65; "Minutes of the Conference of the Executive Board of the International Olympic Committee," 16 June 1961 (Athens): 66, 68; "Minutes of the 58th Session of the International Olympic Committee," 19–21 June 1961 (Athens): 75, 81–82, 84–85; "Minutes of the 61st Session of the International Olympic Committee," 26–28 January 1964 (Landeshaus, Innsbruck): 65. See also "Chto skazali lyzhnia i mishen'?"

102. Elena Vaitsekhovskaia, *Shtrafnoi krug Aleksandra Tikhonova*, 144.

103. "I v shutku, i v ser'ez," *Sovetskaia Belorussiia*, 5 March 1974; ibid., ". . . I pod zanaves—'zoloto'"; "Zharkaia duel'," *Sovetskii sport*, 12 February 1982; "Novaia vysota biatlona."

104. "Biathlon's Skiing, Shooting for the Steady Hand"; Brian Olsen, "Top Guns: Biathletes Train in Skiing and Shooting"; *United States Biathlon Association E-Mail Bulletin* 7, no. 15 (October 2010): 6.

105. Sinitsyn, "Na 'Priz druzhby.'"

106. N. Denisov, "Zolotye medali armeitsev," *Pravda*, 10 February 1961.

107. "Pobedu prinosit metkaia strel'ba," *Krasnaia zvezda*, 14 January 1961; V. Gavrilin, "Lyzhnia vedet v Zakopane," 18 January 1961.

108. V. Staritskii and N. Shagin, "V vozdukhe i na zemle," *Sovetskii sport*, 29 January 1961.

109. "Mariia Komar', Ol'ga Petukhova, Ol'ga Mazokina—obladatel'nitsy 'Zolotykh lyzh *Sovetskogo sporta*,'" *Sovetskii sport*, 9 February 1961.

110. D. Sokolov, "Doroga zimnego dvoebor'ia," *Sovetskii sport*, 15 March 1961.

111. "Zolotoe dubl' Iu. Suutarinena," *Sovetskii sport*, 3 March 1974; Arthur Stegen, e-mail correspondence, 24 July 2010.

112. V. Gavrilin, "Pobeda sovetskikh gonshchikov," *Krasnaia zvezda*, 8 February 1961; *Pravda*, 8 February 1961.

113. *Sovetskii sport*, 5 February 1961. See also *Krasnaia zvezda*, 10 February 1961 [photo].

114. V. Gavrilin, "Gonky vedet patrul'," *Krasnaia zvezda*, 10 February 1961.

115. Niinimaa, 73; Stegen, 107; "World Championship of Winter Biathlon—Umea/Umea (SWE)" [http://Services.biathlonresults.com/Results.aspx?RaceId=BT6061SWRLCH01SMIN] International Biathlon Union website.

116. "Patrul' i estafeta," *Krasnaia zvezda*, 22 March 1961.

117. Headline, *Le Monde*, 1 February 1962 [The Cold War and Sport].

118. *New York Times*, 30 January 1962.

119. "Bar'ery na puti v Shamoni," *Sovetskii sport*, 24 January 1962; *New York Times*, 31 January 1962; "FIS—Statuten respektieren," *Neues Deutschland*, 31 January 1962.

120. *New York Times*, 2 February 1962; La fédéderation international de ski réaffirme sa position: 'Pas de championnats du monde sans l'Allemagne de l'Est,'" *France-Soir*,

2 February 1962.

121. "Les championnats du monde de Chamonix risquent d'être annulés," *Le Monde*, 31 January 1962.

122. "Les championnats du monde de ski," *Le Monde*, 1 February 1962; "Les championnats du monde auront sans doute lieu ailleurs qu'à Chamonix," 3 February 1962; "La crise du ski est au point mort," *France-Soir*, 3 February 1962; "Pas d'arrangement en vue pour Chamonix," 5 February 1962; Robert Daley, "A View that F.I.S. Plan to Save World Title Meet May Be Too Late," *New York Times*, 6 February 1962.

123. "Keine Weltmeisterschaften!" and "Klare Entscheidung in Bern," *Neues Deutschland*, 6 February 1962; "Les championnats du monde deviendront-ils les jeux mondiaux de la F.I.S.," *Le Monde*, 7 February 1962.

124. *New York Times*, 6 February 1962.

125. Louis Tomasini, "Le mur de Berlin coûtera des centaines de millions à Chamonix," *France-Soir*, 6 February 1962. See also "Es bleibt bei der Absage der Ski-Weltmeisterschaften," *Die Welt*, 7 February 1962.

126. "Ski-Meisterschaften gefährdet," *Die Welt*, 1 February 1962; "Visa-Erteilung könnte WM retten," *Neues Deutschland*, 2 February 1962; "Kto ne daet vizy lyzhnakam GDR," *Pravda*, 4 February 1962; "Les championnats du monde de ski auront-ils lieu?" *Le Monde*, 4–5 February 1962; *New York Times*, 5 February 1962; "'Suspense' jusqu'à mardi midi," *Le Monde*, 6 February 1962; "Dernier espoir: de Gaulle, Kennedy, MacMillan," *France-Soir*, 6 February 1962; "Ski-Weltmeisterschaften abgesagt," *Die Welt*, 6 February 1962; "Les Américains: 'Pas de commentaire . . . ,'" and "Les Anglais: 'Quel télégramme?'" *France-Soir*, 7 February 1962; "Obshchestvennost' osuzhdaet," *Sovetskii sport*, 7 February 1962; "Chempionat sorvan," *Krasnaia zvezda*, 7 February 1962; "Vstrecha gornolyzhnikov sorvana," *Izvestiia*, 8 February 1962.

127. Prior to the Chamonix controversy, the Eastern Bloc had already registered protests concerning the location of ice-hockey and table-tennis world championships in the West.

128. *New York Times*, 7 February 1962; "Pas de soviétiques à Chamonix," *Le Monde*, 8 February 1962; "Les pays de rideau de fer solidaires des Allemands de l'Est: l'URSS, la Roumanie, la Tchékoslovaquie n'iront pas à Chamonix," *France-Soir*, 8 February 1962; "UdSSR nicht nach Chamonix," *Neues Deutschland*, 8 February 1962.

129. "Ski nordique et ski alpin," *Le Monde*, 8 February 1962. Also "'Nordische' muβte vertragt werden," *Neues Deutschland*, 6 February 1962.

130. "La préparation des jeux de Chamonix se poursuit en Haute-Savoie," *Le Monde*, 9 February 1962.

131. "La décision d'annuler les championnats du monde sera-t-elle rapportée?" *Le Monde*, 10 February 1962; *New York Times*, 10 February 1962; "Nichts als Eiertänze," *Die Welt*, 12 February 1962; "Marianne Jahn donne â [sic] l'Autriche son premier succès à Chamonix," *Le Monde*, 13 February 1962.

132. A. Kiknadze, "Sport dolzhen sluzhit' delu mira," *Sovetskii sport*, 14 February 1962.

133. D. Romanovich, "Na start vyshli lyzhniki," *Pravda*, 19 February 1962.

134. "Nouvelle réunion à Chamonix," *Le Monde*, 11–12 February 1962; "A Chamonix les jeux mondiaux redeviennent championnats du monde de ski," 17 February 1962; "Championnats du monde quand même!" *France-Soir*, 17 February 1962.

135. K. Smirnov, "Reportazh s finskoi lyzhni," *Sovetskii sport*, 22 December 1961.

136. "Snezhnaia kavelariia idet v ataku."

137. "Poslednii ekzamen pered Zakopane," *Krasnaia zvezda*, 3 February 1962.

138. N. Alekseev, "V Tatrakh, na snezhnykh trassakh," *Krasnaia zvezda*, 17 February 1962.

139. Viktorov, "Tri? Net, chetyre!" 22–23.

140. E.g., B. Fedosov, "Vperedi—Zakopane," *Trud*, 1 February 1962; "Zakopane vstrechaet gostei," 13 February 1962; Ezhi Ivashkevich, "Pismo iz Zakopane," 15 February 1962; "Zakopane zhdet startov," 18 February 1962. See also "Zakopane: Finnland mit Veikko," *Neues Deutschland*, 9 February 1962; "Ab Sonnabend in Blickpunkt: Zakopane," 15 February 1962.

141. "Televidenie," *Pravda*, 22 February 1962; 24 February 1962; 25 February 1962.

142. "Pobeda sovetskikh lyzhnits," *Pravda*, 20 February 1962; "Zoloto, serbero, bronza . . . ," *Sovetskii sport*, 20 February 1962; I. Nemukhin, "Pobeda pomnozhennaia na tri," 20 February 1962; Alevtina Kolchina, "Chetvertyi kilometr," 21 February 1962; K. Zharov, "Zamechatel'nyi uspekh sovetskikh lyzhnits," *Krasnaia zvezda*, 22 February 1962; I. Nemukhin, "Vtoraia zolotaia medal' Alevtiny Kolchinoi: reportazh s trekh tochek," *Sovetskii sport*, 23 February 1962; "Sovetskie lyzhnitsy—chempionki mira," 24 February 1962; I. Nemukhin, "Triumf lyzhnits SSSR," 24 February 1962; L. Romanovich, "Zolotye medali sovetskikh lyzhnits," *Pravda*, 24 February 1962.

143. B. Fedosov, "Nashi lyzhnitsy—geroini Zakopane," *Trud*, 24 February 1962.

144. "Norway Bans Skiers from East Germany," *New York Times*, 13 March 1962; A. Gurkov, "Piatno na snegu," *Sovetskii sport*, 16 March 1962.

145. *New York Times*, 29 March 1962; V. Babkin and A. Sychev, "Vazhnoe reshenie MOK," *Sovetskii sport*, 29 March 1962. Brundage had expressed this opinion in the midst of the World Ski Championships controversy as well: "Our viewpoint is that every nation should have the right to take part at every Olympic gathering." See "IOC-Präsident gegen Diskriminierung," *Neues Deutschland*, 22 February 1962.

146. "Bez chempiona mira," *Sovetskii sport*, 13 January 1962.

147. "Tsena vyderzhki," *Sovetskii sport*, 14 January 1962.

148. "Chto skazali lyzhnia i mishen'?"

149. S. Sergeev, "Snezhnaia pristrelka," *Izvestiia*, 1 February 1962.

150. "Na chempionat mira v Finliandiiu," *Sovetskii sport*, 27 February 1962; "Kon'ki, lyzhi, tennis . . . ," *Pravda*, 27 February 1962.

151. "Zolotoi dubl' Vladimira Melanina," *Sovetskii sport*, 6 March 1962. See also "Start/Finish Area in the 1962 World Championships in Hämeenlinna, FIN," in Niinimaa, 6 [photo].

152. Melanin, "Pora zrelosti."

153. "Vladimir Melanin—chempion mira," *Pravda*, 5 March 1962; I. Nemukhin, "Povtorenie legendy," *Sovetskii sport*, 5 February 1964; Niinimaa, 73; Stegen, 108; "World Championship of Winter Biathlon—Hameenlinna/Hameenlinna (FIN)" [http://services. biathlonresults.com/ Results.aspx?RaceId=BT6162SWRLCH01SMIN] International Biathlon Union website.

154. Cited in "Zolotoi dubl' Vladimira Melanina."

155. Melanin, "Pora zrelosti."

156. "Mariia Komar', Ol'ga Petukhova, Ol'ga Mazokina"; V. Shirokov, "Zolotaia medal' Nikolaia Meshcheriakova," *Pravda*, 11 March 1962; "S pritselom na Insbruk," *Izvestiia*,

10 January 1963.

157. Melanin, "Pora zrelosti."

158. I. Nemukhin and S. Tokarev, "Slagaemye pobedy," *Sovetskii sport*, 11 March 1962. As of 1964, the norms for the All-Union Sports Classification Second Grade in biathlon stipulated that a racer complete the 20-kilometer course in 1:40.00 and hit thirteen out of twenty targets firing a large-bore military rifle, or fourteen out of twenty with a small-caliber firearm. See "Edinaia vsesoiuznaia sportivnaia klassifikatsiia na 1965–1968 gg," *Sovetskii sport*, 29 December 1964. As a point of comparison, by 1973 the same classification demanded that the biathlete complete a 20-kilometer course in 1:36.40 and hit fourteen out of twenty targets with a large-bore rifle, or sixteen out of twenty with a small-bore rifle. See Mokropulo and Sazhin, 62.

7: The Triumph of Soviet Biathlon

1. Viktor Viktorov, "Lyzhniu!" *Ogonek* no. 4 (1857), 20 January 1963: 28–29.

2. Roy Terrell, "The Heroes of Squaw Valley," *Sports Illustrated*, 29 February 1960: 22.

3. Nemukhin and Tokarev, "Slagaemye pobedy."

4. "V. Melanin—trekhkratnyi chempion mira," *Krasnaia zvezda*, 5 February 1963.

5. Melanin, "Pora zrelosti."

6. In 1956, this region became part of the Russian Socialist Federative Soviet Republic as the Karelian Autonomous Soviet Socialist Republic.

7. Jason Lavery, *The History of Finland*, 140–42; Fred Singleton, *A Short History of Finland*, 148–50; Suny, *Soviet Experiment*, 358–59.

8. A. Frenkin, "Siksten Ernberg," *Sovetskii sport*, 8 January 1958. See also V. Viktorov, "Chempion mira," *Ogonek* no. 13 (1398), 28 March 1954: 28–29; Viktorov, "Olimpiiskie medali," no. 7 (1496), 12 February 1956: 30–31; I. Nemukhin, "Oni budut v Lakhti," *Sovetskii sport*, 19 February 1958; N. Smirnov, "'SSSR i Finliandiia—favority v Lakhti,'" 27 February 1958; "Otsenki, prognozy, deistvitel'nost'," 7 March 1958; G. Sergeev, "Na lyzhakh po asfal'tu," 13 November 1958; I. Nemukhin, "Nad Uktusami flagi chetyrekh stran," 11 January 1959; Nemukhin, "Blestiashchaia pobeda Nikolaia Anikina," 13 January 1959; Nemukhin, "Falun—Kortina—Lakhti," 4 January 1960; "V prizovoi troike," 21 February 1960; "Lyzhnia," 1 January 1965; I. Nemukhin and L. Nikolov, "Lyzhnaia dekada," 17 February 1966.

9. V. Viktorov, "Ot '3' do '3,'" *Ogonek* no. 3 (1908), 12 January 1964: 18–19.

10. "Govoriat chempiony," *Sovetskii sport*, 6 January 1960; Viktorov, "Tri? Net, chetyre!" 22–23; "Poslantsy Suomi," *Sovetskii sport*, 23 January 1964.

11. V. Viktorov, "Kolchin—Khakulinen," *Ogonek* no. 6 (1651), 1 February 1959: 22–23; Iu. Kordiiak, "Vstrecha cherez 20 let," *Sovetskii sport*, 23 February 1974; V. Viktorov, "Nasha Olimpiada," *Ogonek* no. 13 (2542), 27 March 1976: 17; V. Viktorov, "Na breiushchem polete," no. 9 (2642), 25 February 1978: 31.

12. Viktorov, "Tri? Net, chetyre!" 23. A pure racer (*chistyi gonshchik*) refers to an athlete who races only cross-country events, in contrast to Nordic combined or biathlon. See I. Nemukhin, "Zeefel'dskie motivy," *Krasnaia zvezda*, 23 January 1964.

13. Donald S. Connery, "Lonely Quest in Lapland," *Sports Illustrated*, 27 January 1964: 47.

14. K. Smirnov, "Finskie biatlonisty pered Zeefel'dom," *Sovetskii sport*, 24 January

1963. Also *Sovetskii sport*, 11 January 1963 [photo and text]; N. Nemukhin, "Tsifry i psik-hologiia," 3 February 1963; V. Andreev, "Snova zolotoi dubl'," 5 February 1963; Nemukhin, "Zeefel'dskie motivy."

15. N. Shagin, "Temp i metkost'," *Sovetskii sport*, 10 January 1963.

16. B. Reznichenko, "Lyzhnia vedet na strel'bishche," *Krasnaia zvezda*, 9 January 1963; Shagin, "Temp i metkost.'"

17. Nemukhin, "Tsifry i psikhologiia."

18. Andreev, "Snova zolotoi dubl'"; Niinimaa, 73; "World Championship of Modern Winter Biathlon Seefeld/Seefeld (AUT)" [http://services.biathlonresults.com/Results.aspx?RaceId=BT6263SWRLCH01SMIN] International Biathlon Union website.

19. *Pravda*, 4 February 1963.

20. "Uspekh, povtorennyi trizhdy," *Izvestiia*, 5 February 1963.

21. "V. Melanin—trekhkratnyi champion mira."

22. Andreev, "Snova zolotoi dubl.'"

23. "Finishiruet estonskaia," *Sovetskii sport*, 21 February 1963 [article and photo]; 22 February 1963 [photo]; 23 February 1963 [photo]; V. Triputen' and V. Gorelov, "Na Kavgolovskikh kholmakh," 28 February 1963; 1 March 63 [photo]; "Snaiperskii klass," 2 March 1963; M. Azernyi, "Veter, veter . . . ," 5 March 1963; 9 March 1963 [photo]; 10 March 1963 [article and photo].

24. O. Kriukov, "U sportsmenov druzhestvennikh armii," *Sovetskii sport*, 20 February 1963. The full title of this series of races was "The First Competitions in Applied-Military Events between Skiers of the Friendly Armies of the Eight Socialist Nations." In attendance were Bulgaria, GDR, China, Mongolia, Poland, USSR, Czechoslovakia and Romania.

25. G. Rukabishnikov, "Na lyzhne—sil'neishchie armeiskie sportsmeny," *Krasnaia zvezda*, 26 February 1963; Z. Firsov and V. Gavrilin, "Gonki patrulei," 1 March 1963; Triputen' and Gorelov, "Na Kavgolovskikh kholmakh"; "Snaiperskii klass."

26. Azernyi, "Veter, veter . . . "; V. Gavrilin, "Tri pervykh mesta—u sovetskikh gonshchikov," *Krasnaia zvezda*, 12 March 1963; "Na lyzhne-voennyi patrul'," 14 March 1963.

27. "God olimpiiskii," *Krasnaia zvezda*, 29 January 1964; V. Novoskol'tsev, "Pobednaia postup'," *Sovetskii sport*, 9 February 1964.

28. "Sportivnaia zima," *Pravda*, 2 February 1961.

29. *Sovetskii sport*, 7 December 1963; 10 December 1963; 11 December 1963; 12 December 1963; 15 December 1963; 17 December 1963; 18 December 1963; 19 December 1963; 26 December 1963; 5 January 1964; 11 January 1964; 15 January 1964; "God olimpiiskii," *Krasnaia zvezda*; "Sportivnaia zima," *Pravda*.

30. "Do beloi olimpiady tri mesiatsa," *Sovetskii sport*, 30 October 1963; "Konkurs olimpiiskikh dogadok," 17 November 1963; "Konkurs olimpiiskikh dogadok," 21 November 1963; "Olimpiiskii teleskop," 22 November 1963; "Olimpiiskii teleskop," 26 November 1963; "Olimpiiskii teleskop," 28 November 1963; "Olimpiiskii teleskop," 29 November 1963; "Do beloi olimpiady ostalos' dva mesiatsa," 29 November 1963; "Olimpiiskii teleskop," 4 December 1963; "Olimpiiskii teleskop," 8 December 1963; "Olimpiiskii teleskop," 11 December 1963; "Olimpiiskii teleskop," 17 December 1963; "Olimpiiskii teleskop," 18 December 1963; "Do beloi olimpiady—rovno mesiats," 29 December 1963; "Olimpiiskii teleskop," 31 December 1963. The weekly magazine *Ogonek* also featured early articles about the Innsbruck Games. See V. Men'shikov, "Insbruk—riadom," *Ogonek* no. 51 (1904), 15 December 1963: 28–29; Petr Sobolev, "Insbruk—most druzhby," *Ogonek* no. 4 (1909),

19 January 1964: 29; V. Men'shikov, "Stolitsa tirolia vstretila gostei," no. 6 (1911), 2 February 1964: 14–15.

31. E.g., *Izvestiia* 5 February 1964; 8 February 1964; 9 February 1964; 11 February 1964.

32. *Pravda,* 10 February 1964.

33. *Sovetskii sport,* 5 February 1964.

34. "Olimpiiskaia komanda SSSR," *Sovetskii sport,* 22 January 1964; S. Tokarev, "Optimal'nyi temp," 8 February 1964; "Prosto Melanin."

35. Gus'kov, *V atake dollar,* 10. *Sports Illustrated* designated Schranz and his countrymen Anderl Molterer, Hias Leitner and Egon Zimmermann "this handsome foursome" in a full-color pictorial prior to the 1960 Winter Olympics. See "Watch for Them in Squaw Valley," *Sports Illustrated,* 15 February 1960: 18–19.

36. Compare Raymond Marcillac, "Sous le soleil, éclatante revanche des Autrichiens qui prennent les trois premières places du slalom géant," *Le Monde,* 17 February 1962; and "D'un sport de l'autre . . . ," *Le Monde,* 22 February 1962. A similar comparison is Robert Daley, "Zimmerman Wins Race in Chamonix," *New York Times,* 16 February 1962; and Arthur J. Olsen, "Ski Sweep Gained by Soviet Women," *New York Times,* 24 February 1962. It is interesting to note that the mirror image of this phenomenon appeared in the Soviet and East German press. After the Eastern Bloc pulled out of Chamonix, there was no further coverage of the Alpine events. Multi-paged daily reports from the Nordic World Championships commenced in *Sovetskii sport* and *Neues Deutschland* the following week.

37. Terrill, "The Heroes of Squaw Valley," 21–22.

38. "Amerikanskie prognozy," *Sovetskii sport,* 26 January 1964. *Sports Illustrated* featured Hakulinen during the Olympic years of 1956 and 1960. See "The 1956 Winter Olympics," 6 February 1956: 38 and 43; "Cross-Country and Combined," 15 February 1960: 24; "Scoreboard 8th Winter Olympic Games," 7 March 1960: 5; Roy Terrill, "The Games Were the Best," 7 March 1960: 16.

39. Nemukhin, "Zeefel'dskie motivy."

40. K. Smirnov, "Iunosheskie mechty veterana," *Sovetskii sport,* 17 December 1963; "Poslantsy Suomi"; Nemukhin, "Zeefel'dskie motivy."

41. "Olympic Form Chart," *Sports Illustrated,* 27 January 1964: 38–39.

42. V. Viktorov, "Al'py—S'erra Nevada—Al'py—," *Ogonek* no. 51 (1904), 15 December 1963: 29; K. Andrianov, "Sportivnyi prazdnik mira," *Pravda,* 29 January 1964; V. Pakhomov, "Tirol' zhivet olimpiadoi," *Krasnaia zvezda,* 8 February 1963.

43. "Bez promakha," *Sovetskii sport,* 17 December 1963; I. Nemukhin and G. Romanov, "Vopreki nepogode," 18 December 1963; I. Bulochkin, "Vernoi lyzhnei," 18 December 1963.

44. I. Nemukhin and G. Romanov, "Vernost' pocherku," *Sovetskii sport,* 8 January 1964.

45. Ibid., 3. The article notes the significant increase in biathletes from other clubs and organizations who made the finals at five All-Union Winter Spartakiadas the previous year.

46. "Predolimpiiskie starty," *Krasnaia zvezda,* 7 January 1964; "Vchera na sostiazaniakh," *Sovetskii sport,* 7 January 1964.

47. "Mirnye vystrely," *Sovetskii sport,* 21 January 1964.

48. "B'etsia puls olimpiady," *Izvestiia,* 5 February 1964.

49. V. Ermakov and V. Men'shikov, "Pod olimpiiskim fakelom," *Pravda*, 5 February 1964; "Zolotaia medal' ofitsera V. Melanina," *Krasnaia zvezda*, 5 February 1964.

50. I. Nemukhin, "Relefy Zeefel'da," *Sovetskii sport*, 15 January 1964.

51. I. Nemukhin, "Povtorenie legendy," *Sovetskii sport*, 5 February 1964.

52. Ibid. The Soviet National Team took this incident seriously. In subsequent races, skiers placed spare bullets inside the stock of the rifle rather than in the cartridge belt. See Vaitsekhovskaia, 62.

53. Friedl Wolfgang and Bertl Neumann, *Offizieler Bericht der IX. Olympischen Winterspiele Innsbruck 1964*, 124–26.

54. Tokarev, "Optimal'nyi temp."

55. To calculate splits between the two competitors, see Wolfgang and Neumann, 125–26.

56. "Biatlon: Zoloto i serebro—nashi [headline]," *Sovetskii sport*, 5 February 1964. Also Ermakov and Men'shakov, "Pod olimpiiskim fakelom"; "Zolotaia medal' ofitsera V. Melanina"; "B'etsia pul's olimpiady"; "Slovo chempionam: Vladimir Melanin," *Sovetskii sport*, 5 February 1964; Nemukhin, "Povtorenie legendy"; Tokarev, "Optimalnyi temp"; "Prosto Melanin."

57. *Ogonek* no. 8 (1913), 16 February 1964: 26–27. See also V. Viktorov, "Dramatizi borb'y," no. 7 (1912), 9 February 1964: 2–3.

58. V. Sadovnikov, "Pochta i biatlon," *Sovetskii sport*, 18 March 1967. A similar stamp honored the female cross-country skiers as well.

59. V. Gavrilin, "Doverie rodnoi partii," *Krasnaia zvezda*, 11 February 1964.

60. Ermakov and Men'shikov, "Pod olimpiiskim fakelom."

61. N. Gerasimov, "'Novoi Oslo?'" *Sovetskii sport*, 21 February 1964.

62. V. Gavrilin, "Khokkeisty SSSR—chempiony olimpiady, mira i evropy," *Krasnaia zvezda*, 10 February 1964.

63. In the 50-kilometer race, Soviet skiers Igor Voronchikin, Baiazhit Gizatullin, Aleksandr Gubin and Ivan Lubinov finished eleventh, twelfth, fourteenth and seventeenth respectively. See Wolfgang and Neumann, 108–9.

64. Iurii Mashin, "Vo slavu rodiny," *Pravda*, 10 February 1964.

65. V. Bai and N. Drachinskii, "Blestiashchii uspekh nashikh sportsmenov!" *Izvestiia*, 11 February 1964; M. Pavlovskii, "Na rodnoi zemle," *Sovetskii sport*, 13 February 1964.

66. "V chest' geroev Beloi Olimpiady," *Sovetskii sport*, 20 February 1964; "Armeitsy na Beloi Olimpiade," *Krasnaia zvezda*, 21 February 1964. Khrushchev was a recreational cross-country skier; he also loved guns and considered himself quite the marksman. See William Taubman, *Khrushchev: The Man and His Era*, 111–12, 134, 189, 627 and photograph facing 557.

67. Tam'iana Papova, "Velikie Otechestvennye. Vladimir Melan'in."

68. Z. Firsov, "E. Mekshilo—chempiona vooruzhennikh sil," *Krasnaia zvezda*, 16 February 1964; N. Shagin, "Trudno i na lyzhne v Kavgolove," *Sovetskii sport*, 18 February 1964; "20 pobednykh vystrelov Nikolaia Puzanova," *Krasnaia zvezda*, 18 February 1964; Z. Firsov, "Na sorevnovaniiakh lyzhnikov," 19 February 1964; Z. Firsov, "S vintovkoi na lyzhne," 22 February 1964; Z. Firsov, "Lyzhniki-Leningradtsy—sil'neishie," 29 February 1964.

69. N. Shagin, "O chem rasskazyvaiut misheni," *Sovetskii sport*, 4 March 1964.

70. Z. Firsov, "Lyzhniki-Leningradtsy—sil'neishie," *Krasnaia zvezda*, 29 February

1964. The All-Union Sport Classification norms for biathlon specified that for the attainment of Third Rank, a biathlete had to ski a 20-kilometer course in 1:51.00 with at least ten hits out of twenty firing a large-bore military rifle, or twelve out of twenty shooting a small-caliber firearm. See "Edinaia vsesoiuznaia sportivnaia klassifikatsiia na 1965–1968 gg," *Sovetskii sport*, 29 December 1964.

71. Shagin, "O chem rasskazyvaiut misheni." The Soviet speed-skating team had similar concerns. See "Rezervy: gde oni?" *Sovetskii sport*, 30 December 1964.

72. Aleksandr Burla, *Pervym budu ia . . .* , 58.

73. Niinimaa, 11–12; Stegen, *Biathlon*, 11.

74. E. Polikanin, "Ot etogo zavisit uspekh," *Sovetskii sport*, 29 January 1965.

75. "Kavgolovo gotovitsia," *Sovetskii sport*, 8 January 1965; "Vnimanie—lyzhi!" 13 January 1965; I. Nemukhin, L. Nikolov and G. Popov, "Obmanutaia stikhiia," 14 January 1965.

76. V. Gavrilin, "Vystrely nad kholmami Kavgolovo," *Krasnaia zvezda*, 13 January 1965; V. Gavrilin, "Pobeda, dobytaia v bor'be," 14 January 1965; V. Gavrilin, "Gonku vedut patruli," 15 January 1965; G. Popov, "Poedinok armeiskikh lyzhnikov," *Sovetskii sport*, 17 January 1965.

77. "Vystrely v tumane," *Krasnaia zvezda*, 23 January 1965.

78. K. Smirnov, "Zakony bol'shoi lyzhni," *Sovetskii sport*, 4 February 1965; "Na lyzhne—biatlonisty," 13 March 1964; "Po finskoi lyzhne," 29 January 1965; K. Smirnov, "Zakony bol'shoi lyzhni," 4 February 1965; "Sneg i ogon," 18 February 1965; "Khakulinen vperedi," 19 February 1965; "Medali, dobytye na lyzhne," 28 February 1965; "Lyzhnia v vesnu," 24 March 1965; K. Smirnov, "Finny prokladyvaiut lyzhniu," 3 November 1965; "Suomi gotovit lyzhi," 2 December 1965.

79. "World Championship of Winter Biathlon Elverum/Elverum (NOR)" [http://services.biathlonresults.com/Results.aspx?RaceId=BT6465SWRLCH01SMIN] International Biathlon Union website; Niinimaa, 74; Stegen, *Biathlon*, 108; "Jordet Wins Biathlon title as Norway Upsets Soviet [sic]," *New York Times* 22, February 1965; "Serebro iz El'veruma," *Sovetskii sport*, 23 February 1965.

80. "Ognevaia estafeta," *Sovetskii sport*, 3 December 1965. See film footage from this relay in Hermann Ohletz's "50 Jahre Faszination," minutes 3:21 to 5:25. The description in this article is from an interview with head coach Evgenii Polikanin, who is informing readers of the changes to biathlon competition at the start of the Second Spartakiada of the USSR scheduled for the 1965–1966 season. For a complete discussion of biathlon targets, see Niinimaa, 43–46; Ralph Kleinekathöfer and Ilmo Kurvinen, "A look back at the history and development of shooting target technology," in Lehotan et al., *50 Years of Biathlon: 1958 to 2008*, 93–100. The rules for the 4 x 7.5-kilometer biathlon relay were modified in subsequent years. The most significant changes were the replacement of target balloons, which had a tendency to burst at random, with glass discs (and then metal silhouettes in 1980) and the reduction of the penalty loop to 150 meters around 1973 or 1974 (not 1978 as Niinimaa suggests). The exact year the penalty loop changed is unclear, although by the time of the 1974 Biathlon World Championships, the distance was definitely 150 meters. See Niinimaa, 19; Fliegner, ed., 400; Burla, 106; The Organizing Committee for the XIth Olympic Winter Games, Sapporo 1972, *Official Report* [http://www.la84foundation.org/6oic/OfficialReports/1972/orw1972pt2.pdf], 263; Mokropulo and Sazhin, 5; "Nadezhdy ne opravdalis," *Sovetskii sport*, 1 March 1974.

81. "Favority—biatlonisty SSSR," *Sovetskii sport*, 21 February 1965; "Serebro iz El'veruma"; Niinimaa, 74; Stegen, *Biathlon*, 108.

82. I. Nemukhin, "V 'olimpiiskom' klimate," *Sovetskii sport*, 20 March 1965. Nemukhin conceded no quarter to the men's ski team. On the occasion of the seventieth anniversary of ski racing in Russia, he praised the women's ski team and biathlete Vladimir Melanin while complaining: "Our men cannot brag equally about brilliant successes." See I. Nemukhin, "Den' rozhdeniia," *Sovetskii sport*, 29 December 1965.

83. "Na lyzhnykh trassakh [. . .]," *Krasnaia zvezda*, 2 March 1965; V. Galaktionov and G. Popov, "Lyzhnye starty na poroge vesny," *Sovetskii sport*, 2 March 1965.

84. "Sport—pomoshchnik kosmonatov [headline]," *Sovetskii sport*, 19 March 1965.

85. Walter Wingo, "Russia's Ladder to the Moon," *Science News-Letter* 84, no. 20, 16 November 1963: 314.

86. Malia, 333; Suny, *Soviet Experiment*, 409.

87. *Sovetskii sport*, 19 March 1965; 20 March 1965; 21 March 1965; 25 March 1965 [photographs]. The newspaper linked skiing to space on the front page of its 1 January 1961 edition with a fanciful rendition of a rocket pulling two skiers into the stratosphere. See *Sovetskii sport*, 1 January 1961.

88. *Sovetskii sport*, 19 March 1965.

89. N. Anikin, "Molodost' strany," *Sovetskii sport*, 25 March 1965.

90. B. Bikbov, "Skorost' i tochnost'," *Sovetskii sport*, 24 March 1965.

91. I. Nemukhin and G. Popov, "Intuitsiia ne podvodit," *Sovetskii sport*, 24 March 1965.

92. Organizers had the option of setting up one or several shooting ranges in 1966 and 1967. However, the distance at each range was a standardized 150 meters. UIPM parameters stipulated that the range or ranges be situated between kilometer 4 and kilometer 18 of a 20-kilometer race and between kilometer 4 and kilometer 13 of a 15-kilometer race for juniors. See Niinimaa, 12–13. By 1968, a single range layout was the norm.

93. P. Zemtsov, "Norvegiia s lyzhami na pleche," *Sovetskii sport*, 15 December 1965.

94. I. Nemukhin and L. Nikolov, "Ukroshchenie skorosti," *Sovetskii sport*, 8 January 1966; Nemukhin and Nikolov, "Dorogaia oshibka," 11 January 1966.

95. E. Polikanin, "Bez riska," *Sovetskii sport*, 19 January 1966. Gundartsev's name is misspelled "Gundortsev" here. His age is also incorrectly given as twenty-two. Gundartsev was born 13 December 1944.

96. Viktor Mamatov had participated in the USSR National Biathlon Championships of 1960, coming in sixteenth. His studies at Novosibirsk Institute kept him from participating with the National Team for five years. See Viktor Mamatov, "Viktor Mamatov: Belated biathlon career," in Lehotan et al., *50 Years of Biathlon: 1958 to 2008*, 145. Mamatov has enjoyed a remarkably long association with Russian and international biathlon. He served as head coach of the Soviet National Team from 1973 through 1976 and again from 1981 to 1985. He was president of the Soviet Biathlon Federation from 1989 to 1991 as well as vice president of the State Committee of the USSR for Physical Culture and Sport from 1987 to 1991; Olympic team leader or deputy leader for Russia's delegations to the 1988, 1992, 1994, 1998 and 2002 Winter Games; vice president of the International Biathlon Union from 1993 to 1998; and since 2010, he has held a variety of positions within the Russian Biathlon Union. He has served as a teacher at the Moscow State Institute of Physical Culture and authored a number of books on biathlon training. After a mishap at a relay finish line

in 1969 that prematurely ended his promising competitive career, Vladimir Gundartsev applied himself to coaching for Dinamo and the National Team from 1974 through 1995.

97. "Taktika nervov," *Sovetskii sport*, 3 February 1966. Jernberg did not participate in either event.

98. "Lotereia v tumane," *Sovetskii sport*, 6 February 1966.

99. "Ne unimaiutsia," *Sovetskii sport*, 5 February 1966.

100. "Biathlon World Championship 1966—Garmisch Partenkirchen/Garmisch Partenkirchen (GER)," International Biathlon Union Data Center [http://services.biathlonresults.com/Results.aspx?RaceId=BT 6555SWRLCH01SMIN]. Hermann Ohletz includes footage from Garmisch-Partenkirchen in his film "50 Jahre Faszination," minutes 5:26 to 7:21 featuring Melanin at the shooting range firing from the prone position and Gundartsev at the finish line of the 20-kilometer race.

101. "Konets bol'shoi chetverki," *Sovetskii sport*, 8 February 1966. The powerful East German team had travelled to Garmisch-Partenkirchen to compete but withdrew in protest after harassment by the West German police. See "Chto zhe topiat v 'kholodnom kolodtse'?" *Sovetskii sport*, 8 February 1966. Both the Romanian and Polish biathlon teams had two top-ten finishes in the 20-kilometer individual race: Poland's Stanisław Szczepaniak and Stanisław Lukasczyk finished in seventh and tenth respectively; Romania's Gheorge Cimpoia in fifth and Nicolae Barbasescu in sixth. In the relay, Romania's team took sixth.

102. I. Nemukhin and L. Nikolov, "Kto delaet pogodu," *Sovetskii sport*, 18 February 1966; Nemukhin and Nikolov, "Mozhno li soglasitsia?" 19 February 1966; Nemukhin and Nikolov, "Podtverzhdenie avtoriteta," 20 February 1966; Nemukhin and Nikolov, "Chudes na svete ne byvaet," 22 February 1966; Nemukhin and Nikolov, "Doroga k p'edestalu," 24 February 1966; Nemukhin and Nikolov, "Rokovoi pod"em," 27 February 1966; Nemukhin and Nikolov, "Krepkaia nit'," 1 March 1966; "Za nashim kruglym stolom," 25 March 1966; V. Viktorov, "Khoziaiki Kholmenkollena," *Ogonek* no. 10 (2019), 6 March 1966: 26–27; V. Viktorov, "Neveselaia lyzhnia," no. 13 (2022), 27 March 1966: 26–27; V. Viktorov, "Lyzhnia poveselela," no. 5 (2066), 29 January 1967: 30–31.

103. I. Nemukhin and L. Nikolov, "Poslednie starty na snegu Oslo," *Sovetskii sport*, 1 March 1966.

104. [Headline] *Sovetskii sport*, 16 February 1966. The official tally reached nine million by the end of the Spartakiada in the middle of March. See *Sovetskii sport*, 15 March 1967.

105. O. Petrov, "V prazdnik o budniakh," *Sovetskii sport*, 16 February 1966.

106. O. Petrov, "Korrektiruiut ognevye rubezhi," *Sovetskii sport*, 18 February 1966.

107. A. Samoilov, "Komu pochet, komu—'krug pocheta,'" *Sovetskii sport*, 18 February 1966.

108. "Lyzhnia perednego kraia," *Sovetskii sport*, 10 March 1966; 12 March 1966 [photo and text]; "Ekzamen na masterstvo," *Pravda*, 10 March 1966; "Spartakiada nazivaet pobeditelei," *Izvestiia*, 11 March 1966.

109. "Vokrug bol'shogo marafona," *Izvestiia*, 13 March 1966; "U kogo krepche nervy," *Sovetskii sport*, 13 March 1966; "Chelovek s ruzh'em," 13 March 1966; 13 March 1966 [photo and text].

110. Burla, 58.

111. "Stal'nye muskuly rodiny," *Sovetskii sport*, 5 December 1965; B. Bikbov, "Pobedeli lyzhniki 'Dinamo,'" 19 February 1966.

112. "Luchshie biatlonisty," *Krasnaia zvezda*, 15 January 1967; "V tiuringii 'Zvez-

dopad,'" 26 January 1967; "Gubernator Kirovskoi oblasti N. I. Shaklein vruchil vdove pro-slavlennogo biatlonista Vladimira Melanina Pochetnuiu medal' Mezhdunarodnogo soiuza biatlonistov," 7 March 2008 [http://www.ako.Kirov.ru/news/Detail.php?ID=8430]; Burla, 67, 73, 152, 180, 198.

    113. Burla, 148–50; Vaitsekhovskaia, 62, 69.

    114. Iu. Riazanov, "Bol'shaia lyzhnia," *Sovetskii sport*, 15 February 1966; Iu. Riaza-nov, "Tsena samostoiatel'nosti," 17 February 1966; 6 March 1966 [photo]; "Ostanovka—po trebovaniiu," 6 March 1966; 15 March 1966 [photo]; Iurii Mashin, "Kryl'ia krepnut v po-lete," 15 March 1966; "Prazdnik sportivnoi zimy," *Izvestiia*, 15 March 1966; Burla, 58.

8: The Era of Aleksandr Tikhonov

    1. "Telekanal ARD poprosil ubrat' reklamnye bannery 'Alexander Tikhonov & MA,'" Sports.ru, 26 September 2009 [http://www.sports.ru/biathlon/34909091.html]; "Pro-gramm: IBU-Weltmeisterschaften Sommerbiathlon 21–27 September 2009 in der DKB-Ski-Arena Oberhof" [competitor's packet, 25 pages].

    2. *Ogonek* no. 11 (3008), 8–15 June 1985: 32 [photo]; Burla, 201, 221; Vaitsekhovs-kaia, 31–32, 82; Khromov, 18; Anastasiia Blagodatskikh, "Biatlon: pobedonosnaia tradit-siia zhiva," *Kalashnikov. Oruzhie, Boepripasy, Snariazhenie* (December 2008): 76–79; Sergei Butov, "Komu flag v ruki? V 2002-m Rostovstev obidelsia," *Sport-Ekspress*, 31 January 2006 [http://www.sport-express.ru/newspaper/2006-01-31/9_1/].

    3. "Delo organizatora pokusheniia na Tuleeva vernuli v prokuraturu," *Lenta.ru: Novosti* 29 January 2007 [http://lenta.ru/news/2007/01/29/tihonov/]; "Glava Soiuza bi-atlonistov otverg obvineniia v pokushenii na Tuleeva," *Lenta.ru: Novosti*, 11 April 2007 [http://lenta.ru/news/2007/04/11/tihonov/]; "Glava Soiuza biatlonistov trebuiut posa-dit' na 5 let za pokushenie na Tuleeva," *Lenta.ru: Novosti*, 31 May 2007 [http://lenta.ru/news/2007/05/31/five/]; "V poslednem slove Tikhonov ne priznal sebia vinovnym v pokushenii na Tuleeva," *Lenta.ru: Novosti*, 23 July 2007 [http://lenta.ru/news/2007/07/23/word/]; "Sud amnistiroval Aleksandra Tikhonova," *Lenta.ru: Novosti*, 23 July 2007 [http://lenta.ru/news/2007/07/23/tihonov/]; Katie Thomas, "In Biathlon, Concerns about Rus-sia's Program," *New York Times*, 23 February 2010 [http://www.nytimes.com/2010/02/23/sports/Olympics23biathlon.html?scp=1&sq=biathlon%20tikhonov&st=cse].

    4. Tikhonov was eleven years old when this race took place on 12 February 1958. See Vaitsekhovskaia, 73.

    5. K. Boitsov, "Nachalo bol'shogo puti," *Sovetskii sport*, 23 January 2002 [http://www.sovsport.ru/gazettaarticle-item/34354].

    6. S. Blizniuk and G. Romanov, "Ostanovka—po trebovaniiu," *Sovetskii sport*, 6 March 1966; I. Nemukhin, "Pora zadumat'sia!" 10 March 1966; Vaitsekhovskaia, 60, 79.

    7. I. Nemukhin, "Sibiriaki operezhaiut favoritov," and photograph with text, *Sovetskii sport*, 11 March 1966.

    8. S. Blizniuk et al., "'Taezhnaia lyzhnia,'" *Sovetskii sport*, 15 March 1966. A general recapitulation of the Spartakiada by the chairman of the Central Council of the Union of Sport Societies and Organizations of the Soviet Union mentions Tikhonov's outstanding record. See Iu. Mashinyi, "Kryl'ia krepnut v polete," *Sovetskii sport*, 15 March 1966. See also "Mnenie sportsmenov," 25 March 1966.

    9. "Informatsionnoe biuro soobshchaet," *Sovetskii sport*, 10 March 1966; Vaitsek-

hovskaia, 34, 41.

10. Burla, 53–56; Vaitsekhovskaia, 24; Boitsov, "Nachalo bol'shogo puti"; Kopylova, "Aleksandra Vasil'evicha Privalova—s iubileem!" As often occurs while tracing Tikhonov's career, there are many variations to this story. In 2002, Tikhonov told Boitsov that he was "walking with crutches" after injuring his leg. In 2008, he told Ivor Lehotan of IBU that he met Privalov in Otepää when he "was out having a slow walk (since I couldn't ski)." Lehotan also indicates that Tikhonov incongruously made a special trip to Otepää "where the biathletes train," although Privalov told Vaitsekhovskaia that both the special cross-country and biathlon teams were training together there. See Ivor Lehotan, "Alexander Tikhonov: Four Olympic Games—four Golds," in Lehotan et al., *50 Years of Biathlon: 1958 to 2008*, 156–57.

11. Boitsov, "Nachalo bol'shogo puti."

12. A. Privalov, "V gonke melochei ne byvaet," *Sovetskii sport*, 17 January 1967.

13. "Dykhanie severa," *Sovetskii sport*, 14 January 1967; Privalov, "V gonke melochei ne byvaet." Safin's given name is sometimes spelled "Rinat."

14. "Na korotkoi volne," *Sovetskii sport*, 31 January 1967.

15. "Na raznykh meridianakh," *Sovetskii sport*, 26 February 1967; S. Gribanov, "Ne begom edinym zhivet biatlon," *Krasnaia zvezda*, 29 January 1967.

16. "Gostepriimnyi Al'tenberg," *Sovetskii sport*, 17 February 1967; B. Sapronenkov, "Takim ia uvidel Grenobl'," 22 February 1967; S. Tosunian, "Lyzhnia mushketerov," *Izvestiia*, 17 February 1967.

17. B. Kaptelkin, "Novaia lyzhnia chempionata," *Sovetskii sport*, 2 February 1967. A lead of thirty seconds in a short 7.5-kilometer race is a substantial margin.

18. Boitsov, "Nachalo bol'shogo puti."

19. Tosunian, "Lyzhnia mushketerov."

20. "UdSSR-Sieg im Biathlon," *Die Welt*, 18 February 1967; "Viktor Mamatov—chempion mira," *Sovetskii sport*, 19 February 1967; "Tak shel k pobede Mamatov," 19 February 1967; "Goresti i radosti zimy," *Ogonek* no. 9 (2070), 26 February 1967: 31; "World Championship Biathlon 1967—Altenberg/Altenberg GER" [http://services. biathlonresults.com/Results.aspx?RaceId=BT6667SWRLCH01SMIN], International Biathlon Union website.

21. "Solntse i metel'," *Sovetskii sport*, 21 February 1967. Results for the relay in Stegen's book indicate Tikhonov was a full four minutes and twenty seconds faster than Sweden's lead-off skier Ohlin. See Stegen, *Biathlon*, 109.

22. E.g., E. Polikanin, "Bez riska," *Sovetskii sport*, 19 January 1966. The logo reappears with Privalov's article about the Spartakiada 20-kilometer individual race, an enormous event with a record-breaking 115 participants. See A. Privalov, "Debiut v trudnoi roli," *Sovetskii sport*, 7 March 1967. Articles in February 1967 concerning the World Biathlon Championships at Altenberg featured that event's "Weltmeisterschaft Biathlon DDR 1967" placard. See "Gostepriimnyi Al'tenberg"; "Lyzhnia i mishen'"; "Tak shel k pobede Mamatov"; "Solntse i metel'."

23. "Biuro spravok," *Sovetskii sport*, 7 March 1967; "Kommentarii k tablitse," 15 March 1967. Competing in biathlon were teams from Moscow and Leningrad; the oblasti of Umurt, Moscow, Gorkii, Perm, Kirov, Cheliabinsk, and Murmansk; and the SSRs of Kazakh, Ukraine, Latvia, Estonia, Belarus, Georgia and Lithuania. Sverdlovsk oblast' competed in all *Spartakiada* events with the exception of hockey and biathlon.

24. S. Tokarev, "Vazhnye melochi," *Sovetskii sport*, 25 March 1967; Tokarev, "Po chuzhim misheniam," 28 March 1967. The 15-kilometer race for juniors had only three shooting stages: two prone and one standing.

25. Tokarev, "Po chuzhim misheniam."

26. Mokropulo and Sazhin, 15; "Tables to Determine Penalty Times in the Biathlon," *Theory and Practice of Physical Culture and Sport* 4–59 (1972) in *Yessis Review of Soviet Physical Education and Sports* 7, no. 2 (June 1973): 56 [abstract].

27. V. Viktorov, "Znakom'tes', ms'e [sic] 'vdrug!'" *Ogonek* no. 8 (2121), 17 February 1968: 27; "Schastlivoi vam lyzhni!" no. 5 (2118), 27 January 1968: 30.

28. "Lyzhnia vedet v Grenobl'," *Krasnaia zvezda*, 12 January 1968. This article states that there were more than 350 competitors on hand to vie for twenty-five positions on the Soviet Olympic Ski Team in cross-country, Nordic combined and biathlon. See also Natal'ia Ufimetseva, "Startoval na lyzhakh iz bochonka," *Media Zavod*, 12 January 2010 [http://www.mediazavod.ru/articles/81425].

29. *Pravda*, 13 February 1968; Wolf-Dieter Roesner, "Biathlon Gold for an Unknown," in Fliegner, ed., 227–28; Boitsov, "Nachalo bol'shogo puti"; Burla, 75–80; Vaitsekhovskaia, 25.

30. *Pravda*, 14 February 1968.

31. Viktorov, "Znakom'tes', ms'e [sic] 'vdrug!'"

32. Burla, 120, 181; *Biathlon in the USSR* [press booklet].

33. Igor' Maslennikov, "I vse za odnogo," *Smena* no. 24 (1118), December 1973: 29; A. Maiskii, "Estafeta polna neozhidannostei," *Izvestiia*, 3 March 1974.

34. V. Gavrilin, "Poryv, vdokhnovenie, masterstvo," *Krasnaia zvezda*, 16 February 1968; 17 February 1968 [photo]; *Pravda*, 16 February 1968; Burla, 81–94; Fliegner, ed., 400; Stegen, *Biathlon*, 110; Aleksandr Kruglikov, "Stat'ia 14 [Nikolai Puzanov]," *Nevskoe vremia* no. 126 (2586), 17 July 2001 [http://www.pressa.spb.ru/newspapers/nevrem/2001/arts/nevrem-2586-art-14.html]; Boitsov, "Nachalo bol'shogo puti."

35. Burla, 82; Fliegner, ed., 400.

36. V. Viktorov, "Vperedi—Sapporo!" *Ogonek* no. 9 (2122), 24 February 1968: 6.

37. Lev Kassel', "Zametki pisatelia," *Pravda*, 20 February 1968. Vedenin went on to win one silver and two gold medals at the 1970 Nordic World Championships and one bronze and two gold medals at the 1972 Sapporo Olympics.

38. Burla, 213–14.

39. William Oscar Johnson, "Brrrracing [sic] for 1980," *Sports Illustrated*, 19 February 1979: 16.

40. Malia, 371.

41. Daryl Gibson, "No More Applause," *Sunday Camera Magazine*, 12 May 1985: 14.

42. Weiner, 18, 380, 385.

43. Burla, 81. In 1968, the UIPM changed the organization's name to *Union Internationale de Pentathlon Moderne et Biathlon*, or UIPMB.

44. Burla, 74, 146–47.

45. Vaitsekhovskaia, 59. Burla's version of this story is a little more fanciful: Tikhonov predicts with uncanny accuracy the race results the night before in Solberg's room: "I want to congratulate you on your bronze medal. . . . Tomorrow you'll be third and I—I will be first. Understood? Excellent! Sweet dreams!" See Burla, 94–95. This version also appears in Mikhail Marin and Anatolii Korshunov, "Aleksandr Tikhonov," *Fizkul'tura i sport* 4 (886), April 1972: 20. Solberg did in fact finish third in the race behind Tikhonov and

Rinnat Safin. See "Biatlon prosit lyzhniu," *Izvestiia*, 27 February 1969. In honor of the biathlon team's outstanding performance at the 1969 Zakopane World Championships, the government distributed a number of medals and titles to the athletes and coaches. See "Nagrady snezhnym snaiperam," *Komsomol'skaia pravda*, 13 March 1969.

46. Kopylova, "Aleksandra Vasil'evicha Pirvalova—s iubileem!"

47. Burla, 103.

48. Niinimaa, 74; Burla, 115.

49. Burla, 116–20; Niinimaa, 74; The Organizing Committee for the XIth Olympic Winter Games, Sapporo 1972, *Official Report*, 486.

50. Aleksei Orlov, "Terpi, Rinnat!" *Avrora* no. 2 (February 1973): 76; Maslennikov, "I vse za odnogo," 28; Marin and Korshunov, 21; Burla, 122–23; Vaitsekhovskaia, 159; Lehotan, "Alexander Tikhonov," 159; Kopylova, "Aleksandra Vasil'evicha Privalova—s iubileem!" Burla puts Tikhonov in tenth place at the exchange with Safin.

51. John Morton, interview, 30 November 2010. At the time of the 1972 Sapporo Olympics, Tikhonov was affiliated with Dinamo sports club, sponsored by KGB and Soviet security services. Mamatov represented Lokomotiv sports club, sponsored by the railway workers' union. Safin skied for the sports organization of the Red Army. For KGB sponsorship of Dinamo, see O. Petrichenko, "Ne sotvori sebe kumira," *Ogonek* no. 12 (March 1987): 14–15.

52. Vaitsekhovskaia, 59, 61.

53. Burla, 16; Vaitsekhovskaia, 67, 100. Film footage of this entire sequence is included in Ohletz's documentary, "50 Jahre Faszination," minutes 8:32 to 9:12. Tikhonov appears to have his rifle in hand as he crosses the finish line, rendering the win legitimate.

54. Igor' Maslennikov et al., "Poslednii boi, on trudnyi samyi," *Sovetskii sport*, 5 March 1974. Also, "A man should know how to shoot, otherwise he ceases to be a man," in "I v shutku, i vser'ez," *Sovetskaia Belorussiia*, 5 March 1974. Although these sound like Hemingway quotations, neither exists in that author's work. *Neues Deutschland* reported yet another variation: "Everyone must know how to shoot . . . [sic] even the little man—in every village." See Horst Schiefelbein, "100000 Minsker feierten Erfolg ihrer Mannschaft," *Neues Deutschland*, 4 March 1974.

55. "Po-Chempionski!" *Izvestiia*, 19 March 1969; "Poedinok," *Trud*, 19 March 1969; Stanislav Tokarev, "Khomo sportivus," *Avrora* no. 11 (November 1976): 58–59; Burla, 108–10; Vaietskhovskaia, 12. This remarkable tale has overtones of Hemingway's short story *The Capital of the World*, in which the main protagonist is skewered by twin knives affixed to the legs of a chair used by his friend to simulate the charge of a bull. See Ernest Hemingway, "The Capital of the World," in *The Complete Short Stories of Ernest Hemingway*, 35–36. The championship in Kirov took place on or just prior to 10 March 1969, a week and a half before the events on the train appeared in the press. See "Zapisnaia knizhka bolel'shchika: biatlon," *Izvestiia*, 11 March 1969.

56. Heikki Ikola, interview by author, 5 July 2011. Ikola was a double silver medalist at the Olympics in 1972 and 1976. He was nominated Finland's Sportsperson of the Year in 1975 and in 1981. See Salokannel, "Heikki Ikola," 155.

57. John Morton, e-mail correspondence, 7 October 2008.

58. Vaitsekhovskaia, 18.

59. John Morton, interview, 30 November 2010; Martin Hagen, interview by author, 23 November 2010; Art Stegen, e-mail correspondence, 25 July 2010.

60. Yuri Brokhin, *The Big Red Machine: The Rise and Fall of Soviet Olympic Champions*, 107–10; James Riordan, "Playing to New Rules: Soviet Sport and Perestroika," in *Soviet Studies* 42, no. 1 (January 1990): 138 and 144, footnote 44; Riordan, "The Rise and Fall of Soviet Olympic Champions," 11, 35–38.

61. John Morton, interview, 30 November 2010.

62. Burla, 5–6.

63. Vaitsekhovskaia, 178.

64. L. Nikolov, "Vmeste i kazhdyi v otdel'nosti," *Sovetskii sport*, 24 February 1974; A. Privalov, "Vpervye na rodnoi zemle," *Sovetskii sport*, 24 February 1974; 26 February 1974 [photo].

9: Minsk

1. Privalov, "Vpervye na rodnoi zemle"; S. Tokarev, "Zelenaia raketa, schastlivaia lyzhnia," *Sovetskii sport*, 27 February 1974; "I znak GTO na grudi," *Pravda*, 27 February 1974.

2. "Lyzhnia dlia bystrykh," *Pravda*, 19 February 1974.

3. M. Zubko, "Falun: starty v tumane," *Izvestiia*, 19 February 1974; Zubko, "'Soversh-enno iskliuchitel'no!'" 22 February 1974.

4. Michael Brady, "Falun Championships Rocks Scandinavia," *Skiing* 22, 7 (April 1974): 15; "Wood Skis Are Dead Says Marty Hall," *Nordic World Magazine* 3, no. 3 (May 1975): 19; Caldwell, *Caldwell on Cross-Country*, 122; Hall and Penfold, 104–8; O. Belousov and S. Luk'ianchikov, *Okhota na zoloto*, 16mm, 22 min. (Belarus'fil'm: Tvorcheskoe ob"edinenie LETAPIS, 1974); Lehotan et al., *50 Years of Biathlon: 1958 to 2008*, 260, 375 [photos].

5. Brady, 15; "Wood Skis Are Dead," 19; Caldwell, *Caldwell on Cross-Country*, 122; Stegen, *Biathlon*, 17–18; Hall and Penfold, 104–8; Leonid Kuzmin, "Investigation of the Most Essential Factors Influencing Ski Glide."

6. A. Kuleshov, "8 chempionskikh, 8 pirzovykh—pobeda!" *Ogonek* no. 8 (2329), 19 February 1972: 32. Although East Germany was runner-up to the USSR in total medals at Sapporo, the special cross-country skiers of the GDR—both men and women—did not manage even a single pedestal spot.

7. L. Lebedev, "Falun prigotovil trudnye trassy," *Pravda*, 16 February 1974; "Lyzhnia dlia bystrykh"; "'Zoloto' vnov' u G. Kulakovoi," 21 February 1974; M. Zubko, "Chempionat finishiroval," *Izvestiia*, 26 February 1974; V. Viktorov, "Esli by ne zhenshchiny," *Ogonek* no. 10 (2435), 2 March 1974: 2–3. East German skiers also won three gold and three silver medals in jumping and Nordic combined at Falun.

8. Doug Gilbert, *The Miracle Machine*, 141–42, photo and text between pages 150 and 152. For Grimmer's career prior to Falun see V. Viktorov, "Pobednaia lyzhnia," *Ogonek* no. 9 (2226), 28 February 1970: 3; L. Sviridov, "Snezhnyi schet," no. 4 (2325), 22 January 1972: 29.

9. Niinimaa, 100, 101. The numbers for the period 1978 through 1998 take into account the seven years that transpired after the collapse of the Soviet Union and the eight after German reunification.

10. Gilbert, *Miracle Machine*, 273; Burla, 125; John Morton, e-mail correspondence, 18 December 2010; Art Stegen, "Recollections of Minsk—1974 Biathlon World Championships."

11. Privalov, "Vpervye na rodnoi zemle." Also M. Pavliuchenkov, "Streliaiushchie

lyzhniki," *Sovetskaia Belorussiia*, 8 January 1974; D. Terekhov, "Kubok BSSR—u 'Burevest-nika,'" 15 February 1974; V. Nemanov, "Zolotoi dubl' sormovicha," 29 January 1974; V. Khachirashvili, "Interv'iu nakanune starta," 26 February 1974; V. Nemanov, "Vse reshila skorost," 1 March 1974.

12. The Technical Biathlon Committee of the UIPMB considered a number of fac-tors in the debate leading up to the switch from large-bore to small-caliber rifles during the 1976 through 1977 competitive season: large-bore biathlon required more expensive rifles, ammunition, targets and ranges than the small-caliber version; it was increasingly difficult to find suitable sites for a large-bore shooting range; many countries prohibited the possession of large-bore rifles; and hearing loss was more extensive as a result of firing these types of rifles. See I. Novikov, "Utro nachinaetsia s kongressa," *Sovetskii sport*, 28 Feb-ruary 1974; Josef Deflorian, "Heavy Calibre or Small Bore Biathlon?" *Union Internationale de Pentathlon Moderne et Biathlon Bulletin* no. 27 (January 1975): 21–22; Blagodatskikh, 76–79; Dieter Anschütz, "The small-bore revolution," in Lehotan et al., *50 Years of Biathlon: 1958 to 2008*, 101–3.

13. Horst Schiefelbein, "Weltmeisterschaft im Biathlon mit 18 Ländern," *Neues Deutschland*, 26 February 1974.

14. "Svetovno p'rvenstvo na biatlonistite," *Robotnichesko delo*, 23 February 1974; "Vintovki pristreliany, lyzhi smazany," *Pravda*, 26 February 1974; Khachirashvili, "Interv'iu nakanune starta"; "Biatlon—u sebia doma," *Sovetskii sport*, 2 March 1974; "V dukhe druzh-by i sportivnogo sopernichestva" and "I v shutku, i vser'ez," *Sovetskaia Belorussiia*, 5 March 1974; Olle Hederén, "Something about the Activity in Biathlon," *Union Internationale de Pentathlon Moderne et Biathlon Bulletin* no. 27 (January 1975): 17–19; Vaitsekhovskaia, 71; V. Khachirashivili, "Nakanune chempionata mira," *Sovetskaia Belorussiia*, 28 January 1982.

15. N. I. Ponomarev, *Sport and Society*, 204.

16. Edelman, 123.

17. Ponomarev, 204, 212.

18. Tokarev, "Khomo sportivus," 63.

19. *Sovetskii sport*, 26 February 1974 [headline].

20. "Budut li v Minske katki i lyzhnye bazy?" *Sovetskii sport*, 2 November 1946; V. Kuznetsov, "Zimniaia spartakiada Belorussii," 21 February 1948; V. Laut et al., "Tsve-tushchaia molodost' Belorussii," 28 December 1948; "Startuiut 800 lyzhnikov—Minsk," 12 February 1949; V. Khachirashvili, "Na samom vysokom urovne," *Sovetskaia Belorussiia*, 19 February 1974; L. Nikolov, "Vmeste i kazhdyi v otdel'nosti," *Sovetskii sport*, 24 February 1974; 26 February 1974; "Vintovki pristreliany, lyzhi smazany"; Stegen, "Recollections of Minsk"; Alexandr [sic] Beliaev, "Raubichi: Crossroads of sport and culture," in Lehotan et al., *50 Years of Biathlon: 1958 to 2008*, 376. Aleksandr Privalov, coach of the Soviet biathlon team, told ski journalist Viktor Viktorov that his athletes had been training on the new courses outside Minsk since the middle of January. See "Turnir streliaiushchikh gonsh-chikov," *Izvestiia*, 26 February 1974.

21. John Morton, interview by author, 30 November 2010.

22. I. Maslennikov et al., "Primite tsvety, gosti Minska!" *Sovetskii sport*, 26 February 1974; "Chempionat mira otkryt," *Sovetskaia Belorussiia*, 26 February 1974. Olga Korbut was certainly the most famous Soviet athlete, and perhaps the world's best-known and most popular female athlete, in 1974. To this day, her name is still inextricably associated with gymnastics.

23. "V dukhe druzhby i sportivnogo sopernichestva"; Belousov and Luk'ianchikov, *Okhota na zoloto*.

24. "I znak GTO na grudi"; M. Suponev, "Romashki rastsvetaiut v fevrale," *Sovetskii sport* 23 February 1974; V. Pshenitsyn, "Dolg platezhom krasen," 28 February 1974; "Sukces młodych dwuboistów ZSRR—Polak Zięda na 10 miejscu," *Trybuna ludu*, 27 February 1974; "Pervoe 'zoloto'—nashe," *Sovetskaia molodezh'*, 27 February 1974; A. Maiskii, "Medali u sil'neishikh," *Izvestiia*, 27 February 1974; "Svetovno p'rvenstvo po biatlon," *Narodna armiia*, 27 February 1974; Tokarev, "Khomo sportivus," 59; Tokarev, "Zelenaia raketa, schastlivaia lyzhnia."

25. A. Maiskii, "Mimo tseli," *Izvestiia*, 1 March 1974.

26. Privalov, "Vpervye na rodnoi zemle."

27. Nemanov, "Zolotoi dubl' sormovicha"; "Turnir streliaiushchikh gonshchikov"; Privalov, "Vpervye na rodnoi zemle"; Suponev, "Romashki rastsvetaiut v fevrale." Izhevsk, located near the foothills of the western Urals, was famous for the production of rifles.

28. Khachirashvili, "Na samom vysokom urovne"; "Vintovki pristreliany, lyzhi smazany"; V. Orlov and V. Nemanov, "Bol'shoi uspekh finskikh gonshchikov," *Sovetskaia Belorussiia*, 28 February 1974. The same warm weather and deteriorating track conditions plagued Falun earlier in the month. See Lebedev, "Falun prigotovil trudnye trassy."

29. "Plokhie dela v khoroshuiu pogodu," *Sovetskii sport*, 28 February 1974.

30. Maiskii, "Mimo tseli."

31. "Ne spitsia treneru . . . ," *Sovetskii sport*, 1 March 1974. As a coach for Dinamo, Glinskii had an enormous influence on Tikhonov's development. They worked together for twelve years until Glinskii's untimely death in an automobile accident in 1978. See Burla, 65, 132–33; Vaitsekhovskaia, 33, 61.

32. Art Stegen, e-mail correspondence, 29 July 2010; Heikki Ikola, interview by author, 5 July 2011.

33. Horst Shiefelbein, "Suutarinen vor allen Favoriten," *Neues Deutschland*, 28 February 1974; "Novini-Minsk," *Narodna armiia*, 28 February 1974. Although Romania's Girnitsa had a stellar performance in this race, the rest of his teammates finished far out of the running in twenty-third, forty-third and fifty-fifth places, out of fifty-seven competitors. See "Gh. Girniță locul doi la proba de 20 km in cadrul campionatelor mondiale de biatlon," *România liberă*, 28 February 1974; "Medal' dlia serzhanta," *Komsomol'skaia pravda*, 28 February 1974.

34. V. Melanin, "Vnimanie, skorost'," *Sovetskii sport*, 1 March 1974. The adjustments in technique necessary for using fiberglass skis may have been a factor at Minsk: "Tikhonov had [fiberglass skis], but I think that he hadn't quite perfected the changes in technique required to use them efficiently." Art Stegen, e-mail correspondence, 8 November 2012.

35. "[. . .] 'shtrafnym krugam,'" *Sovetskii sport*, 5 March 1974; "Do novykh vstrech!" *Sovetskaia Belorussiia*, 5 March 1974; Lavery, 140–42; Singleton, 148–50; Suny, *Soviet Experiment*, 358–59; Stegen, *Biathlon*, notes to photographs between pages 14 and 17.

36. Nemanov, "Vse reshila skorost'."

37. Russell Scott, interview by author, 18 November 2010; Martin Hagen, interview by author, 23 November 2010; Stegen, *Biathlon*, 79. Scott finished tenth in the 10-kilometer sprint, a remarkable result for the beleaguered contingent from the United States. His marksmanship won begrudging praise from *Komsomol'skaia pravda*'s correspondent: "Out of 42 participants only one left the second shooting stage clean, 'five for five [na piat']'—American Russell Scott. But sharpshooting didn't save him. Skis betrayed him. Scott skied too slowly."

See A. Shumskii, "Uroki lyzhnogo sprinta," *Komosmol'skaia pravda*, 1 March 1974.

38. "Nadezhdy ne opravdalis'," *Sovetskii sport*, 1 March 1974; A. Maiskii, "Sprint streliaiushchikh lyzhnikov," *Izvestiia*, 2 March 1974; "Chempion—biatlonist iz GDR," *Sovetskaia molodezh'*, 1 March 1974.

39. A. Striapchii and V. Khachirashvili, "Vse nagrady poluchaiut gosti," *Sovetskaia Belorussiia*, 2 March 1974.

40. Ibid. Besides praising each of the individual biathletes from Finland while describing each stage of the race, the authors were generous to an American skier as well, a rarity in Soviet ski-racing coverage, mentioning Martin Hagen by name for scrambling to second place after the first round of shooting during the opening leg of the relay. *Sovetskii sport* was not so gracious: "The Americans had already fallen behind [by the second leg] and, frankly speaking, were never taken seriously." See I. Maslennikov et al., "Vse kachalos', kak na vesakh," *Sovetskii sport*, 2 March 1974. East Germany's correspondent noted that the Americans were holding on to second place at the ten-kilometer mark. See Horst Schifelbein, "Staffel-Silber an die DDR-Biathlon-Junioren," *Neues Deutschland*, 2 March 1974. Poland's bronze medal made the headlines in *Trybuna ludu*, the official newspaper of the Polish United Workers' Party. See "Brązowy medal sztafety juniorów," *Trybuna ludu*, 2 March 1974.

41. Maslennikov et al., "Vse kachalos', kak na vesakh"; A. Maiskii, "Estafeta polna neozhidannostei," *Izvestiia*, 3 March 1974; V. Dutov and V. Kukushkin, "Intriguiushchii siuzhet estafeti," *Sovetskii molodezh'*, 3 March 1974.

42. ". . . Na nikh by meste," *Sovetskii sport*, 3 March 1974.

43. V. Gundartsev, "Beregite nervy smolodu," *Sovetskii sport*, 2 March 1974.

44. N. Puzanov, "Kto luchshe spravilsia s poteriami," *Sovetskii sport*, 3 March 1974.

45. "Chelovek, u kotorogo vse normal'no," *Sovetskii sport*, 2 March 1974.

46. "Na tret'em rubezhe," *Ogonek* no. 12 (2385), 17 March 1973: 29; Dmitrii Sokolov, "Nikolai Kruglov—starshii. Sil'nii sredi sil'nikh." Privalov and his coaching staff certainly had a good eye for rookie athletes: by the end of his career in 1977, Kruglov had accumulated two Olympic and three world championship gold medals as well as two bronze and three silver world championship awards.

47. V. Orlov, "Pul's chempionata," *Sovetskaia Belorussiia*, 3 March 1974.

48. Belousov and Luk'ianchikov, *Okhota na zoloto*; Niinimaa, 11; "Segodnia—posledniaia gonka," *Komosmol'skaia pravda*, 3 March 1974; *Neues Deutschland*, 3 March 1974 [photo]; Lehotan et al., *50 Years of Biathlon: 1958 to 2008*, 260 [photo]; Stegen, "Recollections of Minsk" [photo].

49. Americans John Morton and Ken Alligood finished in thirty-fourth and thirty-sixth positions respectively, furthering Biakov's humiliation. Only Biakov's name and place is mentioned in the text of *Sovetskii sport*'s coverage, which offered an in-depth analysis of the other three Soviet skiers in the race the day after.

50. I. Maslenikov et al., "Zolotoi dubl' Iu. Suutarinena," *Sovetskii sport*, 3 March 1974.

51. E. Tsar'kov, "Ulybki khudozhnika," *Sovetskaia Belorussiia*, 3 March 1974.

52. V. Khachirashvili, "Zolotoi dubl' Iukhani Suutarinena," *Sovetskaia Belorussiia*, 3 March 1974.

53. Burla, 82.

54. Belousov and Luk'ianchikov, *Okhota na zoloto*. The relationship of hunting, skiing and the military had antecedents in Peter the Great's establishment of the Okhotniki in the eighteenth century. A vignette from a *dokumental'naia povest'* (documentary novel) set dur-

ing the Great Patriotic War illustrates how this notion developed in response to the German invasion. As a group of young women receive training at a school for snipers, one of the sergeants observes: "In peace time, it's true, I would ski in pursuit of furry animals with my little rifle, but war has forced us to hunt fascists." See V. A. Chuvilkin, *Devushki v shineliakh*, 36.

55. I. Maslennikov et al., "Poslednii boi."

56. V. Khachirashvili and V. Orlov, ". . . i pod zanaves—'zoloto,'" *Sovetskaia Belorussiia*, 5 March 1974.

57. Ikola, interview, 5 July 2011. The throngs lining the ski track and crowding into the stadium are visible throughout *Okhota na zoloto*. See also film footage from Minsk in Ohletz and Roggi, "50 Jahre Faszination," minutes 7:53 to 8:31. A photograph of the start of the relay shows spectators overflowing the start-finish area in Lehotan et al., *50 Years of Biathlon: 1958 to 2008*, 376.

58. "Sovjet tok stafettgullet—takket være Tikhonov," *Aftenposten*, 4 March 1974; A. Shumskii, "Pobednyi den'," *Komosmol'skaia pravda*, 5 March 1974; V. Dutov and V. Kukushkin, "'Besproigryshnaia' estafeta," *Sovetskaia molodezh'*, 5 March 1974; Horst Schiefelbein, "100000 Minsker"; Khachirashvili and Orlov, ". . . i pod zanaves—'zoloto'"; Maslennikov et al., "Poslednii boi."

59. John Morton, interview by author, 30 November 2010; Morton, e-mail correspondence, 29 March 2011. The warm response received by Morton was duplicated eight years later when the World Championships returned to Minsk. Reports that the poor performance by the American team inspired partisan Minsk spectators to chant: "U-S-Ah! Ha-Ha-Ha!" as reported in Hubert Mizell, "Ballyhooed Josh Another U.S. Flop," *St. Petersburg Times*, 21 February 1988, were unfounded. "It's a bit of folklore. . . . I never heard that in Minsk," recalls John Ruger, who represented the United States there. John Ruger, e-mail correspondence, 29 May 2011.

60. "I v shutku, i vser'ez"; Maslennikov et al., "Poslednii boi."

61. "Sovjet tok stafettgullet—takket være Tikhonov [Soviets won relay gold—thanks to Tikhonov]," read the page 23 headline in the sports section of *Aftenposten* on 4 March 1974. *Neues Deutschland*'s correspondent, Horst Schiefelbein, concurred: "The hosts had to thank above all the (at present) ten-time world champion Aleksandr Tikhonov for their triumph." See Schiefelbein, "100000 Minsker."

62. Ikola, interview by author, 5 July 2011.

63. "Sovjet tok stafettgullet"; A. Kurashov, "'Zolotoi' kvartet," *Pravda*, 4 March 1974; A. Maiskii, "Zolotaia estafeta," *Izvestiia*, 5 March 1974; Maslennikov et al., "Poslednii boi, on trudnyi samyi"; Khachirashvili and Orlov, ". . . i pod zanaves—'zoloto'"; "I v shutku, i vser'ez"; "Kaleidoskop: biatlon," *Krasnaia zvezda*, 5 March 1974; A. Shcherbakov, "Nakonets-to pobeda!" *Ogonek* no. 11 (2436), 9 March 1974: 29; John Morton, interview by author, 30 November 2010; Stegen, "Recollections of Minsk"; Stegen, e-mail correspondence, 29 July 2010; Stegen, e-mail correspondence, 22 March 2011. Both Stegen and Morton recall that Ikola was furious after the race and, at the awards ceremony, supposedly told the Russians on the podium that the results would be different at the next World Championships in Antholtz-Anterselva, Italy, because they would not have help from a crowd of Soviet spectators there. This was in fact the case: the same Finnish personnel from 1974—Henrik Flöjt, Simo Halonen, Juhani Suutarinen and Ikola—defeated a Soviet team made up of Ushakov, Tikhonov and Kruglov (with Aleksandr Elisarov replacing Kolmakov) in the relay of 1975.

64. John Morton, e-mail correspondence, 29 March 2011.

65. Kurashov, "'Zolotoi' kvartet."

66. Maslennikov et al., "Poslednii boi."

67. Maiskii, "Zolotaia estafeta."

68. Belousov and Luk'ianchikov, *Okhota na zoloto.*

69. Maslennikov et al., "Poslednii boi."

70. Shumskii, "Pobednyi den.'"

71. Maslennikov et al., "Poslednii boi"; Maiskii, "Zolotaia estafeta."

72. Khachirashvili and Orlov, ". . . i pod zanaves—'zoloto.'"

73. Kurashov, "'Zolotoi' kvartet."

74. "Sztafeta biathlnowa ZSRR zdobyła mistrzostwo świata," *Trybuna ludu*, 4 March 1974.

75. Shcherbakov, "Nakonets-to pobeda!" 29.

76. "Chempionat-74," *Sovetskii sport*, 5 March 1974.

77. Belousov and Luk'ianchikov, *Okhota na zoloto.*

78. "Chempionat-74."

79. V. Nemanov, "Pod zanaves—vtorye," *Sovetskaia Belorussiia*, 2 March 1976; S. Leskov, "V roli dogoniaiushchikh . . . [sic]," *Komsomol'skaia pravda*, 14 February 1982; L. Zdanovich, "Chempionat vechaet estafeta," *Izvestiia*, 15 February 1982; Jürgen Fischer, "Frank Ullrich und Junior Ralf Göthel die Besten," *Neues Deutschland*, 15 February 1982; V. Khachirashvili, "I pod zanaves—'zoloto,'" *Sovetskaia Belorussiia*, 16 February 1982; Zdeněk Kašper, "Anniversary World Championships Raubichi 1982" and "Biathlon in the USSR and Byelorussia [sic]," *Union Internationale de Pentathlon Moderne et Biathlon Bulletin* no. 48 (June 1982): 16–18; Edelman, 160–66; A. Shcherbakov, "Vse vidno na belom snegu," *Ogonek* no. 8 (2849), 20 February 1982: 32–33; John Ruger, interview by author, 5 August 2010. As a point of comparison, an unprecedented fifty thousand fans showed up for the first game of the 1972 Team Canada–Team USSR hockey series at the Luzhniki Sports Palace in Moscow. See Brokhin, 169–70.

10: The Fifteenth Winter Olympic Games

1. "Do novykh vstrech!" *Sovetskaiia Belorussiia*, 5 March 1974.

2. Stegen, *Biathlon*, 115–18; Niinimaa, 75; Vladimir Melanin, "Pristupaite smelo!" *Ogonek* no. 1 (2530), 1 January 1976: 21; V. Gavrilin, "Pobezhdaiut sil'nye dukhom," *Krasnaia zvezda*, 7 February 1976; V. Gavrilin, "50 zolotykh nagrad!" 14 February 1976; Boris Khavin, "Okhota za medaliami," *Smena* no. 3 (1169), February 1976: 22; John Moore, "The World Biathlon Championships 1977," *Union Internationale de Pentathlon Moderne et Biathlon Bulletin* no. 35 (April 1977): 8.

3. R. Gallezot, "Development of Biathlon, 1976–1980," *Union Internationale de Pentathlon Moderne et Biathlon Bulletin* no. 45 (December 1980): 20–21; Edgar Fried, "The World Biathlon Championships 1978, Hochfilzen, Tirol, Austria: Twenty Years of Biathlon World Championships," *Union Internationale de Pentathlon Moderne et Biathlon Bulletin* no. 38 (April 1978): 14–15.

4. Niinimaa, 75–77.

5. "Olympic Notebook," CTV Television Network (CTV), 19 February 1988. In the 20-kilometer race at the 1987 Lake Placid World Biathlon Championships, Josh Thompson

of the United States won a silver medal and Jan Matous of Czechoslovakia a bronze behind gold medalist Frank-Peter Roetsch of East Germany. The biathletes of the GDR swept the 10-kilometer event and also won the relay. In 1986 at the Holmenkollen World Biathlon Championships in Norway, Alfred Eder and Franz Schuler of Austria won bronze and silver medals in the individual races. See Niinimaa, 77.

6. East Germany came close to wresting the relay title from the USSR in the decade prior to reunification, winning five world championship relays and placing second to the Soviet squad three times. The team from the GDR also placed second to the Soviet Union at the Olympic relay in 1980. See Niinimaa, 76–77.

7. The Soviet Union managed seventeen medals, including two gold and one silver in the three relays. "Calgary 1988"; "Soviet Skiers Score a Sweep," *New York Times*, 26 February 1988; *Nordic Update* 3, no. 5, 1989: 3.

8. Rafael Reuveny and Aseem Prakash, "The Afghanistan War and the Breakdown of the Soviet Union," 702–3; Milton Beardon, "Afghanistan, Graveyard of Empires," *Foreign Affairs* 80, no. 6 (November–December 2001): 19–23; O'Mahoney, 188.

9. Gregory, 268–72; Suny, *Soviet Experiment*, 444.

10. Malia, 435.

11. Riordan, "Playing to New Rules," 134.

12. Alexei Yurchak, *Everything Was Forever, until It Was No More: The Last Soviet Generation*, 295.

13. Aleksandr Galagan, "Sindrom nedelimosti," *Ogonek* no. 32 (3237), 5–12 August 1988: 18–19; Suny, *Soviet Experiment*, 460; O'Mahoney, 176–77, 180, 188; Yurchak, 31.

14. Riordan, "The Rise and Fall of Soviet Olympic Champions," 26.

15. Ian Johnson, "The New Gold War: Germany Revives Its Communist-Era Athlete Mills as the Global Race for Olympic Glory Heats Up." East Germany and the Soviet Union were in a virtual tie at both Lake Placid and Sarajevo in total medals; the "winner" of these tallies was determined by the number of gold medals won.

16. John Powers, "E. Germans Wonders of Winter Olympics," *Boston Globe*, 22 February 1988; Mark Johnson, "Bloc Party: Scientific Approach Bears Golden Fruit for Soviets, E. Germans," *Dallas Morning News*, 26 February 1988; Johnson, "New Gold War"; Gilbert, *Miracle Machine*, 9, 32.

17. "'Udovletvoritel'no,' ne bole," *Sovetskii sport*, 5 March 1974; Iurii Lushin, "Nasledniki," *Ogonek* no. 15 (2596), 9 April 1977: 28–29; Derick L. Hulme, Jr., *The Political Olympics: Moscow, Afghanistan, and the 1980 U.S. Boycott*, 8.

18. A. H. Beckett and D. A. Cowan, "Misuse of Drugs in Sport," 185.

19. Ivan Waddington and Andy Smith, *An Introduction to Drugs in Sport: Addicted to Winning?* 52; Gilbert, *Miracle Machine*, 194–98; Robert Voy, *Drugs, Sport, and Politics*, 3–11. A 2001 indictment of the East German sports program details the serious side effects, both physical and psychological, of steroid use by athletes in the GDR. See Steven Ungerleider, *Faust's Gold: Inside the East German Doping Machine*.

20. A report presented at the First Permanent World Conference on Anti-Doping in Sport described macabre attempts to avoid detection for doping by East European women, who were artificially inseminated then underwent abortions after two or three months to gain a perceived hormonal boost. It also offered evidence of athletes from both sides of the Iron Curtain who would catheterize themselves with someone else's drug-free urine after flushing their own tainted urine with diuretics. See Mary Ormsby, "Abortion Part of Train-

ing Regimen?" *Toronto Star*, 29 June 1988. For women, the use of anabolic steroids could stimulate the growth of facial hair, the development of lower voices and other "male" characteristics. This situation fostered accusations that Soviet and Eastern Bloc women were, in fact, men and should be subject to gender-verification testing, even though anabolic steroids would have had no effect on chromosomal formulas. See Wiederkehr, 561–66.

21. A. Lemeshenok, "Ne otvernis' ot nas, lakki!" *Sovetskaia Belorussiia*, 24 February 1990.

22. Voy, 66; James Stray-Gundersen, MD, e-mail correspondence, 15 May 2011. Dr. Stray-Gundersen served as director of Sports Science for the United States Cross-Country Team and was team physician and physiologist for the 1988 and 1992 United States Olympic Teams. He was also team physician for the 2002 Norwegian Olympic Team.

23. John Underwood, interview by Mike Adamle, ABC Sports, 20 February 1988.

24. Voy, 66–74; Stray-Gundersen, e-mail correspondence.

25. Stray-Gundersen, e-mail correspondence.

26. Robert Walker and Andrew Brown, "Test Drug Sparks New Fear of Doping," *Calgary Herald* 17 February 1988; Robert Walker, "IOC to Check Drug Threat," 18 February 1988; Walker, "Ex-Coach Offers More Blood-Doping Evidence," 19 February 1988.

27. Walker and Brown, "Test Drug"; Randy Starkman, "New Wonder Drug May Speed Athletes to the Killing Fields," *Toronto Star*, 27 April 1991; Gretchen Vogel, "A Race to the Starting Line," 634; Christie Aschwanden, "Blood Doping Test Cannot Be Cheated"; Waddington and Smith, 95–96; Arthur J. Sytkowski, *Erythropoietin: Blood, Brain and Beyond*, 187. EPO had been on the market since 1986. See Michael Reinsch, "Der kanadische Trainer Hall beschuldigt sowjetische Langläufer des 'Blutdopings,'" *Frankfurter Allgemeine Zeitung*, 18 February 1988.

28. V. Viktorov, "Nasha olimpiada," *Ogonek* no. 31 (2542), 27 March 1976: 17; Trina L. Larsen and Robert T. Green, "Export Opportunities in a Crumbling Economy: The Soviet Union in 1990," 74; Malia, 376–77.

29. Gus'kov, 123, 132, 167, 185.

30. See additional entry under "Austrian Killed in Accident," *Times*, 27 February 1988. The IOC had strict regulations concerning the amount of space that logos could occupy on clothing during Olympic competition. A photograph of the Soviet women's relay team at Calgary shows all four women wearing Adidas ski hats. Gavryliuk has covered the front of her hat with a piece of tape. See "Foto no. 556026." After the 1984 Sarajevo Olympics, Fischer Ski Company of Austria printed a twelve-page full-color brochure, *Olympia-Reportage: Sarajevo '84: 9x Gold 11x Silver 5x Bronze*. It features photographs with text of Fischer-sponsored medal winners, including Soviet cross-country specialists Nikolai Zimiatov, Aleksandr Zav'ialov, Raisa Smetanina, Vladimir Nikitin and Aleksandr Batiuk. The gold-medal Soviet biathlon relay team of Dmitrii Vasiliev, Iuri Kashkarov, Algis Shalna and Sergei Bulygin received its own page under the banner: "The Russian Medal Hunters Settled for Competition between Themselves." Cross-country skiers sponsored by Fischer accounted for a total of nine gold, eleven silver and five bronze medals in Sarajevo. A full-color photograph of multi-medalist Zimiatov (in a distinctive Swix logo hat) also appears on page 2 of a waxing guide published by Swix of Norway after the 1980 Lake Placid Olympics. See *Swix Advanced Waxing for Cross-Country Skiing*. Under a superimposed Soviet flag, the same photo of Zimiatov graces a poster for the 1982 World Ski Championships in Oslo produced by the Norwegian firms Swix, Odlo and Liljedahl. See "SWIX, Official Sup-

plier to World Ski Championships in Oslo 1982/ Fournisseur officiel des Championnats du Monde de ski 1982 à Oslo" [poster].

31. Riordan, *Sport in Soviet Society*, 234; Riordan, "Playing to New Rules," 139, 141–42; Oleg Petrichenko, "Ne sotvori sebe kumira," 14; Marty Hall, interview by author, 11 April 2011.

32. "The Soviets: A Special Report," 3.

33. Garri Kasparov and Valerii Vyzhutovich, "Korolevstvo krivykh zerkal," *Ogonek* no. 3 (3208), 14–21 January 1989: 11.

34. Michael I. Kalinski, "State Sponsored Research on Creatine Supplements and Blood Doping in Elite Soviet Sport," 450.

35. James Riordan, *Sport, Politics and Communism*, 123; Riordan, "The Rise and Fall of Soviet Olympic Champions," 39.

36. Janet Rae Brooks, "Proof Positive," *Salt Lake City Tribune*, 31 August 2003.

37. Kalinski, "State Sponsored Research," 448–49; M. I. Kalinski, C. C. Dunbar, and Z. Szygula, "Evidence of State-Sponsored Blood Doping Research Program in Former Soviet Union," S268.

38. Waddington and Smith, 90, 92.

39. Audrey Mangan, "What Skiing Can Take Away from Armstrong Saga." Wadsworth was reacting to the United States Anti-Doping Agency's report on cyclist Lance Armstrong released on 10 October 2012.

40. Stanislav Tokarev, "Ne proigrat' by cheloveka," *Ogonek* no. 9 (3110), 28 February 1987: 20.

41. Riordan, "Playing to New Rules," 137; Malia, 422.

42. David Leon Moore, "The Games Get Down to Business," *USA Today*, 16 February 1988.

43. Alevtina Kolchina, "Pobedit'!" *Ogonek* no. 1 (2530), 1 January 1976: 21; Oleg Spasskii, "Olimpiiskie skorosti," *Smena* no. 8 (1174), April 1976: 30; V. Viktorov, "Schast'e sportivnoi borb'y," *Ogonek* no. 10 (2747), 1 March 1980: 31.

44. Norman Chad, "Three Years, $409 Million Later, ABC Says Let Games Begin," *Washington Post*, 12 February 1988; Daniel Ruth, "ABC Lines Up Olympic-Size Coverage," *Chicago Sun-Times*, 14 February 1988; Gus'kov, 112–14, 116; John McMillan, "Bidding for Olympic Broadcast Rights: The Competition *before* [sic] the Competition," Table 1.

45. "XV Winter Games: TV Could Have Say in Schedule," *Houston Chronicle*, 23 February 1988; Jack Craig, "TV Paradox: Games Rate; Drama Doesn't," *Boston Globe*, 24 February 1988; Esther B. Fein, "Olympics Rewrite Moscow's Schedule," *New York Times*, 26 February 1988; "Capital Cities' ABC Television Network Stands to Lose over $75m (£42.3m) on Its Coverage of the Calgary Winter Olympics," *Financial Times*, 27 February 1988; Larry Siddons, "ABC Joins Criticism of U.S.; Arledge, McKay Say It's Time to Act," *Record*, 28 February 1988; Dudley Doust, "Winter Olympics: Greed Gives Way to an Exploding . . . Bomba," *Sunday Times*, 28 February 1988; Alain Giraudo, "Les leçons de Calgary," *Le Monde*, 1 March 1988.

46. V. Viktorov, "Pod flagami beloi Olimpiady," *Ogonek* no. 9 (2746), 23 February 1980: 30–31; "Schast'e sportivnoi borb'y."

47. "The Russian Medal Hunters Settled for Competition between Themselves," in *Olympia-Reportage* [no page number]; V. Beskromnyi and V. Dvortsov, "Do svedaniia, Vuchko!" *Ogonek* no. 9 (2954), 25 February 1984: 32, inside back cover; Beskromnyi and Dvortsov, "Olimpiada na pamiat'," *Ogonek* no. 11 (2956), 10 March 1984: 8–10.

48. Kenny Moore, "A Fire Burns Fiercely within Him," *Sports Illustrated*, 6 February 1984: 45.

49. The concept of a World Cup in Nordic skiing evolved from a season-long succession of Alpine ski races held for the first time in the winter of 1966–1967. World Cup race points were awarded according to finish position at each competition then tallied at the end of the season to determine the overall winner. UIPMB established a biathlon world cup series in 1977–1978. Through the end of 1989, biathletes of East Germany won the title nine times. FIS formulated a cross-country skiing version in 1982. Winning the overall World Cup title carried prestige equal to winning an Olympic gold medal in the opinion of many ski-racing aficionados. See Huntford, *Two Planks*, 378–79; Niinimaa, 33–35.

50. Hall, interview, 11 April 2011.

51. Bill Spencer, "1985—The Year of Skating," 3; Iurii Khromov, "Uroki Zefel'da," *Ogonek* no. 10 (3007), 2–9 March 1985: 25–26; Halldor Skard, "Skiskøyting er i skuddet," 4–10.

52. Niinimaa, 15; Kurt Hinze, "The development of skiing techniques in the sport of biathlon," in Lehotan et al., *50 Years of Biathlon: 1958 to 2008*, 84–92.

53. The women's 20-kilometer race was introduced into international competition at the 1978 Nordic World Championships in Lahti, Finland. The event was on the Olympic card for the first time at the 1984 Games of Sarajevo. See V. Viktorov, "Na breiushchem polete," *Ogonek* no. 9 (2642), 25 February 1978: 32.

54. Kevin Cox, "Cross Country Skiing," 24.

55. V. Smirnov, V. Sukhoi and V. Shelkov, "Zolotoi pochin," *Pravda*, 16 February 1988; Michael Reinsch, "Die 'Kraftbeutel' herrschen hinter den Bergen," *Frankfurter Allgemeine Zeitung*, 17 February 1988; John Husar, "Soviets' Nordic Monopoly Grows amid Controversy."

56. V. Gorlov and G. Shchvets, "Sverkai, Olimp, pobedoi!" *Komosmol'skaia pravda*, 17 February 1988.

57. Simoneau comment: Husar, "Soviets' Nordic Monopoly." Panic ensued: Hall, interview, 11 April 2011; Bruno Moravetz, "Von Pulver bis Papp—die Mischung macht's," *Frankfurter Allgemeine Zeitung*, 23 February 1988; Llibert Tarrago, "Du sang-froid sur la neige," *Le Monde*, 24 February 1988. See also Christopher Clarey, "Powder, Crust, Slush."

58. "Wieder ein sowjetischer Langlauf-Doppelsieg Prokururow siegt auf der schwierigen Strecke," *Frankfurter Allgemeine Zeitung*, 16 February 1988.

59. Bruce Patterson, "Canadian Cross-Country Effort Gets 'Lousy' Rating," *Calgary Herald*, 15 February 1988; Patterson, "Cross-Country Classic a Soviet Surprise," *Calgary Herald*, 16 February 1988; Reinsch, "Die 'Kraftbeutel;'" "Logika zavisti," *Sovetskii sport*, 18 February 1988; "Blood-Doping Comments Draw Reprimand for Canadian Coach," *Calgary Herald*, 20 February 1988; "Deset otlichiia," *Robotnichesko delo*, 24 February 1988. The Soviet Ski Team used the ski center at Bakuriani in a similar manner in preparation for the 1960 Squaw Valley Olympics.

60. "Einege Fragen an: Alexej Prokurorow," *Neues Deutschland*, 17 February 1988.

61. Erik Røste, "'Dear Countrymen: We Wish You to Be the Best,'" *Ski sport* no. 9 (1988), excerpted in "The Soviets: A Special Report," 2–3. Røste took the title of his article from a placard over the door of the Soviet training center he was visiting. The strenuous sessions he observed are indicative of the yearly training program for elite athletes in the Soviet Union during the mid- to late 1980s. It is likely that the Soviets could accommodate

such high loads of training because of anabolic steroid use. Stray-Gundersen, e-mail correspondence.

62. John Caldwell, "Secrets from a Soviet Training Camp."

63. "Am UdSSR-Dreifachsieg fehlten nur 20 Sekunden," *Neues Deutschland,* 17 February 1988; Patterson, "Canadian Cross-Country Effort"; Llibert Tarrago, "Débandade suédoise," *Le Monde,* 1 March 1988; "09.01.1988 Kavgolovo 30km C and 10.01.1988 and Kavgolovo Rel 4x10km F" [http://www.fis-ski.com/uk/604/1228.html?event_id=4951&cal_suchsector=CC] FIS website (1 May 2011); "09.01.1988 Leningrad 10km C and 10.01.1988 Leningrad Rel 4x5 km C" [http://www.fis-ski.com/uk/604/1228.html?event_id=4952&cal_suchsector=CC] FIS website.

64. Smirnov, Sukhoi and Shelkov, "Zolotoi pochin"; O. Vikhrev, "Gorit olimpiiskii ogon,'" *Krasnaia zvezda,* 16 February 1988.

65. V. Smirnov, V. Sukhoi and V. Shelkov, "Po lyzhne Kenmora," *Pravda,* 17 February 1988; O. Vikhrev, "Lyzhnia vedet k p'edestalu," *Krasnaia zvezda,* 17 February 1988; Nikolai Bodnaruk, "Chempion—Aleksei Prokurorov," *Izvestiia,* 17 February 1988; V. Vatutin, "U podnozhiia Skalistikh gor," *Trud,* 17 February 1988.

66. Bruce Patterson, "Waxing Chief Is Key to Cross-Country Victory," *Calgary Herald,* 14 February 1988; Nathaniel Brown, e-mail correspondence, 15 May 2011 and 4 July 2011. Nat Brown was wax technician for the United States Biathlon Team at the 1988 Olympics. He has also worked for the national cross-country ski teams of Germany, Sweden and Slovenia over the course of three Olympics and fourteen world championships. His definitive work, *The Complete Guide to Cross-Country Ski Preparation* has gone through two editions, three printings and a Russian translation.

67. "Atmospheric Conditions (at the Stadium)," *Cross Country Ladies—10 Km Classical Unofficial Results/Ski de Fond Femmes—10Km Classique Résultats non officiels,* 14 February 1988: 1; "Atmospheric Conditions (at the Stadium)," *Cross Country Men—30 Km Classical Unofficial Results/Ski de Fond Hommes—30Km Classique Résultats non officiels,* 15 February 1988: 1; "S predelni usiliia k'm titlite," *Robotnichesko delo,* 16 February 1988; "Smarowanie to też sztuka," *Trybuna ludu,* 16 February 1988; Lech Pochwała, "Opinia eksperta: Źle smarowali?" 17 February 1988; "Wieder ein sowjetischer," *Frankfurter Allgemeine Zeitung,* 16 February 1988; Michael Reinsch, "Die 'Kraftbeutel' herrschen hinter den Bergen," 17 February 1988; Llibert Tarrago, "Le bon fart des Soviétiques," *Le Monde,* 16 February 1988; Tarrago, "Du chianti dans la vodka," 17 February 1988; "Dnevnik Olimpiady," *Pravda,* 17 February 1988; Oleg Vikhrev, "Olimpiada nabiraet temp," *Krasnaia zvezda,* 18 February 1988; Liubov' Baranova, "Raduet lyzhnia Kenmora," *Izvestiia,* 22 February 1988; Moravetz, "Von Pulver bis Papp"; Tarrago, "Débandade suédoise."

68. Bruce Patterson, "Cross-Country Classic a Soviet Surprise," *Calgary Herald,* 16 February 1988. I was a spectator out on the course at Canmore during this race as well.

69. "Drug moi—tret'e moe plecho," *Sovetskii sport,* 17 February 1988; "Dnevnik Olimiady," *Pravda,* 17 February 1988.

70. Gorlov and Shchvets, "Sverkai, Olimp, pobedoi!"

71. Vikhrev, "Olimpiada nabiraet temp"; Seth Masia, "Grip and Glide: A Short History of Ski Wax."

72. Brown, e-mail correspondence, 15 May 2011.

73. Brown, e-mail correspondence, 4 and 5 July 2011. After the Olympics, Brown and Jim Galanes, wax technician for the United States Cross-Country Team at Calgary,

acquired one of these wax-testing gadgets. Both were impressed with the innovative think-ing involved in its development but found problems with inconsistent results, especially different melt characteristics based on the small surface area of the testing chips. In ad-dition, there was a questionable relationship between the device and the surface pressure and weight distribution of an actual pair of skis. Nat Brown and Jim Galanes, e-mail cor-respondence, 31 October 2011.

74. "Drug moi."

75. Ibid.; "Einige Fragen an: Alexej Prokurorow."

76. "Lyzhnyi dubl," *Moskovskaia pravda*, 17 February 1988. Footage of the men's 30-kilometer broadcast on 15 February features a striking contrast between the flawless technique of Smirnov and the hit-and-miss steps of Svan as they both ski the same uphill section. See Independent Television (ITV) Olympic Coverage, 15 February 1988. Mogren was among the earliest skiers out on the course in position 18, followed by Prokurorov wearing bib 28. Smirnov was in the back of the field leaving from position 78, followed by Svan in bib 82. See *Cross Country Men—30 Km Classical Unofficial Results*: 1.

77. "Drug moi."

78. "Wieder ein sowjetischer."

79. Hall, interview, 11 April 2011.

80. Esten O. Sæther, "Hold Kjeft—for nå snakker bare dårlige tapere," *Dagblad-Sporten*, 17 February 1988.

81. Marty Hall quoted in Dave Dorr, "'Incident' Centers on Blood Doping," *St. Louis Post-Dispatch*, 19 February 1988.

82. Bruce Patterson, "Controversy Dogs Canadian Coach," *Calgary Herald*, 17 Feb-ruary 1988; Dorr, "'Incident'"; "The Winter Olympics Cross-Country Skiing: Marty the Mouth Has Mellow Side," *Globe and Mail*, 25 February 1988; Randy Starkman, "Random Tests Urged for Distance Skiers," *Toronto Star*, 8 February 1991.

83. "The Definitive Marty Hall" [http://www.xcskiworld.com/news/Features/Hall.htm] XCskiworld website; "Marty the Mouth."

84. Mary Hynes, "Call for Blood Tests Seen in Vain," *Globe and Mail*, 20 February 1987.

85. Hall, interview, 11 April 2011; "The Definitive Marty Hall."

86. Randy Harvey, "U.S. Nordic Skier Suspended for Blood Doping: Kerry Lynch, Considered a Contender for Medal, Will Miss Winter Olympics," *Los Angeles Times*, 20 January 1988 [http://articles.latimes.com/1988-01-20/sports/sp-24958_1_kerry-lynch], *Los Angeles Times* article collections; Husar, "Soviets' Nordic Monopoly"; Voy, 72–73.

87. Tarrago, "Bon sang."

88. "Canadian Draws Officials' Anger," *Calgary Herald*, 17 February 1988. In a spe-cial feature on the blood-doping controversy, the Canadian Broadcasting Corporation an-nounced to viewers that Prokurorov had finished in sixty-seventh place in the World Cup in 1987. Witt Frazier, *CBC News*, 16 February 1988.

89. Prokurorov's best finish in 1987 was first place in the 30-kilometer race at the prestigious Lahti, Finland, World Cup races on 1 March. See "Sila kharaktera," *Trud*, 17 February 1988; "Polzhizni na lyzhakh," *Izvestiia*, 17 February 1988; "Predstavliaem chempiona," *Pravda*, 17 February 1988; "Dr'zki debiutanti," *Robotnichesko delo*, 17 Feb-ruary 1988; "Results: Lahti (FIN) 01.03.1987" [http://www.fis-ski.com/uk/604/610.html?sector=CC&raceid=1960] FIS website.

90. "Soviets, Backed by U.S., Angrily Deny Blood Dope Claims," *St. Petersburg Times*, 17 February 1988; "The Winter Olympics: Officials Condemn Doping Critique," *Globe and Mail*, 17 February 1988; "Cup Standings [1986 and 1987]" [http://www.fis-ski.com/uk/disciplines/cross-country/cupstandings.html?suchen=true&suchcompetitorid=&suchseason=1985&sector=CC&suchgender=M&suchcup=WC&suchnation=&discipline=ALL&search=Search] FIS website. At Davos, Prokurorov finished ninth and Smirnov thirteenth. See "Results, Davos (SUI) 19.12.1987" [http://www.fis-ski.com/uk/604/610.html?sector=CC&raceid=1976] FIS website. At Castelrotto, Smirnov placed eighth and Prokurorov eleventh. See "Results, Castelrotto/Kastelruth (ITA) 15.12.1987" [http://www.fis-ski.com/uk/604/610.html?sector=CC&raceid=1972] FIS website. Smirnov out-skied Gunde Svan to win a 15-kilometer race in Kavgolovo in 1986. See "S pobedoi!" *Ogonek* no. 10 (3059), 1–8 March 1986: 28.

91. Patterson, "'Lousy' Rating."

92. "Blood-Doping Charge Draws a Harsh Reply," *Houston Chronicle*, 17 February 1988.

93. Allan Maki, "Unexpected Soviet Victories Raise Blood-Doping Query," *Calgary Herald*, 16 February 1988.

94. Maki, "Unexpected"; "Winter Olympics: Officials Condemn"; "Soviets, Backed by U.S."; Sandra Bailey, "Soviet Cross Country Performance Questioned," *Washington Post*, 17 February 1988; "Canadian's Doping Allegation," *Times*, 17 February 1988; Nikolai Bodnaruk, "Trudnye shagi k medaliam," *Izvestiia*, 19 February 1988.

95. Hall, interview, 11 April 2011.

96. "Blood-Doping Charge Draws a Harsh Reply."

97. "Canadian Draws Officials' Anger."

98. "Winter Olympics: Officials Condemn"; Sandra Bailey and Leonard Shapiro, "Soviet Cross Country Performance Questioned," *Washington Post*, 17 February 1988; "Soviets, Backed by U.S."

99. Robert Walker and Bruce Patterson, "Jelinek Apologizes for Ski Coach," *Calgary Herald*, 18 February 1988; V. Vatutin, "Komu ne strashen veter," *Trud*, 19 February 1988; "Kto khodit v geroiakh," *Moskovskaia pravda*, 19 February 1988; "FIS distanziert sich von Doping-Vorwürfen," *Neues Deutschland*, 20/21 February 1988; "S blias'ka na pobedite!" *Narodna armiia*, 20 February 1988.

100. Hall, interview, 11 April 2011.

101. Walker and Patterson, "Jelinek Apologizes"; Dorr, "'Incident.'"

102. Kevin Cox, "Coach Not Sorry for Blood-Doping Comment," *Globe and Mail*, 18 February 1988.

103. "A New Uproar," *Boston Globe*, 18 February 1988.

104. Daily Olympic Coverage, CTV, 17 February 1988. However, in this 30-kilometer freestyle race, the next Soviet finisher, Vladimir Sakhnov, finished just behind Harvey in eighth place. See Lahti (FIN) 01.03.1987 [http://www.fis-ski.com/uk/604/610.html?sector=CC&raceid=1960] FIS website.

105. Witt Frazier Report, CBC News, 17 February 1988.

106. Husar, "Soviets' Nordic Monopoly"; Walker and Patterson, "Jelinek Apologizes."

107. Peter Bowers, "Soviets Exhibit a Rush of Blood over Charges of Doping," *Sydney Morning Herald*, 18 February 1988.

108. Michael Reinsch, "Der kanadische Trainer Hall beschuldigt sowjetische Lan-

gläufer des 'Blutdopings,'" *Frankfurter Allgemeine Zeitung*, 18 February 1988.

109. Sæther, "Hold Kjeft."

110. "Coverage of the Winter Olympics," ABC Sports, 20 February 1988.

111. V. Smirnov, V. Sukhoi and V. Shelkov, "'Bravo!' nashim masteram," *Pravda*, 18 February 1988.

112. V. Vatutin, "Rastet schet medaliam," *Trud*, 18 February 1988.

113. Nikolai Bodnaruk, "Kalgari: zdes' sostiazaiutsia, a ne igraiut v igri," *Izvestiia*, 18 February 1988.

114. "Logika zavisti."

115. Vikhrev, "Olimpiada nabiraet temp."

116. Dimit'r Gornenski, "Oshche edna nadprevara," *Robotnichesko delo*, 19 February 1988; "'To glupota,'" *Trybuna ludu*, 18 February 1988.

117. "Dopingu nie ma i nie będzie," *Trybuna ludu*, 18 February 1988.

118. "Szinek az olimpiáról," *Magyar nemzet*, 18 February 1988. On Donike see also Reinsch, "Der kanadische Trainer."

119. Oleg Vikhrev, "Po goriachei lyzhne," *Krasnaia zvezda*, 19 February 1988.

120. "Sam sebia i vysek," *Sovetskii sport*, 19 February 1988.

121. "Blood-Doping Comments Draw Reprimand for Canadian Coach," *Calgary Herald*, 20 February 1988; "Hall Reprimanded by Jelinek, Soviets," *Globe and Mail*, 20 February 1988; Randy Harvey, "Notes: Olympic Flame Leaves Some with a Warm Feeling Inside," *Los Angeles Times*, 21 February 1988 [http://articles.latimes.com/1988-02-21/sports/sp-44177_1_olympic-flame], *Los Angeles Times* article collection.

122. Mikhail Dmitriev, Valerii Kudriavtsev and Igor Obraztsov, "Lovite mig udachi," *Sovetskii sport*, 19 February 1988; "Smelyi poryv Mikhaila Deviat'iarova," 21 February 1988; V. Smirnov, V. Sukhoi and V. Shelkov, "Vstrechi na ulitsakh," *Pravda*, 21 February 1988; Husar, "Soviets' Nordic Monopoly." In 1987, Deviat'iarov finished seventeenth in the FIS World Cup standings. At the Nordic World Championships in Obertsdorf, West Germany, he took third place in the 15-kilometer race and was a member of the silver medal men's 4 x 10-kilometer relay team. See "Predstavliaem chempiona," *Pravda*, 21 February 1988; "Ural'skaia zakalka," *Trud*, 21 February 1988.

123. V. Vatutin, "Poka my vperedi," *Trud*, 21 February 1988; Nikolai Bodnaruk, "Ural'skii kharakter chempiona," *Izvestiia*, 21 February 1988; *Cross Country Men—15 Km Classical Unofficial Results/Ski de Fond Hommes—15Km Classique Résultats non officiels*, 19 February 1988: 1.

124. It is worth noting that a 26 February article in the *New York Times* reported that Moscow's evening news, scheduled for 9:00 p.m., was delayed by two minutes to allow viewers to see the end of the women's relay, an event unprecedented in the USSR, according to the newspaper. However, there is no mention of this two-minute delay in *Ogonek*, *Pravda*, *Komsomol'skaia pravda*, *Moskovskaia pravda*, *Izvestiia*, *Trud*, *Sovetskaia molodezh'*, *Krasnaia zvezda* or *Sovetskii sport*. See "Televidenie s 15 fevralia do 21 fevralia," *Moskovskaia pravda*, 12 February 1988; Liubov' Baranova, "Velikolepnaia dvoika," *Izvestiia*, 16 February 1988; "Televidenie," *Moskovskaia pravda*, 21 February 1988; Fein, "Olympics Rewrite Moscow's Schedule."

125. Oleg Vikhrev, "Zolotye nashi devchata," *Krasnaia zvezda*, 23 February 1988; Vikhrev, "Ves' p'edestal—sovetskii!" 27 February 1988; Mikhail Dmitriev, Valerii Kudriavtsev and Igor Obraztsov, "Svet zavetnoi mechty," *Sovetskii sport*, 23 February 1988;

Obraztsov, "Snezhnye koralevy," 27 February 1988; V. Smirnov, V. Sukhoi and V. Shelkov, "Chetyre serdtsa, kak odno," *Pravda*, 23 February 1988; "Predstavliaem chempionok," 23 February 1988; V. Smirnov and V. Shelkov, "Na p'edestale tol'ko nashi," 27 February 1988; "Predstavliaem chempionku," 27 February 1988; Liubov' Baranova, "Radosti i goresti lyzhni Kenmora," *Izvestiia*, 24 February 1988.

126. "V zerkale pressy: komentarii izlishni," *Sovetskii sport*, 27 February 1988. The Soviet skiers fell apart in the 50-kilometer race on Saturday, 27 February. The top finisher was twelfth. Gold medalists Deviat'iarov and Prokurorov placed twenty-fifth and thirty-eighth respectively. *Cross Country Men—50 Km Free Technique Unofficial Results/Ski de Fond Hommes—50Km style libre Résultats non officiels*, 27 February 1988: 1–3. For more details on Smetanina's career, see A. Korshunov, "V ee glazakh sineve severa," *Sovetskii sport*, 18 February 1988.

127. Mikhail Dmitriev, Valerii Kudriavtsev and Igor' Obraztsov, "Obozhdal by nedel'ku, chinuk!" *Sovetskii sport*, 23 February 1988. A "tight group" refers to bullet holes touching one another inside the bull's-eye of a target, the result of skillful hand-eye coordination. Frank-Peter Roetsch was a triple gold medalist at the 1987 Biathlon World Championships in Lake Placid, New York, and heavily favored to win at the Calgary Olympics. See Bruce Patterson, "Fast Ski Track Awaits Biathlon," *Calgary Herald*, 19 February 1988; Michael Reinsch, "Das Glück des Tüchtigen begleitet Roetsch und verläßt Angerer Drei Fehlschüsse und en Sturz entthronen den Biathlon-König von 1984," *Frankfurter Allgemeine Zeitung*, 22 February 1988.

128. Mikhail Dmitriev, Valerii Kudriavtsev and Igor' Obraztsov, "Zagavor molchaniia?" *Sovetskii sport*, 25 February 1988.

129. V. Gorlov and G. Shchvets, "Reshaet Kalgari zagadki," *Komsomol'skaia pravda*, 25 February 1988.

130. Dmitriev, Kudriavtsev and Obraztsov, "Zagavor molchaniia?" Tarrago, "Du sang-froid sur la neige"; "Erneut stürmte Franz-Peter mit großem Einsatz zu Gold," *Neues Deutschland*, 24 February 1988; Michael Reinsch, "Mit oder ohne Angerer stehen Neuaufbau und Leistungstief bevor," *Frankfurter Allgemeine Zeitung*, 25 February 1988; "Dnevnik Olimpiady," *Pravda*, 26 February 1988.

131. Bruce Patterson, "Soviets Win Sixth Biathlon in a Row," *Calgary Herald*, 27 February 1988; "Soviets Take Sixth Straight Biathlon Relay," *Dallas Morning News*, 27 February 1988; "Soviets Win Biathlon Relay," *Washington Post*, 27 February 1988; "Soviet [sic] Captures Biathlon Relay," *New York Times*, 27 February 1988; "Soviets Win to Extend Olympic Relay Streak," *Houston Chronicle*, 27 February 1988; "Soviets Remain Unbeatable in Biathlon Relay," *Globe and Mail*, 27 February 1988.

132. *Sovetskii sport*, 28 February 1988; *Krasnaia zvezda*, 28 February 1988; *Pravda*, 28 February 1988. A warm Chinook wind during the second week had created spring-like conditions across southern Alberta.

133. Oleg Vikhrev, "Tiazhkoe 'zoloto' Kalgari," *Krasnaia zvezda*, 28 February 1988.

134. "Sobytie nomer odin," *Sovetskii sport*, 28 February 1988.

135. Mikhail Dmitriev, Valerii Kudriavtsev and Igor' Obraztsov, "Khorosho, kogda v serdtse vesna," *Sovetskii sport*, 28 February 1988.

136. V. Vatutin, "Kto sil'nee na finishe," *Trud*, 28 February 1988. *Pravda* made this point as well in the build-up before the race: "The record of the USSR National Team—five gold medals in five Olympics in a row!—can be broken only in the 21st century." See

"Dnevnik Olimpiady," *Pravda*, 26 February 1988. In 1986, the IOC voted to separate the Winter and Summer Olympics, scheduling them in alternating two-year intervals starting in 1994. Thus, the 1992 Winter Olympics were the last to take place in the same year as the summer version. In order to accommodate the new arrangement, Lillehammer, Norway, hosted the 1994 Winter Olympics two years later, followed by the Winter Olympics of 1998 held in Nagano, Japan.

137. Robert Walker, "Ex-Coach Offers More Blood-Doping Evidence," *Calgary Herald*, 19 February 1988.

138. "Gallery Doping Charge Rejected," *Newsday*, 17 February 1988 [*Factiva* Document nday000020020503dk2h02b03]; "Rumanian Incident: Four Conflicting Tales," *New York Times*, 18 February 1988; "Czech Skaters Return Home," *Boston Globe*, 18 February 1988; Robert Walker, "IOC to Check Out Drug Threat," *Calgary Herald*, 18 February 1988; "IOC ermittelt in Sachen der neuen Blutdroge EPO," *Frankfurter Allgemeine Zeitung*, 19 February 1988; "Das IOC will Labors für Vortests bestrafen," 29 February 1988; "Olympic Blood Dopers: The Uncatchable Cheaters," *San Francisco Chronicle*, 19 February 1988; Tony Sarno and Peter Bowers, "Drug Cheats Get New Weapon in Battle for Gold," *Sydney Morning Herald*, 19 February 1988; David Miller, "The Struggle to Keep Track of the Drug Cheats," *Times*, 20 February 1988; "Pole Falls [sic] Drug Test" and "Testing Demanded," *Dallas Morning News*, 21 February 1988; "Nie stosowałem dopingu," *Trybuna ludu*, 22 February 1988; "Antydoping—surowym sędzią," and Marek Daniewski, "Końska dawska," 23 February 1988; Jeff Blair, "Poles Blame Security Lapses for Player's Drugging," *Calgary Herald*, 23 February 1988.

139. Allan Maki, "Canada's Anti-Drug Fight Sparks Conference," *Calgary Herald*, 27 February 1988.

140. Mary Hines, "Cross-Country Skiing Subject to Strict Doping Controls," *Globe and Mail*, 8 November 1988.

141. Mary Ormsby, "Cross-Country Skiers Get Tough Drug Policy: Random Test Could Lead to Lifetime Suspensions," *Toronto Star*, 8 November 1988; Randy Starkman, "Random Tests Urged for Distance Skiers," 8 February 1991; Starkman, "New Wonder Drug May Speed Athletes to the Killing Fields," 27 April 1991; Marty Hall, interview by author, 11 May 2011; Nathaniel Herz, "The 'Opinionated and Controversial' Marty Hall Holds Forth."

142. Erkki Vettenniemi, "Is Norway the New East Germany? Notes on the Post-2001 Image of Norwegian Skiing in Finland," 266–74.

143. Mark McDonald, "Endurance Athletes Say Blood Doping Exists despite Ban," *Dallas Morning News*, 21 February 1992. Stray-Gundersen comments that Tarasov suffered from a transfusion reaction and was placed on dialysis and a respirator at hospital in Annecy as Russian team doctor Lev Markov frantically searched for injectable corticosteroids. CBS Television intended to publicize the situation until IOC President Juan Antonio Samaranch threatened to undermine any of the broadcasting company's future Olympic contracts. Stray-Gundersen, e-mail correspondence. Tarasov survived and went on to win one bronze and two silver medals at the 1993 World Biathlon Championships in Borovetz, Bulgaria; a silver medal in World Championship Team Competition at Canmore, Alberta, in 1994; gold, bronze and silver medals at the 1994 Winter Olympics in Lillehammer, Norway; two gold medals at the 1996 World Biathlon Championships in Ruhpolding, Germany; and a bronze medal as a member of the Russian Biathlon Relay Team at the

1996 Winter Olympics in Nagano, Japan. Skiing for the Soviet Biathlon Team, Tarasov had already won a silver and a bronze medal in the relay and team events at the 1991 World Biathlon Championships in Lahti, Finland. See Niinimaa, 78–79.

144. Oksana Yablokova, "Fans Give Athletes a Hero's Welcome," *Moscow Times*, 27 February 2002 [Factiva Document mostim0020020226dy2r00001]; Tat'iana Bateneva and Evgenii Zuenko, "Zavtrak chempiona. Dopingovye skandaly v professional'nom sporte neizbezhny," *Izvestiia*, 27 February 2002; Anton Uskov, "Lazutina Should Get Her Prize Money—Matvieyenko," *TASS News Agency*, 28 February 2002 [Factiva document tass-000020020301dy2s000rz]; Sarah Karush, "Russians Turn on Country's Olympic Officials," *Hamilton Spectator*, 27 February 2002; Mary Ormsby, "Drug Poses Health Risks for Cheaters at Games," *Toronto Star*, 27 February 2002; "Zhut'!" *Ogonek* no. 8 (4735), February 2002: 6; Mathieu Reeb, "Larissa [sic] Lazutina and Olga Danilova Appeals Dismissed."

145. Ivan Isaev, "Anfisa Reztsova: v sovremennom sporte bez doping nikuda"; Jeff Lee, "Russia's Doping-Plagued Olympic Team Takes Another Hit before Vancouver 2010 Games"; Thomas, "In Biathlon, Concerns about Russia's Program"; Kirill Zhurenkov, "Bronzovyi vek," *Ogonek* no. 8 (1 March 2010): 48–49; Duncan McKay, "Exclusive: Russia Will Adopt 'Zero-Tolerance' Policy towards Drugs Cheats."

Afterword

1. "Moscow Students Applaud Reagan University Speech on Freedom"; Don Oberdorfer, "It's 'Moscow Spring,' Says Reagan: President Praises Gorbachev's Reforms," *Washington Post*, 1 June 1988.

2. "Over Half of Muscovites Like Reagan after Summit"; Suny, *Soviet Experiment*, 460, 465, 471–72; Malia, 445.

3. Niinimaa, 78, 81; "1992 Winter Olympics, Albertville, France, Nordic Skiing."

4. This number does not include seven medals won by Vladimir Smirnov, who skied for Kazakhstan in 1993 and 1995. "Podiums" [http://www.fis-ski.com/uk/604/podiums.html?nation_comp=&nation_place=&place=&category=WSC&place=&season=ALL&sector=CC&nation_place=&gender=M&category=WSC&nbr=4&nation_comp=&discipline=ALL&search=Search] FIS website.

5. Johnson, "The New Gold War."

6. David Ewing Duncan, "So Long, Lance. Next, 21st-Century Doping," *New York Times Sunday Review*, 19 January 2013; Chelsea Little, "'Doping Is Such a Shame Here': Why Skiing's Next Positive Test Won't Come from Scandinavia."

7. Brigid McCarthy, "Nostalgia for the Soviet Union"; Andrei P. Tsygankov, "If Not by Tanks, Then by Banks? The Role of Soft Power in Putin's Foreign Policy," 1089; Vladimir Shlapentokh, "Two Simplified Pictures of Putin's Russia, Both Wrong," 65.

8. "Putin Deplores Collapse of USSR"; Victor Yasmann, "Nostalgia for USSR Increases"; Kharunya Paramaguru, "Behind the Story: *Time*'s Simon Shuster Discusses Putin's Russia."

9. Fiona Hill, "Why Putin Is Invested in the 2014 Winter Olympics in Sochi."

10. Joshua Yaffa, "As Olympics Loom, Sochi Hurries to Be Ready," *New York Times*, 16 November 2008. Putin has recently tried his hand at biathlon in Sochi as well. See "Macho Putin Shows Off Shooting Skills."

11. "Medvedev and Putin Skiing at Rosa Khutor in Sochi"; Tom Balmforth, "Mt.

Elbrus' Slippery Slopes"; Casey O'Malley, "Terrorism on Elbrus"; "Russia 'Foils Winter Olympics Attack Plot'"; Kirit Radia, "Russia Says It Foiled Sochi Olympics Terror Plot." Although unprecedented accreditation and rifle-check protocols were in place at the Biathlon World Cup races in Sochi in early March 2013, the Boston Marathon bombing by two ethnic Chechen brothers on 15 April has fostered heightened concern about security for the Olympics there in 2014. See Chelsea Little, "Biathlon's First Look at Olympic Venue: Exciting, Unfinished, Unusual"; "IBU Video of Rifle Frustrations in Sochi"; Carol Mattlack, "Could Boston Mayhem Hit the Sochi Olympics?"; Phillip Hersh, "Boston Bombing Links Underscore Sochi Olympic Security Concerns."

12. Kathy Lally, "Russia Bets Winter Olympics Will Warm Its Somber Image"; James Hill, "This Year, Moscow's Mayor, a Leader of United Russia, Arranged a Parade in Red Square Featuring Soldiers Dressed in World War II Uniforms"; "Foto nedeli: nochnoi dozor," *Ogonek* no. 26 (9 November 2009): 28–29; "Today's photos—Wednesday, November 4th, 2009"; "November 07, 2011 [photo number 3]"; "In a Grand Display, Russian Soldiers Re-enact Historic World War II March."

13. Anders Besseberg, "Development of IBU finances and marketing," in Lehotan et al., *50 Years of Biathlon: 1958 to 2008*, 115–17. A recent request for updated financial information elicited a terse response from an IBU communication assistant that the organization no longer publishes its yearly budget. IBU, e-mail correspondence, 14 November 2012.

14. Uwe Jentzsch, "From insider sport to audience hit," in Lehotan et al., *50 Years of Biathlon: 1958 to 2008*, 231.

15. "Mikhail Prokhorov: 'Sam pishu uchebnik po biatlonu'" [www.sports.ru/biathlon/90772832.html] Sports.ru website; "SBR v 2011 godu okazhet material'no-tekhnicheskuiu podderzhku na 16,7 milliona rublei"; Vladimir Mozgovoi, "Russian Biathlon Teams' Dismal Performance"; Evgeniia Chakovskaia, "Biathlon Fans Want Prokhorov Shot Down"; Katya Soldak, "Russian Billionaire Mikhail Prokhorov: From Oligarch to President?" Prokhorov and Aleksandr Tikhonov have been at loggerheads over the direction of the RBU. See "Prokhorov predlozhil Tikhonovu vernut'sia v Soiuz biatlonistov Rossii."

16. Anders Besseberg, "Biathlon today: Ready for the future," in Lehotan et al., *50 Years of Biathlon: 1958 to 2008*, 396; ibid., Sigi Heinrich, "Box-office hit and unusual sport," 237–42; ibid., Andreas Lauterbach, "Crazy about a crazy sport," 232–36; Chelsea Little, "In Packed Soccer Stadium in Germany, Biathletes Put on a Show; Burke and Dunklee Tenth at Shalke"; Little, "With Changes in Geopolitics and Sport Itself, U.S. Biathletes' Relay Performance more Notable than Ever."

17. See photo accompanying "Biathlon World Championships 2003" [http://en.wikipedia.org/wiki/Biathlon_World_Championships_2003], Wikipedia website.

18. "The Reverse Side: Of the silver 3 Roubles coin 'Biathlon.'"

19. Boitsov, "'Zolotoi' zalp v Khanty-Mansiiske," 50.

20. Kurakin, "Soviet/Russian biathletes set the pace," 261.

21. Kopylova, "Aleksandra Vasil'evicha Privalova—s iubileem!"

22. Will Leitch, "It's All About TV Ratings."

23. Anderson, "Nelson's 'Ultimate Accolade.'"

24. "America's Lonely Losers," *Newsweek*, 25 February 1980: 95.

Bibliography

Newspapers, Magazines and Periodicals

Artist i stsena (St. Petersburg)
Avrora (Leningrad)
Boston Globe (Massachusetts)
Calgary Herald (Canada)
Chicago Sun Times (Illinois)
Dagbladet (Oslo)
Dallas Morning News (Texas)
Die Welt (Berlin)
Financial Times (London)
France-Soir (Paris)
Frankfurter Allgemeine Zeitung (Frankfurt)
Globe and Mail (Calgary, Canada)
Hamilton Spectator (Ontario, Canada)
Houston Chronicle (Texas)
Illustrated London News (London)
Izvestiia (Moscow)
Journal de St. Pétersbourg (St. Petersburg)
K novoi armii (Moscow)
Komosmol'skaia pravda (Moscow)
Krasnaia niva (Moscow)
Krasnaia zvezda (Moscow)
Krasnyi sport (Moscow)
Le Monde (Paris)
Leningradskaia pravda (Leningrad)
Los Angeles Times (California)
Magyar nemzet (Budapest)
Moskovskaia pravda (Moscow)
Moskovskiia vedomosti (Moscow)
Narodna armiia (Sofia)
Nedelia (Izvestiia) (Moscow)
Neues Deutschland (Berlin)
New World Review (New York)
New York Times (New York)
Niva (St. Petersburg)
Novoe vremia (St. Petersburg)
Ogonek (Moscow)
Pravda (Moscow)
Record (Hackensack, New Jersey)

Reno Gazette (Nevada)
Robotnichesko delo (Sofia)
România liberă (Bucharest)
Salt Lake City Tribune (Utah)
San Francisco Chronicle (California)
Smena (Moscow)
Sovetskaia Belorussiia (Minsk)
Sovetskaia molodezh' (Riga)
Sovetskii sport (Moscow)
Soviet Life (Moscow)
Soviet Russia Today (New York)
Sports Illustrated (New York)
St. Louis Post-Dispatch (Missouri)
St. Petersburg Times (Florida)
Sydney Morning Herald (Australia)
Times (London)
Toronto Star (Ontario, Canada)
Trud (Moscow)
Trybuna ludu (Warsaw)
Union Internationale de Pentathlon Moderne et Biathlon Bulletin (Stockholm)
USA Today (Arlington, Virginia)
Washington Post (District of Columbia)
Yessis Review of Soviet Physical Education and Sports (Fullerton, California)

Books, Articles and Media

"1992 Winter Olympics, Albertville, France, Nordic Skiing" [http://www.databaseolympics.com/games/gamessport.htm?g=42&sp=NOR] databaseOlympics.com website.

Agranovskii, M. A. *Lyzhnyi sport*. Moscow: Fizkul'tura i sport, 1954.

"Akin to Those of the French Chasseur Alpins Who Have Done Good Service in the Vosges: Russian Military Ski-Runners." *Illustrated War News*, 17 March 1915 [Part 32], 31.

Aleksandrov, M. I., and Iu. A. Ranov. *Fizicheskaia kul'tura i sport v SSSR*. Moscow: Fizkul'tura i sport, 1957.

Allen, E. John B. *The Culture and Sport of Skiing from Antiquity to World War II*. Amherst: University of Massachusetts Press, 2007.

———. *From Skisport to Skiing: One Hundred Years of an American Sport, 1840–1940*. Boston: University of Massachusetts Press, 1993.

———. "Leni Riefenstahl and Her Skiing World." In *L'Art et le Sport* 1, ed. Laurent Daniel, 221–30. Biarritz: Atlantica, 2009.

———. "The Longest Race, 3–4 April 1884." *Journal of the New England Ski Museum*, no. 77 (Spring 2010): 32.

Allgemeine Sport-Zeitung XIV (5 February 1893): 127–28.

"America's Lonely Losers." *Newsweek*, 25 February 1980: 94–95.

Andreeva, Tat'iana, and Marina Guseva. *Sport nashikh dedov: stranitsy rossiiskogo sporta v fotografiiakh kontsa XIX—nachala XX veka*. St. Petersburg: Liki Rossii, 2002.

Andrews, James T. *Science for the Masses: The Bolshevik State, Public Science, and the Popu-*

lar Imagination in Soviet Russia, 1917–1934. College Station: Texas A&M University Press, 2003.

Annenskaia, A. *Fritiof Nansen i ego puteshestviia v grenlandiiu i k severnomu poliusu,* 4th ed. St. Petersburg, 1913.

———. *Fritiof Nansen i ego puteshestviia v grenlandiiu i k severnomu poliusu,* 5th ed. Petrograd, 1916.

Antifashistskii Miting Sovetskikh Sportsmenov v Moskve. Moscow: Fizkul'tura i sport, 1942.

Anuchin, D. N. *Frit'of Nansen, ego podvigi i otkrytiia.* Moscow: Russkaia Vedomost', 1896.

Anzulovic, James Venceslav, Jr. "The Russian Record of the Winter War, 1939–1940: An Analytical Study of the War with Finland from 30 November 1939 to 12 March 1940." PhD Dissertation, University of Maryland, 1968.

Artsikhovskii, A. "Lyzhi na Rusi." *Fizkul'tura i sport,* nos. 5–6 (May–June 1946): 8–12.

Aschwanden, Christie. "Blood Doping Test Cannot Be Cheated." *New Scientist,* 2 October 2004 [http://www.newscientist.com/article/dn6456-blood-doping-test-cannot-be-cheated.html] *NewScientist* website.

"Aus Moskau." *Allgemeine Sport-Zeitung,* no. 95 XV Jahrgang, 8 December 1894: 1334.

"Aus Moskau." *Deutscher Wintersport,* nr. 16 Jahrgang 15 (16 February 1906): 213.

Baburina, N. I., et al. *Plakaty voiny i pobedy.* Moscow: Kontakt-Kul'tura, 2005.

Baddeley, John F. *Russia in the "Eighties": Sport and Politics.* London: Longmans, Green, 1921.

Balmforth, Tom. "Mt. Elbrus' Slippery Slopes." 21 February 2011 [http://russiaprofile.org/politics/32843.html]. Russia Profile website.

Barkhatova, Elena, ed. *Russian Constructivist Posters.* Moscow: Avant-Garde, 1992.

Baryshnikov, N. I., V. N. Baryshnikov and B. G. Fedorov. *Finlandiia vo votoroi mirovoi voine.* Leningrad: Lenizdat, 1989.

Bat', L., and A. Deich. *Frit'of Nansen (zhizn' i puteshestviia).* Moscow: Uchpedgiz [Gos. ucheb.-pedagog. izd-vo], 1936.

Bays, Ted. *Nine Thousand Years of Skis: Norwegian Wood to French Plastic.* Mather Monograph Series #1, ed. M. Magnaghi. Ishpeming, MI: National Ski Hall of Fame Press, 1980.

Beardon, Milton. "Afghanistan, Graveyard of Empires." *Foreign Affairs* 80, no. 6 (November–December 2001): 19–23.

Beckett, A. H., and D. A. Cowan. "Misuse of Drugs in Sport." *British Journal of Sports Medicine* 1979, 12:185 [http://www.ncbi.nlm.nih.gov/pmc/articles/PMC1859795/pdf/brjsmed00267-0019.pdf].

Belousov, O., and S. Luk'ianchikov. *Okhota na zoloto.* 16mm, 22 min. Belarus'fil'm: Tvorcheskoe ob"edinenie LETAPIS, 1974.

Belyukov, D., and N. Ershova. "Skiing Development in Russia in the Beginning of the XX Century." In *Winter Sport and Outdoor Life,* 289–93.

Bergman, B. I. *Lyzhnyi sport.* Moscow: Fizkul'tura i sport, 1965.

Bertholet, Denis. *Die Walliser Alpen auf Ski: die 100 schönsten Skitouren und Abfahrten.* Munich: Bruckmann, 1987.

Bezobrazov, S. V. "Lyzhnaia rat'." In *Entsiklopedicheskii slovar',* tom XVIII, ed. K. K. Arsen'ev, T. T. Petrushevskii and S. V. Bezobrazov. St. Petersburg, 1896.

Biathlon in the USSR. Moscow: Sovetsky Sport Publishers, 1987 [Press booklet in English].

"Biathlon's Skiing, Shooting for the Steady Hand." [http://nbcsportsmsnbc.com/

id/10929154/] NBC Sports website.

"Biathlon World Championships 2003." [http://en.wikipedia.org/wiki/Biathlon_World_ Championships_2003] Wikipedia website.

Blagodatskikh, Anastasiia. "Biatlon: pobedonosnaia traditsiia zhiva." *Kalashnikov. Oruzhie, Boepripasy, Snariazhenie* (December 2008): 76–79.

Blinov, G., and I. Prok. "Sport glazami kino." In *Fizicheskaia kul'tura i sport v SSSR*, ed. N. Liubomirov, 96–113. Moscow: Fizkul'tura i sport, 1963.

Boitsov, Konstantin. "Nachalo bol'shogo puti." *Sovetskii sport*, 23 January 2002: 1–3. [http:// www.sovsport.ru/gazettaarticle-item/34354]

Bown, Matthew Cullerne. *Socialist Realist Painting*. New Haven, CT: Yale University Press, 1998.

Brady, M. Michael. "Falun Championships Rocks Scandinavia." *Skiing* 22, no. 7 (April 1974): 15.

———. *Nordic Touring and Cross Country Skiing*. 3rd rev. ed. New York, Philadelphia: Port City Press, 1974.

Brokhin, Yuri. *The Big Red Machine: The Rise and Fall of Soviet Olympic Champions*. Trans. Glenn Garelik and Yuri Brokhin. New York: Random House, 1978.

Brooks, Jeffrey. *Thank You, Comrade Stalin! Soviet Public Culture from Revolution to Cold War*. Princeton, NJ: Princeton University Press, 2000.

Brown, Nathaniel. *The Complete Guide to Cross-Country Ski Preparation*. Seattle, WA: Mountaineers Books, 1999.

Burla, Aleksandr. *Pervym budu ia . . .* Moscow: Fizkul'tura i sport, 1990.

Bush, Richard J. *Reindeer, Dogs and Snow-Shoes: A Journal of Siberian Travel and Explorations Made in the Years 1865, 1866 and 1867*. London: Sampson Low, Son, and Marston, 1871 [http://hdl.handle.net/2027/uc1.b3931109] HathiTrust Digital Library.

Butin, I. M. *Lyzhnyi sport*. Moscow: Prosveshchenie, 1983.

Butov, Sergei. "Komu flag v ruki? V 2002-m Rostovstev obidelsia." *Sport-Ekspress*, 31 January 2006 [http://www.sport-express.ru/newspaper/2006-01-31/9_1/].

Bystrov, V. E., ed. *Sovetskie partizany*. Moscow: 1961.

Caldwell, John. *Caldwell on Cross-Country: Training and Technique for the Serious Skier*. Brattleboro, VT: Stephen Greene Press, 1975.

———. "Secrets from a Soviet Training Camp." *Cross Country Skier*, October 1988 [http:// www.crosscountryskier.com/2005-06/oct_05_features_voices_from_past.html] *Cross Country Skier Magazine* website.

"Calgary 1988." [http://www.olympic.org/calgary-1988-winter-olympics] Olympic.org: Official Website of the Olympic Movement.

Chakovskaia, Evgeniia. "Biathlon Fans Want Prokhorov Shot Down." 1 April 2011 [www. themoscownews.com/sports/20110401/188546362.html] *The Moscow News* website.

Chernoglazova, R. "Zhenshchiny Belorussii v Velikoi Otechestvennoi voine." In *V bor'be i trude*, ed. Tamara Dmitrieva and Vladimir Beliavtsev, 186–210. Minsk: Belarus', 1985.

Chew, Allen F. *The White Death: The Epic of the Soviet-Finnish Winter War*. East Lansing: Michigan State University Press, 1971.

Chubaryan, A. O. "Foreword." In *Stalin and the Soviet-Finnish War, 1939–1940*, ed. E. N. Kulkov et al., trans. Tatyana Sokokina, xv–xviii. London: Frank Cass, 2002.

Chuvilkin, V. A. *Devushki v shineliakh*. Moscow: Moskovskii rabochii, 1982.

Clarey, Christopher. "Powder, Crust, Slush: More to Snow than Snow." *New York Times*, 26 February 2010 [http://www.nytimes.com/2010/02/27/sports/olympics/27iht-OLYCLAREY.html?ref=olympics].

Cohen, Stephen F. "Bukharin, NEP, and the Idea of an Alternative to Stalinism." In *Rethinking the Soviet Experience: Politics and History since 1917*, 71–92. New York: Oxford University Press, 1986.

Conze, Susanne, and Beate Fiesler. "Soviet Women as Comrades-in-Arms." In *The People's War: Responses to World War II in the Soviet Union*, ed. Robert W. Thurston and Bernd Bonwetsch, 211–34. Urbana: University of Illinois Press, 2000.

Cox, Kevin. "Biathlon." In *The Globe and Mail Guide to Calgary 88*, ed. Murray Campbell (February 1988): 28–29.

———. "Cross-Country Skiing." In *The Globe and Mail Guide to Calgary 88*, ed. Murray Campbell (February 1988): 24–25.

Cox, Randi. "All This Can Be Yours!" In *The Landscape of Stalinism: The Art and Ideology of Soviet Space*, ed. Evgeny Dobrenko and Eric Naiman, 125–62. Seattle: University of Washington Press, 2003.

———. "'NEP without Nepmen!' Soviet Advertising and the Transition to Socialism." In *Everyday Life in Early Soviet Russia: Taking the Revolution Inside*, ed. Christina Kiaer and Eric Naiman, 119–52. Bloomington: Indiana University Press, 2006.

Cross Country Ladies 4x5 Km—Relay Free Technique Unofficial Results/Ski de fond femmes relais 4x5 Km—style libre Résultats non officiels. Calgary 1988, XV Olympic Winter Games. 21 February 1988: 1–3 [Race result sheets].

Cross Country Ladies—10 Km Classical Unofficial Results/Ski de fond femmes—10Km Classique Résultats non officiels. Calgary 1988, XV Olympic Winter Games. 14 February 1988: 1–2 [Race result sheets].

Cross Country Men—15 Km Classical Unofficial Results/Ski de fond hommes—15Km Classique Résultats non officiels. Calgary 1988, XV Olympic Winter Games. 19 February 1988: 1–3 [Race result sheets].

Cross Country Men—30 Km classical Unofficial Results/Ski de fond hommes—30Km Classique Résultats non officiels. Calgary 1988, XV Olympic Winter Games. 15 February 1988: 1–3 [Race result sheets].

Cross Country Men—50 Km free technique Unofficial Results/Ski de fond hommes—50Km style libre Résultats non officiels. Calgary 1988, XV Olympic Winter Games. 27 February 1988: 1–5 [Race result sheets].

Davies, Norman. *Europe: A History*. New York: Oxford University Press, 1996.

"The Definitive Marty Hall" [http://www.xcskiworld.com/news/Features/Hall.htm] XCskiworld website.

De Lefreté, G. "Les 'Jeux du Nord.'" *La Vie au Grand Air*, 10 February 1901: 85–86.

"Delo organizatora pokusheniia na Tuleeva vernuli v prokuraturu," Lenta.ru: *Novosti*, 29 January 2007 [http://lenta.ru/news/2007/01/29/tihonov/].

"Der Skilauf im Russischen Heer." *Der Winter* 9 (January 1915): 49–50.

Der Winter 2 (October 1935): 18.

Deutscher Eissport II 8 (14 December 1893): 52.

"Dmitri Shparo—30 let vokrug poliusa" [www.trud.ru/issue/article.php?id=200612072271301] *Trud* website.

Doherty, Thomas. *Projections of War: Hollywood, American Culture, and World War II*.

New York: Columbia University Press, 1993.

Doughty, Robert A., and Ira D. Gruber. *American Military History and the Evolution of Warfare in the Western World.* Lexington, MA: D. C. Heath, 1996.

Edelman, Robert. *Serious Fun: A History of Spectator Sports in the USSR.* New York: Oxford University Press, 1993.

Egupov, L. F. "Takticheskie ustanovki slalomistov." In *Voprosy psikhologii sporta*, ed. A. Ts. Puni, 206–41. Moscow: Fizkul'tura i sport, 1955.

———. "Zapominanie slalomnoi trassy." In *Voprosy psikhologii sporta*, ed. A. Ts. Puni, 154–205. Moscow: Fizkul'tura i sport, 1955.

Eimeleus, K. B. E. E. *Lyzhi v voennom dele.* St. Petersburg: Izdanie Glavnoi Gimnastichesko-Fekhtoval'noi Shkoly, 1912.

Erman, Adolph. *Reise um die Erde durch Nord-Asien and die beiden Oceane in den Jahren 1828, 1829 und 1830 ausgeführt von Adolf Erman: Zweiter Band: Reise von Tobolsk bis zum Ochozker Meere im Jahre 1829.* Berlin: G. Reimer, 1838 [http://hdl.handle.net/2027/ucl.$b557326] HathiTrust Digital Library.

———. *Travels in Siberia: Including excursions northwards, down the Obi, to the Polar Circle, and southwards, to the Chinese frontier*, vol. 1. Trans. W. D. Cooley. London: Longman, Brown, Green, and Longmans, 1848.

Esaian, A. M., ed. *Fizkul'turniki VII s"ezdu sovetov.* Moscow: Otiz-fizkul'tura i turizm, 1935.

Evans, Eric. "Powers That Will Never Be." *Cross Country Skier* (Spring 1987): 48–51.

"Extract of the Minutes of the 55th Session of the International Olympic Committee," 25–28 May 1959 (Munich) LA Foundation Digital Archive [www.la84/foundation.org].

"Extract of the Minutes of the 56th Session of the International Olympic Committee," 15–16 February 1960 (San Francisco) LA Foundation Digital Archive [www.la84/foundation.org].

"Extract of the Minutes of the 57th Session of the International Olympic Committee," 22–23 August 1960 (Rome). LA Foundation Digital Archive [www.la84/foundation.org].

Falkner, Gerd. "The *Deutschen Winterkampfspiele* German National Winter Olympics." In *2002 International Ski History Congress: Selected Papers from the Seminars Held at Park City, Utah, January 20–24, 2002*, ed. E. John B. Allen, 252–57. New Hartford, CT: International Skiing History Association, 2002.

Fedden, Robin. *Alpine Ski Tour: An Account of the High Level Route.* London: Putnam, 1956.

Fédération Internationale de Ski (FIS) website [http://www.fis-ski.com].

Finsch, Otto. *Reise nach West-Sibirien im Jahre 1876.* Berlin: Erich Wallroth, 1879 [http://Hdl.handle.net/2027/mdp.39015069864380] HathiTrust Digital Library.

Firsoff, V. A. *Ski Track on the Battlefield.* New York: A. S. Barnes, 1943.

"Fischer Ski Company. *Olympia-Reportage: Sarajevo '84: 9x Gold 11x Silver 5x Bronze.*" [Advertising brochure, 12 pages].

Fitzpatrick, Sheila. "The Civil War as a Formative Experience." In *Bolshevik Culture: Experiment and Order in the Russian Revolution*, ed. Abbott Gleason, Peter Kenez and Richard Stites, 57–76. Bloomington: Indiana University Press, 1989.

———. "New Perspectives on the Civil War." In *Party, State and Society in the Russian Civil War: Explorations in Social History*, ed. Diane Koenker, William Rosenberg and Ronald Suny, 3–23. Bloomington: Indiana University Press, 1989.

———. "Stalin and the Making of a New Elite, 1928–1939." *Slavic Review* 38, no. 3 (September 1979): 377–402.

Fliegner, Frederick, ed. *1968 United States Olympic Book*. Lausanne: International Olympic Editions, 1969.

Fochler-Hauke, Gustav. *Schi-Jäger am Feind! Von Kampf und Kameradschaft eines Schi-Bataillons in den Winterschlacht in Osten 1941/42*. Heidelberg: Kurt Vowinckel, 1943.

"Foto No. 556026." [http://visualrian.com/images/item/556026%253Fprint%253Dtrue&d ocid=UXiRpfG_OMsIqM&itg=1&w=512&h=351&ei=pi0vTuWEOajiiAL2-dQr&z oom=0&iact=rc&dur=400&page=1&tbnh=90&tbnw=131&start=0&ndsp=33&ved =1t:429,r:4,s:0&tx=44&ty=55] VisualarianRianovosti.

Freeman, Douglas Southall. *Lee's Lieutenants: A Study in Command*. Vol. 1, *Manassas to Malvern Hill*. New York: Charles Scribner's Sons, 1946.

"From Pole to Pole." *Soviet Shipping* 3 (91): 33.

"Gallery Doping Charge Rejected." *Newsday*, 17 February 1988 [*Factiva* Document nday-000020020503dk2h02b03].

Garri, A. *Po sledam Amundsena*. Moscow: Molodaia gvardiia, 1930.

Gavrichkov, L. V. *Lyzhnik-boets*. Moscow: Fizkul'tura i sport, 1940.

Gibson, Daryl. "No More Applause." *Sunday Camera Magazine*, 12 May 1985: 6–9, 11–16.

Gilbert, Daniel. "The Weight at the Plate." *New York Times* [http://www.nytimes.com/2010/08/05/opinion/05gilbert.html?_r=1&hp].

Gilbert, Doug. *The Miracle Machine*. New York: Coward, McCann & Geoghegan, 1980.

Gill, Diane L. "Sport and Exercise Physiology." In *The History of Exercise and Sport Science*, ed. John D. Massengale and Richard A. Swanson, 293–320. Champaign, IL: Human Kinetics, 1997.

Gins, G. K. *Sibir', soiuzniki i Kolchak*. Vol. 2. Peking: Tipo-litografiia Russkoi Dukhovnoi Missii, 1921.

Glantz, David M. "Preface." In *Stalin and the Soviet-Finnish War, 1939–1940*, ed. E. N. Kulkov et al., trans. Tatyana Sokokina, xi–xiv. London: Frank Cass, 2002.

———. *Stumbling Colossus: The Red Army on the Eve of World War*. Lawrence: University of Kansas Press, 1998.

"Glava Soiuza biatlonistov otverg obvineniia v pokushenii na Tuleeva." Lenta.ru: *Novosti*, 11 April 2007 [http://lenta.ru/news/2007/04/11/tihonov/].

"Glava Soiuza biatlonistov trebuiut posadit' na 5 let za pokushenie na Tuleeva." Lenta.ru: *Novosti*, 31 May 2007 [http://lenta.ru/news/2007/05/31/five/].

Gmelin, Johann Georg. *Voyage en Sibérie: Contenant la description des moeurs & usages des peuples de ce pays, le cours des rivières considérables, la situation de chaînes de montagnes, des grandes forêts, des mines, avec tous les faits d'histoire naturelle qui sont particuliers à cette contrée*. Trans. Louis-Félix Guynement de Keralio. Paris: chez Desaint, 1767 [http://hdl.handle.net/2027/hvd.hxijts] HathiTrust Digital Library.

Goksøyr, Matti. "Skis as National Symbols, Ski Tracks as Historical Traits: The Case of Norway." In *2002 International Ski History Congress: Selected Papers from the Seminars Held at Park City, Utah, January 20–24, 2002*, ed. E. John B. Allen, 197–203. New Hartford, CT: International Skiing History Association, 2002.

Gor'kii, A. M. "Perepiska A. M. Gor'kogo s F. Nansenom." In *Arkhiv A. M. Gor'kogo*. Tom VIII: *Perepiska Gor'kogo s zarubezhnymi literatorami*, 290–93. Moscow: Izdatel'stvo Nauk SSSR, 1960.

Graham, Loren R. *Science in Russia and the Soviet Union: A Short History*. Cambridge: Cambridge University Press, 1993.

Grammaticus, Saxo. *Gesta Danorum*. Book V. "The Nine Books of the Danish History of Saxo Grammaticus," trans. Oliver Elton. New York: Norroena Society, 1905 [http://www.ealdriht.org/saxo5ii.html].

Gran, Tryggve. *The Norwegian with Scott: Tryggve Gran's Antarctic Diary, 1910–1913*. Ed. Geoffrey Hattersley-Smith, trans. Ellen Johanne McGhie. London: National Maritime Museum, 1984.

Great Soviet Encyclopedia: A Translation of the 3rd Edition. New York: Macmillan, 1973.

Gregory, Barry. *Mountain and Arctic Warfare: From Alexander to Afghanistan*. Wellingborough, UK: Patrick Stephens, 1989.

"Gubernator Kirovskoi oblasti N. I. Shaklein vruchil vdove proslavlennogo biatlonista Vladimira Melanina Pochetnuiu medal' Mezhdunarodnogo soiuza biatlonistov." 7 March 2008 [http://www.ako.Kirov.ru/news/Detail.php?ID=8430] Kirov.ru website.

Gunter, Georg. *Die deutschen Skijäger von den Anfängen bis 1945*. Friedburg (Dorheim), GER: Podzun-Pallas, 1993.

Gurevicha, M., et al., eds. *Boi v Finliandii: vospominaniia uchastnikov*. Vols. 1 and 2. Moscow: Voennoe izd-vo, 1941.

Gus'kov, S. I. *V atake dollar (mezhdunarodnyi sport i ideologicheskaia bor'ba)*. Moscow: Mysl', 1988.

Gwagnin, Alexander. *Opisanie Moskovii*. Ed. G. G. Kozlova. Moscow: Greko-latinskii kabinet Iu. Shichalina, 1997.

Hall, Marty, and Pam Penfold. *One Stride Ahead: An Expert's Guide to Cross-Country Skiing*. Tulsa: Winchester Press, 1981.

Hargreaves, Jennifer. *Sporting Females: Critical Issues in the History and Sociology of Women's Sports*. London: Routledge, 1994.

Harper, Frank. *Military Ski Manual: A Handbook for Ski and Mountain Troops*. Harrisburg, PA: Military Service Publishing, 1943.

Hartranft, Fritz, and Franz Königer. *Skiführer Haute Route*. Munich: Bergverlag Rudolf Rother, 1983.

Heck, Sandra. "'A Superfluous Appearance?' The Olympic Winter Pentathlon 1948." In *Winter Sport and Outdoor Life*, 184–92.

Hemingway, Ernest. *The Complete Short Stories of Ernest Hemingway*. New York: Simon and Schuster, 1987.

Herberstein, Sigmund von. Bertold Picard, ed. *Description of Moscow and Muscovy*. Trans. J. B. C. Grundy. New York: Barnes & Noble, 1969.

Hersh, Philip. "Boston Bombing Links Underscore Sochi Olympic Security Concerns." 19 April 2013 [articles.chicagotribune.com/2013-04-19/sports/chi-boston-bombing-links-underscore-sochi-security-concerns-20130419_1_sochi-winter-games-metal-detectors-boston-marathon] *Chicago Tribune* website.

Herz, Nathaniel. "The 'Opinionated and Controversial' Marty Hall Holds Forth." 22 October 2012 [fasterskier.com/2012/10/the-opinionated-and-controversial-marty-hall-holds-forth/] FasterSkier.com website.

Hill, Alexander. *The War behind the Eastern Front: The Soviet Partisan Movement in North-West Russia, 1941–1944*. London: Frank Cass, 2005.

Hill, Fiona. "Why Putin Is Invested in the 2014 Winter Olympics in Sochi." 8 February 2013 [http://www.brookings.edu/research/interviews/2013/02/08-putin-sochi-hill] Brookings Institute website.

Hill, James. "This Year, Moscow's Mayor, a Leader of United Russia, Arranged a Parade in Red Square Featuring Soldiers Dressed in World War II Uniforms." In "A Photographer's Journal: Putin's Russia," 1 December 2007 [www.nytimes.com/interactive/2007/11/30/world/europe/20071201_RUSSIA_FEATURE.html] *New York Times* website.

Hirsch, Francine. "Toward an Empire of Nations: Border Making and the Formation of Soviet National Identities." *Russian Review* 59, no. 2 (April 2000): 201–26.

Holquist, Peter. "'Information Is the Alpha and Omega of Our Work': Bolshevik Surveillance in Its Pan-European Context." *Journal of Modern History* 69, no. 3 (September 1997): 415–50.

Hopkirk, Peter. *The Great Game*. New York: Kodansha International, 1992.

Horensma, Pier. *The Soviet Arctic*. London: Routledge, 1991.

Hulme, Derick L., Jr. *The Political Olympics: Moscow, Afghanistan, and the 1980 Olympic Boycott*. New York: Praeger Publishers, 1990.

Huntford, Roland. *The Last Place on Earth*. New York: Modern Library, 1999.

———. *Nansen: The Explorer as Hero*. New York: Barnes & Noble, 1998.

———. *Scott and Amundsen*. New York: Putnam, 1980.

———. *Shackleton*. New York: Atheneum, 1986.

———. *Two Planks and a Passion: The Dramatic History of Skiing*. New York: Continuum, 2008.

Husar, John. "Soviets' Nordic Monopoly Grows Amid Controversy." *Chicago Tribune*, 20 February 1988 [http://articles.chicagotribune.com/1988-02-20/sports/8804010201_1_blood-doping-soviet-press-cross-country-ski-race/2].

Huttunen, Antero. "Naisten ja nuorten ampumahiihdon MM-kisat." *Ampumahiihtäjä*, no. 3 (27 March 1987): 1, 3–4.

Iakovlev, A. *Rual Amundsen*. Moscow: Molodaia gvardiia, 1948.

"IBU Video of Rifle Frustrations in Sochi." 13 March 2013 [blogs.fasterskier.com/biathlon/2013/03/13/ibu-video-of-rifle-frustrations-in-sochi/] FasterSkier.com website.

"In a Grand Display, Russian Soldiers Re-enact Historic World War II March." 7 November 2012 [photoblog.nbcnews.com/_news/2012/11/07/14995153-in-a-grand-display-russian-soldiers-re-enact-historic-world-war-ii-march?lite] NBC News website.

International Biathlon Union website [www.biathlonworld.com/en/].

Isaev, Ivan. "Anfisa Reztsova: v sovremennom sporte bez doping nikuda." *Lyzhnyi sport*, 28 August 2009 [http://www.skisport.ru/news/index.php?news=8539] *Lyzhnyi sport* website.

Iurev, M., and V. Semeniuk. *World War II Russia: The Russian Front*. Trevi Telecommunications and Sovetelexsport, USSR, 1992. VHS format, 30 min.

Izard, Ralph. *The Soviet Olympic Team and Soviet Athletes*. San Francisco: American Russian Institute, 1953.

Johnson, Ian. "The New Gold War: Germany Revives Its Communist-Era Athlete Mills as the Global Race for Olympic Glory Heats Up." *Wall Street Journal Weekend Edition*, Saturday/Sunday 2–3 August 2008.

Johnson, Lonnie R. *Central Europe: Enemies, Neighbors, Friends*. 2nd ed. New York: Oxford University Press, 2002.

Jones, David R. "Forerunners of the Komsomol: Scouting in Imperial Russia." In *Reforming the Tsar's Army: Military Innovation in Imperial Russia from Peter the Great to the Revolution*, ed. David Schimmelpenninck van der Oye and Bruce W. Menning, 56–81. Cambridge: Cambridge University Press, 2004.

Jönsson, Åke. *Nordiska Spelen: Historien om sju vinterspel i Stockholm av olympiskt format 1901 till 1926.* Värnamo, SWE: Bokförlaget Arena, 2001.

Jørgensen, Per. "From Balck to Nurmi: The Olympic Movement and the Nordic Nations." In *The Nordic World: Sport in Society*, ed. Henrik Meinander and J. A. Mangan, 69–99. London: Frank Cass, 1998.

Kalinski, M. I., C. C. Dunbar and Z. Szygula. "Evidence of State-Sponsored Blood Doping Research Program in Former Soviet Union." *Medicine and Science in Sport and Exercise* 35, no. 5, Supplement 1 (May 2003): S268.

Kalinski, Michael I. "State Sponsored Research on Creatine Supplements and Blood Doping in Elite Soviet Sport." *Perspectives in Biology and Medicine* 46, no. 3 (Summer 2003): 445–51.

Karachi, D., and V. Karlinskii. *Pochtovye marki SSSR (1918–1968).* Moscow: Sviaz', 1969.

Keegan, John. *The First World War.* New York: Alfred A. Knopf, 1999.

Keys, Barbara J. *Globalizing Sport: National Rivalry and International Community in the 1930s.* Cambridge, MA: Harvard University Press, 2006.

———. "Soviet Sport and Transnational Mass Culture in the 1930s." *Journal of Contemporary History* 38, no. 3 (3 July 2003): 413–34.

Khmel'nitskaia, I. B. *Sportivnye obshchestva i dosug v stolichnom gorode nachala XX veka: Peterburg i Moskva.* Moscow: Novyi khronograf, 2011.

Khromov, Iu. *Lyzhnyi sport v SSSR.* Moscow: Sovetskii sport, 1987.

"Khronika." *Sanktpeterburgskiia vedomosti.* 16 April 1898.

Khrushchev, Nikita. *Khrushchev Remembers.* Ed. and trans. Strobe Talbott. Boston: Little, Brown, 1970.

Kopylova, Elena. "Aleksandra Vasil'evicha Privalova—s iubileem!" 7 August 2008 [http://www.skisport.ru/news/index.php?news=6599] *Lyzhnyi sport* website.

Krasheninnikov, Stepan. *Opisanie zemli Kamchatki, s prilozheniem raportov, donesenii i drugikh neopublikovannykh materialov.* Ed. L. S. Berg et al. Moscow: Glavsevmorputi, 1949.

———. *Opisanie zemli Kamchatki: v dvukh tomakh.* St. Petersburg: Imperatorskaia akademiia nauk, 1755. Reprint, St. Petersburg: Nauka, Kamshat, 1994.

Krivoshapkin, Mikhail. *Eniseiskii okrug i ego zhizn.* St. Petersburg: Imperatorskoe russkoe geograficheskoe obshchestvo, 1865 [http://hdl.handle.net/2027/nnc1.0035549106].

Krivosheyev, G. F. "Preparation of Trained Reserves for the Soviet Army in the Prewar Years and during the Great Patriotic War." *Soviet Union Military History Journal*, no. 1 (January 1988).

Krüger, Arnd. "Sport in German International Politics, 1918–1945." In *Sport and International Politics: The Impact of Fascism and Communism on Sport*, ed. P. Arnaud and James Riordan, 79–96. New York: Routledge, 1998.

Kruglikov, Aleksandr. "Stat'ia 14 [Nikolai Puzanov]." *Nevskoe vremia*, no. 126 (2586) 17 July 2001 [http://www.pressa.spb.ru/newspapers/nevrem/2001/arts/nevrem-2586-art-14.html].

Kruglov, Aleksandr. "Pervyi iz pervykh." 5 July 2010 [biathlonrus.com/main/2010/24075/] Russian Biathlon Union website.

Kubalski, Mikołaj A. *Voyages en Sibérie recueillis par N.-A.* [sic] *Kubalski.* Tours: A. Mame, 1853 [http://hdl.handle.net/2027/nyp.33433082446869] HathiTrust Digital Library.

Kublitskii, Georgii. *Frit'of Nansen ego zhizn' i neobyknovennye prikliucheniia.* Moscow: Detskaia literatura, 1981.

Kuisma, Suvi. "Womanly Light and Easy on Ski Track—Women's Ski Races in Lahti Ski Games between 1923 and 1952." In *Winter Sport and Outdoor Life,* 121–30.

Kulkov, E. N., and O. A. Rzheshevsky (in Russian) and H. Shukman (in English), eds. *Stalin and the Soviet-Finnish War, 1939–1940.* Trans. Tatyana Sokokina. London: Frank Cass, 2002.

Kul'kov, E. N., and O. A. Rzheshevskii. *Zimniaia voina 1939–1940,* Kniga 2: *I. Stalin i finskaia kampania.* Moscow: Nauka, 1998.

Kurakin, Aleksandr. "O biatlone: istoria razvitiia biatlona" [http://www.biathlonrus.com/biathlon/story/] Russian Biathlon Union website.

Kuzmin, Leonid. "Investigation of the Most Essential Factors Influencing Ski Glide." Luleå University of Technology [http://epubl.ltu.se/1402-1757/2006/03/LTU-LIC-0603-SE.pdf].

Lally, Kathy. "Russia Bets Winter Olympics Will Warm Its Somber Image." *Seattle Times,* 11 February 2013.

Larsen, Trina L., and Robert T. Green. "Export Opportunities in a Crumbling Economy: The Soviet Union in 1990." *Journal of International Marketing* 1, no. 4 (1993): 71–90.

Larson, Edward J. *An Empire of Ice: Scott, Shackleton, and the Heroic Age of Antarctic Science.* New Haven, CT: Yale University Press, 2011.

"Latest from the USSR." British Pathé, 1942 [issue date: 26 March 1942]. 1:59 min., canister: 42/25, film ID: 1322.01, tape: *PM1322* [http://www.britishpathe.com/record.php?id=22542].

Lavery, Jason. *The History of Finland.* Westport, CN: Greenwood Press, 2006.

Lee, Jeff. "Russia's Doping-Plagued Olympic Team Takes Another Hit before Vancouver 2010 Games." *Vancouver Sun,* 26 January 2010 [http://communities.canada.com/vancouversun/blogs/insideolympics/archive/2010/01/26/russia-s-doping-plagued-ski-team-takes-another-hit-before-vancouver-2010-games.aspx] *Vancouver Sun* website.

Leffler, Melvyn P. "The Cold War: What Do 'We Now Know'?" *American Historical Review* 104, no. 2 (April 1999): 501–24.

Lehotan, Ivor, Jozsef Magyar and Peer Lange, eds. *50 Years of Biathlon: 1958 to 2008.* Salzburg: International Biathlon Union, 2008.

Leitch, Will. "It's All about TV Ratings." 17 August 2009 [roomfordebate.blogs.nytimes.com/2009/08/17/going-for-olympic-gold/#will] *New York Times* website.

Lenin, V. I. "I. F. Armand." In *Polnoe Sobranie Sochinenii.* Tom 49, 5th ed., 340–41. Moscow: Izdatel'stvo politicheskoi literatury, 1975.

Lenoe, Matthew. *Closer to the Masses: Stalinist Culture, Social Revolution, and Soviet Newspapers.* Cambridge, MA: Harvard University Press, 2004.

Liebers, Arthur. *The Complete Book of Winter Sports.* New York: Coward-McCann, 1963.

Lincoln, W. Bruce. *Red Victory: A History of the Russian Civil War.* New York: Simon and Schuster, 1989.

Little, Chelsea. "Biathlon's First Look at Olympic Venue: Exciting, Unfinished, Unusual." 8 March 2013 [fasterskier.com/article/biathlons-first-look-at-olympic-venue-exciting-unfinished-unusual/] FasterSkier.com website.

———. "'Doping Is Such a Shame Here': Why Skiing's Next Positive Test Won't Come from

Scandinavia." 7 November 2012 [fasterskier.com/2012/11/doping-is-such-a-shame-here-why-skiings-next-positive-test-wont-come-from-scandinavia/] FasterSkier.com website.

——. "In Packed Soccer Stadium in Germany, Biathletes Put on a Show: Burke and Dunklee Tenth at Shalke." 29 December 2012 [fasterskier.com/article/in-packed-soccer-stadium-in-germany-biathletes-put-on-a-show-burke-and-dunklee-tenth-at-schalke/] FasterSkier.com website.

——. "With Changes in Geopolitics and Sport Itself, U.S. Biathletes' Relay Performance More Notable than Ever." 7 January 2013 [fasterskier.com/article/with-changes-in-geopolitics-and-sport-itself-u-s-biathletes-relay-performance-particularly-notable/] FasterSkier.com website.

Liudskov, P. N. *Lyzhnyi sport.* Moscow: Fizkul'tura i sport, 1953.

Liventsev, V. *Partizanskii krai.* Leningrad: TSK VLSKM, 1951.

Long, John Wendell. *Civil War and Intervention in North Russia, 1918–1920.* PhD dissertation, Columbia University, 1972. Microfilm.

"Lot #308, 'Proletariat, On Your Skis! Fadeev.'" [http://www.postersplease.com/index.php?FAFs=75333d9b6a90d1907e539b7c971996f5&FAFgo=/Auctions/LotDetail&LotID=132&sr=102&t=C&ts=&AID=4] Poster Auctions International website.

Lukashin, Y. *USSR Skiing.* Moscow: Novosti Press Agency Publishing House, 1971.

Lund, Morten. "Arnold Lunn and the Birth of International Downhill Racing in the Bernese Oberland." *Journal of the New England Ski Museum,* no. 87 (Fall 2012): 1, 4–15.

Luther, Carl J. *Schneeschuhläufer im Krieg.* Munich: J. Lindauersche Universitäts-Buchhandlung Schöpping, 1915.

"Lyzhniki Pavlovskogo Polka na Marsovom pole v S. Petersburge: Les soldats du régiment de garde de Pawlowsky sur le champ de Mars à St. Petersbourg." J. J. W. 505 [no date]. [Postcard].

"Macho Putin Shows Off Shooting Skills." 9 March 2012 [au.eurosport.com/biathlon/macho-putin-shows-off_sto3186850/story.shtml] EuroSport.com website.

Magidovich, I. P. *Ocherki po istorii geografecheskikh otkrytii.* Moscow: Prosveshchenie, 1967.

Magnus, Olaus. *Historia de Gentibus Septentrionalibus.* Rome, 1555. Reprint, Westmead, UK: Gregg International Publishers, 1971.

Magocsi, Paul Robert. *A History of Ukraine.* Seattle: University of Washington Press, 1996.

"Major Oscar Schadek," *Allgemeine Sport-Zeitung* XIV (1 January 1893): 27.

Malia, Martin. *The Soviet Tragedy: A History of Socialism in Russia, 1917–1991.* New York: Free Press, 1994.

Mandel, William M. *Soviet Women.* Garden City, NY: Anchor Books, 1975.

Mangan, Audrey. "What Skiing Can Take Away from Armstrong Saga." 12 October 2012 [fasterskier.com/2012/10/what-skiing-can-take-away-from-the-armstrong-saga/] FasterSkier.com website.

"March of Time—One Day of War—Russia." British Pathé, 1943. 20:19 min., canister: DOCS, film ID: 2723.01, tape: *PM2723* [http://www.britishpathe.com/record.php?=84457].

Marin, Mikhail, and Anatolii Korshunov. "Aleksandr Tikhonov." *Fizkul'tura i sport* 4 (886) April 1972: 20–21.

Markov, D. P. and V. G. Kalashnikov. *Lyzhi: Uchebnoe posobie po lyzhnomu sportu.* Moscow: Fizkul'tura i sport, 1944.

Martin, Terry. *Affirmative Action Empire: Nations and Nationalism in the Soviet Union, 1929–1939.* Ithaca, NY: Cornell University Press, 2001.

Martynov, Arkady. "'Metelitsa's Last Address: The Antarctic." *Soviet Woman* 4, 1990: 25–27.

Masia, Seth. "Grip and Glide: A Short History of Ski Wax" [http://skiinghistory.org/skiwax. html] Skiing Heritage: International Skiing History Association website.

Maslennikov, I. B., and V. E. Kaplanskii. *Lyzhnyi sport.* Moscow: Fizkul'tura i sport, 1984.

Matlack, Carol. "Could Boston Mayhem Hit the Sochi Olympics?" 22 April 2013 [www. businessweek.com/articles/2013-04-22/could-boston-mayhem-hit-sochi-olympics] *Business Week* website.

McCannon, John. *Red Arctic: Polar Exploration and the Myth of the North in the Soviet Union, 1932–1939.* New York: Oxford University Press, 1998.

McCarthy, Brigid. "Nostalgia for the Soviet Union." 23 December 2011 [www.theworld. org/2011/12/nostalgia-for-the-soviet-union/] PRI's *The World* website.

McKay, Duncan. "Exclusive: Russia Will Adopt 'Zero-Tolerance' Policy towards Drugs Cheats [sic]." 27 November 2010 [http://www.insidethegames.biz/winter-olympics/2014/11202-exclusive-russia-will-adopt-qzero-toleranceq-policy-to-wards-drugs-cheats] Insidethegames.biz website.

McMillan, John. "Bidding for Olympic Broadcast Rights: The Competition *before* [sic] the Competition." *Negotiation Journal* 7, no. 3 (July 1991): 255–63.

"Medvedev and Putin Skiing at Rosa Khutor in Sochi." Video report, 2011, 1:37 min [http:// en.rian.ru/video/20110218/162671232.html] RIA *Novosti* website.

Meignan, Victor. *De Paris à Pékin par Terre: Sibérie-Mongolie.* Paris: E. Plon, 1877.

——. *From Paris to Pekin over Siberian Snows.* Trans. William Conn. London: W. S. Sonnenschein, 1885.

"Men and Women's Ski Race." [Russian title: "Druzheskie vstrechi sportsmenov (Sportsmen's Friendly Meet)."] British Pathé, 1959. 2:20 min., canister: UN31886, film ID: 2764.31, tape: *PM2764* [http://www.britishpathe.com/record.php?id=65067].

Messerschmidt, Daniel Gottlieb. *Forschungsreise durch Sibirien, 1720–1727: Tagebuchaufzeichnungen ab Nov. 1725, Gesamtregister.* Berlin: Akademie-Verlag, 1977.

——. *Forschungsreise durch Sibirien, 1720–1727: Tagebuchaufzeichnungen Jan. 1723–Mai 1724.* Berlin: Akademie-Verlag, 1964.

Middendorff, Alexander T. von. *Reise in den äussersten Norden und Osten Sibiriens.* Band IV: *Übersicht der Natur Nord- und Ost-Sibiriens, Theil 2.* St. Petersburg: Kaiserlichen Akademie der Wissenschaften, 1874 [http://books.google.com.au/books?id=wK8h AQAAMAAJ&printsec=frontcover&source=gbs_ge_summary_r&cad=0#v=onepa ge&q&f=false].

"Mikhail Prokhorov: 'Sam pishu uchebnik po biatlonu'" [www.sports.ru/biath-lon/90772832.html] Sports.ru website.

"Minutes of the 58th Session of the International Olympic Committee," 19–21 June 1961 (Athens). LA Foundation Digital Archive [www.la84/foundation.org].

"Minutes of the 61st Session of the International Olympic Committee," 26–28 January 1964 (Landeshaus, Innsbruck). LA Foundation Digital Archive [www.la84/foundation. org].

"Minutes of the Conference of the Executive Board of the International Olympic Committee," 16 June 1961 (Athens). LA Foundation Digital Archive [www.la84/foundation. org].

Mokropulo, I. F., and O. I. Sazhin. *Trenirovka lyzhnika-biatlonista*. Moscow: Voenizdat, 1973.

Morton, Henry M. *Soviet Sport: Mirror of Society.* New York: Collier Books, 1963.

"Moscow Students Applaud Reagan University Speech on Freedom." *Reuters News*, 31 May 1988 [*Factiva* document Iba0000020011203dk5v01wog].

Mozgovoi, Vladimir. "Russian Biathlon Teams' Dismal Performance." 18 March 2011 [en. novayagazeta.ru/arts-and-sports/8732.html] *Novaya gazeta* website.

Mudge, Zachariah Atwell. *Fur-clad adventurers; or, Travels in skin-canoes, on dog-sledges, on reindeer, and on snow-shoes, through Alaska, Kamchatka, and Eastern Siberia.* New York: Phillips & Hunt, 1880 [http://hdl.handle.net/2027/mdp.39015065815337] HathiTrust Digital Library.

Murmantseva, V. S. *Sovetskie zhenshchiny v Velikoe Otechestvennoi voine*. Moscow: Mysl', 1974.

Naida, S. F., et al. *Istoriia Grazhdanskoi Voiny v SSSR*, vol. 3. Moscow: 1957.

Nansen, Fridtjof. *Farthest North, being a record of a voyage of exploration of the ship "Fram" 1893–1896, and of a fifteen month's sleigh journey by Dr. Nansen and Lieut. Johansen.* Vols. 1 and 2. New York: Harper & Bros., 1897.

——. *The First Crossing of Greenland*. Vols. 1 and 2. Trans. Hubert Majendie Gepp. London: Longmans, Green, 1890.

——. *Through Siberia the Land of the Future*. Trans. Arthur G. Chater. London: William Heinemann, 1914.

"[Nansen receives order of St. Stanislaus 12 April (sic)]." *Vladivostok*, 19 April 1898.

Nemukhin, I. *Lyzhnia pokoriaetsia smelym*. Moscow: Fizkul'tura i sport, 1963.

Nemukhin, I. A. *Lyzhi—sport sil'nykh i smelykh*. Moscow: Fizkul'tura i sport, 1955.

Niinimaa, Veli M. J. *Double Contest: Biathlon History and Development.* Wals-Himmelreich, AUS: International Biathlon Union and Biathlon Alberta, 1998.

Nilsson, B. H. *Competing in Cross-Country Skiing*. New York: Sterling Publishing, 1974.

Nolte, Claire E. "All for One! One for All! The Federation of Slavic Sokols and the Failure of Neo-Slavism." In *Constructing Nationalities in East Central Europe*, ed. Pieter M. Judson and Marsha L. Rozenblit, 126–40. New York: Berghahn Books, 2005.

——. *The Sokol in the Czech Lands: Training for the Nation*. New York: Palgrave MacMillan, 2002.

"Norsk Nordpolsexpedition." *Morgenbladet*, 12 December 1888 [http://www.nb.no/Avis/programvare/vis_sider.php?publisert=&vis_tiffbild=JA&modus=sok&tittel=URN:NBN:no-nb_digavishefte_8&aarstall=1888&maaned=12&dag=12].

"November 07, 2011 [Photo Number 3]." 7 November 2011 [blogs.voanews.com/photos/2011/11/07/November-07-2011/] Voice of America website.

Novikova, Ekaterina. "Pervyi i edinstvennyi." 8 May 2011 [http://www.biathlonrus.com/main/2011/35861/] Russian Biathlon Union website.

Official Index to the Times, October–December 1939. London: Times Publishing. Reprint, Nendeln, LIE: Kraus Reprint, 1968.

Official Index to the Times, January–March 1940. London: Times Publishing. Reprint, Nendeln, LIE: Kraus Reprint, 1968.

Ohletz, Hermann, and Roggi [sic]. "50 Jahre Faszination." Documentary film, 30 min. In DVD supplement to *50 Years of Biathlon: 1958 to 2008*, ed. Ivor Lehotan, Jozsef Magyar and Peer Lange. Salzburg: International Biathlon Union, 2008.

Olsen, Brian. "Top Guns: Biathletes Train in Skiing and Shooting." *Cross Country Skier Magazine* 24, no. 3 (January 2005): 36–37, 61.

O'Mahoney, Mike. *Sport in the USSR: Physical Culture—Visual Culture.* London: Reaktion Books, 2006.

O'Malley, Casey. "Terrorism on Elbrus." *Backcountry Magazine,* October 2012 [http://www.backcountrymagazine.com/index.php?option=com_content&task=view&id=803&Itemid=52]. *Backcountry* website.

Orenstein, Harold S., trans. *Soviet Documents on the Use of War Experience.* Vol. 1: *The Initial Period of the War, 1941.* London: Frank Cass, 1991.

———. *Soviet Documents on the Use of War Experience.* Vol. 2: *The Winter Campaign, 1941–1942.* London: Frank Cass, 1991.

———. *Soviet Documents on the Use of War Experience.* Vol. 3: *Military Operations, 1941 and 1942.* London: Frank Cass, 1993.

Organizing Committee for the XIth Olympic Winter Games, Sapporo 1972. *Official Report* [http://www.la84foundation.org/6oic/OfficialReports/1972/orw1972pt2.pdf].

"Over Half of Muscovites Like Reagan after Summit." *Reuters News,* 1 June 1988 [*Factiva* document Iba0000020011203dk6101sft].

Pallas, Peter Simon. *Reise durch verschiedene Provinzen des Russischen Reichs.* Vol. 3. St. Petersburg: Kaiserlichen Academie der Wissenschaften, 1776. Reprint, Graz, AUS: Akademische Druck –u. Verlagsanstalt, 1967.

———. *Tafelband.* St. Petersburg: Kaiserlichen Academie der Wissenschaften, 1776. Reprint, Graz, AUS: Akademische Druck –u. Verlagsanstalt, 1967.

———. *Voyages en différentes provinces de l'empire de Russie.* Book 4. Trans. Gauthier de la Peyronie. Paris: Chez Maradan, 1793 [http://hdl.handle.net/2027/nyp.33433000103634] HathiTrust Digital Library.

"Pamiati Valentiny Kuznetsovoi, glavnoi Metelitsy strany." [http://spox.ru/plugins/page/index.php?id=10864] Spox.ru website.

Papova, Tam'iana. "Velikie Otechestvennye. Vladimir Melan'in." 17 June 2013 [biathlonrus.com/main/2013/45286/] Russian Biathlon Union website.

Paramaguru, Kharunya. "Behind the Story: *Time's* Simon Shuster Discusses Putin's Russia." 16 November 2012 [world.time.com/2012/11/16/behind-the-story-times-simon-shuster-discusses-putins-russia].

Parks, Jenifer. "Verbal Gymnastics: Sports, Bureaucracy, and the Soviet Union's Entrance into the Olympic Games, 1946–1952." In *East Plays West: Sport and the Cold War,* ed. Stephen Wagg and David L. Andrews, 27–44. New York: Routledge, 2007.

Pasetskii, V. M. *Frit'of Nansen: 1861–1930.* Moscow: Nauka, 1986.

Pasetskii, V. M., and S. A. Blinov. *Rual Amundsen: 1872–1928.* Moscow: Nauka, 1997.

Peppard, Victor, and James Riordan. *Playing Politics: Soviet Sport Diplomacy to 1992.* Greenwich, CT: JAI Press, Inc., 1993.

Petrov, P. P., and L. M. Subotskii. *Partizanskie byli.* Moscow: Voennoe izdatel'stvo, 1958.

Photographs Nos. 196 and 444, COLL.CNOSF (2). *Le Comité National Olympique et Sportif Français. Collège des fédérations multisport et affinitaires.*

Pimenov, E. K. *Zavoevanie poliusov.* Leningrad: Brokgauz-efron, 1930. University Microfilms International, 1990.

Ponomarev, N. I. *Sport and Society.* Trans. James Riordan. Moscow: Progress Publishers, 1981.

Popova, O. N. *Geroi poliarnoi nochi i vechnykh l'dov Fritiof Nansen.* 4th ed. St Petersburg: 1914.

Portugal'skii, R. M., et al. *Marshal S. K. Timoshenko: Zhizn' i deiatel'nost'.* Moscow: MOF Pobeda—1945 god, 1994.

Pospelov, P. N., et al., eds. *Istoriia Velikoi Otechestvennoi voiny Sovetskogo Soiuza, 1941–1945.* Vols. 1 and 2. Moscow: Voennoe izdatel'stvo ministerstva oborony Soiuza SSR, 1960.

"Programm: IBU-Weltmeisterschaften Sommerbiathlon, 21–27 September 2009, in der DKB-Ski-Arena Oberhof." [Competitor's packet, 25 pages].

Programma pervenstva SSSR po lyzhnomu sportu 1948 g. Sverdlovsk: Ural'skii Rabochii, 1948. [Pamphlet].

"Programma voenno-fizicheskoi podgotovki uchashikhsia nachal'nykh i I–IV klassov nepol'nykh srednykh i srednykh shkol." Moscow: Narkompros RSFSR, 1942. [Pamphlet].

"Prokhorov predlozhil Tikhonovu vernut'sia v Soiuz biatlonistov Rossii." 21 January 2011 [lenta.ru/news/2011/01/21/sbr/] Lenta.ru website.

Pushkin, A. S. "Istoria Pugacheva." In *Sobranie sochinenii v shesti tomakh.* Tom IV, ed. M. A. Tsiavlovskii. Moscow: Akademiia, 1936.

"Putin Deplores Collapse of USSR." *BBC News,* 25 April 2005 [http://news.bbc.co.uk/2/hi/4480745.stm] BBC News website.

Radia, Kirit. "Russia Says It Foiled Sochi Olympics Terror Plot." 10 May 2012 [abcnews.go.com/blogs/headlines/2012/05/Russia-says-it-foiled-sochi-olympics-terror-plot/] ABC News website.

Ramenskaia, T. I. *Lyzhnyi vek Rossii.* Moscow: Sovetskii Sport, 1998.

Readhead, Robert. "Soldiers on Skis." In *Mountain Panorama: A Book of Winter Sports and Climbing,* ed. Max Robinson, 106–16. London: Max Parrish, 1955.

Reeb, Mathieu. "Larissa [sic] Lazutina and Olga Danilova Appeals Dismissed." 24 June 2003 [http://fasterskier.com/2003/06/larissa-lazutina-and-olga-danilova-appeals-dismissed/] FasterSkier.com website.

Rees, E. A. "Stalin and Russian Nationalism." In *Russian Nationalism, Past and Present,* ed. Geoffrey Hosking and Robert Service, 77–106. New York: St. Martin's Press in association with the School of Slavonic and East European Studies, University of London, 1998.

Reese, Roger. *The Soviet Military Experience: A History of the Red Army, 1917–1991.* London: Rutledge, 2000.

———. *Stalin's Reluctant Soldiers: A Social History of the Red Army, 1925–1941.* Lawrence: University Press of Kansas, 1996.

Reuveny, Rafael, and Aseem Prakash. "The Afghanistan War and the Breakdown of the Soviet Union." *Review of International Studies* 25, no. 4 (October 1999): 693–708.

"The Reverse Side: Of the Silver 3 Roubles Coin 'Biathlon.'" [http://www.cbr.ru/eng/banknotes_coins/memorable_coins/current_year_coins/print.asp?file=110415_eng.htm] Central Bank of the Russian Federation website.

Riordan, James. "Playing to New Rules: Soviet Sport and Perestroika." *Soviet Studies* 42, no. 1 (January 1990): 133–45.

———. "The Rise and Fall of Soviet Olympic Champions." *Olimpika: The International Journal of Olympic Studies* 2 (1993): 25–44.

――――. "Soviet Sport and Foreign Policy," *Soviet Studies* 26, no. 3 (July 1974): 322–43.

――――. *Soviet Sport Background to the Olympics.* New York: Washington Mews Books, 1980.

――――. *Sport in Soviet Society: Development of Sport and Physical Education in Russia and the USSR.* Cambridge: Cambridge University Press, 1977.

――――. *Sport, Politics and Communism.* Manchester, UK: Manchester University Press, 1991.

――――. "The Sports Policy of the Soviet Union, 1917–1941." In *Sport and International Politics: The Impact of Fascism and Communism on Sport,* ed. Pierre Arnaud and James Riordan, 67–78. New York: Routledge, 1998.

Roberts, Eric. *High Level Route Chamonix-Zermatt-Saas.* 2nd ed. Swindon, UK: Swindon Press/West Col Productions, 1984.

Romanov, N. N. *Trudnye dorogi k Olimpu.* Moscow: Fizkul'tura i sport, 1987.

Rudenstine, Angelica Zander, ed. *The George Costakis Collection: Russian Avant-Garde Art.* New York: Harry N. Abrams, 1981.

"Russia." British Pathé, 1942 [issue date: 6 July 1942]. 1:46 min., canister: 42/54, film ID: 1328.24, tape: *PM1328* [http://www.britishpathe.com/record.php?=22934].

"Russia 'Foils Winter Olympics Attack Plot.'" 10 May 2012 [www.aljazeera.com/news/europe/2012/05/2012510152623335744.html] Aljazeera website.

"Russian Overcome Winter [sic]." [Ia. Marchenko, et al., eds.] British Pathé, 1944 [?]. 2:02 min., canister: UN231D, film ID: 1623.24, tape ID: *PM1623* [http://www.britishpathe.com/record.php?id=60609].

"Russian Skaters and Skiers at Training." British Pathé, 1961. 1:37 min., canister: UN3572C, film ID: 2637.03, tape: *PM2637* [http://www.britishpathe.com/record.php?id=62641].

"Russian Ski Troops." [Russian title: "Pomoshch' ranenym zimoi (Help for the Wounded in Winter)," ed. I. Veinerovich.] British Pathé, 1943 [?]. 1:51 min., canister UN230G, film ID: 1623.20, tape: *PM1623* [http://www.britishpathe.com/record.php?id=60605].

"Russo-Finish [sic] War—1940 (aka Bryansky Front)." [Russian title: "Brianskii front," ed. A. Solodkov and M. Prudnikov.] British Pathé [no date]. 2:09 min., canister: UN228D, film ID: 628.06, tape: *PM0628* [http://www.britishpathe.com/record.php?id=50928].

"(Russo-Finnish War 1940)." British Pathé [no issue date], unused/unissued material. 2:16 min., canister: UN226E, film ID: 626:13, tape: *PM0626* [http//www.britishpathe.com/record.php?id=50917].

Sæther, Esten O. "Hold Kjeft—for nå snakker bare dårlige tapere." *Dagblad-Sporten,* 17 February 1988.

Sarychev, Gavriil Andreevich. *Account of a Voyage of Discovery to the North-East of Siberia, the Frozen Ocean, and the North-East Sea. By Gawrila Sarytschew, Russian Imperial Major-General to the Expedition. Translated from the Russian, and Embellished with Engravings* (London: Richard Phillips, 1806) [http://hdl.handle.net/2027/mpd.3901] HathiTrust Digital Library.

"SBR v 2011 godu okazhet material'no-tekhnicheskuiu podderzhku na 16,7 milliona rublei." [www.sports.ru/biathlon/130422922.html] Sports.ru website.

Schrenck, Leopold von. *Reisen und Forschungen in Amur-Lande Band III: Die Völker des Amur-Landes.* St. Petersburg: Kaiserlichen Akademie der Wissenschaften, 1881.

Schuster, Alice. "Women's Role in the Soviet Union: Ideology and Reality." *Russian Review* 30, no. 3 (July 1971): 260–67.

Selivanova, I. V., and N. N. Shkol'nyi. *Leningradskie "Okna TASS" 1941–1945 gg.* St. Petersburg: Rossiiskaia natsional'naia biblioteka: 1995.

Semenov, V. *Sredi l'da i nochi.* St. Petersburg: Izdanie P. P. Soikina, 1897.

Serebriakov, V. A. *Lyzhnyi sport.* Moscow: Molodaia gvardiia, 1949.

———. *Lyzhnyi sport v SSSR: Spravochnik za 1952–1954 gg.* Moscow: Fizkul'tura i sport, 1955.

Shaposhnikov, Vladimir. *Na lyzhnoi trasse.* Moscow: Fizkul'tura i sport, 1956.

Shchadenko, E. *Nastavlenie po lyzhnoi podgotovke krasnoi armii,* 2nd ed. Moscow: Voennoe izdatel'stvo, 1945.

Shlapentokh, Vladimir. "Two Simplified Pictures of Putin's Russia, Both Wrong." *World Policy Journal* 22, no. 1 (Spring 2005): 61–72.

Shparo, Dmitrii. "Dvadtsat' chetyre dnia na lyzhakh po dreifuiushchim l'dam arktiki." In *Letopis' severa.* Tom IX, ed. S. V. Slavin, et al., 124–36. Moscow: Mysl', 1979.

———. *K poliusu!* Moscow: Molodaia gvardiia, 1987.

———. "Skiing across the Bering Strait." *Explorers Journal* 76 (1) 1998: 10–13.

———. "To the North Pole on Skis." *Soviet Union* 3 (276) 1973: 55.

Shparo, Dmitrii, and Matvei Shparo. *Challenging Greenland (The Epic Russian Crossing of Greenland).* Trans. Elena Mokrous and Gordon Thomas. Moscow: Vagrius Publishers, 2002.

Shukman, H. "Introduction." In *Stalin and the Soviet-Finnish War, 1939–1940,* ed. E. N. Kulkov et al., trans. Tatyana Sokokina, xix–xxv. London: Frank Cass, 2002.

Siegel, Jennifer. *Endgame: Britain, Russia and the Final Struggle for Central Asia.* London: I. B. Tauris, 2002.

Siegelbaum, Lewis H. *Stakhanovism and the Politics of Productivity in the USSR, 1935–1941.* Cambridge: Cambridge University Press, 1988.

Singleton, Fred. *A Short History of Finland.* Cambridge: Cambridge University Press, 1989.

Singsaas, Marianne. "Laying the First Tracks: Female Skiers at the Turn of the 19th Century." In *Winter Sport and Outdoor Life,* 90–98.

Sinyavsky, Andrei. *Soviet Civilization: A Cultural History.* New York: Arcade Publishing, 1990.

Skard, Halldor. "Skiskøyting er i skuddet." *Trim Trenning* (March 1986): 4–10.

Skard, Halldor, and Olle Larsson. *Langrennsteknikk.* Oslo, NOR: Universitetsforlaget, 1981.

"Skiers Compete for 'Silver Edelweiss' Prize." British Pathé, 1962. 1:18 min., canister: UN3578I, film ID: 2639.21, tape: *PM2639* [http://www.britishpathe.com/record.php?id=62710].

"Skiing Championships near Sverdlovsk." [Russian title: "Na lyzhne pod Sverdlovskom (On the ski tracks near Sverdlovsk)," ed. A. Istomin, Iu. Leongardt, N. Shmakov] British Pathé, 1959. 2:45 min., canister: UN32166, film ID: 2720.23, tape: *PM2720* [http://britishpathe.com/record.php?id=64256].

Skiing in the USSR. Moscow: Sovetsky Sport Publishers, 1987.

Slezkine, Yuri. "The USSR as a Communal Apartment, or How a Socialist State Promoted Ethnic Particularism." *Slavic Review* 53, no. 2 (Summer 1994): 414–52.

Snegirev, Vladimir. *On Skis to the North Pole.* Trans. George Watts. New York: Sphinx Press, 1985.

Snopkov, A., et al., eds. *Shest'sot plakatov.* Moscow: Kontakt-Kul'tura, 2004.

"Snowshoes in Warfare." *Graphic* (3 March 1894): 247–49.

Sokolov, Dmitrii. "Nikolai Kruglov—starshii. Sil'nii sredi sil'nikh." [http://www.skisport. ru/index.php?news=3299] *Lyzhnii sport* website.

Soldak, Katya. "Russian Billionaire Mikhail Prokhorov: From Oligarch to President?" 5 March 2013 [http://www.forbes.com/sites/katyasoldak/2013/03/05/russian-billionaire-mikhail-prokhorov-from-oligarch-to-president/] Forbes Magazine website.

Sörlin, Sverker. "Nature, Skiing and Swedish Nationalism." In *Tribal Identities: Nationalism, Europe, Sport*, ed. J. A. Mangan, 147–63. London: Frank Cass, 1996.

"The Soviets: A Special Report." *Nordic Update* 3, no. 5 (1989): 2–4.

"Soviet Sports Parade (aka Cultural Parade in Red Square)." British Pathé, 1930–1939 [?]. 16:16 min., canister: UN63H, film ID: 474.12, tape: *PM0474* [http://www.british-pathe.com/record.php?id=49840].

Spencer, Bill. "1985—The Year of Skating." *Biathlon Bulletin: United States Biathlon Association* 5, no. 2 (March–April 1985): 3.

"Stafett 4 x 10 km." MPEG-2 XA_TF10-5115. National Library of Sweden Film Archives.

Stalin, J. V. "A Year of Great Change: On the Occasion of the Twelfth Anniversary of the October Revolution." In *Problems of Leninism*, 429–46. Peking: Foreign Language Press, 1982.

Stankevich, V. *Frit'of Nansen: Puteshestviia cherez grenlandiiu k severnomu poliusu i v sibir'.* Berlin: Z. J. Grschebin, 1923.

Starostin, A. *Sport in the USSR*. Moscow: Foreign Languages Publishing House, 1939.

Stegen, Arthur. *Biathlon*. Washington, DC: National Rifle Association of America, 1979.

———. "Recollections of Minsk—1974 Biathlon World Championships." PDF file. Attachment to e-mail correspondence, 25 July 2010. [Twelve pages with thirteen photographs].

Stephen, John J. *The Russian Far East: A History.* Stanford, CA: Stanford University Press, 1994.

Strachan, Hew. *The First World War.* New York: Viking, 2004.

Strekhnin, Iurii. "Dvenadtsatyi prizhok." In *V tylu i na fronte: Zhenshchiny-kommunistki v gody Velikoi Otechestvennoi voiny*, ed. K. K. Iatskevich, 244–72. Moscow: Izdatel'stvo politicheskoi literatury, 1984.

"Sud amnistiroval Aleksandra Tikhonova." Lenta.ru: *Novosti*, 23 July 2007 [http://lenta.ru/news/2007/07/23/tikhonov/].

Sunde, Einar. "Oscar Wergeland: An Apostle for Skiing." In *2002 International Ski History Congress: Selected Papers from the Seminars Held at Park City, Utah, January 20–24, 2002*, ed. E. John B. Allen, 204–16. New Hartford, CT: International Skiing History Association, 2002.

Suny, Ronald Grigor. *The Soviet Experiment: Russia, the USSR, and the Successor States.* New York: Oxford University Press, 1993.

Suny, Ronald Grigor, and Terry Martin. *A State of Nations: Empire and Nation-Making in the Age of Lenin and Stalin.* New York: Oxford University Press, 2001.

"Sweden-Russian Wins Ski-Contest." British Pathé, 1954. 1:14 min., canister: 54/18, film ID: 14432, tape: *PM0144* [http://britishpathe.com/record.php?id=31669].

Swix Advanced Waxing for Cross-Country Skiing. Oslo, NOR: S. & Jul. Sørensen Trykkerier A/S, 1981. [Booklet].

"SWIX, Official Supplier to World Ski Championships in Oslo 1982/ Fournisseur officiel des Championnats du Monde de ski 1982 à Oslo." Oslo, NOR: Ødegaard Reklame NRF. [Poster].

Sytkowski, Arthur J. *Erythropoietin: Blood, Brain and Beyond.* Weinheim, GER: Wiley VCH, 2004.

Tarkhova, N. S., K. M Anderson, P. N. Bobylev, V. L. Vorontsov, V. P. Kozlov, I. I. Kudriavtsev and V. N. Kuzelenkov, eds. *"Zimniaia voina:" Rabota nad oshibkami aprel'–mai 1940 g.* Moscow: Rossiiskii gosudarstvennyi voennyi arkhiv, 2004.

Tarleton, Robert E. "'Bolsheviks of Military Affairs': Stalin's High Commands, 1934–1940." PhD dissertation, University of Washington, 2000.

Taubman, William. *Khrushchev: The Man and His Era.* London: Free Press, 2003.

"Telekanal ARD poprosil ubrat' reklamnye bannery 'Alexander Tikhonov & MA.'" Sports. ru, 26 September 2009 [http://www.sports.ru/biathlon/34909091.html].

[Television Coverage of the Calgary Winter Olympics 1988 from American Broadcasting Company (ABC) Sports, CTV Television Network (CTV), Canadian Broadcasting Corporation (CBC) and Independent Television (ITV)]. Videocassette, 120 min. Private collection.

Thomas, Katie. "In Biathlon, Concerns about Russia's Program." *New York Times*, 23 February 2010 [http://www.nytimes.com/2010/02/23/sports/Olympics23biathlon.html?scp= 1&sq=biathlon%20tikhonov&st=cse].

"Today's Photos—Wednesday, November 4th, 2009" [http://www.militaryphotos.net/forums/showthread.php?168214-Today-s-Photos-Wednesday-November-4th-2009] Militaryphotos.net website.

"'Toil and Sweat' Win Out over 'Amusement.'" *Life* 36, no. 4 (25 January 1954): 128–29.

Trotsky, Lev [Leon]. *Kak vooruzhalas' revoliutsiia (na voennoi rabote).* Vols. I and III. Moscow: 1921. Microfilm, University of Chicago Library.

———. *The Revolution Betrayed.* Trans. Max Eastman. 1937. Reprint, Mineola, NY: Dover, 2004.

Trotter, William R. *A Frozen Hell: The Russo-Finnish War of 1939–1940.* Chapel Hill, NC: Algonquin Books of Chapel Hill, 1991.

Tsygankov, Andrei P. "If Not by Tanks, Then by Banks? The Role of Soft Power in Putin's Foreign Policy." *Europe-Asia Studies* 58, no. 7 (November 2006): 1079–99.

UdSSR Der Wintersport/SSSR Zimnii sport. Moscow: Fizkul'tura i sport, 1963.

Ufimetseva, Natal'ia. "Startoval na lyzhakh iz bochonka." *Media zavod*, 12 January 2010 [http://www.mediazavod.ru/articles/81425] *Media zavod* website.

Ungerleider, Steven. *Faust's Gold: Inside the East German Doping Machine.* New York: St. Martin's Press, 2001.

United States Biathlon Association E-Mail Bulletin 7, no. 15 (October 2010).

Upton, Anthony F. *Finland, 1939–1940.* Cranbury, NJ: Associated University Presses, 1979.

Uskov, Anton. "Lazutina Should Get Her Prize Money—Matvieyenko." *TASS News Agency*, 28 February 2002 [Factiva document tass000020020301dy2s000rz].

"USSR Mountain Ski Championships." British Pathé, 1959. 53 sec., canister: UN3209D, film ID: 2716.27, tape: *PM2716* [http://www.britishpathe.com/record.php?id=64199].

"V boiakh za obespechenie bezopasnosti severozapadnykh granits SSSR. Na Karel'skom peresheike 1939–1940 gg. Lyzhniki v pokhode." Leningrad: Iskusstvo [no date]. [Postcard].

"V boiakh za obespechenie bezopasnosti severozapadnykh granits SSSR. Na Karel'skom peresheike 1939–1940 gg. Vo bremia boev s belofinnami v raione Teriok." Leningrad: Iskusstvo [no date]. [Postcard].

"V. K. Dmitrievskii, *Lyzhnyi kross*." Moscow: Sovetskii khudozhnik [no date]. [Postcard].

"V poslednem slove Tikhonov ne priznal sebia vinovnym v pokushenii na Tuleeva." Lenta. ru: *Novosti*, 23 July 2007[http://lenta.ru/news/2007/07/23/word/].

Vaage, Jacob. "The Norse Started It All." In *The Ski Book*, ed. Morten Lund, Robert Gillen and Michael Bartlett, 194–98. New York: Arbor House Publishing Company, 1982.

Vaitsekhovskaia, Elena. *Shtrafnoi krug Aleksandra Tikhonova*. Moscow: Lyzhnyi sport, 2006.

Van Dyke, Carl. *The Soviet Invasion of Finland, 1939–1940*. London: Frank Cass, 1997.

Vasara, Erkki. "Maintaining a Military Capability: The Finnish Home Guard, European Fashion and Sport for War." In *The Nordic World: Sport in Society*, ed. Henrik Meinander and J. A. Mangan, 157–72. London: Frank Cass, 1998.

Vasil'ev, Dmitrii M. *Na lyzhne*. Moscow: Molodaia Gvardiia, 1956.

Vasil'ev, Nikolai M. "Porazhenie, ravnoe pobede." In *Rasskazy starykh sportsmenov*, ed. P. V. Batyrev and N. M. Vasil'ev, 59–70. Moscow: Fizkul'tura i Sport, 1951.

Vehviläinen, Olli. *Finland in the Second World War: Between Germany and Russia*. Trans. Gerard McAlester. New York: Palgrave, 2002.

"Vertigine Bianca." MPEG-2 XA_TF10-F113. National Library of Sweden Film Archives.

Vettenniemi, Erkki. "Is Norway the New East Germany? Notes on the Post-2001 Image of Norwegian Skiing in Finland." In *Winter Sport and Outdoor Life*, 266–74.

Vikstrem, Ul'ias. *Toivo Antikainen, dokumental'naia povest'*. Petrozavodsk: Iz. Kareliia, 1970.

Vogel, Gretchen. "A Race to the Starting Line." *Science* 305, no. 5684 (30 July 2004): 632–35.

Volkovskii, N. L., ed. *Tainy i uroki zimnei voiny 1939–1940*. St. Petersburg: Poligon, 2000.

Von Hagen, Mark. "From 'Great Patriotic War' to the Second World War: New Perspectives and Future Prospects." In *Stalinism and Nazism: Dictatorships in Comparison*, ed. Ian Kershaw and Moshe Lewin, 237–50. Cambridge: Cambridge University Press, 1997.

Von Thiele, L. F. K. "The Norwegian Olympic Games." *Wide World Magazine* 9 (May 1902–October 1902): 465–73.

Voy, Robert. *Drugs, Sport, and Politics*. Champaign, IL: Leisure Press, 1991.

"Vozrast—sportu ne pomekha!" [http://www.originalskiposters.com/new/poster.php?ID=288] Original Ski Posters.com website.

Waddington, Ivan, and Andy Smith. *An Introduction to Drugs in Sport: Addicted to Winning?* London: Routledge, 2009.

Weiner, Amir. *Making Sense of War: The Second World War and the Fate of the Bolshevik Revolution*. Princeton, NJ: Princeton University Press, 2001.

Weitz, Eric. "Racial Politics without the Concept of Race: Reevaluating Soviet Ethnic and National Purges." *Slavic Review* 61, no. 1 (Spring 2002): 1–29.

"West of Voronezh." British Pathé, 1943 [issue date: 25 March 1943]. 2:10 min., canister: 43/24, film ID: 1079.10, tape: *PM1079* [http://www.britishpathe.com/record. php?id=12203].

Wiederkehr, Stefan. "'We Shall Never Know the Exact Number of Men Who Have Competed in the Olympics Posing as Women': Sports, Gender Verification and the Cold War." *International Journal of the History of Sport* 26, no. 4 (2009): 556–72.

Wingo, Walter. "Russia's Ladder to the Moon." *Science News-Letter* 84, no. 20 (16 November 1963): 314–15.

Winter Sport and Outdoor Life: Papers Presented at the Telemark Conference for Historians of Sports, ed. Halvor Kleppen. Morgedal, NOR: Norsk Skieventyr, 2011.

Wolfgang, Friedl, and Bertl Neumann. *Offizieler Bericht der IX. Olympischen Winterspiele Innsbruck, 1964*. Vienna: Österreichisher Bundesverlag für Unterricht, Wissenschaft und Kunst, 1967 [http://www.la84foundation.org/oic/OfficialReports/1964/orw1964.pdf].

"Wood Skis Are Dead, Says Marty Hall." *Nordic World Magazine* 3, no. 3 (May 1975): 19.

Woodward, Bob. *Cross-Country Ski Conditioning for Exercise Skiers and Citizen Racers*. Chicago: Contemporary Books, 1981.

Wrangel, Ferdinand Petrovich. *Le Nord de la Sibérie: Voyage parmi les peuplades de la Russie asiatique et dans la mer Glaciale*. Trans. Prince Emmanuel Galitzin. Limoges: Eugène Ardant, 1882 [http://hdl.handle.net/2027/wu.89103512703] HathiTrust Digital Library.

Yablokova, Oksana. "Fans Give Athletes a Hero's Welcome." *Moscow Times*, 27 February 2002 [Factiva Document mostim0020020226dy2r00001].

Yasmann, Victor. "Nostalgia for USSR Increases." *Radio Free Europe/ Radio Liberty*, 23 December 2006 [http://www.rferl.org/content/article/1073655.html].

Yurchak, Alexei. *Everything Was Forever, until It Was No More: The Last Soviet Generation*. Princeton, NJ: Princeton University Press, 2006.

Zhaojian, Shan, and Wang Bo, eds. *The Original Place of Skiing—Altay Prefecture of Xinjiang, China*. Xinjiang: Xinjiang People's Publishing House and People's Sports Publishing House, 2011.

"Zimnii perekhod okhotnich'ei komandy. No. 2." Published by Scherer, Nabholz and Co., Moscow 1904. [Postcard].

Zubkova, Elena. *Russia after the War: Hopes, Illusions, and Disappointments, 1945–1957*. Ed. and trans. Hugh Ragsdale. Armonk, NY: M. E. Sharpe, 1998.

Index